Economic Issues

Economic Issues

Selections from *The CQ Researcher*

CQ Press

A Division of Congressional Quarterly Inc.
Washington, D.C.

CQ Press
A Division of Congressional Quarterly Inc.
1255 22nd Street, N.W., Suite 400
Washington, D.C. 20037

(202) 822-1475; (800) 638-1710

www.cqpress.com

∞ The paper used in this publication meets the minimum requirements of the American National Standard for Information Sciences—Permanence of Paper for Printed Library Materials, ANSI Z39.48-1992.

Printed and bound in the United States of America

05 04 03 02 01   5 4 3 2 1

A CQ Press College Division Publication

Director	Brenda Carter
Acquisitions editor	Charisse Kiino
Associate editor	Amy Briggs
Marketing Manager	Rita Mayti
Managing editor	Ann Davies
Production editor	Precious Sherry
Cover designer	Dennis Anderson
Composition	Paul Cederborg
Print buyer	Liza Sanchez
Sales manager	James Headley

Photos: pp. 1, 21, 43, 62, 89, 107, 114, 139, 144, 149, 179, 187, 211 and 212: © AP; pp. 5, 24, 37, 71, 119, 131, and 159: © Reuters.

"At Issue" piece: p. 173: Reprinted with permission of Adam D. Thierer.

Library of Congress Cataloging-in-Publication Data

In process

ISBN: 1-56802-721-4

Contents

MARKETS

Annotated Table of Contents

The 14 *CQ Researcher* articles reprinted in this book have been reproduced essentially as they appeared when first published. In a few cases in which important new development have occurred since an article came out, these developments are mentioned in the following overviews, which highlight the principle issues examined.

A GLOBAL PERSPECTIVE

Transatlantic Tensions

U.S.-European relations, already on a downward slide since the mid-1990s, have deteriorated further since President Bush took office in January 2001. Bush's reluctance to support the Kyoto treaty to curb global warming and his plans to deploy a missile defense system in defiance of a 1970s-era arms-control treaty are the two main friction points. But American positions on many other issues, including the role of NATO peacekeeping initiatives, Europe's evolving trade policies and the U.S. death penalty, also are straining bilateral relations. European critics charge that the United States is misusing its post–Cold War status as the world's sole superpower to impose its will, ignoring the interests of its closest allies.

China Today

China is becoming a more powerful nation — and more willing to spar with the United States over a range of issues. But nothing has the potential to bring the two countries into conflict like Taiwan. While the U.S. officially supports the island's reunification with the mainland, it has warned China not to threaten a takeover if Taiwan seeks independence. Moreover, some American policymakers urge the U.S. to adopt a tougher line against Beijing and to abandon its "one China" policy in favor of one backing Taiwan's right to self-determination. Meanwhile, despite continuing controversy, China's admission to the World Trade Organization in 2001 appears inevitable. While many say WTO membership will turn China into a more open society, others say it could lead to greater political repression.

World Trade

World trade has emerged as a critical issue among Americans concerned about how opening up new markets affects people's lives here and abroad. The debate spilled onto the streets of Seattle and Washington in demonstrations that rivaled the antiwar protests of the 1960s. It reemerged before the recent House vote to normalize trade with China. Critics charge that globalization only benefits corporations that relocate factories in countries with cheap labor and weak environmental laws, worsening working conditions abroad, polluting the environment and threatening American jobs. But proponents say that free trade is the key to improving living and working conditions in developing countries, creating high-paying jobs in the U.S. and protecting the global environment.

Oil Production in the 21st Century

Twenty-five years ago the Organization of Petroleum Exporting Countries struck at the heart of the American economy with an embargo on oil exports to the United States. The resulting rise in energy prices sparked a round of inflation and stagnant economic growth that lasted more than a decade. A quarter-century later, OPEC has once again driven up oil prices by curtailing output, but this time the cartel's stranglehold is much weaker than before. Non-OPEC producers supply much of the oil, and major new deposits in the Caspian Sea region promise to keep the oil spigot open for the foreseeable future. But the good times for consumers will not last forever. In a matter of time the world's oil will run out, and it's far from certain that there will be sufficient alternative energy sources.

International Monetary Fund

In 1997, an economic crisis started in Thailand and quickly spread to Asia and Russia. It soon threatened Brazil and the rest of Latin America. In trying to stabilize the global economy, the International Monetary Fund (IMF) prescribed some painful fiscal medicine. In exchange for the loans it provides to member countries to help them ward off financial crises, the agency required governments to adopt austerity measures, including spending cuts to reduce government deficits and debt and higher interest rates to shore up weak currencies. Many critics say the fund's "cure" has been worse than the disease, causing essentially healthy Asian economies to become weak. Some say the time has come for fundamental reform of the 53-year-old system of oversight provided by the IMF.

MANAGING THE U.S. ECONOMY

Budget Surplus

For the first time in more than 30 years, the U.S. government is taking in more money in taxes than it is spending on federal programs. The expectation that the federal surplus will continue to grow touched off a vigorous debate over how best to use the unanticipated windfall. The Bush administration is giving back part of the surplus to taxpayers in the form of a $1.6 trillion tax cut. Critics say the money should be used for a more modest tax cut, but only after the national debt is paid down and urgently needed social programs are funded. Beyond the political infighting over Bush's tax proposal, lawmakers are at odds over how best to protect the funds needed for Social Security and Medicare.

The Federal Reserve

Alan Greenspan, chairman of the Federal Reserve Board, has been called the most powerful man in America, after the president. As head of the nation's influential central bank, Greenspan and the Fed have played a key role in the nation's nearly 10-year record of uninterrupted economic growth. The Fed effectively sets the interest rates that banks charge for loans, which in turn affects the inflation rate. Defenders of the Fed argued that by acting aggressively to cool down America's booming economy, Greenspan has kept inflation in check and the expansion going. But critics say the rate hikes were an overreaction that unnecessarily dampened economic growth. Other analysts claimed that the Fed has too much power and that its deliberations should be more open to the public.

Deflation Fears

In 1998, just when Americans were ready to declare victory in the war against inflation, a new potential enemy appeared: deflation. Some economists, citing both long-term changes in the global economy and the economic crisis in Asia, warned that the U.S. faced a greater danger of uncontrollably falling prices than the threat of rising prices. Many economists dismissed such fears, and insisted that inflation remained the greater hazard. But jitters over the financial turmoil in Asia led theoreticians and policymakers to reexamine some basic assumptions about how the U.S. and global economies work. In particular, they wondered whether businesses and financial institutions were equipped to avert the problems that can arise from falling prices — including higher unemployment and bankruptcy.

INDUSTRY REGULATION

Energy Policy

Electricity blackouts in California, skyrocketing heating bills and high gasoline prices have raised concerns about energy supplies. The Bush administration says the nation faces an "energy crisis" and calls for boosting domestic supplies of oil, coal and natural gas and building new nuclear power plants. Critics say that focusing more on increasing supply than on reducing demand would only worsen pollution and threaten sensitive habitat while discouraging conservation and a greater reliance on environmentally benign, renewable energy sources, such as solar and wind. But supporters of the president's supply-side energy policy suggest that growth in energy demand is inevitable if Americans are going to maintain and improve their standard of living.

Airline Industry Problems

In the 20 years since Congress deregulated U.S. airlines, supersaver fares, frequent-flyer programs and price wars have changed the way millions of Americans travel. As airline traffic has skyrocketed, so have passenger complaints, airport congestion and allegations of anti-competitive behavior by major airlines. The public outcry grew so loud that Congress considered legislation to force airlines to provide better customer service. But after the companies promised to do better, lawmakers took no action. Meanwhile, because airport construction hasn't kept up with increases in air traffic, many fear air travel may be headed for gridlock as demand outpaces supply, and measures to increase airport competition and construction have met with congressional delays over how they should be funded.

Digital Commerce

Once known mainly for chat rooms, e-mail and pornography, the Internet has rapidly transformed into a powerful commercial selling tool. U.S. business transactions on the World Wide Web totaled $43 billion in 1998 and could rise to $1.3 trillion by 2003. Companies increasingly go online to order parts, schedule shipments and obtain business services. Consumers are clicking on Web sites that sell books, recordings and high-tech equipment. But all of the activity is posing difficult questions for regulators, who must set rules for the thriving marketplace. Among the chief issues are taxing sales in cyberspace, defining appropriate commercial speech used on Web sites and applying antitrust laws to an industry often likened to the Wild West.

MARKETS

Affordable Housing

The long U.S. economic expansion was a boon for housing. Prosperity drove the home-ownership rate to a record 67.7 percent, putting two-thirds of the country's households into their own homes. By all measures, Americans were better housed than at any time in the country's history. Yet, there's a black lining to this silver cloud: For millions of Americans — many of them middle-class families — it has been impossible to find decent, affordable shelter. The stock of existing low-cost housing is shrinking rapidly, while production of modestly priced housing is stalled. Meanwhile, wages at the bottom quarter of the earnings scale haven't kept pace with housing inflation. An economic slowdown isn't expected to drastically ease what some call an affordability crisis.

Auto Industry's Future

Depending on where you sit, the U.S. auto industry's gas tank is either half-full or half-empty. While 1999 sales totaled a record 17 million vehicles, market share has been steadily nibbled away by foreign automakers. Many industry-watchers argue that a fleet of jazzy new Japanese vehicles, especially in the all-important light-truck market, could further erode sales of American cars. But other analysts say the Big Three — GM, Ford and DaimlerChrysler — are answering the threat with their own forward-looking new products. Meanwhile, many analysts predict that the expense of competing in a global marketplace will force foreign and domestic car companies to merge into five or six megafirms. But others say that smaller companies that want to remain independent will thwart the trend toward consolidation.

The Economics of Recycling

In the late 1980s, acting on fears that landfill space was running out, communities across the country began curbside collection of paper, glass, metal and plastic waste. Polls suggest that Americans strongly support recycling, despite the fact that the United States remains the world's leading "throwaway society." But critics say recycling is often a wasted effort, helping consumers' consciences more than the environment or the economy. Markets for recycled materials are notoriously volatile, and it often costs more to recycle waste than it does to simply bury it in a landfill. Recycling supporters, however, say the benefits of recycling far outweigh its drawbacks and predict a strong market for recycled materials in the future.

Preface

How should the United States and the European Union resolve their trade disputes? What are the optimal solutions to ensure adequate energy supplies during a crisis? How can the United States best help its industries in the face of foreign competition? Tough questions like these confront economists and policy analysts every day—and often there are no easy answers. To encourage thoughtful deliberations, *Economic Issues* does not take sides or champion a particular perspective. Instead, by reading these balanced, informed accounts, students can thoroughly and fairly explore opposing sides of some of today's most complex and interesting economic debates. Applying economic principles to real-life problems, students will be challenged to form their own well-informed opinions on such topics as the costs and benefits of globalization, management of the budget surplus and market-based solutions to a variety of social problems.

This reader is a compilation of 14 recent articles from *The CQ Researcher,* a weekly policy brief that brings into focus the often complicated and controversial issues on the public agenda. Rather than being reductive, *The CQ Researcher* makes complex issues less intimidating by explaining difficult concepts in plain English. Offering in-depth, objective and forward-looking reporting on a specific topic, each selection chronicles and analyzes past actions and current debates while looking toward future developments. *Economic Issues* is designed to encourage discussion, to help readers think critically and actively about these vital issues and to facilitate future research. Adding color and depth, real-world examples give a flavor of the substantive detail in a variety of areas while showing how economic issues at all levels—from states to nations and the globe—will affect students' lives and futures.

This collection is organized into four subject areas that cover a wide range of important economic policy concerns. The pieces were chosen to expose students to a variety of subjects, from the personal effects on individuals of a housing shortage to the broader concerns of Federal Reserve operations and policies. We believe this volume will be an attractive supplement for courses in economic policy, political economy, and principles of economics.

The CQ Researcher

The CQ Researcher was founded in 1923 under a different moniker: *Editorial Research Reports.* ERR was sold primarily to newspapers, which used it as a research tool. The magazine was given its current name and a design overhaul in 1991. Today, *The CQ Researcher* is still sold to many newspapers, some of which reprint all or part of each issue. But the audience for the magazine has shifted significantly over the years, and today many libraries subscribe. Students, not journalists, are now the primary audience for *The CQ Researcher.*

People who write for the *Researcher* often compare the experience to that of drafting a college term paper. Indeed, there are many similarities. Each article is as long as many term papers—running about 11,000 words—and each is written by one person, without significant outside help.

Like students, staff writers begin the creative process by choosing a topic. Working with the publication's editors, the writer comes up with a subject that has public policy implications and for which there is at least some controversy. Once a topic is set, the writer embarks on a week or two of intensive research. Articles are clipped, books ordered and information gathered from many sources, including interest groups, universities and the government. Once a writer feels well informed about the subject, he or she begins a series of interviews with experts—academics, officials, lobbyists and people working in the field. Each piece usually requires a minimum of 10 to 15 interviews; some especially complicated subjects call for more. After much reading and interviewing, the writer begins to put the article together.

Chapter Format

Each issue of the *Researcher,* and therefore each selection in this book, is structured in the same way, beginning with an overview of the topic. This introduction touches briefly on the areas that will be explored in greater detail in the rest of the chapter.

Following the introduction is a section that chronicles the important debates in the field. This section is structured around a number of "Issue Questions," such as, "Are the IMF's tough lending policies helping financially strapped countries?" or "Do the environmental benefits of recycling outweigh the costs?" The questions are the core of each selection; they are often highly controversial and usually are the object of much argument among those who work and think in the field. Hence, the answers provided by the writer are never conclusive. Instead, each answer details the whole range of opinion within the field.

Following these questions and answers is the "Background" section, which provides a history of the issue being examined. This look back includes important legislation, executive actions and court decisions from the past. Readers will be able to see how current policy has evolved.

An examination of existing policy (under the heading "Current Situation") follows the background section. Each "Current Situation" provides an overview of important developments that were occurring when the article was published.

Each selection concludes with an "Outlook" section, which gives a sense of what might happen in the near future. This part looks at whether there are any new regulations afoot, anticipates court rulings and considers possible legislative initiatives.

All selections contain other regular features that augment the main text. Each selection includes two or three sidebars that examine issues related to the topic. An "At Issue" page provides opposing answers to a relevant question from two experts. Also included are a chronology that cites important dates and events, and an annotated bibliography that details some of the sources used by the author.

Acknowledgments

We wish to thank the many people who were helpful in making this collection a reality. First is Tom Colin, editor of *The CQ Researcher,* who gave us his enthusiastic support and cooperation as we developed this collection. He and his talented staff of writers have amassed a first-class library of *Researcher* articles, and we are privileged to have access to that rich cache. We also thankfully acknowledge the advice and feedback from the scholars who commented on our plans for the volume. In particular, we thank Richard Ballman at Augustana College, Robert Benedict at the University of Utah, Dan Cothran at Northern Arizona University and James Lindeen at the University of Toledo.

Some readers of this collection may be learning about *The CQ Researcher* for the first time. We expect that many readers will want regular access to this excellent weekly research tool. Anyone interested in subscription information or a no-obligation free trial of the *Researcher* can contact CQ Press at www.cqpress.com or at (800) 638-1710.

We hope that you are as pleased with *Economic Issues* as we are. We welcome your feedback and suggestions for future editions. Please direct comments to Charisse Kiino, in care of CQ Press, 1255 22nd Street, NW, Suite 400, Washington, D.C. 20037, or by email at ckiino@cqpress.com.

— *The Editors of CQ Press*

Contributors

Thomas J. Colin, managing editor, has been a magazine and newspaper journalist for more than 25 years. Before joining Congressional Quarterly in 1991, he was a reporter and editor at the *Miami Herald* and *National Geographic* and editor in chief of *Historic Preservation* magazine. He has degrees from the College of William and Mary (English) and the University of Missouri (journalism).

Adriel Bettelheim covers telecommunications, science and technology for the *CQ Weekly*. Previously, he was Washington correspondent for the *Denver Post* and a business reporter for the *Syracuse Herald-Journal*. He was a member of the *CQ Researcher* team that won the 1999 Society of Professional Journalists Award for Excellence for a 10-part series on health care. He is also the author of *Aging in America A to Z* (CQ Press, 2001). He graduated from Case Western Reserve University with a bachelor's in chemistry.

Christopher Conte, a former reporter and editor for the *Wall Street Journal,* is a freelance writer in Washington, D.C. He covers a wide range of issues as a staff correspondent for *Governing* magazine and also has written extensively about computer networking, transportation, banking and economic and social issues. He previously reported on tax and budget legislation for Congressional Quarterly and on state and local government for newspapers in Vermont. He holds a B.A. from Harvard University.

Mary H. Cooper specializes in environmental, energy and defense issues. Before joining the *CQ Researcher* as a staff writer in 1983, she was a reporter and Washington correspondent for the Rome daily newspaper *l'Unitá*. She is the author of *The Business of Drugs* (CQ Press, 1990). She also is a contract translator-interpreter for the U.S. State Department. Cooper graduated from Hollins College (English).

Kathy Koch specializes in education and social policy issues. She has freelanced in Asia and Africa for various U.S. newspapers, including the *Christian Science Monitor* and *USA Today*. She also covered environmental legislation for the *CQ Weekly* and reported for newspapers in South Florida. She graduated in journalism from the University of North Carolina at Chapel Hill.

David Masci specializes in social policy, religion and foreign affairs. Before joining the *CQ Researcher* as a staff writer in 1996, he was a reporter at CQ's *Daily Monitor* and the *CQ Weekly*. He holds a B.A. in medieval history from Syracuse University and a law degree from George Washington University.

Jane Tanner is a freelance writer in Charlotte, N.C., who writes for Congressional Quarterly, the *New York Times* and Ballard & Tighe Publishers. Her analysis of Florida's prepaid university-tuition program for *Florida Trend* magazine won a first-place feature award from the National Association of Area Business Publications. She is also the author of *A History of a U.S. Navy Aircraft Carrier* (1994). She holds a B.S. in social policy and an M.S. in journalism from Northwestern University.

1 Transatlantic Tensions

Mary H. Cooper

Chants of "Bush assassin!" reverberated in the streets of Madrid, Spain, last month, as thousands of demonstrators greeted President Bush on the first stop of his first official tour of Europe. The placards they waved listed a litany of complaints against U.S. policies, including Bush's call for a missile defense system, his rejection of a treaty to slow global warming and his support for the death penalty.

AP Photo/J. Scott Applewhite

Spain's King Juan Carlos welcomes U.S. National Security Adviser Condoleeza Rice to Zarzuela Palace near Madrid on June 12. Rice was accompanying President Bush on his first trip to Europe since taking office in January. Spain was the first stop on the five-day trip.

The same criticisms were voiced at almost every other stop on the president's five-day trip, both by crowds of young protesters and state officials.

It was hardly the first time Europeans have criticized American policies. Since the end of World War II, when the United States established a permanent presence on the continent as the leading military power in the North Atlantic Treaty Organization (NATO), the transatlantic relationship has been defined by an underlying tension that periodically erupts into anti-American protests. And although the immediate focus of that tension has changed over the years, the basic theme has remained the same — European indignation over what critics there see as American heavy-handedness.

This year the tension has intensified. Since taking over the White House in January, Bush has announced a series of policy changes on arms control, defense and the environment that have triggered European alarm bells. Many observers fear that the new Republican administration and its congressional allies plan to usher in a new era of unilateral policy-making aimed at advancing American interests, regardless of the impact on Europe.

"There is increasing talk in the leading circles in Europe of increased U.S. unilateralism," says Steven Everts, director of the transatlantic program at the Centre for European Reform, an independent think tank in London. "Even among people who would normally consider themselves very Atlanticist, and I put myself in that category, there's a degree of unease, skepticism and opposition about some of the decisions that Bush has taken."

On his European trip, Bush faced strong criticism of several recent policy announcements. In March, the president alarmed many in Europe — where environmental-activist Green parties enjoy growing political power — by reversing a campaign pledge to support mandatory limits on industrial emissions of carbon dioxide and other gases held responsible for global warming. [1] Alarm turned to outrage when Bush then openly renounced the Kyoto Protocol, which the United States and more than 150 other countries signed in 1997. The agreement, which would require the United States to reduce its carbon emissions by 7 percent below 1990 levels by 2012, has yet to be ratified by any major industrial country.

"I think the administration was absolutely right in publicly acknowledging that the United States was not going to meet the target established for it in Kyoto," says Paul R. Portney, president of Resources for the Future, a nonpartisan research organization in Washington, D.C. Indeed, Portney adds, some European countries are unlikely to meet their emissions targets either. "On the other hand, I think it was handled in a rather clumsy fashion."

Plans to develop a missile defense system to protect the United States from ballistic missile attack, expanded by former President Bill Clinton and accelerated by Bush, have also aroused strong opposition in Europe. Critics say such a system would violate the 1972 Anti-Ballistic Missile (ABM) Treaty and thus destabilize the arms-control regime that was carefully developed over the past half century. [2] They also see Bush's rejection of European misgivings about missile defense as yet another sign of American unilateralism, and even unreliability, as an alliance partner.

"On the nuclear front, the United States doesn't wish to be constrained by international law, and it is very clear about that," says Daniel T. Plesch, director of the London-based British American Security Information Council, which studies transatlantic security issues. "There has been a very clear policy drift over a 10-year period in this

From *The CQ Researcher*, July 13, 2001.

EU Invests Most in the United States

The more than half a trillion dollars invested in the United States in 1999 by the 15 members of the European Union was almost twice as much as that invested by all other regions.

Total Foreign Investment in U.S. in 1999
(in $billions)

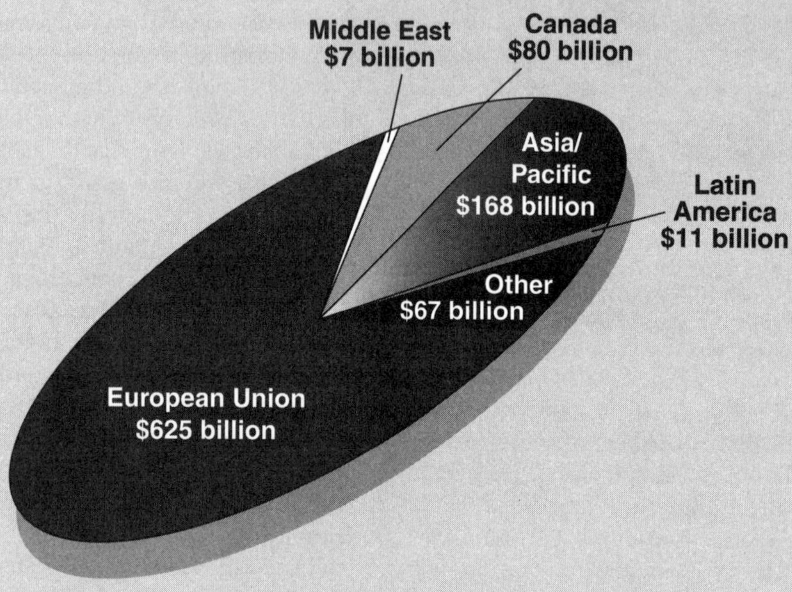

Source: U.S. Department of Commerce, Bureau of Economic Affairs, 1999.

direction, which is to dispense with the rule of law in this area. Of course, the rule of the jungle is suitable if you see yourself as the Lion King, but for the smaller beasts in the forest it's a very alarming prospect."

Similar concerns were voiced by Russian President Vladimir Putin during his first meeting with Bush, on June 16 at Brdo Castle outside Ljubljana, Slovenia. Although Putin's criticism of U.S. missile defense plans was far more muted than expected, the Russian president joined the European chorus when he warned that "unilateral actions" by the United States could worsen relations between the two former Cold War antagonists.

In response to the friction, European leaders who support close transatlantic relations have been trying to quell an anti-American backlash. "There's a tendency sometimes in some circles in Europe to revert to knee-jerk anti-American rhetoric," says Everts, who adds that intemperate remarks by U.S. conservatives merely add fuel to the fire. "I'm still hopeful that there are enough multilateralists or internationalists in Washington who can win the arguments against the neoconservative crowd that seems to have gained power in the Bush administration."

Bush adamantly rejected European charges of American unilateralism. "Unilateralists don't ask opinions of world leaders," he said at a June 13 news conference in Brussels, Belgium, after meeting with NATO leaders. "Sometimes we don't agree, and I readily concede that, but there's a lot more that we agree upon than we disagree about." [3]

The administration's official pronouncements on some of its more controversial policy shifts have softened somewhat since May 24, when Sen. James M. Jeffords of Vermont announced he was abandoning the Republican Party, shifting the majority of the Senate to the Democratic Party for the first time since 1995. No longer able to count on a solid Republican consensus in both houses of Congress, the administration now may have trouble gaining Senate support for parts of Bush's agenda that have aroused negative European public opinion.

Despite his weakened position vis-à-vis Congress, Bush remains steadfast on the main issues that lie behind transatlantic tensions today. For instance, after his stop at NATO headquarters in Brussels, he said, "I have made it clear to our friends and allies that I think it's necessary to set aside the ABM Treaty, but I will do so in close consultation with not only members of NATO and EU [European Union] countries that are not members of NATO, but as well with the Russians."

There are signs that the changing political environment in Washington and the fervent European criticism may have prompted a softening of Bush's stance on global warming. Shortly before leaving for Europe, he backed away from his earlier contention that the existence of global warming was unproven. But the president's shift fell far short of demands by critics at home and abroad who say the United States — which accounts for up to a quarter of the pollutants that cause global warming — must take the lead in curbing emissions.

Many European critics say the administration's stance on global

Europe Unites

*The European Union's expansion reflects its growing political and economic clout. Although the United States continues to deal with individual nations, it increasingly deals with the EU through its administrative headquarters in Brussels. Thirteen nations have applied for membership in the 15-member EU, including six that are currently negotiating terms for joining in the first round of expansion.**

** The six are Cyprus, Czech Republic, Estonia, Hungary, Poland and Slovenia*

Source: European Union

warming, like other sensitive issues, was unnecessarily inflammatory. "Kyoto shows the shortcomings of this administration as much as anything else," says Guillaume Parmentier, director of the French Center on the United States at the French Institute of International Relations in Paris. "Kyoto was not going to be ratified in 1,000 years anyway. Another administration would have hidden behind that fact, but this one decided to make it into a big issue. This put the administration on the spot, and they've had to moderate their language, from saying there was no global warming to saying they have to do something unilaterally. So they've changed tack, and that is the consequence of having adopted a rather unskillful strategy."

European criticism of American policies extends to domestic issues as well, especially the death penalty. Nations with the death penalty are barred from membership in the European Union, and the widespread use of capital punishment in the United States ranks high on the list of anti-American grievances. As a longstanding supporter of the death penalty during his tenure as governor of Texas, Bush was a lightning rod for anti-death penalty protests at each of his stops in Europe.

Over the coming months, as policy-makers in the White House and Congress reassess issues affecting U.S.-European relations, these are some of the questions they will ask:

Are the United States and Europe drifting apart?

During most of the Cold War — which dominated international affairs for the last half of the 20th century — Europe and the United States shared a common security interest that eclipsed lesser disputes and differences. As long as the allies feared a potentially deadly attack from the Soviet Union, issues such as military burden-sharing, arms control and U.S. economic dominance were sometimes hotly debated — but within the context of assumed mutual dependence.

Some observers say that shared interdependence evaporated when the Soviet Union collapsed in December 1991. As a result, they say, today's disputes are weakening the transatlantic bonds. "There's no single factor that is really driving the relationship apart, but there's a growing divergence of perspectives on a lot of different issues," says Ted Galen Carpenter, a foreign policy and defense expert at the conservative Cato Institute in Washington, D.C.

Besides the two main bones of contention — missile defense and global warming — Carpenter cites a virtual laundry list of issues on which U.S. positions are diametrically opposed to the views of many Europeans, including:

- When the Bush administration failed to follow up on Clinton's initiative to improve relations between North and South Korea, the 15-member EU stepped into the void with a delegation of its own. [4]
- Bush's early reluctance to pick up where Clinton left off in brokering Israeli-Palestinian peace negotiations was widely criticized in Europe, where sympathies often lie more closely with the Palestinian cause than with Israel.
- U.S. lack of support for multilateral organizations like the United Nations has roiled European public opinion and led in May to the United States being voted off the U.N. Human Rights Commission and the International Narcotics Control Board. [5]

Carpenter welcomes what he sees as a weakening of the transatlantic tie. "There are lots of little signs of the emergence of a true post-Cold War relationship between Europe and the United States, a relationship that maybe is a little bit more normal between two major centers of power," he says. "In the absence of a major threat to transatlantic interests, I don't think we need the kind of cohesion that we had during the Cold War era, when we did face a very dangerous mutual adversary."

Even the longstanding "special relationship" between the United States and Britain may be on the rocks. [6] Britain has long been ambivalent about its participation in the EU, and it is one of only three members that will not replace its currency with the euro, the union's common currency, next January. British leaders, notably Winston Churchill and Margaret Thatcher, have long emphasized a special Anglo-American bond resulting from a common language and cultural traditions. But the resounding election victory of Prime Minister Tony Blair and his Labor Party over the traditionally Euro-skeptical Conservatives on June 7 may reflect a weakening of British resistance to identifying more closely with the continent. Indeed, Blair has suggested that British adoption of the euro be put to a referendum.

"Britain is getting more and more involved with its continental neighbors," says Everts, of the Centre for European Reform, "and it seems to me that increasing numbers of people in both Washington and London are wondering whether the so-called special relationship will last." Everts contends that the importance of that relationship was always overstated. "I always thought it was more myth than reality. And, anyway, it was always used more by Brits than Americans because America quite frankly has special relationships with a host of countries," he says.

If a special Anglo-American relationship ever existed, Everts says, recent U.S. unilateral policy statements on issues like missile defense and global warming may have undermined it. "People here in the Foreign Office tell me that the game that British diplomacy has played for a long time of aligning itself very closely with America is becoming less attractive to Britain. They feel that the flip side of the coin — having influence in Washington — is becoming more and more difficult, as the way in which U.S. priorities are being shaped becomes less and less amenable to outside influence."

Everts hastens to add, however, that Blair is in no hurry to loosen the transatlantic bond. "People around Tony Blair are still very, very keen to maintain very close relations with Washington," he says, "and do not seem to be particularly worried by the counterclaim that so far, at least, there's little evidence that Britain has a lot of influence in Washington."

Some continental observers also contend that current tensions are hardly serious enough to suggest a permanent erosion of transatlantic ties. "If you put today's disputes into a historical context, we've had much worse difficulties," says Parmentier of the French Center on the United States. He says French President Charles de Gaulle's 1966 decision to pull out of NATO's military command and widespread criticism of the deployment of U.S. intermediate-range nuclear forces in Europe in the 1980s were far more serious rifts, which still failed to drive a lethal wedge between the United States and Europe.

Indeed, Parmentier suggests that the current round of transatlantic bickering may actually be a sign of even closer ties than ever before. "I think what we have at the moment is a crisis that comes out of proximity," he says. "We consider the other side's politics as being domestic politics. We know each other so well that we feel quite comfortable about criticizing each other in a rather hard way. There's no doubt that there are issues that we look upon rather differently, but that's always been true. What's obvious today is that many of these issues are domestic in nature rather than international."

Reuters/Win McNamee

President Bush meets with NATO Secretary-General George Robertson of Great Britain in the Oval Office in March 2001. Government leaders met in Brussels in June to discuss security issues, including the rapid-response force being organized to handle European regional emergencies.

Much of the tension in transatlantic relations may be simply the result of misunderstanding, just as in individual human relations. "Form is as important as substance," says Jacqueline Grapin, president of the European Institute, an independent European-American policy organization in Washington. "When the United States wants or doesn't want something, its leaders should make every effort to present what they want in such a way that is acceptable and not shocking for their partner. If they present it as a fait accompli or as a unilateral measure, it is bound to provoke reactions in public opinion."

After a negative perception has taken root, Grapin says, it is hard for European leaders to change it. "Once public opinion is unleashed in a negative way, European governments and the European Union have no other choice than just to respond to it." She cites the U.S. efforts to dispel European consumers' concerns about the potential health hazards posed by U.S. exports of foods containing genetically modified organisms (GMOs). "Those campaigns were much too strong, much too unilateral and did not take into account European culture. They were counterproductive, because now the European governments themselves are in a difficult position to disseminate information about the reality of the dangers and the non-dangers of certain GMOs."

Does Europe's new rapid-reaction force undermine U.S. military influence in Europe?

Security issues often dominated transatlantic disputes during the Cold War. From NATO's founding in 1949, the United States provided most of the funding, equipment and manpower dedicated to defending Europe and North America against a possible Soviet attack. As the main contributor to the common defense, the United States also assumed the dominant decision-making power in NATO.

Europe's Changing Political Structure

Even as rifts in transatlantic relations are developing over security, environmental and cultural issues, Europe itself is moving closer to the United States in its political organization.

The 15-member European Union (EU) is strengthening its role as a federal entity, assuming many of the powers recently reserved for its member states. Europeans already send their national representatives to the European Parliament and are subject to regulations promulgated by the European Commission, the EU's chief administrative body. Twelve EU countries soon will abandon their pounds, francs and lire in favor of a common currency, the euro.

Even the most prominent holdout on the euro, Britain, may be coming into line. The recent overwhelming re-election of Prime Minister Tony Blair and his Labor Party — defeating conservative anti-EU opponents — may mean that British resistance to identifying more closely with the continent is weakening. Blair has suggested that British adoption of the euro be put to a referendum, perhaps within the next two years.

Meanwhile, the EU is preparing to accept new members from Eastern Europe. At a three-day summit in Goteborg, Sweden, EU leaders agreed to a firm timetable for admitting the first wave of new candidates by the end of 2002. These are likely to include Hungary, the Czech Republic, Estonia, Slovenia and Poland, which are the closest to adopting the laws and achieving the economic stability required of membership. As many as a dozen countries may make the cut, if they meet the union's exacting standards in time.

Several obstacles still stand in the way of the EU's expansion, however. Some small countries fear that new members will tax the EU's budget and dilute their own clout within the organization. On June 7, for example, Irish voters rejected the Treaty of Nice, which opens the way for new countries to join. Major countries also argue over the terms of expansion. Germany, for example, is pushing for neighboring Poland to gain entry before the others.

As the European Union is expanding, NATO also is poised to admit new member states, including several former Soviet allies, under the transatlantic security umbrella.[1] The Czech Republic, Hungary and Poland joined NATO in 1999, while the 10 countries that are seeking admission as early as next year include Bulgaria and Romania. They also include the former Soviet republics of Estonia, Latvia and Lithuania.

Many observers say Europe's move toward a stronger, federated entity cannot help but affect the continent's relations with the United States.

"Europe is changing," says Steven Everts, director of the transatlantic program for the London-based Centre for European Reform. "It's not just an economic union or a trading bloc, but increasingly a political enterprise dealing with external challenges, enlargement and European defense."

[1] See Frank Bruni, "President Urges Expansion of NATO to Russia's Border," *The New York Times*, June 18, 2001.

But as European economies recovered from World War II and then boomed, and the United States began to suffer growing budget deficits, American critics began demanding that European governments shoulder a larger share of the alliance's financial burden. Charging that Europe was taking advantage of American largesse, critics agreed with then-Rep. Patricia Schroeder, D-Colo., and her often-repeated one-liner to Europe: "It's grow-up time."[7]

Burden-sharing remains a thorn in transatlantic relations. "To make sure that NATO remains vibrant and to make sure that the Europeans can adequately participate in their own European security defense initiative, they need to increase their investment in defense efforts," Secretary of State Colin L. Powell recently told the Senate Foreign Relations Committee.[8]

Today, however, the argument has shifted somewhat. Europe is ready to assume more of the burden of its own defense, and indeed is creating a rapid-reaction force made up exclusively of European troops that could be quickly deployed to continental trouble spots like the Balkans. Despite European leaders' insistence that the new European force poses no threat to NATO's current structure, American skeptics worry that the United States is losing its grip over European security.

"The European Union is in the process of creating a military force institutionally distinct from NATO," wrote former Secretary of State Henry Kissinger, warning that the force "could produce the worst of all worlds: disruption of NATO procedures and impairment of allied cooperation without enhanced allied military capability or meaningful European autonomy."[9]

Many Europeans say this attitude leaves them in a no-win position when they are faced, as they were in the Balkan wars, with U.S. reluctance to intervene militarily on the continent. "You can't at the same time say you might not intervene and then say in case you don't go no one else should," says Grapin, who points out the limited size and mandate of the rapid-reaction force. The proposed force would consist of only 60,000 soldiers, compared to NATO's more than 4 million troops, and would act only in Europe or in nearby areas. "Its purpose is conflict resolution and peacekeeping at the local or regional level," she says, with NATO retaining its role as defender of Europe and North America from outside attack. "The purpose is not at all to defend Europe as such. There is no possibility of doing that."

European critics also have little confidence in American commitment to resolving complex ethnic conflicts, citing the U.S. military strategy of bombing military targets from the air while resisting placing troops in the line of fire during NATO's 1999 intervention in Kosovo.

"The United States is frankly perceived to be cowardly," says Plesch, of the British American Security Information Council. "You're so worried about your own people that they have to sit in their barracks hiding, while these guerrilla wars break out all around them. The United States still is certainly regarded as the indispensable ally, but it is regarded as a highly unreliable one and one that needs to be talked to gently, as to a heavily armed, unreliable relative."

Some American observers see development of the European force as an indication that it's time for the United States to reduce its military role in Europe. "It's probably not reasonable to assume that two rather different regions can maintain that kind of solidarity indefinitely when there is no overarching adversary," says Carpenter, of the Cato Institute. "Sooner or later Europe is going to pursue uniquely European interests, and the United States — with its interests in various parts of the world — will not be obsessed with minor developments in Europe, such as the Balkans."

"It's probably not reasonable to assume that two rather different regions can maintain that kind of solidarity indefinitely when there is no overarching adversary. . . . Sooner or later Europe is going to pursue uniquely European interests, and the United States — with its interests in various parts of the world — will not be obsessed with minor developments in Europe, such as the Balkans."

— Ted Galen Carpenter, The Cato Institute

That view seemed to be confirmed by U.S. Defense Secretary Donald Rumsfeld when he said recently that he was "pushing" for withdrawing U.S. troops from NATO-led peacekeeping forces in Bosnia as soon as possible.[10] Some 750 troops were withdrawn earlier this year, reducing U.S. troops in Bosnia to about 3,300 out of the 22,000 NATO peacekeepers currently in the region.

However, the suggestion that the United States might pull its troops out of the Balkans set off vehement criticism in Europe, prompting Secretary of State Powell to reassure European peacekeeping allies. "Secretary Rumsfeld and I know that our presence is still required," he told reporters after a May meeting with NATO foreign ministers. "We went into this together; we'll come out together."[11]

The administration's Balkan policy is still unclear, indicating continued ambivalence toward the EU's emerging defense capability. The administration's Balkan policy is still unclear. The Serb-dominated government of Macedonia has been under attack since February from ethnic Albanian rebels. NATO Secretary-General George Robertson visited Washington in late June to urge U.S. participation in a new alliance brigade being drawn up to oversee the disarmament of the rebels if a peace agreement now in negotiation is reached. During his European tour, Bush said NATO leaders agreed on the need to "face down extremists in Macedonia and elsewhere who seek to use violence to redraw borders or subvert the democratic process." But the administration has not announced what role the United States will play in the NATO force.

There is little indication that tensions over burden-sharing and the U.S. military role in Europe will be resolved anytime soon. "We're happy with the United States being here, and we're happy with the United States calling the shots, as long as the United States is involved," says Parmentier, of the French Center on the United States. "On the other hand, we realize that the United States isn't going to be there every time, and what we don't want is for the U.S. to just lose interest or make proposals while not taking any responsibility on the spot."

Senate Democrats are pressuring the administration to commit troops to the new Macedonia brigade and to assume a leading political role in the crisis. "I remain unconvinced that the EU alone has the credibility or the resources needed to forge a political solution to Macedonia," said Foreign Relations Committee Chairman Joseph R. Biden Jr., D-Del. "It's clear to me that this country must increase its involvement. The stakes in Macedonia are simply too high for us to choose to play a secondary role." [12]

Can the world's two largest trading partners resolve their trade disputes?

Compared with some other facets of the transatlantic relationship, trade and financial ties between Europe and the United States are strong and growing stronger. (*See graph, p. 2.*) The United States and the EU are each other's largest single trading partner, accounting for a fifth of each other's trade in goods and a third of each other's trade in services. Europe annually accounts for more than $1 trillion in total bilateral investment and more than $500 billion in bilateral trade with the United States. [13]

"The transatlantic marketplace is rapidly integrating," says Willard M. Berry, president of the European-American Business Council, a Washington-based membership group comprised of American and European companies that support free trade and investment. He estimates that transatlantic investment has doubled in the past five years alone.

Almost half of all transatlantic trade takes place within companies — another sign of economic integration, he says. "A European company seeking a particular [U.S.] technology will either buy it or make it in a [subsidiary] plant in the United States," he says. "They don't bother to build it in Europe. The same thing goes with U.S. companies. The Italians may have a particular kind of technology in transportation, and the American company will just buy it there."

The bulk of transatlantic trade goes smoothly. "We are each other's most important trading partner and most reliable ally," says Grapin, of the European Institute. "So I think the trade disputes that everybody hears about are not really the most fundamental difficulties that we are going to experience."

She cites the quick resolution this spring of a nine-year trade dispute involving banana exports to Europe. The EU had imposed quotas on banana imports favoring Caribbean and African producers, to the detriment of Chiquita Brands International, an American company that exports bananas from Latin America. The United States subsequently retaliated with punitive tariffs against European luxury imports. EU Trade Commissioner Pascal Lamy and U.S. Trade Representative Robert B. Zoellick finally reached agreement on April 11, resulting in the lifting of some $200 million worth of U.S. sanctions against European exports.

"I think trade conflicts will be resolved because we have two very good negotiators right now," Grapin says. "They know each other well, they know the issues well and they know what they can and cannot do to satisfy their constituencies."

But several fundamental disputes threaten to undermine this increasingly vital relationship. C. Fred Bergsten, director of the Institute for International Economics and a former Treasury official, warns that U.S. retaliatory measures against European import restrictions and European threats to retaliate against U.S. export subsidies worth several billion dollars could lead to a deeper rift unless the Bush administration takes rapid action. "The United States and the European Union are on the brink of a major trade and economic conflict," he writes. [14]

Transatlantic mergers are another potential source of friction. Until recently, such activity was dominated by American firms, prompting fears of an American takeover of European businesses. But with the surge in bilateral investments, transatlantic mergers have boomed in recent years, and the latest buyouts have gone both ways. For instance, French media giant Vivendi Universal SA purchased U.S. publisher Houghton-Mifflin Co., and Deutsche Telekom AG of Germany bought out VoiceStream Wireless Corp., a U.S. mobile telephone company.

Sometimes transatlantic mergers founder over differences in European and American management styles, which reportedly was why negotiators recently dropped a planned transatlantic merger of telecommunications equipment manufacturers Alcatel of France and Lucent, its American counterpart. [15]

But serious differences in merger policy appear to be an emerging source of friction. These differences recently came to light with General Electric Co.'s proposed acquisition of Honeywell International, another American industrial giant. U.S. regulators approved the $45 billion deal, but EU regulators rejected it on July 3 out of concern that the combined business would have too much power in the market for jet engines and other aviation products.

Some experts suggest that U.S.-European relations would benefit if a new institution were created to deal strictly with economic issues like international mergers. "The transatlantic relationship is far too heavily biased toward the security dimension, which really has become a minor part of the relationship," says Parmentier. He proposes establishing a new "Euro-Atlantic political and economic forum," dedicated to trade and other non-security matters. [16] The

Chronology

1940s-1960s

After World War II, the United States and Western Europe cement trade and defense ties.

June 5, 1947
The United States offers massive economic assistance to help rebuild Europe from the ravages of World War II. Over the next three years, the United States disburses some $12.5 billion in aid under the Marshall Plan.

April 4, 1949
In response to Soviet expansion in Eastern Europe, the United States, Canada and their Western European allies form the North Atlantic Treaty Organization — NATO — as a defensive alliance in which each member promises to consider an attack on any other member as an attack on its own territory.

1957
Six European countries — France, Germany, Belgium, the Netherlands, Luxembourg and Italy — sign the Treaties of Rome establishing the European Economic Community — known as the Common Market or the EEC — which lifts trade barriers and lays the groundwork for subsequent European integration.

1966
French President Charles de Gaulle pulls his country out of NATO's military command.

1970s-1980s

Transatlantic relations are strained as a peace movement in Europe opposes the U.S.-Soviet nuclear arms buildup.

1972
The United States and the Soviet Union sign the Anti-Ballistic Missile (ABM) Treaty, agreeing to refrain from building defenses against incoming missiles and thereby removing a key incentive to developing more weapons of mass destruction.

1990s-2000s

The end of the Cold War alters the nature of transatlantic relations.

1991
EEC leaders draw up plans to create a single currency, the euro. In December, the Soviet Union collapses, bringing the Cold War to an end after almost a half-century.

January 1992
Bolstered by new political institutions and new members, the EEC establishes a "single market," eliminating internal border checks on the flow of people, goods, services and capital.

1993
The EEC becomes known as the European Union (EU) under a treaty ratified on Nov. 1.

Dec. 11, 1997
More than 150 countries meeting in Kyoto, Japan, agree to curb or reduce their emissions of carbon dioxide and other gases blamed for global warming. As the world's largest producer of such gases, the United States agrees to cut its emissions by 7 percent below 1990 levels by 2012.

1998
The EU begins negotiations with 13 countries that want to join the union, mostly former Soviet allies in Eastern Europe.

Jan. 1, 1999
Eleven EU members introduce the euro, using both it and their national currencies, such as the French franc and German mark, for most transactions.

December 1999
Meeting in Helsinki, Finland, the European Council decides to field by 2003 a 60,000-man rapid-reaction force to carry out humanitarian and rescue tasks, peacekeeping and crisis management on the European continent. The council describes the new force as "separable but not separate" from NATO and restates the EU's commitment to NATO's collective defense.

March 13, 2001
Bush reveals that he will not seek reductions in U.S. carbon dioxide emissions, reversing himself on a campaign pledge and throwing European leaders into turmoil over the future of the Kyoto treaty to reduce global warming.

June 5, 2001
Bush seeks protection for the beleaguered U.S. steel industry by invoking Section 201 of the 1974 Trade Act, one of several trade actions denounced by European critics as protectionist.

June 12-16, 2001
Bush tours five European capitals on his first official visit to the continent.

Jan. 1, 2002
Twelve European currencies are to be phased out until they are replaced entirely by the euro on July 1, 2002.

Outrage Over the Death Penalty

When Timothy J. McVeigh was executed on June 12, few tears were shed in the United States. The infamous Oklahoma City bomber had been condemned for setting off a truck bomb near the federal building in 1995, killing 168 adults and children. McVeigh had freely acknowledged his guilt and expressed no remorse for his action, and only a few death-penalty opponents protested his execution.

But in Europe McVeigh was widely seen as yet another victim of America's barbarous death penalty. The Council of Europe called his execution "sad, pathetic and wrong." [1] And in the latest of a string of demonstrations denouncing capital punishment, on June 23 thousands of protesters marched through Strasbourg, France, behind a black banner that read "Together Against the Death Penalty." [2]

Europeans tend to oppose all capital punishment as a morally unjustifiable taking of another human's life, even in cases where there is no doubt that the accused is guilty of committing a heinous crime. Opposition often turns to outrage in cases where the condemned is a youthful offender or mentally retarded — or is later found to be innocent.

The death penalty is only one of several transatlantic disputes that have erupted in recent years over a broad range of cultural and moral issues. Europeans, for example, strongly object to eating hormone-treated beef and view genetically modified fruits and vegetables as potentially dangerous to their health. The European Union set off a round of trade disputes in recent years when it tried to block imports of what European environmentalists call "Frankenfoods" from the United States.

Europeans also strongly support their public-health systems and cradle-to-grave welfare benefits; many Americans are suspicious of what they see as "socialized medicine," and U.S. lawmakers drastically slashed government welfare programs during the 1990s. America's gun violence, shockingly depicted by Hollywood, consumption of fast food and seeming oblivion to events and concerns beyond U.S. borders round out the European perception that America is a self-absorbed superpower run amok.

But no issue exemplifies the differences in the worldviews of Americans and Europeans as clearly as the death penalty. While the U.S. Supreme Court lifted its ban on executions in 1976, the European Union requires members to ban the practice. U.S. policy over capital punishment was a constant headache for former U.S. Ambassador to Paris Felix G. Rohatyn. "During my nearly four years in France, no single issue evoked as much passion and as much protest as executions in the United States," he recently wrote. [3]

Some observers view the death penalty debate as a symptom of divergent political trends on the two sides of the Atlantic. "As a whole, America is much more conservative than Europe," says Jacqueline Grapin, president of the European Institute, an independent European-American policy organization in Washington, D.C. "Even the American Democrats are to the right of some of the European centrists in many ways."

> **"As a whole, America is much more conservative than Europe. . . . Even the American Democrats are to the right of some of the European centrists in many ways."**
>
> ***—Jacqueline Grapin, President of the European Institute***

Grapin hastens to add that Europeans often see the worst side of American culture. "They have a perception which is much worse than what the United States really is," she says. "Usually when Europeans come here they are nicely surprised. After all, Europeans like to come here. Many of them send their children here for education, and on an individual basis people like the U.S. very much. But there is a cultural difference, and many Europeans have this perception that the United States has a different value system."

To bridge that gap, Rohatyn calls for a broad, new transatlantic dialogue. "The death penalty, guns, violence in society — these cast a large cloud on America's moral leadership," he wrote. "At a time when our military, economic and political power, our so-called 'hegemony,' is a source of concern to many of our allies, it is important that our moral leadership be sustained."

[1] See Suzanne Daley, "Almost as One, Europe Condemns Execution," *The New York Times*, June 12, 2001.

[2] See Estelle Shirbon, "Thousands March in Silent Death Penalty Protest," Reuters English News Service, June 23, 2001.

[3] Felix G. Rohatyn, "America's Deadly Image," *The New York Times*, Feb. 20, 2001.

absence of such an informal forum, Parmentier says, "makes the United States more likely to see all transatlantic issues through the prism of security, which I think is very detrimental to the relationship in general.

"That's because NATO is the only place where the United States can be certain to be heard, and of course NATO's concern is security," he says. ■

BACKGROUND

Postwar Institutions

Transatlantic relations over the past 50 years developed within an institutional framework that took shape in the aftermath of World War II. Europe lay in ruins, its economies destroyed, many of its government institutions shattered. In this power vacuum, the Soviet Union and the United States, wartime allies in the fight against Nazism, saw an opportunity to help shape the course of Europe's reconstruction according to their own highly divergent models — American democratic capitalism or Soviet authoritarian communism.

The Soviet Union, whose economy was also in ruins, took advantage of its geographic proximity and military strength to ensure the rise of compatible communist regimes in Central Europe, which eventually became part of a larger Soviet bloc that included Poland, Czechoslovakia, Hungary, Bulgaria, Romania and the Baltic republics of Latvia, Lithuania and Estonia. The bloc also included East Germany, the eastern third of the defeated enemy, occupied by Soviet forces at the end of the war.

Lacking the Soviets' geographic advantage but spared the physical devastation of the conflict, the United States brought its overwhelming economic advantage to bear in the emerging contest for Europe that would be known as the Cold War. On June 5, 1947, the United States announced its answer to Soviet expansion — the Marshall Plan.

"Europe's requirements for food and other essential products — principally from America — are so much greater than her present ability to pay that she must have substantial additional help, or face economic, social and political deterioration of a very grave character," said Secretary of State George C. Marshall as he announced the plan in a now-famous Harvard University commencement address. "The remedy lies in breaking the vicious circle and restoring the confidence of the European people in the economic future of their own countries and of Europe as a whole." [17]

At home, the Marshall Plan initially revived an enduring debate between two opposing views on U.S.-European relations. Isolationists, led by Sen. Robert Taft, R-Ohio, argued against the plan as an example of "foreign entanglements" that waste money and could drag the country into another war; internationalists, such as Sen. Arthur Vandenberg, R-Mich., said positive engagement in world affairs was necessary to enhance U.S. security.

Eventually, fear of communism helped the internationalists win out, and on April 2, 1948, Congress passed the European Recovery Act authorizing the Marshall Plan. President Harry S Truman signed the measure into law the very next day.

Over the next three years, the United States provided about $12.5 billion in aid to Europe, much of it in the form of agricultural exports and capital goods needed to rebuild the continent's transportation systems and factories. The plan was a resounding success: By 1952, Western Europe's economic output had increased by a third and its farm output and industrial production were 11 and 40 percent higher, respectively, than before the outbreak of the war.

The Marshall Plan proved equally helpful to the United States. "The Marshal Plan was a limited investment that paid incalculable dividends," wrote Diane B. Kunz, a Yale University associate professor of history. "A situation favorable to American interests was established in Europe. The aid program raised Western Europe from its knees, launched the American challenge to the Soviet Union and bolstered the American economy." [18]

Soviet actions helped garner support for a new U.S.-European security system for Western Europe as well, especially after June 1948, when Soviet forces denied ground access to Berlin, located within their occupation zone. The Berlin blockade sped creation of NATO on April 4, 1949. Within a month, Germany had been divided into Soviet-allied East Germany and West Germany, comprising the areas occupied by Britain, France and the United States. Eastern and Western Europe were also divided by a heavily fortified border, famously described by Winston Churchill as the "iron curtain."

European Integration

As the United States and Western Europe were consolidating transatlantic commercial and security relations, European countries were integrating economically in order to reduce the likelihood of future bloodshed. Championed by French statesman Jean Monnet, European integration initially took the form of a six-member agreement to control the production of coal and steel, the

European Investments Produce U.S. Jobs

The influence of European investments on the U.S. economy is reflected in the 10 states that received the most investments in 1998. The $280 billion invested in those states helped create nearly 2 million jobs.

EU's Favorite States	Jobs Created
California	292,000
New York	246,900
Texas	235,300
North Carolina	182,000
Pennsylvania	173,300
Florida	171,100
Illinois	169,300
New Jersey	164,400
Michigan	163,300
Ohio	154,200

Note: The investments were from the 15 members of the European Union plus Iceland, Liechtenstein, Norway and Switzerland.

Source: European-American Business Council.

essential ingredients of weapons manufacture. In 1952 the European Coal and Steel Community was established under the leadership of French Foreign Minister Robert Schuman and Konrad Adenauer, chancellor of the newly created Federal Republic of Germany. In addition to France and Germany, Belgium, the Netherlands, Luxembourg and Italy were also members.

In 1957 the same six countries signed the Treaties of Rome establishing the European Economic Community (EEC), or Common Market, which lifted trade barriers between member countries. In 1973, Britain, Ireland and Denmark joined the community, followed by Greece in 1981 and Portugal and Spain in 1986.

Today the community, which became known as the European Union under a treaty ratified on Nov. 1, 1993, includes 15 member nations, comprising about 370 million people.

Over the years the EEC gradually increased transborder cooperation and integration by adopting a common agricultural policy, creating a monetary system to stabilize exchange rates and establishing common political institutions. Based primarily in Brussels, these include the directly elected European Parliament, the European Council — which brings together the 15 heads of state or government — and the European Commission, the organization's chief administrative body.

In 1991, EEC leaders drew up plans for creating a single currency, the euro. [19] To be eligible to adopt the euro, member countries had to have stable currencies and achieve limited budget deficits, national debt, inflation and interest rates. In January 1992, the community reached a milestone when it established a "single market," eliminating internal border checks on the flow of people, goods, services and capital. Britain, long the most vocal skeptic of European integration, opted out of the treaty creating the euro and was joined later by Denmark and Sweden.

Europe met its Jan. 1, 1999, target for establishing the euro as the official currency for the 12 countries that agreed to adopt it. Introduced with great fanfare, the euro was initially valued at $1.17 on the U.S. dollar, but its value has since slid to about 85 cents. As the new currency was introduced, member countries were permitted to use both it and their national currencies — such as the French franc and German mark — for most transactions. Beginning next Jan. 1, however, national currencies will be phased out until they are replaced entirely by the euro by next July 1.

Since the end of the Cold War and the adoption of democratic institutions in Eastern European countries formerly allied with the Soviet Union, the EU has adopted modified requirements for new members. Because most applicants have less-developed economies and political institutions, the EU established a set of criteria each applicant must satisfy to gain entry, including: stable institutions guaranteeing democracy, the rule of law and human rights; a functioning market economy; and the ability to take on the obligations of membership, including acceptance of the EU's ongoing unification process.

In 1998, negotiations commenced with six countries considered most likely to meet these criteria first — Cyprus, the Czech Republic, Estonia, Hungary, Poland and Slovenia. A second wave — Bulgaria, Latvia, Lithuania, Romania and Slovakia — was expected to follow. Meanwhile, all candidate countries were included in EU deliberations on the enlargement effort.

Rapid-Reaction Force

The end of the Cold War also prompted the EU to re-examine its defense needs, resulting in plans to develop an exclusively European military force to deal with changing security conditions on the continent. Those plans took on more urgency after the eruption of bloody ethnic wars in the Balkans and the posting in 1995 of 60,000 NATO peacekeeping troops to Bosnia. The deployment prompted a heated debate over the use of alliance forces outside of NATO territory and for purposes that differed from their original defensive role.

Meeting in Helsinki, Finland, in December 1999, the European Council committed to fielding by 2003 a 60,000-man rapid-reaction force capable of carrying out humanitarian and rescue tasks, peacekeeping and crisis management on the European continent. The council was careful to describe the new European force as "separable but not separate" from NATO, and it restated the EU's commitment to collective defense within the NATO alliance.

That commitment was reiterated last December at an EU-U.S. summit in Washington, where then-President Clinton and his European counterparts formulated a "New Transatlantic Agenda." The agenda reaffirmed the "indivisibility" of transatlantic security and of NATO as "the centerpiece of transatlantic security, providing the indispensable link between North America and Europe." For its part, the United States welcomed Europe's new defense initiative, saying it would "strengthen both the EU and the European pillar of the Atlantic alliance. The U.S. looks forward to working with the European Union playing its full role and assuming its full responsibilities on the international scene." [20] ■

CURRENT SITUATION

Missile Defense

Throughout last year's election campaign and during his first months in office, President Bush voiced strong support for the National Missile Defense (NMD) program, a Pentagon effort to develop and deploy a system of ground-, sea- and space-launched missiles capable of destroying incoming ballistic missiles before they can reach the United States. Even though the administration has suggested extending the protective missile defense umbrella over the territory of its allies, the proposal has aroused criticism across the political spectrum in Europe, where it is seen as a major threat to global stability because it would violate the Anti-Ballistic Missile (ABM) treaty signed in 1972 by the United States and the Soviet Union.

Europeans, as well as the Russian government, consider the ABM Treaty the cornerstone of global stability because it removes a major incentive for countries to build more ballistic missiles. Scrapping the treaty, they say, would encourage not only Russia but also China, North Korea and other countries with nuclear weapons to develop more weapons to overcome the new defensive shield.

"The main concern the Europeans have is the reaction of Russia and the potentially destabilizing effect that this project could have on the strategic balance," says Grapin of the European Institute. "What they don't want to see is the strategic balance being destroyed for a project which from their perspective is not absolutely indispensable at this time. There is also a tendency to think that there are many other threats that are really serious but which are not conveyed by missiles, such as terrorism, biotech weapons and the suitcase bomb, which is as dangerous as the missile bomb and is much easier to bring to New York."

Bush acknowledges that the NMD would violate the ABM Treaty, which he dismisses as an anachronism. "The ABM Treaty is a relic of the past," Bush said on June 12 in Madrid, the first stop on his tour. "It prevents freedom-loving people from exploring the future. And that's why we've got to lay it aside." [21] In its place, Bush advocates "missile defense as part of a new strategic framework to address the changing threats of our world." [22]

Although several NATO members — Italy, Spain, Hungary and Poland — support the NMD, most see the administration's push for missile defense in the face of widespread European opposition as yet another example of American unilateralism.

Others are more blunt. "The administration's approach to nuclear policy is not really as unilateralists," says Plesch of the British American Security Information Council. "Unilateralism implies acting in one's own interest, which we all do." Rather, this administration wishes to act aside from the law, he says, "And according to my dictionary that makes them nuclear anarchists. The fundamental tenets of transatlantic nuclear policy are quite deliberately being set aside by this administration."

Bush came under little public criticism over the issue from Western European leaders — and even from Russia's Putin, one of the most outspoken opponents of the project, whom he met in Slovenia on the last day of his five-day tour. [23]

Plesch attributes the muted official statements on missile defense to domestic European politics rather than any implicit softening of opposition. "Officials in the chancelleries of Europe are loath to talk about it explicitly for fear of inciting an even stronger reaction and for fear of inciting Green-left opinion, which is the last thing they want," he says.

Plesch says the new mission for NATO could be the containment of this unilateralist, anarchist strain of American policy. "The alliance is a multilateral framework that the United States does not wish to dispense with, and therefore it becomes a vehicle to keep the United States amongst the majority of civilized nations," he says.

"We do not know how much effect natural fluctuations in climate may have had on warming. . . . We do not know how fast change will occur, or even how some of our actions could impact it. . . . And finally, no one can say with any certainty what constitutes a dangerous level of warming and therefore what level must be avoided."

— President George W. Bush

Bush's Reversal

The Bush administration's unilateral withdrawal from the Kyoto Protocol, signed in 1997 after five years of multilateral negotiations, is the other major source of friction between the United States and Europe. No industrial power in Europe or elsewhere has ratified the treaty, which sets mandated targets for reducing emissions of carbon dioxide and other so-called greenhouse gases responsible for global warming.

After rejecting the treaty and backing away from his campaign promise to support mandatory limits on industrial carbon emissions, Bush further undercut greenhouse-gas reduction efforts on May 17, when he released his new energy plan. It calls for producing more coal, oil and natural gas — the fossil fuels that are the primary source of carbon emissions — while reducing research and development spending for cleaner renewable-energy sources. [24]

The day before he left for Europe, Bush threw down the gauntlet on global warming. "We do not know how much effect natural fluctuations in climate may have had on warming," he said. "We do not know how fast change will occur, or even how some of our actions could impact it. . . . And finally, no one can say with any certainty what constitutes a dangerous level of warming and therefore what level must be avoided." [25] He proposed instead spending millions of dollars in further research on the causes of climate change and new technologies to combat it.

Bush's European counterparts quickly dismissed his proposals and repeated their criticism of his rejection of Kyoto. "We simply agree to disagree," said Swedish Prime Minister Goran Persson after meeting with Bush. "We think Bush has chosen the wrong policies. European Union governments intend to ratify the treaty, and we will try to persuade the rest of the world to follow our example, and not that of the United States." [26]

Bush says the treaty's targets and timetables unfairly disadvantage the United States and pose a threat to the U.S. economy. However, some American critics of Kyoto who agree with some of Bush's points say the administration was wrong to pull out of the Kyoto negotiations.

"If they had only waited a bit," says Portney of Resources for the Future. "They could have said the United States was willing to talk turkey on climate change, maybe even under the rubric of Kyoto, so long as everyone realized those targets and timetables had to go. I wish they had been a little bit more sophisticated about the way they announced what I think many of us knew was the case anyway."

Some American observers suggest that Bush inadvertently played into Europe's hands on global warming, because many European leaders share Bush's view of the Kyoto timetables.

"From the Europeans' standpoint, the ideal outcome was for the Kyoto treaty to collapse, but for Washington to take the blame," wrote Gregg Easterbrook, an environmental expert at the Brookings Institution, a Washington think tank. "Now Europe gets to act outraged while being spared the hard work and cost of actual reform." [27]

At Issue:

Does European defense policy undermine U.S. authority in NATO?

yes

JOHN REDWOOD
CONSERVATIVE MEMBER, BRITISH HOUSE OF COMMONS

FROM A LECTURE AT THE HERITAGE FOUNDATION IN WASHINGTON, D.C., MAY 2, 2001.

The European rapid-reaction force is a European army in the making, and . . . it could become a potential thorn in the side of the NATO alliance.

We British Conservatives can assure you that we believe NATO should be the cornerstone of our defense. We are very grateful for the enormous role the United States has played post-1945 in the defense of the West. It wouldn't have been possible without you. We freely acknowledge that. We see no need to disrupt arrangements that have worked extremely well for more than 50 years.

Our worries come from the detail in the annexes and the presidency report, which form a proper part of the Treaty of Nice. If you read that detailed work . . . you will see that the so-called European rapid-reaction force will have access to 250,000 troops which are currently available for NATO from the European forces.

It will have proportionate backup from European navies and European air forces. It wishes to be able to deploy 60,000 of those troops at any given time a considerable distance from base and will need to strengthen logistics and "deployability," as they call it, in order to do so.

It will have a separate military committee supervising it. It will have a separate political committee supervising it. It is very clear from all of the paperwork so far that the design is that it will be under European control, not under joint European and other NATO-partner control.

There is one genuflection in the treaty to NATO, saying that of course they don't want any of this to disrupt NATO. Everything else written into the treaty is setting up a rival center of power, a rival center of command.

If only I could tell you that all the troops they want for the European force are going to be additional so that I could say at least Europe has now accepted that it needs to make a bigger contribution to the defense of Western Europe, but that is not true. The intention seems to be to call on troops and other forces currently available only for NATO or domestic purposes. . . .

We [Conservatives] cannot live with a European army that is any kind of threat to the NATO alliance. We think there needs to be substantial changes in the way that particular animal is developing.

no

JACQUES DELORS
FORMER PRESIDENT, EUROPEAN COMMISSION

FROM AN ADDRESS DURING A SPEAKING TOUR IN THE UNITED STATES, MARCH 26-APRIL 4, 2001.

I would like to tackle a subject that is currently testing our relationship. This is the European Union's creation of a rapid-reaction force able to fulfill the tasks set out in the European treaties: preventing conflicts, restoring peace, protecting humanitarian action, etc.

The United States has raised concerns that the force will result in disengagement from NATO, duplication of effort and discrimination.

There is no disengagement from the Atlantic Alliance. It could easily be argued that by increasing the resources devoted to defense, the European Union is helping strengthen NATO.

There is no duplication of effort. In seeking to fill the gap that exists in some operational areas, the Europeans are responding to a constant demand from their American partner. Some of these resources — such as intelligence, communications, transport and air cover — are essential for the successful implementation of a military operation.

There is no discrimination. That is a claim made mainly by the European countries that do not belong to the EU. On this point, there should be no ambiguity. The decision to intervene is the responsibility of the European Union. If the countries concerned want to be involved, that is their right, and it is a possibility that is open to them.

In other words, the aim is not to build another military organization alongside NATO. It is, very simply and after consultation within NATO, to make it possible for the European Union to conduct an operation in which its allies, first and foremost the United States, do not intend to participate, while agreeing to it in principle.

On this basis, a consensus has emerged between the United States and the European Union. It is undoubtedly fragile and will be tested by the first crisis requiring intervention either by NATO or by the European rapid-reaction force. Yet I am so convinced of the robustness of the Atlantic Alliance that I do not believe that such a situation could damage transatlantic relationships.

The Europeans have up to now demonstrated both pragmatism and loyalty toward NATO. When, however, I recall the critical observations made by American leaders in 1991 on "the Europeans' inability to cope with the Yugoslav drama," I cannot help but welcome this initiative and the promise it brings of a more tight-knit and responsible European Union.

But the European Institute's Grapin says that assessment is too harsh and predicts that Europe will continue to press for the treaty's ratification, with or without U.S. support. "The Europeans have a real problem with pollution and environmental policies," she says. "They do want to put Kyoto together. They have no choice because they have such a high population density that the environment has become a prime political issue. So the leadership knows that global warming is not an issue that they can just forget about."

Trade Tensions

Though trade issues did not figure prominently in Bush's discussions with European leaders, several simmering disputes threaten to exacerbate transatlantic tensions. A U.S. law granting a $4 billion tax break to domestic exporters tops the list. The EU complained that the law — which grants exporters tax-free profits from goods sold through offshore companies known as foreign sales corporations — amounted to an illegal export subsidy because it provided an unfair competitive advantage to U.S. exporters. A World Trade Organization (WTO) dispute panel agreed, prompting Congress last year to reduce the tax break. But the EU complained that the new version failed to resolve the disparity. Once again, the WTO panel agreed, enabling the EU to impose up to $4 billion in punitive duties on U.S. imports. [28]

Even if the EU decides to take full advantage of the sanction authority, $4 billion is not enough to seriously disrupt U.S. exports to Europe, which totaled more than $150 billion last year. But the penalty far exceeds previous WTO-sanctioned punitive duties that the United States slapped on European cheese, handbags and other luxury items during a recently settled dispute over bananas and another quarrel over a European ban on imports of U.S. hormone-treated beef, which many Europeans deem a health threat.

Some experts, noting the close working relationship between U.S. Trade Representative Zoellick and EC trade negotiator Lamy, downplay the foreign sales corporation dispute. "There is enough goodwill and friendship on both sides that they will be able to resolve these matters," says Grapin, who suggests that the sanctions at both sides' disposal in trade disputes exist as a form of reciprocal deterrence. "Nobody really wants to use it, but it is there in case the other does something that is not good."

> **"From the Europeans' standpoint, the ideal outcome was for the Kyoto treaty to collapse, but for Washington to take the blame."**
>
> ***— Gregg Easterbrook, Visiting Fellow, Brookings Institution***

But others are not so sure there is enough goodwill to dispel the dispute that easily. "The European position has been that the United States should comply with the WTO, and I think for a lot of people in Europe that means the foreign sales corporation program should be terminated," says Berry of the European-American Business Council. "But a lot of the beneficiaries of the program like it. And, of course, if the tax break amounts to a huge amount of money, it's also hard to terminate it and not have your books show a substantial loss. It would be hard for Congress to just cut those companies loose and have them swallow their losses."

The WTO ruling comes as U.S.-EU trade relations already are being strained by a recent Bush administration action on steel imports. On June 5 the administration sought protection for the beleaguered U.S. steel industry by invoking Section 201 of the 1974 Trade Act. It authorizes the government to limit foreign imports while investigators determine whether the imports are being "dumped" on the U.S. market at artificially low prices, to the detriment of domestic producers.

"The U.S. steel industry has been affected by a 50-year legacy of foreign governments' intervention in the market and direct financial support of their steel industries," Bush said as he announced the move. "The result has been significant excess capacity, inefficient production and a glut of steel on world markets." [29]

Bush reportedly took the action to curry favor and support among the steel industry and its unions in his effort to gain congressional approval of so-called fast-track trade authority. It would enable the president to insulate trade agreements from potentially "killer" amendments as they pass through the legislative process. [30] But European steelmakers cried foul, charging that their American counterparts should be forced to undergo the same painful restructuring that they themselves had to endure in a recent wave of European industry privatizations.

As if transatlantic trade tensions were not already high enough, a rift over merger policy poses another threat to U.S.-European ties. The past decade has seen a steady increase in corporate mergers as one facet of a rise in corporate investments on both sides of the Atlantic. Most gained rapid approval by regulators — the Federal Trade Commission and the antitrust division at the U.S. Justice Department and their counterparts at the European Commission.

But General Electric's recent bid to buy Honeywell International has run into a potentially insurmountable obstacle. Although U.S. regulators approved the $45 billion deal, their EU counterparts rejected it on July 3, saying the combined companies — both American — would put European producers at an impossible disadvantage. The EU's unprecedented move could only deepen transatlantic friction.

During an earlier trip to Paris, Commerce Secretary Donald L. Evans had made a public plea to European regulators to OK the deal. "I would like to encourage them to think seriously about how constructive a merger like this could be," he said.

But his statement only made matters worse. "I deplore attempts to misinform the public and to trigger political intervention," said Mario Monti, the EU's commissioner for competition affairs. "This is entirely out of place in an antitrust case and has had no impact on the commission whatsoever. This is a matter of law and economics, not politics." [31]

The official rhetoric over the issue became even more heated after the commission formally rejected the merger, an action that U.S. Treasury Secretary Paul O'Neill denounced as "off the wall." [32] ■

OUTLOOK

Power Shift

Sen. Jeffords' decision to leave the Republican Party and vote with the Democratic Caucus may alter the Bush administration's policies toward Europe in several ways. The president's plan to rapidly develop a missile-defense system, for example, figured among Jeffords' reasons for defecting, and the new chairman of the Senate Armed Services Committee, Carl M. Levin, D-Mich., has taken a more cautious approach to the plan. "I don't think the technology is likely to develop fast enough, even if he decided to violate the treaty," Levin said of Bush's dismissal of the ABM Treaty. "And I think our European allies have responded with caution and concern to such a degree that the president is going to have to look again at the complexities of the issue." [33]

In addition, new Senate Foreign Relations Committee Chairman Biden strongly opposes Defense Secretary Rumsfeld's plan to withdraw U.S. troops from Bosnia. "I firmly believe that Secretary Rumsfeld's analysis of the situation in Bosnia is incorrect and that his policy prescription would be seriously detrimental to the national security interests of the United States," Biden said. "The linchpin to the strategy of pacifying and democratizing Bosnia and Herzegovina is a continued, robust U.S. military presence." [34]

Just how much U.S.-European relations might change as a result of the power shift in the Senate is far from clear. "If Bush is clever, he will take advantage of the change and make himself look like a moderate, sensible sort of person, which could free him from his extremist supporters," says Parmentier, of the French Center on the United States. "On the other hand, it's also possible that it will make partisan relations in Washington even worse."

But some Bush critics in Europe hope that the new Democratic majority in the Senate will help improve transatlantic relations. "Jeffords' defection was clearly a sign of the dangers to Bush of pursuing a rather narrow and fairly right-wing agenda," says Everts of the Centre on European Reform. "The Bush administration may have its reasons for wanting to be tough on Russia, pursue missile defense and junk the Kyoto agreement, but do they really want to do all of this at the same time?

"I think not," he continues, "and I'm quite optimistic that some of the rough edges are going to disappear." ■

Notes

[1] For background, see Mary H. Cooper, "Global Warming Treaty," *The CQ Researcher*, Jan. 26, 2001, pp. 41-64.

[2] For background, see Mary H. Cooper, "Missile Defense," *The CQ Researcher*, Sept. 8, 2000, pp. 689-712.

[3] Bush spoke at a news conference on June 13 after meeting with NATO leaders in Brussels.

[4] See William Drozdiak, "EU Seeks to Fill U.S. Role in Koreas," *The Washington Post*, March 25, 2001. For background, see Kenneth Jost, "Future of Korea," *The CQ Researcher*, May 19, 2000, pp. 425-448.

[5] See Barbara Crossette, "U.S. Is Voted Off Rights Panel of the U.N. for the First Time," *The New York Times*, May 4, 2001.

[6] For background, see Philip M. Seib, "U.S.-British Relations," *The CQ Researcher*, Jan. 30, 1998, pp. 73-96.

[7] See, for example, Cragg Hines, "NATO's Critics Say It's Time to Pull Plug," *Houston Chronicle*, May 28, 1989.

[8] Powell spoke on June 20, 2001, at a hearing of the Senate Foreign Relations Committee.

[9] Henry Kissinger, "An Alliance That Sees

Eye to Eye," *The Washington Post*, Jan. 24, 2001.
[10] See Thomas E. Ricks, "Possible Military Overhaul Outlined," *The Washington Post*, May 18, 2001.
[11] Powell addressed a press briefing in Budapest, Hungary, on May 29, 2001.
[12] Biden spoke at a Senate Foreign Relations Committee hearing on U.S. security interests in Europe held on June 13, 2001.
[13] Statistics provided by the European-American Business Council.
[14] C. Fred Bergsten, "America's Two-Front Conflict," *Foreign Affairs*, March/April 2001, p. 17.
[15] See Allan Sloan, "Lucent, Alcatel Limped into Talks and Bumbled Their Way Out," *The Washington Post*, June 5, 2001.
[16] See Guillaume Parmentier, "Let's Give the Atlantic Trade Partners a Forum for Problem-Solving," *International Herald Tribune*, Jan. 11, 2001.
[17] George C. Marshall, "Against Hunger, Poverty, Desperation and Chaos," commencement address at Harvard University, June 5, 1947.
[18] Diane B. Kunz, "The Marshall Plan Reconsidered," *Foreign Affairs*, May/June 1997, p. 170.
[19] For background, see Mary H. Cooper, "European Monetary Union," *The CQ Researcher*, Nov. 27, 1998, pp. 1025-1048.
[20] Communique issued at the EU-U.S. summit Dec. 17-18, 2000, in Washington, D.C.
[21] See Dana Milbank, "Criticism Greets Bush as Europe Trip Begins," *The Washington Post*, June 13, 2001.
[22] Speaking at a news conference held on June 3, 2001, at NATO headquarters in Brussels following his meeting with heads of the alliance governments.
[23] See Susan B. Glasser, "Putin Is Upbeat on U.S. Ties," *The Washington Post*, June 19, 2001.
[24] For background, see Mary H. Cooper, "Energy Policy," *The CQ Researcher*, May 25, 2001, pp. 441-464.
[25] Bush spoke at a Rose Garden appearance on June 12, 2001.
[26] Quoted in William Drozdiak, " 'We Simply Disagree,' " *The Washington Post*, June 17, 2001.
[27] Gregg Easterbrook, "Europe Builds Itself Up at Bush's Expense," *The New York Times*, June 17, 2001.
[28] See Paul Blustein, "U.S. Loses Trade Case to Europe," *The Washington Post*, June 23, 2001.
[29] From a White House statement, June 5, 2001.
[30] See Geoff Winestock, "EU Escalates Trans-Atlantic Steel Battle," *The Wall Street Journal*, June 12, 2001.
[31] See William Drozdiak, "EU Official Decries Bush Effort on GE-Honeywell," *The Washington Post*, June 19, 2001.
[32] Quoted in Martin Crutsinger, "O'Neill Voices Optimism about U.S. Recovery," Associated Press Newswires, July 5, 2001.
[33] Quoted by Thom Shanker, "Missile Defenses Need More Tests, Key Senator Says," *The New York Times*, June 1, 2001.
[34] Biden spoke on the Senate floor on May 23, 2001.

FOR MORE INFORMATION

British American Security Information Council, 1900 L St., N.W., #401, Washington, D.C. 20036; (202) 347-8340; www.basicint.org. This independent research organization analyzes government policies and promotes public awareness of defense, disarmament, military strategy and nuclear policies in order to foster informed debate.

Cato Institute, 1000 Massachusetts Ave., N.W., Washington, D.C. 20001-5403; (202) 842-0200; www.cato.org. A conservative think tank that promotes limited government, free markets and limited U.S. involvement in European security affairs.

Centre for European Reform, 29 Tufton St., London SW1P 3QL, England; 44-20-72.33.11.99; www.cer.org.uk. An independent think tank that seeks closer British integration into the European Union while keeping strong ties to North America.

European-American Business Council, 1333 H St., N.W., #630, Washington, D.C. 20005; (202) 347-9292; www.eabc.org. Comprised of more than 85 EU and U.S. companies, the council is the leading business association active on transatlantic trade, tax and investment policy issues.

European Institute, 5225 Wisconsin Ave., N.W., #200, Washington, D.C. 20015-2014; (202) 895-1670; www.europeaninstitute.org. A public-policy organization devoted to the betterment of transatlantic relations.

French Center on the United States, French Institute of International Relations, 27, rue de Procession, 75740 Paris Cedex 15, France; 33-1-40.61.60.33; www.ifri.org. The center, run jointly with the Center on the United States and France at the Brookings Institution in Washington, D.C., seeks mutual understanding of the public policies of France and the United States.

Resources for the Future, 1616 P St., N.W., Washington, D.C. 20036; (202) 328-5000; www.rff.org. A research organization that studies the economic, environmental and policy aspects of energy, conservation and the development of natural resources.

Bibliography

Selected Sources Used

Books

Brzezinski, Zbigniew K., *The Grand Chessboard: American Primacy and Its Geostrategic Imperatives*, HarperCollins, 1998.

Former President Jimmy Carter's national security adviser holds that the United States has concentrated its diplomatic energies in Europe while ignoring the need to project its geopolitical presence beyond the region to advance U.S. interests in Eurasia.

Clemens, Walter C. Jr., *America and the World 1898-2025: Achievements, Failures, Alternative Futures*, St. Martin's Press, 2000.

The author, a political science professor at Boston and Harvard universities, examines areas where the United States has succeeded, and where it has failed, in advancing its foreign policy goals over the past century. Much of the book focuses on U.S.-European relations.

Kissinger, Henry, *Does America Need a Foreign Policy? Toward a Diplomacy for the 21st Century*, Simon & Schuster, 2001.

The Republican Party's elder statesman warns that his fellow citizens have become complacent in the belief that the world's lone superpower can afford to ignore the details of diplomacy in defending U.S. interests in Europe and elsewhere.

Articles

Blinken, Antony, "The False Crisis over the Atlantic," *Foreign Affairs*, May/June 2001, pp. 35-48.

Despite prominent displays of anti-American sentiment in Europe, the author contends that the two sides of the Atlantic actually are growing closer culturally, economically and strategically.

Daalder, Ivo H., "Are the United States and Europe Heading for Divorce?" *International Affairs*, summer 2001.

President Bush's first months in office have brought new strains in U.S.-European relations, as the United States focuses on security threats posed by the spread of missile technology and Europe concentrates on its own enlargement and environmental issues.

Lipset, Seymour Martin, "Still the Exceptional Nation?" *The Wilson Quarterly*, winter 2000.

Current strains in transatlantic relations belie the fact that Europe is growing more similar to the United States in its political and economic organization. But strong differences also are emerging, such as the absence in the United States of a strong Green party along the lines of the growing environmental advocacy in Europe.

McAllister, J.F.O., "What Kind of Allies? The U.S. and Europe Are Drifting Apart," *Time*, March 5, 2001.

Since the end of the Cold War removed a key motivation for transatlantic cohesion, a number of critical issues have divided Europe and the United States.

Perlez, Jane, "U.S. Doesn't Want to Join Any NATO Mission Into Macedonia," *The New York Times*, June 16, 2001.

The Bush administration has told its NATO partners that it does not want to take part in a NATO military mission that the Macedonian government has requested for the disarming of ethnic Albanian insurgents, according to senior administration officials.

Serfaty, Simon, "Lasting Liaison," *NATO Review*, spring 2001, pp. 6-8.

Growing mutual skepticism on both sides of the Atlantic should be tempered by a common interest in acknowledging the impact of policies on Russia — "too close to ignore, too big to integrate and too nuclear to offend."

Walker, Martin, "Europe: Superstate or Superpower?" *World Policy Journal*, winter 2000/2001, pp. 7-16.

The United States must adapt its policies to better reflect Europe's economic, political and military integration.

Reports and Studies

Everts, Steven, "Unilateral America, Lightweight Europe? Managing Divergence in Transatlantic Foreign Policy," Centre for European Reform, February 2001.

American policy-makers tend to see "threats" where Europeans see "challenges," a difference in interpretation of world events that helps explain some of the recent transatlantic squabbles over security, trade and such domestic issues as capital punishment.

Mandelbaum, Michael, "NATO Expansion: A Bridge to the Nineteenth Century," Center for Political and Strategic Studies, June 1997.

The admission to NATO of Poland, Hungary and the Czech Republic, and the alliance's planned expansion eastward will bring no benefits to security while it risks precipitating a future confrontation with Russia.

2 China Today

DAVID MASCI

School children rehearse a song for China's anniversary celebration. A parade of 500,000 people and military displays celebrated the 50th anniversary of the People's Republic of China on October 1, 1999.

Last October, the People's Republic of China threw itself a party the likes of which hadn't been seen in Beijing in years.

The mammoth event featured a five-mile-long parade that snaked past President Jiang Zemin and other government leaders gathered in Tiananmen Square to celebrate the PRC's 50th anniversary. Some 90 floats depicted the communist state's recent achievements, from its growing industrial might and improved standard of living to its victories in the Olympics.

But the parade also was intended to showcase China as an up-and-coming military power, a point dramatically made by the more than 10,000 white-gloved soldiers and 400 tanks and other military vehicles. (*See sidebar, p. 27.*)

The display of military might was calculated, says James R. Lilley, a resident fellow at the American Enterprise Institute. "They want us to know that they're not going to be pushed around," he says. "Their intention is clear: neutralize American power in the region and press their territorial claims."

Pressing territorial claims has been a priority for China in recent years. On June 30, 1997, the British followed the dictates of a 19th-century treaty and returned Hong Kong to the PRC. Two and half years later, China took back the island of Macao from another former colonial power, Portugal.

But one major prize remains: Taiwan. Unlike Hong Kong and Macao, the island is a de facto independent state, run by a democratically elected government. Bigger than the state of Maryland, modern Taiwan was founded in 1949 by China's former leader, Chiang Kai-shek, and his Nationalist Party. Chiang and the Nationalists — losers in the civil war that brought the Communists to power — set up a parallel state and proclaimed themselves the legitimate government of all of China.

Until the 1970s, the United States accepted Taiwan as the sole representative of China. But President Richard M. Nixon's groundbreaking visit to the mainland in 1972 set in motion a shift in American policy. Today, the United States recognizes the Communists on the mainland as the legitimate government of China. It also adheres to what is known as the "one China" policy, which maintains that Taiwan should reunite with the mainland, though by peaceful means. [1]

Some experts contend that the "one China" policy is misguided and should be discarded in favor of one that respects the wishes of Taiwan's 26 million people. "Unlike [mainland] China, Taiwan is a democracy, and we need to respect and back up whatever decision [it] makes," says Gary Schmitt, executive director of the Project for the New American Century, a Washington, D.C., think tank that promotes American global leadership. That includes the right to be independent, he says. [2]

Schmitt and others argue that instead of pushing Taiwan into the arms of the PRC, the United States should be telling the government on the mainland that it will defend the island's right to decide its own fate.

But others say that such a move would be terribly irresponsible and not in America's interests. "Our relationship with China is one of the cornerstones of U.S. foreign policy, and siding squarely with Taiwan would destabilize that relationship and the whole region," says Richard Haass, director of foreign policy studies at the Brookings Institution.

"One China" is a viable strategy, according to Haass, because it "allows Taiwan to continue in its present state without antagonizing the Chinese."

Haass and others also argue that mainland China is becoming a more open society, making the prospect of reunification at some point in the future much more appealing to Taiwan. "Economic changes have already transformed China for the better and will continue to do so," Haass says.

Indeed, those who believe that China is becoming a more open society contend its expected entry into the World Trade Organization (WTO) next year should accelerate the process of liberalization. [3]

"Membership will ultimately make China a more transparent society, one that is more accountable to its people," says David Shambaugh, director of the China Policy Program at George Washington University.

The WTO is a multinational coalition that works to lower barriers to international trade. Supporters of China's entry into the organization

From *The CQ Researcher*, August 4, 2000.

argue that increased trade will spur economic growth, creating a middle class that will come to expect greater personal liberty and political freedom.* In addition, supporters say, WTO membership will integrate China further into the world community, pushing the country to adopt international standards, like respect for the rule of law and human rights.

But Margaret Huang, program director for Asia at the Robert F. Kennedy Memorial Center for Human Rights, argues that WTO membership actually may make the Chinese Communists more, not less, repressive. According to Huang, as freer trade forces the government to cede control over the economic sphere, it may feel the need to tighten its hold over political activity. "They may feel more threatened and crack down," she says.

As events in China unfold, here are some of the questions experts are asking:

Should the United States continue to support the "one China" policy?

For the mainland, the meaning of "one China" is simple: Taiwan is a renegade province that must eventually return to the fold. In fact, for most of its 50-year existence, the government in Taipei also envisioned full reunification, though with a Nationalist government at the helm.

But Taiwan now views the "one China" concept more ambiguously. Chen Shui-bian, the island's recently elected president, has said "one China" could have a range of meanings, presumably from some sort of loose association to complete reunification. But Chen, the first non-Nationalist to hold Taiwan's presidency, has not publicly stated his own definition of the term. [4]

Until recently, there was a lot of ambiguity in how the United States publicly viewed the relationship between Taiwan and China. In 1972, the year Nixon made his trip to China, the United States stated that it "acknowledges that all Chinese on either side of the Taiwan Strait maintain there is but one China and that Taiwan is part of China." [5] In other words, America simply affirmed the view held by both sides without saying anything more.

Even in 1979, when the United States officially shifted diplomatic recognition from Taipei to Beijing, the meaning of "one China" remained nebulous.

But in 1998, President Clinton peeled away some of the ambiguity. While on a visit to Shanghai, the mainland's largest city, he asserted what became known as the "three no's," rejecting the idea of Taiwanese independence, two Chinas or membership for the island in any international organizations that require statehood. [6]

"This was a big mistake for the Clinton administration because we put our cards on the table, we picked a side," says Stephen Yates, a senior policy analyst at the Heritage Foundation, a conservative think tank. "When you say 'one China' and spell out what that means the way Clinton did, you're implying that you want reunification as an outcome and are basically accepting Beijing's argument."

Instead, Yates says, the United States should drop the "one China" policy and simply push for a peaceful resolution of the situation. "This should be about process, not outcome," he argues.

Others favor more openly siding with Taiwan. "Supporting the 'one China' policy is living in the past because the situation has changed so dramatically since that policy was developed," says Schmitt of the Project for the New American Century. "Taiwan is now a democracy and, frankly, I don't think [its] heart is in this," he says, referring to the prospect of reunifying with the mainland.

Schmitt says the United States needs to "break out" of its current policy and fully back and defend, with military force if necessary, Taiwan's right to self-determination. "We need to make it clear that it's unacceptable for Beijing to do anything to force Taipei into accepting something [it doesn't] want," he says.

But other China experts think that jettisoning "one China" is foolhardy and dangerous. "One China" is the only policy that will bring any resolution to this problem," says George Washington University's Shambaugh. "An independent Taiwan has no future."

Supporters of "one China" contend that if the United States were to publicly abandon the policy, Taiwan's security would be seriously compromised, even with American support. "Taiwan's long-term security cannot be achieved just through weapons but must come through some sort of accommodation with the People's Republic of China," says David M. Lampton, director of China Studies at the School for Advanced International Studies (SAIS) at Johns Hopkins University.

According to Lampton, mainland China's vast population advantage over Taiwan (1.3 billion people vs. 23 million) and close proximity to the island mean that it will be a serious threat to Taiwan as long as it wants to be. And, Lampton, says, China is unlikely to relinquish its claim to the island anytime soon.

"If China went democratic tomorrow," he says, "[it'd] be as tough on Taiwan as [it is] today because this is a great nationalist issue."

Finally, supporters say, "one China" is the best policy for the United States

---

* A landmark China trade bill approved by the House in May would end the annual congressional review of China's trade status, which is partly based on China's improvements in human rights, and grant the Beijing government permanent normal trade relations as part of its accession to the WTO next year. The proposal has overwhelming support in the Senate and is expected to pass easily on the final vote in September.

Inside the World's Most Populous Nation

Former Chinese leader Mao Zedong once likened his vast nation to "another United Nations." The world's most populous country dwarfs tiny Taiwan, off the southeast coast. China has 31 provinces and two special administrative regions, the islands of Hong Kong and Macao. The largest province is Xinjiang, about three times the size of Spain. The most populous province, Sichuan, has more than 110 million residents, about the same as Japan. China's largest city, Shanghai, has 11 million people. Many provinces, including Guangdong, Hubei, Shandong, Jiangsu and Hunan, all have 50-100 million people, similar to such countries as France and Mexico.

While China is more than 90 percent Han Chinese, each region does have its own cultural and economic flavor. Guangdong, in the south, is known for its freewheeling ways and burgeoning economy. Shanghai is China's cultural and financial center. A number of provinces, like Tibet and Xinjiang, have large pockets of non-Chinese ethnic groups and have been designated as "autonomous regions." Nonetheless, separatist movements are active in both provinces.

While China's 1.3 billion people make up more than one-fifth of the world's population, they only occupy one-fifteenth of the Earth's land. And, since much of the Western part of the country is sparsely inhabited, due to the harsh terrain and climate, more than two-thirds of China's people are crowded into the more prosperous eastern part of the country.

Sources: China Statistical Yearbook, The Economist

because U.S. relations with the mainland are much more important than those with Taiwan. "If we changed this policy, we would cause a serious and fundamental crisis with China," says Nancy Bernkopf Tucker, a professor of history at Georgetown University. "Doing so with such a huge and important country cannot be in the national interest."

Will membership in the World Trade Organization lead to a more open society in China?

Sometime next year, the People's Republic of China will almost certainly join the WTO. Admission will be a major victory for China's Communist government, which spent the last 13 years negotiating terms of entry with the United States and other Western countries.

The WTO is a 135-nation trading club whose members agree to reduce barriers to international commerce. In its bid for membership, China has agreed to significantly lower tariffs on industrial and agricultural goods and reduce existing restrictions on foreign investment.

Supporters of China's application say it will accelerate the country's efforts to develop a modern market economy. U.S. Trade Representative Charlene Barshefsky and other WTO boosters also argue that entry will help China become a more open society. WTO membership will help make China "freer, more open to the world and [more] responsive to the rule of law than it is today," Barshefsky said in May. [7]

"When you inject the seed of capitalism in a place, it naturally breeds openness everywhere," says William

Morley, chief lobbyist for the U.S. Chamber of Commerce, which supports WTO membership for China. Once you give the people economic freedom, they'll begin to want more personal freedom."

Morley predicts that WTO membership will help create a solid middle class that will quickly develop a sense of its rights. "Once people begin enjoying the fruits of their labors," he says, "they inevitably start to demand a greater say in other areas, like politics." And that, adds the Heritage Foundation's Yates, "expands the amount of pressure on the government to become more open and democratic, and to guarantee personal freedom."

Supporters also argue that WTO membership will force China to begin to respect the rule of law, a human rights linchpin in any society. "[WTO membership] will get them much more involved in rules-based behavior," says Johns Hopkins' Lampton, "because without it they won't be able to operate in the international arena."

First, Lampton argues, China will have to develop a more reliable court system to deal with business-related issues such as commercial transactions and intellectual property. But eventually, he says, the openness and reliability will spill over into other areas. "Once you develop a core of people who rely on due process in one realm, they begin to expect it in others," he says.

Finally, WTO supporters contend, freer trade will bring an influx of new ideas and information, via the Internet and a host of other mediums. "This will bring greater access to information, especially information from the West," Morley says. "They will become accustomed to the Western way of doing things, and this will have a profound impact on them."

How profound? No one knows, of course. But according to the American Enterprise Institute's Lilley, the influx of new ideas and information from the outside "could very well help to undermine the current system."

House Minority Whip David Bonior, D-Mich., cautions that accession to the WTO may not ultimately be a positive force for change. "Contrary to the assertions of WTO cheerleaders, the hidden hand of the marketplace will not automatically bring about democratic reforms or social progress," Bonior wrote recently. He argues that it was organized protest, not the marketplace, that won Americans greater labor and other rights in the 20th century. [8]

Indeed, some experts say entry into the WTO might shrink political freedoms. "I think things are going to get worse because the government will tighten political control as it loses more and more authority in the economic sphere," says the Robert F. Kennedy Center's Huang. "There will be more arrests, more crackdowns, more harassment of labor organizers and human rights workers."

Huang predicts additional curtailment of rights and liberties as the opening of the economy leads to massive worker dislocation and other social tensions. "WTO [membership] will lead to millions being laid off as they privatize state-run industries," she says. "The sudden presence of all of these unemployed workers and other changes are going to lead to social upheaval, which will force the government to crack down even more" (*see p. 27*).

And some argue that China will probably try to segregate the system used for international business from the rest of the country's legal infrastructure. "They may well be able to guarantee that commercial law reaches certain standards without changing the way, say, human and labor rights are handled," says Mike Jendrzejczyk, Asia director for Human Rights Watch, an advocacy group that favors China's admittance to the WTO. "My guess is that they'll try." ■

Reuters Photo/Dennis Owen

Farmers shovel fertilizer onto a wheat field outside Beijing. Despite China's aggressive push toward modernization and manufacturing, more than two-thirds of its 1.3 billion people still live in rural areas.

BACKGROUND

East Meets West

Until relatively recently, China took little interest in the outside world.

Chronology

Secure in its venerable culture and society, the so-called Middle Kingdom usually ignored the world beyond its borders.

Even when the Chinese did venture out, their actions would have seemed alien to Western explorers, conquistadors and adventurers. In the early 15th century, for example, Adm. Cheng He took Chinese naval expeditions as far as East Africa. Cheng was not seeking new lands to conquer or even plunder, however. His mission was "to make 'the whole world' into voluntary admirers of the one and only center of civilization." [9]

But China could not remain closed to the outside world forever, and when European powers took an interest in it in the 19th century, the nation was wholly unprepared.

The first major opening came in 1840, when a British fleet arrived in southern China to force the repeal of measures that had outlawed the lucrative, British-controlled opium trade. Outgunned by the English on sea and land, the Chinese swallowed a peace treaty that not only permitted the opium trade but also ceded Hong Kong to the British and opened five ports to foreigners.

The rest of the 19th century was equally difficult for China. Forays by France, Russia and Japan, in addition to Britain, were common. The foreign meddling, coupled with internal strife, weakened the state tremendously.

In 1911, China's last imperial dynasty, the Qing, fell, and a republic was proclaimed under Sun Yat-sen, a Western-educated reformer. But Sun's republic quickly disintegrated into chaos as independent warlords fought for control of the country.

After World War I, Sun's Nationalist Party, known as the Kuomintang, began working to reunite China. Under Sun's successor, Chiang Kai-shek, and aided by the growing Communist Party, the Nationalists began

1900-1939

China's last imperial dynasty topples.

1911
The last Qing emperor abdicates, and Nationalist Party leader Sun Yat-sen becomes president of the new Republic of China.

1927
Civil war begins between the Communists and Nationalists.

1934
The defeated Communists go on "The Long March" into northern China.

1940-1974

The Communists defeat the Nationalists for control of China.

Oct. 1, 1949
The Communists proclaim the People's Republic of China. Chiang and the Nationalists escape to Taiwan.

1960
Mao taps Deng Xiaoping and other pragmatists to reverse the economic damage caused by an experiment in socialism.

1966
Mao launches "The Cultural Revolution" to eliminate Western influence, killing millions.

1972
President Richard M. Nixon visits China; the U.S. recognizes the Communist government.

1975-Present

Mao is replaced by reformers Deng and Jiang.

1976
Mao dies. Deng launches economic reforms.

1979
President Jimmy Carter resumes full diplomatic relations with the People's Republic and breaks ties with Taiwan.

1989
Pro-democracy protests in Tiananmen Square in Beijing are brutally suppressed by Deng. Jiang Zemin becomes Deng's handpicked successor.

1996
China fires practice missiles near Taiwan; the U.S. dispatches two aircraft carriers to the area.

February 1997
Deng dies; Jiang takes over.

June 30, 1997
Britain returns Hong Kong to China.

Dec. 20, 1999
Portugal returns Macao.

February 2000
China threatens to use military force against Taiwan if the island indefinitely delays reunification talks.

May 2000
Chen Shui-bian becomes president of Taiwan and accepts the "one China" policy.

creating a unified Chinese state.

In 1927, Chiang broke with his Communist allies. Although the Nationalists controlled most of the country, the Communists established a substantial military and even administrative presence in parts of China.

Japanese aggression in Manchuria beginning in 1931 distracted the Nationalists. But in 1934, Chiang refocused his attention on the Communists, routing them in most areas under their control. The scattered Communist army retreated for nearly two years, fighting its way through western China to Shaanxi Province in summer 1936. Known as "The Long March," the odyssey established Mao Zedong as the leader of the Communists. [10]

In 1937, Japanese aggression turned into a full-scale invasion of northern and eastern China, prompting the Nationalists and Communists to bury their differences and confront the Japanese together. But Japan's modern military quickly occupied much of the country.

Chairman Mao

After World War II, Chiang and Mao began fighting again. This time, the Communists were stronger. Mao's genius for organizing had enabled the party and its military wing, now called the People's Liberation Army (PLA), to grow tremendously during the war years. [11]

Chiang's undisciplined army was no match for the well-organized PLA, and by 1949 the Nationalists were in severe trouble. On Oct. 1, the Communists formally established the People's Republic of China, and Chiang and about 200,000 followers fled to Taiwan.

During the first decade of his rule, Mao turned China into a socialist state. Agriculture was collectivized and industry was nationalized. China's first five-year plan, in 1953, set out to develop heavy industry, using the Soviet Union as a model. At the same time, Chinese society became more structured and, for many, more inhospitable. For example, peasants and workers were organized into brigades, while many artists, professionals and businessmen were persecuted as enemies of the party. In 1958, the transformation was accelerated in what came to be known as "The Great Leap Forward," which lasted for two years.

Throughout the first decade of Communist rule, China maintained close relations with the Soviets. China's entry into the Korean War against the United States in 1950 strengthened the tie. But as the 1950s came to a close, Sino-Soviet relations grew colder because of ideological differences and territorial disputes. The freeze would last for three decades.

By 1960, Mao and other Chinese leaders recognized that the Great Leap had been a failure. The economy was in a state of crisis. In response, a new group of pragmatic leaders arose, including Deng Xiaoping. They improved the economy by allowing farm and factory managers more control over production. At the same time, Deng strengthened the Communist Party. [12]

Mao, sensing he was being edged from power, began a campaign against what he said were China's increasingly "capitalist" tendencies. During the so-called Cultural Revolution (1966-1976), Mao purged his political opponents, including Deng. Millions of people were killed, including many of China's leading thinkers, politicians and professionals. Many other educated people were sent to remote parts of China to be "re-educated" through manual labor.

Secure once again, Mao, during his remaining years eschewed the bold — and often disastrous — steps that characterized the first 20 years of his rule. A major exception was the building of better relations with the United States, fostered by President Nixon's historic 1972 trip to China. At the time, each country saw the other as a valuable ally against the Soviet Union.

Deng Takes Over

By the time Mao died in 1976, Deng had been rehabilitated. Mao's trusted lieutenant, Premier Zhou Enlai — himself a pragmatic modernizer — had brought Deng back in 1973 to once again help restructure Chinese society.

But Zhou had died eight months before Mao, leaving a huge leadership vacuum. After a relatively brief struggle for power with Mao's widow and her key supporters (known as the Gang of Four), Deng became paramount leader.

Deng quickly launched a series of ambitious reforms. Collective agriculture was scrapped in favor of the old system of family-run farms. Private enterprise, once illegal, was encouraged, leading to the rapid creation of a new business class. China's market was opened to foreign trade and investment.

Important non-economic changes also were undertaken. Couples were restricted to one child to reduce China's huge population, and diplomatic relations were established with the United States and other Western countries.

In the political arena, though, there was a marked absence of change. The Communist Party retained control of the government and restricted citizens' liberty. The limits on freedom of speech and assembly were dramatically revealed to the world in 1989, when tens of thousands of democracy supporters gathered in Beijing's Tiananmen Square to demand change. After vacillating for a number

China Beefs Up Its Military

For the United States, the 1991 war against Iraq vindicated more than a decade of spending on high-tech armaments. Equipped with so-called smart bombs, Patriot surface-to-air missiles and powerful M-I Abrams tanks, American forces led by Gen. Norman Schwartzkopf dispatched Saddam Hussein's military in a matter of days.

But for China's political and military leadership, the conflict over Saddam's invasion of Kuwait was a wake-up call, many defense experts say. "They were very impressed with U.S. power and realized that their military was decades behind ours," says Harvey Feldman, a senior fellow at the Heritage Foundation's Asia Studies Center.

Since then, the Chinese have been trying to catch up, embarking on a massive effort to buy and develop new weapons and professionalize their military. "They clearly want to be able to challenge U.S. power in the Pacific," says James R. Lilley, a resident fellow at the American Enterprise Institute.

Throughout the 1990s, China's military budget has steadily increased, usually growing by 10 percent or more each year. [1] At the same time, President Jiang Zemin ordered the military to divest its substantial business holdings, which at one point comprised an estimated 20,000 companies employing 16 million people. Profits from these businesses — which included hotels, farms and factories — were used for military purposes. But Jiang worried that China's generals were becoming more concerned with the bottom line than combat readiness.

In some military areas, the Chinese have made substantial progress in recent years. For example, they have developed intercontinental ballistic missiles capable of hitting the West Coast of the United States, as well as other possible adversaries such as Russia, India and Japan. "By next year, they should be able to hit any target in our country," Feldman says.

In addition, the Chinese have made strides in efforts to miniaturize nuclear weapons — aided by stolen U.S. technology, American officials charge. "This allows them to put more than one [nuclear] warhead on their long-range missiles," Feldman says.

In most military areas though, China still lags far behind the United States. For instance, while the 3-million-strong People's Liberation Army is the world's biggest fighting force, many of its troops still use weapons from the 1960s and '70s. And training and tactics are also still antiquated. The navy, and to some extent the air force, fare little better by comparison. "They're still completely out of our league," Feldman says. "In an all-out engagement, we would destroy them."

The Chinese are trying to close the gap by buying sophisticated weapons from abroad, especially from the Russians. They already have purchased two Russian *Sovremenny*-class destroyers with the Sunburn anti-ship missile, one of the most effective weapons of its kind. "This is a particularly bad development, because these missiles can threaten our [aircraft] carriers," Lilley says. "They are difficult if not impossible to defend against," says Michael Pillsbury, a Department of Defense consultant on the Chinese military.

In addition, Beijing has bought a number of Russian fighter planes, including the SU-27 and the more advanced SU-30MK. While these aircraft are a substantial improvement over the rest of China's aging air force, they cannot effectively stand up to F-16, F-18 and other front-line American fighter planes, many experts say.

Actually, the Chinese do not expect these and other weapons purchases to put them on a military par with the United States any time soon, Feldman says. Instead, he says, the Chinese just want to be powerful enough to deter the U.S. from intervening if China were to attack Taiwan, which it has threatened to do if the island declares independence.

"Their short-term goal is to be able to hold us off long enough to destroy the military and economic capability of Taiwan," he says. "And you know, I think they're getting there."

[1] Figures cited in Frank Gibney Jr., "Birth of a Superpower," *Time*, June 6, 1999.

of weeks, the government violently crushed the protest, killing thousands, according to some reports. [13]

Tiananmen tarnished the regime's image abroad and at home but had little impact on China's reforms or its rapidly growing economy. By the time Deng died in 1997, China had been transformed from an isolated country with an inefficient state-run economy into an economic powerhouse that many say will be a superpower in the next century. [14]

But Deng's passing also left political uncertainties, including whether party elite would accept his hand-picked successor, Jiang Zemin.

Unlike Mao and Deng, Jiang was not a founding member of the Communist Party. Moreover, he had not served in the military and consequently lacked strong support within the all-powerful PLA.

Still, Jiang has established a relatively strong power base, placing people loyal to him in important government posts. The smooth takeover of Hong Kong and Macao under Jiang's watch, coupled with China's continued economic growth during the Asian financial crisis, also helped ease uncertainties about his leadership. ■

CURRENT SITUATION

Economic Growth

During the early 1990s, China's economy defied gravity. In 1992, for instance, the gross domestic product (GDP) rose a phenomenal 14 percent. Average growth for the decade was an impressive 10 percent. [15]

Deng's market-opening reforms had brought a vibrant and brash form of capitalism to China, transforming the lives of hundreds of millions.

But economic gravity is a powerful force, and in the second half of the 1990s it returned, although not with enough force to stall the economy. From 1995 to 1999, GDP growth steadily slowed, from 10 percent to 7 percent. [16] During this time, however, most developing economies in East Asia were spiraling into a deep recession.

Still, government spending has fueled much of the growth over the last three years, which in turn has driven up China's budget deficit. "They can't keep pumping up the economy with government stimulus," says Nicholas Lardy, a senior fellow at the Brookings Institution and an authority on China's economy. "What they're doing is ultimately unsustainable," he says, noting that 50 percent of government spending now goes to debt repayment.

Growth also has been sustained by overproduction, experts say. Between 1990 and 1998, an estimated 40 percent of the increase in GDP was due to the production of products that were not needed and not sold. "They've built up huge inventories that just go into warehouses," Lardy says. "Last year they produced 30 million televisions and sold 20 million, leaving the remaining 10 million in inventory."

Economic Problems

Moreover, the economy still needs more structural reform. Beijing continues to have a huge presence in many commercial areas, a vestige of once-pervasive communism. Most economists believe the government controls between one-quarter and half of the means of production, making everything from telecommunications equipment to autos.

Economists generally agree that a large share of the state-owned businesses are inefficient holdovers, often employing too many workers making products not up to market standards. "Many of them are just not competitive and are losing a lot of money," says Gary Jefferson, a professor of economics at Brandeis University in Waltham, Mass.

Under premier and economic czar Zhu Rongji, the government has been steadily selling off state-owned businesses. "They've made real progress in shrinking the state's presence in the economy," Jefferson says.

Lardy agrees but feels that Rongji has not moved fast enough, out of the legitimate fear that accelerated privatization will put millions of Chinese out of work and could lead to social upheaval. "They clearly need to speed up the pace here because it's such a terribly inefficient use of resources," he says.

The inefficient state sector is also creating another problem. "Because many of these state enterprises are in financial difficulty, they are putting an enormous strain on the banking system," Jefferson says. Indeed, an estimated 75 percent of the loans made by China's four biggest state banks go to government enterprises. [17] Many of these loans will never be repaid, as both the bankers and company managers well know, Jefferson says. But lending continues because the banks are directed by the government not to let these money-losing firms slide into bankruptcy, he says.

The banking problem is already enormous, Lardy says. As of last year, up to 40 percent of the banking system's $1 trillion in outstanding loans were deemed unrecoverable, largely because of lending to the state sector. [18] "Unless something is done to change this," he says, "the financial system may collapse."

Still, Jefferson sees the overall economic picture as positive. "If international growth rates continue, I predict that China will continue to grow in a stable way," he says, citing healthy exports and continued high levels of foreign investment.

In addition, Jefferson says, China's imminent WTO membership will open the country's markets to more competition, forcing the government to "further accelerate efforts to reduce state participation in the economy. They'll have to move forward rapidly with this if they want to compete." ■

OUTLOOK

Political Change?

In May, President Jiang announced the latest in a long line of efforts to rejuvenate the Chinese Communist

At Issue:

Should Congress link passage of permanent normal trade relations (PNTR) with China to guarantees on human rights reforms?

yes

Mike Jendrzejczyk
Washington director, Asia Division, Human Rights Watch

FROM TESTIMONY BEFORE THE HOUSE COMMITTEE ON INTERNATIONAL RELATIONS, MAY 10, 2000

China has lobbied for several years for an end to the annual review of its trade status under the Jackson-Vanik amendment of the Trade Act of 1974, and as part of the World Trade Organization (WTO) deal President Clinton has pledged to give China permanent normal trade relations status. . . .

Congress should set concrete, meaningful and realistic human rights conditions that China must meet before receiving PNTR. The president should be required to certify that these conditions have been met, and this could happen any time following China's accession to the WTO.

For example, China should be required to:

• Ratify the two United Nations human rights treaties it has signed: the International Covenant on Civil and Political Rights . . . and the International Covenant on Economic, Social and Cultural Rights;

• Take steps to begin dismantling the huge system of "re-education through labor," which allows officials to sentence thousands of citizens to labor camps each year for up to three years without judicial review;

• Open up Tibet and Xinjiang to regular, unhindered access by U.N. human rights and humanitarian agencies, foreign journalists and independent monitors. . . .

Getting China to meet these conditions is possible, if the administration engages in the kind of intensive, high-level negotiations with Beijing it conducted to finalize the trade agreement last November. In light of the failure of the U.N. in Geneva to censure China, it is even more imperative that Congress and the administration agree on meaningful human rights conditions on PNTR as one of the few remaining sources of serious leverage.

To replace the annual trade-status review, we would strongly support creation of a new mechanism, such as a special commission appointed jointly by Congress and the executive branch along the lines of what Rep. [Sander M.] Levin, [D-Mich.,] has proposed. This commission should issue a report annually on China's compliances with international human rights and labor rights norms.

But this should be more than a pro forma process, or it will have no real credibility. Legislation establishing the commission should require a vote by Congress on the commission's findings and recommendations for U.S. bilateral and multilateral policy initiatives. . . .

no

Willard Workman
Vice president for International Affairs, U.S. Chamber of Commerce

WRITTEN FOR *THE CQ RESEARCHER*, JULY 2000

Using trade as a weapon does more than hurt the working people, farmers and business of the United States — it reduces our economic and social influence abroad. We don't just export goods, we export American ideals.

Throughout the United States and around the world, individual liberty and free enterprise go hand in hand. By their very presence and operations, American companies and the expatriate communities that depend on them contribute mightily to economic, political and religious freedom in their host countries. Continuing U.S. company presence abroad is critical to the inculcation of American civic values.

The U.S. business presence in China has resulted in greater job choice for workers, higher wages and living standards, better workplace safety and health standards, improved education and training opportunities and a host of other benefits sought by workers in the United States, China and all over the world. And as hundreds of millions of Chinese people continue to migrate from the interior to the coastal regions to take advantage of these imported economic opportunities, the potential for expanded U.S. economic, social and cultural influence will be historic.

These workers will make more money, read more Western books and periodicals and receive greater exposure to Western ideals of social, economic and political reform than their compatriots who remain isolated. Unilateral restrictions on U.S. firms in China not only imperil U.S. competitiveness in that country but also compromise a principal source of human progress for nearly one-fourth of the world's people.

No moral person can countenance the atrocities that are committed around the world against our fellow human beings, whatever the political, economic, social or religious pretext. Basic human rights are core American values. (We believe just as strongly in the need to combat other man-made scourges, such as terrorism, weapons proliferation and drug trafficking, that plague us.)

But history demonstrates that unilateral economic sanctions not only fail to address these concerns but also make heroes out of the regimes we target and impede, rather than advance, the cause of freedom in those countries.

For all of these reasons — plus the fact that U.S. economic and national security interests demand it — Congress should approve PNTR now.

Party. Jiang's plan, spelled out in a 74-page booklet issued to party cadres, is known as "The Three Represents." [19] According to the president, the party must "always represent the development needs of China's advanced social productive forces, always represent the onward direction of China's advanced culture and always represent the fundamental interests of the largest number of Chinese people." [20]

Jiang reasons that if the party follows his simple advice of devoting itself to the Chinese people, it will prosper long into the future, regardless of economic and other changes taking place.

But many China-watchers claim that "The Three Represents" has the more immediate goal of shoring up the party's stature enough to counter any calls for a multiparty system or some milder form of political liberalization.

"They understand that they have to change if they want to stay in power," says George Washington University's Shambaugh. "They know that they have to root out corruption and become more responsive, more accountable to the people."

Indeed, by all accounts, corruption and other abuses have lowered the party's stature in the eyes of most ordinary Chinese. Protests and even violent riots are not uncommon, especially in the countryside, where poor farmers are often overtaxed by corrupt, local party officials.

Some experts say the Communists may be able to transform themselves sufficiently to retain enough popular support to hang on to power in the coming decades. "Assuming this party stays in power, it will be a very different party in 20 years," says Georgetown's Tucker. "The next generation of leaders will be more internationalist in their thinking and more open to new ideas."

But Brandeis University's Jefferson doubts that "The Three Represents" or any other efforts will restore the party's esteem in the eyes of the people. In the coming decades, he predicts, the Communists will no longer be the undisputed and sole political force in China. "The most likely scenario is that they will evolve much like South Korea or Taiwan has, in the sense that you'll see the ruling party slowly being pressured to allow more and more room for the opposition until there is a real multiparty system," Jefferson says. [21]

The Heritage Foundation's Yates sees a different path to the same outcome. "They will be incapable of changing and will lose power," he says. "I just don't think that they'll transform themselves into some sort of European-style socialist party that allows for competing voices."

The Robert F. Kennedy Center's Huang agrees: "The government will continue to crack down on its citizens and then will lose its mandate and be overthrown."

But Schmitt of the Project for the New American Century is betting that Jiang and the Communists may well hang onto power without significant political liberalization. "They're very determined not to let go, and they've learned a lesson from [Mikhail S.] Gorbachev," whose efforts to promote more political freedom led to the breakup of the Soviet Union and the fall of the Communists.

Schmitt reasons that if China's Communists continue to improve the standard of living (as they have for 20 years), they should be able to keep a lid on efforts to change the country's political system.

"Look, if [Cuban Communist leader] Fidel Castro can hang onto power for 40 years and provide little or nothing to his people," Schmitt asks, "why can't the Chinese Communists go on for decades with a growing and vibrant economy?" ■

Notes

[1] For background, see Kenneth Jost, "Taiwan, China and the U.S.," *The CQ Researcher*, May 24, 1996, pp. 457-480.

[2] For background, see Kenneth Jost, "Democracy in Asia," *The CQ Researcher*, July 24, 1998, pp. 625-648.

[3] For background, see Mary H. Cooper, "World Trade," *The CQ Researcher*, June 9, 2000, pp. 497-520.

[4] John Pomfret, "Taiwan Leader Accepts 'One China' Idea," *The Washington Post*, June 29, 2000.

[5] Quoted in Larry M. Wortzel, "Why the Administration Should Reaffirm the 'Six Assurances' to Taiwan," The Heritage Foundation, March 16, 2000.

[6] *Ibid.*

[7] Speech before the Bretton Woods Committee, a nonpartisan membership group that supports the World Bank and International Monetary Fund, May 16, 2000.

[8] Quoted in David Bonior, "Free for All," *The Washington Post*, Nov. 27, 1999.

[9] Daniel J. Boorstin, *The Discoverers* (1983), p. 192.

[10] Frederica M. Bunge and Rinn-Sup Shinn (eds.), *China: A Country Study* (1981), p. 27.

[11] *Ibid.*, pp. 27-30.

[12] *Ibid.*

[13] Harry Harding, *A Fragile Relationship: The United States and China Since 1972* (1992), pp. 216-224.

[14] For background, see David Masci, "China After Deng," *The CQ Researcher*, June 13, 1997, pp. 505-528.

[15] Karby Leggett, "China Sees a Solid Jump in Growth," *The Wall Street Journal*, July 11, 2000.

[16] *Ibid.*

[17] Cited in Dominic Ziegler, "Now Comes the Hard Part," *The Economist*, April 8, 2000.

[18] Cited in Hugo Restal, "Is China Headed for a Crash?" *The Wall Street Journal*, Sept. 2, 1999.

[19] "The Three Big Thoughts," *The Economist*, June 17, 2000.

[20] Quoted in *Ibid.*

[21] For background, see Kenneth Jost, "The Future of Korea," *The CQ Researcher*, May 19, 2000, pp. 425-448.

Bibliography

Selected Sources Used

Books

Bernstein, Richard, and Ross Munro, *The Coming Conflict with China*, Alfred A. Knopf, 1997.
Veteran journalists Bernstein and Munro argue that China and the United States are headed toward ever worsening relations and possibly war. The problem is that China wants to become the dominant power in Asia and sees America's presence in the region as the primary obstacle.

Soled, Debra E. (ed.), *China: A Nation in Transition*, CQ Press, 1995.
A writer with a special interest in Asia provides a useful introduction to China detailing its history, economy, society, and foreign policy.

Articles

"Can China Change?" *The Economist*, Oct. 2, 1999.
The article asks whether China can continue to develop economically without corresponding political changes. It concludes that if China is to become a more open society, it will almost certainly do so in spite of rather than because of the Communist Party.

Gibney, Frank, "Birth of a Superpower," *Time*, June 7, 1999.
Gibney details China's efforts to modernize its poorly equipped military.

Jost, Kenneth, "Taiwan, China and the U.S.," *The CQ Researcher*, May 24, 1996, pp. 457-480.
A slightly dated but enlightening report argues that Taiwan's surging economic self-confidence and China's increasing assertiveness pose difficult policy choices for the United States.

Lilley, James, and Arthur Waldron, "Taiwan is a 'State.' Get Over It," *The Wall Street Journal*, July 14, 1999.
Lilley and Waldron contend that treating Taiwan as a de facto independent country is the best way for China to bring about reunification.

Masci, David, "China After Deng," *The CQ Researcher*, June 13, 1997.
A report on issues facing China nearly two decades after Deng Xiaoping initiated economic reforms.

Pomfret, John, "Dissidents Back China's WTO Entry," *The Washington Post*, May 11, 2000.
Pomfret details support for China's membership in the World Trade Organization by members of the country's dissident community.

Ziegler, Dominic, "Now Comes the Hard Part," *The Economist*, April 8, 2000.
Ziegler predicts extraordinary and beneficial changes in the country's economy, but he is less certain about China's future political landscape.

Reports and Studies

Wortzel, Larry M., "Why the Administration Should Reaffirm the 'Six Assurances' to Taiwan," The Heritage Foundation, March 16, 2000.
Wortzel, director of the foundation's Asian Studies Center, argues that the United States should work harder to reassure Taiwan and stop trying to "appease" China.

FOR MORE INFORMATION

Council on Foreign Relations, 58 E. 68th St., New York, N.Y. 10021; (212) 434-9400; www.cfr.org. The nonpartisan research organization studies international issues.

Heritage Foundation, Asian Studies Center, 214 Massachusetts Ave. N.E., Washington, D.C. 20002; (202) 546-4400; www.heritage.org. Conducts research and provides information on trade, military policy and other issues that concern the United States and Asia.

Human Rights Watch, 1630 Connecticut Ave., N.W., Suite 500, Washington D.C. 20009; (202) 371-6592; www.hrw.org. The nonpartisan organization monitors human rights violations worldwide.

Project for the New American Century, 1150 17 St., N.W., Suite 510, Washington, D.C. 20036; (202) 293-4983; www.geocities.com/newamericancentury. The educational organization supports American global leadership.

Robert F. Kennedy Memorial Center for Human Rights, 1367 Connecticut Ave., N.W., Suite 200, Washington, D.C. 20036; (202) 463-7575; www.rfkmemorial.org. Investigates and reports on human rights around the world.

U.S.-Asia Institute, 232 E. Capitol St., N.E., Washington, D.C. 20003; (202) 544-3181; www.usasiainstitute.com. Conducts research and sponsors overseas visits and conferences to foster greater cooperation and understanding between the United States and Asian countries.

3 World Trade

MARY H. COOPER

The Qin Shi handbag factory in China's Guangdong Province employs about 1,000 workers to sew Kathie Lee Gifford handbags for Wal-Mart. They toil 12 to 14 hours a day, seven days a week. The workers share metal bunk beds in crowded dormitories. They are allowed outside the fenced compound for only one-and-a-half hours a day.

All this for an average wage of 3 cents an hour — about $3 for a 98-hour workweek. And that's the average. Almost half the workers earn nothing after deductions for room and board. [1]

A 16-year-old girl makes Keds sneakers at a factory in China, which provides about 60 percent of all the shoes sold in the United States.

With such low labor costs, Wal-Mart is able to sell the handbags in the United States for less than $10. In fact, the giant retailer finds overseas manufacturing so profitable that it imports more goods than any other U.S. firm. But it is hardly alone. Nike, RCA and Huffy are just a few of the U.S. manufacturers that lower their labor costs by making goods in China and other developing countries.

Before the House of Representatives voted to normalize trade relations with China last month, members debated more than such arcane matters as tariffs and import taxes. The most contentious issues were appalling working conditions like those at the Qin Shi factory, environmental pollution and the threat to American jobs posed by expanded U.S.-China trade.

World trade has emerged as a critical issue among American voters concerned about how opening up new markets affects ordinary people's lives — here and abroad. The last several months have seen the political debate spill onto the streets of Seattle and Washington, D.C., in demonstrations that have rivaled in intensity the antiwar protests of the 1960s.

From *The CQ Researcher*, June 9, 2000.

The protests have focused on the seemingly inevitable move toward a more global economy — the rapid expansion of international trade, the movement of multinational corporations to low-wage countries and the erosion of national boundaries by advances in telecommunications.

Critics — including labor leaders, human-rights activists and environmentalists — charge that globalization does little more than encourage corporations to relocate factories to countries with the cheapest labor and the weakest environmental laws. But proponents say that free trade, a hallmark of the so-called new economy, will be the key to raising living standards in developing countries, improving working conditions in authoritarian countries and protecting the environment on a global scale.

"The question is not whether trade works or is appropriate," says Jeff Faux, president of the Economic Policy Institute, a Washington, D.C., think tank. "Of course, it is both. The question is, 'What are the rules of this global economy?' Are we going to have rules that protect workers, human rights and the environment the way we have in our own successful history?"

Free-trade champions, including the Clinton administration and business organizations, say such fears are unfounded. Not only will trade expansion, or "liberalization," establish new markets for American exports and thus create new jobs at home, they say, but opening countries like China to American business will inevitably open them to American values as well.

"With more than a billion people, China is the largest new market in the world," President Clinton said in welcoming the House vote. "Our administration has negotiated an agreement which will open China's markets to American products made on American soil — everything from corn to chemicals to computers. We will be exporting, however, more than our products. By this agreement, we will also export more of one of our most cherished values — economic freedom. Bringing China into the World Trade Organization and normalizing trade will strengthen those who fight for the environment, for labor standards, for human rights, for the rule of law." [2]

By granting permanent, normal trade relations (PNTR) with China, the House voted to relinquish its 21-year practice of approving China trade each year after reviewing the country's human rights record. (The Senate is expected to approve the measure by a wide margin this month.) As a result of the bilateral trade agreement reached last Nov. 15, Chinese imports will receive the same favorable tariff treatment the United States extends to all but a handful of countries subject to sanctions for political reasons, such as Cuba, Afghanistan and North Korea. [3]

In return, China agreed to open its markets to a broad array of U.S. farm,

Trade by China, Latin America Increased the Most

Exports from China increased by 15 percent from 1990 to 1998, nearly twice as much as the next-highest increase. Imports by China and Latin America increased the most during the period. Overall, Western Europe had more trade than any other region.

Growth in Value of Trade, 1990-1998

	EXPORTS		IMPORTS	
	Value (in $ Billions)	Percent Change 1990-98	Value (in $ Billions)	Percent Change 1990-98
World	$5,270	6%	$5,465	6%
North America*	897	7	1,152	8
Latin America	276	8	340	14
Western Europe	2,348	5	2,367	4
European Union	2,181	5	2,172	4
Africa	107	1	134	5
Middle East	137	0	144	5
Asia	1,293	7	1,086	5
Japan	388	4	280	2
China	184	15	140	13

** Excluding Mexico*

Source: World Trade Organization

industrial and telecommunications exports and reduce tariffs on those goods. The agreement, together with a similar pact China reached with the 15-member European Union shortly before the House vote, paves the way for China's entry into the 136-member World Trade Organization (WTO), the Geneva-based organization that oversees the global trading system.

In the view of free-trade supporters, history shows that eliminating barriers among countries hastens a fairly predictable process of economic development, one that moves from subsistence farming to industrialization, from authoritarian to democratic political systems and from poverty to modern living standards. "The economic evidence overwhelmingly suggests that other countries have had their wage levels rise over time because of trade," says Robert E. Litan, director of economic studies at the Brookings Institution, a Washington think tank. "Just look at countries that have been closed to trade — the Cubas, the North Koreas and, for that matter, Eastern Europe before the Berlin Wall fell. Countries that were closed obviously have done less well in terms of their wage growth than countries that have opened up. This is not rocket science; it's basic economics."

Likewise, trade boosters say that globalization helps the environment over time because history also shows that societies that are mired in poverty are too concerned about getting enough to eat to do much about curbing pollution.

"In the long term, trade makes everybody richer and better off," says Paul Portney, president of Resources for the Future, a Washington research organization. "When that happens, then people are going to pay attention to the environment."

But skeptics say one need look no further than the North American Free Trade Agreement (NAFTA) to understand how trade expansion has fallen short of those promises. [4] The agreement, which expanded an earlier free-trade area between the United States and Canada to include Mexico, was signed by Republican President George Bush and won congressional approval with Clinton's strong support in 1993. Supporters hailed the agreement as a way to hasten Mexico's economic development and create American jobs as demand for U.S. products rose with Mexican consumers' disposable income.

Less than a decade later, NAFTA is widely perceived as having not lived up to those expectations. Not only have American workers lost jobs as their employers moved production to lower-cost Mexican sites, but the anticipated boost in American exports to Mexico has failed to materialize as economic problems have persisted south of the border.

Additionally, the high concentration of polluting *maquiladoras*, or assembly plants on the Mexican side of the border that churn out goods for export to the United States, has grown even larger, aggravating air and water pollution in U.S. border states. The problems are so serious that a Clinton administration task force recently called for special federal assistance to the border region. [5]

The reason globalization has failed to spread its benefits, critics say, is that it has been promoted and carried forward at the behest of multinational corporations — and their political supporters — with an overriding interest in maximizing profits. Unlike the U.S economy, which is regulated by labor, health and envi-

U.S. Trade Deficit Mushroomed

The nation's balance of trade dropped from its high point, a $12 billion surplus in 1975, to a deficit of more than $271 billion in 1999. As barriers to global trade have fallen, trade has assumed growing importance to the U.S. economy. Supporters of trade liberalization say that encouraging the flow of goods, services and capital among nations benefits everyone, but labor unions say it encourages manufacturers to transfer operations overseas, costing Americans jobs and increasing the deficit.

U.S. Balance of Trade

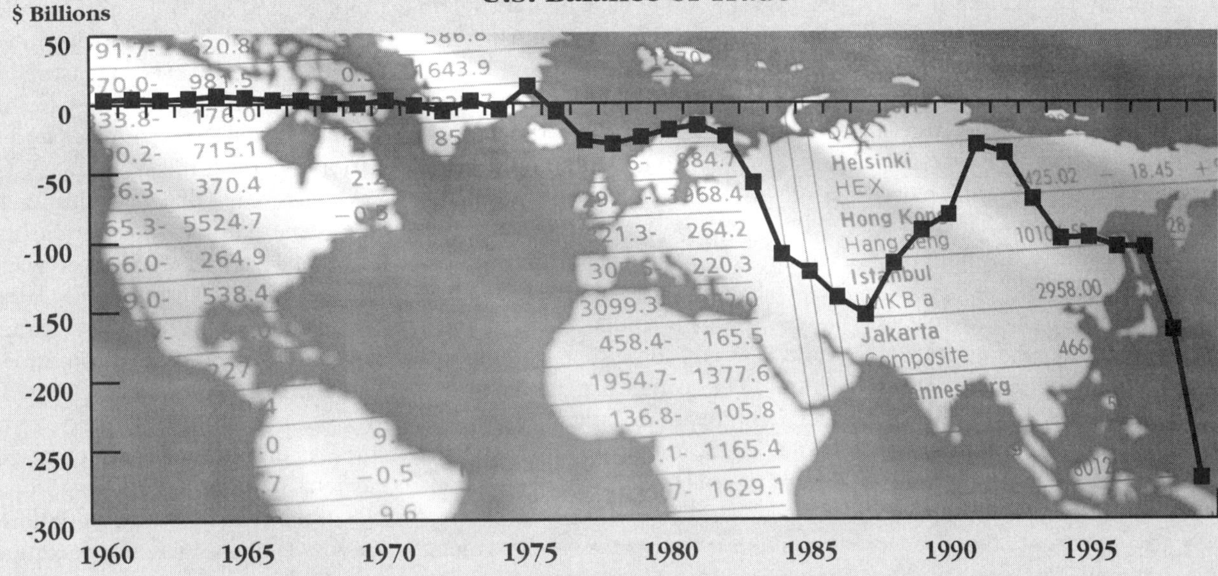

Source: U.S. Department of Commerce

ronmental laws, the global economy is relatively free of such regulatory safeguards.

Indeed, a central mandate of the institutions that govern international trade — the WTO, the International Monetary Fund (IMF) and the World Bank — is to remove obstacles to the international flow of goods and capital. The bank provides economic assistance to poor countries, while the IMF makes loans to countries that agree to make their economies more competitive. [6]

"We are now going to a global economy, but there's no global government, so the rules have been set by these narrow institutions, which are essentially driven by narrow economic and business interests," says Faux of the Economic Policy Institute. "So-called free-trade agreements such as NAFTA, permanent normal trade relations with China and even the WTO itself are actually full of rules that protect investors, such as protections of intellectual property rights."

He and other critics are calling for trade agreements to include rules that guarantee workers' rights and help safeguard the environment.

When tens of thousands of demonstrators disrupted last fall's WTO meeting in Seattle, Clinton acknowledged the protesters' demands by proposing the creation of a working group on trade and labor within the WTO and promising to assess the environmental impact of future trade pacts. But the administration has since remained silent on the issue, and the trade agreement with China contains none of the protections labor and environmental activists sought.

The China agreement is not the last word on the subject of labor and environmental standards, however. Unions, environmental organizations and human-rights activists promise to continue pressing for greater regulation of the world economy.

As policy-makers address the issue, these are some of the questions they are asking:

Is globalization good for American workers?

The United States is enjoying a period of unprecedented prosperity. Now in the longest expansion in history, the booming economy has led to skyrocketing stock prices, enriching many Americans who invested in companies producing computers, software and electronics equipment. Inflation, which historically rises with a booming stock market, has remained low, enabling policy-makers to maintain low interest rates and avoid — so far, at least — the boom-and-bust cycle that has marked industrial development in the past.

Even the federal budget deficit, once a seemingly permanent feature of the political landscape, has vanished under the wave of new tax revenues, leaving politicians arguing over how best to spread the largess. This technology-driven "new economy" has created instant millionaires of dot-com investors and increased the retirement security of millions of working Americans.

Trade has played a big role in America's prosperity. Since the end of World War II, the United States and other countries have reduced tariffs, the taxes on imported goods designed to protect domestic industries from foreign competition. Many countries also have negotiated bilateral and regional free-trade agreements, such as NAFTA, which eliminate tariffs altogether. Today, the value of U.S. exports and imports is equal to one-quarter of total U.S. economic output, more than twice the level just 40 years ago.

A key player in the global economy is the multinational corporation. Worldwide, some 60,000 multinationals and a half-million of their affiliates in various countries account for 25 percent of global output. U.S. multinationals employ about 20 million American workers and 8 million workers in other countries. Foreign multinationals with factories in the United States employ about 5 million Americans. [7]

Globalization has brought benefits to American workers — but at a cost. On the positive side, unemployment, at about 4 percent, is lower than at any time since the late 1960s. Low inflation is protecting the value of workers' paychecks. And for workers with retirement accounts tied to the stock market, the booming economy has increased the prospects of a secure retirement.

But the news is not all good. After rising more than 2 percent a year from the end of World War II to the first energy crisis of 1973, Americans' wages on average have actually fallen over the past quarter-century when inflation is taken into account. Highly skilled workers have held their own, but the lowest-paid workers have seen their incomes plummet. As a result, the income gap between the richest and poorest Americans has widened. [8]

"There's no question that average wages rise as a result of international trade," says the Brookings Institution's Litan. "The only dispute is about whether trade hurts particular portions of the labor force." In his view, increased global trade probably has contributed slightly to the plight of low-income workers, but not nearly as much as immigration, which forces American workers to compete for low-skill jobs, and technological development, which favors skilled workers.

But even those disadvantages have faded since the early 1990s, Litan says. "During the Clinton years, the United States has enjoyed not only rapid economic growth at the average level, but the growth has been broadly distributed across all income classes," he says. "Not only have all workers shared in the prosperity, but throughout this period, the United States has become more and more involved with trade. So to the extent that there has been any depressing effect of trade on wages in the past, it certainly doesn't look like it's had much impact at all in the 1990s."

Some experts emphasize that free trade indirectly benefits all Americans, especially low-income workers, by making available cheap imports, which generally depress prices for consumer goods across the board.

"Openness to imports has helped to keep inflation low, broaden choice and improve consumer prices, especially for basic household necessities," U.S. Trade Representative Charlene Barshevsky said. "This is especially important for the poorest families." [9] That was a strong selling point behind the Trade and Development Act, which Clinton signed into law on May 18. The measure will facilitate imports of low-cost clothing from poor countries in Africa and the Caribbean Basin. [10]

Critics charge that globalization has cost American workers dearly in terms of lost jobs and lower wages. They estimate that free-trade agreements such as NAFTA, for example, have cost hundreds of thousands of American jobs since 1993. "For working people in the United States, NAFTA continues to mean good-paying jobs moving to low-wage countries like Mexico," said Rep. Sherrod Brown, D-Ohio, a leading congressional ally of labor unions and critic of U.S. trade policy. "In 1994, NAFTA's supporters said we would see up to 200,000 new jobs created in the U.S. because of increased trade. Instead, NAFTA has led to the elimination of nearly 204,000 high-paying U.S. manufacturing jobs. [11]

Critics predict the China trade deal will worsen the U.S. trade deficit with China, which reached $69 billion last year, and bleed away even more U.S. jobs. "For every 10 percent increase in U.S. multinational investment in China over the last 20 years," Faux says, "Chinese exports to the United States have risen by 7.3 percent, and U.S. exports to China have decreased by 2 percent."

This lopsided trade pattern, he says, is the result of a deliberate strategy by U.S. multinationals to use China as a low-wage assembly area for products that they then turn around and export to the United States. "Forty percent of the bilateral trade deficit is made up of so-called 'tourist exports'," Faux says. "In this way, U.S. multinationals export raw materials or parts to a production platform in China for input into a good that will be re-exported back into the United States."

Are labor standards the best means of improving the lot of workers in poor countries?

U.S. labor unions are at the forefront of a campaign to include labor standards in both bilateral and multilateral trade agreements to protect foreign workers from exploitation. They contend that conditions in today's global economy mirror those in the United States at the turn of the last century, when rapid industrialization and interstate commerce expanded to create a truly national U.S. economy.

"The enormous transformation of the American economy at that time resulted in the vast movement of people from farm to factory and appalling labor conditions," says David Smith, director of policy for the AFL-CIO. Decades of union activism led to fundamental labor protections.

In 1935, Congress passed the National Labor Relations Act, or Wagner Act, protecting workers' rights to bargain collectively and form unions. Three years later, lawmakers approved the Fair Labor Standards Act, which barred child labor, established the minimum wage and required employers to pay time-and-a-half wages for overtime.

"Our history demonstrates that the process of development requires rules like these," Smith says. "Improvements in working conditions in the United States did not happen because corporations wanted them. We had to establish rules of the game stipulating that you can't send an 11-year-old into the factory, you can't insist that men and women work more than 40 hours a week without overtime compensation and you must allow people who work for you to freely associate and form a union if they wish to. We need those same kinds of rules in the international arena."

Reuters/Jessica Persson

Labor union activists at the U.S. Capitol in April denounce the landmark trade bill with China, which they fear threatens American jobs. Union officials say U.S. companies will move production to cheaper overseas factories.

But government officials in many developing nations strongly oppose inserting labor standards into international trade rules. They argue that standards would place them at an unfair competitive disadvantage because they cannot afford to implement the kinds of workers' rights taken for granted in the industrial world.

"If you ask the trade ministers of many developing countries whether they want labor standards, they adamantly say no," Litan says. "The biggest opposition is the countries themselves. And given that, who in the hell are we to tell them what to do?"

But union supporters say the generic standards they propose need not discriminate against Third World countries. "We're not talking here about exporting the American minimum wage or the Fair Labor Standards Act," Smith says.

He and other proponents say the WTO should incorporate into trade pacts those core labor standards already espoused by the International Labor Organization (ILO), an agency established in 1919 to promote workers' rights. Chief among those standards are workers' right to organize and prohibitions on discrimination, child labor and prison labor.

"We're merely insisting that these basic labor rights ought to be honored," Smith says, "both because it reflects our values and because those standards provide a check on a global race to the bottom."

But some experts warn the push to include labor standards in trade agreements actually may worsen working conditions in developing countries.

"On the surface, it sounds easy to say that everybody should have these minimum standards as a condition for trading with them," Litan says. "But the reality is that a lot of Third World countries either don't have labor laws on their books or, if they do, they don't have the resources to

U.S. and Germany Lead Global Trade

The United States and Germany exported goods worth $1.2 trillion in 1998 and had imports valued at $1.4 trillion, leading the world.

Top 20 Trading Nations

COUNTRY	EXPORTS Value (in $ Billions)	Share of World Market
United States	$682.5	12.6%
Germany	539.7	10.0
Japan	387.9	7.2
France	304.8	5.6
United Kingdom	272.9	5.0
Italy	242.3	4.5
Canada	214.3	4.0
Netherlands	198.7	3.7
China	183.8	3.4
Belgium-Luxembourg	178.5	3.3
Hong Kong	174.9	3.2
South Korea	132.3	2.4
Mexico	117.5	2.2
Singapore	109.9	2.0
Taiwan	109.9	2.0
Spain	109.0	2.0
Sweden	84.7	1.6
Switzerland	78.9	1.5
Russia	73.9	1.4
Malaysia	73.3	1.4

COUNTRY	IMPORTS Value (in $ Billions)	Share of World Market
United States	$944.4	16.8%
Germany	466.6	8.3
United Kingdom	315.2	5.6
France	286.3	5.1
Japan	280.5	5.0
Italy	215.6	3.8
Canada	206.2	3.7
Hong Kong	186.8	3.3
Netherlands	184.2	3.3
Belgium-Luxembourg	166.5	3.0
China	140.2	2.5
Spain	132.8	2.4
Mexico	129.0	2.3
Taiwan	104.2	1.9
Singapore	101.6	1.8
South Korea	93.3	1.7
Switzerland	80.2	1.4
Sweden	68.2	1.2
Austria	68.2	1.2
Australia	64.7	1.2

Source: World Trade Organization

enforce them." Consequently, most work performed in developing countries is unregulated, he says, and "if we put trade sanctions on countries that fail to meet the standards, more of the labor forces of these countries would just go underground, and that would only make working conditions worse for them."

A better way to improve working conditions in the developing world, some free-trade supporters say, is to make it even easier for U.S. multinationals to set up shop there. Because many American firms with overseas factories pay higher wages and provide better working conditions than local employers, they can, by their very presence, raise the expectations of local workers, putting pressure on governments and companies to improve working conditions throughout the economy.

"We employ more than 450 people in our Chinese subsidiary, where salaries are far higher than the average Chinese wage," writes Microsoft Corp. Chairman Bill Gates. "Our compensation and benefits are helping to raise the standard of living." [12]

But the same cannot be said of many other U.S. firms currently producing goods in China. The National Labor Committee (NLC), a human-rights advocacy group, alleges that Nike, the Gap, Liz Claiborne, Kathie Lee Gifford/Wal-Mart and the Walt Disney Co. are among American firms that run sweatshops in China that force workers to toil under prison-like conditions to make such items as car stereos, bikes, shoes, sneakers, clothing, TVs, hats and bags for export to the United States. [13]

Critics charge that the WTO's exclusion of labor standards undermines the interests of workers everywhere. "When there are no ground rules for corporations concerning labor or human rights, a brutal 'race to the bottom' in wages and working conditions is triggered," write Lori Wallach and Michelle Sforza of Public Citizen's Global Trade Watch. "The country that can offer the cheapest production costs 'wins' by merit of production being moved there, but people working in that country — under horrific conditions and paid starvation wages — lose, as do the people in the competing countries.[14]

Don't look to China's dissidents to resolve the debate over labor standards. Harry Wu and Wei Jingsheng, who were persecuted at home before emigrating to the United States, pleaded with lawmakers to reject the China trade agreement on human-rights grounds. "The conditions described in [the NLC] report are rampant throughout China," Wu said. "Let's not pretend that American companies in China care about spreading democracy and human rights. They care about profits and business rights."

But Bao Tong, another prominent dissident who lives in Beijing, disagreed. "I appreciate the efforts of friends and colleagues to help our human-rights situation," he said. "But it doesn't make sense to use trade as a lever. It just doesn't work."[15]

"When there are no ground rules for corporations concerning labor or human rights, a brutal 'race to the bottom' in wages and working conditions is triggered. . . . The country that can offer the cheapest production costs 'wins' by merit of production being moved there, but people working in that country — under horrific conditions and paid starvation wages — lose, as do the people in the competing countries."

— Lori Wallach and Michelle Sforza
Public Citizen's Global Trade Watch

Do existing trade rules undermine environmental quality?

With its central mandate to dismantle remaining barriers to international trade, the WTO has no specific rules aimed at protecting the environment. Member governments are free to enforce whatever environmental laws they choose within their borders.

But if a country restricts trade with another country that it claims violates its own environmental laws, the WTO can — and has — stepped in. On several occasions, the organization has ruled that trade restrictions imposed to protect the environment constitute unacceptable discrimination in international trade.[16]

The first challenge to U.S. environmental laws came soon after the WTO was launched, when Venezuela and Brazil charged that a 1990 amendment to the Clean Air Act requiring oil refiners to make cleaner gasoline discriminated against their gasoline exports to the United States. In January 1996, a WTO dispute panel agreed. To avoid trade sanctions by Venezuela and Brazil, the Environmental Protection Agency (EPA) adopted a less stringent standard for gasoline contaminants.

The United States was the complainant in another prominent trade dispute, this one related to the U.S. cattle industry's practice of treating beef and dairy cattle with hormones. The European Union, sensitized to potential health hazards in their beef supply following Great Britain's "mad cow" scare, banned U.S. exports of hormone-treated beef.[17] In 1997 a WTO panel agreed with the U.S. position that its treated beef posed no risk to human health or the environment.

Perhaps the most controversial case challenging environmental-protection efforts came following a complaint by several Asian countries about a U.S. ban on imports of shrimp from countries that allow fishermen to catch shrimp using methods that kill endangered sea turtles. The turtles are protected under several multilateral environmental agreements, including the 1979 Bonn Convention on Protecting Migratory Species of Wild Animals. However, a WTO panel found the U.S. "turtle-safe" requirements an unacceptable violation of its nondiscrimination rule.

"Unfortunately, our predictions of a movement to the lowest-common denominator on environmental standards have come true," says Brent Blackwelder, president of Friends of the Earth. "Both under NAFTA and the WTO, there have been significant challenges to health and environmental regulations, and in a number of cases, the rulings have gone in favor of the polluter or the weaker standard."

Recent trade agreements, he contends, have been as detrimental to the environment as union supporters say they have been to global working conditions. "The corporate globalization that is going on right now is extremely damaging," Blackwelder says. "Trade agreements are empowering corporations all over the world to go to the utmost corners of the world and exploit resources in a most unsustainable manner."

Blackwelder, who serves on an advisory committee on the environmental impact of trade at the U.S. Trade Representative's office, decries the absence of environmental-protection standards in recent agreements, including the one with China. China is the world's biggest trader in animal parts from such endangered or threatened species as tiger and rhinoceros, and it is the main source of the Asian long-horned beetle, an invasive species that is already destroying trees in parts of the United States.

"There were many opportunities to get some understanding with China on curtailing its trade in endangered species and an agreement not to challenge our efforts to block invasive species," Blackwelder says. "China also is extremely polluted, and our pollution-control equipment could cut that in half. But the agreement was not written to deal with urgent issues like that. It's hard to imagine a greater hostility towards the environment from any administration than we've gotten from this one."

On Nov. 16, President Clinton issued an executive order requiring a review of how future trade agreements would affect the environment. But he and other free-trade supporters insist that trade itself holds out the greatest promise for improving environmental quality throughout the world.

"We are committed to finding solutions which are win-win, that benefit both the economy and the environment — open trade and cutting-edge clean technologies, which I believe will be the next industrial revolution," Clinton said. [18]

Indeed, some observers say the inclusion of environmental standards in trade agreements may actually impede improvements in the global environment.

"I'm willing to consider having environmental issues raised in trade negotiations, but if they become a big obstacle and prevent further trade liberalization, then I think that in the long term we will have set the environment back, not forward," says Portney of Resources for the Future. "If you bollix up trade agreements too much with these issues, the poorer countries that would benefit from enhanced trade will grow less slowly than they would otherwise, and so they'll pay less attention to the environment than they would otherwise." ■

BACKGROUND

Postwar Trade System

The foundation of the world-trade system in place today was laid 56 years ago at the remote New Hampshire mountain resort of Bretton Woods. Representatives of 44 countries met there in the final months of World War II to decide how best to shore up the world economy, laid to waste by conflict, and to protect it from the forces that had helped spark the war in the first place.

Nazism and Germany's aggression against its neighbors in Europe did not arise in a vacuum — rather they came in the wake of severe economic hardship. As the Great Depression destroyed jobs at home, governments of the industrial powers enacted protectionist laws designed to keep out imports that might compete with domestic industries. For every trade barrier thrown up by one country, its trading partners erected retaliatory barriers, setting in motion a process that quickly brought international trade to a standstill and fueled political extremism that erupted in war.

History gave the conferees at Bretton Woods little hope for success. A similar effort to create an international forum for settling disputes, launched in the wake of World War I, had gone nowhere. Despite the ardent support of President Woodrow Wilson, Congress rejected U.S. membership in the League of Nations. Without the crucial imprimatur of the United States, by then a major economic and military power, the League was swept away in the turmoil that sparked World War II.

The decisions made at Bretton Woods proved more lasting. In an effort to prevent the wild swings in currency values that had contributed to financial instability in the 1930s, participants agreed on a fixed-rate exchange system in which the dollar's value was set at one-thirty-fifth of an ounce of gold and other currencies were "pegged" to the dollar.

To oversee the new fixed-rate system, they created the International Monetary Fund, composed of high-ranking government officials from each country that signed the agreement. * A sister organization, the In-

* Though the gold standard was later abandoned, the IMF continues to issue loans to countries with balance-of-payments difficulties.

Chronology

1930s Congress passes key labor laws.

1935
The National Labor Relations Act, or Wagner Act, guarantees workers' rights to bargain collectively and form unions.

1938
The Fair Labor Standards Act bars child labor, establishes the minimum wage and requires employers to pay time-and-a-half wages for overtime.

1940s-1960s

In the wake of World War II, international trade expands under the oversight of multilateral institutions.

May 19, 1948
Twenty-three countries meet in New Hampshire and later establish the General Agreement on Tariffs and Trade (GATT) to set rules governing international trade, the International Monetary Fund (IMF) to oversee exchange rates and the World Bank to assist economic development in poor countries.

1970s-1980s

Key environmental laws take effect in the United States.

1970
The Clean Air Act sets standards for major air pollutants in U.S. cities.

1972
The Clean Water Act requires the removal of pollutants from the nation's waterways.

1973
The Tokyo Round of trade negotiations among about 100 countries begins. The talks, which last for six years, result in an average one-third reduction in customs duties in the world's major industrial markets.

1988
The Trade and Competitiveness Act requires the president to retaliate against countries found to engage in unfair trade practices, such as "dumping" goods in the United States at below-market prices.

1990s-2000s

Trade expansion continues despite growing protests.

1993
Congress approves the North American Free Trade Agreement (NAFTA), expanding an earlier U.S.-Canadian free-trade area to include Mexico.

December 1994
Negotiations to extend NAFTA to all countries in the Western Hemisphere begin at the Summit of the Americas, held in Miami. Talks bog down after Congress refuses to renew the president's "fast-track" trade negotiating authority.

Jan. 1, 1995
The World Trade Organization (WTO), founded by 135 countries to replace the GATT, begins operations, with the mandate of administering trade agreements and settling trade disputes.

January 1996
A WTO dispute panel rules that a 1990 amendment to the Clean Air Act requiring refiners to make cleaner gasoline discriminates against Venezuelan gasoline exports to the United States, prompting the Environmental Protection Agency to adopt a less stringent standard for gasoline contaminants.

1998
A WTO panel rules than a ban by the European Union on imports of hormone-treated beef from the United States violates trade rules because there is no proof that it threatens public health.

Nov. 15, 1999
China and the United States reach an agreement on bilateral trade expansion. The same month, violent demonstrations by globalization opponents disrupt a WTO meeting in Seattle.

Nov. 30 – Dec. 3, 1999
The ninth round of international trade negotiations takes place in Seattle amid massive protests.

May 18, 2000
President Clinton signs the Trade and Development Act, which opens U.S. markets to more goods from Africa, the Caribbean and Central America.

May 24, 2000
After a heated debate, the House approves the China trade bill, paving the way for China's acceptance into the WTO.

ternational Bank for Reconstruction and Development — better known today as the World Bank — was set up to help raise productivity and reduce poverty in developing countries and thus hasten their entry into the world trading system.

A third institution established at Bretton Woods was the General Agreement on Tariffs and Trade, or GATT. The clumsy acronym was chosen for what originally was intended to be simply an agreement until a permanent body, the International Trade Organization, could be established to oversee it. But Congress never approved the permanent body, leaving the GATT bureaucracy, headquartered in Geneva, as the only mechanism for setting the rules of international trade for the next 30 years.

The GATT, initially signed by 23 countries, was formally launched on May 19, 1948, with the mandate to promote the free trade of goods by supporting the elimination of tariffs, import quotas and subsidies that prevented or discouraged imports. Over the years, as the volume of trade and the number of signatories grew, the GATT underwent a number of revisions that were agreed to in multilateral trade talks, known as rounds. These generally lasted for a number of years and produced changes in the rules that gradually reduced allowable tariffs. The Tokyo Round, for example, involved about 100 countries, lasted from 1973-79 and resulted in an average one-third reduction in customs duties in the world's major industrial markets.

The United States, traditionally one of the strongest champions of free trade, came under pressure to curb imports in the 1970s, as the domestic auto, steel and other basic manufacturing industries lost market share to imports from Japan, Europe and other countries. With the 1974 Trade Act, Congress required the executive branch to monitor foreign trade practices and authorized the president to impose tariffs on countries found guilty of unfair trade practices.

Also in 1974, a separate agreement covering trade in textiles went into effect. The Multifibre Arrangement, as it was known, sought to promote free trade in textiles but also allowed countries to retain certain protections for their textile industries, a sector that is especially vulnerable to low-cost competition from developing countries.

CQ Press/Scott Ferrell

U.S. Trade Representative Charlene Barshefsky addresses the press at the World Trade Organization meeting in Seattle last November. Street protests forced the WTO to cancel its opening ceremony.

But as quickly as GATT members tore down tariffs and duties on imports, they often created less visible barriers to trade, such as import license requirements and government subsidies to prop up domestic industries threatened by imports. As a result, entire sectors of a country's economy, such as agriculture, textiles and the fast-growing service sector, remained largely off-limits to trade-liberalizing rules.

Frustrated by the practice of some exporters of "dumping" their goods in the United States at below-market prices, Congress passed the 1988 Trade and Competitiveness Act, which beefed up earlier legislation by requiring the president to retaliate against countries found to engage in dumping and other unfair trade practices.

To deal with those entrenched barriers to trade, GATT members launched another round of negotiations in 1986. Called the Uruguay Round after their location in Punta del Este, Uruguay, the negotiations went on for almost eight years. By their conclusion in 1994, the 125 member countries had agreed to expand the subject of trade rules beyond goods to include services and intellectual property as well. They also agreed to establish the WTO with a stronger legal mandate than the GATT to oversee the expanded trade regime.

As the GATT moved ahead with liberalized trade rules, the United States and other countries proceeded to eliminate remaining trade barriers through a series of free-trade agreements with individual countries or regions. In 1985, the United States signed a free-trade pact with Israel, followed in 1988 by the U.S.-Canada Free

Anti-Globalization Movement Unites Students and Unions

"Make the global economy work! Stop corporate greed!" read the banner being carried down K Street in downtown Washington. A few minutes later, police in riot gear fired several canisters of tear gas to keep the protesters from getting any closer to the White House. When the crowd refused to disperse, armored personnel carriers moved in, and police handcuffed dozens of youthful demonstrators and carted them off to jail in yellow school buses.

The confrontation was one of many between demonstrators and law-enforcement officers that engulfed the capital for two days in mid-April. The catalyst was the annual meeting of the International Monetary Fund (IMF) and the World Bank, the global institutions that oversee exchange rates and provide economic assistance to developing countries, respectively. The same rallying cries had been heard at the violent protests in Seattle during a meeting of the World Trade Organization (WTO) last November.

"The WTO, the IMF and the World Bank are the main institutions that promote corporate greed," Drea, a young woman who had traveled from Montana for the April demonstration, told a reporter. "What's bringing all these people together is the recognition that globalization is just another way to allow multinational companies to exploit people all over the world. We can't just ignore what's happening and let them do it."

AP Photo/Heesoon Yim

A demonstrator protesting World Bank and International Monetary Fund policies is arrested as other demonstrators block a street in Washington, D.C., in September 2000.

Washington hadn't seen such an outpouring of youthful outrage since the late 1960s, when antiwar demonstrators took to the streets. But the anti-globalization forces also seem to include a broader cross-section of the American public. Marching alongside the students were a number of veterans of earlier protests — middle-aged men and women with more than a few gray hairs. A group of elderly ladies wearing plastic rain kerchiefs said they had come from California to march and ask their congresswoman to vote against trade agreements that cost Americans jobs and gut U.S. environmental-protection laws.

But the biggest difference between the antiwar protests and the demonstrations against globalization may be the active participation by labor unions. In the 1960s, student protesters clashed not only with police but also with "hard hats," blue-collar workers who denounced the protesters as unpatriotic slackers.

"There's a new coalition today," says David Smith, director of policy at the AFL-CIO. "In both Seattle and Washington we saw young people, environmentalists and folks from the religious community marching together with trade unionists. This is a powerful and growing popular coalition."

Free-trade advocates wasted no time in dismissing the demonstrators as extremist kooks. A *Wall Street Journal* editorial described the Washington protesters as "this seeming circus — a smorgasbord of save-the-turtles activists, anarchists, egalitarians, Luddites and Marxists." [1] James Pinkerton, a columnist for *Newsday*, wrote of "pasty wastrels taking time off from their studies at Vassar to rage against the machine, their expensive orthodontia bared at the Kevlar-knuckled cops in riot gear." [2]

To Smith, such statements amount to little more than whistling past the graveyard. "I take some of the venom of our critics as a sign that we're on the right track," he says.

Indeed, says Brent Blackwelder, president of Friends of the Earth, multinational corporations will face even greater opposition in the future if they continue to ignore calls to protect the environment and workers' rights.

"The huge demonstrations in Seattle and Washington provided a clear signal to the international globalization institutions that if they keep trying to do business as usual they're going to encounter an ever-growing storm of protest," he says. "People are not going to stand by and see their communities and their quality of life degraded by distant corporate powers. I certainly hope they get the message, because if things don't change I would predict that this is just the initial blip on the radar screen of a growing tidal wave."

---

[1] "Trade Junked," *The Wall Street Journal*, April 21, 2000.

[2] James Pinkerton, "Methinks They Doth Protest Too Much," IntellectualCapital.com, April 20, 2000.

Fair-Trade Movement Targets "Unfair" Labor Practices

At the same time that the Clinton administration and other governments are doing their best to dismantle tariffs and other barriers to trade, citizens' groups and state and local governments are moving just as fast to put them back up again.

It's all part of a movement known generally as "fair trade," and it has the enthusiastic support of those who feel the current trend toward globalization is not the panacea for the world's problems that free-trade advocates say it is.

The initiative harkens back to the 1980s grass-roots campaign to isolate the South African government and its racist policy of apartheid by boycotting American companies doing business there. The effort paid off. Heeding the call of the Rev. Leon Sullivan, who wrote a corporate code of conduct for dealing with South Africa, many American firms pulled out of the country, providing an important impetus for apartheid's eventual repeal in 1991.

Today, fair-trade advocates are trying to put similar pressure on companies to ensure that products they import and sell to the American public are produced in ways that protect workers' rights and the environment.

The movement took root more than a decade ago in Europe, where some importers agreed to buy coffee beans from Central American farmers' cooperatives that distributed proceeds from coffee sales to the farmers themselves. Fair-trade coffee is now available in the United States as well, though it accounts for less than one-tenth of 1 percent of all the coffee consumed in this country.[1]

A more visible expression of the fair-trade movement is the current wave of campus boycotts of athletic shoes, clothing and equipment bearing college logos sold by companies that produce them in sweatshops in the United States and overseas.

The protest effort is coordinated by an international coalition called United Students Against Sweatshops. In 1997, the coalition launched a campaign encouraging students to force their colleges to take responsibility for the conditions under which such products were made. Duke University completed a code of conduct for its suppliers last November, and Brown University followed suit in May.

"The goal of students across the country who are organizing around sweatshop issues is to create widespread change in an industry where insufficient wages and mandatory overtime are common," writes Sarah Jacobson, a coalition activist and a senior at the University of Oregon. "In many Third World and American apparel factories, there have been reports of intimidation of workers who try to speak out. And because it is easy for these factories to cut and run, vanishing across national borders and abandoning workers, many people are hesitant to organize unions or demand a living wage."

A number of state and local governments have selective-purchasing policies that prohibit them from doing business with companies that engage in objectionable practices. Many of these provisions are aimed at punishing companies that do business in countries with repressive governments, such as Myanmar, formerly Burma, and Nigeria. The city of Berkeley, Calif., for instance, has so many purchasing restrictions in place that the city government reportedly has trouble finding adequate supplies.[2]

On May 8, San Francisco went beyond such specific purchasing bans to become the first U.S. city to adopt a general resolution opposing unregulated economic globalization and supporting fair trade, socially responsible investment and sustainable and equitable economic development.

It is uncertain, however, whether other governments will follow suit. The World Trade Organization is considering new trade regulations that would find such fair-trade initiatives in violation of its non-discrimination rules.

[1] See John Burgess, "Deal Brews to Give Fairer Deal to Farmers," *The Washington Post*, May 13, 2000.

[2] See Miles A. Pomper, "Sanctions Slowdown," *Governing*, June 2000, pp. 28-29.

Trade Agreement. In December 1992, President Bush signed NAFTA, which expanded the North American free-trade area to include Mexico.

Hailed by its supporters as the most comprehensive regional free-trade pact ever negotiated, NAFTA became a lightning rod for critics who decried the absence of adequate protections for workers' rights and the environment. These issues were addressed in supplemental, or side, agreements. The North American Agreement on Labor Cooperation created a tri-national secretariat in Dallas to field petitions regarding labor practices. The North American Agreement on Environmental Cooperation created a similar body based in Montreal to promote cooperation on improving environmental protection throughout the continent. Congress eventually approved NAFTA in 1993, and President Clinton signed it into law.

World Trade Organization

By 1990, international trade accounted for an unprecedented

portion of global economic activity. (*See graph, p. 38.*) The volume of world trade was clearly outstripping the GATT's ability to oversee it. For that reason, 135 countries agreed in 1994 to replace the GATT with a new agency, the WTO.

Like its predecessor, the Geneva-based WTO was given the mandate to assure the freest possible flow of trade, administer trade agreements and act as a forum for trade negotiations. Unlike the GATT, it was granted a clear legal mandate to implement trade agreements and settle trade disputes between governments.

Under the new organization's dispute-resolution system, member countries can file complaints against other members with the WTO. If subsequent negotiations fail to resolve a dispute, the matter is turned over to a WTO panel of trade experts who issue a formal decision. A country found guilty of unfair trade practices can legally refuse to comply with the panel's ruling. But if it does, the WTO will allow the petitioner to retaliate with trade sanctions and other potentially costly penalties. Since 1995, more than 150 trade disputes have come before the WTO; of those, more than 100 are still in the process of adjudication or appeal.

From its opening on Jan. 1, 1995, the new trade organization chalked up early achievements reflecting the growing impact of the information-based "new economy" on global trade patterns. With a series of agreements in 1997, many WTO members agreed to lower customs duties on computer and software products, phase out barriers to foreign telecommunications investments and open their markets to foreign banks, securities firms and insurance companies.

Trade's growing importance to domestic prosperity prompted many countries that had shunned affiliation with the GATT to seek membership in the WTO. Among these was China, whose government had encouraged limited foreign investment since the 1970s but resisted the broad liberalization of its vast markets.

On Nov. 15, 1999, China and the United States reached trade-expansion agreement that would facilitate China's entrance into the WTO. The United States agreed to suspend its annual review of China's human-rights record for renewal of China's most-favored nation status. In return, China agreed to open its markets to a broad range of U.S. exports and investments.

The Clinton administration and other free-trade supporters had eagerly anticipated last fall's meeting in Seattle as the launch of a new round of talks that would continue the removal of trade barriers. But the ninth round of multilateral trade negotiations since Bretton Woods, known variously as the Seattle Round or the Millennium Round, got off to a shaky start as demonstrators insisted that trade liberalization not come at the cost of workers' rights and environmental protection.

Negotiators made little headway, leaving the resolution of several major issues for the future:

- Agriculture: Negotiators agreed to begin talks on reducing agricultural export subsidies. Although the European Union continues to protect member nations' farmers from cheap agricultural imports, it is not alone. The United States still subsidizes the production of sugar and other commodities. Trade in genetically modified foods, which the United States and some developing countries support amid skepticism in Europe, will be the subject of a new WTO study group.
- Services: Despite earlier agreements liberalizing trade in financial services, telecommunications and transport, many countries still bar imports of these services. U.S. efforts to start talks on sweeping changes that would open up such trade fell short. Members agreed to the talks, but the goal will not be to end countries' right to exclude services.
- Dumping: Some countries want to make it harder for the United States to implement its anti-dumping laws, which bar imports that are sold below cost on the U.S. market.
- Technology: Members agreed to extend a moratorium in new tariffs on electronic transmissions across borders, but failed to agree on a new set of talks aimed at reducing tariffs on high-tech products.
- WTO transparency: Members agreed to make public WTO documents and decisions, but stopped short of opening up the dispute-resolution process or allow non-governmental organizations to participate in that process.
- Labor standards: Developing countries blocked a U.S. proposal to study the impact of trade on labor standards, arguing that such efforts could enable developed countries to bar Third World imports.
- Poor countries: Members agreed to allow poor, developing countries to phase in WTO requirements over three years. [19] ■

CURRENT SITUATION

New Trade Talks

Supporters of labor and environmental standards are now focusing their efforts at ongoing efforts to expand NAFTA to include other countries of the Western Hemisphere, beginning with Chile. Negotiations on a Free Trade Area of the Americas

(FTAA) began in earnest after the December 1994 Summit of the Americas, held in Miami.

But those talks have bogged down in large part because of Congress' refusal to renew the president's "fast-track" trade negotiating authority when it expired in 1994. Fast-track authority requires lawmakers to vote for or against trade agreements reached by the president within 90 days, with no amendments allowed. The lack of fast track, which Clinton requested and failed to obtain in both 1997 and 1998, has hampered his administration's ability to negotiate trade agreements. In its absence, the Chilean government is reluctant to sign an agreement that may be significantly altered by Congress.

Despite Congress' action, Clinton recently reiterated his determination to meet the goal of achieving a free-trade agreement covering all of North and South America by 2005. "You should not believe that because the legislation didn't pass, that the United States is any less committed to finishing the Free Trade Area of the Americas," he said, "or that, because it didn't pass, any agreement we make in the context of a Free Trade Area of the Americas is less likely to pass Congress." [20]

But union and environmental activists want to make sure than any future agreement the United States enters into contains specific standards to promote workers' rights and environmental quality. "As the administration negotiates the FTAA, they ought to negotiate an obligation to adhere to the ILO core labor standards," says Smith of the AFL-CIO. "That ought to be part of the deal, as well as any other deal that Congress approves."

Including such provisions in the FTAA would mean rewriting NAFTA because it relegated labor standards to side agreements with no enforcement measures. "Under NAFTA, if a Mexican company making goods for export to the United States decides to reduce its labor costs by shooting somebody who wants to start a union or otherwise suppress wages in ways that would be illegal in the United States, it will face no penalties," says the Economic Policy Institute's Faux. "We need to renegotiate NAFTA to force the Mexicans to abide by the core ILO labor standards, include a mechanism for increasing the minimum wage in Mexico as productivity increases and stipulate that violations of labor rights be punishable by trade sanctions."

Consumer Choice

As the debate over the inclusion of enforceable standards in trade agreements continues, there is renewed interest in expanding the use of product labels to promote environmental quality and workers' rights. By identifying products that are made using environmentally friendly methods and under acceptable working conditions, so-called eco-labels enable consumers to exert pressure on manufacturers directly.

"Given the concerns being raised on both the labor and the environmental side," says Portney of Resources for the Future, "one obvious thing we can do is harness market power and allow consumers to vote with their pocketbooks in deciding which conditions they want to see continued and which ones they don't want to see continued."

He advocates labeling as an especially effective tool for promoting environmental protection. "It deals with legitimate national concerns about products, for example the use of genetically modified organisms, which some countries object to." Many Europeans in particular are concerned about the potentially adverse health and environmental effects of so-called "Frankenfoods" and have staged demonstrations against importing such products from the United States. [21]

To be effective, however, labeling programs have to be backed up by a credible certification system. "If the program is self-certified, it's meaningless," Portney says. "You've got to have some organization that's respected for its objectivity. And of course it's also meaningless unless the standards set for qualifying for labels are strict enough to exclude producers that fall short of widely accepted consumer expectations."

Some eco-label programs call for government certification, such as the EPA energy ratings on appliances and the "dolphin-safe" label placed on cans of tuna caught using nets that don't trap and kill dolphins. But even when they are backed by certification, label programs are vulnerable to challenge under international trade rules. In 1991, GATT dispute panels ruled that the U.S. ban on imports of tuna from Mexico, associated with the dolphin-safe program, was illegal. "The dolphin-safe tuna program was great," Friends of the Earth's Blackwelder says, "but since it's come under attack as a result of trade agreements, the label is likely to become meaningless."

More recently, students on many campuses across the country have organized boycotts of Nike and other suppliers of athletic clothing bearing college logos made in Chinese sweatshops. (*See sidebar, p. 43.*) But labor activists say that approach is not enough to protect workers and the environment. "Certainly, well-informed consumers will vote with their feet, and we welcome that," the AFL-CIO's Smith says. "But it's not a substitute for the rule of law and the obligation of governments to adhere to core standards. If you thought that volunteerism would work, all you

At Issue:

Will the U.S.-China trade agreement help workers' rights?

yes

CHARLENE BARSHEFSKY
U.S. Trade Representative

FROM TESTIMONY BEFORE THE SENATE BANKING COMMITTEE, MAY 9, 2000

With respect to reform within China, WTO [World Trade Organization] accession represents a potentially profound and historic shift, building upon — but going much further than — China's domestic reforms to date.

China's domestic reforms have reversed the most damaging policies of the Cultural Revolution and Great Leap Forward. WTO accession will accelerate and deepen this process, altering policies [that] date to the earliest years of the communist era. As it enters the WTO, China will:

- Permit foreigners and all Chinese businesses to import most goods into China;
- Reduce, and in some cases remove entirely, state control over internal distribution of goods and the provision of services;
- Enable foreign businesses to participate in information industries such as telecommunications, including the Internet; and
- Subject its decisions in all areas covered by the WTO to enforcement. . . .

These commitments are a remarkable victory for economic reformers in China. They will give China's people more access to information, and weaken the ability of hard-liners in government to isolate China's public from outside influences and ideas. More deeply, they reflect a judgment that prosperity, security and international respect will not come from the static nationalism, state power and state control over the economy China adopted after the war, but that China's own interests are best served by the advancing economic freedom, engagement with the world and, ultimately, development of the rule of law inherent in the initiative President Truman began in 1948 with the founding of the GATT [General Agreement on Tariffs and Trade].

The WTO accession, therefore, has potential beyond economics and trade: as a means to advance the rule of law in China, and a precedent for willingness to accept international standards of behavior in other fields. That is why many Hong Kong and Chinese activists for democracy and human rights . . . support PNTR [permanent normal trade relations] and see WTO accession as China's most important step toward reform in 20 years. And it is why our support for WTO accession rests on a broader long-term commitment to human rights and freedoms, as well as new opportunities and strengthened guarantees of fairness for Americans.

no

HARRY WU
Executive director, Laogai Research Foundation

FROM TESTIMONY BEFORE THE SENATE COMMERCE, SCIENCE AND TRANSPORTATION COMMITTEE, APRIL 11, 2000.

It has long been fashionable to think, "What is good for Wall Street is good for the United States." Globalization has greatly benefited multinational corporations, and it is true that PNTR [permanent normal trade relations] and WTO entry for China will further help these companies economically. But the other major beneficiary of China's entry into the [WTO] will be the Chinese Communist Party (CCP). The CCP maintains political and economic control in China, and WTO entry will not change that. . . .

Why do the Western capitalists want to rush into China? China has a population of 1.25 billion. This is a lucrative market. . . . But even more importantly, China has a huge, cheap and obedient labor force. In this country there are no free trade unions, all the men and women are controlled by one hand — the communist government. . . .

We've heard many politicians and business people say that doing business in China helps spread American values and business practices. It is true that Chinese businessmen are willing to learn how to be more efficient, but U.S. businesses in China will never be allowed to take steps to improve human rights that go against the fundamental policies of the Communist Party. The Chinese communist government is one of the worst human-rights violators in the world today. In China, there is a national "population-control" policy. . . . If a woman in an American company gives birth to a child without a permit, Chinese law says that she will be fired. There is nothing the American bosses can do. If Chinese workers want to organize an independent trade union in an American company in China, these people would be fired or even arrested. Again, there is nothing the American bosses can do. . . .

In 1994, the Clinton administration delinked human rights and trade. . . . Last month the State Department Human Rights Report admitted that the human-rights situation in China is worsening. The administration intends to introduce a resolution at the Human Rights Commission in Geneva this year. But why not take a stand in Washington, D.C., using our economic leverage? If foreign policy does not contain a moral basis, it is a typical appeasement policy.

From a human-rights standpoint, one can only hope this focus on trade agreements will not completely overshadow the long road that must be traveled towards democracy in China. Perhaps one day, the U.S. government will try to promote human rights in China with the same zeal that it runs after market access.

have to do is look at the history of industrial relations in this country and in Europe to understand that it won't. These things require a commitment by government. Otherwise, all you get is a race to the bottom."

Workers' Anxieties

Amid the emotional debate emanating from the streets of Seattle and Washington and from Congress regarding the China trade vote, opinion polls suggest that Americans are ambivalent about the impact of globalization on their lives.

On the China deal, for example, a recent Gallup Poll indicates Americans are slightly more likely to believe increased trade will benefit the U.S. economy (48 percent) than believe that it would hurt it (37 percent). But 57 percent said that increased trade with China would "mostly hurt" U.S. workers, as opposed to helping them (28 percent). [22]

The popular perception that trade is good for the economy but bad for job security suggests to some analysts that the government needs to beef up assistance to workers who are displaced by economic trends. "We do not handle displacement as well as we should," says Litan of the Brookings Institution. "We ought to do a lot more to promote retraining of workers during their working lives."

In addition, Litan proposes the creation of a new government program that would provide workers with "wage insurance." When workers lose employment and can only find lower-paying jobs, such a program would help make up the difference, encouraging workers to take inferior jobs temporarily and get training for better-paying jobs in the future.

The government also should offer better health insurance coverage for unemployed workers, Litan says. Under current law, displaced workers can receive 18 months' coverage under their former employers' health plans, but they have to pay the entire premium out of pocket.

"If you're a displaced worker today, you can get health insurance, but you can't pay for it," he says. "Subsidizing health insurance for the unemployed is a no-brainer. I'm mystified that the politicians haven't even discussed such a proposal." [23] ■

OUTLOOK

Gore's Balancing Act

The benefits of trade and globalization are one area where the two candidates for this fall's presidential election agree. Both Vice President Al Gore and George W. Bush, the Republican governor of Texas, supported the trade agreement with China and have consistently touted the advantages of globalization for the U.S. economy.

The Clinton administration's unequivocal endorsement of globalization has complicated Gore's standing with the American labor movement, however. Despite their steady decline in membership over the past three decades, unions hold the key not only to Gore's presidential bid but also to Democrats' hopes of regaining the majority of seats in the House. Unions and environmental groups welcomed Gore's strong endorsement last fall of Clinton's executive order requiring environmental-impact reviews of all trade agreements negotiated by the United States, a process Gore promised would "revolutionize the way the environment is dealt with in all future trade talks." [24]

But the emergence of the China trade agreement as the administration's top legislative priority this year forced Gore to straddle the line on that key issue. He declared his support for the trade bill even though it contained no environmental or labor standards and no formal assessment of its impact on those areas.

"I strongly support normal trade relations with China because I believe it is right for America's economy and right for the cause of reform in China," he said on May 22, just two days before the crucial House vote.

Many union leaders, who led the opposition to normalizing trade relations with a country they see as a major threat to American jobs, were outraged at Gore's position. Stephen P. Yokich, head of the United Auto Workers (UAW), said the union was "deeply disappointed" in Gore because he had "tried to have it both ways" on trade.

"Gore is holding hands with the profiteers of the world," Yokich said. He and other union leaders threatened to throw their support behind the presidential candidacy of consumer activist Ralph Nader, leader of the Green Party. Although the likelihood of a Nader victory is next to nil, a defection of union support to his cause could cost Gore critical votes in the West and Midwest, and perhaps the election.

That scenario became less likely, however, when AFL-CIO President John Sweeney renewed the federation's endorsement of Gore after losing its battle to defeat the China trade bill. "The vice president is not the president," Sweeney said, "and this was clearly the president's bill. We saw very little lobbying by the vice president." [25]

However they view the impact of trade on jobs and the environment, most observers agree that the concerns that have colored the debate about globalization did not end with the vote to normalize trade relations with China.

"Every economic system has a politics, and the global economy is going to be no different," says Faux of the Economic Policy Institute. "What we've seen in recent months is just the beginning of a global politics that will accompany a global economy." ■

FOR MORE INFORMATION

American Federation of Labor-Congress of Industrial Organizations (AFL-CIO), 815 16th St., N.W., Washington, D.C. 20006; (202) 637-5000; www.aflcio.org. The union is the leading source of information on the impact of trade on U.S. jobs and on working conditions.

Friends of the Earth, 1025 Vermont Ave., N.W., Washington, D.C. 20005; (202) 783-7400; www.foe.org. This environmental-advocacy group supports the inclusion in international trade agreements of standards to protect the environment.

International Bank for Reconstruction and Development (World Bank), 1818 H St., N.W., Washington, D.C. 20433; (202) 477-1234; www.worldbank.org. The bank provides exhaustive information on environmental protection, agriculture, health and other conditions in the developing world.

International Monetary Fund, 700 19th St., N.W., Washington, D.C. 20431; www.imf.org. The IMF, established in 1948 to oversee exchange rates, is an excellent source of statistics on international trade.

International Trade Administration, U.S. Department of Commerce, 14th St. and Constitution Ave., N.W., No. 3850, Washington, D.C. 20230; Trade information: (800) 872-8723; Publications: (202) 482-5487; www.ita.doc.gov. The ITA implements programs to promote world trade.

World Trade Organization, 154 rue de Lausanne, 1211 Geneva 21, Switzerland; 41-22-739-51-1; www.wto.org. The successor agency to the General Agreement on Tariffs and Trade (GATT), the WTO oversees the world-trade system and hears disputes among its 136 member countries.

Notes

[1] National Labor Committee, "Made in China: The Role of U.S. Companies in Denying Human and Worker Rights," 2000.

[2] From remarks made at the White House on May 24, 2000. For background, see David Masci, "China After Deng," *The CQ Researcher*, June 13, 1997, pp. 505-528, and Kenneth Jost, "Democracy in Asia," *The CQ Researcher*, July 24, 1998, pp. 625-648.

[3] For background, see Kenneth Jost, "Future of Korea," *The CQ Researcher*, May 19, 2000, pp. 425-448, Mary H. Cooper, "Economic Sanctions," *The CQ Researcher*, Oct. 28, 1994, pp. 937-960, and David Masci, "Castro's Next Move," *The CQ Researcher*, Dec. 12, 1997, pp. 1081-1104.

[4] For background, see Mary H. Cooper, "Rethinking NAFTA," *The CQ Researcher*, June 7, 1996, pp. 481-504.

[5] See Glenn Kessler, "U.S. Task Force Targets Poverty Along Mexican Border," *The Washington Post*, May 26, 2000. For background, see David Masci, "Mexico's Future," *The CQ Researcher*, Sept. 19, 1997, pp. 817-840.

[6] For background, see Mary H. Cooper, "International Monetary Fund," *The CQ Researcher*, Jan. 29, 1999, pp. 65-88.

[7] Council of Economic Advisers, Economic Report of the President, February 2000, pp. 202-203.

[8] See Gary Burtless, Robert Z. Lawrence, Robert E. Litan and Robert J. Shapiro, *Globaphobia* (1998), pp. 1-3.

[9] Testifying Feb. 8, 2000, before the House Ways and Means Subcommittee on Trade.

[10] See Lori Nitschke, "Third World Trade Bill Likely to Have Limited Impact," *CQ Weekly*, May 6, 2000, pp. 1020-1027.

[11] From Rep. Brown's Web site, www.house.gov/sherrodbrown.

[12] Bill Gates, "Yes, More Trade with China," *The Washington Post*, May 23, 2000.

[13] National Labor Committee, "Made in China: The Role of U.S. Companies in Denying Human and Worker Rights," May 10, 2000. For background, see Kenneth Jost, "Human Rights," *The CQ Researcher*, Nov. 13, 1998, pp. 977-1000.

[14] Lori Wallach and Michelle Sforza, *Whose Trade Organization?* (1999), p. 174.

[15] Quoted by John Pomfret, "Dissidents Back China's WTO Entry," *The Washington Post*, May 11, 2000.

[16] For details on the WTO's approach to environmental issues, see Gary P. Sampson, "Trade and the Environment," in Miguel Rodriguez Mendoza, Patrick Low and Barbara Kotschwar, eds., *Trade Rules in the Making* (1999), pp. 511-524.

[17] See Suzanne Daley, "Rise in Cases of Mad Cow Disease Alarms Europe," *The New York Times*, May 7, 2000.

[18] Clinton spoke Dec. 1, 1999, before a meeting of trade officials attending the WTO meeting in Seattle.

[19] See Steven Pearlstein, "Key Negotiating Points," *The Washington Post*, Dec. 4, 1999.

[20] Clinton addressed a meeting of the Council of the Americas in Washington on May 2, 2000.

[21] For background, see Kathy Koch, "Food Safety Battle: Organic vs. Biotech," *The CQ Researcher*, Sept. 4, 1998, pp. 761-784.

[22] Jeffrey M. Jones, "Americans Think Increased Trade with China Will Help U.S. Economy but Hurt Workers," The Gallup Organization, May 17, 2000.

[23] For more information, see Burtless et al., *op. cit.*, pp. 127-155.

[24] From a statement issued on Nov. 17, 1999.

[25] Quoted in David S. Broder, "AFL-CIO Lauds Gore for Role in 'President's China Trade Bill," *The Washington Post*, May 26, 2000.

Bibliography

Selected Sources Used

Books

Burtless, Gary, Robert Z. Lawrence, Robert E. Litan and Robert J. Shapiro, *Globaphobia: Confronting Fears about Open Trade*, Brookings Institution, Progressive Policy Institute and Twentieth Century Fund, 1998.
The authors address some common fears about globalization, including its impact on jobs, wages and environmental quality. They conclude that other forces, notably technological development, play a greater role in those areas and suggest that trade offers more benefits than costs over the long run.

Friedman, Thomas L., *The Lexus and the Olive Tree*, Farrar Straus Giroux, 1999.
Globalization is revolutionizing world markets, writes Friedman, a foreign-affairs columnist for *The New York Times*. At the same time, the rapid flow of goods, capital and information — symbolized by the Lexus — threatens the survival of local communities and culture, the olive tree of the book's title.

Mendoza, Miguel Rodriguez, Patrick Low and Barbara Kotschwar, eds., *Trade Rules in the Making: Challenges in Regional and Multilateral Negotiations*, Organization of American States/Brookings Institution Press, 1999.
Chapters by experts treat a broad range of trade issues, including the history of trade and efforts to reduce barriers; the authority of multilateral trade groups, such as the World Trade Organization (WTO), and regional agreements; and prospects for future pacts like the Free Trade Area of the Americas.

Wallach, Lori, and Michelle Sforza, *Whose Trade Organization? Corporate Globalization and the Erosion of Democracy*, Public Citizen, 1999.
This critique of the WTO examines its negative impact on the environment, food-safety standards, labor rights and economic development in the Third World. The head of Public Citizen is consumer advocate Ralph Nader, this year's presidential candidate of the Green Party.

Articles

"Vote for China's Freedom," *The Economist*, May 20-26, 2000.
Given the choice between opening China to trade, investment and outside information and the status quo, members of the House of Representatives should opt for openness as a way to improve workers' rights and economic development in the world's largest market.

Avery, Dennis T., "Clueless in Seattle," *American Outlook*, winter 2000, pp. 31-34.
Instead of protecting workers' rights and the environment, the author charges, the protesters who disrupted the WTO meeting in Seattle inadvertently undermined their own agenda by delaying further trade liberalization, which he contends offers the greatest promise of global progress.

Hornblower, Margot, "The Battle in Seattle," *Time*, Nov. 29, 1999, pp. 40-44.
Written before the WTO meeting in Seattle broke down amid violent street protests against globalization, this article reviews the trade organization's history and the agenda of the coming round of trade talks.

Licking, Ellen, "They're Here, and They're Taking Over," *Business Week*, May 24, 1999.
In the absence of natural predators to keep them in check, exotic species arriving in the United States on the hulls of cargo ships or embedded in shipping pallets threaten widespread environmental damage and exemplify the potential damage posed by free-trade agreements.

Noland, Marcus, "Learning to Love the WTO," *Foreign Affairs*, September/October 1999, pp. 78-92.
Free trade's critics charge that it enables corporations to exploit workers and foul the environment in the developing world. But the author, a senior fellow at the Institute for International Economics, says those accusations often are a cover for less noble, protectionist motives.

Reports and Studies

Burke, James, "U.S. Investment in China Worsens Trade Deficit," Economic Policy Institute, May 2000.
American manufacturers are building factories in China, where they exploit low-wage labor and add to the country's already serious pollution problems in order to make goods for export, largely back to the United States.

World Trade Organization, "Trade and Environment, 1999."
This exhaustive study examines the impact of trade on such worrisome environmental problems as global warming, deforestation and overfishing. The report concludes that government policies are needed to limit the environmental damage resulting from industrial development and trade.

4 Oil Production in the 21st Century

MARY H. COOPER

American motorists got a shock this year: After enjoying several years of cheap gasoline, they were suddenly faced with gas prices that in some parts of the country exceeded $2 a gallon.

Several factors produced this unhappy turn of events. In March 1999, the Organization of Petroleum Exporting Countries (OPEC) began curtailing its output of crude oil in an attempt to halt a glut of global oil supplies that had depressed prices to their lowest level in 30 years.* The move caught American refiners by surprise, leaving them with lower than normal inventories for the U.S. market. At least two major pipeline disruptions added to the shortage of gasoline in the Midwest, where the price boost was most pronounced.

Consumers were quick to blame oil companies, OPEC and the federal government's clean-air requirements for the price hike. Worried about the impact of oil prices on the outcome of this fall's elections, politicians were sensitive to their complaints. The Clinton administration launched a federal investigation into alleged price fixing by the oil companies, while the governors of Illinois and Indiana responded to consumer outrage by suspending the states' gas taxes.

All indications were that the price hike, which propelled the average price for a gallon of regular unleaded gas to $1.68 on June 19, was temporary. By late July, the average price had fallen to $1.60. But in some ways, this summer's gas shortage resembled earlier energy crises. It may also have served as a useful reminder to American consumers that the era of cheap oil will one day come to an end.

Public Broadcasting Service

Just a quarter-century ago, OPEC had the United States and the rest of the industrialized world by the throat, and Saudi Arabian oil minister Sheik Zaki Yamani was as familiar to many Americans as their representatives in Congress. Saudi Arabia and the four other major Middle East members dominated OPEC, controlling more than a third of world oil production.

In October 1973, the oil cartel imposed a total embargo on its exports to the United States and the Netherlands for their support of Israel in the Yom Kippur War. Oil prices skyrocketed. The ensuing inflation and stagnant industrial output spilled over from the U.S. and Dutch economies to infect the entire industrial world. Stagflation became even more deeply entrenched after 1978-79, when the Iranian revolution sparked a second energy crisis and rise in oil prices.

The industrial world responded to OPEC's grip on world oil supplies by searching for alternative sources. By the 1990s, non-OPEC producers such as Britain, Mexico and Norway had enabled importers to reduce their oil dependence on the volatile Persian Gulf. They also launched campaigns to reduce their consumption of oil by raising energy taxes and encouraging energy conservation through improved efficiency of automobiles and appliances. And they sought to develop alternatives to oil such as solar, wind and geothermal energy.

These efforts paid off in the next two decades. Largely by diversifying their sources of foreign oil, the United States and other major consumers have significantly reduced their vulnerability to oil price manipulations by OPEC. Technological advances in exploration and drilling equipment have enabled producers to discover new oil deposits, further relaxing pressure on oil prices posed by growing global demand for oil.

Worries about future energy crises diminished still further when oil reserves under and around the Caspian Sea were opened to outside development after the Soviet Union's collapse in 1991. The former Soviet republics of Azerbaijan, Kazakhstan and Turkmenistan that border the Caspian — and, to a lesser extent, their Central Asia neighbors Tajikistan and Uzbekistan — stand to reap enough earnings from oil and natural gas exports alone to launch them into the modern industrial era in the space of a few years.

"The Caspian is potentially one of the world's most important, new, energy-producing regions," said former Energy Secretary Federico Peña in 1998. "Although the Caspian may never rival the Persian Gulf, Caspian production can have important implications for world energy supplies by increasing world supply and diversifying sources of supply among producing regions of the world." [1]

The oil glut that began in 1997 provided the icing on the cake for oil consumers. But as this summer's gas price hike suggests, Americans would be foolish to gloat over their current

* OPEC members are Algeria, Indonesia, Iran, Iraq, Kuwait, Libya, Nigeria, Qatar, Saudi Arabia, the United Arab Emirates and Venezuela.

Originally published August 7, 1998.
Updated by Mary H. Cooper, August 10, 2000.

Getting Oil Out of the Caspian

Several new pipelines have been proposed to move oil from the landlocked Caspian republics to maritime ports for export. The U.S. favors lines running from Baku, Azerbaijan, to Ceyhan, Turkey, or from Baku to Georgia. Russia prefers a northern pipeline connecting to its own system or to its Black Sea port of Novorossisk. The pipeline sought by the Caspian republics, runnning south to the Persian Gulf, is opposed by the U.S. because it crosses Iran. The route planned by China across Kazakhstan is not controversial.

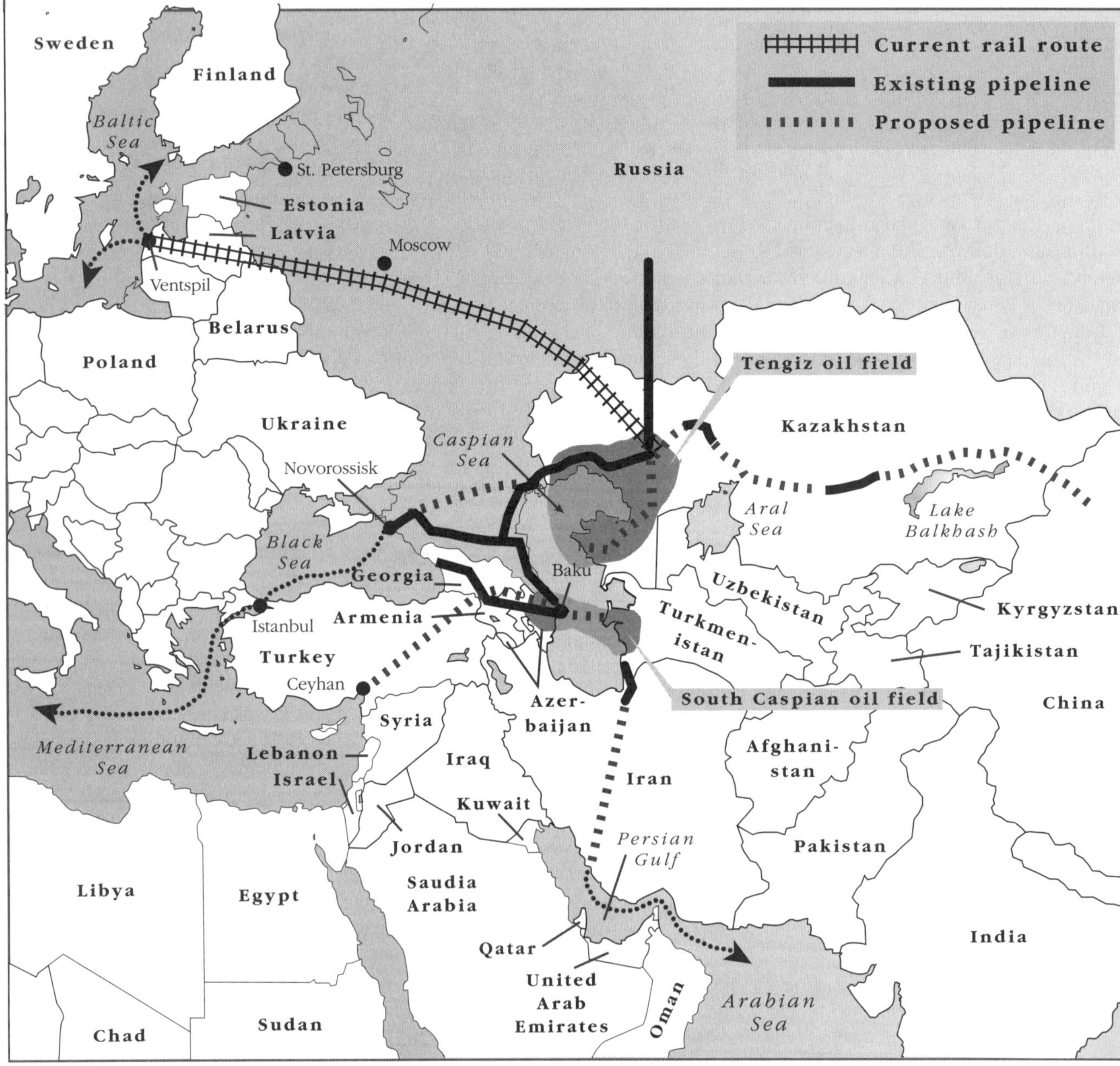

Sources: Energy Information Agency, Fortune Magazine, Parade Magazine

bounty. Even counting Alaska's prolific North Slope oil fields, domestic reserves are falling. The United States now imports more than half of its oil, placing the country at added risk from future disruptions of foreign supplies. [2]

For all its promise, the Caspian Sea region is far from coming on line as a major source of non-OPEC oil. The region's remoteness and legendary political turmoil threaten to postpone or even scuttle the flow of oil before production is fully under way.

Meanwhile, historically low gasoline prices have lulled American motorists into trading in their energy-efficient sub-compact cars for gas-guzzling sport utility vehicles, which now account for almost half of American new car sales. Programs to develop alternatives to oil are losing support in Congress, which has cut the Energy Department's research budget.

America's growing oil consumption also flies in the face of concern that using oil and other fossil fuels is causing a gradual but potentially catastrophic warming of Earth's atmosphere. In December 1997, the United States joined 167 other countries in agreeing to reduce fossil fuel consumption. But in the current climate of energy abundance, support for the Kyoto Protocol has stalled, and the Senate appears highly unlikely to ratify the measure anytime soon.

For much of the 1990s, OPEC members were unable to agree on production cuts to buoy prices. But as consumers discovered this year, it is too soon to write the organization's obituary. OPEC has begun seeking agreement from non-member producers to go along with its efforts to buoy sagging prices. In March 1998, Mexico agreed to join OPEC in cutting production, prompting some oil experts to predict that other countries soon would join in. [3]

Crude Oil Prices Have Been Dropping

World crude oil prices dropped in the 1990s as members of the Organization of Petroleum Exporting Countries resisted OPEC efforts to limit their oil production. Discoveries of new oil sources in non-OPEC nations also have kept prices down.

Source: Energy Information Administration, World Oil Markets 2000.

Even absent a further strengthening of OPEC's ability to manipulate oil prices over the short term, some experts contend that the break in oil prices that prevailed in the 1990s will prove to be temporary. Colin J. Campbell, an oil-industry consultant in Geneva, Switzerland, and author of *The Coming Oil Crisis*, predicts that prices will rise when global oil production reaches its peak, "within the first few years of the next century." After that, he predicts, demand for oil will outpace its supply. "This will be a fundamental turning point, because until now we've always had growing oil production," he says.

As global oil deposits are depleted, OPEC's Middle East producers could be left in control of an increasing portion of world reserves. "We can expect another major price shock around 2000," Campbell said two years ago, "when the Middle East's share of world reserves will be much greater than it is now."

As Americans fire up their gas guzzlers for summer outings, these are some of the questions oil experts are asking:

Has OPEC lost its control over global oil prices?

Through new discoveries and an expanded membership, OPEC's oil reserves have grown over the years. The organization has reached beyond its stronghold in the Persian Gulf — still the main source of the world's oil — to include far-flung producers such as Indonesia and Nigeria. And OPEC's undisputed leader, Saudi Arabia, retains its clout as the world's largest oil producer.

But OPEC's grip over world oil production has slipped in the past 20 years, largely as a result of its own actions. When it set strict quotas in the 1970s

Getting Oil Out of the Caspian . . .

Although some parts of the Caspian region and Central Asia do not hold promise as oil and gas producers, virtually every country in the vast area is likely to play a role in the industry's development. Some will serve as routes for pipelines or railroads and some, because of the threats they pose to the region's political stability, will retard progress. Here are the likely key players:

Armenia — In 1988, the largely Armenian population of Nagorno Karabakh, a province of Azerbaijan, began a six-year rebellion in an effort to become a part of neighboring Armenia. With support from Armenia, the rebels emerged victorious in 1994. Under the truce, Armenia was left in control of the province and other territory comprising 20 percent of Azerbaijan. Peace talks led by the United States, France and Russia, under the aegis of the Organization for Security and Cooperation in Europe, produced a compromise by which Nagorno Karabakh would be an autonomous province of Azerbaijan. After agreeing to these terms, rejected by the province's rebels, Armenian President Levon Ter-Petrossian was forced from office and replaced in March 1998 by Robert Kocharian, a Karabakh native who opposed the compromise. The U.S.-backed proposal to build a pipeline from Baku, Azerbaijan, to the Mediterranean port of Ceyhan, Turkey, would pass through Armenia.

Azerbaijan — Foreign oil companies have already invested heavily in the oil fields centered around the city of Baku. American companies Amoco, Exxon, Pennzoil and Unocal lead a consortium of 11 companies from eight countries — the Azerbaijan International Operating Company — that are drilling for oil for the first time in the country since it gained independence with the Soviet Union's collapse in 1991. President Heidar Aliyev, a former KGB general and member of the Soviet Politburo, took power in a 1993 coup against democratically elected Abullaz Elchibey. Aliyev has survived two attempted coups since then but remains a popular leader who has brought political stability despite the destabilizing effect of the war with Armenia, which ended with the occupation of a fifth of Azerbaijan's territory, including Nagorno Karabakh.[1] Azerbaijan subsequently imposed a trade embargo against Armenia. Under pressure from the Armenian Assembly of America, Congress passed a measure in 1992 barring economic aid to the Azeri government until it takes steps to lift the embargo. An amendment to the Freedom Support Act that provides aid to the former Soviet republics, Section 907, remains in effect despite growing opposition from the Clinton administration and many lawmakers who see it as an obstacle to ensuring U.S. access to Azeri oil.

Georgia — This former Soviet republic has been torn by fighting among several distinct ethnic communities after gaining independence in 1991. President Eduard Shevernadze, a former Soviet foreign minister, has survived two assassination attempts since assuming power in 1992. An oil pipeline links the Azeri oil fields at Baku and the Georgian Black Sea port of Supsa.

Iran — A longstanding oil producer of the Persian Gulf region, Iran also borders the Caspian's southern coast. Because the region's main oil and natural gas deposits lie north of the Iranian coast, Iran's main potential role in the Caspian Sea's oil industry is as a transport link. The Caspian oil producers back construction of a pipeline that would carry the region's oil through Iran to the Persian Gulf for shipment through the Strait of Hormuz to market. The United States, which maintains a unilateral embargo against Iran for its role in supporting international terrorism, adamantly opposes this route. For

that quadrupled oil prices, the cartel sparked a frantic search for alternative sources of oil by the industrial world, which depends on petroleum products for its economic survival.

With the exception of the United States, most industrial countries imported the bulk of their energy supplies. Using sophisticated technology, Britain and Norway soon located and began working oil deposits under the North Sea. *(See story, p. 61.)* The United States and other countries shifted much of their oil demand to these and other non-OPEC producers, which now account for about half of the oil export market. Russia and Norway now are the world's second- and third-largest exporters, after Saudi Arabia.

Until earlier this year, OPEC appeared to have lost its ability to set production quotas among its membership as a way to buoy prices, especially in the fall of 1998, when a global oil glut began depressing prices. As usual, Saudi Arabia took the lead, calling in March of that year for a cut in oil production of 1.2 million barrels a day. But with prices falling — and with them precious oil revenues — many members ignored their quotas and pumped as much oil as the market would bear.

Desperate to reduce output, OPEC has appealed to other producers, which are also feeling the pinch of falling oil revenues. Russia, which has the largest oil reserves of any non-OPEC country and badly needs oil revenues to stave off its deepening financial crisis, attended an OPEC meeting in 1998, giving rise to speculation that it might join the organization.[4] On June 4, 1998 the oil ministers of Saudi Arabia and Venezuela reached an agreement with Mexico to cut production by 450,000 barrels a day, beginning July 1. This agreement had some effect on prices, leading some observers to predict that

. . . Involves Many Actors, Many Ifs

now, some Caspian Sea oil is making its way indirectly through Iran via a swap arrangement by which oil is shipped to refineries in northern Iran, and an equivalent amount of Iranian oil is loaded onto tankers in the Persian Gulf for transport to market.

Kazakhstan — Though only a fraction of this vast and sparsely populated country's territory lies near the Caspian, it holds one of the region's most promising oil and gas deposits — the Tengiz Basin now under development by Chevron and other companies. China plans to build a 1,900-mile pipeline from the basin across Kazakhstan to Xinjiang, China. President Nursultan Nazarbaev, a former first secretary of the Kazakhstan Community Party, was elected after the country declared its independence from the Soviet Union in December 1991. Since then he has consolidated his power by eroding the country's limited representative government.

Kyrgyzstan — Considered to be the most democratic country in Central Asia, Kyrgyzstan is led by Askar Akaev, a former physicist who often quotes Thomas Jefferson. Elected president by the Supreme Soviet in 1990, Akaev won re-election in 1995. The country's oil potential is uncertain.

Russia — Like Iran, Russia stands to play a marginal role in the Caspian's oil production, but a crucial one in transporting the region's oil and gas to market. The first developer of the region's oil a century ago, Russia — and later the Soviet Union — largely abandoned the Caspian fields in favor of other domestic reserves to build its considerable oil industry. Today Russia transports Caspian oil by rail to the Baltic Sea and maintains other oil and gas pipelines, including one from Baku to its Black Sea port of Novorossisk. A proposed pipeline would also link the Tengiz oil field and Novorossisk.

Tajikistan — In 1997, Tajik President Imomali Rakhmonov and opposition forces signed a peace agreement ending a five-year civil war waged among the country's four regional tribes and between the secular government and Islamic militants. One of the poorest of the former Soviet republics, Tajikistan supports a thriving drug trade that has hampered efforts to improve the economy. [2]

Turkmenistan — Saparmurat Niyazov, a former Communist Party leader who became president in 1990, heads an oppressive regime based on a cult of personality. Known as Turkmenbashi — "head of the Turkmen" — Niyazov has banned opposition parties and presides over the legislature. Despite considerable reserves of natural gas and oil under and around the Caspian Sea, mismanagement of the economy has impoverished the country, which borders Afghanistan and Iran. The only existing export outlets for Turkmen gas is through Russian pipelines.

Uzbekistan — With almost 24 million inhabitants, Uzbekistan is the most populous country in the region. Cotton is the country's main product, but the government has announced plans to search for oil and gas under the polluted Aral Sea, drained of much of its water for irrigation. President Islam Karimov, a former communist leader, has introduced limited democratic reforms but faces the growing influence of Islamic militants.

---

[1] See Richard C. Longworth, "Boomtown Baku," *The Bulletin of the Atomic Scientists,* May/June 1998, pp. 34-38.

[2] See Martha Brill Olcott, "The Caspian's False Promise," *Foreign Policy,* summer 1998, pp. 94-113.

OPEC would turn more often to informal agreements of this kind in an effort to regain leverage over the market and stabilize prices around the historical norm of about $20 a barrel.

"OPEC is a major factor in determining world oil prices," said Edward H. Murphy at the time. He is the director of finance, accounting and statistics for the American Petroleum Institute (API), which represents U.S. oil companies. "They have succeeded in reducing production by about 2.1 million barrels a day, or 6 percent, since February. That is a significant factor that has prevented oil prices from falling even further. They're not back up to $20 a barrel, but they'd be a lot lower today in the absence of OPEC's production cuts."

A landmark agreement among OPEC members in March 1999 to restrict production helped propel the price of crude from its 12-year low of $10.72 a barrel in December 1998 to $32.72 on June 28, 2000. Fearful of causing a global recession that eventually would hurt the oil producers themselves by drying up demand for oil, Saudi Arabia unilaterally announced in July that it would increase its output enough to nudge the price of oil back below $30 a barrel.

Does U.S. foreign policy enhance Americans' access to foreign oil?

A fundamental, though infrequently recognized, goal of U.S. foreign policy has been to ensure the access of American businesses and consumers to foreign oil supplies, especially since 1971, when domestic oil production peaked and began its gradual decline. By 1996, the United States — once a leading exporter of crude — was for the first time forced to import half of its oil. Today, imports account for half of U.S. consumption. *(See graph, p. 56.)* As demand for oil continues to rise, the

U.S. Dependence on Imported Oil Growing

U.S. oil imports have been increasing while domestic production has been falling, reflecting decreasing U.S. oil reserves.

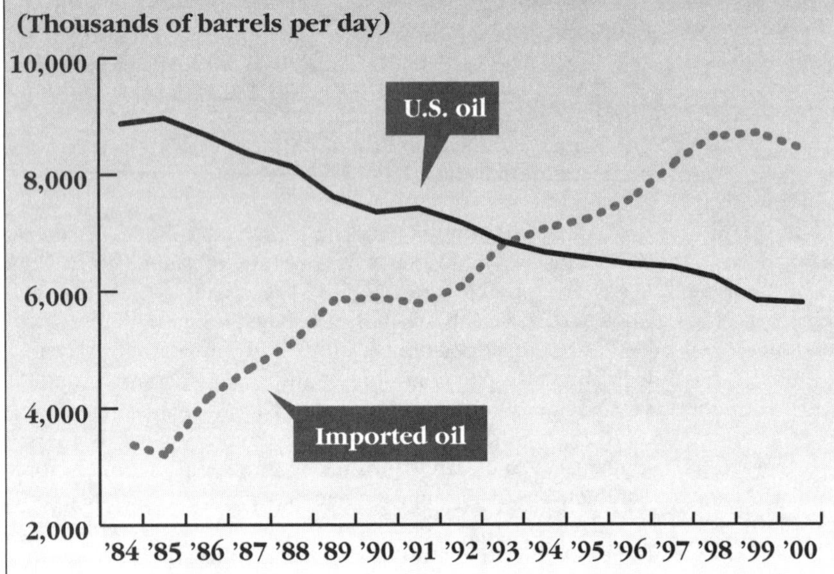

Source: Energy Information Administration, Monthly Energy Review, *June 2000*

United States will likely depend on imports for an ever-growing portion of its oil supply.

Like other industrialized countries, the United States has diversified its sources of foreign oil away from the Middle East since the energy crises of the 1970s. Today, Canada is the leading source of U.S. oil imports, followed by Venezuela. Although U.S. dependence on Persian Gulf oil has fallen from 24 percent of oil imports in 1991 to 21 percent today, the region will remain a vital oil supplier for years to come. But it is also one of the most politically unstable regions, the focus of 50 years of hostilities between Israel and its Arab neighbors and, for the past two decades, of militant Islamic fundamentalism.

Access to oil has figured prominently in the United States' activities in the Middle East throughout this period, most recently in the 1991 Persian Gulf War, when the United States led a United Nations military coalition that forced Iraq to withdraw from neighboring Kuwait. [5]

Of course, access to oil is not the sole U.S. strategic interest in the region. Even during the gulf war, the Bush administration stressed the need to repel Iraq's invasion of Kuwait to maintain the international rule of law. Because Iraq's leader, Saddam Hussein, was suspected of producing nuclear and biological weapons, the United States also sought and obtained Security Council support for a U.N. embargo against Iraq pending the completion of U.N. inspections of Iraqi arsenals. But the Clinton administration's "dual containment" policy toward Iraq and Iran — which together control 20 percent of the world's proven reserves — has implications for U.S. access to the region's oil exports. [6]

Iraq, with 112 billion barrels of proven oil reserves, is second only to Saudi Arabia, with 262 billion barrels. The embargo has exacted a heavy toll on Iraq, depriving it of oil revenues and leaving many Iraqis without adequate food and medical supplies. In December 1996, the embargo was eased to allow Iraq to export just enough oil to pay for food and other essential supplies. This "oil-for-food" provision is to remain in place until the Iraqi government allows U.N. arms inspectors full access to weapons sites.

But some oil-importing countries, notably France, Russia and China, oppose continuing the embargo against Iraq indefinitely. Critics of the embargo welcomed U.N. Secretary General Kofi Annan's role in prodding Saddam Hussein to allow U.N. inspectors greater access to the country in February 1998. Annan signaled a softening of international attitudes toward Iraq by calling the Iraqi leader "a man you can do business with." For his part, Saddam has threatened to take unspecified action to break the embargo if it is not lifted. [7]

Indeed, Iraq is already expanding oil exports in defiance of the U.N. embargo. "The fact that Iraq continues to export sizable amounts of petroleum products illegally — and that the Iraqi government refuses to permit the U.N. to oversee or monitor these sales — strongly suggests that the proceeds from these sales are intended for non-humanitarian purposes," said Under Secretary of State Thomas R. Pickering in 1998. "We are currently seeking ways to make the Iraqi government accountable for this illegal traffic — or to end it through tougher enforcement measures." [8]

Critics say the U.S. efforts are doomed. "American policy [toward Iraq] is nothing more than the desperate embrace of sanctions of diminishing effectiveness punctuated by occasional whining, frequent bluster, political retreat and military paralysis," said Richard Perle, assistant secretary of Defense for international security during the Reagan administration.

Varied Sources Provide U.S. Oil Imports

U.S. oil imports come from a wide range of sources. Four of the top five providers are not Arab nations, and two of the five are not members of the Organization of Petroleum Exporting Countries (list at left). More than half the oil imported by the United States comes from non-OPEC members (list at right).

Top Five U.S. Suppliers

(thousands of barrels per day)

Canada	1,648
Venezuela*	1,480
Saudi Arabia*	1,452
Mexico	1,329
Nigeria*	777

OPEC vs. Non-OPEC Production

(thousands of barrels per day)

Arab OPEC	2,209
Other OPEC	2,501
Non-OPEC	5,799
Total	10,510

* *OPEC members*

Source: Energy Information Administration, Monthly Energy Review, *June 2000*

"The pressure to relax the sanctions, which has already pushed to more than $10 billion per year the amount of revenue Iraq is allowed from the sale of oil, will not subside and will almost certainly increase. The French, Russians and others will continue to agitate for the further relaxation of sanctions, and the United States will almost certainly make further concessions in this regard." [9]

U.S. policy toward Iran, whose 93 billion barrels of proven oil reserves place it fifth in the global ranking of oil powers, elicits similar concerns. Since the 1979 Islamic revolution, the United States has identified Iran as one of the world's leading supporters of international terrorism. With the Iran-Libya Sanctions Act, the United States unilaterally barred American and foreign companies from investing more than $20 million in Iran's energy sector.

But Iran is an important source of Persian Gulf oil, and several foreign companies have defied the ban. Under pressure from Europe, Clinton announced in May 1998 that he would not impose sanctions on three French, Russian and Malaysian companies that invested $2 billion in a natural gas field in Iran.

Meanwhile, U.S. oil companies are losing lucrative oil contracts to overseas competitors. "There's no question that unilateral sanctions against Iran are hurting U.S. companies," said Murphy of the API. "By preventing them from competing in those markets, the sanctions provide a relative advantage to foreign oil companies. That's a real concern of our members. Whether or not there's a fair foreign policy tradeoff, I can't say."

Some critics see a clear clash of interests between U.S. foreign policy in the region and U.S. energy security. "The United States' vilification of Iran, Iraq and Libya makes for strange policy," Campbell said, "especially when you understand we'll be dependent on these three places for oil before long."

The Clinton administration continues to defend its policy of containment toward Iran. "Unilateral sanctions have proven costly to U.S. business," conceded Assistant Secretary of State for Near Eastern Affairs Martin S. Indyk. "However, we believe that Iran poses threats so significant that we have no choice but accept these costs. Economic pressure has an important role in our efforts to convince Iran to cease its efforts to acquire weapons of mass destruction and missiles and to support terrorism." [10]

The U.S. position toward Iran has shown signs of softening since the August 1997 election of President Mohammad Khatami, who has loosened somewhat the strict regime set in place by his militant predecessors by expanding press freedoms and establishing more cordial relations with countries in the Persian Gulf and Europe.

But, citing evidence that Iran's support of terrorism is unchanged, the United States officially has not changed its position on sanctions. On June 17, 1998, however, Secretary of State Madeleine K. Albright held out the possibility of a future improvement in bilateral relations. Although she refrained from proposing specific steps to normalize relations, Albright said, "Obviously, two decades of mistrust cannot be erased overnight. The gap between us remains wide. But it is time to test the possibilities for bridging this gap." [11]

The Caspian Sea region is another area where foreign policy goals may clash with those of energy security. "Our interest in the Caspian is not defined simply by the region's energy resources, but no one doubts their significance," said Stephen Sestanovich, special adviser to the secretary of State for the new independent states. "Energy could become a source of conflict, a lever of control or an obstacle to progress. Or it could become a ticket to prosperity and peace, a secure link to the outside world." [12]

The United States has played an active role in brokering peace talks in some of the region's simmering ethnic battles, such as those between the government of Azerbaijan and leaders of Armenian rebels who occupy the region of Nagorno Karabakh. It also has funneled economic and technical assistance — totaling $372 million in fiscal 1998 — to the newly independent countries of the region, which own potentially huge deposits of oil.

But an existing measure, Section 907 of the 1992 Freedom Support Act, bars the United States from extending this assistance to Azerbaijan. Enacted at the behest of the U.S. Armenian lobby, which claimed that the government of Azerbaijan subjected ethnic Armenians to human rights abuses, the measure has attracted widespread opposition since the extent of Azerbaijan's oil wealth has become more apparent. The Clinton administration also supports the measure's repeal.

Caspian Sea oil cannot reach consumers until a pipeline network is built linking the remote, landlocked region to seaports far away. *(See map, p. 52.)* The most direct route, and possibly the least expensive to construct, would pass through Iran to the Persian Gulf. But U.S. sanctions against Iran stand in the way of that option. Instead, the United States backs a multiple pipeline network that includes the so-called main export pipeline, which would pass through Georgia and NATO ally Turkey to the Turkish port of Ceyhan on the Black Sea, where the oil would be loaded onto tankers and shipped to markets via the Mediterranean Sea.

Some experts say the United States should ease its current opposition to the Iran pipeline option. "If the international oil companies working in Central Asia do not need to start construction of new pipeline routes immediately, the U.S. government should not lock the door prematurely against the prospect of a new pipeline transiting Iran," said Richard W. Murphy, senior fellow for the Middle East at the Council on Foreign Relations. "The routing of new pipelines will have profound political and economic implications for years to come." [13]

Will the United States be ready with alternative energy sources when the oil runs out?

As a finite resource, petroleum will not last forever. Estimates of how long the world has before the oil runs out vary widely. The United States is likely to run out far sooner than many major producers, however. Using about 7 billion barrels of oil products a year, the United States is the world's most voracious oil consumer. And it shows no sign of changing its energy habits. U.S. demand for oil is expected to grow by 20 percent by 2015. [14]

But the crunch is likely to come long before the world exhausts its oil supplies. "The idea of running out of oil, of when the last barrel comes out of the ground, is a red herring," Campbell said. "It misses the point. What's much more relevant is when world production will peak, and that will occur within the first few years of the next century." When that happens, Campbell predicts, oil consumers will be in for a major price shock as production slows.

Campbell says the United States may be especially ill-prepared for the next energy crisis. Even though U.S. oil production started declining in 1971, the United States was never seriously affected because it was able to import its oil from other countries. "This chapter is coming to an end because the other places, too, are getting close to peak production," he said. "There's monumental ignorance in the government and among the public at large on this subject."

Other critics charge that the United States, by holding oil taxes below those of other consuming nations, has encouraged oil consumption with little concern for the consequences. [15] "Part of our energy policy seems to be to keep prices low," said George Yates, chairman of the Independent Petroleum Association of America, whose 8,000 members produce almost half of the nation's domestic crude. "But we have only about 3 million barrels a day worldwide of excess capacity, and that includes Iraq, which is officially out of production because of the embargo. That's a pretty slim margin. It's like operating a factory at 100 percent capacity — you can't go on forever like this."

The development of alternatives to oil has proceeded slowly in the United States. After the energy crises of the 1970s, the federal government funded research and development of renewable energy sources such as solar, wind, geothermal and biomass energy. [16] But as oil prices subsequently fell and Congress turned its attention to reducing the federal budget deficit, support for these efforts dwindled.

According to Energy Under Secretary Ernest Moniz, his department's budgets for energy research and development fell fivefold from 1978 to 1997; privately funded research has also declined. [17] Today, much of the U.S.-developed technology for renewable energy sources is being used more intensively in Europe and Asia — where oil products are heavily taxed — than in the United States.

"The effects of world dependence on Middle Eastern oil means that while the quoted market price per barrel is about $20, the costs associated with keeping shipping lanes open, rogue states in check and terrorists at bay may more than quadruple the price per barrel," said Sen. Richard G. Lugar, R-Ind., before the recent price rise. "Given these costs, the United States may pay more than $100 billion this year for oil from the unstable

Chronology

1960s ***Oil production comes under the growing control of Middle Eastern producers.***

Sept. 14, 1960
Iran, Iraq, Kuwait, Saudi Arabia and Venezuela form the Organization of Petroleum Exporting Countries (OPEC).

1970s ***An Arab embargo leads to oil crises that quadruple the price of oil.***

1970
Domestic oil production peaks at 11.3 million barrels a day in the United States, forcing it to gradually increase its dependence on imports.

October 1973
After OPEC raises oil prices by 70 percent, to $5.11 a barrel, Arab producers impose an embargo on oil exports to the United States and the Netherlands for their support of Israel in the Yom Kippur War. Oil prices soar above $17 a barrel.

1975
The Strategic Petroleum Reserve is created to protect the United States from interruptions in oil supplies. Congress sets fuel-efficiency standards for cars.

December 1978
The Iranian revolution disrupts Persian Gulf oil supplies, causing a second oil shock and deepening inflation in oil-consuming countries.

June 1979
OPEC raises the price of crude from $14.50 to as high as $23.50 a barrel. Gas lines form in the United States.

1980s ***As oil production spreads outside OPEC, prices begin to fall.***

1980
The eight-year Iran-Iraq War begins, compounding the disruption in Gulf oil. By the following January, OPEC's oil price reaches $34 a barrel, more than 10 times the price in 1972.

1986
Oil prices fall to their lowest level since the first oil crisis in 1973.

1990s ***OPEC's inability to control output leads to a global oil glut.***

Aug. 2, 1990
Iraq occupies Kuwait, cutting off 1.6 million barrels of oil a day from the world market. The U.N. imposes an embargo on Iraqi oil exports as well. Panic buying pushes oil prices up from $13 a barrel to $40.

1991
The United States leads a coalition of forces in the Persian Gulf War to drive Iraqi occupying forces out of Kuwait.

December 1991
The Soviet Union dissolves, and the newly independent countries of the Caspian Sea begin opening their oil reserves to exploitation.

1992
Congress passes the Freedom Support Act providing economic assistance to the former Soviet republics. Section 907 of the law prohibits the aid from going to Azerbaijan — a major oil producer — for abuses against ethnic Armenians.

1993
Chevron Corp. invests in Kazakhstan's vast Tengiz oil field, beginning the oil rush in the Caspian Sea region.

1996
The U.S. begins to import more than half the oil it consumes.

December 1996
An "oil-for-food" provision is added to the U.N. embargo against Iraq, allowing the country to export just enough oil to pay for food and other essential supplies. The same year, energy conservation pushes oil consumption in the industrial world below the peak level of 1978.

October 1997
The financial crisis in Asia curbs oil consumption in that part of the world, leading to a glut in world oil supplies.

March 1998
As oil prices plummet to their lowest levels in decades, OPEC reaches an unprecedented agreement with a non-OPEC oil producer — Mexico — to curtail production in an effort to keep oil prices from falling further.

March 1999
OPEC members agree to curtail oil output, propelling the price of crude to more than $30 a barrel by 2000.

Middle East. By contrast, the United States will spend less than $1 billion this year on energy research." [18]

Some analysts find little reason for concern about the United States' energy future. In their view, the technology that has enabled oil producers to discover new deposits and remove more oil from existing wells will continue to advance. "We've made tremendous advances that have made it cheaper to find and produce oil," said Murphy of the API. "If those continue, we're probably looking at oil availability for the indefinite future at today's prices or less."

When the oil crunch does come, Murphy predicts, the technology to provide cheap alternatives will be ready to take up the slack. "My feeling is that long before the use of petroleum is diminished, other sources will be there. In 10 years, all cars may be run with fuel cells instead of gasoline."

Public Broadcasting Service

A replica of the world's first oil well, drilled by "Colonel" Edwin L. Drake in Titusville, Pa., in 1859.

BACKGROUND

OPEC's Power Play

The United States was the world's dominant oil producer for the first half of this century. [19] Outside the United States, world production fell under the control of the world's major oil companies, known as the "Seven Sisters," which acquired the right to extract oil from countries where they operated in exchange for royalties paid to the host governments. So great was their power over the markets that they were able to manipulate the price of crude from their extensive holdings in the Middle East. [20] By the late 1950s, however, they faced growing competition from independent companies and cut their prices.

Because they collected taxes based on oil prices, Persian Gulf countries where the Seven Sisters extracted oil were faced with falling revenues. On Sept. 14, 1960, representatives of Iran, Iraq, Kuwait, Saudi Arabia and Venezuela met in Baghdad, Iraq, and founded OPEC. The fledgling cartel froze oil prices to prevent further erosion in oil revenues. Other producer nations joined OPEC, including Qatar, the United Arab Emirates in the Persian Gulf region, as well as Algeria, Indonesia, Libya and Nigeria. Membership in the organization enabled these countries to set a minimum royalty to be paid by companies for the privilege of extracting oil from their territories. The organization's expansion also helped the Seven Sisters by making it harder for independent companies to undercut them in the host countries.

The new order in oil development began to unravel in 1969, when Libyan strongman Muammar el-Qadaffi forced Occidental Petroleum, an independent American operator in Libya, to cut production. Because Libyan oil was of high quality, it was in high demand, and the cutback created an oil shortage. OPEC decided to profit from the change by raising oil prices. In an effort to stabilize the market, OPEC and the oil companies agreed in 1971 to a new pricing system that allowed for prices to be negotiated every five years.

As Oil Runs Out, Technology Buys Time

The world's supply of "conventional" oil — oil that is easily recovered — is running short of demand. In little more than a decade, some experts predict, global demand will so far exceed supplies of conventional oil that price shocks will occur that may lead to recession or political turmoil.

Faced with this impending shortfall, oil companies are investing heavily in research to improve existing technologies and develop new ones. Some of the work is already paying off. According to Roger N. Anderson, director of petroleum technology research at Columbia University, recent advances in finding and extracting oil may raise world oil production by more than 20 percent by 2010. [1]

Recent advances in oil exploration and extraction include:

4-D Seismic Analysis — As oil and natural gas are extracted from underground deposits, the remaining oil and gas seeps into the layers of rock. Three-dimensional monitoring with seismic instruments helps identify the location of oil deposits but cannot follow the shifting of oil that occurs as the well's contents run down. Anderson and others have developed a "4-D" system that incorporates the added dimension of time and helps drillers determine where the rest of the oil is likely to settle. Recovering this otherwise lost oil can increase the output of a given field by as much as 15 percent. The new technology has been applied at about 60 oil fields worldwide over the past four years.

Steam and Gas Injection — Drillers traditionally abandon wells when the flow of oil slows to a trickle. But scientists now know that this often leaves behind more than half the oil in a given deposit. Pumping steam, natural gas or liquid carbon dioxide into seemingly dry wells can force the remaining oil through porous rock toward a neighboring well, where it can be extracted. Another technique involves pumping water below the deposit, which increases the pressure under the oil, forcing it to the surface. Although steam or gas injection increases oil recovery by up to 15 percent, the high cost of this technique often outweighs the oil's value.

Directional Drilling — Oil wells typically are drilled straight down into the ground. But new technology allows drillers to change direction thousands of meters below ground and bore horizontally through rock in search of deposits a mile or more away from the wellhead. Sensors near the drill bit can detect oil, water and gas by measuring the density of surrounding rock or by measuring minute changes in electrical resistance. Engineers at the surface monitor the drill's progress by computer.

Deep-Water Drilling — Most offshore rigs, such as those along the coasts of Texas and Louisiana, operate at relatively shallow depths. But new technology is enabling drillers to tap into oil deposits under deeper water — currently down to 1,700 meters. Unmanned submarines install equipment on the ocean floor to regulate the flow of oil at high pressure and prevent environmentally devastating blowouts. The oil is then loaded onto tankers at sea or piped ashore or to shallow-water platforms through underwater pipelines. Recently declassified U.S. Navy technology enables geophysicists to detect underwater oil deposits through the sheets of salt and basalt that often hide them from conventional seismic surveys. While deep offshore drilling is very expensive, it is expected to become more widely pursued as conventional oil deposits dry up. Deep-water platforms are already in use off the coast of Newfoundland, Canada, and more are planned for the Gulf of Mexico, the North Sea and the Atlantic Ocean off Brazil and West Africa.

Just how much impact technological advances can have on global oil supplies is a matter of heated debate. Oil companies are optimistic about technology's ability to extend the petroleum era for decades to come. "If you look at the available proved reserves, there are about 1 trillion barrels of oil still in the ground," said Edward H. Murphy, an economist at the American Petroleum Institute. "If we continue to produce 27 billion barrels a year as we do now, that means we have 37 years left." That deadline can be extended, Murphy says, by technological advances. "We only recover 40 percent of production out of a given field today," he said. "So there's substantial room for enhanced recovery."

There's a downside to technology's impact on oil production, however, especially for small domestic producers who depend on the slow but steady flow of oil from marginal wells. "Some technologies mean that the same reserves are depleted more quickly instead of maintaining production over a long period," said George Yates, chairman of the Independent Petroleum Association of America. "So while technology has had a very positive impact on this industry, it's also put more oil on the market, which exacerbates our problems."

Still other experts say technology can only delay for a short time the inevitable demise of our oil-based economy. "Deep-water drilling is capable of producing 100 billion barrels, or about five years of world demand," said Colin J. Campbell, a consultant in Geneva, Switzerland. "It's expensive, and it's viable only in giant fields." He foresees further development of oil deposits under polar ice in Alaska, Russia and Canada, as well as the large deposits of heavy oil in Canada and Venezuela. "But even that won't make a lot of difference," Campbell said. "Whatever the accumulated advances of technology can deliver ought to be incorporated into our estimates of existing oil reserves. It's not something you can keep adding to."

[1] Information in this section is largely based on Roger N. Anderson, "Oil Production in the 21st Century," *Scientific American,* March 1998, pp. 86-91.

Energy Crises of the 1970s

OPEC's new pricing system quickly fell apart, however. Oil was bought from companies in the open market for more than the established price, and OPEC members wanted to share in the profits. After the companies balked at their request, OPEC unilaterally raised the official price by 70 percent in October 1973, to $5.11 a barrel. The same month, the Arab producing countries imposed an oil embargo on the United States and the Netherlands for their support of Israel in the Yom Kippur War. The embargo was later replaced with a cutback in production by all Arab members except Iraq.

"Using oil supply as a political weapon was a new development in the industry and one that did great damage to OPEC's commercial credibility as a reliable supplier," writes Fadhil J. Chalabi, director of the Center for Global Energy Studies in London and acting secretary of OPEC from 1983-88.[21]

Part of the Caspian Sea oil-drilling installation built by Soviet leader Josef Stalin in 1949, about 40 miles east of Baku, Azerbaijan.

The production cutback reduced availability to all oil importers and led to a quadrupling of prices and the decade's first oil shock. The second shock came in the winter of 1978-79 following the Iranian revolution, which led to the ouster of Shah Mohammed Reza Pahlavi and his replacement by the Ayatollah Ruhollah Khomeini's militant Islamic regime.

The revolution caused a disruption of oil from the Persian Gulf that was compounded by the outbreak in 1980 of the Iran-Iraq War. By January 1981, OPEC's oil price had reached $34 a barrel, more than 10 times the price in 1972, before the first oil shock. Taken together, the shocks produced a windfall for OPEC members, whose oil revenues skyrocketed from less than $23 billion in 1972 to more than $280 billion by the end of the decade.

Oil Consumers React

But OPEC's bonanza days were numbered. The United States and other industrial countries reacted strongly to the gasoline rationing, long lines at the pump and double-digit inflation produced by the production cutbacks and price increases. They launched a frantic search for alternative sources of oil and set about trying to reduce their dependence on oil imports by making more fuel-efficient cars, improving energy conservation and developing renewable energy sources.

Over time, the growth in demand for oil slowed. By 1995, industrial nations were consuming only 2 million barrels a day more than they had in 1975. "Put another way," wrote Chalabi, "oil consumption by OECD countries in 1996 was less than at its peak level in 1978, even though their [gross domestic product] had grown by 42 percent during the same period."[22]

The oil consumers' efforts to reduce their reliance on Middle East oil paid off most successfully in the development of new oil fields. Companies shifted their investments to non-OPEC countries such as Mexico and Canada, as well as Britain and Norway, where they developed new platform-drilling technology to exploit the vast deposits under the North Sea. High oil prices also made it feasible to tap the enormous reserves on Alaska's North Slope.

As a result of these efforts, OPEC's share of the global oil market fell by half, from 56 percent in 1975 to just 26 percent in 1995. Although non-OPEC countries possess only a quarter of the world's oil reserves, they now account for 60 percent of global production.

CURRENT SITUATION

OPEC's Dilemma

Despite the industrial nations' success in reducing their dependence on Middle East oil, OPEC has continued to reap enormous profits from oil exports. The revenues from oil sales have enabled many member countries to invest in other industries to help diversify their economies in preparation for the day when they will no longer be able to rely on petroleum exports.

But the glut in oil supplies that began in 1997 dealt a serious blow to countries that still depend heavily on oil exports, both within and outside OPEC. Even Saudi Arabia felt the pinch of falling oil revenues.

The economic crisis encouraged cheating on the part of some OPEC members, further undermining the organization's clout. Venezuela was said to be the most flagrant offender, and called on fellow OPEC members to abandon quotas altogether in favor of other strategies to win market share. Algeria, Iran, Libya and Nigeria also routinely ignored the production quotas to prevent further erosion of the oil revenues they depend on for economic survival. [23]

In a desperate effort to slow production, OPEC for the first time called on non-member producer countries to cooperate with its quota system. In March 1998, Mexico agreed to cut oil output, and Norway later agreed to curb production as well. Russia has expressed interest in joining OPEC and attended the organization's June 1998 meeting in Geneva as an observer. The March agreement sent oil prices up by 13 percent, to almost $17 a barrel. But prices soon dropped back to around $14, suggesting that the market was not confident that OPEC could hold production down for long.

Some U.S. oil-company representatives supported OPEC's campaign to hold the line on output and prices. "I'm hoping that by including nonmembers, OPEC can exercise some restraint on oil production," said Yates of the Independent Petroleum Association. "Restraint, coupled with higher prices, will mean fewer oil wells being abandoned in the United States. It also means new wells will be drilled to find additional oil, which will make us better able to meet demand in the future. OPEC's really the American consumer's friend right now."

©Digital Stock

Oil companies are investing heavily in research to improve exploration and drilling technology, because conventional methods may be unable to meet demand in the near future.

But many analysts question OPEC's ability over the long term to control the global market, which has changed in fundamental ways over the past two decades. "What's dominating the market today is the advance of technology, which is having a significant impact on the industry's ability to explore and produce oil in areas they were forbidden from exploring before," said Murphy of the API. Another change is the willingness of countries such as Venezuela, where the oil business was once run by state-owned companies, to have foreign, private companies come in and produce their oil. Finally, the former Soviet republics in the Caspian may have a major impact on world markets when the region's oil starts to flow. "OPEC is a bystander in this region," Murphy said.

OPEC's difficulties have led some experts to predict its eventual demise. "OPEC, as such, is disintegrating," Campbell said. Indeed, OPEC members know that drastically raising prices to solve their current dilemma will backfire on them in the end. "They remember what happened after the last shock," he said, "and they fear that if they put up the price they will lose their market share, and if that happens that they will lose everything."

In Campbell's view, however, the five leading Middle Eastern producers — Iran, Iraq, Kuwait, Saudi Arabia and Abu Dhabi (one of seven emirates comprising the United Arab Emirates) — have nothing to worry about. "They don't realize that the situation is very different today," he said. He calculated that by about 2002 world production of conventional oil — that which is easily recoverable — would peak, sending prices upward once again.

"Unlike the 1970s, when a flood of new oil production followed the price shocks," he said, "there are very few new oil deposits being found, with the exception of the Caspian." Campbell predicted that Middle Eastern producers, with about half the world's remaining conventional oil reserves, will see their share of recoverable oil rise substantially by 2000.

At that point, he said, "the Middle Eastern countries will recognize their control."

Cheap Oil

Campbell's prediction appears to be borne out by the current oil price hike. Until this year, however, oil-producing countries, including the petroleum-rich kingdoms of the Middle East, were suffering as a result of low oil prices. Most depend on oil exports for the bulk of their revenue. Saudi Arabia saw its oil revenues drop from $43 billion to about $29 billion between 1997 and 1998. As a result, King Fahd's government was forced to borrow $2 billion from Saudi banks to fund public programs and cut its budget by at least 10 percent. [24]

The bad news for oil producers may have a silver lining over the longer term. As autocratic regimes in the Middle East are forced to reduce their generous health, education and welfare programs, social unrest may quicken the pace of economic and political reforms. Pressure for reform has surfaced in a number of the region's oil states, including Saudi Arabia and the other gulf states, as well as Syria and Iran. [25]

Oil producers outside the Middle East have had problems as well. Before the recent price rise, unexpectedly low oil revenues forced Mexico, a major source of U.S. oil imports, to undergo a number of painful spending cuts. Nigeria, in the midst of chronic political turmoil, faces an even graver plight. In this poor West African country, earnings from oil exports provide a vital buffer against widespread poverty. For Russia, low oil prices of recent years have only added to the country's serious economic crisis. Only Britain and Norway, with the most diversified industrial economies among the major foreign exporters, were able to absorb the loss of oil revenues without major disruption.

In the United States, which now imports more than half its oil, the recent spike in oil prices appears to have had little impact on energy consumption and the economy. Sales of gas-guzzling SUVs and other large vehicles continue apace, and inflation remains in check. The main beneficiaries of the price rise are U.S. oil companies, which have recovered from their poor financial performance of the late 1990s. Both Exxon Mobil Corp. and the Chevron Corp., the two largest U.S. oil companies, registered record earnings in the second quarter of 2000. [26]

Most analysts predict that oil prices will remain unstable for the foreseeable future, a trend that may discourage major new investments in domestic output. Low crude oil prices of recent years have dampened the incentive for oil companies to look for new domestic deposits and to maintain production in existing fields with marginal output. According to the API's Murphy, the number of drilling rigs used to search for oil and gas fell by 31 percent over the average used for that purpose in the 1990s. "This drilling data should, we believe, be of major concern to those interested in this country's energy future," he said. "Oil drilling at these rates is inadequate to maintain U.S. crude oil production levels, particularly in the lower 48 states." [27]

Many smaller American oil companies are in especially bad shape. As a group, the 8,000 independent oil companies suffered a 25 percent drop in revenues in 1998. These include many companies that extract natural gas as well as oil. Natural gas prices have been largely unaffected by the oil glut. "But some of our members produce only oil," explained Yates of the Independent Petroleum Association. "For them, the impact of low oil prices is extremely dramatic. You have to go back to the 1930s for corresponding prices, and then they had to call out the Texas Rangers to bring order to the market." *

Many small companies face bankruptcy. "The worst off are those with marginal production," Yates said. "There are thousands of these mom-and-pop operations." As large oil fields have run dry in the United States, many of the 500,000 wells operated by the association's members produce just two or three barrels of crude a day. "Most of these marginal wells could go on producing forever, but not at a loss, so they are being abandoned," Yates said. "This is a very serious issue, because the oil we don't produce domestically we have to import. And it's not just the oil producers who are affected,

* In 1931, an oil glut in Texas and Oklahoma drove down oil prices, prompting Texas Gov. Ross Sterling to send the Texas Rangers into the East Texas oil fields to enforce a production cutback.

At Issue:

Should the United States ease its sanctions against Iran to improve international access to Caspian Sea oil?

S. FREDERICK STARR
Chairman, Central Asia Institute, Nitze School of Advanced International Studies, Johns Hopkins University

FROM TESTIMONY BEFORE THE HOUSE INTERNATIONAL RELATIONS SUBCOMMITTEE ON ASIA AND THE PACIFIC, FEB. 12, 1998.

Two presidential directives in 1995 and the Iran-Libya Sanctions Act of 1996 cut off all significant American and foreign investment in Iran's petroleum industry, including pipelines. The purpose was to pressure Iran into dropping its support for terrorism, abandoning programs to develop atomic weapons and [stopping its] meddling in the Middle East peace process. However laudable the aims, the burden of these measures falls disproportionately on Azerbaijan, Kazakhstan and Turkmenistan, for it prevents them from exporting their gas and oil by one of the obvious alternative routes to Russia, namely, Iran. The U.S. position has been to argue that this would not be in the Central Asians' own interest, but none of our friends there agree.

Now, let us suppose that the U.S. sanctions [remained] in place for a long time and [were] truly effective. Over time, so we have argued, planners and financial markets would adjust to this reality. They would construct the east-west pipeline and thus give Central Asians access to secure export routes bypassing both Iran and Russia.

But this is not happening. French, Indonesian and Russian firms are already investing in the construction of oil facilities and pipelines in Iran, and the U.S. seems disinclined to intervene against them. Iran itself is busy constructing a line linking Turkmenistan and Turkey. Turkmenistan and Kazakhstan have worked out swap deals with Tehran, by which Central Asia ships its crude oil to Iran's north and Iran then exports the same quantity of its own oil from the south. In short, the American quarantine of 1995-6 is not holding. . . .

[The United States could] adopt a "wait and see" posture toward Iran, one that would be cautious but less categorical than our current policy. It would replace an "all or nothing" approach with one that recognizes the existence of a large number of finely calibrated positions between these two extremes. . . . On balance, it seems to me that [this alternative] holds the most promise for achieving a balance between U.S. objectives in Central Asia, in the Caspian basin and in Iran. . . .

[I]t is no longer possible to treat U.S. policy toward Central Asia and toward Iran as totally separate from one another. Our Iranian policy, however just its goals, has a powerful and, for the most part, negative impact on our ability to achieve our stated objectives in Central Asia and the Caspian basin.

SEN. SAM BROWNBACK, R-KAN.

FROM TESTIMONY BEFORE THE SENATE FOREIGN RELATIONS SUBCOMMITTEE ON INTERNATIONAL ECONOMIC POLICY, EXPORT AND TRADE PROMOTION, OCT. 23, 1997.

The countries of the South Caucasus and Central Asia — Armenia, Azerbaijan, Georgia, Kazakhstan, Kyrgyzstan, Tajikistan, Turkmenistan and Uzbekistan — are at a historic crossroads in their history: They are independent, they are at the juncture of many of today's major world forces, they are rich in natural resources and they are looking to the United States for support. . . .

First of all, these countries are a major force in containing the spread northward of anti-Western Iranian extremism. Though Iranian activity in the region has been less blatant than elsewhere in the world, they are working very hard to bring the region into their sphere of influence and economic control.

Secondly, the Caspian Sea basin contains proven oil and gas reserves which, potentially, could rank third in the world after the Middle East and Russia and exceed $4 trillion in value. Investment in this region could ultimately reduce U.S. dependence on oil imports from the volatile Persian Gulf and could provide regional supplies as an alternative to Iranian sources. . . .

The independence of the region could indeed well depend on the successful construction of pipelines on an east-west axis through non-Russian as well as non-Iranian territory. Both Russian and Iranian rhetoric on this issue shows clearly that these countries see the connection between pipelines free of Russian and Iranian control and their domination over the region. And it is no coincidence that we are seeing an intense rapprochement between these two countries.

Time is of an essence here. We have the opportunity to help these countries rebuild themselves from the ground up and to encourage them to continue their strong independent stances, especially in relation to Iran and the spread of extremist, anti-Western fundamentalism, which is one of the most clear and present dangers facing the United States today.

The window of opportunity has been closed even further by the recent investment by the French company Total . . . in the Iranian South Pars offshore gas field. It is vital that the [Clinton] administration hold strong on implementing existing sanctions and on discouraging our allies from following the despicable example of Total. If the floodgates open through Iran, the eastern Caspian will certainly fall into the Eastern sphere of dominance, and the South Caucasus will lose out on its opportunity to prosper as producer of oil and as a pivotal transit point from East to West.

because as imports grow, so does the trade deficit." In May 2000, the U.S. trade deficit hit a record $31.04 billion as imports grew and exports fell.[28]

Caspian Treasure

As petroleum deposits are depleted in coming years, prices are likely to rise more dramatically, formally ending the era of cheap oil. With few major new fields expected to be found, oil companies are in hot competition to develop the potentially huge reserves under and around the landlocked Caspian Sea, which lies between southern Russia and northern Iran. Estimates of the volume of crude oil in the region range up to 200 billion barrels — more than a quarter of the Middle East's reserves.

The region's oil has been known about for centuries. Marco Polo remarked on the seepage of oil around the Caspian Sea during his travels along the Silk Road, the ancient trade route between Europe and the Far East. Swedish businessmen Ludwig and Robert Nobel began developing oil fields in Baku, on the western coast of the Caspian Sea, more than 120 years ago.[29] The Soviet Union, with large oil reserves in other parts of the country, did little to develop the Caspian fields because most of the oil was trapped under water or salt formations and too hard to extract.

Modern technology now places the Caspian's oil within reach, and oil companies have descended on the sparsely populated region since 1991 to gain a foothold in what may be the world's last oil boom. One of the first Western companies in the region was Chevron Corp., which in 1993 began investing in Kazakhstan's Tengiz oil field in and around the northeastern Caspian. Numerous other companies have since invested in the region as well. A consortium of other companies, including Exxon Mobil and eight other international companies recently discovered a mammoth deposit in the Caspian Sea field of Kashagan off the Kazak coast that may hold up to 50 billion barrels of oil.[30]

©Digital Stock

New pipelines are needed to move crude oil from the landlocked Caspian Sea region to deep-water ports where it can be loaded onto tankers and shipped to markets.

The main obstacle to the development of Caspian oil is the volatile political situation throughout the region. The Soviet Union's dissolution in 1991 transformed the former Soviet republics of Azerbaijan, Kazakhstan and Turkmenistan, which also border the Caspian, into independent countries. With no democratic tradition, ethnic divisions that rival those of the former Yugoslavia and virtually undeveloped economies, the Caspian is a region that journalist Richard C. Longworth described as "Bosnia with oil."

"In this oil-soaked cockpit, the prospects for both wealth and trouble are simply stupendous," he wrote. "The Caucasus is a land of ancient vendettas and warring tribes that makes the Balkans look straightforward by comparison, and the Caspian is where this bloody region meets Central Asia and the

Middle East. It's where Orthodox Christianity meets both Sunni and Shi'ite Islam, where Iranians traveling north have met Russians coming south. It's an area once ruled by Iran, then by Russia, now contested by Turkey, whose language and civilization dominate the region." [31]

FOR MORE INFORMATION

Energy Information Administration, U.S. Department of Energy, 1000 Independence Ave. S.W., #2G051, Washington, D.C. 20585; (202) 586-5214; www.eia.doe.gov. The EIA collects and publishes data on domestic production, imports, distribution and prices of crude oil and refined petroleum products.

American Petroleum Institute, 1220 L St. N.W., Washington, D.C. 20005; (202) 682-8000; www.api.org. This membership organization of U.S. producers, refiners, marketers and transporters of oil and related products provides information on the industry.

Independent Petroleum Association of America, 1101 16th St. N.W., 2nd Floor, Washington, D.C. 20036; (202) 857-4722; www.ipaa.org. Members are independent oil and gas producers and others involved in domestic oil and gas production.

International Energy Agency, 9, rue de la Federation, 75739 Paris Cedex 15, France; (33-1) 40.57.65.51; www.iea.org. Created in the wake of the energy crises of the 1970s, the IEA monitors global oil production and helps consumer countries coordinate strategies to avoid supply disruptions.

Pipelines and Politics

The Caspian region's political turmoil exacerbates another significant obstacle to developing Caspian oil: transportation problems. Once the crude is extracted, it must travel thousands of miles to reach ports where it can be loaded onto tankers and shipped to markets. Some oil from the Tengiz field already reaches the Baltic Sea by rail. But rail shipment is expensive and increases the risk of oil spills. [32] The only alternative under consideration is to build pipelines. Three are already being developed. The problem is where to build the next ones.

China plans a 1,900-mile pipeline from Tengiz across Kazakhstan into China. But all the routes from the Caspian to Western markets have political drawbacks. The most direct route to open sea, and the one desired by the Caspian countries, is through Iran to the Persian Gulf. But the United States opposes that route because it would defy U.S. sanctions against Iran and make Caspian oil hostage to political instability in the gulf.

Although Secretary Albright waived the sanctions against three foreign companies that invested in Iranian oil fields in May 1998, the move apparently did not signal a change in policy. "We continue to oppose trans-Iran pipelines for Caspian energy exports in the strongest terms," said Sestanovich of the State Department. [33]

Russia has proposed a route that would carry oil from the eastern Caspian to the Russian port of Novorossisk on the Black Sea, which already serves as the terminus for an existing pipeline from Baku. Turkey opposes this and other new pipelines that would terminate at the Black Sea because the oil must then be shipped through the narrow Bosporus strait, which passes through Istanbul, to reach the Mediterranean. Some 4,000 tankers already pass through the 17-mile-long passage each year, negotiating four 45-degree turns on their way and posing the risk of disastrous oil spills. Another planned pipeline, linking Turkmenistan to Pakistan, is on hold pending resolution of Afghanistan's protracted civil war.

The Clinton administration supports a network of multiple oil and gas pipelines to make it less likely that a supply interruption in one would cut off the entire region's oil flow. It is pushing strongly for a pipeline stretching from the Caspian port of Baku, Azerbaijan, through Georgia to the Mediterranean port of Ceyhan in Turkey, a NATO ally.

The region's political turmoil leads some observers to question the ability of the Caspian region to meet the growing global demand for oil. "The Caspian states are not necessarily plunging into a maelstrom in which corrupt regimes will be challenged either by secret drug lords or social unrest," wrote Martha Brill Olcott, a senior associate at the Carnegie Endowment for International Peace and professor of political science at Colgate University. "But the possibility of such chaos cannot be precluded. Each of these states faces difficult political transitions in the next five to 10 years, while peak oil production and the economic benefits that it promises are unlikely to be realized in the region until 2010." [34]

Other obstacles to the region's ascendance as a leading oil provider spring from its geological limitations. "The Caspian is the only place in the world right now with significant promise," Campbell said. "But there's been some exaggerated talk about its real potential." He estimates that the region may contain only 50 billion barrels. "Even that is stretching credibility a little bit," he says. "And that's if it comes in, which as of today is not something to count on."

With Caspian deposits perhaps equivalent in volume to those under the North Sea, Campbell said, offshore production could total up to 4 million barrels a day by 2025. "Although that's valuable and not to be dismissed," he said, "it's unlikely to make much of an impact on the peak of global oil production," which he says will occur within the next few years. ■

OUTLOOK

Will Prices Rise?

OPEC surprised its critics in 1999 when it succeeded in curbing production output, eliminating the world oil glut and forcing the price of oil above $30 a barrel by 2000. They were aided by rising demand, as economic recovery took hold in Asia and the appetite for oil products continued to grow in the United States.

Gasoline prices in the United States peaked in mid-summer and appear likely to decline even more in coming months. Saudi Arabia is leading a call to increase OPEC output in an effort to prevent a global energy crisis.

Some economists predict that oil prices will continue to subside in the immediate future because the world has already begun to wean itself from petroleum products.

"The industrial world uses 42 percent less oil to produce an extra unit of [gross domestic product] than it needed in 1973," wrote Lester C. Thurow, an economics professor at the Massachusetts Institute of Technology. "Transportation still depends upon oil, but fuel cells look as if they are about to arrive. When they do, early in the next century, oil demand will begin to fall even in this, its primary market." As a result, Thurow predicted, oil "prices will be low for the foreseeable future." [35]

Other experts are equally convinced that oil prices are headed in the opposite direction. In Campbell's view, the world is in for an oil shock that will make the energy crises of the 1970s pale in comparison. "There will be an initial price shock around 2000, with a doubling or perhaps a tripling of prices," he said in 1998. "Although the roof won't fall in overnight, long-term shortages will force a change in attitude about energy consumption."

The price rise will spur development of renewable energy sources, Campbell predicted. "But it's hard to picture this being done at a rate and a scale to enable renewables to act as substitutes for the way we've used cheap oil up to now."

In Campbell's view, the United States will play a crucial role in determining the global response to what he sees as the coming oil crisis. "There is an enormous danger that the United States, with its peculiar Middle East policies, may misunderstand this situation and perceive the price hikes to be a politically hostile act by Iran or Iraq," he said.

"But at the heart of the matter, the coming oil crisis isn't about politics; its simply about the distribution of a resource that events during the Jurassic Period dictated." ■

Notes

[1] Peña testified April 30, 1998, before the House International Relations Committee. Peña announced on April 6 he would resign this summer, and President Clinton nominated U.N. Representative Bill Richardson as the next Energy secretary. The Senate Energy and Natural Resources Committee voted 18-0 on July 29 to approve Richardson's nomination. The Senate approved Richardson on July 31.

[2] For background, see Mary H. Cooper, "Oil Imports," *The CQ Researcher,* Aug. 23, 1991, pp. 585-608.

[3] For background, see Rodman D. Griffin, "Mexico's Emergence," *The CQ Researcher,* July 19, 1991, pp. 497-520.

[4] For background, see David Masci, "U.S.-Russian Relations," *The CQ Researcher,* May 22, 1998, pp. 457-480, and Mary H. Cooper, "Russia's Political Future, *The CQ Researcher,* May 3, 1996, pp. 385-408.

[5] For background, see Patrick G. Marshall, "Calculating the Costs of the Gulf War," *Editorial Research Reports,* March 15, 1991, pp. 145-156.

[6] See James Kim and Chris Woodyard, "Glut Knocks Oil Costs Down, but It Won't Last," *USA Today,* Feb. 26, 1998.

[7] See "Saddam Seeks End to U.N. Embargo This Year," *The Washington Post,* July 18, 1998.

[8] Pickering testified May 21, 1998, before a joint hearing of the Senate Energy and Natural Resources and Foreign Relations committees.

[9] Perle testified at the May 21 hearing before the Senate Energy and Foreign Relations committees.

[10] Indyk testified May 14, 1998, before the Senate Foreign Relations Subcommittee on Near Eastern and South Asian Affairs.

[11] Albright spoke before the Asia Society in New York City. See Thomas W. Lippman, "Albright Offers Iran Possibility of Normal Ties," *The Washington Post,* June 18, 1998.

[12] Sestanovich testified July 8, 1998, before the Senate Foreign Relations Subcommittee on International Economic Policy, Export and Trade Promotion.

[13] Murphy testified May 14, 1998, before the Senate Foreign Relations Subcommittee on Near Eastern and South Asian Affairs.

[14] See Tad Szulc, "Will We Run Out of Gas?" *Parade Magazine,* July 19, 1998, pp. 4-6.

[15] For background, see Mary H. Cooper, "Transportation Policy," *The CQ Researcher,* July 4, 1997, pp. 577-600.

[16] For background, see Mary H. Cooper, "Renewable Energy," *The CQ Researcher,* Nov. 7, 1997, pp. 961-984.

[17] Moniz testified Feb. 5, 1998, before the House Commerce Subcommittee on Energy and Power.

[18] Lugar, chairman of the Senate Agriculture, Nutrition and Forestry Committee, spoke before the committee on Nov. 13, 1997.

[19] For background, see Cooper, *ibid.*

[20] Unless otherwise noted, information in this section is based on Fadhil J. Chalabi, "OPEC: An Obituary," *Foreign Policy,*

winter 1997-98, pp. 126-140.
[21] Chalabi, *op. cit.,* p. 130.
[22] *Ibid,* p. 133. The Organization for Economic Cooperation and Development represents the leading industrial nations.
[23] *Ibid,* p. 136.
[24] See Youssef M. Ibrahim, "Falling Oil Prices Pinch Several Producing Nations," *The New York Times,* June 23, 1998.
[25] See "When Gulf States Tighten Their Belts," *The Economist,* March 14, 1998, pp. 49-50.
[26] See "2 Oil Giants Register Record Earnings," *The New York Times,* July 26, 2000.
[27] Murphy spoke July 15, 1998, at an American Petroleum Institute press conference in Washington.
[28] See Edward Alden, "U.S. Trade Deficit Hits Record Levels in May: Reaches US$31B," *Financial Times,* July 26, 2000.
[29] For background on early oil development in the Caspian region, see Daniel Yergin, *The Prize* (1991), pp. 56-65. Another Nobel brother, Alfred, invented dynamite. Their father, Immanuel, invented the underwater mine.
[30] See Hugh Pope, "New Caspian Well Yields Substantial Oil and Gas," *The Wall Street Journal,* July 25, 2000.
[31] See Richard C. Longworth, "Boomtown Baku," *The Bulletin of the Atomic Scientists,* May/June 1998, p. 35.
[32] For background, see Mary H. Cooper, "Oil Spills," *The CQ Researcher,* Jan. 17, 1992, pp. 25-48.
[33] From July 8, 1998, testimony before the Senate Foreign Relations Subcommittee on International Economic Policy, Export and Trade Promotion.
[34] Martha Brill Olcott, "The Caspian's False Promise," *Foreign Policy,* summer 1998, p. 110.
[35] Lester C. Thurow, "Oil Prices No longer Hold Us Hostage," *USA Today,* May 26, 1998.

Bibliography

Selected Sources Used

Books

Adelman, M. A., *The Genie Out of the Bottle: World Oil Since 1970,* MIT Press, 1995.
The author, a leading petroleum economist, builds on his earlier analyses of the global oil trade with this review of events encompassing OPEC's rise to power over oil production and its more recent decline.

Campbell, Colin J., *The Coming Oil Crisis,* Multi-Science Publishing and Petroconsultants, 1997.
A former geologist for Texaco and Amoco predicts that global oil production will peak within the next few years. It is at this point, he writes, not when supplies are close to exhaustion, that oil prices will rise significantly.

Yergin, Daniel, *The Prize: The Epic Quest for Oil, Money & Power,* Simon & Schuster, 1991,
This sweeping history of the oil industry takes the reader from the first oil well in 1859 in Titusville, Pa., through the rise of OPEC and the West's reaction to the energy crises of the 1970s.

Articles

"Asia: The Cloning of America," *Energy Investor,* June/July 1998, pp. 2-3.
Despite its current economic crisis, Asia remains a leading consumer of oil. With rapid industrialization in much of the continent, Asia already uses 70 percent of all newly discovered oil, and its demand for oil can only be expected to grow in coming decades.

Chalabi, Fadhil J., "OPEC: An Obituary," *Foreign Policy,* winter 1997-98, pp. 126-140.
A former OPEC official writes that the formerly omnipotent cartel will continue to lose its control over global oil production and prices because oil-consuming countries have found alternative sources of oil. To survive, the organization's members must introduce economic reforms and change its quota system to reflect changes in the global oil market.

Coy, Peter, Gary McWilliams and John Rossant, "The New Economics of Oil," *Business Week,* Nov. 3, 1997, pp. 140-144.
The authors conclude that today's low oil prices may continue for decades as technological advances make it easier than ever to produce oil.

Longworth, Richard C., "Boomtown Baku," *The Bulletin of the Atomic Scientists,* May/June 1998, pp. 34-38.
Political turmoil in the oil-rich countries bordering the Caspian Sea makes the region the equivalent of "Bosnia with oil," writes journalist Longworth. U.S. policies, especially those favoring Armenian separatists in Azerbaijan, work against U.S. oil companies' efforts to develop the region's oil.

Olcott, Martha Brill, "The Caspian's False Promise," *Foreign Policy,* summer 1998, pp. 94-113.
A Colgate University professor of political science describes the obstacles to oil development in the Caspian Sea region, the most promising new source of oil today. Poverty, ethnic rivalries and economic mismanagement since the region gained independence with the Soviet Union's collapse in 1991 may derail plans for large-scale oil exports.

"Preventing the Next Oil Crunch," *Scientific American,* March 1998, pp. 77-95.
Four articles describe the problems associated with falling oil reserves. Technological advances will stretch out the petroleum age, but price hikes are likely as oil reserves drop and extraction becomes increasingly costly.

"When Gulf States Tighten Their Belts," *The Economist,* March 14, 1998, pp. 49-50.
The collapse in oil prices since early this year has drastically curtailed revenues in the rich kingdoms of the Persian Gulf. Because they depend so heavily on income from oil exports, these countries are having to reduce spending on social programs and hasten economic reforms.

Reports and Studies

Energy Information Administration, Petroleum Supply Monthly, May 1998.
This publication of the U.S. Department of Energy provides updated statistics on global oil supplies and imports and exports, as well as prices and a breakdown of oil products. Historical tables show changes in supplies and prices since the early 1980s.

International Energy Agency, *Oil Market Report,* July 9, 1998.
The Paris-based IEA, created in response to the 1970s' energy crises, monitors the global oil market and helps consuming countries overcome supply disruptions. The latest report concludes that the current oil glut and low prices are likely to continue until consumer nations draw down their record high oil stocks.

5 International Monetary Fund

MARY H. COOPER

They were known as the Asian tigers. Hong Kong, Singapore, South Korea and Taiwan had enjoyed such an economic boom that — together with Japan, Indonesia, Malaysia and Thailand — they had transformed East Asia into one of the world's fastest-growing regions and hottest destinations for foreign money.

Then, almost overnight, the tigers lost their roar. The beginning of the end came on July 2, 1997, when Thailand devalued its currency, causing skittish foreign investors to lose confidence in the country's economic prospects and withdraw their holdings.

Despite emergency infusions of cash from the International Monetary Fund (IMF) and other lenders, the flight of overseas capital spread throughout the region. Banks failed and economies fell like dominoes as investors pulled out of one Asian country after another.

As international investors grew increasingly pessimistic about emerging markets, the "Asian contagion" continued to spread. Last summer, it infected the Russian economy, and by September it was threatening Brazil and the rest of Latin America.

To many observers, the economic chaos claimed another potential victim: the IMF itself. In trying to calm the global economy, the low-profile agency was thrust into an acrimonious international debate over the way it had tried to stabilize the global financial system.

Indeed, the austerity methods the IMF used to staunch capital flight sparked criticism from some unexpected quarters. Harvard University economist Jeffrey Sachs, who had helped Russia dismantle its state-run economy, called the IMF the "Typhoid Mary of emerging markets, spreading recessions in country after country." [1]

From *The CQ Researcher,* January 29, 1999.

Reuters

And Joseph E. Stiglitz, chief economist of the World Bank, issued an unusually harsh assessment of the IMF's performance. Stiglitz suggested that the austerity measures required by the IMF — including the imposition of high interest rates — helped spread the Asian crisis even to well-managed economies. "Many countries that have . . . as reasonable economic policies . . . as you will find have been very adversely affected," he said. "The recognition that the contagion that occurs affects countries whether or not they have undertaken undue risks is a reality that has to be confronted." [2]

IMF Managing Director Michel Camdessus has defended the fund's actions, saying they will work over the long term. "The International Monetary Fund has come under heavy criticism in recent months both for its handling of global financial contagion and its proposals for defending against future crises," he wrote recently. "While many of the critics have offered constructive advice, at times the discourse has lost sight of the facts — and the true significance of the proposed remedies." [3]

Launched in 1945 to help stabilize the war-torn global economy, the IMF today provides short-term loans to its 182 member countries when they face temporary balance-of-payments problems caused by insufficient reserves of foreign exchange to pay off overseas creditors.

The IMF doesn't just hand out loans on demand but may require the recipient government to institute policy changes to improve its economy. In that way, the IMF seeks to ensure that the loan will be repaid and to reduce the risk of future crises. To help Mexico and other Latin American countries overcome a serious debt crisis in the 1980s, the IMF required higher interest rates to shore up investor confidence in local currencies, government spending cuts to reduce deficits and privatization of unprofitable state-owned enterprises. [4]

When the Asian financial crisis erupted in 1997, the IMF imposed similar conditions on governments that appealed for IMF loans. But the stringent spending cuts and high interest rates drove those troubled economies into further difficulties. Because businesses could no longer afford to borrow money, factories shut down and workers lost their jobs. Moreover, the region's already weak social programs were unable to prevent a sharp decline in living standards. Today, despite some signs of improvement, especially in Thailand and South Korea, recession afflicts the region, with depressed output, widespread unemployment and, in some cases, high inflation.

"The IMF has a difficult challenge in Asia," says Robert Manning, an Asia specialist at the Council on Foreign Relations. "They have put up more than $120 billion, and there has been no discernible uptick in the region's performance. But you have to consider another question. Where would the region be today without the IMF?"

The answer to that question, some critics say, is clear. "The world would be a lot better off without the IMF," says Mark Weisbrot, research director of the Preamble Center, an economic-policy think tank in Washington. Like other left-leaning critics, Weisbrot blames the IMF — and the

Economic Trouble in Developing Countries

Economic output plummeted throughout much of East Asia after Thailand devalued its currency in July 1997. The "Asian contagion" then spread to Russia and Brazil.

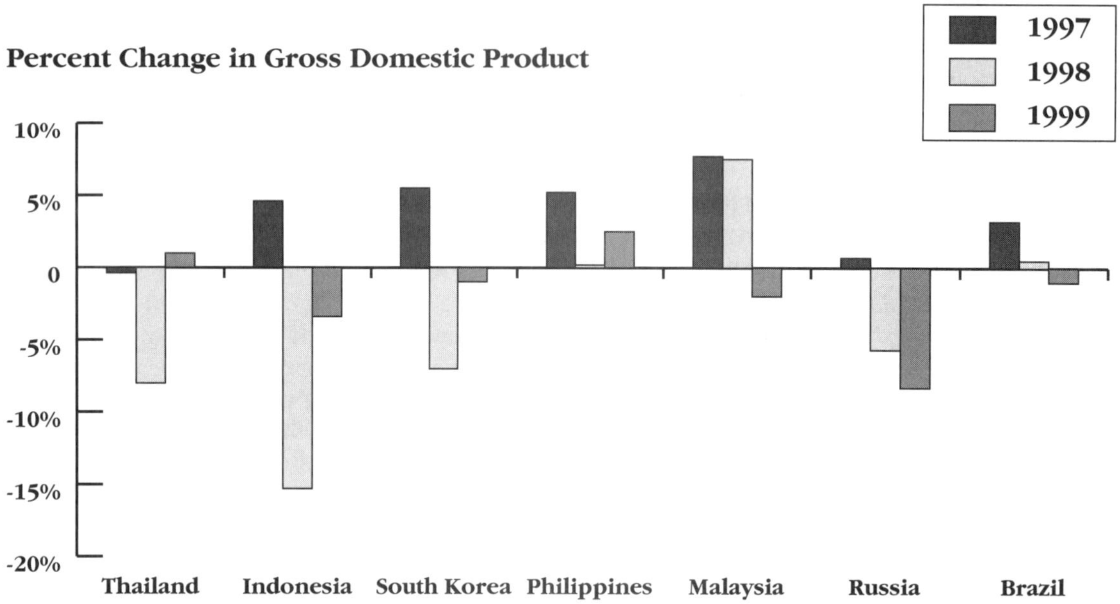

Source: International Monetary Fund

U.S. Treasury Department, its main ally — for impoverishing millions of already poor people in countries where it has required austerity measures in exchange for loans. "The IMF is like a medieval doctor who applies leeches and bleeds patients until they hopefully get better," he says, "but often they don't."

Opposition to the IMF's policies is no less scathing on the right, where critics charge that the fund undermines the workings of the free market by bailing out inefficient governments. "The idea that you need to pay for economic reforms has been proven time and time again to be incorrect," says Bryan T. Johnson, a policy analyst at the Heritage Foundation. "Transferring wealth from countries that have it to countries that don't have it is not a way to create and generate wealth in less-developed countries."

In this view, IMF lending poses a "moral hazard," a term insurance companies use to describe the risk that policyholders will fail to adequately protect their property once it is insured. Similarly, critics say, by holding out the promise of help to governments that fail to adopt sound economic policies, the IMF discourages countries from adopting such policies in the first place.

"The problem in these countries is that people aren't free to work" because their governments fail to embrace free-market policies, Johnson says. "Establishing economic policies that allow people to work doesn't cost money."

Voicing another common complaint from conservatives, many congressional Republicans have long decried what they see as the IMF's lack of accountability to the United States, its biggest donor. As evidence mounted that the IMF's interventions in Asia and other regions had failed to resolve economic crises, lawmakers delayed action on the Clinton administration's request last year for $17.9 billion to help replenish the IMF's coffers. Congress finally approved the funding measure after attaching requirements that the IMF open more of its activities to public scrutiny.

Even fund officials acknowledge that changes are needed if the IMF can be expected to forestall economic crises in the future. "We can surely do better in reducing the frequency and intensity of emerging-market financial crises . . . than we have in the last five years," said American economist Stanley Fischer, the IMF's deputy managing director. [5]

In an unusual self-criticism, the IMF has admitted to mistakes in its handling of the crisis in Asia. "[B]oth the fund and outsiders erred in some ways that could have been avoided at the time," the agency conceded in a recent report. Moreover, earlier crises "might have led one to predict a much sharper slowdown in growth than was initially projected in the Asian crisis countries." [6]

Fischer added that the rapid spread of financial crises around the world in recent years "has led to the most serious rethinking of the structure of the international financial system since the breakdown of the Bretton Woods system in 1971" (*see p. 78*). The Clinton administration also has called for a "new architecture" to strengthen the system's ability to cope with the rapid flow of capital that has accompanied economic globalization (*see p. 84*).

As policy-makers consider revisions to the IMF and other institutions charged with ensuring the global economy's health, these are some of the questions they are asking:

Are the IMF's tough lending policies helping financially strapped countries?

Throughout its history, the IMF has advised governments receiving short-term loans on ways to improve their financial health. In the 1980s, the agency required indebted countries in Latin America to adopt strict austerity measures as a condition for receiving IMF loans. Since then, "conditionality" — requiring recipient governments to take steps to strengthen their economies before receiving loans — has been a prominent characteristic of IMF lending practices.

When Asian countries turned to the IMF for help in 1997, the agency's conditions for short-term loans included the familiar prescription handed out during the Latin American debt crisis: To shore up currency values and attract foreign capital, governments were required to raise interest rates. To reduce deficits, they were to cut government spending. To raise revenues, they had to improve tax collection.

Unlike Latin America, however, Asia did not respond readily to the IMF's bitter medicine. Indeed, the region's economies sank into severe recession. Although the IMF now says it made some mistakes, it generally defends its policies in Asia as necessary to the region's recovery from the financial crisis. "If you have cancer, chemotherapy doesn't make you feel better in the short term, but it may nevertheless be essential for a successful cure," explained Michael Mussa, director of the agency's research department. [7]

But many analysts now say that the IMF's "chemotherapy," which may work in countries with large trade and budget deficits, was overkill for Asia, where economic policies were generally sound. "These countries were growing at very healthy rates before the crisis," Weisbrot says. "They were running budget surpluses and had some of the world's highest savings rates. There is not any excuse in the world to try and put them through the wringer. It was completely outrageous."

Asia expert Manning agrees that the IMF's prescription for Asia was faulty, at least initially. "In the beginning of the crisis, they were almost mechanically applying some of the formulas they'd used for Latin America," he says, "but the budget and other problems typical of Latin America didn't exist in Asia."

When its policies failed to help Asia's ailing economies, the IMF relaxed its conditions somewhat, resulting in some economic improvement, at least in Thailand and South Korea. "To the IMF's credit, they did revise their stance," Manning says. "Of course, that also raises the question of whether they knew what they were doing in the first place."

That question is particularly relevant, critics say, in the IMF's program for Russia, which last Aug. 17 devalued the ruble and defaulted on $40 billion in domestic treasury debt. [8]

When the Soviet Union collapsed in 1991, the IMF faced perhaps its most challenging task ever: helping Russia and the other successor republics enter the global free-market system by privatizing state-owned enterprises and opening their economies to foreign investment and trade.

Even after receiving billions of dollars from the IMF and other donors, the Russian economy remained in a shambles. Foreign trade had virtually ground to a halt, many profitable businesses were in the hands of criminals and the standard of living of ordinary Russians was arguably lower than at any time since World War II.

The IMF suspended its lending to Russia, raising further questions about the agency's ability to solve financial crises. "Russia is clearly the most destructive example of IMF policy failures," Weisbrot says, citing the halving of Russia's gross domestic product (GDP) and falling life expectancy over the past few years. "They have tried to transform this economy in the space of just a few years from a planned economy to their kind of textbook, idealized version of a market economy, and it's been a complete disaster."

How the IMF Works

Membership in the International Monetary Fund is voluntary and open to any country that controls its own foreign policy and agrees to abide by the fund's charter. Among other things, members promise to maintain uniform exchange rates. The IMF currently has 182 members, including Russia and other former Soviet republics. [1]

Central to the fund's mission is the smooth flow of money around the world, a flow that has increased in volume with the expansion of world trade and international investment. Because there are almost as many different currencies in circulation as there are IMF members, currency exchanges occur with virtually every shipment of goods across borders. [2] A wine merchant in Brazil, for example, wishing to buy a shipment of Chianti from an Italian vineyard would run into trouble if he tried to pay in Brazilian reals. But because both Italy and Brazil have made their currencies convertible as part of their commitment to the IMF, the transaction can take place after the merchant exchanges his reals for lire.

The IMF also acts as a kind of credit union. Upon joining, each country contributes a certain amount of money, called a quota subscription. The quota goes into a pool that the IMF draws from to lend to members in financial difficulty. The amount of the contribution, which is based on the country's annual economic output, determines how much it can borrow from the IMF. The quota amount also determines each member's clout in formulating IMF policy.

The United States, the world's largest economy, contributes the most — 18 percent of the total, or about $35 billion; the island nation of Palau, which joined in 1997, contributes the least, about $3.8 million. Likewise, the United States has the strongest voice in setting IMF policies, with more than 265,000 votes, or 18 percent of the total; Palau has 272 votes.

Each member has a representative and an alternate on the Board of Governors, the IMF's top policy-making group. Typically finance ministers or central bank heads, they meet annually. During the rest of the year, the board members relay their governments' positions on day-to-day IMF operations to members of the decision-making Executive Board in Washington. The board's chairman — currently Michel Camdessus of France — is also the IMF's managing director, who by tradition is not an American. (The president of the World Bank, the IMF's sister institution, is traditionally an American.) A staff of about 2,600 people from 122 countries, including battalions of economists, carry out IMF policies.

The fund's main objective is to prevent financial crises. "The IMF has a key role in crisis prevention," says Shailendra J. Anjaria, the fund's external relations director. "In fact, if the IMF does a good job with crisis prevention, it will not be called upon as frequently as it might otherwise to provide large financing packages. Prevention is better than cure. It's also less costly to prevent a fire than to fight a fire."

The main tool used by the IMF to prevent financial crises is surveillance, which it carries out by analyzing all member countries' economic data and suggesting any changes it feels will improve economic conditions. To make it easier to assess those conditions, the IMF recently adopted uniform standards members must use in reporting economic and financial data, including taxation and government expenditures.

"It is very important for the public and for markets to have a consistent and coherent notion of where the money is coming in and where it is going out," Anjaria explains. The IMF's aim, he says, is to "encourage countries to become more transparent and follow coherent standards that can be understood all over the world."

The IMF also has begun publicizing its assessments of economic conditions in member countries. "If markets are better informed, they can make better decisions and are not caught by surprise," Anjaria adds. As a result, "there is less destruction when there is a change in the situation than if the markets were caught by surprise."

When preventive measures fail and member countries encounter difficulties in paying overseas creditors, the IMF will provide short-term loans to help them meet their financial obligations on condition that they adopt economic policies prescribed by the IMF. Before the Asian crisis erupted in mid-1997, the fund provided five- and 10-year loans, each limited to the recipient country's quota. In 1997 it added a two-and-a-half-year loan. Although the new, short-term loan must be repaid earlier and carries a slightly higher interest rate than the other types, the amount is not limited to the recipient's contribution to the IMF. To date, South Korea, Russia and Brazil have received IMF credit under the new terms.

Very few countries have defaulted on IMF loans. Even Russia, which is behind on many of its foreign debts, is current on its IMF obligations. The reason, Anjaria explains, is that other lenders look to a country's record with the IMF before extending credit.

"Countries are very anxious to be current with the IMF," he says, "because if they didn't pay $1 billion back to the IMF, they wouldn't get $100 billion from other places."

---

[1] Material in this section is based on David D. Driscoll, "What Is the International Monetary Fund," September 1998, available on the IMF's Web site at www.imf.org.

[2] Eleven European countries recently adopted a single currency, the euro. For background, see Mary H. Cooper, "European Monetary Union," *The CQ Researcher*, Nov. 27, 1998, pp. 1025-1048.

In Russia, many critics say, the IMF compounded excessive optimism over the economy's potential for rapid change with a failure to perceive the political repercussions of its reform prescription. "The IMF didn't pay enough attention to how the actual policies they were pursuing were being implemented on the ground in Moscow," says Thomas Graham, a senior associate at the Carnegie Endowment for International Peace and a former U.S. diplomat in Moscow. "They came up with a program that they thought made sense from an economic standpoint but did not consider whether there would be sufficient political backing to get the various parts of the program approved by the Russian parliament. Therefore, a lot of things they proposed simply did not work out in reality because of opposition within the broader political framework of the population as a whole."

Particularly noxious to many Russians was the IMF's call for privatization of state-owned businesses and sweeping budget cuts in a country accustomed to generous government benefits. "I think most Russians now accept privatization as a necessity," Graham says. "But there were concerns about the way the program that was devised by the Russian government in consultation with Western advisers and the IMF played itself out in practice, the way it appeared to enrich a very small group of politically well-connected businessmen and financiers."

Shailendra J. Anjaria, the IMF's director of external relations, defends the IMF's program for Russia as a long-term effort that entails no less than the rebuilding of the nation-state and its institutions, which collapsed with the Soviet Union. "Those who felt that reforms could be achieved overnight will perhaps be disappointed," he says. "But that does not mean that the reforms were not needed or are not needed now."

"While many of the critics have offered constructive advice, at times the discourse has lost sight of the facts — and the true significance of the proposed remedies."

— Michel Camdessus, IMF Managing Director

Critics see the IMF's role in Brazil, the latest victim of the international financial crisis, as equally destructive. "Brazil is going into a recession right now and largely as a result of policies imposing extremely high interest rates, of around 36-40 percent in a country where inflation is running at only 3-4 percent," Weisbrot says. "If we had such policies [in the United States], we'd be in a depression today."

But here, too, IMF supporters say the criticism is misplaced. "The IMF does not impose policies," said C. Fred Bergsten, director of the Institute for International Economics, a nonprofit think tank in Washington. "It works them out with the countries. Brazil's high interest rates were put in place by Brazil a year ago. You can't blame it on the IMF." [9]

Is the IMF up to the task of dealing with financial crises on its own?

The seemingly relentless spread of the financial crisis from Asia to Russia and possibly to Latin America over the past year and a half has left many observers wondering whether the IMF is still able to do its job.

Computerized trading has made it increasingly easy for international investors to buy and sell stocks, bonds and other securities 24 hours a day, and liberalized markets have greatly expanded their access to countries around the world. While all this facilitates the free flow of capital by making it easier for investors to quickly move their money from one country to another, it makes it harder for the IMF to keep an eye on things and avert crises before it's too late.

"The reason that dealing with economic problems is more difficult today than it was 25 or 50 years ago is that the world is more integrated," Anjaria says. "Economies also are more integrated with each other, and there is a belief very strongly held in all parts of the world that markets

Did Malaysia Shoot Itself in the Foot . . .

When panicky investors began pulling their money out of one East Asian country after another in mid-1997, one nation refused to stand by and wait for disaster to strike. Malaysia simply slammed the door shut. On Sept. 1, 1998, it adopted currency controls that barred foreigners from withdrawing their funds for a year after investment and pegged the currency, the ringgit, to the U.S. dollar.

"The free-market system has failed and failed disastrously," declared Prime Minister Mahathir Mohamad. "The only way that we can manage the economy is to insulate us ... from speculators." [1]

Mahathir's solution to the Asian financial crisis dismayed the International Monetary Fund (IMF) and other supporters of global economic integration. It reminded them of the beggar-thy-neighbor policies of the 1930s, when countries refused to exchange their currencies, contributing to the international tensions that eventually ignited World War II. Preventing a repetition of that scenario was the impetus behind the IMF's creation 54 years ago and the gradual liberalization of international capital flows that followed.

"If the capital is well-used for productive investment rather than for real estate and other speculative investment, it adds to a country's wealth potential and improves its standard of living," says Shailendra J. Anjaria, the IMF's director of external relations. "The most important thing is that the capital flow be sustainable and stable." For countries to enjoy these benefits, he says, they must adopt sound economic policies and have strong, well-run financial institutions. "I don't think that there is any disagreement whatsoever that under those conditions capital liberalization is helpful and not hurtful." [2]

But some economists say that capital controls are a legitimate policy alternative, at least in situations like Malaysia's. Rather than allow the depletion of its capital reserves and accept the painful austerity measures linked to IMF loans, Malaysia sought to prevent its economy, already suffering its first recession in more than a decade, from plunging even further.

Indeed, private lenders, who have yet to return to much of Asia, recently extended a $1.35 billion loan to Malaysia. [3] That development cheers Mark Weisbrot, research director of the Preamble Center in Washington. "Here's a country that's already been put on the bad list by the IMF for adopting currency controls and had their bond rating reduced to near junk-bond status in world markets," he says. "They went to the big U.S. banks and told them to give them the loan or get out of their country, and it worked. It shows how much the IMF and these other colonial institutions really depend on the very active collaboration of the leadership of countries" that turned to the IMF for help as the crisis spread.

In addition to the new infusion of private loans, Malaysia has enjoyed low inflation, a widening trade surplus and rising consumption. But the jury is still out on the long-term impact of its currency controls. Industrial production declined in the third quarter of 1998, indicating a possible deepening of Malaysia's recession. [4]

In adopting capital controls, Mahathir may have taken his cue from China, which does not allow the free conversion of its currency although it is a member of the IMF. China's economic insulation from the economic collapse around it has enabled the economy to continue to grow, though perhaps not by the stunning 7.8 percent reported by the government for 1998. "The Chinese have control over their banking system, and they don't have massive foreign ownership of stocks," Weisbrot says. "They have all the tools they need to run their own economy."

While other Asian governments turned to the IMF for help and cut back public spending, China embarked on a stimulus program, including massive subsidies for construction and factory expansion. "Some of the things they're building won't be used for years, but so what?" Weisbrot says. "They're keeping their economy from sinking into the swamp that everyone else is sinking into. This is just because they're one of the only independent countries in the world."

Other experts say China is merely postponing an inevitable reckoning with economic reality. "China has a

must be kept open, even when there is a crisis."

The IMF has tried to improve its ability to prevent and cure financial crises by encouraging member countries to provide consistent and timely data on their economic conditions. (*See story, p. 74.*) Some economists call for expanding the agency's power as well. Billionaire investor George Soros has proposed transforming the IMF into a global central bank, ready to bail out countries with much larger infusions of money than the IMF currently has at its disposal. [10]

Soros also has proposed the creation of an "international credit insurance corporation" to provide prompt infusions of capital into countries threatened by the kind of sudden withdrawal of private capital experienced during the Asian crisis. This new entity would work much as a doctor gives a blood transfusion to an accident victim. "The most urgent need is to arrest the reverse flow of capital," Soros wrote. "That would ensure the continued allegiance of the periphery to the global capitalist system, which would in turn reassure the financial centers . . . and moderate the

. . . When It Adopted Currency Controls?

financial system as weak as any in Asia," says Robert Manning, a specialist on Asia at the Council on Foreign Relations. "Because they're so nervous about unemployment and instability, they're simply having the banks gin up more loans to state-owned enterprises. But they are digging themselves into an even deeper hole, and the next two or three years are going to be very dicey for China."

But as austerity measures have failed to quickly restore economic health to Asia, many economists are reconsidering the suitability of some form of currency controls. Massachusetts Institute of Technology economist Paul Krugman, for example, warns that the postwar liberalization of financial markets and move to full currency convertibility may have gone too far. "[I]n bringing back the virtues of old-fashioned capitalism, we also brought back some of its vices, most notably a vulnerability both to instability and sustained economic slumps," he wrote. "[I]t is hard to avoid concluding that sooner or later we will have to turn the clock at least part of the way back: to limit capital flows for countries that are unsuitable for either currency unions [such as the European Monetary Union] or free floating." [5]

Not all currency controls are the same, however. By adopting such strict controls after investors were already pulling out of Malaysia, Mahathir may have caused unnecessary long-term harm to the economy. "Malaysia stopped currency from leaving the country after it had already left," Manning says. "So instead of actually stopping currency from leaving, they're making it harder for currency to come in. Malaysia is using every trick in the book to get capital, but over the longer term it's not going to be very productive for them."

Many economists endorse the more modest controls adopted by Chile as a better way to discourage capital flight that stops short of scaring away investors interested in long-term investment. Instead of directly banning the withdrawal of foreign capital, Chile in 1991 began phasing in a tax on capital investments that were withdrawn from the country after less than one year. "Overall, the international system has an interest in creating a tax regime that motivates capital to make long-term investments in the real economy, rather than one that rewards speculators for destabilizing currency markets," writes Ethan B. Kapstein, a political scientist at the University of Minnesota. But he warns against imposing the kind of strict controls that Malaysia has adopted. "This might make sense for some countries at particular moments in their development, but as a general rule it would do considerable harm to the world economy. It would freeze a good share of trade and investment flows, lowering growth rates and creating new sources of conflict." [6]

For the time being, capital controls have ceased to be a burning issue for some economists, who point out that even Chile abandoned its controls last fall. "The question of capital controls on inflows was a relevant issue for debate and discussion among economists at a time when there was a lot of capital sloshing around in the world," says Anjaria. But the amount of private capital invested in developing countries has shrunk dramatically since 1997, when it totaled $286 billion. "Today you're not going to worry about whether to keep capital out or not because none is coming in," Anjaria says. "So I think that debate for the time being can be put on the back burner, and what we can do is help countries build stronger financial systems so that they can deal with the flow of capital when capital does decide to return."

---

[1] Quoted by Sheila McNulty, "Mahathir Introduces Strict Currency Curbs," *The* (London) *Financial Times*, Sept. 2, 1998.

[2] For background, see also Shailendra J. Anjaria, "The Capital Truth," *Foreign Affairs*, November/December 1998, pp. 142-143.

[3] See "12 Banks to Lend Malaysia $1.35 Billion at a Low Rate," *The New York Times*, Dec. 30, 1998.

[4] See "Malaysia's Industrial Output Tumbled," *The Wall Street Journal*, Jan. 12, 1999.

[5] Paul Krugman, "The Return of Depression Economics," *Foreign Affairs*, January/February 1999, pp. 71, 74.

[6] Ethan B. Kapstein, "A Global Third Way: Social Justice and the World Economy," *World Policy Journal*, winter 1998/99, p. 33.

ensuing recession." [11]

In a similar vein, the IMF's Fischer has called for the agency to become the world's official "lender of last resort," making larger loans available to troubled countries than the fund currently can afford to make. To reduce the "moral hazard" of rescuing any needy government, Fischer recommends limiting IMF loans to countries that follow sound economic policies. "These changes should not result in an increase in IMF lending," Fischer said. "For if the reforms succeed, there will be fewer international crises, and fewer occasions for crisis lending. And that, surely, is a goal we all share." [12]

Critics of IMF lending policies naturally look askance at proposals to expand the agency's authority. "In an ideal world, it may be that we would need a central bank for the global economy if it did at least as good a job as the Federal Reserve does in the United States," says Weisbrot, who points out that Alan Greenspan, chairman of the U.S. central bank, is at least indirectly answerable to the American public for his policies. "But at the international level, institutions like the IMF are accountable only to the most powerful actors in the world economy, which are big corporations and the U.S. Treasury Department."

Weisbrot is far more supportive of alternative proposals to expand the role of regional, rather than global, institutions. Japan, for example, proposed the creation of a new Asian Monetary Fund, to be funded largely by Japan and limited to the countries of East Asia. "I'm very much in favor of that approach," he says. "Japan has an interest in economic growth throughout that region because that's where most of its exports go. It's much better than having one country control the whole world economy, as the United States does through the IMF." The regional approach is opposed by the United States and other developed countries that fear it would undermine the IMF's leadership role.

Some critics of the IMF say it should be abolished altogether. "The IMF and the World Bank believe they can stop these short-term economic crises by simply transferring wealth from institutions to countries that need it," says Johnson of the Heritage Foundation. "But that ignores the central reason why these countries have put themselves in a situation where there is little or no foreign investment coming in and why they aren't achieving economic growth. The reason is that those governments have bad economic policies."

Far from encouraging governments to improve their policies, in Johnson's view, IMF lending programs inevitably lead them to put off government spending cuts and other painful policy adjustments, in spite of the agency's strict conditionality. "If you look at all the major IMF recipients over the last 50 years, you will see that a country that becomes an IMF recipient is much more likely to become a long-term recipient of assistance than countries that didn't get IMF aid," Johnson says. "Once you become a recipient of aid, you become addicted to it."

But most economists say that abolishing the IMF is not the answer to today's financial instability. Even Russia, which critics call the most conspicuous example of poor management by the IMF, may have benefited from the agency's technical assistance. "I think those who argue that Russia would be in better shape now without the IMF are wrong," says the Carnegie Endowment's Graham. "In the absence of an IMF, there would have been an even greater decline in economic activity, and the Russians wouldn't have the knowledge base they have now to apply to what is still a very difficult situation."

While acknowledging the need for some changes to the IMF in light of the changing global financial system, IMF spokesman Anjaria urges caution. "Because the Asian crisis had a strong element of contagion and spread unexpectedly, because the economic downturns were deeper than people initially expected and because some people were waiting for instant results, there was initially a flurry of frantic calls for reforming everything under the sun," he says. "I think that as the Asian situation stabilizes, people will be looking at reform in a more considered and reflective way." ■

BACKGROUND

Visionaries at Work

The International Monetary Fund was founded as part of a new international system set up to help restore financial stability and expand world trade in the aftermath of World War II. Meeting in Bretton Woods, N.H., in July 1944, delegates of the United States and 43 other countries devised a system of fixed exchange rates in which participating currencies were pegged to the dollar, which in turn was linked to gold. [13]

The IMF, which began operations in May 1946, was set up to monitor the new regime's performance and support the convertibility of member countries' currencies. Its founders hoped that it could prevent the kind of sudden variations in exchange rates that had made governments reluctant to allow their currencies to be exchanged for foreign currency and contributed to the tensions leading up to the outbreak of hostilities.

At the same time that the IMF was established, the International Bank for Reconstruction and Development, better known as the World Bank, was set up. The IMF's sister institution was created to provide assistance in long-term development, initially to war-torn Europe and later to developing countries. With a loan to Belgium in 1952, the IMF began extending short-term loans to member countries having trouble meeting their financial obligations to other members. The loans are made available on condition that the recipient country's government undertakes economic reforms to eliminate the causes of its balance-of-payments problem.

The global fixed-rate system collapsed in 1971, when President Richard M. Nixon abandoned the gold standard, allowing the dollar to fluctuate in value. However, the IMF continued to play an important role in the rapidly expanding global economy when member countries voted to enlarge its mandate. In addition to supporting the convertibility of exchange rates, the IMF began to more closely oversee economic policies that influence the balance of payments in member

Chronology

1940s-1960s

After World War II, industrial countries join in an effort to rebuild the international financial system.

July 1944
Meeting in Bretton Woods, N.H., delegates of 44 countries set the stage for establishing the International Monetary Fund (IMF), to oversee the system of fixed exchange rates based on the gold standard, and the World Bank, to assist needy countries with long-term development assistance.

Dec. 27, 1945
Twenty-nine nations sign the articles of agreement formally creating the IMF, which opens its headquarters in Washington, D.C., the following May.

1952
Belgium becomes the first country to receive a short-term loan from the IMF, to help it meet a temporary balance-of-payments problem. As a condition for the loan, the IMF requires Belgium to make policy changes to help prevent such problems from arising in the future.

1970s

Although the Bretton Woods system of fixed exchange rates falls apart, the IMF expands its role in stabilizing the global financial system.

1971
President Richard M. Nixon takes the dollar off the gold standard, allowing the currency's value to float against other currencies.

1980s

Debt crises in Latin America prompt the IMF to impose stricter conditions on its loans.

1982
After borrowing heavily from foreign banks to finance economic development, Mexico is unable to repay its loans on time, sparking a debt crisis that spreads throughout the region. In exchange for loans to Latin American countries, the IMF requires austerity measures, such as budget cuts and tax increases.

1990s

The rapid expansion of international capital investments poses a new challenge to the IMF's oversight role.

December 1991
With the Soviet Union's collapse, Russia and the other successor republics begin the difficult task of transforming their economies, with technical and financial assistance from the IMF.

July 2, 1997
The Asian financial crisis begins in Thailand when the government, short of foreign exchange, devalues its currency, the baht.

Aug. 20, 1997
The IMF arranges a $17.2 billion loan package for Thailand, requiring the government to curtail spending and adopt other austerity measures.

Oct. 31, 1997
The IMF arranges a $42 billion loan for Indonesia.

Dec. 3, 1997
The IMF arranges a $58 billion rescue for South Korea.

May 21, 1998
Indonesian strongman Suharto resigns after riots break out to protest the government's removal of price subsidies on consumer goods.

July 20, 1998
The IMF assembles $22.6 billion in loans for Russia, following an earlier $10 billion package.

Aug. 17, 1998
Russia devalues the ruble and defaults on some debts. The IMF suspends payments to Russia.

September 1998
Malaysian Prime Minister Mahathir Mohamad imposes strict capital controls to curb speculation on the country's currency. Chile abandons the tax on foreign investment it introduced in 1991, as the volume of private investment capital flowing to developing countries continues to plunge.

Oct. 21, 1998
President Clinton signs into law a $17.9 billion funding increase for the IMF. The measure calls on the IMF to provide more information on its operations.

Nov. 13, 1998
In an attempt to prevent the spread of the Asian crisis to Latin America, the IMF and the Clinton administration unveil a $41.5 billion loan package for Brazil.

Jan. 19, 1999
Days after devaluing the real, Brazil abandons the currency's fixed rate, relying on high interest rates to buoy its value.

Is Debt Relief the Answer?

Many developing countries are so deep in debt to foreign creditors that they are unlikely to free themselves without help. Some economists call on creditors to offer these countries some form of debt relief, either by stretching out repayment deadlines or by forgiving debt outright.

The IMF and the World Bank have identified 41 "highly indebted poor countries" (HIPC) that are unlikely to pay off their creditors without help (*see map*). The IMF has helped put together special debt-relief packages for seven of the HIPC countries — Bolivia, Burkina Faso, Ivory Coast, Guyana, Mali, Mozambique and Uganda — which owe foreign creditors, including the IMF, a total of $3 billion.

But the IMF accounts for only about 10 percent of outstanding debt in the poor countries it has singled out for relief. Its main role is getting the foreign governments, banks and other creditors to agree to the terms of debt relief. "The HIPC initiative has been a significant source of debt relief for the countries that have already been approved," says Shailendra J. Anjaria, the IMF's director of external relations. "In addition, similar mechanisms have been extended to take care of Honduras and Nicaragua," the two Central American countries that were hardest hit by Hurricane Mitch last fall.

Russia, which fell victim to the Asian financial crisis last August, also has asked for debt relief. The government of President Boris Yeltsin announced in January that it could pay only about half of its foreign debt obligations this year without help. But many economists warn that offering extensive debt relief to any but the poorest countries would backfire. They note, for example, that Russia's plight is not as hopeless as that of war-torn Mozambique.

"Don't forget that today the reality is that private flows of capital, including not only loans but also direct investment, which can boost developing country economies in a very healthy way, are far more important than official loans," Anjaria says. "If you create an artificial incentive for countries not to repay their debt on time, you're not going to be able to attract private capital."

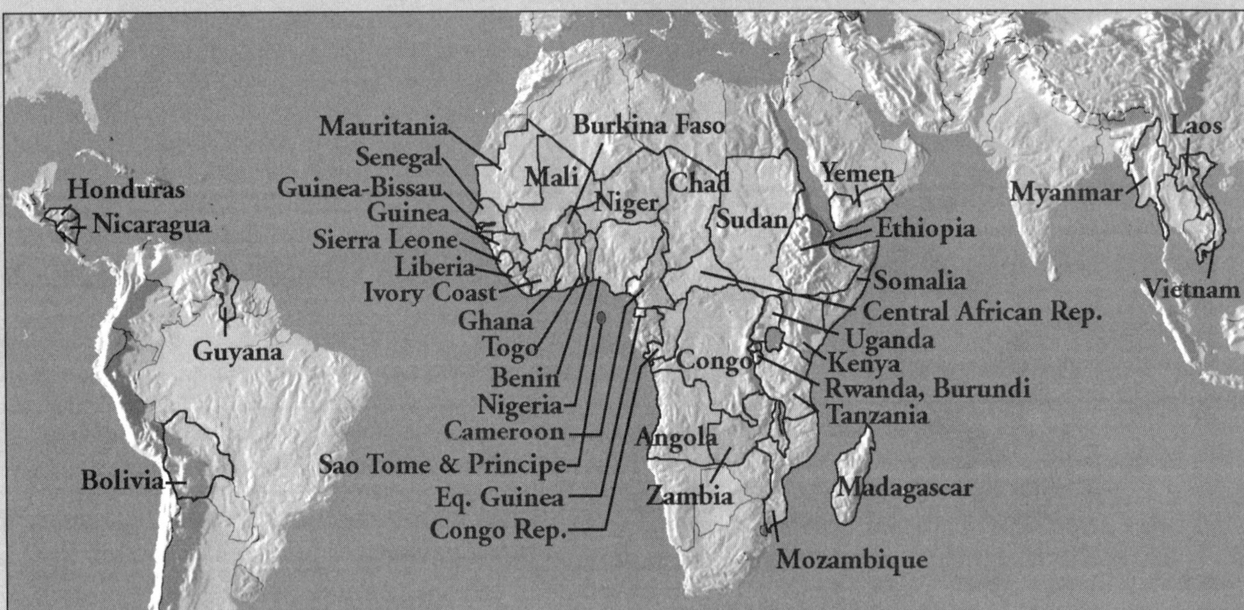

International Monetary Fund

countries and to provide policy advice as well as short-term loans to reverse imbalances.

The 1980s saw the expansion of private international lending, which was encouraged by President Ronald Reagan's downplaying of the IMF and other public institutions in favor of "the magic of the marketplace." But Reagan softened his antagonism toward the IMF when the 1982 Mexican crisis made it clear that private funding alone was insufficient to prevent a major economic disaster. The administration supported an $8.4 billion increase in the U.S. contribution to the IMF, which Congress approved in 1983.

The IMF played a key role in helping Mexico and other Latin American countries overcome the debt crisis, which threatened major commercial banks in the United States and other lending countries. To increase levels of foreign exchange needed to pay off their debts, the Latin American countries had to boost their exports and curb their imports. To this end they adopted sweeping reforms aimed at reducing government spending, raising taxes and raising interest rates to limit domestic borrowing. In Mexico and other countries where unprofitable state-owned enterprises contributed to budget deficits, privatization was another important element of the IMF's prescription for "structural adjustment."

To avoid widespread bank failures at home, the U.S. government provided short-term loans that enabled Mexico to pay off its immediate debts to banks. The IMF also provided some short-term financing, but its main role was to monitor the debtor nations' progress in improving their financial conditions. It was up to the debtor countries and their commercial bank creditors to negotiate new terms for the repayment of loans. In some cases, banks wrote off loans; in others, they accepted reduced payments.

The collapse of the Soviet Union and its allies in Eastern Europe in the early 1990s presented the IMF with a new challenge — providing technical assistance and funding to help successor governments in the region transform their state-run economies into free-market economies able to participate actively in the global trade system. The IMF funding went to so-called transition economies that accepted IMF advice on such matters as privatizing industries, setting up efficient tax-collection systems and adopting legal guarantees for foreign investors.

Crisis in Asia

The financial crisis that erupted in Asia in 1997 soon proved to be different from previous upheavals the IMF had dealt with. Runs on currencies in Mexico and other countries had been reversed after painful cuts in government spending and tax increases required by the IMF to qualify for its loans. Investor confidence was restored as sounder economic policies took effect, and foreign capital once again flowed into many countries receiving IMF loans, enabling businesses to expand and hire workers and consumers to purchase goods and services.

By 1997, however, the sheer volume of foreign capital investments and the ease with which investors could shift their money from one country to another had grown enormously. International capital flows from private sources to developing countries stood at $286 billion before the Asian crisis erupted, according to the IMF. That was far more than the capital coming from governments and multilateral institutions, which amounted to about $50 billion. Unlike foreign direct investments in production facilities, such as factories or power plants, capital investments in securities are highly liquid and can be quickly withdrawn at the first sign of trouble.

Among the most attractive targets for foreign investors since the early 1980s were the fast-growing, export-driven economies of East and Southeast Asia. Lured by the promise of high returns, investors largely ignored the warning signs of impending debt problems resulting from unrestrained lending and consumption throughout much of the region.

A favorite investment target was Thailand, even after it became clear that its currency, the baht, was overvalued. When the Thai government finally devalued the baht in July 1997, foreign investors, fearful that the booming economies of East Asia were primed for a fall, panicked and withdrew their money not only from Thailand but also from other countries, touching off a financial domino effect. The fall in value of currencies, real estate and stocks discouraged would-be private investors, driving away sources of new lending. The Asian contagion spread from Thailand to Indonesia, South Korea, Malaysia and the Philippines.

Battered East Asian countries tried to prop up their currencies by raising interest rates, hoping that investors seeking attractive returns would keep their money there. But these efforts failed to staunch the outflow of capital. Meanwhile, the high interest rates drove businesses into bankruptcy and workers into unemployment. Because most East Asian countries lacked the kind of social safety net that shields jobless workers from poverty in more developed countries, standards of living plummeted throughout the region. The crisis also deepened a recession in Japan, a key export market for the troubled Asian countries. [14]

IMF in Action

The IMF stepped into the Asian financial crisis with loan packages aimed at enabling the affected countries to pay off their most pressing debts. Those loans, which amounted to $57 billion for South Korea alone, came with the usual strings attached — mainly higher interest rates, cuts in government spending and higher taxes — in an effort to restore investor confidence and inflows of private capital.

But the IMF prescription failed to revive the Asian economies quickly, prompting criticism of the IMF for misdiagnosing the region's problems. The IMF later acknowledged that some of its conditions were too harsh and relaxed them somewhat.

Concerns about the IMF's effectiveness intensified on Aug. 17, 1998, when the Russian government devalued the ruble, dismissed the economic reformers who had worked with Western advisers since 1992 and imposed a 90-day moratorium on the repayment of foreign debts held by Russian banks. Russia's action caused stock markets around the world to plummet and prompted the IMF to cut off further payments to Russia, which had been mired in recession for more than six years. The IMF and other donors had provided billions of dollars to help Russia transform its economy, including a three-year, $10 billion IMF loan program in 1996 and a $22.6 billion rescue plan announced in July.

Another indication of the global financial system's vulnerability to sudden shifts of private capital came last fall, when the near collapse of a single U.S.-based hedge fund, Long-Term Capital Management, threatened to undermine the entire system. Fearing widespread panic if the $125 billion fund were allowed to default, the Federal Reserve Bank of New York arranged the fund's rescue by 14 banks and brokerage firms on Sept. 23.

By last fall, the financial crisis threatened to infect Brazil, whose currency, the real, was considered greatly overvalued. In September and October investors withdrew about $30 billion — more than a third of Brazil's hard-currency reserves. Because Brazil is Latin America's leading economic power and the eighth largest in the world, policy-makers feared that the spread of the Asian contagion to Brazil would infect the entire region and beyond.

To prevent that, the IMF and the Clinton administration put together a massive, $41.5 billion rescue package for Brazil, whose president, Fernando Henrique Cardoso, had recently won re-election on a campaign promise to drastically reduce the growing budget deficit. ■

CURRENT SITUATION

U.S. Policy

Efforts to stem the global financial crisis have been led not only by IMF Managing Director Camdessus but also by U.S. Treasury Secretary Robert E. Rubin. Because voting in the IMF is based on the size of each member's contribution, or quota, the United States enjoys an 18 percent weighted vote in the 182-member fund. Because that is much more than any other single member — and because of the United States' traditional leadership role in the IMF — the United States has overwhelming influence over the organization's lending policies.

To many observers, the close working relationship between the IMF and the U.S. Treasury is symbiotic. The IMF enjoys the visible support of the holder of the world's leading reserve currency, the dollar, while the United States can advance its global economic interests behind the shield of a multilateral agency that acts on behalf of 181 other countries. "The critics don't seem to get it," Manning says. "The IMF is very useful to the United States because it lets somebody else do the dirty work."

But many critics contend that the IMF poses a threat to U.S. sovereignty by requiring the Treasury to pay billions of dollars to an organization that is not accountable to American taxpayers. Some conservatives also object to the IMF because they view it as meddling in the free market, which would fare much better, they say, if left to its own devices. In this view, countries that fail to adopt sound economic policies are lulled into complacency by the assurance of IMF assistance.

But criticism of the IMF is not limited to the right end of the political spectrum. "I'm opposed to the IMF because it's a completely unaccountable, colonial institution that plays an overwhelmingly destructive role in the world economy," Weisbrot says. "And I don't see them changing anytime soon."

Before Congress approved $17.9 billion in funding for the IMF last year, lawmakers held a series of hearings on IMF operations. As a result of these hearings, Congress required the IMF to make public more of its deliberations. For example, the funding bill calls for IMF materials to be made available for an annual audit by the U.S. General Accounting Office. It also requires the Treasury secretary and Fed Chairman Greenspan to certify that the IMF's leading members have agreed to support greater transparency in IMF operations, including the discussions leading up to policy-making decisions related to the fund's loan programs.

But there are limits to what the IMF can make public, Anjaria says, because member countries are loath to release all their current economic data for fear of frightening investors. "The IMF is dealing with very sensitive policy matters, such as external debt, exchange rates and interest-rate policy," he says. "I think a lot more can be done to improve transparency in these areas [after the fact], but during the decision-making process a certain degree of confidentiality will need to be maintained simply

At Issue:

Is the International Monetary Fund up to dealing with the financial crises of struggling countries?

yes

ROBERT E. RUBIN
U.S. TREASURY SECRETARY

FROM TESTIMONY BEFORE THE HOUSE BANKING AND FINANCIAL SERVICES COMMITTEE, SEPT. 16, 1998.

The United States has strongly supported the International Monetary Fund as the central institution in the effort to resolve the financial crises in Asia. The IMF programs have been focused on promoting reform in countries in crisis to address the problems that gave rise to the financial instability, combined with financial assistance if necessary. The IMF is the right institution to be at the center of this effort for three important reasons. First, it has the expertise to shape effective reform programs. Second, it can obtain reforms in crisis countries that no assisting nation could obtain. Finally, the IMF internationalizes the burden.

The IMF-led reform programs have been facing an unprecedented situation of enormous complexity. A number of countries have had great difficulties at the same time, and events in one country have greatly affected currencies, trade and investment flows and confidence in others. There have been enormous capital flows into countries with large amounts of private-sector debt and badly flawed financial sectors. There are no simple answers and no guarantees, and in our view, the judgments made by the IMF during this crisis have been largely sensible with subsequent adjustments as circumstances warrants. It is important to remember that problems in these countries are not a function of the IMF, but of the underlying crises.

Countries that have adhered to IMF-led reform programs — specifically the Philippines, Korea and Thailand — have begun to see signs of a return to stability. Although there is clearly a great deal of work yet to do, in Korea and Thailand, currencies have appreciated and interest rates have come down below pre-crisis levels. I have no doubt the situation over the past year would have been much worse without the work of the IMF. . . .

Russia, where the IMF has played an active role in trying to promote financial stability, is in great difficulty. . . . Russia made significant progress in reforming its economy over the last several years, particularly in privatization and trade liberalization. However, the Russian government this summer proved unable to adequately carry forward the necessary reforms. We all knew there was a real risk that this wouldn't work, but it was a risk well worth taking. . . .

Indonesia is another example of a country that simply did not take ownership of reform. In all countries in crisis, and this has been demonstrated throughout the past year, the politics of reform must keep pace with the policies of reform.

no

GEORGE SOROS
CHAIRMAN, SOROS FUND MANAGEMENT LCC

FROM TESTIMONY BEFORE THE HOUSE BANKING AND FINANCIAL SERVICES COMMITTEE, SEPT. 15, 1998.

This hearing is very timely because the global capitalist system which has been responsible for the remarkable prosperity of this country in the last decade is coming apart at the seams. . . .

[One] major factor working for the disintegration of the global capitalist system is the evident inability of the international monetary authorities to hold it together. IMF programs do not seem to be working. . . . The response of the governments [of the seven leading industrial countries] to the Russian crisis was woefully inadequate, and the loss of control was quite scary. Financial markets are rather peculiar in this respect: They resent any kind of government interference but they hold a belief deep down that if conditions get really rough the authorities will step in. This belief has now been shaken. . . .

There is much talk about imposing market discipline, but imposing market discipline means imposing instability, and how much instability can society take? Market discipline needs to be supplemented by another discipline: Maintaining stability in financial markets ought to be the objective of public policy. This is the general principle that I should like to propose.

Despite the prevailing belief in free markets, this principle has already been accepted and implemented on a national scale. We have the Federal Reserve and other financial authorities whose mandate is to prevent a breakdown in our domestic financial markets and, if necessary, act as lenders of last resort. I am confident that they are capable of carrying out their mandate. But we are sadly lacking in the appropriate financial authorities in the international arena. We have the Bretton Woods institutions — the IMF and the World Bank — which have tried valiantly to adapt themselves to rapidly changing circumstances.

Admittedly, the IMF programs have not been successful in the current global financial crisis; its mission and its methods of operation need to be reconsidered. I believe additional institutions may be necessary. At the beginning of this year I proposed establishing an International Credit Insurance Corporation, but at that time it was not yet clear that the reverse flow of capital would become such a serious problem, and my proposal fell flat. I believe its time has now come.

because that is the practice in all countries at the national level, including the United States."

In any case, the reform measure may have little impact on IMF operations. "A lot of people may be surprised to learn that Congress can pass as many laws as it wants to [concerning the IMF]," Johnson says, "but there's no enforcement mechanism to back them up." The U.S. representative to the fund can exercise the power of "voice and vote" on the fund's executive board, but nearly all decisions are reached by consensus, and very few come to a vote. For that reason, Johnson says, "The IMF doesn't have to listen to anything the United States puts into law."

Indeed, some observers say Congress has little say at all in dealing with the global financial system. "Congress has become irrelevant," writes Robert B. Reich, Clinton's Labor secretary from 1993-97. For all the criticism of the IMF last year, Reich explains, Congress finally approved the funding increase. "They didn't want to be blamed for the global economy collapsing. But they don't know exactly what the IMF is doing with all that money or how it comes up with the strings it attaches." [15]

Is Asia Recovering?

Supporters of IMF policies today point to signs that the crisis in Asia may have bottomed out. "If you look at the performance of Thailand, Korea and Indonesia, there are many signs of stabilization and gradual turnaround," Anjaria says. South Korea, for example, has recently repaid, on schedule, $3.8 billion in loans from the IMF. Another sign of improvement in South Korea is the return of private capital; foreign investment in the country reached a record $8.85 billion last year. [16]

The IMF now predicts that South Korea will turn last year's 5 percent decline in output into economic growth of more than 3 percent in 1999. Output in the other four countries in the region most affected by the crisis — Indonesia, Malaysia, the Philippines and Thailand — is expected to continue to decline, but only by 1.4 percent, compared with 10.6 percent in 1998. [17] "Clearly, there is a turnaround, and the economic formula which the IMF recommended is bearing fruit," Anjaria says. "In fact, the general conclusion that one can draw is that where countries implement sound economic policies and are serious about reforms, confidence returns faster than where they do not."

But critics say the IMF's assessment of Asian economies is far too rosy, particularly in the case of South Korea, where one of the goals of the IMF program was to lessen the influence of the corporate conglomerates known as *chaebols*. "You have to wonder if they know what they're talking about," Manning says, citing South Korea as an example of poor underlying economic conditions. "I'm not sure Korea has hit bottom yet because of its huge corporate debt. Because the banks are afraid that the whole financial system will go down, they continue to lend to the *chaebols*. As a result, the *chaebols* are actually playing a larger role in the Korean economy than they did before the crisis."

Unlike Latin America, Manning says, where earlier crises involved government-to-government debt, the Asian crisis primarily has involved private-sector loans to private-sector creditors. "So in countries like Indonesia, South Korea, Thailand, probably Malaysia and even Japan, you've got hundreds if not thousands of borrowers, and the challenge is how to write off the debt and clear the books. You're not going to get significant amounts of capital coming back in until you sort that out."

As a result, Manning expects the crisis to continue to plague most of Asia for several years. "Beginning at the end of 1997, we're looking at three to five years, possibly longer in some cases," he says. Although Manning predicts that South Korea and Thailand may begin to grow later this year or next, "Indonesia is a basket case, it's on the edge of chaos, so it's going to be quite a while before they turn around."

Russia and Brazil

Russia remains mired in a deep recession and has seen private investment dry up since last August's ruble devaluation. But its long-term prospects are positive, in the IMF's view. "The unfortunate actions of Aug. 17," Anjaria says, "should not obscure from our vision the fact that Russia is a major economic power with a great deal of potential for economic growth, for improving the standard of living of its people and for contributing to world economic stability."

Some observers agree with the IMF's assessment of Russia's long-term prospects. "It would be a mistake to look at the past six or seven years as a total failure just because of what happened in August," Graham says. "The IMF did some valuable things for Russia by helping educate a whole layer of Russian officials as to how an advanced Western economy functions. If you look at where the country was seven years ago and compare that to where it is now, overall it is in better shape, at least in terms of knowledge of what it needs to do and eliminating some of the adverse aspects of the Soviet system. They've got a long way to go, but we all realized this intellectually in 1992. Then we became victims of our own enthusiasm and hoped that it would go much more rapidly than it did, which makes the situation now look much worse than it is, in fact."

Some critics dismiss the IMF's relatively optimistic assessment of current conditions because it ignores the impact of its policies on the poor in countries with IMF programs. "The impact in Indonesia is the worst of all," Weisbrot says. "The country is in a terrible depression, and there are people who are reduced to living on bark, leaves and insects." Indeed, following the May 1997 resignation of President Suharto, violence has erupted in several regions.

Even among countries that are thus far unaffected by the current financial crisis, Weisbrot says, adoption of IMF programs in the past has lowered living standards, especially for the poor. "In the 1960s and '70s, Mexico and other Latin American countries grew at a per capita rate of more than 3 percent," Weisbrot says. "Since the 1980s, those economies have been stagnant. So even by the IMF's own measure of success, which is economic growth, the era of structural adjustment has been a miserable, miserable failure."

Latin America's ability to avoid contagion by the current crisis depends on the outcome of Brazil's recent brush with financial ruin. The country's troubles sprang mainly from chronically high budget deficits and fears that it will be unable to pay its debts. Despite last fall's rescue package, put together by the IMF and the United States, the Brazilian government raised interest rates in a futile effort to retain foreign capital after the Brazilian Congress refused to approve some of President Cardoso's budget cuts. After a state governor announced in January that his state would be unable to repay a loan to the federal government, investors pulled billions of dollars out of the country, severely depleting its foreign currency reserves.

In a desperate effort to staunch the outflow of capital, the Brazilian government announced on Jan. 13 that it had devalued the real. When that failed to buoy confidence in the currency, the government announced six days later that it had abandoned the real's dollar-pegged fixed rate and would allow the real to float on global markets, relying on even higher interest rates to buoy its value and attract foreign investors. But that move, strongly supported by the IMF and the Clinton administration, could result in a further devaluation of the real, touching off inflation and eroding living standards. Such a development would make it even harder for Cardoso to convince Brazilian lawmakers to approve the reform measures he says are needed to set the economy right.

Cardoso's move paid off on Jan. 20, when Brazil's lower house approved the most contoversial element of his austerity program, a pension-reform plan that was considered certain to win swift passage by the Senate. [18]

The specter of a Brazilian collapse bodes ill for the U.S. and European economies, which have been largely spared the ill effects of the ongoing crisis. Brazil alone buys 20 percent of U.S. exports and is the United States' 11th-largest market. A Brazilian recession would hurt American exporters, who have already seen a contraction in exports as a result of the recessions in Asia. Because other countries in Latin America have close economic ties to Brazil, it is likely that a crisis in that country would quickly spread throughout the region, further reducing demand for U.S. and European exports. ■

OUTLOOK

A "New Architecture"?

Since the Asian financial crisis began a year and a half ago, many economists and politicians have called for a fundamental review of the global financial system and the institutions that oversee it. Computerization of financial markets, expansion of trade and the rapid integration of economies around the world, they say, have radically changed the global economy, leaving the IMF and other postwar institutions unable to ensure financial stability.

In addition to exercising its considerable leverage in the IMF, the Clinton administration has also called for restructuring of the global financial system to make it less vulnerable to the kinds of shocks it has received over the past 18 months.

"I have called on the world community to act to adapt the architecture of the international financial system for the new realities of the 21st century, the 24-hour-a-day, high-tech markets, with $1.5 trillion a day in currency exchanges," Clinton said in November. "That is many, many times the total value of goods and services traded in any given day. And that is at the bottom of a lot of the challenges we're facing today: How do we continue to support the necessary free flow of capital so that we can have the trade, the investments we need and avoid the enormous impact that a financial collapse can have when the money being traded on its own is so much greater than the total value of goods and services being traded or investments being made?" [19]

But critics say the administration has failed, in fact, to answer the very question Clinton posed, limiting itself to vague calls to come up with a "new architecture." "I think it's irresponsible to just say that as a throw-away line, as Rubin has done in several speeches," Manning says. "The real flaw is in short-term capital flows, where you've got some 25-year-old kid pushing buttons in New York or Singapore and taking down all sorts of currencies."

Some critics say the Clinton administration's failure to take a more active role in overhauling the global financial structure has undermined the United States' traditional leadership in this arena. "The Clinton administration has dropped the ball on this," says Johnson of the Heritage Foundation. "The first Bretton Woods conference was pushed by the United States, and we had a strong leadership position there. The administration has completely ignored this issue."

Meanwhile, British Prime Minister Tony Blair has called on the seven highly industrialized nations — the G-7 — to convene a contemporary version of the Bretton Woods conclave that created the IMF and World Bank. Some of the IMF's strongest critics would like to see such a conference abolish the fund and the bank altogether. "We need a multilateral institution in today's global economy, but I don't think it needs to be a money-lending institution," Johnson says. "It should be mainly a negotiating forum that allows countries to come together to reduce barriers to trade and investment."

But the IMF's Anjaria doubts that a new Bretton Woods-type conference would bring about such a radical overhaul of global financial systems. "As the Asian situation stabilizes, people will be looking at the issue of reform more calmly," he says. "One cannot look for instant solutions to these very complex issues. They will take time to resolve." ■

FOR MORE INFORMATION

Council on Foreign Relations, 1779 Massachusetts Ave. N.W., Washington, D.C. 20036; (202) 518-3400; www.foreignrelations.org. This nonprofit research organization is among several groups studying proposals to strengthen the international financial system.

Heritage Foundation, 214 Massachusetts Ave. N.E., Washington, D.C. 20002-4999; (202) 546-4400; www.heritage.org. This think tank promotes free-market economic policies and is highly critical of the International Monetary Fund's role in the global economy.

Institute for International Economics, 11 Dupont Circle N.W., Washington, D.C. 20036-1207; (202) 328-9000; www.iie.com. This nonprofit, nonpartisan research institution is devoted to the study of international economic policy.

International Monetary Fund, 700 19th St. N.W., Washington, D.C. 20431; (202) 623-7000; www.imf.org. The 182-member multilateral organization provides loans to member countries facing balance-of-payment difficulties.

Preamble Center, 2040 S St. N.W., Washington, D.C. 20009; (202) 265-3263; www.preamble.org. This independent research and education organization studies a broad array of policy issues, including the impact of multilateral agreements on the world economy.

Notes

[1] Jeffrey D. Sachs, "With Friends like IMF...," *The* (Cleveland) *Plain Dealer*, June 6, 1998.

[2] Stiglitz spoke at a press briefing at the World Bank's Washington headquarters on Dec. 2, 1998.

[3] Michel Camdessus, "The IMF and Its Critics," *The Washington Post*, Nov. 10, 1998.

[4] For background, see David Masci, "Mexico's Future," *The CQ Researcher*, Sept. 19, 1997, pp. 817-840.

[5] Fischer spoke at a joint meeting of the American Economic Association and the American Finance Association in New York City on Jan. 3, 1999.

[6] Timothy Lane et al., "IMF-Supported Programs in Indonesia, Korea and Thailand: A Preliminary Assessment," International Monetary Fund, January 1999, p. 54.

[7] Mussa spoke at an IMF press conference on Dec. 21, 1998.

[8] For background, see David Masci, "U.S.-Russian Relations," *The CQ Researcher*, May 22, 1998, pp. 457-480; Mary H. Cooper, "Russia's Political future," *The CQ Researcher*, May 3, 1996, pp. 385-408 and Mary H. Cooper, "Aid to Russia," *The CQ Researcher*, March 12, 1993, pp. 217-240.

[9] Bergsten spoke on National Public Radio's "The Diane Rehm Show" on Nov. 19, 1998.

[10] George Soros, "To Avert the Next Crisis," *The* (London) *Financial Times*, Jan. 4, 1999.

[11] George Soros, *The Crisis of Global Capitalism* (1998), p. 176.

[12] Fischer spoke at a joint meeting of the American Economic Association and the American Finance Association in New York City on Jan. 3, 1999.

[13] Information in this section is based in part on Martin Feldstein, "Refocusing the IMF," *Foreign Affairs*, March/April 1998. For background, see also Mary H. Cooper, "Bretton Woods Forty Years Later," *Editorial Research Reports*, June 22, 1984, pp. 449-468.

[14] For background, see Christopher Conte, "Deflation Fears," *The CQ Researcher*, Feb. 13, 1998, pp. 121-144.

[15] Robert B. Reich, "Trial Ties Up Senate? Don't Worry, Congress Is Irrelevant," *USA Today*, Jan. 7, 1999.

[16] See "Foreign Investors Flock to Korea," *The Wall Street Journal*, Jan. 5, 1999.

[17] See International Monetary Fund, "World Economic Outlook and International Capital Markets: Interim Assessment," December 1998, p. 83.

[18] See Anthony Faiola, "Brazilian House Adopts Reform Bill," *The Washington Post*, Jan. 21, 1999.

[19] Clinton spoke at a meeting of the President's Export Council on Nov. 10, 1998.

Bibliography

Selected Sources Used

Books

Soros, George, "The Crisis of Global Capitalism [Open Society Endangered]," *Public Affairs*, 1998.

An international financier writes that the private capital flows that have made him a billionaire have grown to the point where the IMF is no longer able to prevent crises when investors suddenly withdraw their funds from a country. He proposes the creation of a new "international credit insurance corporation" to provide additional loans to developing governments that face liquidity crises.

Articles

Feldstein, Martin, "Refocusing the IMF," *Foreign Affairs*, March/April 1998, pp. 20-33.

A Harvard University economist criticizes the IMF for meddling excessively in the political affairs of governments that turn to it for short-term loans.

Fischer, Stanley, "The Asian Crisis and the Changing Role of the IMF," *Finance & Development*, June 1998, pp. 2-5.

The IMF's deputy managing director reviews the institution's transformation over the past half-century and its response to the current economic crisis. He calls for increased oversight of member-country policies to avert similar disasters in the future.

Krugman, Paul, "The Return of Depression Economics," *Foreign Affairs*, January/February 1999, pp. 56-74.

The author, an economist at the Massachusetts Institute of Technology, finds alarming similarities between the current economic crisis with the Great Depression of the 1930s. Continuation of the IMF's austerity measures, he writes, may bring about another global recession.

Madrick, Jeff, "The IMF Approach: The Half-Learned Lessons of History," *World Policy Journal*, fall 1998, pp. 39-55.

The best way to restore investor confidence in Asia and renew private capital flows to the region, writes Madrick, author of *The End of Affluence*, is to lower interest rates — not raise them as the IMF has required.

"Should the IMF Be Bigger or Smaller or Somewhere in Between?" *The Economist*, Oct. 10, 1998.

Calls for the IMF to become the world's "lender of last resort" by greatly increasing the amount of money member countries contribute to its lending pool would merely discourage governments from adopting painful but sound economic policies, the article suggests.

Wade, Robert, "The Coming Fight over Capital Flows," *Foreign Policy*, winter 1998-99, pp. 41-54.

The United States views the Asian crisis as the result of faulty policies in the countries involved. To many observers in Europe and Asia, however, it resulted from excessive liberalization of capital markets championed by the United States and the IMF. The author argues for a more permissive system that would allow for the coexistence of different types of national economic policies.

Reports and Studies

Bergsten, C. Fred, "Reviving the 'Asian Monetary Fund,'" *International Economics Policy Briefs*, Institute for International Economics, December 1998.

In 1997, Japan proposed the creation of an Asian Monetary Fund to help deal with the spreading Asian financial crisis. The idea was rejected because it was seen as a threat to the IMF's leadership role. The director of the Institute for International Economics proposes an Asia Pacific Monetary Fund to complement the IMF's work in the region by providing more effective oversight and intervention.

International Monetary Fund, *World Economic Outlook and International Capital Markets: Interim Assessment*, January 1999.

The fund issued this combined update of reports issued in the fall to reflect the "unusual turbulence" in financial markets that occurred in the final quarter of 1998. While it identified signs of recovery in a few countries hit by the Asian financial crisis, the report concludes that it is "premature to consider the difficulties to be over."

Johnson, Bryan T., and Brett D. Schaefer, "IMF Reform? Setting the Record Straight," *The Heritage Foundation Backgrounder*, Nov. 25, 1998.

Although the IMF funding measure signed into law last fall requires the IMF to provide more information about its activities, these analysts at the Heritage Foundation say it doesn't go far enough. They call on Congress to promote a new international conference aimed at reforming, if not eliminating, the IMF and its practice of "bailing out" governments with poor economic policies.

Lane, Timothy, et al., "IMF-Supported Programs in Indonesia, Korea, and Thailand: A Preliminary Assessment," International Monetary Fund, January 1999.

In this review of its lending policies in three of the hardest-hit Asian countries since 1997, the IMF admits to some mistakes in its handling of the region's crisis.

6 Budget Surplus

MARY H. COOPER

Imagine that you won the lottery. What would you do with the money? Buy a snazzy new car? Fly to the Caribbean? Pay off those credit-card debts? Or would you salt away your new fortune for your retirement or your kids' college education?

Unfortunately, few of us will ever face such a quandary. But that's exactly what lawmakers in Washington must deal with on our behalf as they argue over what to do with the burgeoning federal budget surplus.

AP Photos/Dennis Cook

House Minority Leader Richard A. Gephardt, D-Mo., criticizes President Bush's proposed budget at a news conference on Feb. 28, calling it "too good to be true."

Since 1998, the government has been taking in more money in tax revenues than it has been spending on defense, education and other federal services. This year, the surplus is expected to hit a record $281 billion. And the Congressional Budget Office (CBO) projects the budget windfall could reach $5.6 trillion by 2011, even if the economy experiences a recession in the coming decade. (*See graph, p. 90.*)

A federal budget surplus is almost as rare as a winning lottery ticket. The last one occurred more than 30 years ago, in 1969. Most of us are more accustomed to budget deficits, which grew to a record $290 billion in 1992 before the booming economy of the 1990s wiped them out.

"This is a startling and in some ways unique opportunity," says Alicia H. Munnell, a professor at Boston College and a former Treasury official and economic adviser to President Bill Clinton. "Indeed, as recently as the late 1990s, we were projecting deficits for the budget going forward."

President Bush and his fellow Republicans in Congress want to "give back" the surplus to taxpayers. In their view, the surplus is simply the result of excessive taxation. "A surplus, after all, is an overcharge of American taxpayers," Bush said. "And on your behalf, I am asking for a refund." [1]

Reflecting that view, Bush proposed tax cuts totaling $1.6 trillion over the next 10 years, together with a promise to hold down government spending during the same period. The Republican-dominated House quickly approved the core of Bush's plan, a bill to cut income tax rates by $958.2 billion through 2011. The House also has approved the other main elements of the plan — repealing the estate tax and abolishing the "marriage penalty," which requires many married couples to pay more in taxes than they would if they were single.

Critics of Bush's plan say it unfairly favors the wealthy. They propose a much smaller tax cut, targeted more heavily toward moderate- and low-income taxpayers. They also want to use more of the surplus to pay off the national debt and increase spending on needed government programs — such as expanded prescription-drug coverage for the elderly and helping the 43 million Americans who lack health insurance.

Reflecting those concerns, the Senate approved a smaller $1.2 trillion tax cut as well as spending increases for education, defense and other programs.

Many Democrats, and some moderate Republicans, say the surplus projections are too uncertain to commit the nation to Bush's tax cut — the deepest in 20 years. "Estimates can be wrong by very, very substantial amounts," says Richard Kogan, a budget expert at the Center on Budget and Policy Priorities. "Many underlying factors relating to the state of the economy can make all the difference in the world, and, by that, I mean hundreds of billions of dollars in a given year."

Indeed, the nonpartisan CBO emphasizes that its future surplus projections "represent the midrange of possible outcomes," that "considerable uncertainty surrounds those projections" and that "actual budgetary outcomes will almost certainly differ from CBO's baseline projections." [2]

Supporters of Bush's tax plan say it allows for the uncertainty. "The budget was built on very cautious economic assumptions," says John F. Cogan, a senior fellow at Stanford University's Hoover Institution who has advised the president on tax and budget policy. "Those assumptions allow for a significant slowdown in economic activity in the current year and assume modest economic growth over the long term."

The surplus projections have made converts of some former opponents of massive tax cuts, including Rudolph Penner, CBO director from 1983-87 and now a senior fellow at the Urban Institute, a nonprofit social policy research organization. "I've changed my mind on the tax cut," he explains. "Just the sheer size of the upward adjustment in the surplus

---

From *The CQ Researcher,* April 13, 2001.

Falling Debt, Rising Surplus

In 2011, under existing taxing and spending policies, the national debt would be about one-quarter of its current $3.4 trillion total, and the probable surplus would be about $900 billion.

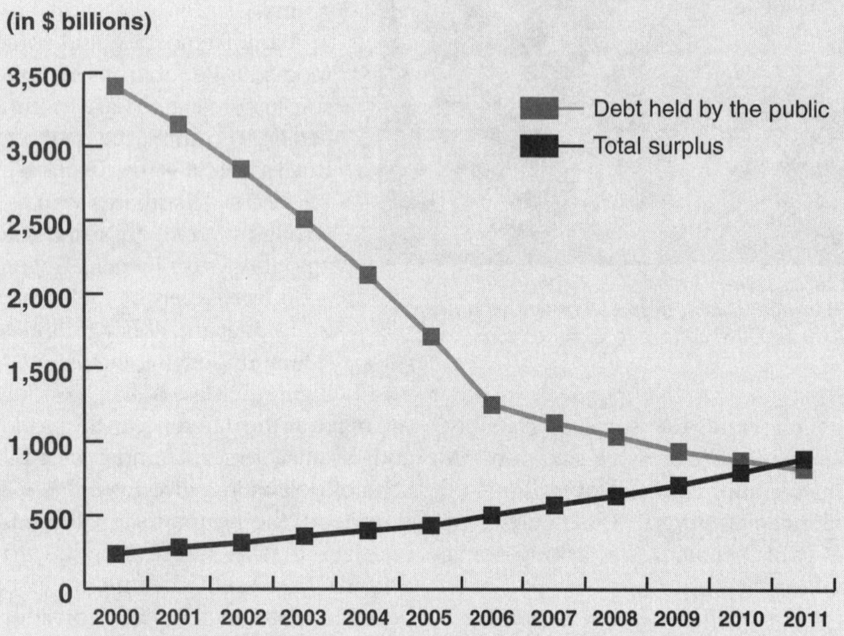

Source: Congressional Budget Office

projections makes a tax cut less risky now."

Still, many lawmakers say the surplus projections are too unreliable to commit the country to a 10-year tax cut with no strings attached. A number of lawmakers propose enacting mechanisms called "triggers" or "circuit breakers" that would defer or halt the president's tax cuts if the surplus failed to materialize. Bush opposes such mechanisms because, he says, they would kick in at just the time a tax stimulus is most needed — when the economy is in a downturn.

But critics point out that many economic factors can affect the surplus. Just as the economic boom of the past decade produced the excess revenues that created the surplus, the current economic slowdown may well reduce the size of projected surpluses in coming years, they say. Indeed, since Bush presented his economic blueprint in January, manufacturing activity has fallen, unemployment has risen and consumer confidence — a key indicator of future spending — has wavered.

The most visible sign of trouble is the drop in stock prices, led by the technology-dominated Nasdaq Composite Index, which is now at its lowest point in two years. The trend spread to other sectors as well, officially ending Wall Street's longest-running bull market on March 12.

Three successive interest-rate cuts by the Federal Reserve Board since the beginning of the year have failed to halt the slowdown or buoy investor confidence. A protracted slowdown would reduce incomes — and therefore income-tax revenues — causing the surplus to be smaller than projected only weeks ago.

It remains to be seen whether the debacle on Wall Street will continue, pitching the U.S. economy into a recession for the first time in a decade. Because most of Bush's tax cut would not take effect for several years, as the economy continued to weaken in recent weeks, many lawmakers on both sides of the aisle began to support some form of immediate tax relief to stimulate the economy, such as a Senate proposal to return $85 billion in surplus revenues to taxpayers this year.

But many argue that a tax cut at this point could not head off a recession. "It's probably far too late for that now," Penner says.

Administration officials offer inconsistent assessments of the current economic situation. The president warns that failure to enact his tax plan will threaten the economy. "We have been hearing too much troubling economic news," Bush said on March 17 in his weekly radio address. "It is only common sense to give our economy a boost during a slowdown." But administration officials also predict that the 10-year surplus will exceed even the CBO's current rosy projections. [3]

Meanwhile, critics of Bush's tax plan fear the surplus could disappear just as quickly as it materialized, especially if the current slowdown turns into a full-blown recession.

"There is the danger of overcommitting on projected surpluses and finding ourselves back in deficits within a few years, or at least having to use the Social Security and Medicare surpluses to pay for other spending," said Peter Peterson, president of the Concord Coalition, a nonpartisan group that advocates fiscal responsibility. "This would risk a return to the vicious spend-and-borrow cycle, which we have now happily gotten beyond." [4]

Tax-cut supporters argue that the economy will grow fast enough over the long run to protect the surplus from a recession. "Even if we had a recession, you could pretty much be sure that we'd still have a surplus," says Kevin A. Hassett, an economist at the American Enterprise Institute, a conservative think tank in Washington. "The CBO found that a recession would only knock off about $140 billion of the [projected] $5.6 trillion surplus. I think that's pretty reliable."

Perhaps reflecting confusion about the state of the economy, Americans appear to be ambivalent about how best to use the budget surplus. In one recent poll, a majority of respondents said they supported Bush's plan to split the surplus among tax cuts, debt reduction and other purposes, even though more than half also said Bush's plan favors the wealthy and wouldn't do much for them personally.[5] In another poll, a majority of Americans wanted the Senate to either change Bush's $1.6 trillion tax cut or reject it altogether.[6]

Other studies suggest that the public's ambivalence arises from ignorance of how the economy works. According to a Louis Harris study, only half of adult Americans — and just 14 percent of students — are familiar with the federal budget process. "No wonder President Bush feels confident he can sell his mega tax cut — essentially a huge gift to the wealthy — as a 'refund' to blue-collar workers," opines the *Los Angeles Times*.[7]

As lawmakers and economists continue their debate over what to do with the federal budget surplus amid a weakening economy, these are some of the questions they are asking:

Can we afford the tax cut proposed by President Bush?

Bush has placed a deep, across-the-board tax cut at the top of his policy agenda. His proposal, which he outlined on Feb. 27 during his first address to a joint session of Congress, would "cost" $1.6 trillion over the next 10 years. That is, the federal government would receive $1.6 trillion less in tax revenues if Congress passes Bush's proposed tax-law changes than it would under current law.

The president and his supporters say the federal government can easily afford such a cut because it is far less than the CBO's projected $5.6 trillion budget surplus over the decade. After tax cuts, $4 trillion would still be left in government coffers as of 2011. Furthermore, Bush promised, by holding spending increases to 4 percent a year, his administration could pay off most of the federal debt, reform Social Security and still have $1 trillion of the surplus left over for a "contingency fund" to cover unexpected needs and new priorities.

"This tax relief package is sound fiscal and economic policy," said Treasury Secretary Paul H. O'Neill. "It fits easily within our budget framework, leaving a $1.4 trillion cushion

How CBO Predicts the Surplus

Federal budget law requires the Congressional Budget Office (CBO) to base its surplus projections on the assumption that current policies will remain unchanged for the next 10 years. The shaded area below shows the range of possible surplus projections from 2001-2006. The darker area represents the most likely outcome; the lighter areas represent outcomes that are less likely but still possible. Such projections provide a baseline against which economists can measure what actually happens to the surplus after Congress implements changes. "Actual budgetary outcomes will differ from CBO's baseline projections as a result of changing economics and congressional action," the agency says.

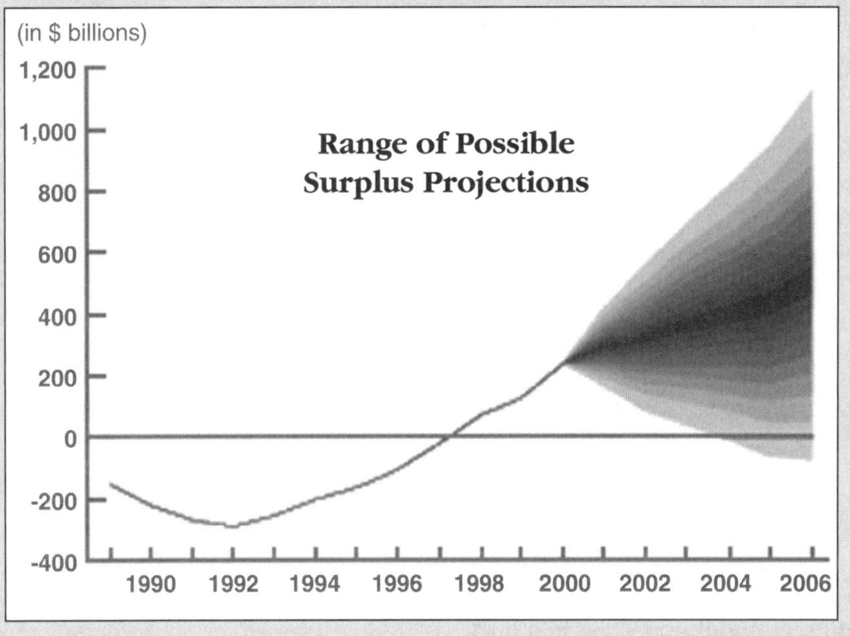

Source: Congressional Budget Office, "The Budget and Economic Outlook: Fiscal Years 2002-2011," January 2001

over the next 10 years to service the debt, to address priorities, beginning with Medicare reform and to handle unexpected needs. I like to refer to it as the Goldilocks tax relief plan — not too big, not too small, just right." [8]

Cogan, who helped draft the president's tax and budget plans, says they are based on cautious assumptions about future economic growth. "The budget assumes a 3.1 percent growth rate in the economy after adjusting for inflation over the 10-year period," he says. "In only one decade in the 20th century did the growth rate fall below 3 percent, and that was in the 1930s. So this is a budget that's built on cautious economic assumptions."

Those assumptions also are different from those used to formulate shorter-term projections, such as monthly changes in interest rates, inflation or unemployment, not to mention the stock market fluctuations that are now the subject of daily news headlines.

"When you look out over a period as long as 10 years, the most important factor is productivity growth," explains Barry Anderson, CBO deputy director. "We've had growth in productivity for the past five or six years, but it's damn hard to measure."

So Anderson is not especially worried about the impact of recent dips in short-term economic indicators on his agency's long-term surplus projections.

"You expect there to be ups and downs in the near term," he says. "I think it's fair to say that nothing has shaken us to the point we feel we've made a mistake. Maybe we won't have 3 percent growth over 10 years. Maybe it will be more like 2.9 percent or 3.1 percent. But nothing we've seen so far tells us we're not in the right ballpark."

But critics who say the country can ill afford Bush's plan emphasize that the tax cut is based on projected surpluses that may never materialize. "The CBO in its latest report has done an unusually forthright job of explaining exactly how wrong its own estimates can be," says Kogan of the Center on Budget and Policy Priorities. "The range of uncertainty is spectacularly large."

The CBO report is candid about the uncertainty. "Looking forward five or 10 years allows the Congress to consider the longer-term implications of policy changes," it states. "But it also increases the likelihood that the budgetary decisions will be made on the basis of projections that later turn out to have been far wrong." [9]

The $5.6 trillion surplus is the CBO's mid-range estimate. Under the agency's most optimistic scenario, the surplus could be far greater. But under its worst-case scenario, the government would be back in the red before the end of 2003 (*See graph, p. 91.*) When they drew up their forecasts, CBO analysts had no way of knowing what changes Congress might make to current tax and spending policies over the next decade. Also, federal budget law requires the CBO to base its surplus projections on the assumption that current policies will remain in force unchanged for the next 10 years — an unlikely scenario, the CBO says.

But even if the CBO surplus projections prove accurate, critics say, the Bush tax cut leaves no money to pay for needed government programs. "As long as we've got surpluses to burn, we could do a lot to ameliorate problems of poverty and near-poverty, especially for working families who are struggling, and at very low cost," says Kogan, who advocates investing the surplus in education and infrastructure, such as bridges and roads.

Critics also point out that U.S. tax rates are among the lowest in the industrialized world. Tax revenues in the United States amount to about a third of the nation's economic output, or gross domestic product (GDP). In most other developed countries, tax revenues amount to 40-50 percent of GDP. [10]

Some experts say the tax cut would cost far more than the $1.6 trillion the administration claims. Henry Aaron, an economist at the Brookings Institution, says the cost would likely exceed $2.5 trillion, because Congress would be forced to change the current tax code to keep a large number of taxpayers from having to pay the alternative minimum tax (AMT) — a levy added to the tax code to keep the wealthiest taxpayers from using loopholes to avoid paying taxes altogether. Because changes under the Bush plan would unfairly force a large number of middle-income taxpayers to pay the AMT, most analysts expect Congress to scale back that provision.

In addition to the size of the Bush tax cut, critics target its shape. If enacted in its present form, the tax cut would allow the richest 1 percent of taxpayers to receive up to 45 percent of the tax benefits. The poorest 60 percent of taxpayers would get less than 13 percent of the benefits. [11] If the nation can afford a tax cut, critics say, it should be more equitably distributed. "I think we should have a tax cut, but I'm concerned about the magnitude of the cut," says Munnell, now director of the Center for Retirement Research. "And I'm very disgusted with the distribution. It's absolutely gross to give [more than 40] percent of a tax cut to the top 1 percent of households."

The recent free-fall in stock prices and other signs of economic trouble have altered the debate somewhat. For his part, President Bush appears to say his tax plan is equally appropriate in good times and bad. During last year's presidential election campaign, as the economy continued to grow at a 5 percent annual rate, Bush presented his tax-cut plan as a fair payback to the wealthiest taxpayers who had contributed disproportionately to the ever-growing surplus. But today, the president and his supporters say the tax cut is necessary to ward off a recession.

"We must put more money in the hands of consumers in the short term and restore confidence and optimism for the long term," Bush said in a recent speech. "We need an immediate stimulus for our economy and a pro-growth environment for years to come." [12]

Indeed, some conservatives argue that weakened economic conditions call for an even bigger tax cut. "Most people would agree that Bush's tax cut is inadequate and needs to be a lot bigger to deal with a slumping stock market, the decline in consumer confidence and more bankruptcies," says Stephen Moore, president of the Club for Growth, a tax-cut advocacy group. A self-described supply-side economist, Moore believes tax cuts are the best way to encourage businesses and wealthy individuals to invest, which in turn boosts economic activity, incomes and tax revenues. "This could be a lot worse recession than a lot of people first thought," he says, "and I'm just a big believer that [high taxes] are really one of the primary impediments to growth right now."

Whatever the eventual impact of tax cuts, critics of Bush's plan warn that a faltering economy threatens the surplus, because lower incomes mean less tax revenue flowing into government coffers. And that would make it harder to pay for other Bush priorities such as a multibillion-dollar missile defense system and the elimination of the estate tax, a doubling of the $500 child credit and marriage-penalty relief — not to mention more than $100 billion in payments that farm interests are requesting over the decade to help farmers survive low grain prices. [13]

Stock Image

Critics of President Bush's tax plan fear a recession could erode the budget surplus, jeopardizing programs for elderly Americans such as Social Security and Medicare. But tax-cut supporters say the economy is strong enough to protect the surplus from a recession.

Relying on tax cuts to stimulate the economy reminds many critics of a similarly large tax cut enacted during President Ronald Reagan's first year in office, together with large boosts in defense and other spending, pushing the budget into deficit for the next 17 years. "One of the reasons we're so skeptical of these frothy, blue-sky projections is that we remember all too well 1981 and how long it has taken us to turn this big battleship around and get to surplus," said Rep. John M. Spratt Jr., D-S.C., ranking member of the House Budget Committee. "Doggone it, we don't want to backslide into the hole we just dug ourselves out of." [14]

Should paying down the national debt be the top priority for spending the budget surplus?

Ever since the surplus appeared in 1998, policymakers have debated what to do with the extra money. The Clinton administration placed a high priority on paying down the national debt that had accrued during 17 years of deficit spending. Like a family borrowing to purchase a new car, the government — starting with the Reagan administration — was forced to borrow money to finance the nation's military, highway maintenance and other federal programs.

Many budget experts say paying down the federal debt is simply a matter of prudent fiscal policy and should remain budget-writers' top priority.

U.S. Revenues Outpace Outlays

In the last fiscal year, the U.S. government collected $236 billion more in taxes — mostly paid by individuals — and fees than it spent on federal programs. Entitlements and other mandatory spending programs — such as Social Security and Medicare — make up 56 percent of the government's annual outlays.

Tax Revenues (in $ billions)

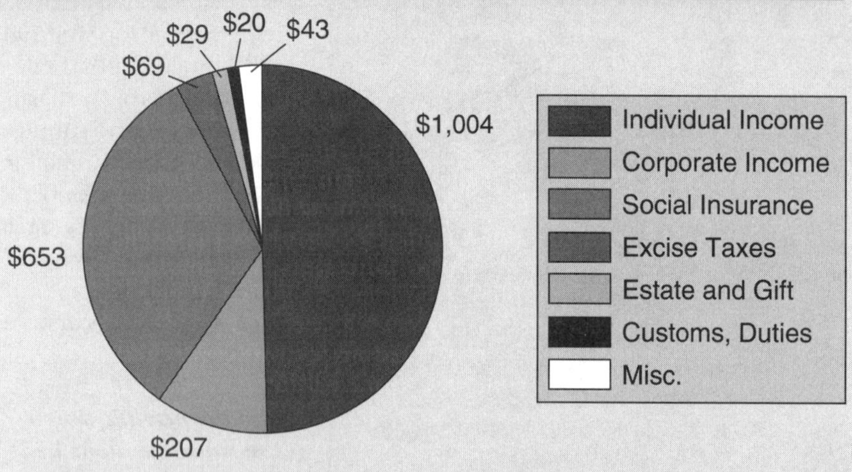

Outlays (in $ billions)

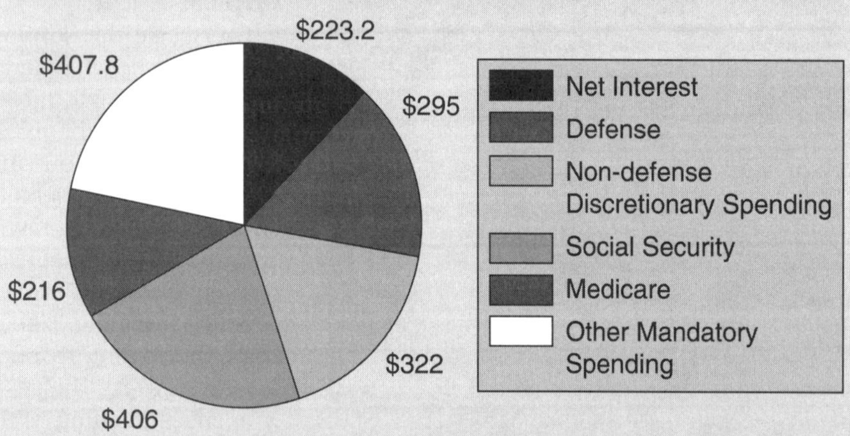

Income vs. Outlays (for fiscal 2000, in $ billions)

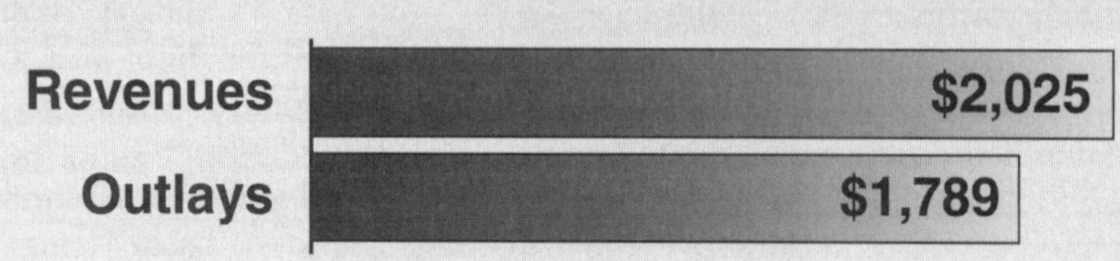

Source: Congressional Budget Office

"There's a fundamental difference between spending money and saving money," says Kogan of the Center on Budget and Policy Priorities. Paying down the debt, he says, "is mathematically and conceptually identical to paying down your credit-card debt or mortgage." In his view, reducing the debt is a form of saving, because it increases net wealth without increasing current consumption. "The whole discussion of reducing debt comes down to a tradeoff between consuming now and consuming later," Kogan says. "The question is, how much saving do we as a nation want to do?"

But under the new administration's budget plan, debt repayment takes a back seat to tax cuts, its top priority for using the surplus. "It is important to be reducing the government's net indebtedness, but one should not look at that as a goal to be achieved over and above all other goals," says Bush budget adviser Cogan. "Using part of the surplus for tax cuts can be of very long-term benefit to the economy." The Bush plan calls for using 28 percent of the surplus for the tax cut.

But Bush's budget-writers say they still plan to pay down as much debt as possible. "The debate has given short shrift to President Bush's debt-reduction plans," Cogan says. "The amount of debt reduction that would be achieved by the president's plan is historically large." The Bush plan, he says, would pay off all of the $2 trillion of the national debt that will mature over the next 10 years.

The $1.2 trillion of debt left outstanding in 2011, Cogan says, would consist of securities considered "non-tradable," such as savings bonds and special-issue Treasury bills that holders are unlikely to sell before they mature unless they are offered a premium.

"If you try to reduce the debt at a faster rate over the decade than the Bush plan proposes, then you'd have to begin buying up debt in advance

Financing the National Debt

Until recently, the federal government typically spent more money every year on defense, education and other federal programs than it received in revenues, chiefly individual income taxes.

In 1992, the budget deficit reached $290 billion, a record in dollar terms. In 1998, however, annual tax revenues began to exceed annual expenditures, thanks to the booming economy. This year, the surplus is expected to reach a record $281 billion. But previous years of deficit spending have left a substantial national debt — $3.4 trillion — that has not yet been paid off.

The government finances the national debt by borrowing from the public, a practice begun in 1791 by the first secretary of the Treasury, Alexander Hamilton, to pay off bills from the Revolution. The Treasury Department borrows money through the sale of various securities, such as U.S. Savings Bonds, which workers can buy through payroll savings plans. The Treasury Department also holds public auctions each month, where T-bills, bonds and notes are sold to the highest bidder. All Treasury securities are backed by the "full faith and credit" of the U.S. government, which has never defaulted on any of its obligations. As a result, Treasury securities are considered among the safest investments in the world.

Different Treasury securities mature, or come due, at different times. There are, for example, 30-year securities, two-year notes and one-year, six-month and three-month bills. When these portions of the national debt come due, the Treasury must either raise cash by taxation or borrow more money to pay off the bondholder.

Total Treasury borrowing makes up the outstanding public debt, or the equivalent of an individual's credit card balance. Since the national debt peaked in 1997 at around $3.8 trillion, budget surpluses have reduced the overall obligation to about $3.4 trillion. That means that there are $3.4 trillion worth of bonds, notes and other Treasury securities in the hands of investors.

The Treasury also borrows from certain government trust funds that are running surpluses. For example, it issues special-issue securities to the Social Security trust fund as a way to invest the excess revenues from workers' payroll contributions until they are needed to pay for retiree benefits.

"Essentially, Social Security ends up with $100 billion more than it needs [every year] and it has to invest that money in something, so it invests the money in special-issue Treasuries," explains Alicia H. Munnell, an assistant Treasury secretary during the Clinton administration who now directs the Center for Retirement Research at Boston College. "That way, the trust fund has $100 billion of special-issue Treasuries, and the Treasury has $100 billion of cash."

of its maturation," Cogan says. "Then you are faced with the question of how much of a premium the government would have to pay to retire that debt. We want to have a sustainable policy of debt reduction that reduces the debt on schedule."

Conservative economists also worry that making debt payoff rather than tax cuts the first priority of budget planning ignores the problem of what to do with the surplus that would still remain in the government's hands after paying off the debt.

In the absence of a tax cut, says AEI's Hassett, the government would have to do something else with the remaining surplus. "If they just hold the money in Washington, then very quickly we're going to be in a world where the government is buying up private assets," he says. "Otherwise, the money would just be sitting in a box somewhere."

Hassett estimates that if the remaining surplus were invested in private securities, by 2020 the government would own $20 trillion in stocks. "So the Democrats' position is only sensible if they're also willing to defend having the government own 25 to 50 percent of the private economy," he says.

Alan Greenspan, chairman of the Federal Reserve, agrees. "At zero debt, the continuing budget surpluses now projected under current law imply a major accumulation of private assets by the federal government," he told the House Budget Committee on March 2. "Such an accumulation would make the federal government a significant factor in our nation's capital markets and would risk significant distortion in the allocation of capital to its most productive uses. . . . I doubt that it is possible to secure and sustain institutional arrangements that would insulate federal investment decisions, over the long run, from political pressures." [15]

Advocates of paying down the debt say this fear is unfounded. "Alan Greenspan has done a brilliant job in terms of monetary policy, but on this issue I think he is absolutely wrong," says former Clinton economic adviser Munnell. "What he's done is extraordinarily dangerous, because he has taken this secondary issue, which is really one of corporate governance, and elevated it to primary importance that now drives the debate on tax cuts."

Munnell worries that the publicity surrounding these concerns will undermine the fiscally prudent goal of boosting national saving. "This has profound implications, because it would mean you're making this macroeconomic decision about how much to save on the basis of the very secondary issue of who's going to invest the funds," she says. "I find it just extraordinarily disturbing that [Greenspan's] pronouncements on this subject have gotten so much credibility."

Conservative economists like to point out that eliminating the national debt does not ensure economic prosperity. The only time that has happened in U.S. history was in January 1835, during Andrew Jackson's presidency. "After the Treasury retired every penny of debt, we actually went into a bit of a depression," Moore says. "So there's no pot of gold at the end of that rainbow. Just because you're debt-free doesn't necessarily mean that your economy is going to be in good shape. Growth is really the key to solving our debt problem, and I think a tax cut would provide much more of a stimulus to investment than a small reduction in the national debt."

Some budget experts say that completely eliminating the federal debt is a bad idea under any circumstances. The United States sells debt in the form of Treasury securities, large quantities of which are held not only by Americans, but also by foreign investors, including foreign governments.

"Paying off all the national debt would put us in an unknown world in two respects," says former CBO Director Penner. "First, we'd have to run monetary policy in a different way if we didn't have debt to buy and sell to influence the money supply. Secondly, debt is a product that foreigners buy because it's a secure investment. And, we are dependent on about $1 billion a day coming in from abroad."

The sudden increase in the surplus has made Penner a convert on the question of budget priorities. "I was in the camp that was all in favor of paying off the debt," he says. "But now that there's some probability that it will actually be paid off, I've become nervous about it. I don't want to save quite as much as a lot of budget people do. That's why I now favor a tax cut."

Should the Social Security and Medicare trust funds be kept in a "lockbox" for future retirees?

The Social Security system, the national retirement plan founded in 1935, is funded entirely by payroll tax contributions to a trust fund, the Federal Old-Age and Survivors Insurance Trust Fund. [16]

Another trust fund was set up in 1965 to pay for Medicare, the national health insurance system for those over age 65. Both funds currently hold more assets than they disburse to elderly Americans, but they are expected to run out of money within the next few decades, as the large Baby Boom generation retires and instead of paying into the system becomes eligible for benefits.

Although a recent report indicated that both trust funds are in better financial shape than previously believed, it predicted that, unless changes are made to the two programs, the Social Security trust fund would be exhausted in 2038, and the Medicare trust fund would go broke in 2029. [17]

Like other federal trust funds, Social Security and Medicare were set up to collect and disburse money for specific goals established by law. But when they receive payroll taxes or other income that is not currently needed to pay benefits, the excess is lent to the Treasury, which can use the money to help pay for other programs or, when the government is running a surplus as it is today, retire outstanding debt held by the public.

"In the old days, when we had deficits in the rest of the budget, the Treasury would borrow the surpluses in the Social Security trust fund and use them to pay for submarines, food stamps, the salaries of FBI agents and other expenditures of the non-Social Security part of the budget," Munnell explains. "Now, [thanks to the surplus] all those costs are being covered by general revenues. So when the Treasury borrows the money from the Social Security trust fund, it is using those monies to pay down the federal debt."

Lawmakers from both political parties have suggested setting aside Medicare and Social Security surpluses in a "lockbox" — a legislative mechanism prohibiting the funds from being used for other purposes — to ensure that the benefits will be there for the Baby Boomers when they retire, beginning in 2011. In February, the House voted to set aside the Medicare surplus, projected to exceed $400 billion over the next decade, as well as the $2.6 trillion surplus projected for Social Security. Current rules protect the Social Security surplus from all uses except paying down the national debt. The new lockbox proposals, which the Senate rejected on March 13, would have placed the Medicare surplus under similar restrictions.

Critics say such proposals are based on faulty assumptions. "Substantively, the lockbox is kind of a phony issue," Penner says. "People talk as though if the rest of the government borrows from the Social Security or Medicare trust fund that somehow the payment of benefits in the future becomes less certain. That's obviously nonsense, because it's no worse for the trust funds to buy government debt than it is for me to buy government debt and put it in my IRA. The securities in the trust funds don't represent a debt that they owe, but an asset that they hold."

Critics of Bush's budget say the administration is inconsistent when it calls for using the Medicare surplus to pay for tax cuts or other programs unrelated to Medicare. Of Medicare's two

How to Outsmart a Recession

The recent economic slowdown, coupled with President Bush's proposed tax cuts, has rekindled a longstanding debate: Which policy tools are most effective in averting a recession?

Policy-makers have two key ways to keep the economy growing slowly and steadily: monetary policy, which involves changing interest rates and the money supply; and fiscal policy, which involves changing tax and spending levels.

Supporters of Bush's plan — which calls for a $1.6 trillion tax cut and a 4 percent cap on spending increases over the next 10 years — argue that fiscal restraint is the most effective tool for stimulating the economy. "The best way to use the tax code to promote strong economic growth is to lower tax rates," says John F. Cogan, a senior fellow at Stanford University's Hoover Institution who has advised Bush on tax and budget policy. "Reducing tax rates will increase work effort and the returns to entrepreneurship, and that will lead to greater economic growth."

Supply-side economists like Cogan concede that the tax cuts and spending limits envisioned by Bush will benefit higher-income taxpayers first, because they pay more in taxes than lower-income Americans. But eventually, the supply-siders argue, the cuts benefit lower-income workers as well, through the higher employment that will follow.

Critics deride the supply-siders' "trickle-down" theory. They often cite economist John Maynard Keynes, who advocated the use of fiscal policy to stimulate the "demand" side of the economic equation. Increasing government spending for selected social programs would raise the incomes of all consumers, who then can purchase more goods and services, which in turn stimulates production and creates new jobs.

"An important part of this debate is over the purpose of tax cuts," says Stephen Moore, president of The Club for Growth, a tax-cut advocacy group. "The Keynesians say the purpose of tax cuts is to cause an increase in demand for products by increasing consumer spending. Supply-siders say the purpose of a tax cut is to give businesses an incentive to hire more workers and to invest more in capital equipment and for individuals to have more of an incentive to save."

Policy-makers also manipulate interest rates to steady the economy. Lower rates tend to stimulate economic growth by reducing the cost of borrowing: for companies seeking new plants, equipment and workers, and for individuals wanting to borrow money to buy houses, cars and other goods. Higher interest rates tend to slow economic growth, which can be desirable to dampen inflation.

Unlike fiscal policy, which is determined by Congress, monetary policy is in the hands of Alan Greenspan — chairman of the Federal Reserve, the nation's central bank — and the Fed's 12-member Open Market Committee.[1] The Fed has lowered interest rates by a half-percentage point three times this year in an effort to slow the economy's slide toward recession.

The Fed manipulates interest rates by raising or lowering the federal funds rate — the rate for overnight loans between banks, which in turn raises or lowers the rates banks charge businesses and consumers for loans. But in Moore's view, the Fed's role is vastly overstated. "There is a great myth out there that the Fed controls interest rates," he says. "Its actions actually follow market interest rates because the Fed is too small a player to create interest rates. The Fed's real impact is its ability to print money, which has the impact of lowering interest rates. But printing money can also create inflation, and if you get inflation on top of slow growth, then all you get is stagflation, as we had in the 1970s."

Keynesian economists dispute this view. "Keynes argued that monetary policy was more effective than fiscal policy and that most of the time you simply wanted to let the central bank change interest rates as a way of fine-tuning the economy," says Richard Kogan, a budget expert at the Center on Budget and Policy Priorities. "He also argued that only in exceptional circumstances did you need to make deliberate fiscal policy changes, that you wanted automatic stabilizers, such as unemployment compensation, and that you'd be perfectly willing to let revenues fall during economic downturns and rise in economic booms. That kind of automatic fiscal policy reinforces monetary policy and works as quickly, or even more quickly, than monetary policy."

But some economists say the kind of deliberate fiscal policy-making inherent in Bush's tax-cut plan is an unwieldy tool for avoiding recession. For fiscal policy to be effective, they say, it has to take effect quickly.

"If you could pass a tax bill fast and get money into people's pockets fast, it would actually be very helpful," says Alicia Munnell, an assistant Treasury secretary in the Clinton administration. "The reason fiscal policy isn't so good at averting recessions is that we dither around for so long. I actually like the idea of fiscal policy, and there's nothing wrong with it intrinsically. It's just that the political reality is that it takes forever to get it done."

Munnell argues that Bush's tax proposal would provide little fiscal stimulus because it is phased in over 10 years and is geared toward higher-income taxpayers. "It's not even going to the people who are going to spend the money," she says. "It all goes to the high-income people who are going to save huge amounts, so its stimulative effect is less than it would have been if it were distributed more equitably."

[1] For background, see David Masci, "The Federal Reserve," *The CQ Researcher*, Sept. 1, 2000, pp. 673-688.

parts, only the Hospital Insurance fund, which pays for seniors' hospital stays, enjoys a surplus, expected to reach $400 billion over the next 10 years; and that is expected to be overwhelmed by a deficit in the other part, Supplemental Medical Insurance, which pays for doctor visits.

"In a long life of seeing peculiar arguments, I must say that this one is among the most bizarre," said Aaron of the Brookings Institution. "The administration points to the long-term financing problems of Medicare as one reason for prompt reform of that program, a sentiment I completely endorse.

"At the same time," he continued, "it argues that the admittedly inadequate reserves of the Hospital Insurance fund should be available to underwrite tax cuts or on-budget spending increases. But one cannot have it both ways. A system whose parlous long-term financial state supports prompt reform is not a system whose reserves can be treated as an on-budget piggy-bank." [18]

Lockboxes aside, concern about the future solvency of Social Security and Medicare has cropped up again in the context of Bush's budget proposals, which call for reforming both programs. To avoid bankrupting the Social Security trust fund when the Boomers retire, Bush wants to enable workers to invest part of their Social Security payroll taxes in private accounts, much like a 401(k). He has left the details of Social Security reform to be worked out by a special presidential commission, whose recommendations will not be known until the fall. The administration's proposals for Medicare reform are also vague, but are expected to give private insurers a bigger role.

"While the short-term financial status of both Social Security and Medicare has improved somewhat since last year's report, our long-term analysis highlights a real threat to the retirement security of future generations," said O'Neill. "[This] has led us to conclude that both programs need to be reformed and strengthened at the earliest opportunity." [19]

But critics say privatizing even a portion of Social Security would be a betrayal of the public trust. "With privatization, all the money you save throughout your life is gambled," says Franco Modigliani, a professor emeritus at the Massachusetts Institute of Technology's graduate program in economics and 1985 Nobel economics laureate. "Only on the day you retire will you see how you come out, rich or poor. How do you like that idea? I am completely against individual accounts, which I think are the most deadly thing for old people that one can imagine."

Instead, Modigliani proposes investing the Social Security trust fund — on behalf of all beneficiaries — in an index fund comprised of stocks and bonds. Because index funds mimic the broader market and thus avoid the potentially corrupting effect of having the government pick investments, Modigliani says his plan offers two benefits: It would not only enable the trust fund to pay for the Boomers' retirement but also allow for a substantial cut in payroll taxes, which are especially onerous for lower-income workers.

"I want people to know for sure what their pensions will be," he says. "That requires a common fund with a government guarantee." [20] ■

BACKGROUND

Rivers of Red Ink

The current budget surplus, which emerged in fiscal 1998, is a fiscal rarity that caught policy-makers off guard. Indeed, for most of the 20th century, budget numbers were posted in red ink. [21]

The century started off well enough — with revenues closely tracking expenditures — until the United States entered War World I, plunging the budget into a massive deficit that reached the equivalent of 16 percent of the gross domestic product (GDP). Within a few years, however, the economic growth spurt during the Roaring '20s eliminated the deficit. Indeed, it produced enough tax revenues to keep the budget in surplus for 11 years running — the century's longest period of uninterrupted surpluses.

However, surpluses gave way to deficits after the 1929 stock market crash and the Great Depression, which dragged on for most of the 1930s. As industries closed down and people were thrown out of work, tax revenues plummeted. At the same time, federal spending increased, as President Franklin D. Roosevelt introduced sweeping new social programs that became the foundation of the country's welfare system. For instance, the landmark 1935 Social Security Act, the centerpiece of Roosevelt's New Deal, provided federal retirement income and disability benefits for American workers.

But no sooner did the budget return to balance in the late 1930s than World War II broke out. The war required a sudden and massive infusion of federal dollars for weapons and troops that far outstripped tax revenues. By 1942, the budget deficit amounted to 30 percent of GDP, a level unmatched at any time in the nation's history. But like the previous deficit, this second one quickly dissipated during the postwar economic boom, which produced a flood of federal tax revenues. The record deficit turned into a record surplus, reaching almost 5 percent of GDP by the late 1940s.

Chronology

1920s-1930s

New Deal adds social programs to the federal budget.

1937
Social Security takes effect under President Franklin D. Roosevelt's New Deal. The program is funded entirely by payroll tax contributions to the Federal Old-Age and Survivors Insurance Trust Fund.

1940s-1960s

Wartime budgets deficits alternate with peacetime surpluses.

1942
World War II drives the budget deficit to 30 percent of gross domestic product (GDP), a level unmatched at any time in the nation's history. After the war, an economic boom produces a flood of federal tax revenues, turning the record deficit into a record surplus that is almost 5 percent of GDP by the late 1940s.

1963
Congress enacts a large tax cut proposed by President John F. Kennedy. The cut, coupled with increased spending for War on Poverty social-welfare programs, results in a period of rapid economic growth.

1965
Medicare, the national health insurance system for people over 65, goes into effect.

1970s-1980s

As the postwar boom nearly grinds to a halt, deficit spending increases the national debt.

1981
The Economic Recovery Tax Act, proposed by newly elected President Ronald Reagan, cuts income tax rates by 25 percent.

1982
Congress gives Reagan hefty increases in federal spending, especially for defense. As the economy sinks into a deep recession, federal spending increases due to high interest rates, which raise interest payments on the national debt, and higher spending for entitlements and other mandatory programs.

1985
In an effort to reduce the widening deficit, Congress passes the 1985 Gramm-Rudman-Hollings law, which specifies deficit targets and mandates spending cuts if the targets go unmet. The law fails to meet expectations, however, as lawmakers find ways to bypass the spending curbs.

1990s

The U.S. economy enjoys its longest expansion in history.

1990
The Budget Enforcement Act, containing stronger caps on spending, helps slow growth in federal spending.

March 1991
The current economic expansion, the longest in U.S. history, begins.

1992
The deficit hits $290 billion, or nearly 5 percent of GDP.

1998
The federal budget, which has run a deficit for almost 30 years, begins to show a surplus.

2000s

Prospects for the budget surplus grow uncertain as the economy suddenly weakens.

2001
The surplus is expected to exceed $281 billion, a record. The Congressional Budget Office (CBO) projects the surplus will be $5.6 trillion by 2011, even if the economy experiences a recession during the next decade.

March 2001
Congressional debate focuses on President Bush's plan to cut taxes across the board by $1.6 trillion by 2011 while holding annual spending increases to 4 percent.

2020s-2030s

Retiring baby boom generation puts pressure on basic retiree benefit programs.

2029
Medicare is expected to run out of money unless current laws are changed.

2038
Social Security will run out of money in the absence of financing-reform measures.

For the next two decades, a series of recessions — as well as U.S. involvement in the Korean War (1950-53) and the Vietnam conflict (1955-73) — resulted in periods of deficit spending, though nothing like the earlier wartime experiences. In 1963, faced with an economic slowdown and a maximum tax rate of more than 90 percent, President John F. Kennedy proposed a large tax cut and increased spending for social welfare programs — known as the War on Poverty. Rapid economic growth ensued. However, the high productivity growth that marked the 1950s and '60s was followed by stagflation — high inflation and slow growth — during most of the '70s. The resulting series of downturns prompted calls for a cut in the federal income tax.

Deficit Spending

In 1981, in one of his first official acts as president, Reagan made good on his campaign promise of a sweeping, 25 percent cut in federal income tax rates. Congress overwhelmingly approved the Economic Recovery Tax Act that year. It was based on the supply-side theory that lower tax rates would encourage investment, create new jobs and ultimately improve the lot of lower- and middle-income workers — a theory critics derided as "trickle-down" economics. Confident that his tax cuts would boost economic growth to 5.2 percent in 1982, Reagan also called for hefty increases in federal spending, especially for defense, while seeking deep cuts in other federal programs.

But the next year the economy contracted by 2 percent, producing a deep recession and an unemployment rate of more than 10 percent. Interest payments on the national debt shot up because of high interest rates, and higher spending for entitlements and other mandatory programs also boosted federal outlays.

To reduce the widening deficit, Congress enacted the 1985 Gramm-Rudman-Hollings law, which mandated spending cuts if specified deficit targets went unmet. But the economy failed to rally sufficiently to provide adequate tax revenues for basic federal programs. Lawmakers found ways to bypass the spending curbs, and Gramm-Rudman, as the law was called, failed to live up to its promise.

The combination of lower tax revenues and higher federal spending pushed the budget into a protracted deficit. In 1990, the deficit worsened with the onset of a recession and expenses associated with the Persian Gulf War (1990-91). By 1992, the deficit had widened to about $350 billion, or nearly 5 percent of GDP.

The 1990 Budget Enforcement Act, enacted during the administration of President George Bush, contained tougher caps on discretionary spending for programs such as defense and education, whose funding is determined by Congress on a yearly basis. Entitlements, such as Medicare and Social Security, are mandatory programs whose funding and benefits are not subject to annual congressional appropriations. The new law's "pay-as-you-go" provision required any new entitlement spending or tax cuts to be paid for with matching cuts in other spending or tax increases.

The 1990 caps, renewed in 1993 and 1997, helped slow growth in federal spending from 21.2 percent of GDP in 1989 to 18.7 percent by 1999 — the lowest level since 1974. Low inflation during the 1990s helped hold down outlays, as did a decline in spending for defense and other discretionary programs, which fell from 9 percent to 6.3 percent of GDP over the same period.

The budget caps, together with the "peace dividend" produced by the end of the Cold War and mounting bipartisan concern over the potential impact of successive record deficits, made it politically easier for lawmakers to hold spending in check. [22]

Surprise Surplus

Nevertheless, as recently as 1995, budget forecasters were projecting federal deficits of 3 percent of GDP "as far as the eye can see." [23] They had failed to recognize a significant increase in tax revenues that would quickly propel the federal budget out of the red within three years.

Almost a third of the revenue increase came from a tripling of taxable capital gains, the profits made on selling stocks and other securities, especially high-technology stocks, whose values boomed during the second half of the 1990s. Another major boost to tax revenues came from a rise in personal incomes over the same period, which boosted many taxpayers into higher tax brackets.

The sudden boost in tax revenues, combined with steady spending levels, effectively wiped out within three years what had been considered a chronic pattern of deficit spending. When the surplus suddenly materialized in 1998, it took many economists by surprise.

"The surplus exists because revenue is higher than spending," says Kogan of the Center on Budget and Policy Priorities. "Revenue as a share of GDP is now above 20 percent, while spending as a share of GDP is down to 18 percent. So we've got a surplus of about 2.6 percent of GDP. That is expected to continue growing at least through this decade, until the baby boomers begin to retire."

Many other positive economic trends that contributed to the budget surplus took shape during the Clinton administration (1993-2001): Bipartisan concern over the budget deficit helped keep public spending down and free-trade agreements boosted not only imports of foreign goods but also exports of U.S. goods.

Finally, Clinton's 1993 deficit-reduction package of tax increases and spending cuts helped bring about lower interest rates, booming stock prices and rising tax revenues. During the eight years of the Clinton administration, the record $290 billion federal budget deficit was transformed into last year's $237 billion surplus. [24] ■

Majority of Public Supports Bush's Plan

More than half of the American public favors President Bush's proposal to use a third of the budget surplus to cut taxes, a third to reduce the debt and a third for other government programs. However, nearly three times as many Americans say the highest priority should be spending on Social Security and Medicare, not cutting taxes.

Do you favor President Bush's plan for using the budget surplus?

Favor	*57%*
Oppose	*36%*

Is it possible to preserve Social Security and Medicare, increase education spending and cut taxes by $1.6 trillion, as Bush has proposed?

Possible to do all	*48%*
Not possible	*43%*

Do you prefer Bush's plan for the surplus or the Democrats'?

President Bush's	*49%*
Democrats in Congress	*41%*

What should be the highest priority for spending the surplus?

Protecting Social Security and Medicare	*53%*
Cutting taxes	*19%*
Paying off national debt	*14%*

Source: CBS News/New York Times Poll, March 8-12, 2001

CURRENT SITUATION

Capitol Hill Action

President Bush's budget and tax-cut agenda faces an uncertain future on Capitol Hill. In March, the Republican-dominated House approved the tax cut, a reduction in the marriage penalty, an increase in the child tax credit and a limit on the alternative minimum tax. On April 5, the House completed action on the president's tax plan by also approving his proposal to repeal the controversial estate tax.

The president's $1.9 trillion 2002 budget blueprint makes room for the full tax cut and would hold government spending — the other side of the budget equation — down to a 4 percent increase. The plan calls for $660.6 billion in discretionary spending, almost half of that for non-defense programs. [25] On March 28, the House approved the president's budget outline by a largely partisan vote, 222-205.

But the prospects dimmed for easy passage of Bush's tax and spending plans when they reached the Senate, which is evenly divided between Democrats and Republicans. On April 4, the Senate dealt the president an unexpected blow when it voted to reduce the $1.6 trillion cut by nearly a third in order to make more money available for debt reduction and education programs. On April 6, senators adopted, 65-35, a fiscal 2002 budget resolution that would provide for $1.2 trillion in tax cuts over 10 years. It will be up to a Senate-House conference committee to decide on the final version of the budget blueprint.

Supporters of Bush's plan continue to emphasize the need for a large tax cut, especially in light of the flagging economy.

State Surpluses Dried Up Quickly

In 1997, James S. Gilmore III overwhelmingly won his bid to become Virginia's new governor on a single promise — "No more car tax!" At the time, the nation's economic boom had translated into higher local tax revenues, filling state coffers. In one of its first legislative actions, the General Assembly approved Gilmore's plan to phase out the unpopular tax by 2002.

Today, barely three years later, the car tax is once again the focus of Virginia political debate. But this time the issue is pitting Gilmore against members of the General Assembly, including many of his fellow Republicans. As revenues have plummeted with the slowing economy in recent months, members of the legislature proposed delaying the plan to phase out the car tax to ensure that state spending priorities would be adequately funded.

After Gilmore balked at a delay, the legislature took the unprecedented step of adjourning in February without approving a new budget. Then, to make room for the planned phaseout, Gilmore ordered $421 million in spending cuts and proposed tapping the state's retirement fund to cover this year's pay raises for public employees.

The rancorous political impasse in Virginia is just one example of the way the sudden economic slowdown is playing out in the states.

"Virginia is a classic example of what happened in the mid- and late 1990s, when the states really spent a lot of money because the revenues were so strong," says Stephen Moore, president of The Club for Growth, a group that supports tax cuts as a way to spur economic growth. "Since Gilmore took over, Virginia's budget has gone up 10 percent every year, so they've had this big gold rush of spending, and now they're saying they can't afford to complete the phaseout of the car tax."

Like Virginia, many states may now have to trim spending or raise taxes to compensate for revenue shortfalls. Although the states enjoyed record surpluses and tax-revenue growth for most of 2000, tax receipts suddenly contracted in most states during the last quarter. The National Conference of State Legislatures reported in February that 18 states expected to take in less revenue this year than they had budgeted for. And the National Association of State Budget Officers said about half the states expected revenues to come in even lower next year. [1]

State budgets are not completely analogous to the federal budget. "The states tend to go through more boom-and-bust cycles than the federal government," Moore says. "State tax systems are much more oriented toward consumption patterns, which are much more sensitive to changes in consumer behavior, whereas incomes don't tend to vary as much from year to year," he says. "But this is one sign that revenue growth is really slowing."

The state budget crunch may provide a cautionary tale for federal lawmakers as they consider President Bush's proposal to cut federal income taxes by $1.6 trillion over the next 10 years. Virginia's surplus dried up in just three years; the Bush tax cut is based on projections that the federal budget surplus will reach $5.6 trillion by 2011.

[1] National Conference of State Legislatures, "State Fiscal Outlook for 2001: February Update," Feb. 28, 2001. See William Claiborne, "From Surpluses to Spending Cuts," *The Washington Post*, March 11, 2002.

"Whether you're a supply-sider, like myself, or a traditional old Keynesian, if this isn't the right time to cut taxes, when is?" asks Moore of the Club for Growth. (*See sidebar, p. 97.*) "The states call surpluses rainy-day funds. I keep telling members of Congress, look outside your window, it's raining out. This isn't a time to be running big budget surpluses when the economy is weak and the tax burden is high."

Indeed, Moore says weakened economic conditions appear to be improving the odds that the president's budget plan will eventually prevail.

"In a perverse sort of way, Bush has benefited from the weak economy in the sense that it makes the case a lot stronger for his tax cut," he says. "When I was working on the plan a year and a half ago, criticism of the Bush plan was that it would overheat the economy because we had 5 percent growth. So now the case for a real strong tax-cut stimulus is very persuasive, and I wouldn't be surprised if this tax cut gets bigger, not smaller, over the next few months as it goes through the Senate and then back to the House."

On the spending side of the budget proposal, some Bush supporters worry that even the Republican-dominated Congress will torpedo the surplus by failing to maintain the president's tight, 4 percent growth limit. "People should be wary that if we don't use this surplus to either fix Social Security or have a big tax cut, it will go straight into spending on pork-barrel projects," says AEI economist Hassett.

The president cannot count on the Republicans' numerical advantage in Congress, he says, because party loyalty has little bearing on government-spending decisions. "Sure, Republicans want to cut back government spending," Hassett says, "but they don't want to cut it in their districts."

At Issue:

Is President Bush's tax-cut proposal the best way to spend the budget surplus?

yes

REP. DICK ARMEY
R-TEXAS, HOUSE MAJORITY LEADER

FROM A SPEECH BEFORE THE HOUSE, MARCH 8, 2001

The American people are paying the highest taxes in peacetime history. Families pay more in taxes than they do on food, clothing and shelter combined. We have had 15 years of tax-rate increases and retroactive tax hikes. Americans now work one hour and 57 minutes out of each working day just to pay taxes to Washington. The American people are working hard. They produced these huge tax surpluses. They have earned some relief. They now deserve something, this year. . . .

[T]he American people are nervous. They see the economy slowing, they see their neighbors losing their jobs, they see their 401(k)s and their mutual funds shrinking, while their energy bills double, triple and even, in California, quadruple. Their credit-card debts are going up. They expect us to do something. . . .

Over the next 10 years, taxpayers will be overcharged by a staggering $5.6 trillion. Even after paying down the payable debt, and funding all our priorities, Washington will still be awash in cash surpluses. If we do not get that money out of town, it will either be spent or it will be used to start buying into the private economy. Either way, the government will grow and personal freedom will suffer, unless we get our fiscal house in order now. We need to get that money out of Washington and in the pockets of the American people, and we need to do this as soon as possible. . . .

Eight years ago, President Clinton raised taxes, retroactively. Two years ago, he vetoed $792 billion worth of tax reduction that would have stimulated this economy and would have helped to avoid the current malaise. He later vetoed marriage tax relief. He vetoed death-tax relief. . . . And last year some in the House Democrat leadership actually opposed our bill to promote retirement savings, a bill that passed with over 400 votes. Obviously, the Beltway liberal elites just do not want tax relief. They have delayed and obstructed long enough. The time for action, Mr. Speaker, is now. . . .

But [a tax cut] is not all we should do. We are going to eliminate the unfair marriage-penalty tax. We are going to eliminate the immoral death tax. We are going to promote retirement savings. We are going to help people afford health insurance. And as we fight for fairness, we should not be bound by some artificial number. We should do what is right for the American people. Because, Mr. Speaker, it is their money. They earned it. They produced it. It is theirs.

no

REP. RICHARD A. GEPHARDT
R-MO., HOUSE MINORITY LEADER

FROM A SPEECH BEFORE THE HOUSE, MARCH 8, 2001

I think that it is wrong to be taking up a tax bill without a budget — in fact, without even spending a moment deciding what the budget will say.

[We] are making decisions that will make it difficult . . . to make other decisions that we might want to make in the budget: How much debt we are going to pay down, how much we are going to assign to defense or education or health care or all the other functions that are in the budget?

So the cart is in front of the horse, and we should be waiting for this tax bill until we have considered the budget.

A second reason . . . is because the forecasts that are the premise for this tax-cut bill so often are wrong. In fact, [the Congressional Budget Office] recently said that they are always wrong. Now, sometimes they are better than we thought they were going to be; sometimes they are worse. . . .

The president has talked very dramatically about what he wants to do in education. Query: Will we have the funds to do what he wants to do, what we want to do, in education? Will we be able to take care of Medicare and Social Security? . . .

We all voted two weeks ago to put Medicare in a lockbox. The budget the president sent that encompasses the tax bill, part of which is on the floor today, invades the Medicare Trust Fund. The lockbox has already been picked if we vote for this kind of a tax bill.

Do we really want to do that? I do not think so.

Then there is the issue of fairness. If we are going to deliver tax relief, let us deliver it to the people who most need it.

We have 12 million families in this country with 24 million children who will not get one red cent out of the Republican tax cut. They pay payroll taxes. They do not pay a lot of income taxes. . . .

Finally, let me simply say this: President Bush . . . said he wants to be the uniter and not the divider. . . .

The president, my friends on the other side of the aisle, could easily sit down with the Democrats on the Committee on Ways and Means, and we could reach an honest com promise on taxes.

Everybody in this chamber is for tax cuts. It is a question of how much they cost and to whom they go.

Democratic "Triggers"

Congressional Democrats, meanwhile, are building their case for what they say is a more cautious approach to spending the surplus. To avoid sending the government back into the red if a recession suddenly dries up tax revenues, many Democrats, and some moderate Republicans, propose enacting a "trigger" mechanism to ensure that tax cuts and spending levels are made only if the projected budget surpluses over the next 10 years materialize.

Bush rejects triggers because, he says, they would undermine investor confidence about the long-term reliability of his tax cuts and thus weaken their stimulative impact. "Immediate tax relief is good news, but tax relief that gets yanked away next year is not such good news," the president told Michigan business executives in March. "We must rebuild business confidence and market confidence and consumer confidence through a permanently improved business environment." [26]

Former CBO head Penner says that trigger mechanisms are not needed. "I think all the talk about triggers and what we should do if the surpluses aren't as big as we expect really underestimates the ability of the Congress to adjust," he says. "I don't want to argue that it would be easy to raise taxes and cut spending in the future, but we spent most of the 1980s doing it. Lawmakers have shown that they can get together if they have to."

Other critics say that instead of relying on 10-year surplus projections that may never materialize, tax cuts should be considered annually. That would prevent the budget from going back into the red, they argue.

"Congress should legislate tax cuts only when surpluses are in hand or, at least, when they are imminent," writes Brookings economist Aaron. "If the economy performs as well as the Bush administration and many economists expect it to perform, revenues will be sufficient to support large tax cuts." [27]

Democrats have proposed an alternative tax cut they claim would stimulate the economy while offering more relief to lower-income taxpayers. Under the proposal, presented on March 28 by Senate Minority Leader Tom Daschle of South Dakota and Sen. Joseph I. Lieberman of Connecticut, every American who pays payroll taxes would receive a check for $300 this year. The $60 billion plan also would permanently lower the 15 percent income-tax rate to 10 percent.

While he didn't reject the Democrats' proposal outright, Bush warned that it was not an acceptable substitute for his more sweeping 10-year proposal.

"Our economy needs more than a pick-me-up, more than a one-time boost," he said. "Our economic health depends on people feeling comfort and confidence about long-term decisions." [28] ■

OUTLOOK

Eye on the Economy

The direction of the budget debate over the next few months will depend on the health of the economy. If it dips into a recession, many Republicans may call for even bigger tax cuts than Bush has proposed as a way of stimulating the economy. Democrats can be expected to call for more immediate relief to middle-income workers.

The latest economic data offer conflicting signals about the economy's direction. Economic growth slowed to a sluggish 1 percent in the last three months of 2000, but the total for the year was 5 percent, still the highest pace in 16 years. The manufacturing sector, which was the first sector to suffer a contraction last year, now appears to be gaining strength, along with construction and consumer confidence. [29]

On the other hand, continuing stock market turbulence suggests that the economy may still be in for a rough ride in coming months.

"None of us knows how bad this economy is going to be," says Moore of the Club for Growth. "For all I know, it could turn around next week."

Such uncertainty calls for rapid passage of Bush's tax plan, he says. "We need to cut tax rates, because, in this global economy tax policy is one of the ways countries compete." In that sense, Moore says, the budget debate "doesn't necessarily have anything to do with rich people versus poor people. It's about whether investors all over the world will find the United States an attractive place to invest."

If the economy fails to recover significantly in coming months, the CBO may reduce the surplus estimates on which the tax cut is based. But CBO Deputy Director Anderson doubts that a revision will be necessary when the agency updates its surplus projections, probably in July or August.

"It is quite possible that the stock market may tank even worse than it's done so far," he says, "but if it comes back in the next six months or so that might not have any effect at all on the long-term projections.

"As of today, I haven't seen anything that would really shake our fundamental projections over the 10 years." ■

Notes

[1] From a national radio address on March 3, 2001.
[2] Congressional Budget Office, "The Budget and Economic Outlook: Fiscal Years 2002-2011," January 2001, p. xvii.
[3] See Glenn Kessler and Juliet Eilperin, "Downturn May Dim Outlook for Surplus," *The Washington Post*, March 21, 2001.
[4] Peterson spoke at a news conference on budget policy held in Washington on March 12, 2001.
[5] *The New York Times*/CBS News poll was conducted March 8-12. See Richard L. Berke and Janet Elder, "60 Percent Favor Bush, but Economy Is Major Concern," *The New York Times*, March 14, 2001.
[6] Jonathan Weisman and Judy Keen, "Many Want Smaller Cut," *USA Today*, March 13, 2001.
[7] Harris Interactive, "Standards in Economics," for the National Council on Economics Education, April 18, 1999. See also "Add Economics to the Three Rs," *Los Angeles Times*, March 13, 2001.
[8] O'Neill testified March 1, 2001, before the House Budget Committee.
[9] Congressional Budget Office, *op. cit.*, p. 94.
[10] See Office of Management and Budget, "A Citizen's Guide to the Federal Budget: Budget of the United States Government, Fiscal Year 2001."
[11] See David E. Rosenbaum, "Doing the Math on Bush's Tax Cut," *The New York Times*, March 4, 2001.
[12] From a speech in Kalamazoo, Mich., March 7, 2001.
[13] See Dan Morgan, "Farm Interests Put Squeeze on Bush Budget Plan," *The Washington Post*, March 15, 2001.
[14] Quoted in Juliet Eilperin and Glenn Kessler, "House Panel Adopts Bush Budget," *The Washington Post*, March 22, 2001.
[15] Testifying March 2, 2001, before the House Budget Committee.
[16] For background, see Adriel Bettelheim, "Saving Social Security," *The CQ Researcher*, Oct. 2, 1998, pp. 857-880.
[17] Social Security Administration and Department of Health and Human Services, "The 2001 Annual Report of the Board of Trustees of the Federal Old-Age and Survivors Insurance and Disability Insurance Trust Funds," March 19, 2001.
[18] Testifying March 7, 2001, before the Senate Finance Committee.
[19] Testifying March 20, 2001, at a joint hearing of the House Ways and Means and Senate Finance committees.
[20] For details, see Franco Modigliani, Marialuisa Ceprini and Arun S. Muralidhar, "A Better Solution to the Social Security Crisis: Funding with a Common Portfolio," a discussion paper available from MIT's Sloan School of Management at 1010 Memorial Dr., #20-B, Cambridge, Mass. 02138.
[21] Unless otherwise noted, information in this section is based on June E. O'Neill, "The Story of the Surplus," *Policy Review*, June/July 2000, pp. 3-18.
[22] For background, see Adriel Bettelheim, "Partisan Politics," *The CQ Researcher*, March 19, 1999, pp. 233-246.
[23] *Ibid.*, p. 9.
[24] See Jonathan Weisman, "The Clinton Legacy: Good Luck Was Put to Good Use," *USA Today*, Jan. 1, 2001.
[25] See Daniel J. Parks, "Bush's Budget Now Before the Senate, Where Moderates Wield the Critical Votes," *CQ Weekly*, March 31, 2001, pp. 711-713.
[26] From a March 27 speech to business executives in Kalamazoo, Mich.
[27] Henry J. Aaron, "Don't Trust Those Triggers," *The Washington Post*, March 27, 2001.
[28] From the president's March 27 speech.
[29] See George Hager, "Reports Show Signs of Economic Comeback," *USA Today*, April 3, 2001.

FOR MORE INFORMATION

Center on Budget and Policy Priorities, 820 1st St., N.E., #510, Washington, D.C. 20002; (202) 408-1080; www.cbpp.org. A nonpartisan research organization that analyzes the impact of government policies and programs on low- and moderate-income people.

The Club for Growth, 1776 K St., N.W., #300, Washington, D.C. 20006; (202) 955-5500; www.clubforgrowth.org. The club's mission is to help support political candidates who are advocates of former President Ronald Reagan's vision of limited government and lower taxes.

Concord Coalition, 1819 H St., N.W., #800, Washington, D.C. 20006; (202) 467-6222; www.concordcoalition.org. A nonpartisan, grass-roots organization that advocates fiscal responsibility and ensuring that funding for Social Security, Medicare and Medicaid is secure for all generations.

Congressional Budget Office, 402 Ford House Office Building, Washington, D.C. 20515; (202) 226-2700; www.cbo.gov. A nonpartisan office that provides the House and Senate with budget-related information and analyses of alternative fiscal policies.

Office of Management and Budget, Dwight D. Eisenhower Executive Office Bldg., #252, Washington, D.C. 20503; (202) 395-4840; www.whitehouse.gov/omb. Prepares the president's annual budget, helps develop the government's fiscal program and oversees the budget's administration.

Bibliography

Selected Sources Used

Books

Aaron, Henry J., and Robert D. Reischauer, eds., *Setting National Priorities: The 2000 Election and Beyond*, Brookings Institution, 1999.
As congressional debate focuses on tax-cut proposals, two scholars argue that a number of core federal programs, including defense and Social Security, need an infusion of spending increases if they are to satisfy future needs.

Hassett, Kevin A., and R. Glenn Hubbard, *The Magic Mountain: A Guide to Defining and Using a Budget Surplus*, The AEI Press, 1999.
Economists at the conservative American Enterprise Institute review the history of budget-making in the United States and analyze proposals for using the mounting surplus.

Articles

"Bush's Budget Dilemma," *The Economist*, April 10, 2000.
The Senate's recent approval of a $1.2 billion tax cut casts doubt on the prospects for the president's tax and spending proposals.

Muris, Timothy J., "Ronald Reagan and the Rise of Large Deficits," *The Independent Review*, winter 2000, pp. 365-376.
Contrary to common perception, writes a professor at George Mason University Law School, President Ronald Reagan's 1981 tax cut was designed to curb projected deficits, not enrich wealthy taxpayers.

O'Neill, June E., "The Story of the Surplus," *Policy Review*, June/July 2000, pp. 3-18.
A former director of the Congressional Budget Office (CBO) describes the history of budget deficits and surpluses since the nation's beginnings and considers the implications for tax and spending policy.

Waller, Douglas, "What Is That Oink, Oink?" *Time*, Feb. 19, 2001, pp. 30-32.
After President Bush proposed cutting income taxes by $1.6 trillion by 2011, Democrats proposed a smaller, $900 billion cut, while some Republicans would add other tax cuts, bringing the total to $2.9 trillion or more.

Woodward, Bob, "Behind the Boom," *The Washington Post Magazine*, Nov. 12, 2000, pp. 8-25.
A review of the Clinton presidency illustrates how the combined efforts of a Democratic president and a Republican chairman of the Federal Reserve Board, Alan Greenspan, helped fuel the longest economic expansion in U.S. history.

Reports and Studies

Congressional Budget Office, "The Budget and Economic Outlook: Fiscal Years 2002-2011," January 2001.
The nonpartisan CBO projects that the budget surplus will total $5.6 trillion over the decade, despite the recent downturn in the economy.

Greenstein, Robert, "Can the New Surplus Projections Accommodate a Large Tax Cut?" Center on Budget and Policy Priorities, Jan. 4, 2001.
The president's proposed tax cut would leave no money to pay for needed reforms of the Social Security and Medicare programs or for prescription-drug coverage and expanded health insurance, according to an analysis by the president of a think tank.

Liu, Liquun, Andrew J. Rettenmaier and Thomas R. Saving, "Saving the Surplus," National Center for Policy Analysis, January 2001.
The authors compare the impact of using the current surplus in the Social Security trust fund to pay down the national debt with allowing workers to invest part of their payroll taxes in personal retirement accounts, a reform proposal advocated by President Bush.

McIntyre, Robert S., and Wendy J. Ray, "Bad Policy, Bad Medicine: Bush Plans for Taxes and Prescription Drugs Unfair to Working Families and Seniors," USAction and Citizens for Tax Justice, February 2001.
The president's proposed tax plan would unfairly benefit the wealthiest taxpayers and cost more than the total amount of money needed to pay for a comprehensive prescription-drug benefit for all seniors covered by Medicare.

Office of Management and Budget, "A Blueprint for New Beginnings: A Responsible Budget for America's Priorities," Feb. 28, 2001.
President Bush's 10-year budget plan outlines the new administration's proposals for using the federal budget surplus, including a $1.6 trillion tax cut, debt reduction and spending increases for education and defense.

Office of Management and Budget, "A Citizen's Guide to the Federal Budget: Budget of the United States Government, Fiscal Year 2001."
The OMB presents a detailed but highly readable primer on the process of collecting taxes and spending revenues.

7 The Federal Reserve

David Masci

To most watchers of the U.S. economy, Federal Reserve System Chairman Alan Greenspan walks on water. Indeed, according to a 1998 article in *The New Republic*, one New York brokerage house even set up a small shrine to the Fed chairman that its brokers could visit for "inspiration."

The story turned out to be untrue. But amazingly, until it was debunked almost no one doubted it. Such is the awe in which Greenspan is held.

Nearly 10 years into the longest period of continuous economic growth in U.S. history — a boom the former jazz clarinetist is widely credited with sustaining — Greenspan is perceived by many bankers, brokers and economists as nothing less than a divine force protecting the American economy from inflation and recession. [1]

Greenspan's every utterance is pored over by analysts hungry for the slightest new insight into his thinking. The curiosity builds in the days leading up to the meetings of the Fed's policy-making arm — the Federal Open Market Committee (FOMC) — which influences nationwide interest rates.

Depending on whether the FOMC raises or lowers the "federal funds rate" — the rate banks charge each other for loans — millions of mortgages or car loans could suddenly become cheaper or more expensive, because lending institutions pass the extra cost or savings from a change in interest rates on to consumers.

Just as significantly, a committee decision one way or another can lead to a rally or rout on Wall Street, because interest rates affect corporate profits, and hence stock prices.

AP Photo/Beth A. Keiser

Exuberant traders flash "buy" and "sell" hand signals in the Eurodollar pit at the Chicago Mercantile Exchange in reaction to news on Oct. 5, 1999, that the Federal Reserve Board would not raise interest rates.

The Street's reaction to the latest FOMC meeting, on Aug. 22, was fairly typical. In the days leading up to the meeting, pundits confidently — and correctly — predicted that because the economy appeared to be cooling off, the committee would not raise interest rates. Reacting to the predictions, and later to the actual decision, the stock market racked up substantial gains. [2]

FOMC meetings and comments by Greenspan receive close scrutiny for another reason: their positive impact on inflation. Indeed, the Federal Reserve's successful oversight of monetary policy has given it unparalleled credibility in the history of central banking. Almost a decade of economic growth has been attributed, in large part, to the Fed's use of interest rates to keep inflation in check. For example, when sizzling economic growth and low unemployment threatened to overheat the economy and spark inflation in recent years, the Fed raised rates six times in a one-year period — with barely a whimper from bankers and economists. [3]

"They've done just an excellent job keeping inflation low, which has allowed the expansion to continue," says Wayne Angell, chief economist at Bear Sterns, a New York brokerage, and former member of the Fed's Board of Governors.

But some observers say that the bank overreacted to the threat of inflation with the back-to-back rate hikes, and that in its zeal to prevent price increases it will dampen future economic growth.

"We don't have to slow the economy down in order to prevent inflation," says Stephen Moore, a fellow at the Cato Institute.

Also, says Christian Welles, an economist at the Economic Policy Institute (EPI), instead of focusing so much on inflation, the Fed "should worry more about trying to raise wages, which would improve the lot of American workers."

Angell and other Fed supporters counter that the bank's fear of rising prices and reaction to a revved-up economy is legitimate. "The threat of inflation should not be taken lightly," he says. "If inflation were allowed to inch up, it would get out of control and would destroy this [economic] expansion."

In addition to the Fed's aggressive inflation fighting, some analysts are uncomfortable with the enormous influence the bank has acquired in recent decades. They say it should stop trying to micromanage the economy and focus on its core mission: keeping the dollar stable.

"We've ceded much too much

From *The CQ Researcher*, September 1, 2000.

How the Fed Works

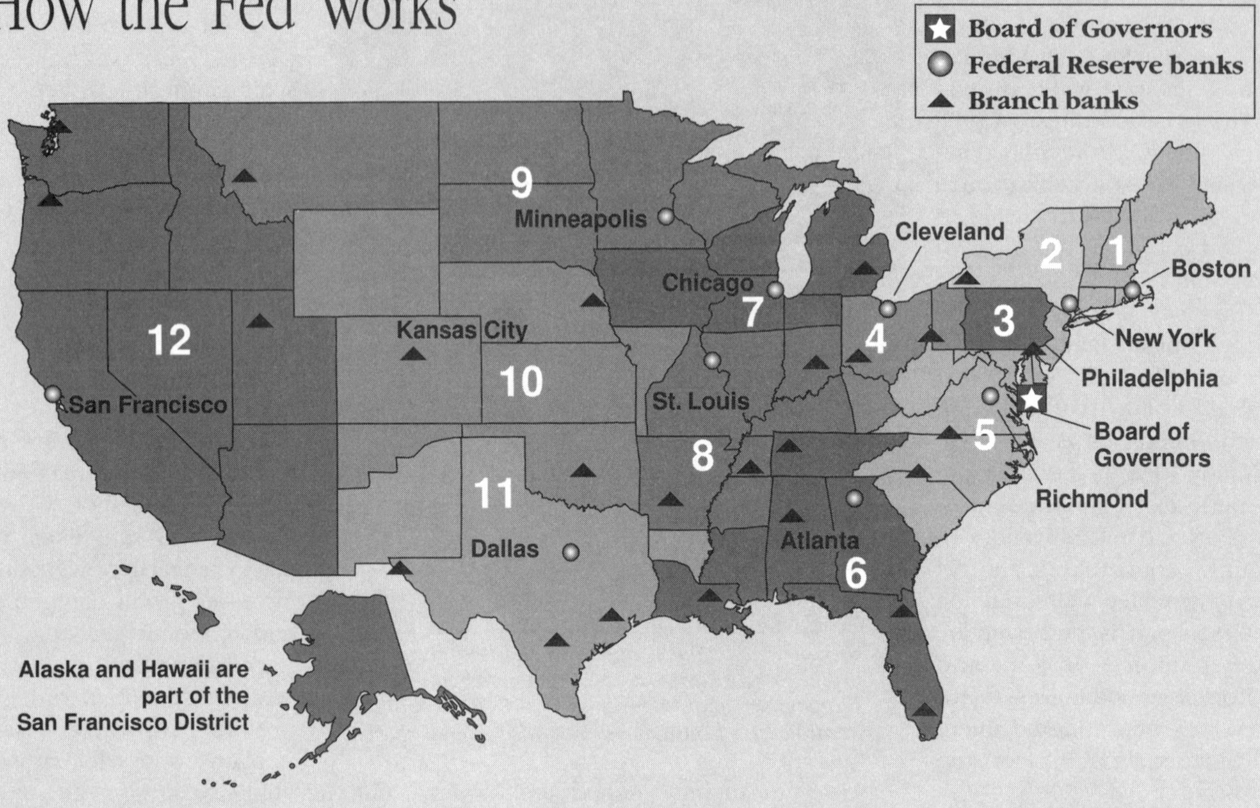

The Federal Reserve System controls the flow of money and credit in the U.S. economy. But most Americans know little about the institution that has the greatest impact on their pocketbooks. Indeed, during a Senate Banking Committee meeting earlier this year, Chairman Phil Gramm, R-Texas, told Alan Greenspan, "Millions of people . . . don't know that there is a Federal Reserve bank, much less that you're chairman of it." [1]

As the nation's central bank, the Fed sets monetary policy to maintain economic stability and keep inflation in check. Congress added to its list of duties in 1978, mandating that the Fed try to create economic conditions that will lead to full employment.

The Fed consists of 12 regional Reserve banks, which serve as the Fed's operating arms, regulating the flow of coin and currency and making loans to other banks. The Federal Reserve System is run by a Board of Governors that supervises the 12 regional banks. Appointed by the president, the seven board members serve 14-year terms. From this group, the president appoints a chairman and vice chairman to four-year, renewable terms.

The Fed's greatest responsibility is to set a benchmark for the "federal funds rate" — the interest rate at which banks lend money to each other. That target rate is set by the 12-member Federal Open Market Committee, which generally meets eight times a year.

The committee is comprised of all seven members of the Board of Governors and five of the 12 regional bank presidents. Its decisions to raise or lower interest rates can send the stock market soaring or plummeting. Financial analysts spend the weeks before each scheduled meeting trying to predict what the committee will do.

The committee meets in private but releases a summary of its deliberations. But it didn't start announcing its interest-rate decisions until 1994, when pressure from Congress forced it to be more open. [2] Some Fed-watchers contend the committee is still too secretive.

"These meetings should be held in public because these are very important decisions these people are taking, and we should be able to see what they're doing and why," says Dean Baker, co-director of the Center for Economic and Policy Research.

But authors David B. Sicilia and Jeffrey L. Cruikshank argue in their recent book, *The Greenspan Effect*, "If investors were privy to the central bank's policy deliberations in real time . . . the financial markets would be in a continual state of turmoil. . . . This would not be the stuff of stability, which, after all, the Fed was invented to promote."

[1] John M. Berry, "Pay Down Debt First, Greenspan Urges; Best Use of Surplus Is to Reduce Red Ink, Fed Chief Says," *The Washington Post*, Jan. 27, 2000, p. E1.

[2] "Fed's Growing Candor Has Little Effect on Markets — Study," "Capital Markets Report," March 23, 2000.

responsibility for economic policy to the Fed," says Tom Schlesinger, executive director of the Financial Market Center, a nonprofit research institute in Philomont, Va. Still others say Greenspan should refrain from speaking out on subjects that don't directly involve monetary policy, like trade and immigration.

At the very least, Schlesinger and other critics argue, the Fed should be subject to more oversight from Con gress and the White House. "Our elected officials have fallen down when it comes to overseeing and interacting with the Fed," he says.

But some analysts are comfortable with the institution's broad policymaking role. "Sure, the Fed has great power and influence, but it's there because people have confidence that Greenspan and the others understand how the economy works and will protect it," says Roger Kubarych, a senior fellow for international economics and finance at the Council on Foreign Relations, a think tank.

Moreover, others warn, more meddling in the Fed's business by elected officials could politicize monetary policy, which could prove disastrous both for the economy and the Fed's now steady policy-making. They contend Congress or the White House could push the Fed to heat up the economy right before an election in an effort to woo voters with sudden prosperity. That could lead to boom-and-bust economic cycles.

As the Federal Reserve helps to bring the American economy into the 21st century, debates over the institution's wisdom and influence will continue. Here are some of the questions that today's Fed-watchers are asking:

Has the Federal Reserve overreacted to the threat of inflation by raising interest rates too high?

For more than 20 years, keeping the inflation rate under control has been the Federal Reserve's overriding concern. Greenspan and his predecessor, Paul Volcker, both vowed to ensure that double-digit price increases — so common in the 1970s — never return.

So far, the Fed has kept its word. In the past two decades, inflation has remained relatively low, breaking the 5 percent barrier only once since 1982. And since 1992, the yearly rate of inflation has never been higher than 3 percent. *(See graph, p. 110.)*

Still, Greenspan and other observers warn, the dragon of high inflation may have been weakened, but it has not been slain. They contend that the robust American economy — which has been growing for 114 consecutive months — actually might reinvigorate inflation.

The problem, the Fed says, is not that the economy has been growing for so long, but that it is doing so at a very high rate for a developed nation like the United States. In the past few years, the nation's gross domestic product (GDP) has increased dramatically, rising 4.6 percent from 1997 to 1999 and 5 percent in the first half of 2000. [4]

The recent economic activity has led to significant job creation and the lowest unemployment rates in a generation. Currently, only 4 percent of Americans are jobless, making the U.S. labor market unusually tight.

Low unemployment traditionally drives up wages as employers offer higher salaries to attract new workers and keep the ones they already have. Higher wages mean more money chasing fewer goods and services, which in turn means higher inflation.

In its efforts to dampen economic growth, the Fed has raised short-term interest rates six times since June 1999, from 4.7 percent to 6.5 percent. By making it more expensive for both individuals and businesses to borrow money, the central bank aims to make consumers less likely to borrow money to purchase goods and businesses more cautious about borrowing to expand operations. [5] The Fed has been inching rates up in the hope that the economy will continue growing, but at a less rapid pace, between 3.5 percent and 4 percent. [6]

Many economists applaud the Fed's recent moves. "There is a real threat of inflation, and we can't be complacent about it," says Robert Shiller, a professor of economics at Yale University. "Their concern about it is well-placed."

Shiller argues that vigilance against inflation is necessary because rising prices erode Americans' savings and their underlying confidence in the economy. "Look, even 3 percent inflation is bad because over 30 years a rate like that will double prices," he says.

But others say the Federal Reserve overreacted in raising interest rates over the last 15 months, arguing that it was too conservative in its estimates of how much the economy can grow without triggering inflation. In fact, they say the Fed should reverse at least some of the rate hikes to keep growth at its current high level.

"This idea that we can only sustain a growth rate of 3 or 3.5 percent is wrong," Cato's Moore says. "We've had high growth for a number of years without high inflation," he points out. "In fact, I think we can have almost unlimited growth without inflation."

According to Moore, high growth rates are possible because even though a revved-up economy will lead to higher wages, it will also produce more goods and services for workers to purchase. "Inflation is caused by more dollars chasing too few goods," he says. "But when there is high economic growth, more goods are produced, evening things out."

Other critics dismiss the Fed's fear of low unemployment.

Determining the "Inflation Rate"

The Consumer Price Index (CPI) — often called "the inflation rate" — measures the percentage change over time in prices paid by urban consumers for goods and services. As the most broadly based measure of inflation, the CPI reflects the government's effectiveness in keeping the economy healthy. The Federal Reserve Board is widely credited with keeping inflation rates low and allowing the nation's economic expansion to continue.*

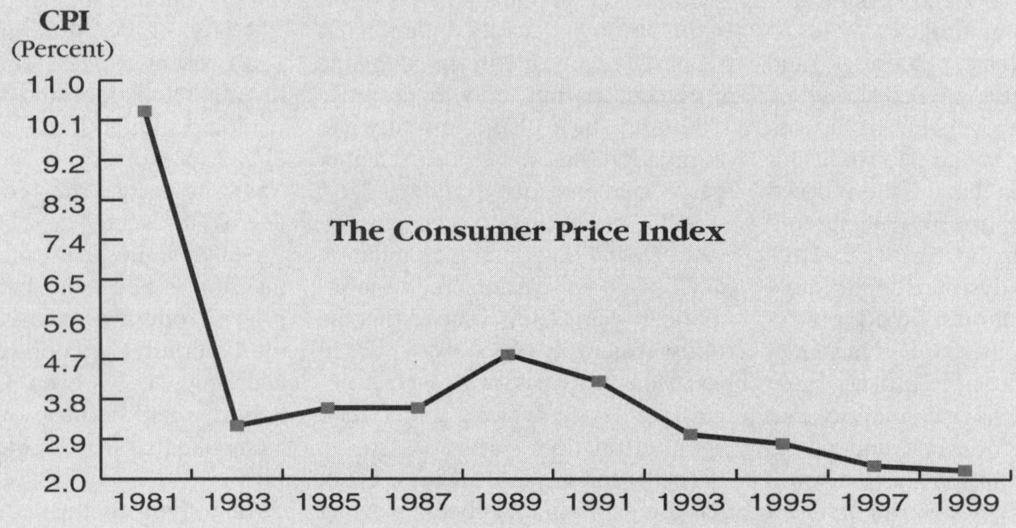

** Prices used to calculate the CPI are collected from about 23,000 retail and service establishments in 87 urban areas around the nation.*

Source: U.S. Bureau of Labor Statistics

"Even though we have low unemployment, this really is not a tight labor market because U.S. businesses can [build plants] elsewhere in the world when they need workers, or they can import them," says Alan Tonelson, a research fellow at the U.S. Business and Industrial Council Educational Foundation and author of *Race to the Bottom*, a new book on globalization.

Finally, some critics argue that the bank's obsession with controlling inflation to the exclusion of other issues is misguided. "The Fed has a mandate to look not just at inflation but at inflation, employment and growth — and balance all three — when making monetary policy," the EPI's Welles says.

He argues the bank should make wage growth a priority. "Higher wage growth would put more money in the pockets of workers," he says, adding that such a policy would be better for America, even if it did lead to slight increases in inflation. "The current policy of keeping wages low hurts workers and only adds to corporate profits."

But Fed supporters counter that the bank is not opposed to wage growth at all. "It just wants wages to grow in line with productivity," says Ralph Bryant, a senior fellow at the Brookings Institution, a think tank. "They want workers to be paid more for producing more." Otherwise, Bryant says, workers will have more money to spend on fewer goods, leading to inflation.

Fed supporters also dispute the argument that because the economy has grown at less than 5 percent over the past few years without significant increases in inflation, there is no reason to assume it can continue to do so. "You can't just indefinitely let the economy rip, because history tells us that when that happens, inflation always eventually picks up," says Richard Berner, chief U.S. economist at Morgan Stanley, a New York brokerage firm.

Indeed, Berner points out, so far this year consumer prices have risen 3.6 percent (annualized), compared with 2.2 percent in 1999. If the increase in prices is not halted, he says, the country could find itself with runaway inflation, which would require a huge interest-rate hike and a recession to tame.

"We can stop it now, when it's relatively easy and painless to deal with, or we can stop it later, when the cost would be much greater," Berner says.

Does the Federal Reserve have too much influence?

On the evening of Dec. 5, 1996, Greenspan arrived at the Washington Hilton to give a speech — "The Challenge of Central Banking in a Democracy" — one of dozens he delivers each year. Nothing about the event seemed special.

And yet, when Greenspan uttered two words — "irrational exuberance" — he set off a panic in global markets. The words were imbedded in a question about the high-flying stock market: "How do we know when irrational exuberance has unduly escalated asset prices?" the chairman asked. To the tea-leaf readers who scrutinize Greenspan's every utterance, he seemed to be saying that "irrational exuberance" had inflated stock — and that something had to be done.

The following day stock markets around the world plunged. In the United States, the Dow Jones Industrial Average lost 2.2 percent of its value and another 3 percent over the course of the following week. [7]

For many financial analysts, the lesson from the "irrational exuberance" episode is clear: The Fed has too much influence on the markets and the overall economy.

"A lot of people think that the Federal Reserve and Alan Greenspan should be running the economy — stimulating it when it's slow, cooling it down when it's too fast," Cato's Moore says. "But who gave Alan Greenspan and the other people at the Fed — all of whom are unelected — the authority to micromanage the economy?"

Moore believes that the central bank should concern itself with one issue alone: "It should have one mission, and that's to keep the dollar stable. Everything else should be left to people we voted into office."

Moreover, critics contend, Greenspan has expanded his role beyond management of the economy to influencing the political debate. "I was deeply concerned when Greenspan came out and made a statement in favor of Permanent Normalized Trade Relations (PNTR) with China," says Tonelson of the U.S. Business and Industry Council. "He doesn't have a mandate to try to influence Congress or anything like that."

Former Fed Chairman Paul Volcker threw the economy into severe recession in the early 1980s when he dramatically raised interest rates, but his bitter medicine succeeded in reducing double-digit inflation.

Critics of the Fed's influence say that, at the very least, the bank should be more accountable to Congress and the administration. "It's so powerful that it's basically like a fourth branch of government," says the Financial Market Center's Schlesinger. "The Fed raises and spends money without congressional appropriation, and so it needs to be monitored very closely by Congress."

A good start, Schlesinger says, would be for Congress to carefully question Greenspan about Fed policy during his twice yearly appearances before the House and Senate Banking committees. "Right now, these are vacuous events where Greenspan is lavished with praise and asked softball questions," he says. "They need to ask him real questions, tough questions, so they can find out what's really going on inside this institution."

But other Fed-watchers want the Federal Reserve to be influential and at least somewhat independent of the political process. "Sure, it has a lot of power, but we need a central bank that is powerful, that is capable of taking concrete steps," says Dean Baker, co-director of the Center for Economic and Policy Research, a think tank.

The Fed also needs to be independent from shifting political winds, supporters of the status quo say. "You don't want Congress or anyone else micromanaging the Fed," says Allan Meltzer, a visiting scholar at the American Enterprise Institute (AEI). "When you leave politicians with their hands on the money supply, they use it to their advantage at election time. That's no way to run our monetary policy."

Actually, supporters say, the Fed is not quite as independent as some critics maintain. For instance, they point out, seven of the 12 members of its influential interest-rate-setting Federal Open Market Committee are appointed by the president and approved by Congress.

"The Federal Reserve always takes the political process into account," the Brookings Institution's Bryant says. "So even if they have indepen-

Chronology

dence in setting interest rates, their overall goals are set in part by Congress and the administration." ■

BACKGROUND

A Shaky Start

The Federal Reserve is not the nation's first central bank, but its third. Two years after the ratification of the Constitution in 1789, Congress created the Bank of the United States (BUS). Chartered for 20 years and endowed with $10 million in capital, the BUS acted as an in-house bank for the federal government, holding its deposits and receiving payments.

The bank also worked to keep the currency stable and inflation low, a policy that earned it the enmity of many farmers. They were deeply in debt and wanted high inflation, which would make paying off their loans easier.

After a long and difficult fight, the BUS charter was not renewed when it expired in 1811. But in 1816, high inflation following the War of 1812 prompted Congress to resurrect the bank for another 20 years.

In 1829, Andrew Jackson ran for president promising to dismantle the second BUS. As a populist, Jackson viewed the bank as undemocratic because it left monetary policy in the hands of a few unelected financiers. In 1832, Jackson vetoed a bill that would have renewed the bank's charter. The following year, his Treasury Department withdrew the government's money from the BUS, effectively ending its role as the nation's central bank.[8]

For the next eight decades, the United States operated without a central bank. State-chartered banks issued paper currency, generally of little or

1900-1960

The Federal Reserve System is established and, over the years, strengthened.

1907
Financier J.P. Morgan helps save New York City from bankruptcy, prompting the federal government to begin seriously considering the need for a central bank.

1913
Congress passes the Federal Reserve Act, creating the Federal Reserve System.

1919
Following World War I, the Fed raises interest rates, throwing the country into a recession.

1929
The stock market crashes, and the Federal Reserve tightens credit, worsening the situation.

1935
Congress passes the Banking Act, which centralizes control over the 12 regional banks, vesting more power in the Board of Governors.

1947
Postwar inflation peaks at 14.4 percent.

1960-Present

Inflation shocks of the late 1960s and '70s lead the Fed to make price stability its main priority.

1974
Inflation hits 12 percent.

1979
President Jimmy Carter appoints Paul Volcker as Fed chairman. Volcker begins raising interest rates to bring down inflation.

1980
Inflation reaches 13.5 percent, the highest level since 1947.

1981
The Fed raises interest rates to 20 percent to tame inflation.

1983
Volcker's policies bring inflation down to 3.2 percent.

June 1987
Volcker resigns, and Republican President Ronald Reagan appoints Alan Greenspan, also a Republican, as Fed chairman.

October 1987
The stock market crashes. Quick intervention by the Fed helps reassure markets and mitigate the impact of the crash.

1996
Greenspan makes his infamous "irrational exuberance" remark, sending markets plummeting.

June 1999
The Fed makes the first of six interest-rate increases in an effort to slow the economy.

January 2000
President Clinton nominates Greenspan for a fourth term. The early nomination suggests that Clinton was seeking to calm fears that the economy was in trouble.

Aug. 22, 2000
The Fed decides not to raise interest rates at its Open Market Committee meeting, sparking a rally on Wall Street.

no value. By the end of the 19th century, the situation had deteriorated to the point where the nation's richest men were occasionally called upon to intervene and prevent financial collapse. In 1895, for instance, financier J.P. Morgan put together a consortium of financiers to bail out the Treasury. In 1907, Morgan came to the rescue again, this time saving New York City from bankruptcy. [9]

Morgan's 1907 rescue prompted lawmakers and others to argue that a new central bank was needed to promote monetary stability. But the idea languished until Woodrow Wilson was elected president in 1912. Wilson, who favored a more activist role for government, became a powerful ally in the fight for a new central bank.

In 1913, Congress passed the Federal Reserve Act, establishing the Fed system that remains in place today. The institution was headquartered in Washington, but to placate populist critics who worried about too much power in too few hands, 12 semiautonomous regional banks were created. *(See map, p. 108.)*

The Federal Reserve was given a dual mission: help keep private banks liquid during financial panics and maintain a stable currency. To help the Fed carry out its mission, the law required private banks that joined the Federal Reserve System to place a percentage of their deposits with the reserve bank in their region. The private banks could then borrow money from the Fed. By raising or lowering interest rates on the money it lent, the Fed could tighten or loosen credit in the banking system.

In its early years, the Fed made a number of huge mistakes. The first occurred in 1919, just after the World War I, when the bank raised interest rates almost overnight from 4 percent to 7 percent. By tightening credit so drastically, the Fed drove the economy into recession. It soon lowered rates, and by 1922 the country was booming.

In the early 1930s, the Fed made the same mistake, tightening the money supply again. With the economy already reeling from the stock market crash of 1929 and a banking crisis that followed, the policy only made the situation worse, helping to deepen the Depression. [10]

In 1935, Congress gave the Federal Reserve Board (now called the Board of Governors) more power over the Fed's 12 regional banks. Lawmakers also created the Federal Open Market Committee, which became the institution's primary policy-making body.

War Against Inflation

Following the Depression and the World War II, the nation entered into a new period of sustained economic growth. But in the late 1960s and '70s, the Fed faced new challenges. The steady growth that had largely marked the first two decades after World War II was interrupted by a number of recessions. By the mid-1970s, the nation found itself fighting both rising inflation and unemployment. To spur employment, Fed Chairman Arthur Burns lowered interest rates. But loosening credit just stoked inflation, as more money began to circulate in the economy.

By the late '70s, annual inflation rates had reached double digits. In 1979, a desperate President Jimmy Carter appointed Volcker to chair the Fed. To dampen inflationary pressures, Volcker dramatically raised interest rates. By the early '80s, the prime rate had reached 20 percent, significantly tightening credit and the flow of money. [11]

Volcker's moves threw the U.S. economy into a severe recession, driving up the unemployment rate beyond 10 percent and battering corporate profits. [12] But the bitter medicine worked. Inflation rates dropped from 10.3 percent in 1981 to 6.2 percent the following year and 3.2 percent in 1983. [13]

By 1983, the economy was once again growing, and Volcker was being lauded as a savior. He retired after completing his second term in 1987, and President Ronald Reagan appointed Greenspan.

Greenspan had no opportunity to rest on his predecessor's laurels. Less than five months after his appointment, on Oct. 19 — "Black Tuesday — the stock market crashed. In one day the U.S. market lost 22.6 percent of its value — or twice the loss on the first day of the 1929 crash.

The following morning, Greenspan announced that the Fed would put as much money into the banking system as needed to prevent it from collapsing. The move calmed the markets, and by the end of the year stock prices were as high as they had been before the crash.

Greenspan's decisive response to the Black Tuesday crisis quickly established him as a worthy successor to Volcker. "He really showed his mettle in his handling of this, and it helped to create the phenomenal credibility he enjoys today," says Kubarych of the Council on Foreign Relations.

The 13 years following the 1987 crash have witnessed low inflation and unemployment as well as largely steady and strong growth. As a result, the chairman's reputation as a good economic steward has reached almost mythic proportions. ■

CURRENT SITUATION

The Man at the Top

Republicans and Democrats agree on few things, but Alan Greenspan is one of them. The praise sometimes gets outlandish. During a GOP presidential debate in December 1999, Sen. John McCain, R-Ariz., joked that if the 74-year-old Greenspan died, "I'd prop him up and put a pair of dark glasses on him and keep him as long as I could." [14]

The accolades extend beyond the corridors of power. Arlington Heights, a Chicago suburb, renamed a street after the chairman, although only for a month. "He's guided the economic policy of our country," said Mayor Arlene Mulder. "Arlington Heights, like every other community, has benefited." [15]

AP Photo/Chris Gardner

SIGN OF THE TIMES: Only 4 percent of Americans are jobless, making the U.S. labor market unusually tight — and the Fed extremely nervous. Low unemployment drives up wages as employers offer higher salaries to attract workers. Higher wages mean more money chasing fewer goods and services, which in turn means higher inflation.

During his nearly 14-year tenure as Fed chairman, Greenspan has been credited with steering the nation through its longest economic boom — a boom that shows few signs of ending as it enters its 10th year.* The successful stewardship of the economy has given the chairman a reputation as a wise man and seer who is incapable of mistakes. "Some sort of myth has been created about him to the point where he's achieved a status that is unprecedented and almost unthinkable in American financial history," Tonelson of the U.S. Business and Industrial Council says. "He's become larger than life."

Although few would deny Greenspan his plaudits, some are concerned that the cult around him might hurt financial markets. "Greenspan has personalized monetary policy to such an extent that it would scare people if he weren't correct so often," says the Council on Foreign Relation's Kubarych.

The danger, Kubarych and others say, is that investors will trust Greenspan too much and won't scrutinize his actions carefully enough. "He's the best Fed chairman we've ever had, but he's only human," the AEI's Meltzer says. "He has made mistakes in the past and he will make them in the future."

Greenspan has not always been the oracle he is today. When he was first appointed, for example, *Business Week* commented, "Greenspan's skill at maneuvering through the political minefields of Washington remains a big question." [16]

Unlike previous Fed chairmen — many of whom hailed from government and academia — Greenspan had spent most of his professional life in the business world, as the successful head of his own financial consulting firm in New York. He only received his Ph.D. in economics at age 53.

Indeed, the chairman began his career far from banking or finance. After two years at New York's prestigious Julliard School of Music, Greenspan joined a swing band, playing clarinet and saxophone. After a year as a professional musician, he decided that his true calling lay elsewhere and enrolled in New York University's business economics program in 1946; he received his B.S. in 1948 and his master's degree two years later.

Before becoming Fed chairman, Greenspan made two forays into public life. In 1968, he served as a domestic policy adviser for Richard Nixon during his successful bid for the presidency. Six years later, Greenspan was tapped to head the Council of Economic Advisers — the president's in-house economics team. He served until 1977.

Throughout his years in both public and private life, Greenspan has always been a highly analytical and detail-oriented thinker. He examines reams of economic data until trends and patterns begin to emerge. A friend once described him as the "kind of person who knew how many thousand flathead bolts were used in a 1964 Chevrolet, and what it would do to the national economy if you took out three of them." [17]

Fed-watchers wonder whether Greenspan's success as chairman is due to his sharp mind or just being at the right place at the right time. Whatever the truth, Greenspan is

* President Clinton nominated Greenspan in January to a fourth four-year-term.

At Issue:

Is the Fed too aggressive in its inflation-fighting policy?

JEFF FAUX
President, Economic Policy Institute, April 2000; www.epinet.org

FROM NEWSDAY, APRIL 18, 2000

yes

One would think that engineering an economic slowdown in an election year would make incumbent politicians nervous. Yet Fed Chairman Alan Greenspan's deity-like status on Wall Street puts him above reproach in Washington. In the last few months he has lectured an intimidated and fawning Congress that he is administering the pain for our own good — taking away the punch bowl before America's booming consumer-spending party expands beyond the capacity of the economy to produce, and sets off a wage-price spiral that can only be stopped with a recession.

When Greenspan warns of inflationary risks, it brings to mind the double-digit nightmare that destroyed Jimmy Carter's presidency. Yet the inflation of the 1970s was not caused by an overheated domestic economy, but by the rise in global energy prices that — as is the case today — originated outside the United States. Nor was the previous bout of politically troublesome inflation due to overheated domestic demand; it was the result of Lyndon Johnson's refusal to raise taxes to pay for the Vietnam War. . . .

In the tradition of the opaque institution he heads, Greenspan is a master at obscuring his motivations. But the simplest explanation for his recent attempt to suppress economic growth is not so much a fear of inflation but a determination to protect corporate profits by keeping wages down.

Regardless of what Greenspan might be thinking, both Wall Street and Washington should remember that he is not infallible. To his credit, he halted the stock market crash of 1987 by encouraging New York banks to keep lending to stock buyers. But he also was slow to ease rates when growth leveled off in the early 1990s, a failure that plunged us into a recession and cost the senior George Bush his presidency.

It would be tragic to repeat that mistake. Tight labor markets and rising wages are good for America. They encourage companies to make labor-saving capital investments and improve efficiency. They make work pay for the poor whose welfare safety nets are being dismantled. And, of course, they increase working family incomes, restraining the widening income and wealth gaps that threaten social stability. . . .

Congress should not be running monetary policy, but neither should it stand by and let Alan Greenspan decide the country's economic priorities. The message to maintain economic growth should be loud and clear.

Otherwise, the congressional chorus who chanted Greenspan's praises this spring may be singing a different tune come November.

ALAN GREENSPAN
Chairman, Federal Reserve Board

TESTIMONY BEFORE SENATE COMMITTEE ON BANKING, HOUSING AND URBAN AFFAIRS, JULY 20, 2000

no

The Federal Reserve has been confronting a complex set of challenges in judging the stance of policy that will best contribute to sustaining the strong and long-running expansion of our economy. The challenges will be no less in coming months as we judge whether ongoing adjustments in supply and demand will be sufficient to prevent distortions that would undermine the economy's extraordinary performance.

For some time now, the growth of aggregate demand has exceeded the expansion of production potential. Technological innovations have boosted the growth rate of potential, but as I noted in my testimony last February, the effects of this process also have spurred aggregate demand. It has been clear to us that, with labor markets already quite tight, a continuing disparity between the growth of demand and potential supply would produce disruptive imbalances.

A key element in this disparity has been the very rapid growth of consumption resulting from the effects on spending of the remarkable rise in household wealth. However, the growth in household spending has slowed noticeably this spring from the unusually rapid pace observed late in 1999 and early this year. . . .

The last decade has been a remarkable period of expansion for our economy. Federal Reserve policy through this period has been required to react to a constantly evolving set of economic forces, often at variance with historical relationships, changing federal funds rates when events appeared to threaten our prosperity, and refraining from action when that appeared warranted. Early in the expansion, for example, we kept rates unusually low for an extended period, when financial-sector fragility held back the economy. Most recently we have needed to raise rates to relatively high levels in real terms in response to the side effects of accelerating growth and related demand-supply imbalances. Variations in the stance of policy — or keeping it the same — in response to evolving forces are made in the framework of an unchanging objective — to foster as best we can those financial conditions most likely to promote sustained economic expansion at the highest rate possible. Maximum sustainable growth, as history so amply demonstrates, requires price stability. Irrespective of the complexities of economic change, our primary goal is to find those policies that best contribute to a non-inflationary environment and hence to growth. The Federal Reserve, I trust, will always remain vigilant in pursuit of that goal.

likely to leave a huge vacuum when he retires. "The president who eventually has to replace him will be hard-pressed to find someone close to him in stature — and probably won't," Tonelson of the U.S. Business and Industrial Council says. ■

OUTLOOK

A Soft Landing?

For more than a year, Greenspan and the Fed have been steadily raising interest rates in small increments in an effort to gradually slow the economy. Their goal is what financial analysts refer to as a "soft landing," an economy with slower but steady growth, coupled with low inflation.

Until recently, it seemed that Fed actions had not produced the desired effect. GDP growth for the second quarter was a strong 5.2 percent, while unemployment remained at a very low 4 percent. Most important, inflation for the first half of the year had risen to 3.2 percent.

In the last few months, though, new signs have emerged that Greenspan's plan may be producing results. While the economy is still growing much faster than the Fed would like, consumer spending — a leading engine for growth — slowed to an annual rate of 3 percent in the second quarter, down from 7.6 percent in the first three months of 2000. [18] In addition, even though jobless claims are low, fewer new jobs are being created in the private sector — another sign that the economy may be slowing. [19]

Some analysts worry, however, that the economy has underlying problems that won't be solved by the Fed's tinkering with interest rates. The Center for Economic and Policy Research's Baker believes that trouble on Wall Street will turn the hoped for soft landing into a crash landing.

"I think the stock market is woefully overvalued and that this bubble is going to burst, and sooner rather than later," he says. When that happens, Baker says, the dollar also will plummet in value, since much of the currency's strength is based on high levels of foreign investment in the American stock market.

A fall in the dollar would likely lead to significant increases in inflation, as consumers were forced to use more dollars to buy the same product.

"I could see the dollar losing 20 percent to 25 percent of its value, which will be very inflationary," Baker says.

But many economists and other Fed-watchers see the recent statistics as evidence that the Federal Reserve will be able to successfully steer the economy into a period of slower, sustained growth. "I think most of the evidence points to the economy slowing down in the way the Fed wants it to," the Financial Market Center's Schlesinger says. "I can't imagine [Greenspan] will push us into recession yet."

Others agree, adding that the Fed can safely slow down the economy because it is too strong to fall into recession. "The U.S. economy, for all its faults, has so many underlying strengths, is such a juggernaut, that I don't see us coming to an abrupt stop any time soon," Tonelson says. "So while a slowdown is very realistic, a recession right now is not."

Still, Schlesinger says, while the short-term prospects for a soft landing may be good, a recession may not be avoidable for much longer.

"You need so much luck to avoid a recession that it may be asking too much for mere mortals, even if they are Alan Greenspan, to keep an economy recession-free for much longer than a decade," Schlesinger says. ■

Notes

[1] For background, see Christopher Conte, "Deflation Fears," *The CQ Researcher*, Feb. 13, 1998, pp. 121-144.

[2] For background, see Kenneth Jost, "The Stock Market," *The CQ Researcher*, May 2, 1997, pp. 385-408.

[3] For background, see Mary H. Cooper, "Jobs in the '90s," *The CQ Researcher*, Feb. 28, 1992, pp. 169-192.

[4] The Department of Commerce, www.commerce.gov.

[5] For background, see Richard L. Worsnop, "Consumer Debt," *The CQ Researcher*, Nov. 15, 1996, pp. 1009-1032.

[6] Richard W. Stevenson, "Federal Reserve Calls a Time Out on Raising Interest Rates," *The New York Times*, June 29, 2000.

[7] Figures cited in David B. Sicilia and Jeffrey L. Cruikshank, *The Greenspan Effect: Words That Move the World's Markets* (2000), pp. 59-61.

[8] William Greider, *Secrets of the Temple: How the Federal Reserve Runs the Country* (1987), p. 254.

[9] John Steele Gordon, *The Great Game: The Emergence of Wall Street as a World Power, 1653-2000* (1999), pp. 190-193.

[10] Greider, *op. cit.*, pp. 300-303.

[11] Gordon, *op. cit.*, p. 287.

[12] *Ibid.*

[13] Bureau of Labor Statistics.

[14] Quoted in John M. Berry, "Rising Campaign Rhetoric Over a Reappointment," *The Washington Post*, Dec. 21, 1999.

[15] Quoted in Dave Newbart, "Greenspan Gets Street in Suburb," *Chicago Sun-Times*, July 6, 2000.

[16] Quoted in Sicilia and Cruikshank, *op. cit.*, p. 8.

[17] Quoted in *ibid.*, p. 5.

[18] Figures cited in Yochi J. Dreazen, "Fed Survey Shows Signs of Cooling," *The Wall Street Journal*, Aug. 10, 2000.

[19] Figures cited in David Leonheardt, "Job Growth Slows, Suggesting Fed May Not Raise Interest Rates, *The New York Times*, Aug. 5, 2000.

Bibliography

Selected Sources Used

Books

Beckner, Steven K., *Back from the Brink: The Greenspan Years*, John Wiley and Sons, 1996.
Beckner, a broadcast journalist, offers a detailed account of Fed Chairman Alan Greenspan's first decade in office. Beckner's examination of Greenspan's reaction to the 1987 stock market crash is particularly enlightening.

Greider, William, *Secrets of the Temple: How the Federal Reserve Runs the Country*, Touchstone Books, 1987.
Greider, a writer for *Rolling Stone*, chronicles the Federal Reserve's history, focusing on the institution's years under Chairman Paul Volcker. Greider is very critical of Volcker's tough inflation-fighting policies.

Lindsey, Lawrence B., *Economic Puppetmasters: Lessons from the Halls of Power*, AEI Press, 1999.
Lindsey, who served on the Federal Reserve's Board of Governors, gives a good overview of what Greenspan and other central bankers think about the conduct of monetary policy.

Sicilia, David B., and Jeffrey L. Cruikshank, *The Greenspan Effect: Words that Move the World's Markets*, McGraw-Hill, 2000.
Sicilia and Cruikshank, both business consultants, explore Chairman Greenspan's thoughts on everything from inflation to Social Security.

Articles

"Almighty Alan Greenspan," *The Economist*, Jan. 8, 2000.
The article urges U.S. policy-makers to make the Fed less reliant on Greenspan's credibility by giving it clearer goals and requiring greater transparency.

Greenwald, John, "Who's Raising Your Rates? The Federal Open Market Committee, That's Who," *Time*, May 29, 2000.
Greenwald explores the workings of the Federal Open Market Committee, which he describes as "the second most powerful group of appointees in Washington — behind only the Supreme Court."

Ignatius, David, "Alan Sunshine," *The Washington Post*, May 19, 1999.
Ignatius, a columnist for *The Washington Post*, applauds recent moves at the Fed toward greater openness.

Miller, Rich, "Greenspan's Dilemma: The More Confident Investors Are In Him, the Harder His Job Becomes," *Business Week*, April 3, 2000.
Miller ponders whether Greenspan's credibility is actually making his job harder. Because investors believe so strongly in his ability to manage the economy, he claims, they continue to pour money into an already overheated stock market.

FOR MORE INFORMATION

American Enterprise Institute, Economic Policy Studies, 1150 17th St. N.W., Washington, D.C. 20036; (202) 862-5800; www.aei.org. The institute conducts research on monetary policy and related issues.

Brookings Institution, Economic Studies Program, 1775 Massachusetts Ave. N.W., Washington, D.C. 20036; (202) 797-6000; www.brookings.org. The program sponsors research and publishes studies on domestic and international economic issues.

Cato Institute, 1000 Massachusetts Ave. N.W., Washington, D.C. 20001; (202) 842-0200; www.cato.org. A public policy research organization that advocates limited government and individual liberty.

Council on Foreign Relations, 1779 Massachusetts Ave. N.W., Washington, D.C. 20036; (202) 518-3400; www.foreignrelations.org. Promotes understanding of U.S. foreign policy and international affairs.

Economic Policy Institute, 1660 L St. N.W., Suite 1200, Washington, D.C. 20036; (202) 775-8810; www.epinet.org. The institute conducts research on economic issues, including income distribution and industrial competitiveness.

8 Deflation Fears

CHRISTOPHER CONTE

To some economists, last year's 1.2 percent drop in wholesale prices was like a warning shot across the bow of the American economy.

"In the new era, the risk is deflation, not inflation," warns Edward C. Yardeni, chief economist for the investment banking firm Deutsche Morgan Grenfell.

For a generation of Americans who have grown accustomed to seeing prices increase year after year, it is hard to imagine that overall prices could turn downward, but a number of economists agree with Yardeni. They cite, among other things, plunging prices for manufactured goods ranging from semiconductors to toys, sharp drops in real estate and stock markets throughout Asia and falling prices for commodities like gold, which some analysts consider a good gauge of future price trends.

Many economists dismiss fears of deflation — which is defined as a general decline in the price of goods and services. In fact, they argue that the underlying economic forces still point toward renewed inflation rather than deflation. But these analysts concede that prices have been unexpectedly calm.

As a result, economists have begun to ask whether the United States could be more vulnerable than they thought to the risks associated with stagnant or falling prices — risks such as declining corporate profits, rising debt burdens, tumbling prices for stocks and real estate, faltering financial institutions and rising unemployment. If financial institutions and policy-makers don't understand these risks and prepare for them, a downturn in prices could push the economy into a recession, they say.

If overall prices do start falling in the United States, it would represent a major turn in economic history. The nation last experienced deflation in 1954, when the Consumer Price Index (CPI) dropped 0.5 percent. But there hasn't been a severe case of deflation since the Depression. At its worst point, from 1929 to 1933, prices fell, on average, 6.7 percent per year. [1]

From *The CQ Researcher,* February 13, 1998.

Reuters

Traders at the Philadelphia stock exchange in Manila react to a selloff on Wall Street and Asian markets.

Economists have differing explanations for why deflation could be a problem in the near future. Many note that prices are dropping around the world for a broad swath of raw materials and for manufactured goods ranging from automobiles to semiconductors. This, they argue, suggests that global supply is climbing much more rapidly than demand. "Thanks to a building binge throughout Asia, continuing economic expansion in the U.S. and the recovering economies in Europe, production everywhere is running ahead of consumption," *Business Week* magazine warned last November. [2]

The imbalance has been magnified because demand for goods and services is relatively slack in the advanced, industrial countries. "In Europe and the U.S., population growth has slowed down," says Neil Johnson, an economic consultant based in Toronto, Canada. "And with populations aging in Japan, Europe and the U.S., more people are becoming concerned about preserving their assets," and thus are saving more and spending less.

Some economists view government policy as a more important factor. Eager to keep inflation under control, the United States, Europe, Japan and Canada all have been restraining growth in the money supply, and they may have gone too far, these analysts say. Supply-side economist Jude Wanniski is probably the most fervent advocate of this view. *(See story, p. 124.)* Wanniski contends the Federal Reserve is not providing enough money to meet the needs of the economy. He says this "shortage of liquidity" is driving down prices and could bankrupt many enterprises. "The [economy] is trying to finance sound transactions, but cannot," he says.

Whatever the cause of deflation, economists generally agree that falling prices, by themselves, do not necessarily pose a serious economic threat. If price declines are mild, companies can cope with disappointing earnings by cutting costs, improving productivity or increasing sales. But a steep decline in prices could be more troublesome because companies operating close to the margin could see their profits disappear altogether.

Deflation would be most worrisome, though, if it spreads to banks. In a serious bout of deflation, many debtors may find themselves unable to pay back their loans. At the same time, steep declines in real estate and stock prices could reduce the value of assets that banks hold as collateral. Ultimately, the losses might leave banks unable to extend new loans, even to creditworthy borrowers. That could send the economy into a tailspin.

"It is possible to imagine a vicious circle developing between falling asset prices, falling prices in the shops, rising real debt levels and downwardly spiralling expectations, reminiscent of what happened in the 1930s," British econo-

Are We There Yet?

Has the U.S. economy entered a deflationary period? Judging from the Consumer Price Index (CPI), the most commonly used measure of price changes, it appears to be close but not quite there. The CPI rose 1.7 percent in 1997, about half as much as it had climbed the previous year. This seemed to continue a long-term trend; overall price increases have been slowing since 1980. (*See graph.*)

But while most economists believe the CPI is the best gauge of inflation, they admit it isn't perfect. In fact, the evidence suggests the United States is probably much closer to an overall decline in prices than the index suggests.

In 1996, a group of experts appointed by the Senate Finance Committee concluded that the CPI overstates increases in the cost of living by about 1.1 percentage points — and possibly by as much as 1.6 percentage points. If that is true, last year's 1.7 percent increase in the CPI actually could have represented an increase of just 0.6 percent or, if the upward bias is as high as the panel believes possible, an almost invisible 0.1 percent rise.

Changes in the Consumer Price Index

Although consumer prices have climbed in every year since 1954, the annual increases have generally slowed since 1980.

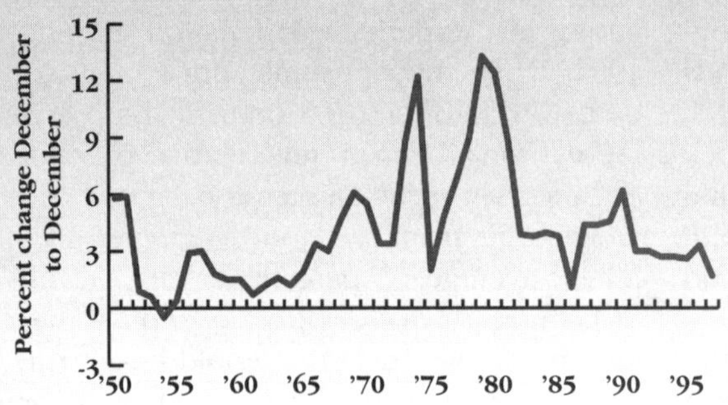

Source: Bureau of Labor Statistics

The Boskin Commission, as it was known, cited several reasons why the CPI may overstate the actual increase in living costs.[1] First, it noted that the CPI measures changes in the price of a fixed "basket" of goods, and therefore fails to capture the common consumer practice of substituting cheaper goods for more expensive ones when prices rise.

Perhaps the most important failing of the CPI may be that it does not account for improvements in the quality of goods. A refrigerator may cost more today than it did 10 years ago, for instance, but it probably is more energy efficient. Some of the price increase, then, reflects the fact that consumers are getting something more than they did in the past. Similarly, medical care is certainly more expensive than it used to be, but a significant portion of the higher cost reflects the fact that doctors and hospitals can test for and treat afflictions they could not handle in the past.

The challenge of measuring price changes becomes even greater when one considers that new products are coming to market at an unprecedented pace. How can statisticians compare the price of a computer today with the price of one manufactured even a year or two ago that had considerably fewer capabilities?

Federal Reserve Chairman Alan Greenspan pondered these issues in a speech on Jan. 3. "For most purposes, biases of a few tenths in annual inflation rates do not matter when inflation is high," Greenspan noted. "They do matter when, as now, inflation has become so low that policy-makers need to consider at what point effective price stability has been reached."[2]

Greenspan, along with many economists, believes the economy's current condition can best be described as "disinflation," not deflation. Disinflation is defined as a situation where the overall price level is still increasing, but at a slower rate than it previously had.

The Fed chairman's interest is more than academic. If the economy slips into deflation, the central bank might find it more difficult to respond adequately. One problem is that the Fed cannot reduce interest rates below zero, so it is limited in how far it could go in combating severe deflation.

In addition, the currently happy combination of low inflation and low unemployment might become more difficult to maintain. Workers in the U.S. have accepted very modest wage increases in recent years, but it's doubtful they would acquiesce to outright wage cuts. In a deflationary situation, then, the level of real wages — wages adjusted for price changes — would rise. And that would put employers, already hit by declining prices for their goods, in a financial bind. The result could be an increase in unemployment that the Fed would be powerless to combat.

"A little deflation is worse than a little inflation," concludes James O'Sullivan, a vice president at J.P. Morgan, an international banking company.

Not so, argues Greenspan. Policy-makers should strive to achieve perfect price stability, not a little inflation or a little deflation, he said Jan. 3. Nevertheless, he added, "We central bankers need to better judge how to assess our performance in achieving and maintaining that objective in light of the uncertainties surrounding the accuracy of our measured price indexes."

---

[1] The committee's chairman was former presidential economic adviser Michael J. Boskin. See *Final Report of the Advisory Commission to Study the Consumer Price Index*, December 1996.

[2] Remarks at the annual meeting of the American Economic Association and the American Finance Association, Chicago, Ill., Jan. 3, 1998; available online at http://www.bog.frb.fed.us.

mist Roger Bootle writes in his 1997 book, *The Death of Inflation*. "If consumers expect prices to fall, then they defer purchases, which puts more downward pressure on prices. Falling prices raise the real value of debt and force debtors to cut back on their spending. Some debtors inevitably go under, thereby endangering financial institutions and the banking system, which depresses confidence further." [3]

Japan and several developing countries in Asia appear close to this kind of damaging deflation. Thailand, Indonesia, Malaysia and South Korea, for instance, are suffering from excess production capacity. "All the countries there tried to build capacity in the same industries at once, resulting in far too much capacity in such industries as autos and high-tech," says David Wyss, chief economist for Standard & Poor's DRI, an economic consulting and information company. "The problem has been exacerbated by a tendency to build landmark projects, such as high-rise office buildings, that have little economic justification."

Japan and Thailand also have seen speculative booms in real estate turn to busts, with devastating effects on the balance sheets of financial institutions. In Japan, real estate prices have plunged about 65 percent since the bubble burst in the early 1990s. Shares traded on the Japanese stock market have lost almost 60 percent of their value. The Japanese economy has been stagnant in the wake of this "kakadu hakai," or "price destruction," and some analysts believe the country could slip back into recession if sharply diminished investor and consumer confidence produces a very sharp slowdown among its Asian trading partners. [4]

Deflation has hit Asian financial institutions particularly hard. The International Monetary Fund estimates that problem loans at South Korean banks equaled almost 70 percent of the banks' capital at the end of 1996, even after taking account of reserves held to cover possible losses. While reliable information for 1997 isn't yet available, the situation clearly has worsened. In Japan, the 19 largest banks have bad loans totaling an estimated $400 billion, or 14 percent of all their outstanding credit. Insolvent or close to it, many lenders throughout the region are unable to extend loans. [5]

Supply-sider Wanniski likens these institutions to canaries in a mine, arguing they are just the first victims of global deflation. But many others say the Asian financial institutions brought on their own problems by lending lavishly to ventures that lacked economic merit. In South Korea, critics say, banks failed to assess lending risks objectively because they had too many close ties to their corporate borrowers. In Indonesia, loans were channeled to friends and family members of President Suharto regardless of whether the underlying projects made sense economically.

"In too many places, corruption has replaced communism as the greatest threat to world order," says Rep. Jim Leach, R-Iowa, chairman of the House Banking Committee. "In many countries, banks are particularly vulnerable to inside thievery for the same reason Willy Sutton stuck them up from outside — that's where the money is."

In contrast to Asia, the United States appears for the moment to be relatively safe from a devastating downturn in prices. The service sector, which represents about 75 percent of U.S. economic output, faces relatively little foreign competition. Perhaps as a result, prices for services are climbing about 3 percent a year. Because manufacturing represents such a small portion of the economy, prices for manufactured goods would have to drop precipitously to drag down the entire Consumer Price Index, notes James O'Sullivan, a vice president at J.P. Morgan & Co., an international banking company.

Moreover, wages in the U.S. are showing signs of picking up, not declining as one would expect in a deflationary period. The Commerce Department reported that real, or inflation-adjusted, average hourly earnings rose 2.2 percent in 1997, a modest increase but still the largest in a decade.

The money supply also is growing at a healthy pace, suggesting — though not proving — that lack of liquidity may not be a serious problem. One monetary measure, M2, rose at a 5 percent rate in January, its fastest pace since the start of the 1990s, while another, M3, was increasing at an 8 percent clip, the strongest rise since the mid-1980s. * "Deflation will not occur when money supply growth is accelerating," declares Mark Zandi, chief economist for Regional Financial Associates, an economic consulting firm in West Chester, Pa.

Even if prices remain stable or start to decline, U.S. companies appear fairly well-equipped to thrive. After-tax corporate profits were rising at better than a 10 percent annual rate in the third quarter of 1997, the most recent period for which data are available. While final figures for 1997 won't be available from the Commerce Department until March, it appears that corporations chalked up their fifth consecutive year of double-digit profit increases.

In addition, corporate-debt burdens in the U.S. generally are falling. Many companies have taken advantage of

---

* M2 consists of cash and balances in checking and savings accounts, certificates of deposit less than $100,000 and money-market funds. M3 is a broader measure of money, consisting of everything in M2 plus, among other things, large-denomination certificates of deposit and balances held in institutional money-market funds.

strong earnings and the rising stock market to pay back loans, and others have aggressively refinanced their loans at today's lower interest rates. As a result, pretax profits last year totaled almost six times net interest expenses, the highest level in more than 25 years, according to John Lonski of Moody's Investors Service. "You don't see anywhere near as many leveraged buyouts as you did in the late 1980s," Lonski adds. "Today, mergers and acquisitions are much more likely to improve balance sheets."

Similarly, U.S. banks have significantly strengthened their financial position. Partly as a result of tough regulations imposed in the wake of the savings and loan crisis of the 1980s, their ratio of past-due loans and other non-performing assets dropped to less than 1 percent of their total assets in September 1997 from more than 3 percent at the end of 1991. According to the Federal Deposit Insurance Corporation, U.S. banks currently hold almost $2 in reserve for every $1 in problem loans. And while their total 1997 profits have not yet been reported, they appear likely to set a new record, exceeding the previous high mark, $52.4 billion, recorded in 1996. "The U.S. banking system is well-capitalized, and we aren't seeing much speculative activity," says Paul Kasriel, chief U.S. economist for Chicago-based Northern Trust Co.

None of the current economic indicators are conclusive, however. Economists agree that the underlying forces at work today will only show up in the official statistics after a delay of uncertain duration. Moreover, the measures themselves are inexact. Economists generally agree, for instance, that the Consumer Price Index probably overstates the real inflation rate by at least 1 percentage point. (*See story, p. 120.*) The biggest uncertainty, however, involves how the current world situation will play out. While most economists believe the crisis in Asia will slow the U.S. economy only slightly, nobody knows for sure how long the crisis will last and how widespread its effects will be.

As the situation in Asia demonstrates, the increased integration of the global economy adds another layer of complexity to the challenges policy-makers face. What is the connection between deflationary developments in Asia and current trends in the U.S. economy? What responsibility does the U.S. have to help Asia out of its crisis? And what would be the appropriate policy stance if Asia stands on the brink of serious deflation while the United States still faces a strong threat of renewed inflation? All these issues come into play as policy-makers in the U.S. confront two major policy questions:

Should the Federal Reserve loosen the monetary reins to fight deflation, or keep them tight to prevent inflation?

Federal Reserve Chairman Alan Greenspan has signaled that the central bank stands ready, if necessary, to switch from its long-standing preoccupation with inflation to an anti-deflation stance. "A persistent deflation in the prices of currently produced goods and services — just like a persistent increase in these prices — necessarily is, at its root, a monetary phenomenon," Greenspan told the American Economic Association on Jan. 3.[6]

The Fed chairman discounted the threat of deflation, and he suggested that he would be most worried by a steep drop in real estate or stock prices, which he said might occur for any number of reasons, "some of which may be only tangentially related to the state of the economy and monetary policy." Nevertheless, his statement clearly established that if the Fed perceives deflation to be a threat, it will ease monetary policy — that is, pump more money into the economy and reduce interest rates — just as it has long battled inflation by constraining the money supply and raising interest rates.

Economists generally agree that easier money is a solution to deflation, though there is some disagreement about how it helps. Traditionalists believe that expanding the money supply increases the level of aggregate demand by encouraging spending. Supply-siders, who say efforts to manipulate demand don't work, argue that loosening the monetary reins simply provides needed liquidity.

In his speech, Greenspan pointedly refused to abandon the view held by most central bank officials that inflation remains the primary economic danger in the United States. The Fed's policy-making arm, the Federal Open Market Committee, summarized this position at a meeting held Sept. 30, 1997. Warning that the economy could not continue growing as fast as it had been without causing prices to rise, and fretting that labor markets were so tight that employers would have to start bidding up wages to attract workers, the panel said, "The risks to the economy [appear] to be strongly tilted toward rising inflation."

Accordingly, the committee voted to maintain interest rates at their current levels but to lean toward tightening monetary policy in the event additional upward pressure on prices became evident. Some participants actually were ready to raise rates immediately, and decided to postpone action only because "a policy tightening was not anticipated at this time and such an action might therefore have unintended adverse effects on financial markets."[7]

Asia's economic troubles changed the equation by diminishing the near-term threat of inflation. "The Asia crisis will produce such a wave of cheap imports that it will have a dampening effect on goods prices," says Dan Laufenberg, chief U.S. economist for American Express Financial Advisers in Minneapolis, Minn. At the same time, economic weakness in Asia will reduce demand for U.S. exports, slowing the U.S. economy and further easing potential pressures on prices here. "Before Asia, the Fed would have had to tighten" monetary policy, suggests Wyss of Standard & Poor's DRI. "This does their job for them."

Many economists, however, believe the good news on inflation will be short-lived. At the December Fed meeting, William Broaddus, president of the Federal Reserve Bank of Atlanta, argued that the central bank should tighten the monetary reins modestly in light of "persisting strength in aggregate demand for goods and services." Broaddus "recognized the case for holding policy steady given recent developments in East Asian economies and financial markets," according to minutes of the meeting. But he argued that a "slight firming" would "provide valuable insurance" against the risk that inflation would accelerate and require "a sharper policy response" later. The majority disagreed, and in fact voted to adopt a "symmetric" policy stance — that is, to be just as ready to ease as to tighten the monetary reins — instead of leaning toward a tighter policy. [8]

Some argue that the Fed should take the threat of deflation more seriously. "The Fed should ease," declares Philip Braverman, chief economist for DKB Securities (USA) Corp. in New York. "It is no longer appropriate to operate on the assumption that just because the U.S. economy is operating at a high rate of capacity, inflation is a threat. We have become part of a global economy, and there is a lot of excess capacity globally. To fight a rearguard action against a nonexistent enemy [inflation] creates more of a risk of deflation."

Even some economists who believe inflation remains the bigger long-term danger predict that governments may have to abandon the fight against inflation to prevent bankruptcies and financial-system failures in places like South Korea, Thailand and Indonesia from spreading to China or beyond. Stephen Roach, chief economist for the investment banking and securities firm Morgan Stanley Dean Witter, predicts that the Fed and central banks in other advanced, industrial countries will have to reduce interest rates to increase liquidity and keep financial weaknesses from spreading.

The financial crisis in Asia has reduced the threat of renewed inflation in the U.S., but Federal Reserve Chairman Alan Greenspan worries that inflationary pressures may soon reappear.

While these steps may be necessary to shore up the world's financial system, Roach says, they will leave the global economic system awash in money. The resulting low level of interest rates will heat up the U.S. economy at just the time restraint will be needed to prevent it from growing too fast, Roach suggests. "We are sewing the seeds of the next inflation," he concludes.

Should the International Monetary Fund rescue Asian countries that face deflation?

While the ultimate responsibility for preventing deflation or inflation may rest with the Federal Reserve and other central banks, the frontline job of fighting today's most serious deflation crisis has fallen to the International Monetary Fund. The IMF last year arranged more than $100 billion in emergency credits to help South Korea, Thailand and Indonesia stay afloat after foreign investors fled those countries amid falling prices and widespread insolvency.

Help from the IMF comes with strings attached. The international organization has exacted commitments from recipient countries to shut down insolvent institutions, to strengthen financial regulation and public disclosure laws, and to open their markets to foreign financial institutions. It also has required countries to tighten monetary policy and drive up interest rates in order to defend their currencies and attract skittish foreign investors back.

IMF programs have been attacked by some for being too lenient and by others for being too stringent. Critics who say the organization is too indulgent warn that the IMF, in effect, is letting investors and financial institutions that made bad decisions off the hook. This could encourage worse behavior in the future, these critics contend.

"A free-market economy has a very efficient way of dealing with misjudgment, excess and failure. It's called bankruptcy," argues James K. Glassman, a resident fellow at the

In Wanniski's School of Economics . . .

In an era of economic uncertainty — of money that is worth one thing today and something else tomorrow, of fluctuating exchange rates, of economic theories that often fail to predict what will happen or when it will happen — is there any reliable guidepost for policy-makers?

Jude Wanniski, a former *Wall Street Journal* editor, economic consultant and leading proponent of "supply-side" economics, [1] believes he has found one, and it's as old as the hills: gold. Unfortunately, he complains, almost nobody else — not even his philosophical compatriots — fully appreciates its importance. As a result, he contends, policy-makers have been fiddling while a serious, deflationary fire has started to burn.

Jude Wanniski

Though his background is in journalism, Wanniski considers himself a "classical" economist. In his world, gold is a "proxy for everything that has a price," a universal yardstick for measuring the value of things. "All you need to know about gold is that from the dawn of civilization, it has been used by ordinary people to measure other goods and services," he says. "It has been the numeraire, and it still is."

Money, on the other hand, can rise and fall in value depending on government policy. If a government prints too much money — that is, more than people actually need to carry out the myriad transactions that make up the economy — prices rise and you have inflation. In this situation, the value of money declines, since each dollar will buy less today than it did yesterday. On the other hand, if the government does not print enough money, prices fall and you have deflation. Deflation implies a rising value of money since each dollar will buy more today than it did yesterday.

Since the real value of gold does not change, Wanniski argues, fluctuations in its dollar price indicate whether policy-makers are printing too much or too little money. In his view, a rising price of gold indicates there is too much money in circulation; unless the government removes this "surplus liquidity," all prices will ratchet up. A falling price of gold, on the other hand, indicates that there is too little money in circulation; unless the government prints money to offset this "shortage of liquidity," prices will fall. [2]

Beginning in late 1996, the price of gold started falling from around $385 an ounce; by the end of 1997, the price had dropped below $300 an ounce. Wanniski had begun warning that the economy was entering a deflationary period around February 1997. As the financial crisis unfolded in Asia later in the year, he claimed vindication for his theories.

According to Wanniski, Asia's problems were made in America. In the early 1990s, he says, the dollar price of gold rose from $350 to $385, suggesting there was too much money in circulation. (Wanniski says tax increases in 1993 had reduced demand for money, [3] and that the Federal Reserve failed to mop up the resulting excess.) Asian countries that tied their currencies to the dollar had to inflate to maintain parity with the dollar, and Asian banks, in turn, "were forced" to push the resulting surplus of reserves into risky loans.

The price of gold started falling in late 1996, signaling there now was a shortage of money. (Wanniski says the shortage became more acute when Congress approved tax cuts in 1997.) Asian central banks had to withdraw money

American Enterprise Institute and a columnist for *The Washington Post.* "Lenders, investors, managers and sometimes employees and politicians all take part of the hit — and assets pass from weak hands to strong. Everyone learns important lessons and starts afresh. But by rushing to the rescue, the IMF is preventing this cleansing process." [9]

The IMF's supporters reply that the Asia crisis has swelled far beyond the lenders and borrowers who made bad investments. The sudden and massive withdrawal of investors from Asia has "the hallmarks of a classic market mania," a panic that damages well-managed companies and financial institutions along with poorly run ones, argues Laura D'Andrea Tyson, an economist at the University of California at Berkeley and former economic adviser to President Clinton.

Only government action, Tyson adds, can correct such a problem. "Once destabilized, markets are not self-equilibrating," she says. "Government intervention is required to provide the public good of monetary stability on which normal economic transactions depend." She adds that the United States has "substantial economic, democracy and security inter-

. . . Gold Is The Answer

from the system to push their currencies down along with the dollar, a move that choked off those who had borrowed a few years earlier when funds were more readily available.

Why is Wanniski almost alone in this analysis? For one thing, many analysts doubt his assertion that gold is a perfectly reliable indicator of price trends. "Gold moves for a lot of reasons other than whether there's inflation or deflation," argues Frederick Mishkin, an economist at Columbia University's Graduate School of Business. "Its price is influenced by what's happening in our ability to mine it and the cost of doing so, what [non-monetary] uses it can be put to and whether central banks want to hold it or not."

The latter point may be especially important. Central banks hold huge stockpiles of gold, but they have no real use for them since governments do not back their currencies with gold anymore. As a result, central banks have been shedding their gold supplies; governments sold about 6 percent of their gold holdings between 1989 and 1996, contributing to gold's slide in value from an all-time high of $850 an ounce in 1980. [4]

Even if gold is a good gauge of whether inflationary or deflationary pressures are present in the economy, it's unclear what the optimum or equilibrium price of gold should be. Federal Reserve Chairman Alan Greenspan, who at times has said a rising price of gold can signal incipient inflation, noted at a 1997 congressional hearing that the price of gold, despite falling that year, remained nine times higher than it was a generation ago. [5]

Wanniski, for his part, suggests that $350 would be the optimal price of gold; he admits the figure is a bit subjective, but notes that gold has averaged about $350 an ounce since 1975, suggesting that debtors and creditors have become "comfortable" with that price.

Many U.S. analysts — including Wanniski's supply-side compatriots — dismiss his warnings about deflation because falling prices do not seem to be causing much trouble in the United States, at least not yet. They blame Asia's problems on unsound banking practices, not on mistakes by the Federal Reserve. "By general agreement among practically all my supply-side colleagues, the economic wreckage around the world that [I] attribute to the Fed's deflation is being attributed to a general outbreak of stupidity among Asian and Latin bankers," Wanniski complains.

Eventually, Wanniski believes, the deflationary disease may spread to the point that Federal Reserve policy-makers cannot ignore it. At that point, they will add money to the system, he predicts. But in the meantime, a lot of deflationary dislocation could be avoided, he says, if the central bank simply would maintain a constant dollar price for gold.

Life would be simpler for central bankers, too, he maintains. They would not have to try to figure out whether aggregate supply and demand are in balance, whether labor markets are too tight to sustain stable wages, whether rising productivity is increasing the economy's growth potential or most of the other complex issues that preoccupy economists today.

"Gold gives all the power to the marketplace. It is the most democratic of all monetary policies," Wanniski says. "It takes all discretion away from the central bank, which today has too much power over the people of the world." [6]

[1] Supply-siders believe traditional economists put too much emphasis on the demand side of the supply-and-demand equation. They say economic policies should focus on maximizing the output of goods and services (primarily through tax policies that reward investment), rather than on increasing or reducing demand.

[2] See Jude Wanniski, "The Optimum Price of Gold," *The Wall Street Journal,* Jan. 7, 1998, p. A22.

[3] For background, see *1993 CQ Almanac*, pp. 107-139.

[4] See Richard W. Stevenson, "The Gold Standard: Spinning Gold Into Dross," *The New York Times,* Dec. 28, 1997; Section 4, p. 5.

[5] Testimony before the House Banking and Financial Services Committee, Nov. 4, 1997.

[6] Wanniski explains his views in detail on his consulting company's Web site: http://www.polyconomics.com/

ests in Asia, all of which would be jeopardized by a prolonged depression there." According to Tyson, these interests include preventing financial weakness in Asia from spreading to other emerging markets. [10]

The IMF, for its part, contends that the conditions it imposes on countries it assists are enough to discourage other countries from engaging in risky lending and investment behavior. But another set of critics argues that at least one of those conditions — that countries maintain tight money in order to bolster their currencies — may be exactly the wrong medicine for economies on the brink of runaway deflation.

The IMF contends that loose-money policies in the early 1990s contributed to Asia's problems; it says Thailand, for instance, allowed "overheating pressures" to produce large trade deficits and artificial surges in stock prices, or "bubbles." Critics counter that the Asian countries were not living beyond their means. They note that the countries now in trouble all had budget surpluses and low inflation. According to these analysts, trade deficits in these countries reflected softening export prices, not overconsumption, and the run-up in stock and other prices stemmed from huge foreign investment, not from errors in monetary policy.

All this suggests that Asia does not need tight money and some of the other disciplinary actions sought by the IMF, they conclude. "The region does not need wanton budget cutting, credit tightening and emergency bank closures," says Jeffrey D. Sachs, director of the Harvard Institute for International Development. "It needs stable or even slightly expansionary monetary and fiscal policies to counterbalance the decline in foreign loans."

Sachs likens IMF-imposed tight money policies to moves by U.S. banks to tighten credit in 1933 rather than lend money to banks to help them calm frightened crowds that were lining up to withdraw their funds. At the time, close to 10,000 banks suspended operations, lending dried up and the economy spiraled downward into the Depression. If policy-makers today would take the opposite approach, moving to increase liquidity rather than restrict it with higher interest rates and emergency bank closures, Asia's underlying strengths — high savings, budget surpluses, flexible labor markets, low taxation — will reassert themselves and the region will be able quickly to resume rapid economic growth, Sachs contends. [11]

Supply-sider Wanniski agrees that easier money is the answer to Asia's crisis, but he argues that the loosening should begin in Washington at the Federal Reserve. According to Wanniski, the Fed started Asia's tailspin by letting the dollar appreciate in value against gold, and Asian countries imported the deflation because their currencies were tied to the U.S. greenback. Further tightening now will only worsen the situation, he concludes, asserting that IMF Director Michel Camdessus and his deputy, Stanley Fisher, "are a menace to the world." ■

BACKGROUND

The End of Inflation?

Even before the Asia crisis catapulted deflation into the headlines, policy-makers and analysts were debating whether profound economic changes have eliminated the danger of inflation and made declining prices the greater risk today.

The mainstream view holds that inflation may be down, but it definitely isn't out. (*See "At Issue," p. 127.*) In fact, traditionalists believe the U.S. economy is very close to the point at which inflation will be triggered by "excess" demand in the labor market.

Economists use two measures to determine whether there is excess demand. One approach is to compare the actual and "potential" growth rates of the economy. Potential growth is presumed to equal the sum of the growth in the labor force plus any gains in productivity, or output per worker. Currently, the labor force is projected to grow about 1 percent a year, and productivity is thought to be rising somewhere between 1 percent and 1.5 percent. Therefore, the potential growth rate is assumed to be somewhere between 2 percent and 2.5 percent.

The other gauge of excess demand is what economists awkwardly call NAIRU, or the "non-accelerating inflation rate of unemployment." Over time, economists have noted that inflation tends to accelerate when joblessness drops below a certain level. In the decade that ended in the early 1990s, economists generally believed NAIRU was around 6 percent. Since then, they say, it may have slipped to perhaps 5.5 percent, perhaps because of demographic changes, adjustments in government programs (welfare reform, for instance) or other factors.

By either measure, the U.S. economy currently is in the inflation danger zone. Preliminary estimates by the Commerce Department show that the gross domestic product, a standard measure of the size of the nation's economy, rose 3.8 percent last year, well ahead of its presumed long-run potential. The Bureau of Labor Statistics reports that the unemployment rate dropped to just 4.7 percent in December and January, its lowest level since 1969. Yet even though the economy crossed these thresholds, consumer price inflation slowed to 1.7 percent from 3.3 percent a year earlier, and it shows no signs of picking up.

Some economists attribute the unexpected price moderation to temporary factors. For one thing, the labor force has been growing about twice as rapidly as would be expected based on growth of the adult population, easing much of the strain in labor markets. "It is as if demand is calling forth its own supply," says Federal Reserve Governor Laurence H. Meyer. Chairman Greenspan argues, however, that the current rate of labor-force growth can't be sustained. He notes that more than half of the 2 million net new hires each year are being drawn from the ranks of the unemployed or from among those who had not been actively seeking work, two sources of labor that eventually will dry up. [12]

Many economists believe the United States has nearly reached the bottom of the well, and that labor markets are beginning to tighten significantly. As a result, they expect wage increases to start putting more pressure on prices. Still, they have expected that to happen for some time, and wages remain fairly quiescent. The 2.2 percent jump in average hourly earnings in 1997 was considered unusually mild, though it did

At Issue:

Is the nation on the verge of a new period of inflation?

yes

MARK ZANDI
Chief economist, Regional Financial Associates, West Chester, Pa.

WRITTEN FOR *THE CQ RESEARCHER*, JANUARY 1998.

Claims that the economy is on the verge of outright deflation are misplaced. Not only will there be no deflation this year, but inflation will accelerate by year's end. Much of the deceleration in inflation during the past year is the result of a number of what will prove to be temporary events.

Energy prices, for example, have been pummeled by a myriad of factors, including the financial and economic woes in Asia, resumption of Iraqi exports, the recently announced increase in OPEC production quotas and the warm winter in the Northern Hemisphere. It is unlikely world energy markets will make it through the year without another disruption of Iraqi oil exports, however. Asian oil demand may even rise somewhat in coming months since many Asian buyers probably have been holding off buying dollar-denominated oil as long as possible in the hope that their very depressed currencies make at least a partial comeback.

Falling import prices also have contributed to weaker inflation during the past year. The dollar's seemingly inexorable rise will come to an end in coming months as the Asian currency and financial crisis finally subsides. As investors deem Asian financial markets have hit bottom — and there is increasing speculation that this may soon be at hand — the dollar will lose some of its luster as a global safe haven.

Collapsing computer prices also have been a major constraint on inflation. Personal computer prices fell by 12 percent during the past year. But it is hard to expect similar declines this year. Margins in the industry have fallen enough to suggest that a significant shakeout may soon occur. That eventually will limit the rate of future price declines.

A further deceleration in the cost of health care also was an important constraint on inflation last year. Health care cost inflation is expected to accelerate this year as the process of moving over to managed care is largely over.

Inflation also will continue to get a lift from stronger growth in labor costs. Labor markets are acutely tight, and at the economy's current rate of growth they will grow tighter. Moreover, productivity will not increase enough to offset rising compensation costs, as employers will have to hire less than qualified labor in the tight labor market.

All this suggests that consumer price inflation will accelerate from just under 2 percent currently to near 3 percent a year from now. While this is still very modest inflation by nearly any standard of the past quarter-century, it is inflation nonetheless.

no

EDWARD YARDENI
Chief economist, Deutsche Morgan Grenfell, New York, N.Y.

WRITTEN FOR *THE CQ RESEARCHER*, JANUARY 1998.

The forces of disinflation are permanent, not transitory, in my opinion.

The end of the Cold War marked the beginning of intense global competition. The U.S. economy has adapted better than the Continental European and Japanese economies to the competitive challenges, and the dollar reflects this situation. In both Europe and Japan, market structures remain too rigid, with too much government intervention in the form of excessive regulation, protection and subsidies. Consequently, the uncompetitive economies of Europe and Japan are weak.

The Europeans and Japanese are deregulating and restructuring their economies, but too slowly. Interest rates remain very low over there, especially compared with rates available in the U.S. So, the dollar is strong, and will likely remain strong. Indeed, the weak deutsche mark and yen are the only reasons that there is any growth in Europe and Japan at all. These countries need weak currencies to keep out of recessions. The Japanese financial system is still a mess. Huge loan losses have yet to be fully realized. A strong dollar should continue to be an important source of disinflation.

Why aren't wages rising at a faster pace with the unemployment rate so low? The favorite explanation is that the Federal Reserve's models didn't include variables for job insecurity, but that the models should soon be back on track once job insecurity goes away. I disagree. Job security may improve, but we all face much greater business insecurity because markets are becoming more competitive globally as a result of the end of the Cold War trade barriers, and domestically as a result of ongoing restructuring, deregulation and privatization. We can all look forward to keeping our jobs as long as our companies don't fail.

The Fed's inflation models also seem to be missing variables to capture how price security is keeping a lid on wages. Workers and consumers are becoming increasingly secure about price stability. They perceive that prices are not rising fast enough to threaten their financial well-being, so they aren't very militant about wages.

My bottom line is that the forces of disinflation remain very much intact. They are not temporary; they are permanent. Tight labor markets are not inflationary because global competition is keeping a lid on prices and lowering workers' inflationary expectations.

represent an acceleration from the 0.5 percent gain in 1996.

Meyer and Greenspan believe that workers may have held back on wage demands because they feel unusually insecure about their jobs. In 1991, at the bottom of the last recession, a poll by International Survey Research Corp. found that 25 percent of workers feared they would be laid off. In 1996, even though the economy had been growing for five years and unemployment had dropped to 5.3 percent from 7.3 percent, the portion of workers who were worried about layoffs had grown to 46 percent, the survey firm found.

Similarly, while labor contracts in the past rarely exceeded three years, it is not uncommon today to have five-year or even six-year contracts — and many of the new contracts emphasize job security in lieu of substantial wage increases. [13]

Greenspan attributes heightened job insecurity in part to efforts by companies to reduce their work forces by farming certain functions to outside contractors. [14] Technological change also may play a role, he suggests, by leading workers to fear that unless they upgrade their skills continuously they won't remain employable. Whatever the cause, the Fed chairman questions how much longer wage demands will remain suppressed. "There is a limit to the value of additional job security people are willing to acquire in exchange for lesser increases in living standards," he says. [15]

Traditionalists also believe that sedate health-care costs have brought temporary relief from inflation, but that prices could start jumping soon. A number of economists argue, for instance, that health maintenance organizations by now have squeezed much of the fat out of doctor and hospital bills, and will have more trouble restraining cost increases in the future. [16]

Similarly, economists question how much longer the dollar can continue rising against foreign currencies, a trend that has cut the price of imports and brought additional price relief to U.S. consumers. For much of 1997, analysts were predicting the dollar would halt its rise as imports enlarged the U.S. trade deficit. With the wave of currency depreciations in Asia, they have postponed predictions of a falling dollar, but they still say the dollar cannot keep rising forever.

A New Paradigm

While many economists predict that "temporary" factors masking inflation eventually will disappear and forces pushing prices upward will reassert themselves, one group of analysts argues that inflation poses no threat for the foreseeable future.

Their theory, dubbed the "new paradigm," holds that two major new forces — increased global competition and a significant, though as yet unmeasured, rise in productivity — will prevent renewed inflation and enable the economy to expand much faster than the 2.5 percent annual growth rate commonly assumed to be its upper limit. If true, these new theories suggest that the Federal Reserve's continuing focus on inflation is, at the very least, unnecessarily restraining growth and, at worst, actually could push the economy into a deflationary downturn.

A new economic era began with the end of the Cold War, argues economist Yardeni of Deutsche Morgan Grenfell. He believes the end of the U.S.-Soviet confrontation eliminated an "unprecedented trade barrier." Now that the conflict is over, trade is flourishing — even between the West and China, which remains communist but is eagerly pushing economic integration with the rest of the world. According to Yardeni, the sum of all nations' exports rose 70 percent between 1989 and 1995 to a record $5.1 trillion. He predicts that total will double to $10 trillion by 2000.

As a result, manufacturers who previously could raise prices easily because they were relatively sheltered, now are exposed to much more competition. That means they can't increase prices — even if tight labor markets are forcing them to raise wages. To remain profitable, Yardeni says, they instead must increase sales volume, constantly develop new products and find ways to operate more efficiently.

"The new era is inherently deflationary," he says. "To offset these deflationary pressures, companies must sell more units of their products and services. The best way to do so is to cut costs, lower prices, improve quality and innovate."

The argument, though tantalizing, is controversial. Paul Krugman, an economist at the Massachusetts Institute of Technology, disagrees that global trade is having such a decisive impact. He argues that the service sector, which now comprises the bulk of the U.S. economy, is largely insulated from foreign competition. Even many U.S. manufacturers don't compete head-to-head with foreigners, Krugman suggests. "Seen any Chinese refrigerators lately?" he asks. [17]

Van Bussman, corporate economist for Chrysler Corp., buttresses Krugman's point. Around the world, automobile manufacturers will be able to produce 80 million cars a year by 2000 — 25 percent, or 20 million cars, more than projected sales. But U.S. companies will escape much of the heightened competition. Most new foreign manufacturers produce primarily sub-compact cars, but there is no excess capacity to produce the vehicles most important to U.S. automakers — sport-utility vehicles, pickups and minivans. "We are somewhat buffered from excess capacity," Bussman says.

The other main plank of the new paradigm theory — that gains in productivity have increased the economy's growth potential — also is hotly disputed among economists. "New paradigm" theorists believe that computer technology has enormously increased the efficiency of U.S. production. The computer industry itself is their favorite example. Computer prices have been declining at double-digit rates every year, and most analysts project they will continue falling indefinitely. Yet profits remain strong, thanks to constant innovation and increasing sales. "Everybody asks how can we keep this up, but the light at the end of the tunnel keeps moving ahead with every long-range plan," notes Rich O'Brien, corporate economist for Texas Instruments.

Some analysts believe computers also may be enhancing productivity in countless other industries. "What we may be observing in the current environment is a number of key technologies, some even mature, finally interacting to create significant new opportunities for value creation," says Greenspan. For instance, advances in laser technology and fiber optics have converged to create a revolution in telecommunications, and new software innovations have made it possible to take advantage of significantly increased computer capacity to create the Internet. [18]

Greenspan notes that in high-tech industries, the lead time required to bring new production facilities on line is much shorter than in the days when manufacturing required heavy equipment such as open-hearth steel furnaces. As a result, output today can be increased quickly to meet rising demand, and the kind of bottlenecks and capacity shortages that led to rising prices and economic slowdown in the past are less likely. Greenspan notes, for instance, that the ratio of unfilled orders to shipments of nondefense capital goods has declined by 30 percent in the last six years. [19]

Dell Computers

Computer prices have been declining at double-digit rates in recent years, yet industry profits remain strong, thanks to constant innovation and increasing sales.

Many economists scoff at the notion that computers have increased productivity. They note that economic statistics have not yet detected a quantum leap in productivity. Computers have increased productivity in some respects, these analysts say, but may actually reduce it in others. "Don't forget that rapid turnover of hardware and software keeps us perpetually in the learning mode, that people spend countless hours mindlessly exploring the Internet and playing amusing computer games, and that most of us suffer more from information overload than from information shortage," says Alan Blinder, a Princeton University economist and former vice-chairman of the Federal Reserve Board. "A productivity miracle based on the computer may be just around the corner. . . . But, if so, it is around the next corner, not the last one." [20]

The bottom line is that the new paradigm remains unproven — a situation that Greenspan says justifies the central bank's reluctance to relax its vigilance concerning inflation. "Is it possible that there is something fundamentally new about this current period?" he asks. "Yes, it is possible. Markets may have become more efficient, competition is more global, and information technology has doubtless enhanced the stability of business operations. But regrettably, history is strewn with visions of such 'new eras' that, in the end, have proven to be a mirage. In short, history counsels caution." [21] ■

CURRENT SITUATION

Japan's Bubble Bursts

While the United States ponders whether inflation is still a threat, Asia appears to be near — if not already into — a period of destructive deflation. Different countries in the region are suffering many of the ailments commonly associated with deflation — plunging asset prices, bankruptcies, badly damaged financial systems, chary consumers and stagnant or declining economies. Nobody yet knows how far the region may fall.

Just as the stock market crash of 1929 is often considered the opening event of the Depression, Asia's deflation of the 1990s began when Japan's so-called bubble economy burst in 1990-91, sending greatly overvalued real estate and stock markets plummeting. According to many economists, the decline was a classic bust following a speculative boom.

Between 1988 and 1990, Japanese land and stock prices had more than doubled in what Geoffrey P. Miller, director of the Center for the Study of Central Banks at New York University Law School, describes as "possibly the largest speculative event in the history of the world." Miller blames the speculative surge in part on an easy-money policy pursued in the late 1980s by the Bank of Japan. Japan had come under intense pressure from the U.S. to allow more American imports into its market. In response, the Japanese central bank slashed interest rates in 1986 and 1987, and then held them low through 1989 in an effort to stimulate domestic demand for imports. [22]

The resulting surge in credit sent the Japanese stock and real estate markets soaring, pushing prices well above what most analysts considered the true value of the assets. The bubble soon became self-inflating: Rising real estate prices increased the value of collateral held for loans, thus encouraging even more lending; much of the new credit helped finance purchases of stock, driving up the Japanese stock market; then, high-priced securities were used as collateral to buy more property.

By the beginning of 1989, Miller says, Japanese "share markets" accounted for more than 42 percent of the value of all markets worldwide, up from 15 percent in 1980. A year later, the Bank of Japan finally concluded the situation had gotten out of hand. It started tightening the monetary reins. Rising interest rates choked off the credit binge, and the house of cards fell. Real estate and stock prices plunged. Banks staggered under a crushing load of bad debt — a problem that persists to this day.

In January, the Japanese Finance Ministry reported that bad or questionable loans still exceed $575 billion, an amount equal to about 16 percent of Japan's gross domestic product. By comparison, the U.S. savings and loan debacle of the 1980s cost the U.S. government about $150 billion to clean up. [23]

Asset deflation has seriously damaged the Japanese economy. Bank lending has contracted. Tokyo and other cities are littered with half-finished or abandoned office buildings and hotels. New investment has dropped sharply, as many companies are burdened with inventories they can't unload. Even though interest rates have dropped about as far as they can go — the Bank of Japan's official rate is just 0.5 percent — the economy hasn't been able to muster more than 1 percent growth in any year since 1992.

Interest rates at rock bottom are one of the classic symptoms of deflation. So is moribund consumer demand; in a serious deflation, consumers stop buying, either because they have lost confidence or because they see prices falling and decide to hold off purchases in hope that prices will fall further still. In the case of Japan, however, the lack of consumer demand may reflect an even more fundamental flaw in the country's economy: Archaic laws and byzantine regulations prevent the emergence of a vibrant consumer sector.

For instance, if a Japanese bank wants to open a branch, it must obtain permission from the Ministry of Finance in Tokyo. The Ministry of Health requires 21 separate approvals if a store wishes to sell meat, fish, milk, bread or frozen foods. Regulations sought and vigorously promoted by small-retailer associations make it extremely difficult to open a large store; prospective investors must file as many as 75 applications relating to 26 different government permits to open a large, multipurpose store. [24]

Many economists in the West believe this system artificially suppresses consumption. "Japan has a world-class manufacturing sector tied to a Third World service sector," says Wyss of Standard & Poor's DRI. "Its service sector is not generating demand for manufactured goods."

Unable or unwilling to consume at a rate that matches its productive capacity, Japan has invested much of its enormous cash surplus overseas. That has produced income that helps cushion the country from the most harmful effects of deflation; unlike some of its East Asian neighbors, Japan appears unlikely for the foreseeable future to go bankrupt and require emergency financial assistance from the International Monetary Fund. But Japanese investment has contributed to deflationary pressures elsewhere, as some of the country's Asian neighbors have learned.

The Asia Crisis

The financial crisis that gripped Thailand, Indonesia and South Korea in 1997 began, ironically, with the remarkable success that those countries and their neighbors achieved in attracting foreign investment. In the early 1990s, investment prospects in the advanced economies dimmed considerably in the wake of deflation in Japan and disappointing economic growth in Europe. Looking for better returns, international investors became enthralled with East Asian nations, whose economies were growing at an astounding 9 percent annual rate after adjusting for inflation. Such growth not only was well above the rate experienced in advanced economies, it probably was higher than ever experienced before by economies of comparable size, according to the International Monetary Fund. [25]

The World Bank estimates that net capital flows into the Asia Pacific region exploded from just $25 billion in 1990 to $110 billion by 1996. In retrospect, analysts say, that was more than the countries could handle. [26]

"Financial markets were swamped," Robert Hormats, vice chairman of the investment banking and securities firm Goldman Sachs, told the House Banking Committee in November. "Pressures to lend to politically favored projects (particularly commercial real estate) that had little economic justification, lax credit standards, weak supervisory regimes and in some cases inadequate bank capital were among the problems."

Compounding the trouble, many Asian banks sought to take advantage of relatively low U.S. interest rates by borrowing dollars on international financial markets and then lending in their local currencies. That strategy paid off for a while, as the interest-rate differential favored Asian banks. But the dollar began rising in value against Asian currencies in mid-1995, making it harder for the Asian banks to repay their loans.

Some economists trace the rise in the dollar to actions by the Federal Reserve. The Fed, concerned that inflation would soon hit the U.S., had tightened monetary policy in November 1994 and February 1995. Other analysts say the dollar started rising because international investors, impressed with the U.S. economy and concerned about economic stagnation in Europe and Asia, were flocking to the dollar.

Reuters

An investment boom in Thailand in the early 1990s led to many construction projects that were not economically viable.

Whatever the cause, the effect was to weaken Asian banks. But the rising value of the dollar hurt the East Asian economies in other ways as well. Most had long maintained a fixed relationship between the value of their currencies and that of the dollar. When the dollar went up beginning in 1995, they therefore had to increase the value of their own currencies, which required tightening their own monetary policies and increasing domestic interest rates. This made their exports relatively more expensive in global trade.

Falling prices, especially in the glutted global electronics market, reduced their exports further. Soon, the countries were chalking up swelling trade deficits. But the East Asians were hamstrung in dealing with this situation.

Normally, a trade deficit causes a country's currency to decline in value. That reduces the price of its exports, making them more competitive internationally. Eventually, exports rise until they are closer to being in balance with imports. The East Asians, however, resisted letting their currencies depreciate because that would have meant abandoning the link to the dollar, a step that would have shaken investors' confidence. But they also were reluctant to defend the currencies because that would have required them to tighten monetary policy and raise interest rates, which would further weaken their already troubled financial institutions.

While the East Asians struggled with this quandary, international investors became alarmed that large trade deficits eventually would force them to let their currencies fall. By mid-1997, investors were heading for the exits. Suddenly, borrowers in Thailand, Indonesia and South Korea could not roll over their international loans, and widespread bankruptcy became a serious threat.

Deflation had turned to panic. By December, Sherry Cooper, chief economist for Nesbitt Burns, a Canadian investment firm, said glumly: "One-third of the global economy is near paralysis." ■

OUTLOOK

Global Uncertainty

Asian economies are expected to slow sharply in 1998, and the problems in that region will reverberate around the world. But forecasters predict the impact beyond the South Pacific will be manageable if the rescue effort led by the International Monetary Fund succeeds in restoring investor confidence so that capital starts flowing back into the troubled region soon.

The longer-term outlook, however, may depend on a number of as-yet-unknown variables — in particular, whether the United States and other advanced countries take steps to strengthen the world's financial system.

As recently as May 1997, the IMF was projecting that most Asian economies would expand at a healthy rate. But just seven months later, the outlook seemed considerably less rosy. The table below, which compares the IMF's May 1997 and December 1997 forecasts for growth in real gross domestic product for countries at the center of the Asian maelstrom, shows how prospects for 1998 have dimmed: [27]

	May Forecast	December Forecast
Thailand	7.0%	0.0%
Indonesia	7.5	2.0
Malaysia	7.9	2.5
Philippines	6.4	3.8
Japan	2.9	1.1
South Korea	6.3	2.5

For the world economy as a whole, the IMF said, growth will slow in 1998 to about 3 percent after adjustment for price changes, compared with 4 percent in 1996 and '97. But the U.S. economy will be affected only slightly; the IMF projected in December that this country's GDP will rise 2.4 percent, just 0.2 percentage point less than previously projected.

While the Asian slowdown will reduce demand for U.S. exports to that region, the overall impact on the United States is expected to be modest because exports represent only 10 percent of total U.S. GDP, and only about one-third of American exports go to Asia. Moreover, some of the harm to the U.S. economy will be offset by the stimulative effect of lower interest rates. Given concerns in the U.S. about the threat of inflation, many analysts believe a modest slowdown such as the IMF projected would actually be beneficial. [28]

The situation could turn out worse, however. The IMF assumed in its forecast that the net flow of capital into Asia will drop by two-thirds, or $67 billion, in 1998. For all developing countries, the decline could be about $78 billion. But if Asian governments fail to convince investors that they have made substantial reforms, new foreign investment could fall by as much as $100 billion, according to the IMF. [29]

Moreover, Japan remains a major question mark. U.S. officials generally have been disappointed in the Tokyo government's response to its own deflationary difficulties. Prime Minister Ryutaro Hashimoto took what they considered a step in the right direction on Jan. 12 by proposing a $227 billion financial-stabilization plan to clean up the nation's banking problems, along with a $15 billion income-tax cut. That marked a significant departure for the Japanese government.

The Hashimoto administration previously had played down the nation's continuing banking difficulties. And as recently as April 1997, it actually had increased taxes, boosting the nation's sales tax to 5 percent from 3 percent and letting some $17 billion in income-tax breaks expire. Japanese officials have resisted tax cuts because the government's budget deficit already is equal to about 3 percent of GDP, and the country faces mounting fiscal demands because the Japanese population is aging.

Despite the change of direction, some Western analysts questioned whether Hashimoto's proposals will be enough to turn the country's economy around. They noted that the Tokyo government remains reluctant to shut down failed banks, and some suggested the tax cut would be too small to spark strong growth.

China, meanwhile, remains perhaps the biggest wild card in the Asia crisis. By all appearances, it has escaped the turmoil affecting its neighbors. But analysts say its financial system may be just as shaky as theirs. Chinese banks have extended tens of billions of dollars in loans to state-owned enterprises that are given little chance of being able to make good on the credit any time soon.

"If China's citizens ever grow concerned about the stability of its banks and decided to save in shoe boxes under the bed instead of in state-sanctioned banks, China would face a full-fledged banking disaster," warns Greg Mastel, vice president of public relations for the Economic Strategy Institute in Washington. [30]

Such lingering dangers undoubtedly helped persuade the Clinton administration to seek congressional backing for plans to bolster the International Monetary Fund. The international organization says Asian rescue efforts have left it short of funds to address future crises. The White House is asking Congress to appropriate about $14.5 billion to cover the U.S. share of an international plan to replenish IMF funds, plus another $3.5 billion as part of a new $25 billion IMF program, the New Arrangements

Chronology

1980s The United States and other advanced, industrial countries push policies that lead to heavy investment and rapid growth throughout Asia.

1985
The major industrial countries agree to drive down the value of the dollar against other major currencies. The Plaza Accord, as it is known, leads to a boom in exports from East Asian countries whose currencies are pegged to the dollar.

1986-1987
Under pressure from the U.S. to buy more American goods, the Bank of Japan cuts interest rates, encouraging a boom in the Japanese real estate and stock markets.

1990-1996 Japan falters, but its East Asian neighbors grow rapidly, as foreign investment more than quadruples in just six years.

1990
Japan's stock and real estate markets plummet, as the Bank of Japan tightens monetary policy to ward off excessive speculation. The Japanese economy becomes mired in bad debt and sluggish growth.

1994
China devalues its currency, the yuan, by about 40 percent, making Chinese goods more competitive but undermining exports from countries whose currencies are tied to the dollar.

1995
The U.S. dollar starts rising in foreign exchange markets, partly as a result of steps by the Federal Reserve to raise U.S. interest rates and partly because investors decide the U.S. may be a better credit risk than countries in Asia.

1997 Financial crisis grips Asia.

January-June
Thailand's exports slacken as the country's currency, the baht, appreciates along with the dollar and as prices fall in the glutted electronic market. Investors, worried that Thais won't be able to repay their debt, start moving out of Thai currency and into the U.S. dollar. The Thai government uses its dollar reserves to buy baht in an effort to maintain its value, drawing them down to a dangerously low point.

July
Thailand abandons its effort to defend the baht, which promptly falls almost 20 percent in value. Shaken investors start converting their funds throughout East Asia to the dollar, putting downward pressure on other regional currencies. They also balk at rolling over loans to Asian borrowers.

August
The International Monetary Fund arranges a $17 billion emergency line of credit to keep Thailand solvent. The country agrees, in turn, to shut down insolvent financial institutions and to tighten monetary policy. On Aug. 28, stock markets plunge all across Asia.

October
The International Monetary Fund orchestrates a $40 billion rescue package for Indonesia, again requiring financial-sector and policy reforms in return. Financial fears spread through Asia and beyond. The Hong Kong stock market loses nearly one-quarter of its value Oct. 23-28. The U.S. stock market plunges 7.2 percent on Oct. 27, although it quickly recovers.

Nov. 1-21
New financial weaknesses surface in Japan. Sanyo Securities, a major stock brokerage, declares bankruptcy on Nov. 3. Hokkaido Takushoku, the country's 10th-largest bank, fails on Nov. 16. Yamaichi, the country's largest securities firm, folds on Nov. 21.

Nov. 24-Dec. 3
Concerns mount about the financial health of South Korea. The country's currency, the won, collapses on Nov. 17, and the IMF announces a $57 billion rescue package on Dec. 3.

Dec. 17
The Japanese government, in a significant policy reversal, announces that it will propose new spending to shore up banks, as well as income tax cuts designed to help pull its economy out of the doldrums.

Dec. 31
Financier George Soros, saying that the Asia crisis is far from over, warns we are "on the verge of global deflation."

Trade Deficits and Free Trade

The last time the United States and the rest of the world encountered serious deflation, during the Depression, Congress enacted the highly protectionist Smoot-Hawley Act. Some people worry that Congress may make a similar mistake today.

Backers of the 1930 law, which increased tariffs on more than 20,000 imports, were trying to shore up failing American industries and prevent unemployment from rising. But European countries quickly retaliated with tariff increases of their own. The result was a sharp contraction in global trade, which analysts generally agreed aggravated the Depression. [1]

A turn toward protectionism today would be very worrisome to countries like Thailand, South Korea, Malaysia and Indonesia, whose hopes of economic recovery hinge in part on their ability to gain badly needed foreign cash by exporting goods to the United States and other advanced economies. But proponents of liberalized trade say the U.S. would be a big loser, too.

As yet, there are few signs of a decisive move toward protectionism in the United States. But that could change if, as expected, America's trade deficit grows as a result of the Asian crisis. American exports to the region are expected to drop this year and next, as the economic slowdown in that region reduces demand for American products. Imports from Asia, meanwhile, will increase as the depreciation of Asian currencies makes goods from the region cheaper here. As a result, says David Hale, chief global economist for Zurich Kemper Investments, the American merchandise trade gap could grow to $250 billion or even $300 billion by 1999, compared with $191.2 billion in 1996.

A larger trade deficit isn't necessarily bad news, Hale insists. With the U.S. economy already operating at a "full-employment" level, the nation does not seem to be suffering in international trade. Instead of hurting the U.S., cheaper imports could act as a potential "inflation safety valve" by reducing prices for goods consumed here, Hale says. But he concedes that many people won't see it that way. "The problem with trade deficits is political," Hale says. "Many Americans perceive the trade deficit to be a source of job losses or slower wage growth, not an inflation brake which permits a stronger and longer expansion." [2]

The biggest test of the U.S. stance on trade this year will come in congressional debates over the Clinton administration's request for "fast-track" trade negotiating authority. Under fast-track, Congress agrees to restrict itself to voting only to accept or reject a negotiated trade agreement within a specified period of time and without amendments. U.S. presidents had such authority for most years from 1974 to 1994, when it was allowed to expire. The administration wants it now to negotiate a free-trade pact with Chile, as well as to advance broader efforts to liberalize trade in the Americas and between the U.S. and East Asian countries.

Proponents say that few countries would negotiate trade pacts with the United States if they knew Congress could amend any agreement after negotiations conclude. "Access to fast-track is a critical element to the success of any negotiating strategy," argued Thomas J. Donohue, president and chief executive of the U.S. Chamber of Commerce. "As anyone in business knows, you do not waste your time making deals with negotiators who are not in a position to commit their principals . . . to an agreement." [3]

Critics of fast-track — most notably the AFL-CIO and such prominent Democrats as House Minority Leader Richard A. Gephardt, D-Mo. — say they do not oppose free trade. But they insist that any trade pact should require other countries to strengthen their labor and environmental laws before letting them compete more directly with the U.S. Otherwise, the critics say, foreign companies will have too great an advantage.

Brookings Institution scholars Robert Z. Lawrence and Robert E. Litan argue in response that free trade hasn't cost Americans any jobs. "Lower trade barriers promote faster growth in the standard of living for Americans," Lawrence and Litan argue. "Broader export markets enable U.S. companies to reap larger returns on their innovations. Lower trade barriers here, meanwhile, enhance competitive pressure on our firms to innovation. In addition, U.S. firms increasingly rely on imported high-tech capital equipment and know-how, which accelerates the growth of productivity and living standards here." [4]

Both sides agree on one point: Fast-track legislation faces tough going in Congress. The Clinton administration had hoped to win the authority last year but yanked it in the face of strong opposition, mainly from House Democrats. A bigger trade deficit arising from the Asian financial crisis won't make the task any easier. [5]

---

[1] Gary H. Stern, "Achieving Economic Stability: Lessons from the Crash of 1929," *Federal Reserve Bank of Minneapolis 1987 Annual Report;* available online at http://woodrow.mpls.frb.fed.us/pubs/ar/ar1987.html.

[2] Testimony before the House Banking and Financial Services Committee, Nov. 4, 1997.

[3] Testimony before the House Ways and Means Committee, Sept. 30, 1997.

[4] Robert Z. Lawrence and Robert E. Litan, "Globaphobia: The Wrong Debate Over Trade Policy," Brookings Institution Policy Brief No. 24 (1997); available online at http://www.brook.edu/ES/POLICY/Polbrf24.htm.

[5] For a compilation of news stories, background reports and position statements on fast-track legislation, see the U.S. Information Agency Web site: http://www.usia.gov/topical/econ/fasttrak/

to Borrow, that would supplement other loan programs.[31]

President Clinton argued in his State of the Union address on Jan. 27 that IMF rescues such as the emergency Asia packages are in America's own self-interest. "First, these countries are our customers," the president said. "If they sink into recession, they won't be able to buy the goods we'd like to sell them. Second, they're also our competitors, so if their currencies lose their value and go down, then the price of their goods will drop, flooding our market and others with much cheaper goods, which makes it a lot tougher for our people to compete. And finally, they are our strategic partners. Their stability bolsters our security."

FOR MORE INFORMATION

American Enterprise Institute, 1150 Seventeenth Street N.W., Washington, D.C. 20036; (202) 862-5800; fax: (202) 862-7177; http://www.aei.org. This conservative-leaning think tank publishes studies on numerous domestic and international issues. Scholars John Makin and Lawrence Lindsey have written a number of articles on the Asian financial crisis and the threat of deflation.

Brookings Institution, 1775 Massachusetts Ave. N.W., Washington, D.C. 20036; (202) 797-6000; fax: (202) 797-6004; e-mail: brookinfo@brook.edu; http://www.brook.edu. This private, nonpartisan research organization has produced numerous studies of domestic and international economics, including a number of discussion papers on Asian countries such as South Korea, Japan and China.

Economic Policy Institute, 1660 L Street N.W., Suite 1200, Washington, D.C. 20036; 1-800-EPI-4844 [in Washington, D.C.: (202) 775-8810]; e-mail: economic@cais.com; http://www.epinet.org. This liberal leaning think-tank offers analysis of a wide range of economic issues, with particular emphasis on matters affecting the distribution of income, social policy, living standards and working conditions.

Institute for International Economics, 11 Dupont Circle N.W., Washington, D.C. 20036-1207; Phone: 202-328-9000; Fax: 202-328-5432; e-mail: bcoulton@iie.com; http://www.iie.com. This private, nonprofit, nonpartisan research institution has been analyzing international economic problems and proposing policy responses to them in speeches, books and working papers since 1981.

Fundamental Reform

No matter how the immediate crisis is resolved, the coming years are almost certain to see considerable discussion about whether the world's financial system needs fundamental reform. Financial institutions are the lifeblood of any economy, but they play an especially important role in a time of deflation, when borrowers can come under severe stress. If financial institutions scrutinize borrowers carefully and lend only to the best credit risks, the chances of serious dislocation can be minimized; but if they lend carelessly to unqualified borrowers, they can damage themselves and thereby magnify deflation.

Many analysts believe financial institutions are the weak link in today's global economy. "During the past 15 years, there has been an epidemic of banking crises in the developing world," notes C. Fred Bergsten, director of the Washington-based Institute for International Economics. Bergsten says that in at least 57 cases during the period, banking systems lost all or almost all of their capital, and that in a dozen cases countries ended up losing 10 percent or more of their gross domestic product. Overall, he says, banking crises in the developing world have cost governments at least $250 billion to clean up.[32]

Morris Goldstein, a colleague of Bergsten, attributes these problems to a litany of financial-system deficiencies familiar to those who have watched the current Asian crisis unfold: excessive government involvement in the banking industry; weak disclosure, accounting and legal frameworks for banking; too much lending to bank owners, managers and their affiliated companies; inadequate bank capital; and official safety nets that protect bank owners and creditors from the consequences of misdeeds that render their institutions insolvent.[33]

While all of these weaknesses should be corrected, reform should begin by requiring far more public disclosure by financial institutions, according to many economists. "The ability of financial markets to work efficiently in channeling resources to their most effective uses stands or falls by the quality of information available to market participants," explained Deputy Treasury Secretary Lawrence H. Summers in testimony to the House Banking and Financial Services Committee in November 1997. "In addition, imprudent or illegal behavior is much less likely where individuals and firms know that their actions will in time be revealed."

While Summers suggested that the international community should encourage individual countries to strengthen their own banking laws, financier George Soros suggests a bigger role for international institutions like the IMF. In December 1997, Soros proposed establishing a new sister institution to the IMF that would guarantee international loans for a "modest fee." This International Credit Insurance Corporation would require countries that seek international credit to provide data on all borrowings from within their borders, public or private. The authority then would set a ceiling on how much it would be willing to insure, thereby preventing runaway investment.

"The private sector is ill-suited to allocate international credit," Soros explained. "It provides either too much or too little. It does not have the information with which to form a balanced judgment. Moreover, it is not concerned with maintaining macroeconomic balance in borrowing countries. Its goals are to maximize profit and minimize risk. This makes it move in a herdlike fashion." [34]

The Soros proposal hasn't attracted many backers, though that could change if deflationary pressures grow or the world experiences more financial crises. In any event, his comments underscore the blend of opportunity and danger that countries face in the evolving global economy. Financial markets can almost instantaneously move capital anywhere in the world. As a result, economic output is rising, new products are coming to market at an unprecedented rate and prices are remarkably restrained. But the gains may not seem worthwhile if institutions, public and private, fail to adjust to a new environment of flat or even declining prices.

"Around the world, we have been witnessing the emergence of a truly global economy, one in which trade, investment, capital, information and know-how can flow ever more freely," Summers told the Banking and Financial Services Committee. But, he cautioned, "being a member of a more integrated world brings risks as well as opportunities." ■

Notes

[1] *The McGraw-Hill Encyclopedia of Economics,* 2nd edition (1994), p. 531.

[2] "The Threat of Deflation," *Business Week,* Nov. 10, 1997, pp. 55-59.

[3] Roger Bootle, *The Death of Inflation* (1997), p. 10.

[4] See Martin Feldstein, "Japan's Folly Drags Asia Down," *The Wall Street Journal,* Nov. 25, 1997.

[5] The figures on Korea's banking situation are from International Monetary Fund, *World Economic Outlook, Interim Assessment,* December 1997, p. 23; figures on bad loans in Japanese banks are from Robert Edelstein and Jean-Michel Paul, "How to Get Japan Back on its Feet," *The Wall Street Journal,* Dec. 11, 1997.

[6] Alan Greenspan, remarks at the annual meeting of the American Economic Association and the American Finance Association, Chicago, Ill., Jan. 3, 1998; available online at http://www.bog.frb.fed.us.

[7] Federal Reserve Board, Federal Open Market Committee minutes, meeting of Sept. 30, 1997; available online at http://www.bog.frb.fed.us.

[8] Federal Reserve Board, Federal Open Market Committee minutes, meeting of Dec. 16, 1997; available online at http://www.bog.frb.fed.us.

[9] James K. Glassman, "Who Needs the IMF?," *The Washington Post,* Dec. 12, 1997.

[10] Laura D'Andrea Tyson, "Leadership in a Crisis," *The Washington Post,* Jan. 22, 1998, p. A21.

[11] Jeffrey D. Sachs, "The Wrong Medicine for Asia," *The New York Times,* Nov. 3, 1997.

[12] Laurence H. Meyer, remarks at the Forecasters Club of New York, April 24, 1997; Alan Greenspan, Monetary Policy Testimony and Report to the Congress, July 22, 1997; available online at http://www.bog.frb.fed.us.

[13] Alan Greenspan, Monetary Policy Testimony and Report to the Congress, Feb. 26, 1997; available online at http://www.bog.frb.fed.us. For background, see "Labor Movement's Future," *The CQ Researcher,* June 28, 1996, pp. 553-576.

[14] For background, see "Contingent Work Force," *The CQ Researcher,* Oct. 24, 1997, pp. 937-960.

[15] From Feb. 26, 1997, remarks, *op. cit.*

[16] For background, see "Patients' Rights," *The CQ Researcher,* Feb. 6, 1998, pp. 97-120.

[17] Paul Krugman, "How Fast Can the Economy Grow?" *Harvard Business Review,* July-August 1997, pp. 123-129.

[18] Alan Greenspan, Monetary Policy Testimony and Report to Congress, July 22, 1997; available online at http://www.bog.frb.fed.us.

[19] *Ibid.*

[20] Alan S. Blinder, "The Speed Limit: Fact and Fancy in the Growth Debate," *The American Prospect,* No. 34, September-October 1997, pp. 57-62.

[21] Alan Greenspan, Monetary Policy Testimony and Report to the Congress, Feb. 26, 1997; available online at http://www.bog.frb.fed.us.

[22] Geoffrey P. Miller, "The Role of a Central Bank in a Bubble Economy," to be published in the *Journal of Legal Studies* in June 1998; available online at http://www.gold-eagle.com/editorials/cscb002f.html.

[23] The estimates of problem loans in Japanese banks come from Bloomberg News and were quoted in Sandra Sugawara, "Japan's Lawmakers Get Stabilization, Tax Cut Proposals," *The Washington Post,* Jan. 13, 1998, p. D1. The estimates of the cost of the U.S. savings and loan bailout were cited in Frederick S. Mishkin, *The Economics of Money, Banking and Financial Markets,* Fifth Edition (1998), p. 318.

[24] Lucien Elington, "Government Regulation, Productivity, and Trade Tensions: Are 'Lifetime Employment' and Seniority Endangered?" May 1995; available online at http://www.indiana.edu/~japan/digest8.html.

[25] International Monetary Fund, *op. cit.,* p. 3. Much of the analysis in the section concerning the Asian financial crisis is based on this report.

[26] Figures on investment flows in Asia quoted by Alan Greenspan, remarks to the Economic Club of New York, Dec. 2, 1997; available online at http://www.bog.frb.fed.us).

[27] International Monetary Fund, *op. cit.,* p. 53.

[28] See Alan Greenspan, testimony before the Senate Budget Committee, Jan. 29, 1998; available online at http://www.bog.frb.fed.us.

[29] International Monetary Fund, *op. cit.,* pp. 54, 59.

[30] Greg Mastel, "A China the World Could Bank On," *The Washington Post,* Dec. 29, 1997, p. A17. For background, see "China After Deng," *The CQ Researcher,* June 13, 1997, pp. 505-528.

[31] See *CQ Weekly Report,* Jan. 10, 1998, pp. 64-65, and Jan. 31, 1998, pp. 232-235.

[32] C. Fred Bergsten in Morris Goldstein, ed., *The Case for an International Banking Standard* (1997), p. vii.

[33] *Ibid.*

[34] George Soros, "Avoiding a Breakdown," *Financial Times,* Dec. 31, 1997.

Bibliography

Selected Sources Used

Books and Reports

Bootle, Roger, *The Death of Inflation: Surviving and Thriving in the Zero Era*, Nicholas Brealey Publishing, 1997.

Bootle, a former lecturer at Oxford and well-known British commentator on economics, argues that the inflation-ridden era of the last 40 years was an aberration, but one so imprinted in our minds that economists and policy-makers alike can't see that fundamental changes in the global economy are making deflation a much greater threat today than inflation.

International Monetary Fund, *World Economic Outlook, Interim Assessment*, December 1997.

This report chronicles how Asia's powerhouse economies got into trouble, examines the implications of the crisis for other countries and explains the reasoning behind IMF loan packages to the region. The report, along with much more information on global economic conditions, can be obtained from the International Monetary Fund, Washington, D.C. 20431; 202-623-7300; fax: 202-623-6278; Web site: http://www.imf.org.

Mishkin, Frederic S., *The Economics of Money, Banking and Financial Markets* (Fifth Edition), Addison-Wesley, 1998.

This popular textbook by a former Federal Reserve economist provides a wealth of information on practically every important event in recent financial history. Mishkin, who is a professor of economics at Columbia University's Graduate School of Business, presents a detailed theory for why banking crises will continue to occur unless reforms are made to improve the flow of information to all participants in the financial system.

Articles

Blinder, Alan S., "The Speed Limit: Fact and Fancy in the Growth Debate," *The American Prospect*, No. 34, September-October 1997, pp. 57-62. Available online at http://epn.org/prospect/34/34blinfs.html.

Blinder, a Princeton economist, former vice chairman of the Federal Reserve Board and member of President Clinton's original Council of Economic Advisers, forcefully disputes the "new paradigm" theories that the economy now can grow much faster than previously believed without rekindling inflation. "Much as we might wish otherwise, it just ain't so," he says, offering a strong defense of the Federal Reserve's stance on monetary policy.

Mandel, Michael, Pete Engardio, Emily Thornton and Christopher Farrell, "The Threat of Deflation," *Business Week*, Nov. 10, 1997, pp. 55-59.

Much of the current debate about deflation began after *Business Week* published this article. Arguing that the world's capacity to produce goods far exceeds demand, the magazine suggests that the world has become "dangerously dependent on the U.S. as the consumer of last resort." If the U.S. economy falters, it concludes, "the world could end up with all sellers and no buyers — and on a path that leads to a devastating deflation."

Shephard, Stephen B., "The New Economy: What it Really Means," *Business Week*, Nov. 17, 1997, pp. 38-49.

In this commentary, *Business Week's* editor-in-chief lays out the case that global economic integration and the revolution in information technology are combining to "raise Americans' standard of living, create jobs, spur entrepreneurial effort — and do all this without boosting inflation."

"Will the World Slump?" *The Economist*, Nov. 15, 1997, pp. 15-16.

While acknowledging that Asia's "acute financial fragility" poses a serious threat to the global economy, *The Economist* says any problems associated with excess production capacity could be overcome by easing monetary policy. "Deflation, when it happens, exposes not the flaw in capitalism but the incompetence of central banks and governments," the magazine concludes.

On-Line Resources

Cents Financial Journal, Electronic Publishing Company, http://lp-llc.com/cents.

Until recently, a layman trying to fathom economic trends had few options between sifting through the mountain of raw statistics ground out by the government and reading journalistic analyses that often are incomplete. Now there's a useful alternative in cyberspace. The Electronic Publishing Company in California compiles analyses of current trends by leading economists and strategists.

Dr. Ed Yardeni's Economics Network, http://www.yardeni.com.

The prolific chief economist for Deutsche Morgan Grenfell maintains this comprehensive Web site full of data, analysis and arguments supporting the thesis that the global economy has entered an inflation-free "new era."

Federal Reserve Board, http://www.bog.frb.fed.us.

Sometimes criticized as an aloof and unresponsive institution, the nation's central bank provides a wealth of information about its operations and the ideas that lie behind its conduct of monetary policy. Particularly noteworthy are its twice-annual monetary-policy reports to Congress and the minutes of its policy-making arm, the Federal Open Market Committee. Federal Reserve Chairman Alan Greenspan's speeches and congressional testimony also offer insights into the workings of the economy.

9 Energy Policy

MARY H. COOPER

Rolling blackouts in California, skyrocketing utility bills and the prospect that gasoline may top the $2 mark again this summer are a few of the signs that the United States faces troubled times on the energy front.

AP Photo/*San Francisco Examiner*, Pico Van

Tina Kharsa uses a flashlight to search for people, after two elderly people trapped in an elevator were rescued by San Francisco firefighters during a rolling blackout in January 2001 in San Francisco.

To boost energy supplies, President Bush unveiled a new energy plan on May 17 that promotes opening public lands to new oil and natural gas drilling and relying more heavily on coal and nuclear power to generate electricity. The plan also stresses the need for new refineries, generating plants, pipelines and transmission lines to speed delivery to customers. (*See box, p. 143.*) "If we fail to act, Americans will face more and more widespread blackouts," Bush said. "America cannot allow that to be our future, and we will not."

Indeed, Energy Secretary Spencer Abraham has said, "America faces a major energy-supply crisis over the next two decades. The failure to meet this challenge will threaten our nation's economic prosperity, compromise our national security and literally alter the way we live our lives." [1]

The last time public figures routinely invoked the term "crisis" to describe the nation's energy situation was during the late 1970s, after Arab oil producers, angered by U.S. support of Israel, embargoed oil exports to the United States. As supplies dried up, prices skyrocketed, gasoline was rationed and drivers sat in long lines at the pump. Then-President Jimmy Carter told Americans that the days of cheap and abundant energy were over and introduced a series of energy conservation and efficiency measures to reduce demand.

From *The CQ Researcher*, May 25, 2001.

But many experts say today's energy problems are not as serious as they were three decades ago — or as the Bush administration implies. "We have an energy problem, but I think the rhetoric is a little bit overblown," says Paul R. Portney, president of Resources for the Future, a nonpartisan research group. "There are some reasons why the country needs to pay pretty close attention to energy issues. We're very short on refining capacity, and there's an inability to move electricity from those parts of the country where it is abundant to those parts where it's scarce. But I don't think we have a crisis here."

In fact, although the United States is even more dependent on foreign sources of oil now than it was three decades ago, there is no immediate lack of crude oil. The current energy shortage is largely the result of extremely low energy prices in the late 1990s, which discouraged oil and gas companies from building new refineries and pipelines to process and deliver their products. Meanwhile, demand was skyrocketing in the United States, where a robust economy and a growing population boosted energy consumption.

By this past winter, natural gas suppliers couldn't keep up with demand for home heating fuel, sparking in some cases a doubling or tripling of utility bills in the Midwest and Northeast. Oil refineries also found it hard to keep up with growing demand, so gasoline prices at the pump began to creep up.

California's electricity shortage stems largely from a flawed utility-deregulation plan passed in 1996, which unfettered wholesale prices but capped what utilities could charge retail customers. When demand for electricity began to outpace supply last fall and early this year, suppliers raised their prices, and utilities — unable to pass those costs on to consumers — began imposing a series of rolling, or staggered, blackouts that are only expected to get worse as warmer weather triggers air-conditioner use.

In formulating a response to the nation's energy problems, President Bush and Vice President Dick Cheney — both former oil company executives — are focusing more heavily on increasing supply than on reducing demand. Focusing on the supply side of the energy equation finds enthusiastic support among fossil-fuel producers. "We are essentially maxed out at our refineries, [and] have to rely on net imports to meet customer demand," says Red Cavaney, president of the American Petroleum Institute, the oil industry's chief lobbying arm. "If Congress and the administration don't address some of these outstanding conditions, we will, in short order, certainly have a crisis."

Supporters of supply-side energy policy suggest that growth in energy demand is inevitable if Americans are going to maintain and improve their

Americans Favor Investing in New Energy Sources

Americans say investing in new energy sources, such as solar, wind and fuel cells, is the best way to deal with the country's energy problems. They also showed strong support for more energy efficiency. But a majority opposed oil drilling in Alaska's Arctic National Wildlife Refuge.

Which of the following ways to deal with the energy situation do you generally favor or oppose?

	Support	Oppose
Invest in new sources of energy	91%	6%
Mandate more energy-efficient appliances	87	12
Mandate more energy-efficient new buildings	86	12
Mandate more energy-efficient cars	85	14
Invest in new power-generating plants	83	13
Foster a government partnership with auto industry to produce more energy-efficient cars	76	22
Invest in more electrical transmission lines	69	23
Invest in more natural gas pipelines	64	29
Drill for natural gas on federal lands	63	33
Increase use of nuclear power to generate electricity	48	44
Explore for oil in Arctic National Wildlife Refuge	38	57

Source: Gallup Organization, based on national telephone poll of 1,005 adults 18 and over, May 5-7, 2001

standard of living. "Over the last decade we adopted a 'negawatt' philosophy — we thought we could diet ourselves into abundance," says Fred Smith, president of the Competitive Enterprise Institute, which advocates free enterprise and limited government. "Now we're beginning to suffer from energy anorexia."

Days after taking office in January, Bush asked former oil industry executive Cheney to chair a task force to formulate a new national energy policy. The panel did not hold public hearings, but instead met privately with leaders of the petroleum industry and several Cabinet members with ties to the oil industry. The final report called for shifting the focus of national energy policy to increasing production of fossil fuels.

Reducing demand — a key focus of U.S. policy since the 1970s — plays a far smaller role in Bush's proposals. The new policy calls for tax breaks to encourage purchases of "hybrid" cars that use less fuel because they run on a combination of gasoline and electricity.

Underlining the shift away from conservation, Cheney recently said, "Conservation may be a sign of personal virtue, but it is not a sufficient basis for a sound, comprehensive energy policy." [2] Citing Energy Department projections that the United States would need at least 1,300 new power plants over the next 20 years, Cheney said, "As a country, we have demanded more and more energy. But we have not brought online the supplies needed to meet that demand."

Even before the task force made its recommendations, the broad outlines of Bush's energy policy were made clear in his budget request for fiscal 2002, which begins Oct. 1. If Congress approves the president's budget, federal spending on most energy-conservation programs would plummet. Although research on technologies to reduce harmful coal emissions would receive more funding, programs encouraging conservation and energy efficiency would lose significant funding, as would research into emerging technologies to produce energy from non-polluting, renewable sources, such as wind, solar and geothermal.

Supporters of renewable energy say the cuts would come at a time when promising new technologies are on the verge of becoming economically viable alternatives to fossil fuels. "The worldwide markets for wind and photovoltaics have grown substantially over the last year," says Bobi A. Garrett, associate director for planning and technology management at the National Renewable Energy Laboratory in Golden, Colo. Photovoltaic cells harness solar energy by converting light into electricity.

Cutting funds for research in renewables also may hurt the prospects of the United States becoming more independent from imported energy and from having to import the technology to develop our own renewable-energy resources, says Garrett. Already, Japan has pulled ahead of the United States in production of photovoltaic technology, and Denmark and Germany are leaders in the production of wind generators, a field once dominated by the United States.

"I'd hate to see us [become] dependent on foreign sources of technology to tap our own indigenous resources," Garrett says. "There is no one energy source that will be the answer. They all are going to be part of our portfolio, but they all need sustained commitment to bring them forward."

Critics also say Bush's focus on increasing energy supplies comes at the expense of the environment. "Everyone needs to recognize that energy and environmental policy are two sides of the same coin," wrote Bill Richardson, Energy secretary from 1998 to 2001. "We need to emphasize supply and demand in equal measure. This balance will be the true recipe for success." [3]

As Congress takes up Bush's new energy plan, these are some of the issues lawmakers will consider:

Rising Demand for Electricity

The amount of electricity used in the United States more than doubled from 1970 to 1999, largely due to industrial and retail expansion, construction of larger houses and the rising use of computers. By 2020 usage will have tripled, according to Energy Department projections.

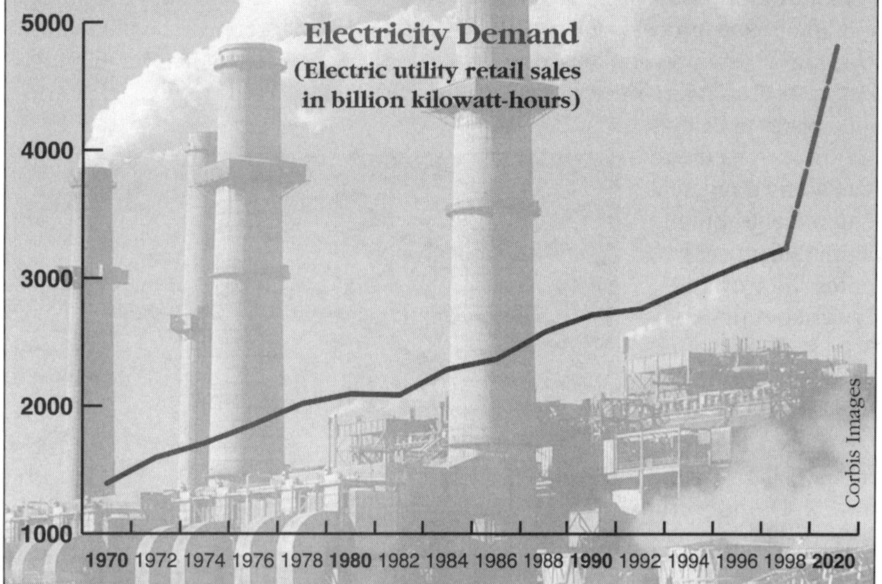

Source: Energy Information Administration Annual Energy Review, 1999

Is the federal government doing enough to relieve California's electricity shortage?

In 1996, California became one of the first states to dismantle decades-old regulations governing the electric utility industry. [4] A new law freed suppliers — mainly coal- and natural gas-burning power plants both inside and outside of the state — to charge California utilities whatever the market would bear for their electricity. To protect consumers, however, the law capped the prices utilities could charge their customers.

But deregulation arrived at the same time that the booming state economy and a growing population were increasing demand for electricity. While providers demanded increasingly high prices for electricity, utilities were barred from passing those costs on to consumers.

California's biggest utilities — Pacific Gas & Electric (PG&E) and Southern California Edison — went into debt, forcing the state government to buy electricity on the high-priced spot market to prevent widespread blackouts. By May 7, the General Assembly — in what would be the biggest municipal bond sale in U.S. history — was forced to adopt a plan to sell $13.4 billion in bonds to pay for the state's electricity needs.

"The California law is very flawed," says Howard Gruenspecht, a senior researcher at Resources for the Future and former Department of Energy official. "Unlike any other [deregulation] laws, it guaranteed a relatively modest price to the end user, which didn't allow the utilities to enter into long-term contracts for power."

In addition, California's lengthy building-permit process delayed construction of new power plants, even in the face of escalating demand. "You can build plants in California that meet the state's environmental requirements, but the permitting process requires a lot of time," Gruenspecht says. "That's another difference between California and other states."

To keep the lights on in California, the state's Democratic governor, Gray Davis, announced price hikes, designed to curb demand by 10 percent, and agreed to buy Southern California Edison's transmission-line network to help keep the troubled company afloat. PG&E, meanwhile, abandoned negotiations with the state and declared bankruptcy under Chapter 11.

But Davis, along with many consumer advocates and California lawmakers, says the electricity shortage is so serious, and likely to worsen in coming months, that the federal government should intervene. On May 22, the state's Democratic leaders and the City of Oakland filed suit in federal appeals court, seeking to force the Federal Energy Regulatory Commission (FERC) to exercise its responsibility to ensure "just and reasonable" electricity rates by capping wholesale prices. The state has repeatedly complained that out-of-state electricity providers overcharge utilities during power shortages.

FERC, with administration support, has refrained from aggressively intervening in what it considers a local problem best left to market forces to sort out. "Market prices are sending the right signals to both sellers and buyers," said FERC Chairman Curt L. Hébert Jr. "Market prices will increase supply, promote delivery, enhance infrastructure and reduce demand, thus correcting the current imbalance."[5]

Corbis Images

President Bush has proposed cutting funding for research into wind generators and other technologies that produce energy from non-polluting, renewable sources.

The agency has declined to investigate most allegations of price gouging by electricity wholesalers, except for a few charges related to periods when the state's electricity supplies were dangerously low. FERC's investigations quickly prompted one of California's leading electricity suppliers, Williams Co. of Tulsa, Okla., to refund $8 million to the state.[6]

Conservatives oppose additional price caps, pointing out that limiting retail prices got California into its current predicament. "The so-called price gouging was nothing more than an artifact of the price caps," says Smith of the Competitive Enterprise Institute. "Whatever may or may not have happened in the prices charged, California [made] it almost impossible for Californians to get a good deal on electricity purchases."

Smith says charges of price gouging will only make the situation worse. "California now has proven that selling electricity to Californians is dangerous," he says. "Countries that go around shooting their farmers find themselves going hungry, and if you're shooting electricity producers by criminalizing their behavior, then you're in real trouble."

But the signal that power suppliers are receiving from FERC may not be the same one the agency is trying to send. If California consumers get no relief from rolling blackouts, popular support for a state ballot initiative to reregulate the state's utility industry may escalate, further discouraging power producers from building new capacity.

"People who are considering building a power plant are not really looking at what prices are today, they're looking at what prices will be when their power plant gets built," says Gruenspecht. "If FERC's actions today are raising the specter of a state takeover via ballot initiative, that signal is not going to make people want to build power plants." Thus, FERC's actions may actually be counterproductive, he adds. "That's the challenge that FERC faces."

As summer approaches, electricity shortages are only likely to become more frequent. On May 7, high temperatures and temporary power-plant closures forced the state's energy

The President's Energy Plan

The national energy plan unveiled by President Bush on May 17 proposes 105 initiatives ranging from relaxing regulations on oil and gas exploration to providing $4 billion in tax credits for a new generation of fuel-efficient cars. The sweeping plan adopts most of the proposals recommended by an energy task force chaired by Vice President Dick Cheney. The major recommendations include:

Oil and Natural Gas

- Opening 2,000 acres of the Arctic National Wildlife Refuge (ANWR) and other federal lands in the Rocky Mountains to drilling for new oil and gas deposits;
- Changing the tax code to provide incentives for new production;
- Reviewing laws and regulations limiting offshore exploration and drilling;
- Considering allowing polluted urban areas to share supplies of reformulated gasoline at times of shortage;
- Easing regulations and simplifying permitting procedures to encourage construction of new oil refineries and natural gas pipelines;
- Building a new pipeline to deliver natural gas from Alaska to the Lower 48 states;
- Increasing the amount of oil stored in the Strategic Petroleum Reserve;
- Reviewing current sanctions that penalize oil companies that deal with Iran, Iraq and Libya, all major oil producers;

Coal

- Spending $2 billion on research into new "clean-coal" technologies aimed at reducing emissions from coal-fired power plants;
- Reviewing clean-air regulations limiting emissions from coal-fired plants;
- Allowing coal-fired plants to engage in emissions trading: enabling plants that exceed allowable limits on emissions of sulfur dioxide, nitrogen oxides and mercury to lawfully keep running by buying pollution credits from cleaner plants;

Electricity

- Building at least 1,300 new power plants in the next 20 years — about one a week — and modernizing others;
- Empowering the Federal Energy Regulatory Commission (FERC) to clear the way for new electricity transmission lines by extending the agency's existing power of "eminent domain" — which currently allows it to seize private land only for natural gas pipelines;
- Easing regulations to facilitate the transfer of electricity from out-of-state generators to California;
- Studying the feasibility of nationalizing the electricity grid to remove bottlenecks;

Nuclear Power

- Streamlining power-plant licensing and relicensing procedures;
- Offering tax credits to encourage nuclear power;
- Providing a "deep geologic repository" for storing nuclear waste;
- Developing technologies for reprocessing spent fuel;

Hydropower

- Streamlining relicensing procedures for hydroelectric plants;

Renewable Energy and Coservation

- Using royalties from drilling in ANWR to fund research of alternative fuels;
- Considering changes in the Corporate Average Fuel Economy (CAFE) standards, pending completion of a National Academy of Sciences study in July;
- Increasing funding for research into biofuels, made from crop waste;
- Providing tax incentives to promote energy conservation and efficiency programs, as well as renewable energy sources like wind and solar power;
- Providing new tax credits for purchasing "hybrid" cars that run on a combination of gasoline and electricity.

managers to resume rolling blackouts for the first time since late March. But judging from the Bush administration's energy proposals and the actions it has taken to date, California cannot hope for aggressive action from Washington to solve its electricity shortage.

The president in early May ordered federal employees to conserve at least 10 percent of their energy use in California. Beyond that, the administration has made it clear that California is on its own.

"They haven't built any electric power plants in the last 10 years," Cheney complained. "And today they've got rolling blackouts because they don't have enough electricity; they've got rising prices; they've got a whole complex of problems caused by relying only on conservation and not doing anything about the supply side of the equation." [7]

Should environmental regulations be relaxed to ensure adequate energy supplies?

Energy production and consumption are leading sources of environmental degradation, and environmental policy since the 1970s has focused largely on curtailing energy-related pollution.[8] To reduce the smog, tainted water and other harmful effects of energy use, laws and regulations have mandated cleaner-burning gasoline, scrubbers on coal-fired power plants, stricter fuel-efficiency standards for automobiles and offshore drilling bans.

Conservatives have long blamed environmental regulations for hindering economic progress. Now they are blaming the nation's energy woes on the Clinton administration's emphasis on environmental protection over energy production. "The energy issue is not only about a clean environment, it's about cleaning up the messes and mistakes created by an administration that failed for eight long years to provide this country with a coherent energy policy," said House Republican Conference Chairman. J.C. Watts Jr., R-Okla. "Now this country is waking up to the nightmare of a full-blown energy crisis, complete with blackouts and high gas prices." [9]

AP Photo/Michael Conroy

The sport utility vehicle (SUV) has become the symbol of American consumers' energy extravagance, even in the face of rising gasoline prices. About 20 percent of all new cars purchased in America today are SUVs, despite gasoline prices that this month reached their highest recorded level ever.

Reversal or relaxation of numerous environmental-protection measures is a key component of Bush's energy-policy goals. Most of these regulations are aimed at curtailing air, ground and water pollution caused by the extraction and use of fossil fuels — oil, coal and natural gas — which the administration has identified as essential ingredients of the country's energy mix.

Shortly after taking office, Bush abandoned a campaign promise to mandate reductions in power-plant emissions of carbon dioxide and renounced the Kyoto Protocol, an international treaty aimed at reducing pollutant emissions that contribute to global warming. [10] In addition, the president wants to open many protected public lands to oil and gas exploration, including federal lands in the Rocky Mountains and the Arctic National Wildlife Refuge (ANWR), as well as certain offshore areas currently closed to drilling. He also has rolled back several Clinton administration environmental regulations, including a rule requiring more efficient air-conditioners. [11]

Bush allowed for certain exceptions to another Clinton regulation — a ban on road-building in 58 million acres of national forests, which would essentially prevent oil and gas drilling companies as well as mining and timber interests from exploiting those lands. Bush also has called for greater reliance on coal — the country's most abundant fossil fuel and the leading source of electrical power, but also the main source of acid rain and much of the air pollution in the Northeast.

Not surprisingly, the fossil fuel industries support the administration's outspoken endorsement of their products and say environmental regulations are partly to blame for the fact that the United States today must import 57 percent of its oil. "A major obstacle has been the inability to have access to federal government lands, where the prime resource reserves are located," says Cavaney of the American Petroleum Institute. "That's true of both crude oil and natural gas."

The difficulty of obtaining drilling permits is another significant problem, he says. "It's a combination of both areas that are off-limits, either through moratoria or through executive orders, plus the difficulty of obtaining permits," he says. "Those delays have the effect of significantly increasing the cost."

Obtaining permits to build new power plants is another difficulty, and Cheney's task force recommended relaxing regulations governing that process, citing Energy Department forecasts suggesting that 1,300 new plants will be needed to satisfy growing consumer demand by 2020.

Bush's early moves on energy and the environment have raised concern beyond the environmental-protection community. "In order to solve the challenge of climate change, we must develop new domestic sources, such as coal, using clean-coal technologies, while also engaging in bold initiatives to develop new technologies in the area of energy conservation, energy efficiency and renewable energy," said Sen. Robert C. Byrd, D-W.Va., who represents the nation's leading coal-producing state. "I am concerned, based on preliminary reports, that the administration's plan may not reflect such a balanced and far-sighted perspective." [12]

Even before the administration released its new policy recommendations, congressional Democrats released an alternative energy proposal on May 15. It calls for more support for conservation, the release of crude oil from the Strategic Petroleum Reserve to alleviate supply shortages and the imposition of price caps on wholesale electricity prices in California to prevent price gouging by power providers.

In apparent anticipation of a backlash by Democrats and environmental advocates against its endorsement of fossil fuels, the administration has toned down its rhetoric calling for immediate drilling in the ANWR. The Bush plan also made a bow toward the use of less-polluting fuels and measures to reduce energy-related pollution. For example, the report recommended new tax credits to encourage consumers to buy "hybrid" cars that run on both gasoline and electricity, and Cheney did not rule out raising federal fuel-economy standards that are a high priority among environmentalists.

Some conservatives chastise Bush for not going far enough to suspend environmental regulations in the quest for energy independence. "Confused is the best way I could describe this policy," says Smith of the Competitive Enterprise Institute. "On the one hand, it looks like we will have an affordable energy policy and do everything possible to make it easier for Americans to have abundant energy for the future, which is a policy I happen to like.

"But on the other hand, it seems we're going to a pristine Earth policy that somehow we can have gourmet dinners every night, but we're never going to wash any dishes. There's an insane attitude in America today that the messy side of life can be somehow legislated away, and unfortunately politicians are often willing to promise people that."

Some experts say policy-makers should make a greater effort to reconcile the often-conflicting goals of protecting the environment and ensuring adequate energy supplies. They say certain government policies have discouraged construction of new power plants and refineries and overloaded the gasoline-distribution system. Among those are emissions standards for coal-fired power plants and refineries and regulations requiring different types of cleaner-burning gasoline in different cities — what Portney of Resources for the Future calls the "balkanization of fuels" in the United States.

"I'm not suggesting that any of these regulations were wrong," he says. "But I think it wasn't done as part of a more conscious and coordinated effort to integrate environmental and energy decision-making."

Should nuclear power play a bigger role in the nation's energy mix?

In the early 1970s, nuclear energy appeared to offer a virtually inexhaustible source of pollution-free electricity. The United States has ample uranium deposits, and nuclear power generators emit almost no harmful pollutants — as long as they run as intended.

But after a reactor vessel at the Three Mile Island nuclear plant near Harrisburg, Pa., sprang a leak in 1979, plant construction ground to a halt nationwide. Although the accident caused no apparent harm, there was widespread concern over the potentially disastrous radioactive contamination of air and water posed by nuclear energy. That fear only mounted in the wake of the devastating 1986 nuclear plant explosion in Chernobyl, Ukraine, which caused long-lasting radioactive pollution of the immediate area and contaminated some food supplies in neighboring countries. Plus, policy-makers have been at a political impasse for years over where to store a mounting backlog of radioactive waste from the nation's 103 operating reactors. [13]

The last order for a new nuclear plant in the United States was placed in 1978, and it was later canceled. But the threat of electricity shortages and the rising cost of natural gas — the leading source of electricity in newer power plants — have prompted a flurry of applications to extend expiring nuclear plant operating licenses. [14]

In endorsing greater use of nuclear power, Cheney on April 30 called it one of the "cleanest methods of power generation that we know." If the nation is serious about environmental protection, he said, "then we must seriously question the wisdom of backing away from what is, as a matter of record, a safe, clean and very plentiful energy source."

Industry spokesmen say Bush's plan to increase nuclear power generation is long overdue. "One of the strengths of the U.S. electricity infrastructure has long been its diversity of fuel sources, and we believe that we must have that diversity moving forward," says Steve Kerekes, a spokesman for the Nuclear Energy Institute, the leading industry association. "That diversity must, should and will include nuclear energy."

Opponents of nuclear power contend that it is far from safe. "Nuclear generation does not create the same emissions as fossil fuel generation, but it has its own set of risks and safety issues," says Alan Nogee, director of the clean energy program of the Union of Concerned Scientists (UCS) in Cambridge, Mass. "Nuclear plants inherently have a risk of catastrophic accidents that could kill or injure tens of thousands of people and make large areas uninhabitable and produce waste that remains in the environment and harmful for tens, if not hundreds, of thousands of years."

The nuclear power industry and the federal Nuclear Regulatory Commission (NRC) say nuclear power is safe. They point to a 10-fold drop in the plant malfunction rate, which has declined from about five automatic scrams, or shutdowns, per plant per year in the mid-1980s to less than one in 2000. "The plants are operating more safely now than ever," says Victor Dricks, a spokesman for the commission.

But critics say the accident rate is likely to rise again as existing plants age and deteriorate. "All these plants are approaching 40 years, which is their original licensed lifetime," says David Lochbaum, a nuclear safety engineer at the Union of Concerned Scientists. "The accidents at Three Mile Island [and] Chernobyl occurred in the facilities' first year of operation, or break-in phase. The other time [nuclear] technology becomes at risk is during the wear-out phase. If there are cracks in piping or other signs of aging, we may not find them until they actually fail and cause an accident."

Lochbaum charges that safety inspections are actually becoming less frequent over time. "As people get older, we tend to see doctors more often to maintain a level of health that we deem to be adequate," he says. "But as these nuclear power plants get older they're getting fewer and fewer safety checks, and the only reason is money."

Dricks rejects Lochbaum's reasoning. "That analogy is not a good one," he says. "A well-maintained machine will last a long time, and the initial 40-year license granted by the NRC for most of these plants was chosen as a regulatory limit, not because of any technical limitation. There's a process in place that seeks a 20-year license extension to demonstrate that the effects of aging are well understood and can be managed. So there's no reason to believe that the aging of the plant is going to be reflected in degraded performance. In fact, the [improved] shutdown numbers demonstrate the opposite."

Even critics concede that new technology promises to alleviate some of the safety concerns associated with nuclear power. So-called "pebble-bed" nuclear plants, being developed in South Africa, substitute helium for the water now used in existing plants to cool the reactor core and spin the electricity-producing turbine. "Most of the low-level radioactive waste that's generated at plants today comes from the cleanup of water or, once water is contaminated or spilled, what it touches and then contaminates through association," Lochbaum says. "By only using helium throughout that loop, the volume of low-level waste generated is reduced almost to zero, which is clearly a good thing." The pebble-bed technology also allows plant operators to load smaller amounts of fuel into the reactor at a time, reducing the risk of a catastrophic accident.

Despite these technological improvements, critics say there are safer clean-energy alternatives to nuclear power. "We can avoid those risks as well as avoid problems of fossil-fuel emission if we invest in improving our energy efficiency and in developing clean, renewable energy resources like solar, wind, geothermal and biomass power," Nogee says. According to a 1997 study by UCS and other organizations, increased investment in energy efficiency, advanced natural gas technology and renewables would allow the United States to phase out both nuclear and coal electricity generation by 2030. [15] ■

BACKGROUND

Energy Crisis

Endowed with abundant supplies of oil, coal and natural gas, the United States was able to power its growing economy on its own well into the 20th century. Even as the explosion of automobile ownership boosted demand for gasoline, cheap fuel was readily available from both domestic sources and Mideast oil fields, then controlled mostly by U.S. and European oil companies.

By 1970, however, the days of cheap energy were numbered. The United States had begun importing oil in the late 1950s, as domestic production approached its peak. Middle Eastern countries had regained ownership and control of their oil resources just as domestic oil

Chronology

1970s *Oil-price spikes thrust energy policy to the top of the policy agenda.*

October 1973
Arab members of the Organization of Petroleum Exporting Countries (OPEC) embargo oil shipments to the United States in retaliation for its support of Israel in the Middle East conflict.

1975
Congress creates the Strategic Petroleum Reserve, a federally owned stockpile of crude oil, to cushion the blow of future oil-supply emergencies.

1977
President Jimmy Carter declares a national energy crisis and calls for a series of policy changes to reduce demand that defines national energy policy for the next several decades. The Department of Energy Organization Act creates the Federal Energy Regulatory Commission (FERC) to replace the Federal Power Commission.

1979
A reactor vessel at the Three Mile Island nuclear plant near Harrisburg, Pa., springs a leak, raising safety concerns that eventually halt new nuclear plant construction. Gasoline shortages produce long lines of motorists at gas stations.

1980s *Deregulation of the energy sector begins to take hold amid the continuing unpredictability of foreign oil supplies.*

January 1981
Oil prices reach $34 a barrel after the 1978-79 Iranian Revolution and the 1980 outbreak of the Iran-Iraq War disrupt the flow of oil from the Persian Gulf.

1986
A devastating explosion at a nuclear power plant in Chernobyl, Ukraine, exacerbates safety concerns surrounding nuclear energy.

July 1989
Congress lifts remaining controls from domestic production of natural gas.

1990s *A booming economy masks the impact of tightening energy supplies.*

1990
Amendments to the 1970 Clean Air Act mandate cleaner-burning fuels in several heavily polluted cities, eventually forcing refineries to produce 16 different types of fuels and straining their ability to maintain reliable delivery of gasoline supplies to some urban areas.

1992
The Energy Policy Act opens the door for deregulation of the last heavily regulated energy sector, electric utilities.

1996
California becomes one of the first states to introduce electric utility deregulation with a law that unfetters wholesale prices but caps rates that utilities may charge retail customers. FERC requires utilities to open their transmission lines to competing electricity generators.

December 1998
World crude oil prices reach a temporary all-time low of $10 a barrel.

2000s *A new administration with extensive ties to the oil industry shifts the policy focus from energy conservation to production.*

July 2000
Gasoline prices exceed $2 a gallon in Chicago and some other Midwestern cities. Oil companies blame low refinery capacity and growing demand.

October 2000
A series of rolling blackouts begins to hit California, as financially strapped utilities are unable to meet the state's burgeoning demand for power.

Jan. 29, 2001
Nine days after his inauguration, Vice President Dick Cheney convenes an energy task force to formulate the new administration's energy policy.

May 17, 2001
Declaring that the nation is in the midst of the worst energy "crisis" since the late 1970s, President Bush unveils his energy policy proposal, based primarily on increasing production of fossil fuels and nuclear power.

producers were extracting the last of the most accessible oil reserves. The era of cheap oil came to an end in October 1973, when Arab members of the Organization of Petroleum Exporting Countries (OPEC) embargoed oil shipments to the United States in retaliation for its support of Israel in the Middle East conflict.

President Richard M. Nixon introduced a gasoline allocation system to distribute fuel evenly around the country. But the system merely produced long gas lines at the pump as American drivers, unaccustomed to shortages and expensive gasoline, resorted to panic buying.

To soften the blow of future interruptions in foreign oil supplies, Congress in 1975 created the Strategic Petroleum Reserve, a federally owned stockpile of crude oil.

In 1977, President Jimmy Carter declared a national energy crisis and set in motion a series of policy changes based primarily on reducing demand that would define energy policy for the next several decades. To help wean the country from its dependence on foreign oil, Congress also approved sweeping new rules calling for the doubling of auto-fuel efficiency as well as more efficient buildings and appliances. Consumers abandoned their gas-guzzlers for gasoline-sipping Hondas and Toyotas, causing the near collapse of the U.S. auto industry.

Finally, Congress passed a slew of tax incentives aimed at prompting the development of alternative energy sources, including renewable sources then in their infancy.

On the supply side, the energy crisis prompted the development of oil production in Alaska's Prudhoe Bay beginning in the late 1970s.

The country suffered a second oil shock during the winter of 1978-79, after the Iranian Revolution disrupted oil flows from the Persian Gulf. That crisis deepened in 1980 with the outbreak of the Iran-Iraq War. By January 1981, oil prices had reached $34 a barrel.

After the energy crises of the 1970s, the United States and other industrial nations diversified their sources of oil away from the volatile Middle East to alternative areas, such as the North Sea, Mexico and Venezuela, reducing OPEC's ability to control global oil prices. In fact, energy independence was one of the goals that spurred development of nuclear energy. First introduced in the late 1950s, nuclear power plant construction grew in the '60s and accelerated in the wake of the first energy crisis. But after the 1979 accident at Pennsylvania's Three Mile Island, interest in expanding nuclear power waned.

Despite major conservation measures, U.S. reliance on foreign oil continued to grow during the 1980s and '90s, as did the nation's overall energy consumption. But concern about energy supplies gave way to worries about the environmental impact of energy use, such as acid rain, urban smog and water pollution. Urban smog, caused mainly by coal-fired power plants and auto tailpipe emissions, was the focus of the 1990 amendments to the Clean Air Act, which required cleaner-burning fuels in several heavily polluted cities.

Some local jurisdictions introduced even tougher standards requiring a variety of different fuel formulations. By the end of the 1990s, the nation's refineries were producing 16 different types of fuels, each in three different grades.

Energy Deregulation

Deregulation, another trend that began in the 1970s and accelerated with the support of President Ronald Reagan, profoundly impacted the nation's energy outlook. The first energy sector outside the petroleum industry to feel the loosening of federal controls was natural gas. Although the 1978 Natural Gas Policy Act left intact a system of price caps based on the location and depth of natural gas wells, FERC gradually eased those restrictions through several rulemaking changes. Finally, in July 1989, Congress formally lifted remaining controls from domestic production of natural gas.

The push to deregulate the energy industry continued under Reagan's successor, President George Bush. While it upheld much of Carter's emphasis on conservation and renewable-energy development, the 1992 Energy Policy Act also opened the door for deregulation of the last heavily regulated energy sector — electric utilities. The industry had been heavily regulated since the Public Utilities Holding Company Act of 1935, passed after claims that electricity providers were fixing prices.

The law essentially had offered the industry a trade-off similar to one it had offered the telephone industry: In return for treating electric utilities as "natural monopolies" protected from outside competition, the companies had to accept limits on the prices they charged their customers.

Awakened to concerns about energy availability by the energy crises of the 1970s, Congress began exposing the industry to limited competition. The 1978 Public Utility Regulatory Policies Act required utilities to buy at least some of their power from outside sources. The Energy Policy Act of 1992 took this trend a step further by allowing new, unregulated power producers to sell electricity to utilities. Four years later, FERC issued a new rule requiring utilities to open their transmission lines to competing generators as well.

It was up to the states, however, to decide whether or not to adopt broader utility deregulation. Lured by the promise that deregulation would lower electricity prices, just as telecommunications deregulation had lowered telephone long-distance rates, many states embraced utility deregulation. In 1996, New Hampshire launched a pilot program to allow competition. The same year, California became the first state to open the retail side of the industry to competition. Arizona, Massachusetts, Pennsylvania and Rhode Island quickly followed suit.

By 1998, President Clinton endorsed deregulation as part of his comprehensive national energy strategy.

AP Photos/Steven Senne

Activists at Harvard University toss students' resumés into an oil barrel, urging classmates to avoid applying for jobs with oil companies that plan to drill in the Arctic National Wildlife Refuge, as President Bush has proposed.

Recent Shortages

Several trends converged in the late 1990s to produce shortages and high prices across a number of energy sectors, culminating in the Bush administration's call for sweeping change in energy policy.

First came a sudden rise in oil prices. By the mid-'90s, thanks to competition from other oil-supplying nations, OPEC was no longer capable of controlling oil prices. By December 1998, world crude oil prices had reached an all-time low of $10 a barrel.

Lulled into complacency by affordable gasoline and a strong economy, many consumers had long abandoned their concerns about energy conservation and had traded their gasoline-conserving Hondas and Toyotas for a new type of vehicle, the gas-guzzling sport utility vehicle (SUV). Amid the nation's longest sustained period of economic prosperity, sales of the wildly popular SUVs skyrocketed, as did sales of home computers and usage of the Internet — all contributing to escalating energy consumption.

In mid-2000, however, Americans had a rude awakening when OPEC producers cut exports, and the price of a barrel of oil more than tripled to $35. At the same time, a series of refinery shutdowns resulted in tight supplies, and gasoline prices rose to their highest levels since 1990. In some cities, gasoline topped the $2 mark, prompting some governors to temporarily suspend gasoline taxes to soften the blow to consumers.

But in retrospect, the governors need hardly have acted. Not only did a record number of motorists hit the road over the July 4 holiday, just as gasoline prices reached their peak, but prices quickly fell back to the $1.50 range as refineries came back on line and increased supplies.

The booming economy had helped cushion the impact of the gas price spike on consumers. For one thing, after accounting for inflation, last year's $35 per barrel peak paled beside earlier price spikes, which in today's dollars reached $40 a barrel in the mid-1970s and more than $70 a barrel in the early '80s. Perhaps more important, American consumers had become less sensitive to oil-price changes: Americans now spend just 3 percent of their after-tax income on fuel, half what they spent in the '70s.

No sooner had gasoline prices returned to their earlier levels than shortages and price hikes struck another energy sector — California's electricity market. By last fall, utilities were unable to purchase all the power they needed to provide electricity to San Diego; by early this year the crunch had spread to San Francisco and other mar-

Major U.S. Energy Sources

The nation's continuing vulnerability to disruptions in energy supplies stems largely from its dependence on foreign oil to meet many energy needs. Since the 1970s, however, America has tried to diversify its energy sources.

Here is a brief description of all major energy sources in the United States.[1]

Petroleum: Until the 1950s, the United States produced virtually all the oil it consumed, but domestic oil production in the Lower 48 states began declining after peaking in 1970. In the late 1970s, drilling in Alaska's Prudhoe Bay helped slow down the decline, but that source also peaked in 1988.

Since 1992, the nation has imported more oil than it has produced. By 2000, imports accounted for 57 percent of oil consumption. Crude oil, used to make products ranging from home heating oil to plastics, is primarily refined into gasoline. Transportation accounts for two-thirds of all U.S. petroleum use.

Corbis Images

President Bush's national energy policy calls for reviewing laws limiting offshore oil exploration and drilling.

Oil prices remain relatively low in the United States, despite recent increases. Last year, oil prices rose from $17 a barrel in 1999 to about $27; the Organization of Petroleum Exporting Countries (OPEC) is trying to stabilize prices close to the $27 level by controlling output. Last summer's spike in gasoline prices was not due to high prices for crude oil but to temporary supply disruptions caused by a shortage of refinery capacity, coupled with rising demand. Since 1995, gasoline demand has risen by 11 percent, while refinery capacity has grown by only 8 percent. No major refineries have been built since 1976, and refineries are working at near capacity.

A series of refinery shutdowns contributed to the current price hikes. Their re-entry into service is expected to help bring prices back down in the coming months.

Natural gas: A mixture of methane, ethane and propane, natural gas often is extracted from the same underground deposits as oil. Until the late 1980s, the United States was virtually self-sufficient in gas, but rapidly rising demand has required the country to import growing amounts of the fuel, mostly from Canada. More than half the domestic gas production is centered in Texas, Oklahoma and Louisiana, but new technology has allowed for offshore drilling for gas, which now accounts for about a fifth of all domestic supplies.

kets. Four blackouts ensued, costing the state more than $1 billion in lost production.[16] In March, Gov. Davis announced a 40 percent rate hike to help slow consumption, in an effort to prevent further blackouts.

Natural gas soon became the third energy sector hit with shortages and price increases in recent months. Low prices had discouraged natural gas production in recent years, leaving the supply system vulnerable to increases in demand that have resulted from the nation's increasing reliance on gas to fuel new electric power generators.

An aging pipeline system also left the natural gas market vulnerable to supply interruptions. Those trends have converged over the past year, with natural-gas prices increasing by almost 70 percent. Homeowners in the Northeast and Midwest who use natural gas to heat their homes were especially hard hit by the unusually cold weather in December and January, when utility bills in some areas tripled over the previous winter. ■

CURRENT SITUATION

Bush's Plan

President Bush released his long-awaited national energy plan on May 17. "To protect the environment,

Industry is the biggest consumer of natural gas, but most new, independent electric power producers also use gas because it generates fewer pollutants than coal, the traditional source of electrical power. Gas also has replaced oil in many parts of the country for use in home heating, and small amounts also are being used to power vehicles. Natural gas prices are about double what they were early last year, in part because the nation's gas pipeline network has not kept up with rising demand. A sudden increase in demand during a cold snap last winter resulted in a tripling of utility bills in parts of the Northeast. In response to rising demand, the number of gas-drilling rigs in operation has more than doubled over the past two years, to about 900.

Coal: The United States possesses vast reserves of coal — enough to satisfy the nation's demand for an estimated 250 years. The U.S. is the world's second-leading coal producer, after China. In recent decades, coal production — once confined to the deep mines of West Virginia and Kentucky — has expanded to include surface mines throughout a broad area west of the Mississippi River.

The cheapest fossil fuel, coal has been the nation's largest domestic energy source since the late 1800s, except for the period 1952-82, when oil and natural gas led the way in domestic energy production. Today coal accounts for a third of all domestic energy production, and just over half of all electricity generated.

About 90 percent of the coal mined in this country is used to generate electricity. But despite research into "clean-coal" technology, coal is the most polluting of all major fuels. Coal burning is the main cause of acid rain, while coal-mining techniques like mountaintop removal cause water pollution.

Nuclear energy: Electricity-generating nuclear plants first came on line in the U.S. in the late 1950s. Nuclear now accounts for about one-fifth of the nation's electricity. In the decade before the 1979 accident at Pennsylvania's Three Mile Island nuclear facility, orders for new reactors skyrocketed, and nuclear power was widely considered to be the most promising future source of inexpensive electricity. Orders ceased after the accident, however, and the number of nuclear reactors in operation has fallen from a peak of 112 in 1990 to 103.

Further development of nuclear power has been stymied by concerns about the potentially catastrophic impact of a major nuclear plant accident and a long-running political impasse over where to build a permanent repository for deadly radioactive waste.

Renewable energy: Unlike finite energy sources, such as fossil fuels, renewable energy sources like water, wind, solar and underground steam are virtually inexhaustible. With the exception of hydropower, which requires the construction of massive dams that can flood vast areas and disrupt fish migration, energy production from renewable sources poses far less of a threat to the environment. Unlike fossil fuels, which are the main source of carbon dioxide and other greenhouse gases believed to cause global warming, renewable energy production is virtually emission-free.

But because of high startup costs, development of renewable energy sources has depended largely on government funding. Today, wind energy in particular is mixed with traditional sources of electricity. But U.S. government spending on research and development has lagged behind that of other countries. Denmark and Germany are leaders in windmill technology, while Japan has become the leader in solar photovoltaics. Taken as a whole, renewable energy sources account for less than 10 percent of the nation's electrical power.

[1] Unless otherwise noted, information in this section is based on Energy Information Administration, "Energy in the United States: A Brief History and Current Trends," 1999.

to meet our growing energy needs, to improve our quality of life, America needs an energy plan that faces up to our energy challenges and meets them," he said. "Vice President Cheney and many members of my Cabinet spent months analyzing our problems and seeking solutions. The result is a comprehensive series of more than 100 recommendations that light the way to a brighter future through energy that is abundant and reliable, cleaner and more affordable. The plan addresses all three key aspects of the energy equation: demand, supply and the means to match them."

The president's eight-chapter report — the result of three months of secretive consultations between administration officials and industry representatives — encourages increasing production of traditional energy sources.

But both Bush and Cheney downplay the importance of renewables in the overall energy mix, saying they would be unlikely to account for more than 6 percent of total energy supplies by 2020. In addition, the budget Bush submitted to Congress in April called for a 50 percent cut in spending for research into renewable-energy sources and a 28 percent cut in funding for a research partnership with U.S. automakers seeking ways to produce cleaner and more efficient cars and trucks.

While Cheney's task force was preparing its report, Republican lawmakers began introducing measures of

U.S. Nuclear Power Plants

The 103 nuclear reactors with operating licenses in the United States provide about 20 percent of the nation's electricity.

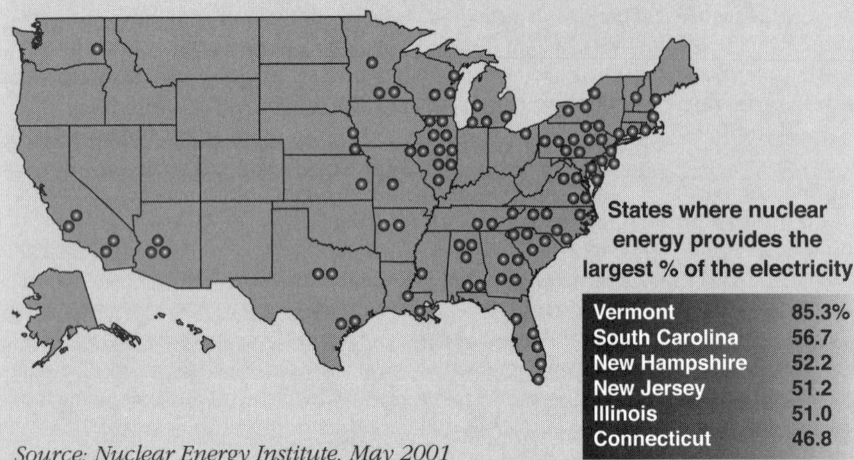

Source: Nuclear Energy Institute, May 2001

their own. In February, Sen. Frank H. Murkowski, R-Alaska, chairman of the Senate Energy and Natural Resources Committee, introduced a bill that would allow drilling for oil and gas in the ANWR and provide tax incentives to encourage energy production throughout the country.

Reps. W.J. "Billy" Tauzin, R-La., and Joe L. Barton, R-Texas, are preparing another measure aimed at boosting production of fossil fuels and nuclear power, as well as renewable-energy sources. Barton also authored a bill that would help alleviate California's blackouts by allowing states to ask for temporary waivers of regulations limiting harmful power-plant emissions.

Congressional Democrats and environmentalists have decried the Bush administration's emphasis on boosting supplies of traditional energy sources, which they say threaten the environment.

"We cannot drill our way out of this problem," said Senate Minority Leader Tom Daschle, D-S.D., "and we cannot use our coming energy challenges as justification for an all-out assault on the environment." [17] On May 15, Daschle joined other Democratic senators in introducing a comprehensive energy bill that would increase domestic production of energy and reduce demand by improving energy efficiency.

The Democrats' plan would force the federal government to intervene in California's electricity crunch by capping wholesale power prices and ordering refunds to customers for overcharges they have already paid. The plan also would:

- offer tax credits of up to $4,000 for the purchase of energy-efficient cars and houses;
- tighten fuel-efficiency standards for SUVs and light trucks, and
- release oil from the Strategic Petroleum Reserve to help overcome any fuel shortages and reduce upward pressure on gasoline prices. [18]

Critics complain that Bush's proposed cutbacks for programs supporting the development of clean energy and conservation couldn't be coming at a worse time.

"This is the wrong message to send out at this time," says Edgar A. De Meo, a consultant in renewable energy in Palo Alto, Calif. "Technologies like wind energy are just now getting off the ground. Government underwriting of research work makes all the difference in whether or not renewable-energy companies can stay in business."

"It's not a very good time to be cutting back," agrees Portney of Resources for the Future. "If we're really committed, as the administration still says it is, to reducing carbon emissions over the long term, you could make a pretty good case for continuing that research."

However, supporters of the administration's focus on traditional fuels say it's the only realistic way to ensure adequate energy supplies over the long term. "There are risks associated with using energy," says Smith of the Competitive Enterprise Institute. "But there are massive risks associated with not having energy to use, too. Environmental policy has almost never faced up to that challenge.

"Environmentalists are now saying they're in favor of power plants, but the only power plants they will allow are some kind of green power or natural gas," he says. "They're not willing to consider coal or nuclear, and those two options are essential."

State Actions

One of the most controversial recommendations by Bush's energy task force is the proposal to take away from the states the authority for deciding the site of long-distance electricity transmission lines. Bush would give that authority to FERC. The agency has long enjoyed the power to condemn private land to build interstate natural gas pipelines, but extending the power of eminent

At Issue:

Should protected public lands be opened to oil and gas development?

yes

MARK RUBIN
GENERAL MANAGER, AMERICAN PETROLEUM INSTITUTE

FROM TESTIMONY BEFORE SENATE ENERGY AND NATURAL RESOURCES COMMITTEE, APRIL 3, 2001

To ensure reliable and secure sources of oil, we have no choice but to diversify the sources of our supplies both domestic and foreign, and to increase both. To do this, we must remove the barriers that currently impede the U.S. oil and natural gas industry's ability to compete both domestically and abroad.

What is access to government lands? The U.S. oil and gas industry does not ask to drill on parklands or in wilderness areas set aside by Congress. Rather, we seek access to areas offshore, in Alaska and in the American West that have been designated by Congress for "multiple use" so numerous activities can take place there.

Most of these multiple-use areas are simply vast expanses of nondescript federal lands. [But just because] they lack the beauty and grandeur of the Grand Canyon or the Grand Tetons does not mean that we treat them with less respect than we do any other lands entrusted to us. Most people driving near or hiking in one of these areas would be hard-pressed to locate one of our facilities, once the drilling rig is removed. Safety and environmental protection are critical concerns, regardless of the location of drilling. And where our contractual obligations with the government require us to, we return the land to its original condition once drilling and production cease.

Yet, despite our record of sound stewardship, President Clinton used his executive powers under the Antiquities Act to bar oil and gas exploration and other activities on vast regions of government lands.

For example, the designation of the Grand Staircase-Escalante Monument in Utah in 1996 summarily withdrew promising valid oil and gas leases on state lands without giving notice to or consulting with state and local authorities or affected communities. Likewise, the U.S. Forest Service recently banned our companies from exploring for oil and natural gas on promising government lands when it published rules to bar road building on nearly 60 million acres in the forest system that . . . could hold 11 trillion cubic feet of natural gas.

Moreover, Congress has refused to authorize exploration on the small section of the Arctic National Wildlife Refuge (ANWR) specifically set aside for exploration in 1980. DOE's Energy Information Administration estimates that the ANWR coastal plain contains between 5.7 billion and 16 billion barrels of technically recoverable oil. The coastal plain provides the best prospect in North America for a new, giant Prudhoe Bay-sized oil field.

no

DAVID J. HAYES
FORMER DEPUTY SECRETARY, DEPARTMENT OF THE INTERIOR

FROM TESTIMONY BEFORE SENATE ENERGY AND NATURAL RESOURCES COMMITTEE, APRIL 3, 2001

Our nation has a long history of restricting oil and gas leasing on sensitive landscapes. We would not accept drilling for oil or gas in our national parks or in many other treasured public lands. Because we have made this policy choice, our nation loses the energy potential associated with the extraordinary geothermal resources in Yellowstone Park, the potential hydropower available if we were to flood the Grand Canyon or potential oil or gas production from the red rock canyons of Bryce or Zion or from the Indian ruins at Mesa Verde.

But in all of these cases we have recognized, and are honoring, competing values associated with conserving these lands in their natural state.

Against this historic backdrop, President Clinton set aside approximately 5 million acres of public lands as national monuments that must be protected from further development. The United States Geological Survey recently confirmed that only five out of the 21 national monuments had moderate-to-high probability for the occurrence of oil and gas resources. . . .

[R]eversing public-policy decisions and seeking to open up protected lands for new oil and gas production . . . would raise fundamental public-policy issues. It would not be responsible, in my view, to assert that there are economically and politically realistic opportunities to increase oil and gas production on our public lands so as to achieve domestic "energy independence."

Our nation is consuming 9.6 million barrels of oil per day. While domestic production on public lands has held its own in recent years, we have been importing more than 50 percent of our nation's oil needs for many years. Even if we were able to reverse the long-term declining trend of domestic oil production and greatly increase our oil production on federal lands, there is no plausible scenario by which new oil production from our federal lands could enable the United States to become independent of the foreign oil markets, or even to reduce our oil imports to less than 50 percent of our total needs.

A balanced energy policy is needed — one that continues to address supply-side needs by promoting responsible oil and gas development on public and private lands, provides incentives for the development of renewable energy sources and gives equal weight to demand-side issues by addressing energy-efficiency and energy conservation needs.

domain to include power lines is expected to run into stiff opposition from the states, with backing from land-rights organizations and environmentalists.

Public opposition has thwarted construction of new power lines in several states. Even in power-strapped California, a plan to expand an existing transmission line to help move power from the Pacific Northwest to San Diego and other southern cities has been stalled. [19]

A drought in the Pacific Northwest has compounded California's power shortage, since hydroelectric power from Oregon and Washington is a vital source of electricity throughout much of the West. Snowpack in the Cascade and Rocky Mountain ranges, which produces water for the Grand Coulee and five other dams on the Columbia River, was far below average last winter, reducing the dams' ability to generate power.

After watching California's ongoing electricity woes, many states are slowing or even reversing plans to deregulate their electricity markets. To date, 24 states and the District of Columbia have taken steps to restructure their electric utility industries. But according to a recent survey of state energy officials, many are reconsidering their plans out of concern that they, too, may be vulnerable to summer blackouts. [20]

Outside California, New York City is the area most vulnerable to electricity shortages this summer. New York was one of the first states to deregulate its electric utilities. To forestall the need for brownouts as the summer air-conditioning season approaches, the state's power authority is trying to complete construction of 11 new "mini" power plants in and around the city by June 1. But the new gas-fired plants have run into opposition from residents who say the facilities will worsen their neighborhoods' already poor air quality; two plants have been put on hold pending completion of an environmental-impact study.

Both states are tightening the screws on power providers found to be taking advantage of electricity shortages by gouging ratepayers. Some California lawmakers propose making price-gouging by energy providers a felony carrying stiff fines and even a jail sentence. New York already has a procedure for fining and publicly identifying power providers that overcharge utilities during power shortages. [21]

In the Midwest, the administration's call for expanded oil and gas drilling on federal lands may lend support to a plan by Michigan's Republican governor, John M. Engler. He wants to allow drilling for oil and gas under Lake Michigan and Lake Huron using new directional, or "slant," drilling techniques that enable drillers to reach untapped underwater reserves from the shore. Michigan is one of eight Great Lakes states that bar drilling from platform rigs in the water. [22]

Voluntary Efforts

Critics of environmental regulations have long asserted that they stymie economic growth by posing too heavy a financial burden on industry. But in recent years a number of companies, including some of those with the highest regulatory costs, have voluntarily adopted measures to lessen the impact of their heavy energy use on the environment. Oil giant BP Amoco, for example, now promotes solar energy and is developing cleaner blends of gasoline. It also reduced its carbon emissions by 5 percent in the late 1990s and expects to reduce them by an additional 5 percent by the end of 2003.

Even some U.S. utilities, among the world's biggest fossil-fuel consumers, have drawn up plans to curb their greenhouse emissions. Entergy Corp. of New Orleans, the nation's third-largest utility measured by production of electricity, has promised to limit carbon emissions from its 25 gas-, oil- and coal-fired plants for the next five years. [23] Even after Bush abandoned his earlier promise to mandate curbs in industrial carbon emissions, Ford Motor Co. reiterated its voluntary commitment to increase the average fuel economy of its sport utility vehicles by 25 percent by 2005. [24]

Some critics of the administration's new energy plan say it will undercut such voluntary efforts and make it even harder for the United States to reduce its emissions of "greenhouse" gases — those believed to contribute to global warming.

"To the extent that [the plan] creates new subsidies for fossil fuels and nuclear power, and would reduce research and development of renewables," says the UCS's Nogee, "it will make it more expensive for companies to undertake voluntary actions."

Supporters of deregulation say the voluntary emission cutbacks were merely a poor business decision. "When Bush announced that he wasn't going to do something foolish in this area [of greenhouse gas emissions], these guys panicked because their investments were stupid," says Smith of the Competitive Enterprise Institute. "The only way we're going to have a brighter, more comfortable, safer, more mobile world is to have a lot more energy use, and the only way you can have more energy use over the next decade is to have more coal and other fossil fuels." ■

OUTLOOK

Policy Prospects

Congressional supporters of Bush's energy proposals hope to act on them quickly. Sen. Murkowski, a champion of opening ANWR to oil and gas drilling, on May 23 held the first in a series of hearings on the Bush plan and other energy policy proposals. If the committee finishes its work in time, Majority Leader Trent Lott, R-Miss., has vowed to call the measure up for a vote of the full Senate before the July 4 holiday. But the ANWR proposal, along with many other elements of the energy plan, face an uphill battle in Congress, where Democrats and several moderate Republicans say it is skewed too heavily toward increasing traditional energy supplies and places too little emphasis on conservation and alternative energy sources.

"We think the president's plan makes the wrong choices for America and for the American people," said House Minority Leader Richard A. Gephardt of Missouri at a May 17 news conference. "It was crafted behind closed doors with a lot of input from energy executives and in a highly secretive way that doesn't serve the public interest."

Gephardt also echoed growing criticism from California politicians that the administration is ignoring their immediate plight by refusing to prevent ratepayers from price gouging by power providers. The president's plan "focuses on drilling and production at the expense of our environment and conservation," Gephardt added, "and it does nothing to help people who need relief right now."

Long, Hot Summer?

The nation's energy crunch will become even more apparent in coming weeks, as consumers turn on air-conditioners and hit the road for long-awaited vacations. Motorists have been warned that gasoline may exceed $2 a gallon; by mid-May, self-serve regular already averaged $1.95 in California. But gasoline prices have begun to fall on the commodities markets, promising a return of more affordable gas for consumers likely by this fall. [25]

Electricity supplies, however, are likely to remain tight for the foreseeable future. Brownouts and temporary blackouts appear likely to strike California and perhaps New York City this summer. "California is getting the big press right now," says energy consultant De Meo, "but this is on the verge of happening in a number of places."

But in most other parts of the country, tight energy supplies are more likely to be expressed in higher utility bills than in flickering lights, experts say. Almost all of the new plants being built today are fueled by natural gas, says Gruenspecht of Resources for the Future, which is more expensive than energy from coal-fired plants. "Most people may be looking at electricity prices being higher," he says, "but that doesn't get you to a California type of situation."

While some parts of the country face worsening power shortages and higher utility bills, many analysts expect deregulation to pay off over time, especially if states avoid California's mistake of capping retail, but not wholesale, prices. "Moving toward competition will certainly allow for more efficient pricing," Gruenspecht says. "One of the problems in California is that there's no price responsiveness, in that demand doesn't really change with price."

In the short term, the nation's energy problems are likely to act as a brake on economic growth. The Federal Reserve reported in early May that "energy costs that have risen sharply" pose a threat of inflation and helped explain the economic slowdown of recent months. [26]

But over the long term, Gruenspecht predicts, the energy industry will initially benefit from further deregulation, and consumers will see the effects over time in lower prices for goods and services, as manufacturers and retailers pass on their energy savings. ■

Notes

[1] Abraham addressed a meeting on energy policy at the U.S. Chamber of Commerce in Washington, D.C., March 19, 2001.

[2] Cheney addressed a meeting of The Associated Press in Toronto on April 30, 2001.

[3] Bill Richardson, "Old Fuels and Poor Policy," *The New York Times*, May 5, 2001.

[4] For background, see Adriel Bettelheim, "Utility Deregulation," *The CQ Researcher*, Jan. 14, 2000, pp. 1-16.

[5] Testifying before the House Energy and Commerce Subcommittee on Energy and Air Quality, May 1, 2001.

[6] See Peter Behr, "Energy Overcharge Case Settled," *The Washington Post*, May 1, 2001.

[7] Cheney was interviewed on May 8, 2001, by CNN.

[8] For background, see Mary H. Cooper, "Energy and the Environment," *The CQ Researcher*, March 3, 2000, pp. 161-184.

[9] Statement, May 9, 2001.

[10] For background, see Mary H. Cooper, "Global Warming Treaty," *The CQ Researcher*, Jan. 26, 2001, pp. 41-64.

[11] See Peter Behr, "Air Conditioner Energy Standard to Be Relaxed," *The Washington Post*, April 14, 2001.

[12] From a Senate floor speech on May 4, 2001.

[13] For background, see Mary H. Cooper, "The Politics of Energy," *The CQ Researcher*, March 5, 1999, pp. 185-208. A forthcoming issue will examine the problem of nuclear waste: Brian Hansen, "Nuclear Waste Disposal," *The CQ Researcher*, June 8, 2001.

[14] See Matthew L. Wald, "Industry Gives Nuclear Power a Second Look," *The New York Times*, April 24, 2001.
[15] Alliance to Save Energy, American Council for an Energy-Efficient Economy, Natural Resources Defense Council, Tellus Institute and Union of Concerned Scientists, "Energy Innovations: A Prosperous Path to a Clean Environment," 1997.
[16] See Christopher Plameri, "The Future of California," *Business Week*, April 30, 2001.
[17] From a news conference held on March 22, 2001.
[18] See Philip Shenon, "Sensing a Bush Liability, Democrats Push an Energy Plan," *The New York Times*, May 16, 2001.
[19] See John Fialka, "States Protest Bush's Plan for Siting Power Lines," *The Wall Street Journal*, May 15, 2001.
[20] See Neela Banerjee, "States' Plans to Deregulate Get Second Look," *The New York Times*, May 2, 2001.
[21] See Andrew Caffrey, "States Try to Deter Power Price Gouging," *The Wall Street Journal*," April 30, 2001.
[22] See William Claiborne, "Risks, Benefits of Lake Drilling Argued," *The Washington Post*, May 4, 2001.
[23] See John J. Fialka, "Utilities Make Own Plans for CO_2 Curbs," *The Wall Street Journal*, May 4, 2001.
[24] See Keith Bradsher, "Ford Tries to Burnish Image by Looking to Cut Emissions," *The Washington Post*, May 4, 2001.
[25] See "Gasoline Falls 4% as Price Peak Seen," *Los Angeles Times*, May 15, 2001.
[26] The Federal Reserve's latest portrait of regional economic activity, known as the "beige book," was issued on May 2, 2001.

FOR MORE INFORMATION

American Council for an Energy-Efficient Economy, 1001 Connecticut Ave., N.W., Suite 801, Washington, D.C. 20036; (202) 429-0063; www.aceee.org. Dedicated to advancing energy efficiency as a means of promoting both economic prosperity and environmental protection.

Competitive Enterprise Institute, 1001 Connecticut Ave., N.W., Suite 1250, Washington, D.C. 20036; (202) 331-1010; www.cei.org. This conservative research group advocates broader deregulation of energy markets and more domestic energy production.

Energy Information Administration, U.S. Department of Energy, 1000 Independence Ave., S.W., Washington, D.C. 20585; (202) 586-8800; www.eia.doe.gov. Collects and publishes a vast compendium of information on national and international energy trends and production.

League of Conservation Voters, 1920 L St., N.W., Suite 800, Washington D.C. 20036; (202) 785-8683; www.lcv.org. Supports candidates who call for strong environmental-protection measures. It is highly critical of the Bush administration's new energy proposals.

National BioEnergy Industries Association, 1616 H St., N.W., 8th Floor, Washington, D.C. 20006; (202) 628-7745; www.bioenergy.org. Represents landowners, foresters, equipment manufacturers and others involved in developing technologies to generate electricity from wood and other plant waste, or biomass.

National Coal Council, 1730 M St. N.W., Suite 907, Washington, D.C. 20036; (202) 223-1191. Represents coal producers and transporters. www.nationalcoalcouncil.org.

Resources for the Future, 1616 P St., N.W., Washington, D.C. 20036; (202) 328-5000; www.rff.org. Conducts studies on the economic and policy aspects of energy and the development of natural resources.

Nuclear Energy Institute, 1776 I St., N.W., Suite 400, Washington, D.C. 20006; (202) 739-8000; www.nei.org. Promotes expansion of the nuclear energy industry in the United States and worldwide.

Solar Energy Industries Association, 1616 H St., N.W., 8th Floor, Washington, D.C. 20006; (202) 628-7745; www.seia.org. Represents industries with interests in the production and use of solar energy and monitors legislation and regulations on renewable energy.

Union of Concerned Scientists, 2 Brattle Square, Cambridge, Mass. 02238; (617) 547-5552; www.ucsusa.org. Supports the development of non-fossil fuels to help improve air quality and reduce emissions of greenhouse gases implicated in global warming.

Bibliography

Selected Sources Used

Articles

Ball, Philip, "Power Cells Get Warm," ***Nature*****, April 19, 2001.**

A new type of fuel cell, developed at the California Institute of Technology, may speed the arrival on the market of electric cars. The new prototype converts hydrogen to electricity more efficiently than existing cells, which are too costly and heavy to be seriously considered as viable alternatives to the internal-combustion engine.

Fineman, Howard, and Michael Isikoff, "Big Energy at the Table," ***Newsweek*****, May 14, 2001, pp. 18-22.**

Vice President Dick Cheney's energy task force reflects the fossil-fuels industries' growing clout in Washington. "Not since the rise of the railroads more than a century ago has a single industry placed so many foot soldiers at the top of a new administration," the authors write.

McCarthy, Terry, "War Over Arctic Oil," ***Time*****, Feb. 19, 2001, pp. 24-29.**

The Bush administration's proposal to open part of the Arctic National Wildlife Refuge (ANWR) to oil drilling may prove to be the most controversial feature of its new energy policy.

Palmeri, Christopher, "The Future of California," ***Business Week*****, April 30, 2001.**

The Golden State's electricity crisis, which has sent its biggest utility into bankruptcy and resulted in a series of rolling blackouts, may spill over state borders. California accounts for 14 percent of U.S. economic output, and a major downturn there — which could result from continued electricity shortages — may worsen the nation's current economic slowdown.

Roberts, Paul, "Bad Sports," ***Harper's Magazine*****, April 1, 2001.**

Sport utility vehicles are among the most popular cars in America, accounting for about a third of the 17 million cars purchased. They are also the biggest, most energy-inefficient vehicles to hit the road in decades and serve as an emblem of enduring consumer tastes for extravagance even at a time of rising gasoline prices.

Reports and Studies

Citizens Coal Council, Hoosier Environmental Council and Clean Air Task Force, "Laid to Waste: The Dirty Secret of Combustion Waste from America's Power Plants," February 2000.

Three environmental groups dispute the efficacy of "clean-coal" technology and current environmental regulations in reducing the negative impact of electricity generation on air and water quality.

Energy Information Administration, U.S. Department of Energy, "Annual Energy Outlook 2001, With Projections to 2020," December 2000.

The EIA, an independent statistical and analytical agency within the Energy Department, assesses the current status of all energy sources. Its projections of the nation's demand for energy over the next two decades are widely cited in the Bush administration's new energy policy proposals.

Energy Information Administration, U.S. Department of Energy, "Energy in the United States: A Brief History and Current Trends," 1999.

This report examines the development of various U.S. energy sources and the forces that have determined their place in the overall energy mix. Growing demand, environmental concerns and prices are among the main determinants of energy-technology development.

Energy Information Administration, U.S. Department of Energy, "Renewable Energy Annual 2000, With Data for 1999," March 2001.

This overview contains detailed information about the various technologies currently being developed to harness energy from the sun, wind, plants and underground steam. Renewable sources, chiefly hydroelectric power and biomass, now account for less than 10 percent of total U.S. energy consumption.

League of Conservation Voters, "Bush and the Environment: A Citizen's Guide to the First 100 Days," April 24, 2001.

The league, a nonprofit group that supports the election of environmentally concerned candidates to public office, presents a critical review of President Bush's record on energy and the environment to date.

Nuclear Energy Institute, "Nuclear Energy: The Renaissance Revealed; A Strategic Direction for the 21st Century," May 2000.

Written by the nuclear industry's main lobbying organization, this report describes the history of nuclear power in this country. Although it presents a sympathetic view of nuclear power, the report reviews ongoing issues that hamper its further development, including environmental concerns and ongoing disagreement over where to dispose of radioactive waste.

10 Airline Industry Problems

KATHY KOCH

At their lakeside home outside Ithaca, N.Y., Alfred E. Kahn and his wife eagerly anticipated a long-planned family reunion last summer. Four different sets of children and grandchildren were flying in from around the country.

They almost didn't make it.

"Four separate flights in a row, all in one week, were canceled," Kahn recalls. "It was disgraceful."

But Kahn was philosophical about the snafus. As chairman of the Civil Aeronautics Board (CAB) in the 1970s, the man known as the "father of airline deregulation" helped usher in the boom in airline travel — and the congestion that came with it.

"Airline deregulation has led to a great increase in air travel," he says. "For instance, my college-age grandkids can visit because of frequent-flyer miles. So, overall, I'm happy with deregulation, since our principal purpose was to make airline travel affordable for people of limited means.

"However, airline managements are not doing as good a job as they should," Kahn adds. "There have been some very severe problems for passengers."

Kahn, now a professor emeritus of economics at Cornell University, was one of 11 experts who in July completed a study for Congress on airline competition. "The industry is far more effectively competitive than it was under regulation," he says, "and travelers are saving between $16 billion and $18 billion a year in discounted airfares."

But the expert panel — assembled by the National Research Council (NRC), an arm of the National Academy of Sciences — also found worrisome anti-competitive behavior.

"Even with the many benefits

From *The CQ Researcher*, September 24, 1999.

Reuters/Brian Snyder

brought about by deregulation, we noted some alarming trends against healthy rivalry," said panel chairman and Harvard economics Professor John R. Meyer. "Specific action needs to be taken to counter them. We must preserve vigorous competition and prohibit unfair exclusionary practices meant solely to eliminate competition." [1]

In the two decades since deregulation, the airline industry has overhauled itself, changing the way millions of Americans travel. Supersaver fares, frequent-flyer programs and price wars transformed flying from a luxury for the rich to transportation for the masses. "Airlines have become the Greyhound buses of the '90s," says former United Airlines flight attendant Diane Agnello.

Indeed, since deregulation in October 1978, average airfares have dropped 36 percent while passenger volume has more than doubled, from 275 million travelers to 614 million in 1998. Travelers today have more flights to choose from, and air travel is safer than ever. The number of fatal accidents on U.S. aircraft declined from an average of 0.0135 per million miles flown during the 40 years before deregulation to 0.0009 per million miles during the 20 years since 1978, according to the Air Transport Association of America (ATA).

And despite a rough-and-tumble shakeout period in the early 1990s, the industry today has never been healthier, with major carriers earning record profits the last four years.

But as profits and passenger loads have risen, so have complaints about poor service and airport congestion and concerns about anti-competitive behavior by major airlines.

Last year, nearly 10,000 passengers complained to the Department of Transportation (DOT) about overbooked flights, unexplained and uncompensated delays, lost baggage and misleading ticketing practices. The public outcry reached a crescendo after a blizzard in Detroit led to a horrific New Year's weekend for thousands of Northwest Airlines passengers. They were stranded for up to 11 hours on aircraft without food, water or functioning toilets.

Then in February 1999, a massive "sickout" by American Airlines pilots left some small cities without any air service at all, highlighting another post-deregulation fact of life: Increased competition hasn't trickled down to many small communities served by virtual airline monopolies. As a result, regional passengers not only fly on less sophisticated aircraft but also pay more per mile than passengers flying between major cities on larger, safer aircraft.

Deregulation has been "an unmitigated disaster for most rural areas and smaller communities," said Sen. Byron L. Dorgan, D-N.D., in introducing legislation on Feb. 5 that would provide federal grants to help smaller communities attract new air service.

Business travelers, too, complain that they have not benefited from deregulation. Because they usually do not stay over on a Saturday night and often cannot book ahead, business travelers frequently pay pre-

Is Airport Funding Keeping Up With Demand?

Nearly a billion passengers are expected to fly on U.S. carriers annually within a decade — a 60 percent increase (top graph) over 1996 levels. But airport construction funding declined steeply from 1992 to 1995, then flattened for two years before starting up in 1998. The General Accounting Office says the country spends $3 billion less per year on airport infrastructure than is needed to keep up with the increased demand for air travel.

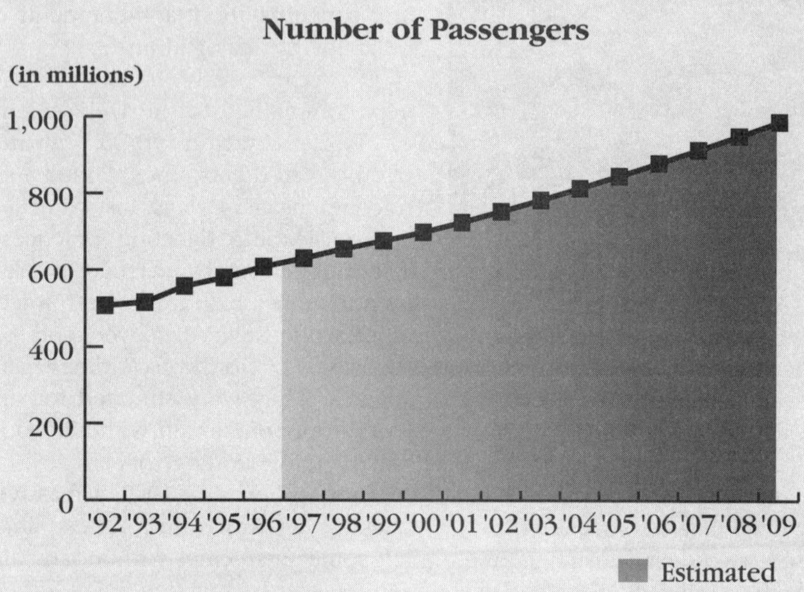

Sources: Federal Aviation Administration (no. of passengers); American Association of Airport Executives (funding).

mium fares. A recent American Express report found that the typical round-trip business fare was $962 — 50 percent higher than in February 1996.

"Discounts [for some passengers] are being taken out of the hides of those who must pay unrestricted fares, usually business travelers," says Kahn. "It's reasonable to have differentiation between fares, but these have become so extreme. The only remedy is competition. But clearly competition is not fully effective."

To fight back, corporations have begun negotiating directly with airlines for lower airfares. Frontier Airlines, in Denver, has negotiated 2,600 such contracts with corporations. Frontier's contracts are non-exclusive, but many major carriers only grant discounts to companies that sign exclusive contracts.

Some businesses banded together in 1996 to form the Business Travelers Coalition (BTC), which has conducted two airline-competition summits. "We realized we had a pretty major competition problem in the airline industry," says Chairman Kevin Mitchell.

Pressure from the BTC and low-fare carriers prompted the DOT to propose new rules prohibiting anti-competitive behavior by airlines. And in a landmark suit this spring, the Department of Justice charged American Airlines with predatory pricing.

By last spring, frustration with the airline industry had boiled over into Congress. At high-profile hearings in Charleston, S.C., and Des Moines, Iowa, the Senate Commerce, Science and Transportation Committee heard horror stories about poor passenger service and small communities where reasonably priced air service has disappeared.

Lawmakers introduced 13 passenger bills of rights early this year, including two proposals supported by presidential candidates — Vice

President Al Gore and Sen. John McCain, R-Ariz., chairman of the commerce committee. Other measures sought to increase airline competition and boost service to small towns.

"We all know the major airlines are dominating the industry more and more every day, and the consumer has suffered," McCain said.

Meanwhile, flight delays surged to record levels last spring and summer under the increased demand for air travel. The delays were so bad in July at the nation's busiest airport, Chicago's O'Hare, that United and American airlines doled out bonus miles to their frequent-flyer customers who had passed through the airport.

Airport congestion is costing the airlines $2.5 billion a year and the American people more than $7 billion in lost productivity, complained Rep. Bud Shuster, R-Pa., chairman of the House Committee on Transportation and Infrastructure. [2] In fact, he noted in April, air-traffic controllers experienced more than 100 "significant system failures" last year because their computer systems are "taxed to their limit."

Like Shuster, the airlines complain that the federal government has not funded airport expansion or updated its air-traffic control system fast enough to keep up with the burgeoning air travel.

"We're working with the air-traffic control system of the 1960s in the 1990s," said Gerald Greenwald, chairman of United Airlines. "It's like gaining 60 pounds and still trying to wear your favorite suit." [3]

Shuster wants to double the amount of money available for airport expansion, but his proposal is tied up in a battle over whether federal airport taxes should be earmarked for airport construction, and thus rendered unavailable for other budgetary uses. The House has agreed, but the measure is stalemated in the Senate.

Meanwhile, nearly a billion passengers a year are expected to fly on U.S. carriers within a decade — a 60 percent increase, the Federal Aviation Administration (FAA) predicts. But the General Accounting Office (GAO) says the country spends $3 billion less per year on airport infrastructure than is needed to keep up with the increasing demand.

"Without prompt action, the United States' aviation system is headed toward gridlock shortly after the turn of the century," the National Civil Aviation Review Commission (NCARC) warned in a December 1997 report.

The passenger bill of rights proposals were forestalled after a closed-door meeting on June 17 between key congressional leaders and airline executives. The airlines promised to police themselves, and legislators gave them a year to show improvement.

But some lawmakers, start-up airlines and passenger groups say the industry's problems are too profound to be fixed by a voluntary program. What is needed, they say, is aggressive, mandatory remediation to correct serious, systemic flaws.

As policy-makers and airlines debate the dilemma, here are the questions being asked:

Are air carriers using anti-competitive practices to block competition?

Critics say anti-competitive behavior by major carriers has bankrupted dozens of new, low-fare airlines. The critics say the big carriers squeeze newcomers by flooding a market with cheap seats and increasing frequent-flyer benefits and travel-agency commissions just on routes served by new competitors. Moreover, the critics say, the big carriers require their corporate clients to sign exclusive contracts, and they refuse to let newcomers sublease their gates and counter space.

For an example of the "unfair exclusionary behavior" used by airlines to block competition, a DOT white paper on airline competition cites actions taken by Northwest Airlines in early 1996. [4] According to the DOT, Northwest offered 1,200 low-priced seats on its Detroit to Philadelphia route. But after a low-fare competitor, Spirit Airlines, offered 12,000 seats, Northwest flooded the route with 50,000 cheap seats, losing $1.7 million in the process. Spirit soon left the market.

Then, the DOT says, Northwest slashed the number of low-fare seats available on the route to 900 — fewer than it had offered initially. Northwest also increased the number of expensive seats available on the route from 400 to a whopping 12,260.

"There is growing concern that major carriers are willing to lose money — lots of it — in the short run to drive off competition, selling so many seats at low fares that the airline's strategy is economically rational only if it forces out competition from low-fare, start-up airlines," DOT Secretary Rodney E. Slater said on April 6, 1998, as he unveiled DOT's proposed guidelines on predatory pricing.

"When tens of thousands of cheap seats are dumped into a market," says the BTC's Mitchell, "the message to potential new entrants and their investors is vividly clear: Enter this market, or any other in this major airline's system, and you will receive the same overwhelming response."

Citing the Northwest-Spirit case, Mitchell says, "When there is such a massive, overwhelming, take-no-prisoners response to new entries, and the airline is losing money, that's not healthy competition. That kind of response is so far afield of a normal, healthy, competitive response that it's not even funny."

Kahn agrees, noting that federal

antitrust rules clearly differentiate between acceptable and unacceptable ways of competing. Still, while he applauds the DOT's efforts to draft guidelines, he says spotting anti-competitive behavior won't be easy.

David A. Fuscus, vice president of communications for the Air Transport Association (ATA), describes the airline business as one of the most competitive in America — "a very, very tough business, with low margins and very high fixed costs." Airlines are out fighting for market share every day, he says.

"But predatory practices are properly illegal," Fuscus points out. "We don't think it's necessary for airlines to engage in that to be tough competitors."

In the ATA's view, Spirit left the Detroit-Philadelphia market because it had decided to focus on leisure markets like Florida, Atlantic City and Myrtle Beach, S.C.

In its predatory-pricing case against American Airlines, the Justice Department charged the company with repeatedly flooding its routes with below-cost seats to drive Vanguard Airlines out of American's Dallas-Fort Worth hub. Once the upstart company withdrew or reduced its services, American re-established high fares and reduced service, the suit claims.

"American crossed a fundamental line," Department of Justice antitrust chief Joel Klein said at a May 13 press conference announcing the suit. "It operated at a loss for one reason — to kill off a competitor so that it could then more than recoup those short-term losses through monopoly prices." [5]

For instance, after Vanguard dropped its Dallas-to-Wichita route, American increased its prices on that route by 50 percent, the suit said. Elsewhere, American used similar tactics with Sun Jet and Western Pacific, the suit said.

American Airlines officials said the Justice Department's allegations "go against the very essence of free-market competition." American merely matched its competitors' prices and added capacity to meet the increased demand, a company press release said. "American is confident its actions will prove to be nothing more than those of any tough competitor in a highly competitive industry," the release said. The government is trying to use antitrust laws "to create a special class of competitors [start-ups] to be protected from competition."

Michael Boyd, an aviation consultant in Evergreen, Colo., calls the legal assault on American "ridiculous, stupid and political. The DOJ has taken convenient circumstances and twisted them around to make American Airlines look like Darth Vader."

"Have there been predatory practices out there? Absolutely," Boyd concedes. "But predation is not the major reason start-ups have gone out of business. Most [failed] because they priced their own products below cost — some at absolutely pirate fares — and the major carriers merely matched them. If predation is defined as pricing your product below cost, the start-ups are the ones that have engaged in predatory practices."

ATA's Fuscus concurs that unfair competition did not force start-ups out of business. "Of the 130 airlines that have failed since deregulation, not a single one failed because of predatory practices," he says, citing a June 30, 1998, study. [6] "The study shows they failed because of lack of financing, bad business decisions, bad business plans, etc."

The study's author, Aviation Institute Director Darryl Jenkins, said that if the Justice Department's suit prevails, it will have a "chilling and devastating effect on American business, because you will no longer be able to match a competitor's price." [7]

Should Congress pass a bill of rights for passengers?

In June, as pressure mounted on Congress to pass a passenger bill of rights, airline executives met with Sen. McCain and other key members of his committee. Afterwards, they announced that the airlines had promised to institute a voluntary "Customers First" program.

Under the program, to go into effect by Dec. 15, the airlines promise to inform passengers of the lowest fare available when quoting prices, notify them about delays and create customer-service programs within each airline to handle complaints. Senators agreed not to pursue legislation on passengers' rights for at least a year while they monitored implementation of the program.

Consumer groups were furious that a deal was struck without them. "I was astonished that passenger-rights activists in Congress would negotiate a private arrangement with the industry and actually agree to block their own legislation," says Paul Hudson, executive director of the Aviation Consumer Action Project, founded by Ralph Nader in 1971. "With friends like that, airline passengers don't need enemies."

The Customer First program doesn't go nearly far enough to fix the industry, Hudson says, pointing out that the passenger bills of rights would have covered only 10 percent of what needs to be done.

His group favors a comprehensive airline competition and consumer-protection act. "We believe there should be a federal anti-price-gouging rule like they have for international flights," says Hudson.

"Airlines can charge you whatever the market will bear on domestic fares," he says, because unlike other industries they are exempt from state and local price-gouging laws. "So, on short- and medium-haul flights major carriers are sometimes charging from

U.S. Has Oldest Planes Among Industrialized Nations

The planes in the U.S. passenger fleet are several years older, on average, than the planes flown by other industrialized nations.

Average Age of Fleet

Over 15 Years Old		*10-15 Years Old*		*Under 10 Years Old*	
Congo	31.9	Canada	14.9	Egypt	9.9
Peru	28.6	U.S.	14.4	New Zealand	9.7
Nigeria	27.7	Denmark	12.8	France	9.5
Venezuela	26.7	Spain	12.8	Japan	9.2
Colombia	20.3	Israel	12.3	United Kingdom	9.2
Mexico	19.3	Ireland	12.2	Sweden	9.0
South Africa	19.1	Brazil	12.0	Italy	8.9
Argentina	19.0	Finland	11.4	Germany	6.5
Russia	17.9	India	11.4	Singapore	5.3
Iran	16.5	Belgium	10.9	Switzerland	4.9

Source: Airclaims Inc. (www.airclaims.co.uk)

8 to 20 times the break-even point. It would be like an oil company charging you $8 to $20 for a gallon of gas," Hudson says. "Oil companies would never be allowed to do that under state and local laws."

Hal Salfen, director of consumer affairs at the International Airline Passengers Association (IAPA), predicts that passenger-rights legislation will land back in Congress' lap. "We absolutely still need a bill of rights," he says. "The voluntary program did not address the real issues, like treatment of passengers, overbooking, delayed flights and information about what the passenger is entitled to if a flight is delayed or canceled."

But aviation consultant Boyd calls the passenger rights bills "idiocy" because none would have changed the way consumers are treated.

"The politicians are responding to consumer anger," and justifiably so, Boyd says, but the passenger rights proposals would have been impossible to implement. One required airlines to notify consumers when there will be a delay, and another mandated that passengers receive lost baggage within 24 hours. "Sometimes it's impossible to do those things," he says.

Boyd doesn't think customer service will improve anytime soon. "Airlines are dancing to the tune of their stock prices, not the consumer," he says. "Unfortunately, complaining to DOT is about as effective as howling at the moon." The DOT only tabulates complaints and puts the totals on its Web site, he says.

The solution is for consumers to "vote with their feet," he says. "In 90 percent of cases, there is another airline you could fly."

The Washington-based Economic Strategy Institute argues in a recent report that the various bill of rights proposals would produce poorer customer service, higher fares, lower efficiency and reduced airline profitability that might create incentives that conflict with safety objectives.[8]

Similarly, the ATA says passenger rights bills would drive up ticket prices and distract attention from the biggest cause of delays, the FAA's outdated air-traffic control system and insufficient government spending on airport expansion.

Fuscus says consumers should give the Customer First plan a chance to work. "It is an aggressive program that will be effective," he insists. "We recognize there are problems, and we're working hard to solve them."

Fuscus admits the airlines haven't done a very good job of explaining delays and cancellations to passengers. "It's just common sense that if you explain to people the reason for delays, they will be more willing to accept it," he says.

By far, most delays last summer were due to problems updating the air-traffic control system, which the FAA runs, not the airlines, Fuscus points out. "And the volume of traffic is just so high," he adds. "Deregulation fostered this explosion in air travel, but the government hasn't moved quickly enough to make improvements in the air-traffic control system to handle the increased traffic."

The IAPA's Salfen blames some of the delays on overcrowding caused by the "hub-and-spoke" system adopted by airlines after deregulation. Hubbing is the practice of sending most of a carrier's flights through a city that serves as the company's base of operations and maintenance in a region. For maximum efficiency, airlines schedule most traffic during the "peak" hours of 8-10:30 a.m. and 4-6:30 p.m., when packed flights depart within minutes of each other.

"To compete with each other, the airlines schedule flights too closely together during these peak periods," says Salfen. "Then, once they are delayed, it mushrooms and quickly disintegrates."

Besides obsolete air-traffic control equipment, others blame insufficient federal funding for airport expansion and poor management of publicly run airports. Privatized airports would be motivated to run flights on time, control costs and maintain high levels of customer satisfaction, argue both the Reason Public Policy Institute and the Cato Institute.

Over the past four years, while annual airline passenger trips increased 16 percent, annual investment in airport development decreased 23 percent, according to a recent study by Charles Barclay, president of the American Association of Airport Executives (AAAE). But Barclay doesn't see privatization as the answer. "Only federal government leadership can see to it that we build the efficient, high-capacity, national airport system America will need in the future to successfully compete," he wrote. [9]

But Mitchell says consumers should not have to wait for more airports to be built before they are treated courteously by the airlines. "You don't have this problem with Southwest Airlines, where customer service is key," he says. "By contrast, other airlines will just tell you to take a hike. You don't need more airports to fix that. That's just an excuse."

Mitchell thinks the voluntary program will die on the vine. "Unfortunately, the culture of the airlines is to not take any initiative in Washington as real or genuine, but rather to kill it or delay it," he says.

However, Mitchell still prefers what he calls an industry-based solution. "I would like it to work, because the day Congress begins to legislate customer service is a bad day in this country."

Are airlines sacrificing safety for profits?

Although the airlines' safety record has improved since deregulation, safety advocates worry that increased competition, fare wars and increasingly crowded skies — all fed by deregulation — are tempting airlines to sacrifice safety for profitability.

Former DOT Inspector General Mary Schiavo, author of the best-selling aviation safety exposé *Flying Blind, Flying Safe*, warned consumers to avoid the airlines that sacrificed safety for profitability after deregulation. [10]

Schiavo said the May 1996 crash into the Florida Everglades of a ValuJet airliner was a deadly example of such declining standards. After deregulation, "some carriers literally let maintenance and safety go, and that was absolutely the cause of the ValuJet crash," Schiavo said. [11]

A ValuJet subcontractor and three maintenance workers were indicted on July 13 in connection with the crash, which killed 109 people. It was caused by a fire that started in a cargo hold illegally carrying oxygen canisters.

Schiavo charged the FAA with responsibility for the declining safety standards, because after deregulation it "acted as though it was a partner with the airlines in guaranteeing profitability . . . when it should have been an independent safety monitor." [12]

The ValuJet crash focused a national spotlight on the FAA's oversight of new, low-fare airlines, which proliferated after deregulation. Many safety advocates complained that some start-ups were using 20- and 30-year-old aircraft and less experienced mechanics than the major carriers.

But Boyd says, "Except for ValuJet, which was eventually shut down, other start-ups are very concerned about safety. If you only have four aircraft, you can't afford to lose one."

He does not think major carriers are sacrificing safety for profits. Neither does Salfen. "They are sacrificing service and convenience for profits," he says, "but not safety."

After the ValuJet crash, the FAA beefed up inspections of new carriers and ordered smoke detectors and sprinkler systems installed in all cargo holds by 2001.

That's not fast enough for the National Air Disaster Alliance (NADA), which lobbies for safer air travel. "The airlines will have had five years since the ValuJet crash," complains NADA President Gail Dunham. "The airlines don't want to put a smoke detector in aircraft they are about to retire," she says. "But why shouldn't they? What public building in the U.S. does not require a smoke detector?"

"Safety is definitely being compromised for profits," she continues. If it weren't, she insists, there would already be smoke detectors and fire-suppression equipment in every cargo hold, more aircraft would have Doppler radar, there would be a $70 smoke hood* for each passenger, and all 737s would have updated flight recorders.

Updated flight recorders on 737s have been the National Transportation Safety Board's (NTSB) No. 1 aviation safety recommendation for seven years, she says. "The airlines don't

* A smoke hood is a portable device with a 10-minute oxygen supply. Most air crash victims succumb to smoke in a crash involving a fire.

want to do it," she says, "because Boeing doesn't want anyone to record the rudder anomalies on the 737s, which are a known design flaw."

Dunham claims it's not just a case of bureaucratic foot-dragging. "The FAA is not proactive on safety issues," she says. "They do what the industry wants them to do when the industry wants them to do it. We have corporate government in Washington these days."

FAA spokeswoman Alison Duquette says the agency has "only one mandate: aviation safety." She points out that in the first FAA reauthorization bill to come up following the ValuJet crash, Congress eliminated the agency's dual mandate. Before then the department had been ordered to both promote the aviation industry and protect the safety of the flying public.

"People who charge that the FAA is run by the airlines truly don't know much about the airline industry and certainly don't know much about the FAA and its relationship with the industry," says John Meenan, ATA's senior vice president for industry policy.

Nevertheless, 43 safety measures recommended by the NTSB following air crash investigations are still pending at the FAA, Dunham points out. "Our members represent families of victims from more than 50 airplane crashes, many of which have been very much preventable disasters," she says. "It's real tough to live with the loss of a loved one when you find that out."

Duquette says over the last 10 years the FAA has "responded favorably" to 90 percent of the urgent recommendations sent to them by the NTSB, and to 84 percent of the rest.

Dunham admits that accident rates were higher before deregulation but says today's airplanes could be even safer, if not for cost-cutting concerns. "Since deregulation, every time the airlines make a safety decision, they insist on a cost-benefit analysis," she says.

Departures Shot Up After Deregulation

The number of airline departures increased by two-thirds in the two decades after deregulation in 1978. Deregulation made air travel accessible to the masses through supersaver fares, frequent-flyer programs and price wars.

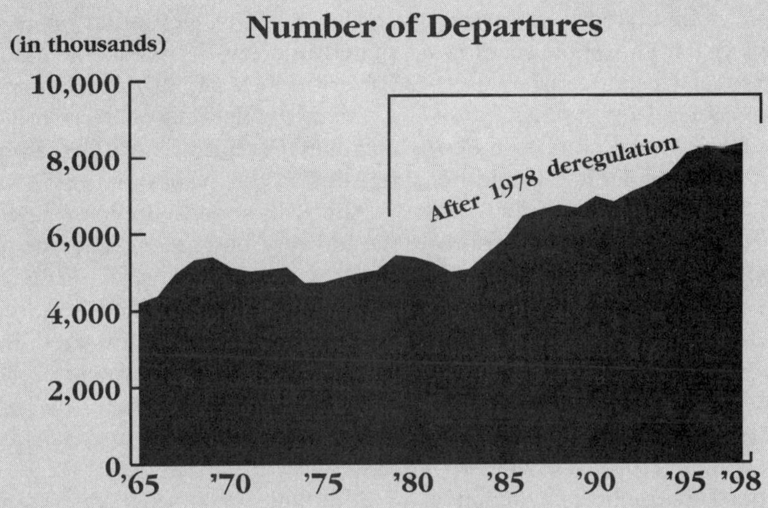

Source: Air Transport Association, Sept. 17, 1999

"That's ridiculous," says ATA's Fuscus. "The safety record of our members in the U.S. is unsurpassed. American skies are the safest in the world." There was not a single U.S. air fatality in 1998, he points out.*

Meenan says the industry believes safety is best advanced through "a systematic, well-thought out, well-executed program." ATA favors "looking at where we can get the most safety benefit, not just from the dollars involved but also from the human resources needed to achieve it. If you give people too many things to do in a total hodgepodge way, you're not going to get a good-quality product.

"If you really want to improve safety, the last thing to be doing is responding to today's 'culture of fear,' in which you take an incident, blow it into proportions that are not warranted and start hurling resources at it," he says.

Airlines began voluntarily installing smoke detectors and fire-suppression equipment in cargo holds before the FAA made it mandatory, Meenan says. Some cargo holds already had smoke detectors, but others didn't because the holds were designed to be airtight, he says.

Other safety advocates question why the U.S. airline fleet is the oldest of any industrialized European country. (*See table, p. 163.*) But, Meenan says, "Our experience suggests that by careful maintenance these aircraft are not necessarily life-limited."

However, increasing concerns about deteriorating wiring in aging aircraft prompted the FAA to establish an agency-industry task force to look into the problem. Investigations

* Fuscus does not count the Swissair crash of an American-made MD-11 off Nova Scotia on Sept. 2, 1998, which killed 229 passengers, because it was not American-owned and the crash did not occur on U.S. soil. The cause of the crash is still under investigation.

of two recent crashes — TWA Flight 800 in July 1996 and the Swissair jet last September — have raised questions as to whether electrical arcing or sparks from old wiring could have caused catastrophic explosions or fires. A number of other on-board fires have been linked to old wiring in recent years. FAA spokesman Les Dorr says that if a serious safety problem is uncovered by the FAA-industry task force, due to report in September 2000, "the agency would not hesitate to order it repaired."

The NTSB has found wiring problems on all but one of 25 jets it inspected during the last two years as part of its investigation into the TWA tragedy, when the plane exploded off Long Island soon after takeoff from John F. Kennedy International Airport, killing 230.

A House oversight subcommittee held a hearing on Sept. 15 on aging wiring problems. And a week later, the nation's top wiring experts met for a four-day conference on wiring and other aging-aircraft issues in Albuquerque, N.M.

Former Defense Department wire and cable specialist Edward Block says he has been trying for years to bring the problem of aging aircraft wiring "out of the closet," but that the industry and the FAA have resisted because it would be prohibitively expensive to replace it all. A typical passenger jet contains more than 150 miles of electrical wiring. ■

BACKGROUND

Impact of Deregulation

Until 1978, the airlines were among the nation's most heavily regulated industries. The CAB was involved in setting prices, determining routes and controlling which carriers were certified to enter a market and when they could leave. The thousands of regulations had pretty much excluded new market entrants for 40 years, says Kahn.

The Airline Deregulation Act, signed into law by President Jimmy Carter on Oct. 24, 1978, ended government regulation of airline routes and rates, but not airline safety, which remains in the hands of the FAA.

Almost as soon as the ink was dry, the industry entered a turbulent period of dramatic restructuring, in which carriers established hundreds of new routes and eliminated less profitable ones. Companies lost astronomical sums of money, and old-line carriers like Pan American and Eastern folded. [13]

Although most observers agree that deregulation has created a far more competitive market, many worry about trends since deregulation that may lead to more consolidation. Some argue that the "hub and spoke" system, the biggest change in the airline industry since deregulation, limits competition.

At hub airports, passengers can transfer to flights to other cities within the hub region, to cities in other parts of the country or to points abroad. Airlines schedule "banks" of flights into and out of hubs at key "rush hour" periods, when dozens of planes arrive within minutes of each other so passengers can quickly transfer to other planes.

Airlines say hubbing enables them to serve far more markets with the same-size fleet than they could if they offered only direct, point-to-point service. The system also allows airlines to retain passengers all the way to their final destinations, rather than handing them off to other carriers for portions of their trips. Many travelers also prefer to stay with a single airline.

The hub system also allows carriers to achieve higher "load factors" (percentage of seats filled) on "spoke" flights to and from small cities within the hub region. A small city of 100,000 residents, for example, may not generate enough passengers to any single destination to make a point-to-point flight economical. But it may generate enough passengers to a dozen different destinations to fill a high percentage of seats on a spoke flight to a hub.

However, the system does have disadvantages. Ground service personnel are often idle between flight banks. Plus, bad weather at a hub can delay flights in a carrier's whole system.

Critics say the system reduces competition because it allows one airline to dominate flights in and out of the hub. "It's much like what happened with the railroads in the last century," says Hudson of the Aviation Consumers Action Project. "Choke points developed at Mississippi River bridges. It got so outrageous that the Interstate Commerce Commission was created to set railroad rates. Hub airports are the Mississippi bridges of the 1990s, and he who controls them is going to do very well."

But Boyd points out that airlines — not airports — create hubs by creating all the traffic. "Accusing airlines of dominating hubs is like accusing Neiman Marcus of dominating Neiman Marcus stores," he says. ■

Barriers to Competition?

Others say it is not so much the hub system that bars new entrants from getting a foothold at large hubs, but lingering remnants of the regulatory framework. Those barriers

Chronology

1930s

The federal government takes an active role in coordinating airline routes and regulating competition among carriers.

1938
The Civil Aeronautics Act establishes the Civil Aeronautics Administration as an independent agency with responsibility for the "encouragement and development" of civil aviation.

1960s-1970s

The airline industry is freed from economic — but not safety — regulation.

1969
To reduce noise around airports served by large jumbo jets, Congress limits the number of takeoffs and landings, or "slots," at New York's LaGuardia and Kennedy airports, Washington's National and Chicago's O'Hare airports.

1978
On Oct. 24, President Jimmy Carter signs the Airline Deregulation Act, designed to spur competition, efficiency, innovation and low prices.

1980s

Airlines scramble to reorganize. Carriers establish hundreds of new routes and eliminate less profitable ones. A slew of new companies start up, while many older airlines go bankrupt. Code-sharing becomes a common practice between major carriers and regional airlines that feed traffic into their hub cities.

Feb. 17, 1981
President Ronald Reagan orders federal agencies not to issue new regulations or modify existing ones unless the potential economic benefits of the change outweigh the potential costs.

1986
DOT's "buy-sell rule" allows major air carriers to keep their slots at major U.S. airports and to buy, sell, lease or trade them.

1990s

After a couple of tough years, the airlines start to turn a healthy profit, as airfares go down and air traffic reaches record high levels amid a nationwide economic recovery. Passenger complaints about poor service skyrocket, even as the nation celebrates the benefits of 20 years of airline deregulation.

1996
In May, a ValuJet aircraft crashes into the Florida Everglades, killing 109 people, and becomes an example of declining FAA oversight standards for start-up airlines. FAA beefs up inspections of new carriers and orders smoke detectors and sprinklers installed in all cargo holds by 2001. Two months later TWA Flight 800 explodes after takeoff from JFK International Airport. After terrorism is ruled out, the focus shifts to aging wiring as a potential cause.

1998
On April 6 the Department of Transportation unveils proposed guidelines for detecting predatory pricing. On April 14 the government announces its "Safer Skies" safety agenda designed to bring about a fivefold reduction in fatal air accidents. In June the House asks the National Research Council to study the competitive issues facing the airline industry while the DOT re-examines its new, predatory-pricing regulations.

1999
Congress hears increasing complaints about airline service, especially after a New Year's snowstorm leaves thousands of Northwest Airlines passengers trapped inside aircraft on the Detroit tarmac for up to 11 hours. In March the Senate Commerce, Science and Transportation Committee holds hearings on service in Charleston, S.C., and Des Moines, Iowa. Some 13 passenger bills of rights are introduced in Congress. In June the House passes an FAA reauthorization bill that would increase airport expansion funds dramatically but would keep them off-budget. Senate hawks balk at the off-budget proposal and block it indefinitely. The airlines propose a voluntary improvement proposal, and the Senate backs off its plan to impose a passenger bill of rights.

July 13, 1999
A ValuJet subcontractor and three maintenance workers are indicted in connection with the 1996 crash, caused by a fire started after illegally stored oxygen canisters exploded in a cargo hold.

Will Global Airline Alliances Hurt Consumers?

Paul Hudson is worried about the future of airline travel. He says the international marketing alliances now being formed by airlines are just the beginning of problems for consumers. In the near future, predicts Hudson, executive director of the Aviation Consumers Action Project, three or four mega-airlines will provide global airline service.

"If these alliances go through as originally conceived, we'll possibly have only four major airlines in the world within a few years," Hudson says. "Everyone will have to line up with one of these alliances or they would be really out in the cold."

"You don't have to look farther than the U.S. market to become alarmed," agrees Kevin Mitchell, chairman of the Business Travelers Coalition (BTC). "Just last year we had proposals by Continental and Northwest, Delta and United, and American and US Airways. They wanted to form three alliances that would have controlled 82 percent of the domestic air travel market. And that is extremely scary."

But government and airline officials say that rather than leading to increased consolidation, international alliances are merely extending to international travelers the same benefits — increased service at lower prices — enjoyed by domestic travelers since the domestic industry was deregulated in 1978. International aviation is still highly regulated by hundreds of restrictive bilateral trade agreements that prevent international air travelers from enjoying the benefits of a deregulated global market, they say.

Those protectionist policies prohibit foreign carriers from making multiple stops inside another country or owning controlling portions of foreign airlines. Such rules also prohibit U.S. airlines from merging with foreign airlines, precluding the kind of efficiencies and economies of scale that other globalizing industries enjoy.

To get around such restrictions, airlines have formed global alliances — essentially joint ventures in which companies share flight codes, coordinate schedules and baggage-handling and honor one another's frequent-flyer programs.

But consumer groups and some industry-watchers fear that while international alliances may allow greater efficiencies and produce lower ticket prices in the short run, they pave the way for global consolidation of the industry and possibly higher prices in the future.

"Any industry that is globalizing wants to gain efficiencies," says Mitchell, "and the airlines are being hamstrung by these [international] ownership laws. So, while I understand the momentum behind them, I think these alliances are very, very problematic.

"They are just proxies for mergers," he continues, "but they don't receive the same competitive and antitrust scrutiny that mergers would receive."

Indeed, U.S. officials for years have encouraged such international alliances by promising antitrust immunity for

include perimeter rules limiting distances planes can fly from an airport; controls on slots (takeoffs and landings); and exclusive gate-leasing contracts granted to some airlines by some airport authorities. A March GAO report found that airfares at 10 "gate-constrained" and "slot-constrained" airports were "consistently higher than at airports of comparable size without constraints." [14]

Two researchers have estimated that perimeter rules and slot controls cost air travelers about $1 billion a year in higher airfares. [15] Congress adopted the perimeter rule known as the Wright amendment when the Dallas-Fort Worth airport was built 15 years ago. Named after its sponsor, then-House Speaker Jim Wright, D-Texas, it restricts any flights originating at the old airport, called Love Field, from flying beyond the five contiguous states. Thus airlines using the new airport are protected from competition on long-haul flights from any airlines operating out of Love Field. The researchers estimate the amendment raises local fares by up to 75 percent.

Similarly, perimeter rules prohibit flights longer than 1,500 miles at New York's LaGuardia Airport and longer than 1,250 miles at Washington's Reagan National. The rules were designed to reduce noise levels in surrounding neighborhoods by blocking noisier long-haul jets. As a result, airfares at the two airports are 15-25 percent higher than they would be without the rules, the two researchers contend.

Finally, since 1969 Congress has limited the number of slots, or takeoffs and landings, at four of the nation's busiest airports — LaGuardia, Kennedy, Reagan National and O'Hare. Slot controls were initially designed to reduce congestion, but some say they have barred new airlines from landing. As a result, fares at the four airports are 10-15 percent higher than comparable flights elsewhere, say the researchers.

In 1986, the DOT instituted the "buy-sell rule," under which the department no longer allocated landing and takeoff slots but grandfathered in existing air carriers' slots. By allowing carriers to buy, sell, lease or trade slots, the new rule boosted the major carriers' control of airport slots from 78 percent to 98 percent, says Mitchell, and they guard them jealously. "If they can't use all their slots for their big jets, they park a com-

alliances between U.S. carriers and foreign national carriers — if the foreign carrier's home country adopts liberalized "open skies" aviation policies. Negotiators reasoned that the negative impact of the short-term (usually five years) antitrust exemptions would be outweighed by the longer-term benefits of the increased competition engendered by the open skies agreements.

But such antitrust immunized code-sharing alliances have raised the eyebrows of consumer groups like Mitchell's, and even former American Airlines CEO Robert L. Crandall calls them a "fraud." "[The government] should simply not renew [the alliances]," Crandall told a reporter in 1998. "Nobody should have antitrust immunity. There should be no code-sharing." [1]

Aviation consultant Michael Boyd of Evergreen, Colo., sees benefits in some alliances and anti-competitive impacts in others. An alliance between Northwest and the Dutch-owned KLM airline, he contends, has been "almost without exception beneficial for everyone involved. It opened up new markets for KLM and for Northwest, and gave the consumer a wider range of choices."

Boyd does not think alliances will promote airline consolidation, at least in the short term. "These alliances are not much of a threat incrementally. Most have totally different route systems and disparate management styles," he says, citing United Airlines' new Star Alliance, which includes Germany's Lufthansa, the Scandinavian airline SAS, Thai Airways, Air Canada, Air New Zealand, the Japanese airline ANA, plus airlines from Australia and Brazil. "Look at all the bulls in that herd," he says. "Who's going to run it?"

As for alliances "turning into some kind of monolith, I don't think we're there and I don't think we will be there for some time," he says. "It's too complex."

Alfred E. Kahn, a professor emeritus of economics at Cornell University and one of the architects of airline deregulation, fears the airlines may be trying to position themselves for the day when international restrictions on ownership are lifted. "If we do achieve our ideal, which is to move to a world where international restrictions are eliminated so anybody can fly anywhere, then the alliances may have eliminated the possibility for more competition between carriers," Kahn says.

But David A. Fuscus, vice president of communications for the Air Transport Association (ATA), doesn't think alliances present anti-competitive worries. "They are a way for an airline to expand its route system without the huge infrastructure investments necessary if you are going to do it as a single airline," he says. "We think it's just another form of competition and that it's healthy."

Will alliances eventually lead to only three or four mega-carriers covering the globe? "That's silly," he says.

[1] Quoted in Don Phillips, "Airline chairman landing after turbulent quarter-century," *Austin American-Statesman*, May 24, 1998.

muter jet there to babysit the slot so they won't lose it."

The end result, he says, is that slots at certain busy airports at peak periods are prohibitively expensive. "There's no way a low-fare carrier could afford one of those slots," he says.

Others say major carriers hoard gates and counter space at their hub airports to keep competitors out, but Boyd says that's "a myth. With almost no exceptions, lack of gates has never kept an airline out of a market."

Antitrust Protection

When Kahn was planning airline deregulation, it was assumed that antitrust laws would be strenuously applied to suppress predatory practices. "Antitrust law becomes much more important when you abandon regulation," Kahn says. But subsequent appointees to the federal judiciary and the Supreme Court would interpret antitrust laws so narrowly that it would become nearly impossible to prosecute a predatory-pricing case, he says.

"The Sherman Act has essentially been gutted by Supreme Court and federal judges primarily appointed by the Reagan and Bush administrations," Kahn says. "The courts have almost written predation out of the antitrust laws."

Kahn says the courts argue that if entry into an industry is legally possible, predators cannot succeed, because the minute they try to raise prices after forcing a competitor out of a market, lower-priced competitors will re-enter the market. "But they are not taking into account the high economic barriers to market entry that exist in the airline industry," he says.

The courts also failed to consider the chilling effect of such predatory practices, Kahn says. "Clearly, one purpose of this kind of behavior is not just to drive somebody out of a market but to send a signal to people about what will happen to them if they try to challenge the company elsewhere."

Luckily, he says, when Congress deregulated the industry it granted the DOT authority to protect consumers against anti-competitive practices. Unlike the Department of Justice, the DOT can act pre-emptively to block predatory practices, says Kahn. "To rely solely on the Justice Department to protect competition in air transport would have been an immense mistake," he says.

Low-Fare Explosion

The development since deregulation that perhaps has most significantly contributed to airline competition has been the phenomenal growth of low-fare leader Southwest Airlines. Southwest "snuck up on the major carriers by staying off their radar screens," says Mitchell. By using only secondary airports and flying point-to-point, it quietly grew to 300 aircraft and today is considered a major airline.

Deregulation opened the airline business to dozens of other newcomers, just as Congress intended. In 1978, there were 36 carriers certified to operate aircraft seating 61 or more passengers. By 1984, there were 123. The number declined in the late '80s as weaker airlines went out of business or were absorbed by stronger companies. By 1993, the number began to rise again as new, no-frills airlines began to emerge.

The new airlines often used aircraft, pilots, mechanics and other airline employees from bankrupt carriers. Boyd insists that many low-fare carriers in the early 1990s were unsafe because of government inaction and a concerted effort to cover up their unsafe conditions.

"Two months prior to the ValuJet crash the DOT published a glowing report about how safe these new airlines were, and how they had saved the consumer $6 billion," Boyd remembers. "It was an election year, and the administration was bragging that these new airlines were part of its program to enhance competition in the airline industry."

But the administration's numbers were skewed, he says, because they included Southwest, which had an impeccable safety record but was too large to be considered a start-up by then. "Southwest represented 98 percent of the total traffic mix in that report," says Boyd.

"The FAA knew at the time that these airlines were unsafe," he says. An internal FAA report recommending that ValuJet be shut down — dated nearly three months before the crash — was ordered buried by FAA officials, the report's author later testified at NTSB hearings on the crash. There was no NTSB follow-up investigation of his allegation.

The FAA's Duquette would not address Boyd's criticism specifically, but she points out that during the months following the ValuJet crash the agency beefed up its oversight of start-up airlines' use of outside maintenance contractors and assigned its best inspectors to new entrants.

ValuJet was grounded two months after the crash and was cleared to resume domestic service in September of the same year after the company revised and strengthened its maintenance procedures.

Nevertheless, the ValuJet crash was a seminal event in post-deregulation history. It not only focused attention on the FAA's poor policing of start-ups but also led some consumers to avoid the new carriers. "The FAA looked very, very bad," Mitchell says, "and the whole low-fare segment got painted with that same brush."

Then Schiavo fanned the public's fears when immediately after the crash she said that she had "avoided flying on ValuJet," and sometimes "skipped conferences because I would not fly on marginal airlines." [16]

Mitchell claims the major carriers then went on an "aggressive public relations campaign implying that low-fare carriers were not safe. That campaign had an impact and has stuck."

The major carriers then took advantage of the public's unease about start-ups and began flooding low-fare carrier markets with cheap seats, he continues. "It was thought that Delta had made a strategic error in allowing ValuJet to get a foothold in its Atlanta hub," he says. "Their mantra became, 'There will be no more ValuJets.' That's when this whole era of systematic predation really began."

Code-Sharing Trend

Another post-deregulation trend that some say has diminished airline competition is known as "code-sharing." It enables small carriers that partner with big carriers to share the larger partners' two-letter code identifying its flights in computer reservation systems. Thus the smaller carrier's flights appear as "through" flights rather than as connecting flights, which normally appear lower in the computer listings. The regional carriers are also allowed to tie into their larger partners' marketing and frequent-flyer programs, and schedules are coordinated for convenient connections.

Code-sharing has also gone global. Many U.S. and foreign airlines now have code-sharing agreements, called global alliances, that enable them to expand their services internationally. (*See story, p. 168.*)

Code-sharing has led the major airlines to rely increasingly on both regional airlines and global alliances, two trends that have exacerbated labor tensions between major carriers and their employees. Regional airline employees are pushing for wages and benefits comparable to those paid by the major carriers, and mainline unions worry that carriers will increasingly rely on lower-paid regional and international employees, threatening their salaries and job security.

Such fears erupted in February

when American Airlines bought Reno Air. The regional airline's pilots earned significantly less than American pilots, who staged a massive sickout, disrupting more than 6,700 flights. The action prompted a court-ordered $45.5-million fine against the union, which finally reached a settlement with American on July 16.

The downward pressure on wages and benefits could not be coming at a worse time for some union members, many of whom were hoping to reap the benefits of the record profits currently being enjoyed by the industry. Airline unions accepted substantial reductions in pay and benefits in the early 1990s, when the industry was sustaining heavy losses. Now they were hoping to recoup some of those losses. ■

CURRENT SITUATION

DOT Guidelines

When the DOT proposed its predatory-pricing guidelines, "the industry came down on them like a ton of bricks," remembers Kahn. "Congress found itself torn between pressure from the industry and complaints from constituents, particularly business travelers."

The House ordered the NRC study while the DOT began reviewing the more than 6,000 comments it received from the public about its proposed rule. The ATA calls the DOT's guidelines an attempt to "re-regulate" the industry that will hinder competition and keep airfares artificially high.

The DOT's analysis of industry competition is "biased and erroneous," and based on a "misleading analysis of fare trends in a very few selected segments," the group argues in a 26-page response to the department's airline competition white paper justifying the guidelines.

"Competition is significantly greater today than when the industry was deregulated," the ATA paper said, plus prices are lower and barriers to entry are low, "except for government constraints imposed at a very few airports."

Hudson claims the DOT guidelines would outlaw price wars by establishing a floor on airfares. "They would protect new carriers from having to dramatically lower fares to gain market share and would prohibit existing carriers from meeting price competition," says Hudson. "That's not competition."

Instead, Hudson's group wants the DOT to require airlines to lock in low fares for "a reasonable period of time, like six months or more," and prohibit flooding routes with new flights when a new carrier comes in.

But Mitchell insists the guidelines do not set a floor on fares. "The policy is not designed to dampen competitive response to new entries," he says, but to improve investor confidence in low-fare carriers. "And it really is the low-fare segment of the industry that has [competitive] pricing," he says.

Adam D. Thierer, a scholar at the Heritage Foundation, finds the DOT's plan inefficient and ineffective. It will "only ensure a return to the stagnant, cartel-like markets that existed before liberalization," Thierer wrote.[17]

The best way to increase competition and consumer protection is through further deregulation, increased foreign competition, privatizing airports and allowing market-based pricing at airports for takeoff times, slots and gates, Thierer says.

Meanwhile, confusion reigns while the DOT guidelines are being revised, and the Justice Department suit against American wends its way through the courts. Major carriers don't know how hard they can compete, and low-fare carriers don't know how much they'll be protected.

Congress to Act?

When Congress considers increasing federal funds for airport expansion, competition is expected to be a major issue. The NRC report has given legislators plenty to think about, especially since it says that the DOT's predation guidelines could stifle competition rather than encourage it. The council was unanimous, however, in recommending that policy-makers could boost airline competition by:

- Encouraging airports to curtail exclusive gate-leasing contracts by linking federal aid for airport construction to airports' progress in increasing gate access.
- Monitoring the bonuses airlines give travel agents to steer business in their direction.
- Allowing more competition from foreign carriers in domestic markets.
- Screening proposed domestic and international alliances and partnerships to ensure they do not adversely affect competition.
- Replacing slot controls and perimeter rules with "congestion fees," or higher taxes on peak-period travel, to divert traffic from congested airports to less crowded nearby airports.

Economists have recommended airport-congestion fees for 30 years, Kahn says. "But the airports just haven't done it. It's insane. They should vary their charges based on peak use, like we do for electric power and telephones. But because airports are owned and subsidized by governments, they don't care about pricing their services intelligently."

Legislation pending in the Senate and House would tinker with the slot rules. The Senate bill increases slots at Reagan National and O'Hare. The House bill would slowly phase out slots at Chicago and the two New York airports, and add six slots at Reagan National.

"That would certainly increase competition," says Mitchell. "Having access to those lucrative business markets can be the difference between profit and loss for a new entrant."

But the battle over slots won't be pretty. Neighbors of already-congested airports oppose additional flights and would energetically oppose unlimited flights. And airlines enjoying grandfathered slot rights would undoubtedly strongly resist losing them.

"This is big money, and it's a big, big issue," says Todd Hauptli, senior vice president of policy and government affairs for the American Association of Airport Executives. "These airlines will cut each others' throats when they are fighting over slots, particularly at places like O'Hare, where American and United both have a major presence."

Pressure to boost airline competition is also coming from businessmen, members of Congress and small-town constituents. "Members from upstate New York complain that it's cheaper for them to fly to Paris than to Washington, D.C.," says a House aviation subcommittee staffer.

Another ugly battle looms over funds for airport expansion. A House-approved bill introduced by Rep. Shuster would double the amount of money available for airport construction and protect it from "raids" for other budgetary purposes by holding the funds "off-budget."

Shuster has long argued that it is immoral to tax passengers for airport construction and then not use it for those purposes. "This bill forces the government to preserve aviation ticket taxes for aviation improvements," Shuster said on June 15.

For years more money has been collected in federal airport taxes than has been spent on airports, creating an estimated $8 billion cash reserve in the airport trust fund. "In the past, it was used to mask the true size of the [federal] deficit," says Fuscus. "Now they want to keep it in the budget because it makes the surplus look larger."

The Senate bill maintains current airport construction spending, but Senate budget hawks adamantly oppose placing airport funds off-budget.

Given the $3 billion annual shortfall in airport construction funds cited by the GAO and the huge increase in air travel projected within the next decade, Hauptli hopes conferees can quickly reach a compromise that will release more funds for airport expansion.

"The number of passengers traveling each year is expected to rise from 618 million to 1 billion in less than a decade," he says. "That's like taking the entire U.S. population and layering it on top of an already crowded, congested and delayed system.

"We need longer runways, more gates and more facilities," he says. "It takes a long time to build all that stuff. We've got to start now."

Meanwhile, on Sept. 15 several major airlines unveiled the details of their voluntary Customers First programs. But Sen. Ron Wyden, D-Ore., who had sponsored a "passenger rights" bill earlier, called the airlines' voluntary programs "toothless gobbledygook" because many of the provisions would not be legally binding.

Wyden offered two amendments to the DOT appropriations bill being considered by the Senate. One provision would have required airlines to reveal when they overbook a flight, and the other would require airlines to quote passengers the lowest fare available when they request it. In a voice vote, senators agreed to ask the DOT to investigate airlines' lowest-fare and overbooking practices. They also passed a watered-down "sense of the Senate" resolution that overbooking or not giving passengers the cheapest fare when requested should be considered a deceptive trade practice. ■

OUTLOOK

No Relief in Sight?

Several pending proposals would establish federal grants to help small and medium-sized cities attract more air service.

The ATA strongly opposes efforts to influence where air carriers establish routes. "Airlines go into communities because they think they can make money there," says Fuscus. "If communities have enough passengers, airlines will vie for the chance to carry them."

Others contend that overcrowding at major airports and poor service in smaller towns could be relieved by using more "regional jets" — a popular new class of faster, quieter jets with 40-70 seats. "Regional jets are the future for small and medium-sized airports," says Hudson, but "powerful forces" are blocking their increased use at regional airports.

"The major carriers and large airports have a huge investment in the big hub airports," he says. "They don't want long-distance flights going in and out of these secondary airports because it will reduce their traffic and thus their revenues."

At Issue:

Should the government do more to remedy anti-competitive practices in the airline industry?

RODNEY E. SLATER
Secretary of Transportation

FROM "PROPOSED GUIDELINES ON UNFAIR COMPETITIVE PRACTICES IN THE AIRLINE INDUSTRY," APRIL 6, 1998.

yes

This year is the 20th anniversary of airline deregulation. Looking back, deregulation has been good for both airlines and consumers. . . . In the deregulated environment, the industry and government working together have made the aviation system more efficient, delivering better service at lower prices for the hundreds of millions of us who fly every year.

The purpose of deregulation was to make the airline industry competitive and make air travel affordable. But competition only works if it exists. So, today we are proposing a set of guidelines on unfair competitive practices to ensure that deregulation works for another 20 years.

There is growing concern that major carriers are willing to lose money — lots of it — in the short run to drive off competition; selling so many seats at low fares that the airline's strategy is economically rational only if it forces out competition from low-fare, start-up airlines. The start-ups say these anti-competitive practices are driving them out of markets, especially at the nation's busiest airports. Some say they have been driven out of business altogether by these practices. . . .

[T]he policy statement I am proposing today defines what kind of competitive behavior is unfair and exclusionary. And the department will consider taking enforcement action against such conduct. This policy is not intended to ensure the success of any start-up carrier, but rather to ensure a level playing field. Consumers deserve a pro-competitive standard that helps ensure affordable airfares and accessible service. To provide a level playing field, we must preserve vigorous competition and prohibit unfair exclusionary practices meant solely to eliminate that competition. . . .

We will consider that a major carrier is engaging in unfair exclusionary practices if, in response to entry by a new carrier into one or more of its local hub markets, it pursues a strategy of price cuts or capacity increases, or both, that either (1) causes it to forgo more revenue than all of the new entrant's capacity could have diverted from it, or (2) results in substantially lower operating profits — or greater operating losses — in the short run than would a reasonable alternative strategy for competing with the new entrant. . . .

Let me be clear: This is not an effort to re-regulate commercial aviation. We are encouraging vigorous competition. Major airlines do not want to go back to the days of regulation, and neither do we.

ADAM D. THIERER
Alex C. Walker Fellow in Economic Policy, The Heritage Foundation

FROM "20TH ANNIVERSARY OF AIRLINE DEREGULATION: CAUSE FOR CELEBRATION, NOT RE-REGULATION," APRIL 22, 1998. EXCERPTED WITH PERMISSION.

no

Despite years of falling prices, increased travel options, and vigorous industry competition, some federal policy-makers appear to be on the brink of abandoning the incredibly successful 20-year experiment in airline competition following deregulation in the 1970s. [The Department of Transportation's (DOT) proposed guidelines] to remedy alleged anti-competitive practices within the industry . . . specifically target efforts by major carriers to offer consumers significant discounts in order to compete with smaller carriers or new entrants. If such fare wars hurt the smaller companies or drive them from the market, DOT will take action against the larger carriers.

The DOT claims that these steps will "ensure that free-market principles and competition continue to thrive in commercial aviation," and says that its proposed enforcement policy "does not attempt to regulate the market in any way." The reality, however, is far different. . . . As James L. Gattuso, vice president for public policy and management at the Competitive Enterprise Institute (CEI), observes, "The message is, don't compete too hard; don't lower your prices too much." In short, the DOT's proposed enforcement policy is tantamount to reintroducing federal bureaucracy and regulation into the airline market, which would have a chilling effect on competition by discouraging fare wars that result in significant savings for consumers.

Surprisingly, threats of renewed DOT regulation of the airline industry have been met with casual acceptance or, worse, general approval on Capitol Hill. In an attempt to counter such calls for re-regulation, some legislators have even suggested that increased subsidization of small carriers or new industry entrants is the best way to bring more competition to the industry, thereby ensuring price competition and lower fares. Such calls for the re-regulation or increased subsidization of the aviation industry are unjustified. . . .

New regulations or subsidies will not alleviate any of the perceived problems that the DOT or some members of Congress fear may arise. Reintroducing bureaucratic regulation into the airline marketplace will only ensure a return to the stagnant, cartel-like markets that existed before liberalization. There are better solutions to many of the problems the DOT addresses in its enforcement policy — solutions that do not require the re-regulation of airline routes and rates.

Travel Agents Fighting for Survival

Travelers buying airline ticket these days are confronted by a maze of puzzling prices, seemingly ridiculous restrictions and inexplicable inconsistencies.

Short trips often cost more than longer ones, traditionally expensive last-minute fares are sometimes offered at bargain-basement prices and passengers on the same flight have often paid wildly differing amounts. As a result, infrequent travelers are confused, and business passengers complain they're been price-gouged.

A recent National Research Council (NRC) report found that the spread between the lowest and highest prices paid for airline seats widened during the 1990s. In 1992, passengers paying the highest price for an airline ticket paid twice as much as the average ticket price. By 1998, the highest-priced tickets — usually those bought by business travelers — were nearly three times as high as the lowest-priced fares, the NRC found. [1]

Adding to the confusion, prices quoted by travel agents can differ widely from prices quoted by airlines, according to a 1997 survey by the U.S. Public Interest Research Group (USPIRG). The nonprofit group compared price quotes from travel agents and airlines for trips between 73 different city pairs among 28 cities. They found that the fares quoted by the two groups could vary by up to $1,000 or more — even when the traveler asked for the lowest prices available.

Even more confusing are the sudden up-and-down changes in last-minute airfares, which traditionally have been the most expensive tickets a passenger could buy. The sharp decreases are the result of the new airline practice of quickly selling off seats about to go unused by discounting them dramatically and advertising them on the Internet.

Some cyber-savvy travelers are searching the Internet for travel bargains, but aviation consultant Michael Boyd of Evergreen, Colo., says they would be better off using a travel agent. "Anybody who books a flight through the Internet is a fool," says the blunt-talking Boyd. "A good travel agent can save you a lot more money than you can save on the Internet."

The USPIRG survey found overwhelmingly that travel agents quoted lower fares far more often than the airlines did.

But that may not be the case too much longer, say some industry-watchers. Because airlines can now market directly to consumers through the Internet, they don't need travel agents to market their product anymore, Boyd says.

The retailing of airline tickets is rapidly shifting from the days when travel agents sold most airlines' seats. "Fifteen or 20 years ago, travel agents had enormous power and were arrogant, condescending extortionists," he says. "They would tell an airline, 'Either you find a seat for my customer or I won't book any more of your flights.'

"Today, they can't pull that stunt," Boyd continues, because now the consumer usually has a frequent-flyer card and tells the travel agent which airline he wants to fly.

"Now the role of the travel agent has changed," says Boyd. "Now they are the folks looking out for the consumer's best interest, by helping them find the lowest possible fare."

"Now the airlines view travel agents as the last consumer bulwark, and they want them dead. D-E-A-D, dead, gone," he says.

Paul Ruden, executive vice president of the American Society of Travel Agents, says that airlines "certainly are doing what they can to disable travel agents."

"The airlines clearly no longer believe they need an intermediary to sell their product," Ruden says. He told

Pilots' unions also oppose large carriers becoming too dependent on regional jets because pilots are paid less to fly the smaller craft. Some pilots' contracts actually limit the number of regional jets carriers can own, which Hudson says should be banned as a restraint of trade.

But John Mazor, a spokesman for the Airline Pilots Association, says pilots are not trying to block the purchase of regional jets outright but to limit the number airlines buy. "Regional jets should not replace bigger jets but should be used to enhance and cross-feed the larger jets," he says.

Boyd strongly disagrees with Hudson's prediction that regional jets will help small and medium-sized communities obtain better or cheaper air service. "They are the wave of the future in terms of mega-carriers making money, yes," says Boyd, "but not for increasing service to small towns. These airplanes are way too expensive to fly to small communities where traffic is low."

In fact, small towns will actually lose service because of regional jets, Boyd insists, because airlines are replacing the less expensive turboprops now used to serve small towns with regional jets. "When airlines get rid of their turboprops, they will eventually pull out of the small towns," he says.

Hudson says national planning is needed to better distribute air service, much as basic planning in the rail and the highway system prevented gridlock and high prices, he says.

Salfen agrees. "Somewhere down the road, the airlines will have to sit down and realistically schedule their

Congress last spring that airlines have adopted a "pattern of policies and practices" designed to prevent the traveling public from receiving "neutral, comparative information . . . about cheaper alternatives." The airlines' goal, he said, is to force the public to deal directly with "biased sources of information provided by the airlines themselves." [2]

Among other things, Ruden says, the airlines have slashed travel agents' traditional commissions by more than 30 percent and refuse to pay agents more than $5 for any ticket they sell via the Internet. Even as airlines are increasingly selling tickets on the Internet, he says, "they don't want travel agents setting up Web sites and selling tickets from them."

After their commissions were cut, many agents were forced to charge customers "transaction fees" to cover operating costs. But millions of customers refused to pay the new fees and decided to buy tickets directly from the airlines, contributing to the closure of 12 percent of the nation's independent travel agencies between 1995 and 1998, Ruden said.

Some airlines have also begun paying higher "bonus" commissions to travel agents who steer customers in their direction on certain routes, especially those served by low-cost competitors. The NRC report said this practice could threaten consumers' access to unbiased information about lower-priced airfares.

All of these tactics put the consumer "right where the airlines want him — bereft of a neutral source of information to deal with a bewildering array of complex air fares and services," Ruden said.

Boyd is not optimistic that anything can be done to halt the trend. "I don't think there's any way to protect the travel agency business. The airlines have the right to retail their product any way they want to. The only answer is for consumers to insist on using them."

So far, says Ruden, consumers seem to be doing just that. Travel agents sold 80 percent of airline tickets during the last five years, he points out. "So far most of the Internet business is coming from those who already bought their tickets directly from the airlines. But eventually sales on the Internet are bound to cut into travel agents' business."

As more travel agents go out of business, he predicted, consumer alternatives will decrease, "resulting in significantly higher consumer travel costs."

"There are billions at stake here," says Ruden. "And the airlines will get a huge windfall without ever having to raise prices."

David A. Fuscus, vice president of communications for the Air Transport Association, which represents the nation's major passenger air carriers, says there's "no organized effort to get rid of travel agents."

"We paid travel agents over $6 billion in commissions last year," he says. "Travel agents will always be a big part of our business. There will always be a large market out there for certain consumers who prefer to use travel agents."

Yet the airlines definitely hope to expand the percentage of tickets they sell directly to consumers via the Internet, he says. Last year airlines sold only about 3-4 percent of their tickets on the Internet, he pointed out.

"Are we interested in increasing that in the future?" he asks. "You bet. Any time we can bring down our costs, we will."

---

[1] John R. Meyer, et al., "Entry and Competition in the U.S. Airline Industry: Issues and Opportunities," Transportation Research Board, National Research Council, July 1999, p. E-4.

[2] Testimony before Senate Commerce Committee, March 11, 1999.

flights in and out of particular airports," he says.

Meanwhile, an increasing number of economists and aviation experts say the quickest way to boost competition is to allow foreign airlines to operate within the U.S. "If we could get competitors from abroad, it would break the major carriers' stranglehold," says Mitchell. For instance, British airline magnate Richard Branson of Virgin Atlantic has proposed expanding his airline into the U.S.

Mitchell acknowledges that opening the domestic market to foreign airlines will be tough, but he says it may gain momentum now that the NRC has recommended it. "Sen. McCain is interested in the subject and told me that he would consider hearings on it," Mitchell says.

But Fuscus doesn't see foreign carriers operating inside the United States because of national-security concerns. The Defense Department opposes foreign ownership of U.S. carriers because in wartime they want to control U.S. airspace and requisition commercial aircraft for troop transport. "It's so far out of the realm that we don't spend an awful lot of time looking at it," he says.

Others say airline congestion may be relieved by the growth of the Internet and cheaper long-distance phone services. "Telecommunications may supplant the business trip, or once you start exchanging information, it may whet the appetite to see people," Southwest CEO Herb Kelleher said recently. "I don't know which is right." [18]

But most observers do not see much immediate relief for harried airline passengers. In fact, many predict the problems will get worse before they get better. "The financial interests of the large carriers and large airports are lined up to keep at least moderate crowding at the major airports," Hudson says.

"Poor service is not going to go away," says Mitchell, "because with the advent of the Internet the airlines can quickly get rid of seats about to go empty." And the airlines' periodic passenger-appeasement efforts won't fix systemic problems plaguing the industry, he says.

"The systems, processes and procedures were never designed to anticipate a situation in which every seat is filled from Monday to Friday," he says. "That's what we are having on a sustained basis, and the system is breaking down and backing up," he says. "But you can't fix one piece of it without getting to the root causes." ■

FOR MORE INFORMATION

Air Transport Association of America, 1301 Pennsylvania Ave. N.W., Suite 1100, Washington, D.C. 20004; (202) 626-4000; www.air-transport.org. This trade organization representing U.S. scheduled air carriers promotes aviation safety and monitors legislation and regulations affecting the airlines industry.

American Association of Airport Executives, 601 Madison St., Alexandria, Va. 22314; (703) 824-0500; www.airportnet.org. This organization of airport managers and consultants monitors legislation and regulations affecting the construction and management of airports.

Aviation Consumer Action Project, 529 14th St., Suite 1265, N.W., Washington, D.C. 20045; (202) 638-4000; www.acap1971.org. This consumer advocacy group, founded in 1971 by Ralph Nader, represents the interests of airline passengers before Congress and federal agencies.

Business Travel Coalition, 3177 Colony Lane, Suite 200, Plymouth Meeting, Pa. 19462; (610) 834-3750; http://btc-online.com. This coalition of large corporations and small businesses lobbies Congress and regulatory agencies to lower business travel costs by increasing airline industry competition.

National Air Disaster Alliance and Foundation, 2020 Pennsylvania, N.W., PMB 315, Washington, D.C. 20006-1846; (888) 444-6232; www.planesafe.org. This nonprofit organization, whose members include the families of airplane crash victims, advocates for improved safety and security on airlines.

Notes

[1] National Research Council, press release, July 30, 1999.

[2] Bud Shuster, "A Yes to Aviation Investment and Safety," *The Washington Post*, Op-Ed, April 15, 1999.

[3] Quoted in David Field, "UAL chief: United trying to fix glitches," *USA Today*, May 4, 1999.

[4] "Competition in the U.S. Domestic Airline Industry: The Need for a Policy to Prevent Unfair Practices," Department of Transportation, August 1998.

[5] Quoted in Glen Johnson, "American Air Faces Antitrust Charge," AP Online, May 14, 1999.

[6] Darryl Jenkins, "An Examination of Why New Entrant Airlines Fail," Aviation Institute, The George Washington University, June 30, 1998.

[7] Johnson, *op. cit.*

[8] "Implications for Customer Service, Competition, and Airline Operations of 'Passenger Bill of Rights' Legislation," Economic Strategy Institute, July 23, 1999.

[9] Charles M. Barclay, "America's Future in Airport Infrastructure," American Association of Airport Executives, July 21, 1999.

[10] Interview with Kyodo News Service, July 26, 1999.

[11] "Air passengers must look after own safety: Schiavo," *Japan Transportation Scan*, (Kyodo News International), Aug. 2, 1999.

[12] *Ibid.*

[13] For background on deregulation, see Richard L. Worsnop, "Airline Safety," *The CQ Researcher*, Oct. 8, 1993, pp. 865-888.

[14] "Airline Deregulation, Changes in Airfares, Service Quality and Barriers to Entry," General Accounting Office, March 1999.

[15] Steven A. Morrison and Clifford Winston, "Foul Regulatory Weather Grounds Airline Competition," *The Wall Street Journal*, Dec. 3, 1997.

[16] Quoted in John Merline, "How Safe Are Cut-rate Airlines?" *Investor's Business Daily*, May 23, 1996.

[17] Adam D. Thierer, "20th Anniversary of Airline Deregulation: Cause for Celebration, Not Re-regulation," Heritage Foundation, April 22, 1998.

[18] Quoted in "Southwest CEO tops this year, magazine says," *USA Today*, July 12, 1999.

Bibliography

Selected Sources Used

Books

Petzinger, Thomas, Jr., *Hard Landing*, Random House, 1995.
The Wall Street Journal reporter and editor tells the stories of the chief executive officers who oversaw the restructuring of the airline industry following deregulation.

Schiavo, Mary, with Sabra Chartrand, *Flying Blind, Flying Safe*, Avon Books, 1997.
The former Federal Aviation Administration (FAA) inspector general claims the agency has a slapdash approach to safety inspections and a "tombstone mentality" of enforcing regulations after disasters instead of before.

Articles

"Air passengers must look after own safety: Schiavo," *Japan Transportation Scan*, (Kyodo News International), Aug. 2, 1999.
Former FAA Inspector General Mary Schiavo says the May 1996 ValuJet crash was a deadly example of declining FAA safety standards.

Morrison, Steven A., and Clifford Winston, "Foul Regulatory Weather Grounds Airline Competition," *The Wall Street Journal*, Dec. 3, 1997.
Two economists estimate that government-imposed perimeter rules and slot controls cost air travelers about $1 billion a year in higher air fares.

Shuster, Bud, "A Yes to Aviation Investment and Safety," *The Washington, Post*, April 15, 1999.
Airport congestion is costing the airlines $2.5 billion a year in extra costs and the American people more than $7 billion in lost productivity, complains the chairman of the House Committee on Transportation and Infrastructure.

Stoller, Gary, "Most Jets Inspected Show Wire Troubles," *USA Today*, Sept. 13, 1999.
The National Transportation Safety Board has found wiring problems on nearly all of the two dozen jets it inspected during the last two years as part of its investigation into the TWA Flight 800 crash.

Reports and Studies

***Airline Deregulation, Changes in Airfares, Service Quality and Barriers to Entry*, General Accounting Office, March 1999.**
The GAO finds that airfares are consistently higher at "gate-constrained" and "slot-constrained" airports than at airports of comparable size without constraints.

Barclay, Charles M., "America's Future in Airport Infrastructure," American Association of Airport Executives, July 21, 1999.
The president of the AAAE points out that over the past four years, while annual airline passenger trips increased 16 percent, annual investment in airport development decreased 23 percent. But Barclay doesn't see airport privatization as the answer.

***Competition in the U.S. Domestic Airline Industry: The Need for a Policy to Prevent Unfair Practices*, Department of Transportation, August 1998.**
This DOT white paper on airline competition gives examples of what it calls "unfair exclusionary behavior" used by airlines to block competition from new airlines.

***Implications for Customer Service, Competition, and Airline Operations of 'Passenger Bill of Rights' Legislation*, Economic Strategy Institute, July 23, 1999.**
The Washington-based institute argues that passenger bills of rights would produce poorer customer service, higher fares, lower efficiency and reduced airline profitability, which might create incentives that conflict with safety objectives.

Jenkins, Darryl, "An Examination of Why New Entrant Airlines Fail," The George Washington University, June 30, 1998.
The director of the Aviation Institute finds that the 130 airlines that have failed since deregulation failed because of lack of financing, bad business decisions and poor business plans, not predatory pricing.

Meyer, John R., et al., "Entry and Competition in the U.S. Airline Industry: Issues and Opportunities," National Research Council, July 1999.
The council finds alarming trends against healthy rivalry within the airline industry. To encourage more competition, the council recommends that the government encourage airports to curtail exclusive gate-leasing contracts, monitor the bonuses airlines give travel agents to steer business in their direction, allow foreign carriers to compete in domestic markets and other changes.

Thierer, Adam D., "20th Anniversary of Airline Deregulation: Cause for Celebration, Not Re-regulation," The Heritage Foundation, April 22, 1998.
Thierer, a fellow in economic policy at the foundation, says deregulation has resulted in more flights at cheaper prices and that the government should lift the last of the government controls over airline travel.

11 Digital Commerce

ADRIEL BETTELHEIM

Illinois manufacturer Arnie Koldenhoven went looking for a few tons of steel coils recently — but not in the usual places. Instead of poring over price lists from local mills or comparison shopping by phone, the president of Arrowhead Steel simply clicked on a new Internet auction site fast becoming the talk of the steel industry.

Almost instantly, Koldenhoven was presented with a choice of three suppliers. He keyed in his bid and within minutes was linked with Weirton Steel, a West Virginia company that unloads its surplus stock online.

"It's kind of the next step in our business," says Koldenhoven, who makes parts for cars, office furniture and high-tech equipment. "Fifteen years ago, the fax machine relieved us from having to rely entirely on the mail or phone calls. This will make us even more efficient — and help us handle more material in less time."

Business-to-business transactions like Koldenhoven's are fueling a dramatic surge in U.S. Internet commerce, transforming the World Wide Web from a domain of chat rooms, weather reports and pornography into a powerful selling tool. Indeed, Forrester Research in Cambridge, Mass., estimates that Internet business trade will explode from $43 billion in 1998 to $1.3 trillion by 2003 — 9 percent of all business sales in the United States.

Companies increasingly are using the Internet for everything from scheduling truck and rail shipments to ordering parts and designing telecommunications equipment. The online transactions save time and cut costs by reducing the need for expensive sales staffs, in-house computer networks and voluminous paper records. [1]

From *The CQ Researcher,* February 5, 1999.

Industry experts foresee many more Internet business applications within the next five years. Farms will be able to take round-the-clock orders for crops from food processors and grocery chains. Utilities will use the Web to buy most of their electricity and gas and to schedule shipments. Construction firms and government agencies will bid out contracts online. Drug and medical supply companies will use the Internet to replenish hospital chains.

The availability of more goods is being accompanied by a profusion of new services, thanks to the vast array of customized software available on the Internet. The technology allows a Wall Street company to connect with a client in Japan using a real-time translation service. An energy trader in Houston can route a telephone call to the Middle East through an online transcription service and get a text version of his conversation delivered via e-mail. And Web-based auctions like the one Koldenhoven used are bringing together small- and medium-sized businesses from every corner of the world.

"It's not sexy, but it's where the action is," says Forrester business analyst Steve Bell. "We're at a point where the number of businesses online has reached critical mass, meaning the market is going to grow dramatically."

But many problems loom. Sticky questions about how to tax goods and services in the borderless realm of cyberspace could imperil future state and municipal tax collections. The government has yet to define what is appropriate online speech — a particularly touchy issue in a medium where pornography is widely available and annual sales of X-rated material exceed $900 million, according to best estimates. [2] Moreover, politicians and government regulators appear to be uncertain how to protect users against online fraud and unscrupulous business practices.

The rise of business-to-business transactions has generally been overshadowed by the incessantly hyped boom in consumer-driven Internet purchases. Online sales to individuals have turned electronic retailers like bookseller Amazon.com and eBay, the popular consumer auction service, into household names — and stock market darlings. Internet retailers accounted for at least $3 billion in sales during the recent holiday shopping season.

Surprisingly, however, consumer transactions account for less than one-quarter of Internet commerce (and only a tiny fraction of all retail sales). The lion's share of online commerce is business-to-business transactions. According to Zona Research, in Redwood City, Calif., they account for 77 percent of online sales and will be the driving force behind significantly greater use of the Internet in the next decade.

"We're seeing the emergence of online market-makers, who can act as intermediates between buyers and sellers, offer a contract, coordinate bids, do language services and arrange shipping, all in one place," says Zona chief economist Jack Staff. "It makes doing business more efficient, with less potential for mistakes."

The dynamic environment is prompting intense jockeying by computer companies that provide links to the Internet and offer software and consulting for digital commerce. In one notable move, America Online Inc. (AOL) struck an agreement to

Surge Expected in U.S. Online Commerce

The total value of Internet commerce in the United States is expected to grow from less than $50 billion in 1998 to more than $1.3 trillion by 2003. Computers and electronics will continue to lead the field, but quantum increases are expected in transactions involving motor vehicles, petrochemicals and other industries.

Value of U.S. Internet Commerce (In $ Billions)

Industry Sectors	1998	1999	2000	2001	2002	2003
COMPUTING & ELECTRONICS	$19.7	$50.4	$121.4	$229.1	$319.1	$395.3
MOTOR VEHICLES	3.7	9.3	22.7	53.2	114.3	212.9
PETROCHEMICALS	4.7	10.3	22.6	48.0	96.8	178.3
UTILITIES	7.1	15.4	32.2	62.9	110.6	169.5
PAPER & OFFICE PRODUCTS	1.3	2.9	6.4	14.3	31.1	65.2
SHIPPING & WAREHOUSING	1.2	2.9	6.8	15.4	32.7	61.6
FOOD & AGRICULTURE	0.3	3.0	6.3	13.1	26.7	53.6
CONSUMER GOODS	1.4	2.9	6.1	12.7	26.0	51.9
PHARMACEUTICAL & MEDICAL	0.6	1.4	3.5	8.5	20.0	44.1
AEROSPACE & DEFENSE	2.5	6.6	14.8	25.6	34.0	38.2
CONSTRUCTION	0.4	1.6	3.4	7.0	14.2	28.6
HEAVY INDUSTRIES	0.1	1.3	2.5	4.7	8.7	15.8
INDUSTRIAL EQUIPMENT	14.1	1.3	2.4	4.5	8.5	15.8
TOTAL (IN $ BILLIONS)	$43.1	$109.3	$251.1	$499.0	$842.7	$1,330.8

Source: Forester Research Inc.

acquire Netscape Communications Corp. in a complicated $4.2 billion deal that also involves Sun Microsystems. AOL — an online service primarily known for its chat rooms, e-mail and news and weather reports — hopes to gain the 70 million people who surf the Internet using Netscape's browser software, then help small and large businesses to create virtual shops to sell to them.

"It will allow more [business] partners to get to market faster," AOL President and Chief Operating Officer Robert Pittman told reporters after the deal was announced. "Simply put, what we are doing is we are going to companies that are expert at building brick-and-mortar stores and giving them the tools they need to build virtual stores."

Assuming the deal is completed, the enlarged AOL will join elite company. It will directly compete with computer industry colossus Microsoft Corp., whose Windows software has become the industry standard for personal computers. Both will try to grab market share from IBM Corp., regarded as the current digital commerce market leader because of its sophisticated software products and consulting services. [3]

Another significant deal is AT&T's proposed $31.8 billion acquisition of cable television giant Tele-Communications Inc. (TCI). The combination, if approved by federal authorities, would create a new outlet for obtaining high-speed Internet access through TCI's cable systems. That would make it easier for computer users to make transactions and transfer large amounts of digital data.[4]

The various deals envision a day within the next decade when high-capacity digital networks provide a seamless link in cyberspace. Consumers and business people will be able to click on the Internet from their televisions, watch TV shows on their desktop computers and make phone calls from either device. The services will be brought to offices and homes by satellite, wireless, microwave, cable TV and telephone technologies, all linked in one giant network.

But such innovations are posing difficult questions for regulators and lawmakers. Should companies have to pay sales taxes on the goods and services they purchase online, as they would in face-to-face transactions? If not, will a de facto tax-free zone in cyberspace siphon business away from traditional merchants and erode local governments' tax bases? Can the federal government regulate advertising claims and the type of speech used in Internet marketing? Could sensitive information exchanged in electronic transactions —say, a company's sales estimates or an individual's medical records — fall into the hands of unscrupulous operators?

Digital commerce currently is free from most government interference, and the Clinton administration hopes it stays that way. The White House last November released a lengthy policy report that called for no new regulations on electronic transactions. Instead, it urged Internet companies to regulate themselves. President Clinton also called on government agencies to develop incentives for private companies to create high-speed networks that carry voice, video and data transmissions faster.

Congress has taken a similar tack, passing legislation last year by Sen. Ron Wyden, D-Ore., and Rep. Christopher Cox., R-Calif., that places a three-year moratorium on states and localities imposing new taxes on Internet transactions and establishes a panel to study ways to create a uniform tax. "To subject the Internet to a crazy-quilt of inconsistent local and state taxes would have a chilling effect on the growth of that marketplace," Wyden says.

"To subject the Internet to a crazy-quilt of inconsistent local and state taxes would have a chilling effect on the growth of that marketplace."

— Sen. Ron Wyden, D-Ore.

Many policy analysts believe the minimalist approach makes sense. They note past efforts to regulate prices and entry in industries such as transportation wound up stifling competition and not serving the public interest. Indeed, the analysts say the whole point of digital commerce is to decentralize business entrepreneurship, empowering citizens while reducing the power of governments.

"Policy-makers should let markets, rather than governments, address any problems associated with digital technology," Brookings Institution economics scholar Robert Litan and Cato Institute Chairman William Niskanen argue in their 1998 book *Going Digital*. "The digital revolution is overwhelmingly a private-sector phenomenon and should remain so."

But critics say there are many legitimate areas for regulation, such as privacy and security, and argue more should be done to protect consumers in the lawless frontier of cyberspace. Some Web sites, such as the popular GeoCities site, have drawn fire from the Federal Trade Commission (FTC) for compiling personal information about users and distributing it to third parties. Hackers also have infiltrated commercial Web sites, forcing companies to create firewalls, identity cards and user passwords to secure their networks.[5]

"On certain issues, the administration is just not doing enough," says Marc Rotenberg, director of the Washington-based Electronic Privacy Information Center, a nonprofit group that addresses Internet issues. "It can be fairly asked whether the administration's policy was based on self-regulation or on promoting business interests."

More difficult questions face Clinton administration antitrust officials, who must develop rules for the rapidly changing market. The Department of Justice says it's willing to move against high-tech market abuses that limit innovation, reduce quality or raise prices, and currently is pressing a closely watched federal antitrust suit against Microsoft. The suit charges the Redmond, Wash., corporation with violating a 1995 federal court decree by allegedly requiring computer manufacturers to license Microsoft's new Internet browsing software as an integral part of the company's Windows operating system.

However, administration officials acknowledge that making broad rules for the digital market isn't always clear-cut. Indeed, in still maturing industries, where the next great product seems to appear each week, it's difficult to agree on what constitutes market domination or unfair trade practices. Justice Department officials concede that they may have to take a less paternalistic view and tolerate some joint ventures and near-monopoly conditions until enough competitors emerge. The officials haven't signaled, for instance, whether they will challenge the AOL-Netscape merger — a combination some critics believe limits consumer choice and concentrates power in the market for Internet browsers and gateways.

Assistant Attorney General Joel Klein, the Justice Department's antitrust chief, told a recent Brookings Institution telecommunications conference that antitrust enforcement in high-tech industries should be "modest in scope and surgical in application," adding that each case is different and has to be appraised on its merits. "I'm not here to tackle big corporations or get in the way of economic efficiencies," Klein said.

As government officials ponder responses to the rapid changes coming to the digital marketplace, these are some of the questions that are being asked:

The FCC "hasn't made the Internet the object of its smothering affection yet, but it's just a matter of time. It is in the nature of regulators to find new things to regulate."

— Rep. Michael G. Oxley, R-Ohio

Should the government take a hands-off approach to regulating digital commerce?

"We will do nothing that undermines the capacity of emerging technologies to lift the lives of ordinary Americans," President Clinton, flanked by digital-commerce executives, declared on Nov. 30 at a White House event showcasing his administration's Internet policy.

Clinton essentially favors a hands-off policy when it comes to the Internet, viewing it as a global medium that creates high-paying jobs and now accounts for up to one-third of the nation's annual economic growth, according to Department of Commerce estimates. The White House — and many in Congress —believe regulations would only stifle creativity and create obstacles to further growth. Instead, they are calling on Internet companies to police themselves and adopt voluntary good-business standards that ensure fair pricing and access.

But self-regulation may not be easy. The Internet's very omnipresence and the host of cyberspace issues up for discussion make it difficult for politicians to avoid adopting some guidelines for the marketplace.

The fear of cyberspace predators capturing and selling personal information has fueled calls for privacy laws and stronger encryption software to scramble users' data.

The profusion of Internet pornography twice prompted Congress to pass laws intended to protect minors from viewing cyberporn and questionable speech, though the first effort was struck down as unconstitutional. And even the White House has backed laws making it a crime to develop technologies that could help people circumvent copyright laws or steal intellectual property.

Ira Magaziner — architect of President Clinton's failed health-care plan and, until recently, the administration's Internet czar — insists government, in general, must show restraint and have faith that market forces will correct abuses. In a recent interview in *The New Republic*, Magaziner termed the Internet "as close to a pure marketplace as we've seen," where consumers have access to an almost limitless number of sellers. Competition is assured because a worldwide set of vendors exists, and the barriers to setting up a Web site are comparatively low. In short, buyers and sellers, acting in their own self-interest, will ensure the market prospers and grows, he says. [6]

Others are more skeptical. Privacy advocates say technological advances have made it increasingly easy for online marketers to collect information about individuals and businesses and store it in databases. One way is through the use of "cookies," bits of computer code that can be deposited on a user's computer hard drive to track everything the person does on a Web site. While a cookie can't uncover a user's name or e-mail address, it has an effect similar to following someone down the aisles of a store: It profiles buying habits and stores the information in a database. Later, the information can be used to sell the person something.

Other technologies collect information as people charge groceries, make toll-free phone calls and fill out warranty cards. And as software gets more sophisticated — and databases are linked — the opportunities for surveillance grow. Rotenberg of the Electronic Privacy Information Center says online consumers and businesses will be increasingly vulnerable to security breaches because transactions are typically routed through a number of computers. At any one connection, data can be intercepted and downloaded by a third party.

"Privacy legislation usually comes in response to new technologies, and I'd like to see that apply across the Internet," Rotenberg says. "There are measures to protect cable subscribers, prevent junk faxes and curb telemarketers. I'd like to see an end to the double standard for the Internet."

The current lack of U.S. Internet privacy laws could trigger a trade dispute with European countries, which have adopted strong consumer privacy laws that address the Internet's potential to be a medium for fraud and other problems. A European Union accord that went into effect last year requires any countries or companies that trade personal data with Europe to recognize the tougher standards. That could affect U.S. banks, travel companies and Internet merchants, which now can move large amounts of consumer data around the world without being subject to similar laws.

"[Europe] has given an ultimatum to Washington: Adopt strong privacy laws, or stand the risk of losing countless billions of dollars of business," Simon Davies, director general of Privacy International, a London-based advocacy group, wrote recently in *The Daily Telegraph*. [7]

The Department of Commerce has tried to broker a compromise, encouraging U.S. companies to adopt voluntary privacy codes in return for European grants of immunity from their privacy laws. But European governments have resisted, and the dispute may head to the courts if both sides can't reach mutually acceptable protections.

A related privacy debate surrounds U.S. export controls on encryption software. There are no limits on the

Not Taxing Internet Sales Could Cost Billions

If the federal government doesn't require Internet commerce to be taxed, consumers may take their business to cyberspace, hurting local merchants and eroding communities' tax bases. The potential loss in tax revenue by 2003 could be 20 percent of current local sales taxes, according to some estimates.

Potential Sales-Tax Losses From Electronic Commerce

States	Total U.S. Sales Tax Revenue 1996 ($Billions)	Potential Tax Loss From 20% Decline ($Billions)
Less-Populated States (< 2 million)	$7.2	$1.4
Populated States (2-4 million)	14.1	2.8
More-Populated States (4-7 million)	29.5	5.9
Most-Populated States (> 7 million)	72.2	14.4

Sources: National League of Cities, National Conference of State Legislatures, National Governors' Association

High-Income Families Spend Most Online

Households that earned over $50,000 in 1998 accounted for nearly three-quarters of total online retail spending, compared with only about half of all U.S. retail spending. Affluent households will continue to dominate online spending in the next decade, though less so.

Percentage of Household Online Spending

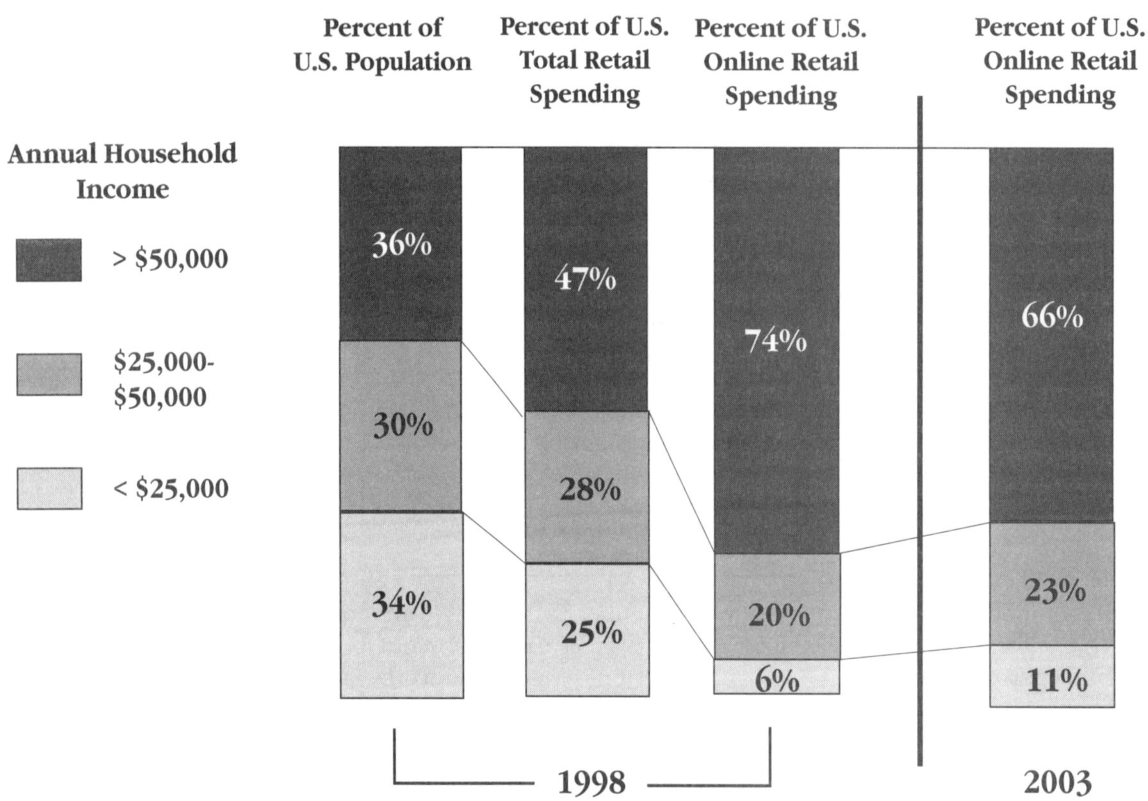

Source: Forrester Research Inc., November 1998

use of encryption technology in the United States, and many digital marketers use the most powerful software available to scramble sensitive data into unreadable code. However, the Clinton administration limits the foreign sale of the most powerful encryption programs, fearing they will fall into the hands of America's enemies. Some in Congress are urging the administration to loosen the restrictions and help boost global electronic commerce. The administration has granted a few exceptions — such as for electronic-banking software — but so far is resisting lifting the ban.

Another subject of growing debate is the potential of the Federal Communications Commission (FCC) to regulate the Internet. Many lawmakers are calling for a broad overhaul of the agency's oversight powers, precisely so it won't be able to impose rules hindering electronic commerce.

The FCC "hasn't made the Internet the object of its smothering affection yet, but it's just a matter of time," Rep. Michael G. Oxley, R-Ohio, a member of the House Commerce Telecommunications Subcommittee, said earlier this year. "It is in the nature of regulators to find new things to regulate."

Many in Congress blame FCC regulations for preventing the increased competition in the phone market that was promised in the Telecommunications Act of 1996. Specifically, lawmakers say the FCC makes it more difficult for phone companies to introduce new high-bandwidth digital services. Regulators on the federal and state levels say the problem rests with local phone companies that have been slow to open their monopoly markets.

Though the FCC has shown some interest in regulating the Internet, it could more immediately find itself setting rules for accessing the global network. A pending case would allow GTE Corp., Bell Atlantic Corp. and other local phone companies to build high-speed data networks with some restrictions. America Online also has asked the agency to require AT&T to give rival Internet providers access to the high-speed networks it plans to build as part of its acquisition of TCI.

One area of Internet commerce where lawmakers favor more regulation is the sending of "spam," or unsolicited e-mail. Online marketers frequently send unauthorized bulk e-mails, angering users and prompting comparisons to aggressive telemarketing phone schemes. Congress is contemplating rules that would better identify commercial e-mail and allow computer users to opt out of receiving the messages. The Ralph Nader-affiliated Consumer Project on Technology has suggested that unsolicited e-mail be tagged to discourage scam artists or pornographers from disguising the messages they send. However, Magaziner and some Clinton administration officials think such proposals could discriminate against computer users who want to receive without any strings attached.

"There are a lot of ways the government can get involved in regulation, but one has to keep in mind the larger issue of where the industry and technology is," says economist Staff. "This is a nascent technology, and we have a long tradition of encouraging industries through little or no regulation. The Clinton administration should be taking a laissez-faire approach; they don't have much of a choice."

Should taxes be levied on Internet transactions?

A computer user in New York City logs on to the World Wide Web using an Alexandria, Va.-based Internet service provider and finds the home page for Amazon.com in Seattle. The user decides to send a book as a gift to a relative in Georgia, paying for the purchase with an online banking service in Charlotte, N.C. Which state gets to tax the transaction?

Currently, none. The ability of digital commerce to hopscotch borders has created a set of difficult policy questions for governments. Simply put, the nation's 30,000 taxing authorities — cities, counties, special taxing districts — want to collect a cut of surging Internet sales but lack a simplified system to levy taxes. Internet merchants fear taxes will scare away potential customers and argue digital commerce will be stymied by myriad local tax laws.

Congress, apparently unwilling to referee the dispute, last October passed the Internet Tax Freedom Act, which imposes a three-year moratorium on new Internet taxes. The measure also created a 19-member advisory commission of businesspersons and state leaders to try to devise a uniform taxing policy by 2001. The law, signed by a supportive President Clinton as part of the omnibus appropriations package passed in the final days of the 105th Congress, grandfathered already-passed taxes on Internet transactions in 11 states and Washington, D.C. [8]

Taxation is perhaps the most controversial issue surrounding digital commerce and one filled with legal implications. Online sellers technically are subject to the same taxes as other businesses. But because the Internet has no single location, it's difficult to establish the precise place where a transaction takes place. Also, the items being sold aren't necessarily physical goods, but screenfuls of information that might more appropriately be categorized as a "service." Some states make this distinction, choosing not to tax downloaded software and Internet access the way they tax other telecommunications services. Other states do. The muddled picture extends to foreign trade, where goods are often subject to tariffs but services aren't. All of this is forcing would-be regulators to reappraise their basic definition of commerce. [9]

"The problem with existing state and local tax structures is that they are horse-and-buggy laws that were developed to address a manufacturing-based economy," says R. Scot Grierson, senior manager for state and local taxes at KPMG Peat Marwick in Costa Mesa, Calif. "They are not readily applied to sophisticated electronic technologies."

There are some legal precedents for taxing long-distance sales. A long-running dispute between states and mail-order companies led to a U.S. Supreme Court decision (in *Quill Corp. v. North Dakota*) that usually prevents states from collecting sales tax on interstate transactions. A state's sales tax can generally be collected only when the buyer and seller have a physical presence in the state — for instance, if the retailer has a headquarters, outlet or warehouse in the state. The question is whether a similar standard should apply to Internet commerce.

James McQuivey, senior analyst at Forrester Research, believes Congress acted correctly because it would be

The Art of the Personalized Pitch

Customers of the Internet music retailer CDNow get more than a screenful of new album releases when they click on its Web site. The popular service also offers them a personalized "Wish List" of recommended purchases based on their stated preferences, past buys and ratings on artists and CDs. The company says the feature essentially creates an individualized music store for each of its 600,000 customers.

Other cyberspace ventures, including bookseller Amazon.com and the Web portal Excite Inc., also use one-on-one pitches to boost sales. At a time when regulators and lawmakers view the Internet as a mass medium, digital marketers increasingly are personalizing it by targeting ads and features at individual users. In the process, they are challenging the decades-old notion that mass marketing is the most effective way to reach consumers.

"I don't think it will mean the death of advertising because ads are too entrenched in our culture," says senior analyst James McQuivey of Forrester Research in Cambridge, Mass. "But you could see selling becoming more specialized. Automakers are excited about using the Internet to show customers individual models and let them try out different options. They'll be able to suggest that drivers in regions with icy or wet weather consider anti-lock brakes."

When Jupiter Communications surveyed 25 top online merchants last year, the New York market researcher found 40 percent already were offering personalized features, and 93 percent intended to have some form of personalization on their Web sites by the end of 1999. Experts say that while aggressive pricing is perhaps the single, biggest factor involved in getting people to make their first online purchases, customized services keep them coming back and allow retailers to develop loyal followings.[1]

McQuivey credits Amazon.com with perfecting the personalized pitch by establishing a popular feature that recommends book titles as potential purchases based on users' interests. The feature is built around a technology called "collaborative filtering," which uses mathematical formulas to predict what customers will buy based on previous purchases, stated preferences and the preferences of other people who bought the same title.

Dell Computer Corp., one of the most successful high-tech online retailers, has used personalization to create more than 1,500 customized home pages for its most loyal customers so that they have fast access to special sales and billing information.

American Airlines' Frequent-Flyer program creates personal profiles of members to accelerate online booking. The profiles contain members' home airports, frequently flown routes and seating and meal preferences. And Kmart recently introduced www.thatperfectgift.com to encourage holiday shoppers to build a Christmas gift list and help them select appropriate items.

The personalization extends beyond individual sites to the Internet portals that serve as gateways to the online shopping bazaar. The portals use software to match a user's stated interest with selected advertising. For example, someone who uses a portal to access a site about Colorado vacations may be presented with a banner ad for skis. Excite, Yahoo! and other portals also offer personalized services, such as weather reports and horoscopes.

Despite the appeal, not everyone is enamored with personalization. Some users worry about their purchasing profiles getting swapped among online retailers. The concerns have prompted Netscape's and Microsoft's popular browsers to offer features that turn off "cookies," the data files that track Web surfers' online movements. Other software allows users to list sites from which they will accept cookies. And a San Diego service called The Anonymizer allows people to surf the Web and send e-mail anonymously.

"Ultimately, this will make transactions more efficient, but I still think people will go out shopping for the experience," says Forrester's McQuivey. "There's nothing like testing out how a leather chair feels, or trying on clothes, in person."

[1] For background, see Robert Hof, Heather Green and Linda Himelstein, "Now It's Your Web," *Business Week*, Oct. 5, 1998, pp. 164-176.

unfair and burdensome to require out-of-state firms to comply with thousands of local tax rates that could lead to multiple taxation. "You hope this is something that could be phased in slowly because the industry is still evolving," McQuivey says.

But critics say putting off the tax issue has serious implications. States believe keeping the Internet tax-free, even for a few more years, could spell economic ruin. Sales taxes account for as much as 40 percent of all state revenues. The National Governors' Association estimates that if sales over the Internet reach $300 billion by 2002, as has been projected, states and local governments will lose up to $20 billion in potential revenues. That would amount to more than 15 percent of current total sales taxes.

"States first need to adopt uniform tax definitions and a single tax rate per state," says Raymond Scheppach, the association's executive director. "Once that is settled, they can come to Congress to get the right to compel out-of-state sellers to collect the tax."

The association agreed, nonetheless, to the three-year moratorium so state governments could try to establish a single tax or a simplified system to apply to Internet sales. A pilot program is under way in Washington, Idaho and Utah, with more studies planned with the National Tax Association.

One possible solution would involve states applying a single tax, say 5 percent, to online sales. The states would then redistribute proceeds to local governments in proportion to their share of statewide sales-tax collections from local businesses. The local governments would no longer be able to design their own sales taxes. And online merchants wouldn't have to deal with myriad local tax rates and definitions of what is taxable.

Austan Goolsbee, a professor of economics at the University of Chicago Graduate School of Business, says there already is strong evidence that customers are flocking to the Internet for the tax advantages. A recent study Goolsbee completed on the purchasing habits of online consumers found that the number of online shoppers and the dollar amounts they spend would decline 25 percent and 30 percent, respectively, if they were charged sales tax.

"People who live in locations with high sales taxes are significantly more likely to buy things over the Internet," Goolsbee says. [10]

Critics also note that the Internet's current tax-free status widens the so-called "digital divide" between information haves and have-nots. The critics cite market surveys showing that approximately 80 percent of U.S. households with incomes over $100,000 have personal computers, while PCs are only found in 25 percent of households with incomes below $30,000. Thus, a person with a credit card, a computer and an Internet-access account can avoid taxation on goods and services that would be taxed for someone who bought them from a neighborhood store.

AP Photo/Greg Gibson

Cisco Systems President John Chambers addresses a conference on Internet commerce last Nov. 30 in Washington. President Clinton and eBay CEO Meg Whitman are at left.

"Sales-tax liability [will] be more and more concentrated among the lowest-income segments of the population," Michael Mazerov and Iris Lav of the Washington-based Center on Budget and Policy Priorities wrote in a lengthy critique of the tax moratorium last year. The two analysts believe states will likely raise sales taxes to make up for revenues lost to the Internet, and that the moratorium gives online merchants less incentive to embrace a uniform policy on Internet taxation.

The 19-member commission that will have a major say in any new taxes on the Internet was designed to have equal numbers of industry and government representatives. But local government agencies are complaining that the group is unfairly tilted in favor of big business, with representatives from corporations like Time Warner, MCI Worldcom and Netscape. Peat Marwick's Grierson says skepticism is mounting over whether the commission will recommend widespread changes or keep the status quo.

The commission "is still missing some business representation from Main Street," Grierson says. "Hopefully, they'll make some recommendations to solve this, but there's a chance they'll leave things as is."

Should the government try to regulate Internet content?

Thousands of Internet surfers logged onto the Internet in September when the House made public intimate details of President Clinton's sexual affair with Monica Lewinsky, as contained in a report by independent counsel Kenneth Starr.

At the same time, a House Commerce subcommittee was approving legislation that could make it a federal offense for a commercial Web site to publish sexually graphic content if it were deemed harmful to minors under age 17. [11] The apparent contradiction illustrated the dilemma over whether to regulate Internet content, a debate that could affect the future of commercial speech on the World Wide Web.

The legislation was eventually passed by Congress as the Child Online Protection Act and signed into law as part of the $500 billion omnibus appropriations bill last October. It would set penalties of up to six months in prison and a fine of $50,000 for businesses that make any indecent online communications for commercial purposes. On Feb. 1, a federal judge in Philadelphia, heeding arguments by civil liberties groups that the law could result in the censoring of free speech, issued a preliminary injunction blocking the statute from taking effect. Judge Lowell Reed, who had issued a temporary restraining order in November so the arguments could be heard, said the fears were "reasonable, given the breadth of the statute." The U.S. Department of Justice, which defended the law, said it was reviewing the decision. The groups claim the statute violates First Amendment guarantees of free speech and is a form of censorship.

The suit is more than just a free-speech battle. The outcome will help define the parameters of commercial speech on the Internet and could have a significant effect on digital marketers of all stripes, from medical Web sites and art dealers to online booksellers and, of course, the robust Internet pornography business. [12]

The law marks the second time Congress has tried to limit access to adult online material. The first attempt, included in the 1996 Telecommunications Act, was invalidated by the U.S. Supreme Court a year later because justices ruled portions of the law were too broad and could restrict speech in cyberspace. The Department of Justice, which is defending the new law, says it is much more narrowly written and only applies to commercial Web sites. The 1996 measure applied to all online material, including e-mail.

"It is not appropriate that there is still no legal protection for children from indecent material," says Ohio Rep. Oxley, the lead sponsor of the measure in the House. Oxley and other supporters say making the Internet more family-friendly will only enhance the medium's economic, educational and societal potential. And they note the statute is especially timely because recent congressional legislation mandates that school classrooms and libraries be wired to the Internet.

It's easy for anyone to come across pornography on the Internet. Literally tens of thousands of adult Web sites are in operation, selling live video sex, raunchy videotapes and sexual paraphernalia. Many use alluring but nonsexual search terms —such as "red light" and "Monica Lewinsky" — to snag casual Internet surfers using browsers. Forrester Research says online pornography accounted for an estimated $925 million in sales last year, and that revenues are growing 30-40 percent per year.

Opponents of the new law contend it's potentially harmful to more than just the pornography business. "The [new] law will seriously stifle the creativity and new business models that are starting to thrive on the Web," Christopher Hansen, an attorney for the American Civil Liberties Union (ACLU) and one of the lead lawyers challenging the law, said before preliminary hearings in the case began last month.

Specifically, opponents object to a provision in the law that requires an electronic-verification system to be put in front of any questionable material. Such a gateway — for instance, a credit-card verification device intended to establish that the person accessing the site is an adult — would be expensive to implement and could be unreliable, Hansen argues. The nuisance of being checked could also drive away potential customers, he adds.

The law makes exceptions for works that have political, scientific or artistic merit. But some online businesses say it will be difficult to decide what is appropriate for children and worry that it will be applied too broadly.

The Internet industry has tried to address the pornography problem itself by offering technology that can block objectionable material on home computers. Microsoft offers filtering software on its Web browser that allows parents to block adult Web sites. AOL has set up a children's viewing zone. The companies, eager not to appear to be defending pornography, say they would prefer to leave regulation of cyberspace in the hands of consumers, though they might favor a narrowly written law specifically targeting hard-core online pornographers.

Other industries have broader concerns. Christopher Finan, president of the American Booksellers Foundation for Free Expression, one of the groups challenging the new law, wrote recently in *Newsday* that the law could restrict transmission of obstetrical and gynecological information on medical Web sites, or limit whether an art dealer can place paintings of nudes on the Internet. Booksellers, led by Powell's Books of Portland, Ore., worry it will restrict sales of some material dealing with alternative sexual lifestyles or pornography.

"Opposing this law doesn't mean that plaintiffs do not care about the problem of unintended exposure of minors to inappropriate material," Finan says. "But if bookstores and other businesses cannot post material about sexual topics that is of interest to adults, then Oxley's law will make the Internet fit only for children." [13] ■

BACKGROUND

Bell's Vision

When Alexander Graham Bell demonstrated the first telephone at Philadelphia's Centennial Exhibi-

Chronology

1930s-1950s

Early computers process and record data electrically and make computational decisions based on wiring and information encoded in their circuitry.

1939
John Vincent Atanasoff builds an electronic digital computer in Ames, Iowa, using concepts that later become central to the development of modern computers.

1946
Engineers at the University of Pennsylvania begin operating the first digital computer: ENIAC (electronic numerical integrator and computer).

1948
Scientists at Bell Labs introduce the transistor.

1958
Texas Instruments scientists invent the integrated circuit, a group of transistors implanted on a single chip of silicon.

1960s-1980s

The advent of the microprocessor ushers in the era of the personal computer. The nascent Internet takes shape, though it is largely restricted to government and academic use.

1969
The U.S. Department of Defense Advanced Research Projects Agency completes ARPAnet, a computer network designed to withstand nuclear attacks that allows messages and data to be sent coast-to-coast.

1971
Intel introduces the 4004, the first microprocessor. The device puts computer memory and processing ability on a single silicon chip, shrinking personal computers to desktop size.

1975
An early personal computer, MITS' Altair, is sold as a mail-order kit for $397.

1983
Radio Shack introduces the first laptop computer.

1986
The National Science Foundation develops NSFNET, a successor to ARPAnet that links supercomputers around the country and that allows scientists to exchange data and send electronic messages.

1989
Scientists at the European Center for Nuclear Research (CERN) in Switzerland develop a method of requesting Web files and documents, called hypertext transmission protocol (HTTP). This marks the beginning of the World Wide Web.

1990s

Internet use explodes with the advent of browsers and the privatization of government networks. A new form of business, digital commerce, allows businesses and consumers to buy and sell online.

1993
Mosaic, an early Web browser that works with the most widely used computers, is developed by the National Center for Supercomputing Applications. The National Science Foundation begins privatizing its network.

1994
More than 10,000 Web sites are in operation; about 3.2 million host computers are connected to the Internet. Developers of Mosaic move to Silicon Valley and establish Netscape, maker of the Navigator Web browser. Microsoft agrees with the U.S. Department of Justice to abandon several business practices that help it dominate the market for PC operating systems.

1995
The first commercial Web sites begin to appear. About 45 million people worldwide now have access to the Internet. Microsoft declares it will focus product development on the Internet market, soon unveiling its Explorer browser that competes with Navigator.

1997
America Online acquires rival Internet service CompuServe in a three-way deal. The company soon announces it has 10 million members worldwide. The Justice Department launches a suit against Microsoft for violating its decree and engaging in anti-competitive behavior to grab a dominant share of the Web browser market.

1998
Mergers and consolidations hit the industry as forecasts of digital commerce increase. AOL, with 14 million subscribers, says it will buy ailing Netscape. Microsoft focuses on more electronic-commerce offerings. The value of online transactions rises to more than $30 billion.

tion in 1876, many sensed the device would bring dramatic changes to everyday life. But Bell and others viewed it, first and foremost, as a tool of commerce. The idea of personal coast-to-coast communication apparently was never considered. After all, the then-dominant telegraph wasn't used in homes.

The digital commerce boom of the 1990s is helping fulfill Bell's vision. The ability to send large volumes of information over wires — specifically, fiber-optic cable — is shifting business away from traditional merchants and service providers. Now, business contracts, sales orders and inventory requirements can be translated into digital code that can be blasted around the world at the speed of light.

The modern era of electronic commerce began in the 1960s, when several industry groups began to develop electronic data interchange (EDI) systems. These networks used a common computer language to transmit large volumes of business data over phone lines. Spinoff applications soon followed. Banks realized the advantages of linking remote sites to centralized data centers and began introducing credit-card processing systems in the early 1970s. These systems married the latest integrated banking services with new technology, speeding up transaction times and making shopping more convenient.

Another wave of development came in the mid-1980s with the introduction of automated teller machines (ATMs) at banks around the country. Consumers at first balked at using the contraptions, preferring the comfort of making deposits and withdrawals in person. But the ATMs foreshadowed Internet commerce by demonstrating how secure networks could allow people to access individual bank accounts via host computers.

Internet Pioneers

The advent of the World Wide Web in 1989 and the commercialization of the Internet in 1991 brought digital commerce into full bloom. Companies set up early Web sites to advertise products, recruit workers or build brand loyalty among customers. Not surprisingly, the sites were especially popular among people with technology backgrounds, who could hunt for jobs in the booming computer industry or access technical data for their home computers. The strength of advertising on the Web grew as casual computer users began gradually surfing the Internet with improved browser software — which uses search terms to steer people to particular sites — and more formal entry points like the Netscape or Yahoo! portals.

The earliest sites were drab by today's standards. Many contained just words, without graphics, pictures or links to other sites. A number catered to specific audiences, such as the Wire Networks' Women's Wire, a women-only site launched in 1994 with $1.2 million in seed capital that now competes with more than a dozen similar Web publications.

Gradually, Web software and marketing became more sophisticated. Cisco Systems Corp., a San Jose, Calif., maker of telecommunications network equipment, set up one of the first sophisticated electronic commerce sites in summer 1996. The site allowed engineers to use the site like an electronic drafting table to design products online using Cisco hardware. They then could place orders for the devices they had created, as well as check on invoices and account information. Online sales for the first year totaled just over $100 million; the company now handles in excess of $3 billion in Internet orders annually.

Another high-tech company that gravitated to the Web early is Dell Computer Corp., which now reaps about $2.2 billion a year in online sales — nearly 15 percent of the company's total revenues. The Round Rock, Texas, company began posting sales literature and technical support information for its personal computers on its Web site in 1994. In mid-1996 it installed software that allowed customers to configure their own computers and order them online. The orders still had to be retyped into computers that ran the rest of Dell's business. But the success — early orders ran about $100,000 per week — convinced Dell, and eventually other computer makers, that the Internet was a successful tool for personalizing business.

Pornographers also were online pioneers. Starnet Communications of Vancouver, B.C., was among the first to use its Web site to show live erotic videos in 1995. Seattle-based Interactive Entertainment Group took the concept further, leasing adult entertainment to some 1,400 Web sites and building its business to approximately $50 million in revenues last year. Despite the continued growth prospects for pornography, Forrester Research says some operators are turning their attention to the next wave: Internet gambling.[14]

The Online Boom

More mainstream consumer sites started to flourish in the mid-1990s as computer tinkerers began to develop variations on online commerce. In 1995, Pierre Omidyar, a French-born Silicon Valley computer programmer, set up a home page called Web Auction to help his girlfriend sell Pez dispensers. The goal was to create an automated service

Shopping Was Never Like This

Click on an Internet Web site, and chances are you'll find an opportunity for interactive digital commerce. Increasingly sophisticated software — and forecasts of a trillion dollar online economy by the next decade — have made the World Wide Web a veritable shopping bazaar. The following examples reflect just a fraction of the products and services available online:

Real Estate — The real estate brokerage Coldwell Banker offers a service called Personal Retriever on its Web site (www.coldwellbanker.com) that creates a portfolio of house listings in specified locales. The user goes through a menu that asks about the time frame for the transaction, the user's price range, annual income, age and number of kids. Then the user enters particulars about the desired house, such as the number of bedrooms and baths. The Web site returns with house listings that meet the criteria, and offers updates by e-mail.

A search for seacoast property near Rockland, Maine, reveals one shortcoming: The properties are limited to Coldwell Banker listings, and currently there are no properties for sale. Moving up the coast, the Web site reveals two properties in Hancock County that fall into the price range. If a listing looks particularly inviting, the user can then click on a mortgage calculator to determine monthly payments.

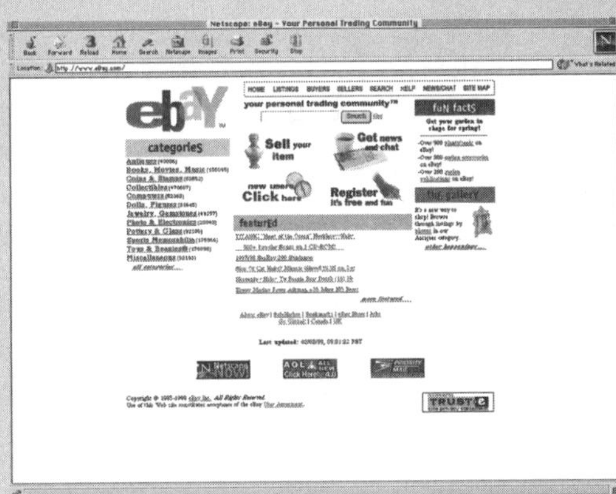

Auctions — The popular eBay auction site (www.eBay.com) offers thousands of items, from baseball cards to weapons, in a traditional auction format. Users who register and receive a password can bid on items, ask the seller questions and contact other potential bidders. One recent auction in the coins and stamps category featured a 1930 U.S. Standing Liberty Quarter with a rare error —the die was rotated 10 percent in the wrong direction. The first bid was for the minimum required, $1. But over the next five days, 17 bidders upped the ante to $52. The consensus seemed to be that the coin would be a unique addition to any collection.

Some of eBay's auction items might raise eyebrows. The erotica section features listings for nearly 7,000 X-rated books, videos, magazines and adult toys — some accompanied by snapshots of the items. eBay recently announced it was adopting new measures to beef up security on the site, but they may not fully address the sale of such material on the site.[1]

Natural Gas — One of the promising commercial Web sites is Altra Energy Technologies' Altranet (www.altranet.com). This Houston-based Web site is a pioneer in digital energy trading, allowing commodities brokers and utilities to strike deals for natural gas shipments, schedule them on pipelines and check market prices. Forrester Research estimates $4.9 billion of natural gas was traded online last year. When registered users with IDs post a deal on the Web site, it is instantly displayed to other traders on the network. When a dealer sees a favorable deal, he clicks a "data cell" and hits the entry key, and the transaction is consummated. The Web site eliminates the need to rely on market makers or other middlemen, who arrange shipments but sometimes have unreliable or questionable pricing.

Wine — Some digital commerce sites offer know-how and helpful suggestions but aren't always practical. The Virtual Vineyard site (www.virtualvineyard.com) is a hit with wine fans, who enjoy the advice and 24-hour ordering features. A gift selector prompts users by asking for the type of gift, the occasion and the price. A recent inquiry into Valentine's Day wine suggestions in the $20-$40 price range turned up three recommendations. The A.R. Lenoble Blanc de Blancs Grand Cru Champagne for $26.95 looked promising, and the accompanying tasting chart detailed its intensity, body, acidity and complexity. However, a request to ship the product to a Maryland address was unsuccessful because the state prohibits shipment of wine direct to consumers. When an alternate address in Washington, D.C., was provided, the service added $8.95 for shipping and advised it will take 10 to 15 days for the wine to arrive.

[1] For background, see Lisa Napoli, "Net Auctioning Has Dark Side," *The New York Times*, Jan. 18, 1999.

that allowed an unlimited number of sellers to auction items 24 hours a day — and collect a small fee for each sale. The venture proved hugely successful with pack rats and collectors and became eBay, which now holds a dominant position in online auctions over competitors such as Yahoo! and Home Shopping Network's First Auction.

"We've really seen three waves of development in electronic commerce sites," says Zona Research economist Staff. "The first was in the early and mid-1990s, when companies wanted to save paperwork and money and put their catalogs online. The second wave, which is happening now, consists of companies that are using the sites to make sales above and beyond the traditional methods. The third wave, which we're starting to see with the auctions, is using the Web as a market maker and serving as an intermediary between buyers and sellers. This is creating transactions that wouldn't have otherwise taken place."

The Internet's myriad applications have made it by far the most rapidly adopted technology in this century. Radio had been in existence for 50 years before 50 million people tuned in. Television took 13 years to reach that point. Sixteen years after the first home computer kits came out in the mid-1970s, 50 million people owned PCs. But once it was opened to the general public, the Internet broke that barrier in four years. [15]

But large corporations still have technical concerns. Because the Internet is a public network that connects smaller networks and service providers, there is no single entity to ensure that a message leaving one point arrives at its destination. For this reason, some businesses have set up "extranets," or virtual private networks on the Internet, that limit access to a prequalified set of businesses. One example is Automotive Network Exchange (ANX), which links Chrysler Corp., Ford Motor Co. and General Motors Corp. with their regular parts suppliers and distribution channels.

Some retailers view the Web as a way of expanding sales to a younger, more affluent audience. Celebrity homemaker Martha Stewart, who launched a site in 1997, surveyed 4,700 customers who responded to an online questionnaire and found the average age was 30 with an income of $65,000. By contrast, readers of her magazine, *Martha Stewart Living*, averaged 41 and $58,000 in income. [16]

But some studies suggest it will be difficult to expand online shopping's allure without offering price breaks. New York-based Jupiter Communications surveyed 50,000 households last year and found that 65 percent of the people with Internet access who browsed or surfed the Web didn't make purchases. Instead, they often checked prices on goods and services, then purchased them from traditional retailers and service providers. The vast majority said online prices — not privacy concerns — were the major barrier to buying something, hinting that off-line businesses were more flexible and willing to deal.

"Aggressive pricing on select items will get customers in the door, and is a crucial step to help win the next phase of the customer acquisition battle," says Jupiter analyst Evan Cohen. "Vendors shouldn't slash prices across the board, but strategic discounting will help." ■

CURRENT SITUATION

Business Worries

As the Internet influences more aspects of daily life, the potential for problems and legislative remedies increases. Soon Internet-related provisions will be part of banking, agriculture and education bills. Senate Judiciary Committee Chairman Orrin G. Hatch, R-Utah, has raised the prospect that criminal and civil rights codes may be amended during the current Congress to address electronic privacy concerns. And the Web already has been a focus of recent copyright and trade legislation.

But lawmakers may find it difficult to define priorities because consumer and business use of the Internet involves different sets of political considerations. Surveys show consumers generally want new laws to protect their online privacy and safeguard against fraud. But such an interventionist approach doesn't please online businesses, which tend to believe in letting the market solve its own problems.

"Businesses tend to work with established partners again and again — they know each other, they can install software to authenticate who everyone is," says Forrester analyst Bell. "It's actually in their interest to provide lots of sensitive information to a supplier or client. They have fewer concerns [about privacy] than an online consumer."

Even so, market-based solutions could prove elusive because not everyone views digital commerce as a cure-all. This is particularly true in financial services and banking, where the rise of discount online brokerages has given investors the option of bypassing brokers and other traditional middlemen.

The tensions were evident last October, when Merrill Lynch & Co. Vice Chairman John Steffens called online trading a "threat to Americans' financial lives" and compared it with gambling. Steffens was frustrated by the rise of brokerages like Charles Schwab and E*Trade, which offer do-it-yourself investing for nominal fees and have eaten into traditional brokerages' commissions. Soon after, Merrill Lynch made its extensive database of corporate investment research available free on

At Issue:

Should Congress permanently ban new state and local taxes on Internet commerce?

yes

ADAM THIERER
WALKER FELLOW IN ECONOMIC POLICY, THE HERITAGE FOUNDATION

FROM "SPARE INTERNET FROM TAXATION?" THE WASHINGTON TIMES, JULY 11, 1997. REPRINTED WITH PERMISSION.

Show me an untaxed corner of the economy, and I'll show you a politician eager to plunder a "new source of revenue." So it is with the Internet, which has America's 30,000 state and local taxing jurisdictions drooling with anticipation at the thought of shaving a slice from this promising new industry.

Absent from their calculations is the fact that subjecting interactive technologies to 30,000 different sets of tax collectors would hobble one of the fastest-growing segments of the U.S. economy. . . .

[T]here is another barrier to local officials taxing the Internet: the U.S. Constitution. The Founding Fathers wisely included a section in the Constitution that prevents states and localities from taxing interstate commerce, which is exactly what electronically transmitted information is. When a good or service enters the stream of interstate commerce, the "Commerce Clause" gives Congress the power to prohibit state or local actions that interfere with the free flow of that commerce.

While the founders could not have envisioned the development of modern, technologically advanced sectors of the economy such as the Internet, the Constitutional framework they outlined for basic commercial activities still applies. State and local officials may not like it, but their taxing authority ends at the geographical boundaries of their jurisdictions.

Moreover, even if states and localities had the proper authority to tax the Internet, they would run into a host of practical problems. Electronically transferred information travels across the Internet far too quickly for regulators to monitor and, more importantly, does so in a way that respects no geographic boundaries. It is virtually impossible to know the points at which the billions of daily Internet transactions begin and end. Consequently, state and local attempts to tax such intangible electronic commerce would result in a confusing and overlapping set of tax laws. . . .

The proliferation of satellite-based technologies and the wireless transmission of information will only add to the confusion. As an increasing amount of Internet traffic is transmitted wirelessly across the United States and around the world, the jurisdictional claims of states and localities certainly will lose credibility. States and localities will have to be content with taxing firms that provide Internet services within their jurisdictions. Anything more than that becomes legally and logistically problematic.

no

RAYMOND C. SCHEPPACH
EXECUTIVE DIRECTOR, NATIONAL GOVERNORS' ASSOCIATION

FROM TESTIMONY BEFORE SENATE FINANCE COMMITTEE, JULY 16, 1998.

Today, only 11 states have taxes on Internet access. . . . Nevertheless, congressional committees continue to consider legislation to address the "problem" of state and local taxes potentially threatening the future growth and development of the Internet. . . .

The fear that 30,000 taxing jurisdictions could threaten the development of the Internet is an unfounded one. Most transactions take place between two parties — a buyer and a seller. Occasionally multiple parties are involved, but it is nearly always a small and manageable number. The only taxes that could be involved in such a transaction are the taxes of the states and cities in which those parties are located. In fact, in nearly every case, the purchaser's location alone determines the tax consequences of a transaction. The concern that multiple jurisdictions will somehow be taxing single transactions has yet to be demonstrated. Before federal legislation is adopted to prevent such a problem, there should be some evidence of a problem. . . .

We have noticed that none of these proposed bills to protect the Internet has included restrictions on federal taxing authority, for instance, the collection of the federal airline ticket tax for tickets sold over the Internet. Apparently what is good for the states and cities is not good for the federal government. We also notice that at the same time there is pressure to stop state and local taxation of Internet access, the federal subscriber line charge on individual telephone lines increases by the number of lines into a household. Thus, if a family decides to get a second line to permit them to make greater use of the Internet, the federal tax on that line is $5.40 per month, compared with $3.50 for the primary phone line. . . .

Today, more than 90 percent of most products are sold in stores, and if products are sold in a state that has a sales tax on that particular product, those sales are taxed. These taxes are what pay for the schools and hospitals, police services and roads that our citizens depend on. . . . However, if a product is sold into a state by a vendor with no physical presence in a state, the sales tax is not collected. The tax is due, but it can't be collected. This unfairness must be corrected, and our proposal for a streamlined, simplified sales tax with uniform definitions of goods and services across all participating states, simplified audit and collection procedures and one sales tax rate per state is designed to make the sales tax collective by remote vendors. . . .

Following the Leaders

The pending purchase of Netscape Communications Corp. by America Online Inc. — and concurrent strategic moves by Microsoft Corp. — will influence the direction of digital commerce for years to come. Here's why these three firms are so important to the online industry:

Netscape — Marc Andreessen and other engineers who developed the early Mosaic Web browser founded the company in California's Silicon Valley just five years ago. Netscape's Navigator browser, first shipped in late 1994, quickly became the preferred tool for computer users to surf the Internet. However, it has steadily lost market share to Microsoft's Explorer, a rival Web browser first introduced in 1996 that is included with Microsoft's Windows PC operating system. Netscape now distributes its browser for free (it is used by approximately 70 million people) and generates most of its revenues from selling digital-commerce and other software to corporations. The electronic-commerce software enables companies to create Web pages and process electronic transactions.

America Online — The Herndon, Va., company was founded as Quantum Computer Services in 1985 and has grown into the world's biggest Internet company, with 14 million subscribers. It acts as a combination service provider and portal, connecting people to the World Wide Web, providing e-mail and chat rooms and offering news, entertainment and commercial services. Now it wants to make the Internet more of a two-way medium, in which businesses interact directly with computer users. By absorbing Netscape and working with partner Sun Microsystems Inc., AOL wants to develop a full line of digital-commerce software and services and, ultimately, a new programming language to get around Microsoft's dominance of desktop computing. This could lead to the development of small devices that bring digital commerce and AOL services to people, without the need for a PC.

Microsoft — The 800-pound gorilla of the personal computer industry was founded in 1975 by Bill Gates and high school classmate Paul Allen. The Redmond, Wash., firm has become a market force through its Windows operating system, which runs in more than 90 percent of the personal computers sold today. Windows is the route most desktop computer users take to connect with the Internet. However, Microsoft has been slow to establish a presence in digital commerce. Gates is trying to build up market share with MSN, an online service that competes with AOL, and digital-commerce offerings that sell cars, travel and real estate. Microsoft also owns the Sidewalk network of local Web sites, which list entertainment and feature digital Yellow Pages. The company is the target of a U.S. Department of Justice antitrust suit. It charges that Microsoft violated terms of a 1995 court decree by using its market power in operating system software to boost its share of the browser market, at Netscape's expense. The company says it was only trying to improve its product offerings and give customers more for their money. The outcome will be significant; if Microsoft loses, some believe the government will force it to include rivals' browsers and other products on Windows — or even break up the company. If Microsoft loses, it is expected to appeal, meaning the case will likely drag on for years.

the Internet, hoping to steer more business to its brokers. [17]

Complaints about online trading have prompted the Securities and Exchange Commission (SEC) to pay more attention to the sector. The SEC has been flooded by hundreds of complaints from investors, who noted discrepancies between the stock prices quoted on their computer screens and what they ended up paying. SEC Chairman Arthur Levitt recently cautioned small investors who have flocked to the Internet to approach electronic investing with care. [18]

Fighting Fraud

Other financial-services professionals are worried about Internet rivals eroding their core business. Bankers note that E*Trade now offers online mortgages, insurance and credit cards. Charles Schwab is adding insurance and electronic bill payments to its Internet services. Industry-watchers wonder whether new electronic intermediaries handling vast amounts of customer information will be regulated the same way as banks and other financial institutions. They also question whether a surge in electronic cash transactions will make it difficult to monitor spending and lead to fraud and money-laundering.

Concerns about fraud also extend to the electronic auction services that are proving increasingly popular in the digital market. The services are built around the idea that businesses are as eager to bid on machine parts and computer equipment as consumers who seek Beanie Babies and sports memorabilia. [19]

However, the potential for abuse is great. Buyers can be victimized by sellers who don't deliver the advertised goods. Sellers also can fall victim to prank bids, or buyers who collaborate to lower prices. In one scenario, a buyer can make a very high bid on an auction item to scare off all other bidders, then withdraw it, allowing a collaborator to then come in with a much lower offer. Because many auctions are conducted anonymously, enforcement is difficult.

The FTC is looking at strengthening anti-fraud measures, particularly as they relate to international transactions. FTC Bureau of Consumer Protection Director Jodie Bernstein says the agency wants to "promote global understanding of the issues at stake and develop a thoughtful, proactive approach . . . for Internet retailing to reach its full potential."

However, electronic retailers appear content to try to safeguard themselves. eBay adopts a Better Business Bureau-style approach by asking buyers to evaluate sellers' promptness and honesty, then posting the evaluations on the site. "The point is to have reputation follow you electronically, whether it is good or bad," says eBay Chief Executive Officer Margaret Whitman.

Those measures may not be enough, however. The New York City Department of Consumer Affairs recently launched a fraud investigation into whether people who use eBay falsely labeled some sports memorabilia as "one-of-a-kind." The probe could decide whether an Internet auction service is accountable for unscrupulous clients. [20]

Other business-to-business sites utilize bank credit verification systems to check sellers' identities and credit. And Internet companies like Netscape are developing more transaction-security software, hoping to demonstrate to would-be regulators that the industry is serious about policing itself.

One area where Internet companies may not be able to escape looming regulation is in the market for their very own stocks. Electronic retailers' shares have soared to unprecedented highs as investors realize the digital commerce market's potential. By mid-January, eBay's stock had risen 1,500 percent from its initial public offering price last September. Amazon.com's stock price doubled roughly twice a month before losing more than half its market value over eight trading days in January. The company had been valued at $29 billion — more than Sears, Roebuck & Co. — even though it hasn't turned a profit since its inception three-and-a-half years ago.

The National Association of Securities Dealers and the Securities and Exchange Commission (SEC) both have brought enforcement actions against speculators manipulating stock prices. And the Nasdaq stock exchange is working with the SEC to consider ways to limit volatility in the Internet sector, perhaps by changing the way initial public offerings (IPOs) are brought to market.

"There is a fair amount of downside risk for both market participants and investors with these kinds of swings," Nasdaq spokesman Scott Peterson said recently. [21] ■

OUTLOOK

No Government Action?

While digital commerce grows at a breathtaking pace, the status quo of non-regulation persists on the Internet. That is likely to continue, in the opinion of many analysts, because government's cumbersome rule-making process and long-term planning can't possibly keep up with a surging market that defies most growth predictions.

Digital commerce's ability to confound even the high-tech experts was evident during the recent holiday season, when the Marketing Corporation of America estimated that U.S. consumers spent $8.2 billion online. That was nearly seven times the amount that it estimated was spent in 1997, and considerably more than pre-holiday industry estimates of from $2.3 billion to $3.5 billion. [22]

The marketing group says it arrived at the number by interviewing 2,000 online merchants and consumers. Craig Johnson, director of the group's electronic retail practice, says forecasts can underestimate totals because they rely on incomplete data from online merchants, or rely too much on consumer surveys that tend to overstate purchases.

It's difficult to even assess the size of the digital market that government is considering regulating. Estimates of total U.S. business and consumer purchases last year range from $31 billion to $51 billion, depending on the methodology used. Even calculating the number of people with online access varies widely: Media Metrix pegs the number of Americans connected to the Web at about 56.8 million, while the Marketing Corporation of America says it's more like 102 million.

The numbers are likely to surge further with the advent of programming technology that bypasses personal computers and links the Internet to small, handheld devices not unlike pagers. The intelligent devices will allow motorists to download driving directions from the Web while in their cars, check their stock portfolios on the subway or be reminded to pick up milk on the way home. And their cost will make the Internet — and digital commerce — available to an entirely different segment of the population that can't afford PCs.

All of the market uncertainty may

provide a good argument for government to avoid intervening until the market matures. *Going Digital* authors Litan and Niskanen point to the history of high-definition television — another technology with the potential to dominate the 21st century that surged on the scene in the 1980s, tempting regulators to set rules. The Bush administration had a choice of setting industry standards for HDTV transmitters and sets or allowing 20 or so domestic manufacturers to hash out rules for the market. The White House took a hands-off approach, prompting the companies to develop better technologies that eventually led to today's crisp, cinema-quality pictures.

"It is important not to assume that government action may be required to resolve every uncertainty or technological incompatibility associated with electronic commerce," the authors write. "Markets can do a far better job, more quickly, than can governments." ■

FOR MORE INFORMATION

American Electronics Association, 601 Pennsylvania Ave. N.W., North Building, #600, Washington, D.C. 20004; (202) 682-9110, www.aeanet.org. This trade group for software, electronic, telecommunications and information technology companies concentrates on trade issues, including export controls of Internet-related products.

Electronic Privacy Information Center,1718 Connecticut Ave. N.W., Suite 200, Washington, D.C. 20009; (202) 483-1140, www.epic.org. This civil liberties group focuses on computer privacy, encryption, information access and other cyberspace issues.

Internet Society, 1775 Wiehle Ave., Suite 102, Reston, Va. 20190; (703) 326-9880, www.isoc.org. A research and educational organization that promotes further development and availability of the Internet and its associated technologies.

Progress and Freedom Foundation, 1301 K St. N.W., Suite 550E, Washington, D.C. 20005; (202) 289-8928, www.pff.org. This conservative-leaning think tank studies how the digital revolution and Internet use affect public policy.

Notes

[1] See "Special Report: The Internet," *The Wall Street Journal*, Dec. 7, 1998, pp. R1-32.

[2] For background, see Charles S. Clark, "Regulating the Internet," *The CQ Researcher*, June 30, 1995, pp. 561-584.

[3] See Jared Sandberg, "Net Gain," and Steven Levy, "Xmas.com," *Newsweek*, Dec. 7, 1998, pp. 46-57.

[4] See Stephen Labaton, "AT&T Passes Hurdle in Plan to Buy TCI," *The New York Times*, Dec. 31, 1998, p. C1.

[5] For background, see David Masci, "Internet Privacy," *The CQ Researcher*, Nov. 6, 1998, pp. 953-976.

[6] Quoted in John Judis, "online Magaziner," *The New Republic*, Dec. 28, 1998, p. 27.

[7] Simon Davies, *The Daily Telegraph*, Jan. 21, 1999, p. 6.

[8] For background, see Eileen Shanahan, "www.taxfree.com," *Governing*, December 1998, pp. 34-38.

[9] For background, see "The Disappearing Taxpayer" and "Taxes Slip Through the Net," *The Economist*, May 31, 1997, pp. 15, 22.

[10] Austan Goolsbee, "In a World Without Borders: The Impact of Taxes on Internet Commerce," Working Paper, University of Chicago, 1998.

[11] See Alan Ota, "On-Line Smut Curb Criticized As Too Tough," *CQ Weekly*, Sept. 19, 1998, p. 2499.

[12] See Pamela Mendels, "online Smut Law Heads Into Court," *The New York Times*, Jan. 18, 1999, p. C3.

[13] See Christopher Finan, "New Internet Law Is Wrong for Adults," *Newsday*, Nov. 10, 1998, p. A45.

[14] See Sharon Waxman, "King of the World Wild Web," *The Washington Post*, Jan. 6, 1999, p. C1. For background, see Richard L. Worsnop, "Gambling Under Attack," *The CQ Researcher*, Sept. 6, 1996, pp. 769-792.

[15] See Mary Meeker and Sharon Pearson, "Morgan Stanley U.S. Investment Research: Internet Retail," Morgan Stanley & Co., May 28. 1997, p. 2-2-2-6.

[16] See Martha Stewart, "My Big Bet on the Net," *Newsweek*, Dec. 7, 1998, p. 53.

[17] For background, see Fred Vogelstein, "online Traders Beware!" *U.S. News & World Report*, Jan. 18, 1999, p. 41.

[18] See Stephen Labaton, "On-Line Trades Rise and So Do The Complaints," *The New York Times*, Jan. 28, 1999, p. A1.

[19] See Claudia Deutsch, "Business Explore online Auctions for Equipment, Parts," *The New York Times*, June 1, 1998.

[20] See Donna De La Cruz, "Web Site eBay Under Investigation," *The Associated Press*, Jan. 27, 1999.

[21] Quoted in Jennifer Files, "Internet Shares Climb to Higher Territory," *Dallas Morning News*, Jan. 12, 1999, p. 1D.

[22] See Maryann Jones Thompson, "New Total for online Holiday Shopping: $8 Billion," *The Industry Standard*, Jan. 15, 1999, www.thestandard.net.

Bibliography

Selected Sources Used

Books

Case, John, *Digital Future*, William Morrow, 1985.
A dated but revealing look at the evolution of the personal-computer market and how it began to affect delivery of goods and services, as it was happening.

Kalakota, Ravi, and Andrew Whinston, *Frontiers of Electronic Commerce*, Addison-Wesley, 1996.
A good overview of the emerging electronic-commerce market, with special attention to the way the Internet works, available technologies and regulations. Somewhat technical, but accessible to general readers.

Litan, Robert, and William Niskanen, *Going Digital!* Brookings Institution Press and Cato Institute, 1998.
Two respected policy analysts outline what they think U.S. lawmakers must do to assure that Information Age technology benefits the global economy. Both favor limited government intervention in digital-commerce markets.

Shurkin, Joel, *Engines of the Mind*, W.W. Norton, 1996.
A respected science writer outlines the evolution of the computer, focusing on the people who developed innovations like the transistor. He does not take up the Internet or digital commerce.

Articles

Hof, Robert, Heather Green and Linda Himelstein, "Now It's Your Web," *Business Week*, Oct. 5, 1998, pp. 164-176.
This overview explains how the Internet is moving toward one-to-one marketing, changing the way all companies will do business.

Judis, John, "Ira's Impractical Plan for the Internet," *The New Republic*, Dec. 28, 1998, pp. 27-32.
This profile of White House adviser Ira Magaziner includes the pros and cons of his plan calling for less government regulation of the Internet.

Sandberg, Jared, "Net Gain," *Newsweek*, Dec. 7, 1998, pp. 46-49.
America Online's deal to acquire Netscape is a high-stakes gamble on the Internet, digital commerce and how technology will affect Americans' lives, Sandberg says.

"Selling Points," *The Wall Street Journal Reports*, Dec. 7, 1998, pp. R1-R32.
A series of articles examining where Internet commerce is succeeding, barriers to further growth and what marketers are learning about online buying habits.

"The Disappearing Taxpayer," *The Economist*, May 31, 1997, p. 15.
The development of digital commerce raises the question of whether governments should continue to levy taxes in a world in which companies, assets and people are mobile.

Walker, Leslie, and Stephanie Stoughton, "Click! Click! Click!" *The Washington Post*, Nov. 22, 1998, p. H1.
A consumer's guide to online shopping and how Web-based buyers' services are still evolving.

Reports and Studies

***Is The New Global Economy Leaving State-Local Tax Structures Behind?* National League of Cities, National Conference of State Legislatures, National Governors' Association, 1998.**
The rise of digital commerce poses potential threats to the current state-local tax structure, argue three trade groups for local and state governments in this policy paper.

***Online Retail Strategies*, Forrester Research, 1998.**
This leading new-media market-research firm tracks digital commerce's growth spiral, analyzes retail categories and sizes up the potential market.

***The Emerging Digital Economy*, Technology Administration, U.S. Department of Commerce, 1998.**
This Clinton administration policy paper outlines reasons for minimal government intervention in Internet transactions and provides a history of electronic commerce.

12 Affordable Housing

JANE TANNER

Carrie Slick has always dreamed of owning her own home. But her $24,500 salary as director of social work at a nursing home barely covers her rent, food, gasoline and car and student loans. Without help, she fears she will never be able to afford the down payment on a house, at least not in her hometown — booming Charlotte, N.C., where affordable housing is scarce.

R. Thomas Jones

Rental apartments for low- and very-low-income residents offer a view of the mountains in San Jose, Calif.

That's why she joined more than a dozen other would-be homeowners at a recent Saturday seminar on buying a home, sponsored by the nonprofit Charlotte Mecklenburg Housing Partnership. Largely funded by local banks, the group helps moderate-income people analyze their household budgets and learn about title searches and mortgage interest rates.

Above all, the partnership helps with down payments. In Slick's case, it will help her come up with the $2,000 she needs once she saves $1,000. "Financially, this is probably the only way I can do it," Slick says.

Throughout the nation, working Americans like Slick are struggling with high housing costs:

- In New York City, working families unable to keep up with high rents are among the hundreds of residents crowding into homeless shelters, many sleeping on the floor. A public school teacher was among those heading off to work after a sleepless night at a Bronx family shelter. "I'm just letting you know how discouraged I am," she said. "At 8:21 a.m., I have to be fresh for 61 New York City public schoolchildren." [1]
- In Rochester, Minn., a shortage of low-cost housing is partly blamed for the scarcity of home health-care workers. At $7 to $9 dollars an hour, they don't earn enough to qualify for the affordable housing being built by local nonprofits. [2] The city's famed Mayo Clinic is so desperate for workers that it has committed $5 million to help build 875 moderately priced homes and townhouses.
- In California's Silicon Valley — the nation's priciest housing market — the Santa Clara Transit Authority is desperately trying to help its bus drivers and light-rail operators find homes. The median home price in the area is $505,000, and two-bedroom apartments rent for an average $2,000 a month.

Although the nation has just enjoyed the longest economic expansion in history, housing advocates say U.S. housing woes are so severe that they are affecting middle-class Americans as well as the chronically poor.

"It goes beyond the lowest income groups to the people who could afford more [upscale] housing but must move farther and farther from their jobs to get what they want," says housing economist Robert Sheehan. Among those hardest hit are public school teachers, police officers and municipal workers.

Some 5.4 million families — nearly 13 million people — have critical housing needs, according to the U.S. Department of Housing and Urban Development (HUD). [3] Most have incomes below 50 percent of the median income for their area; don't receive government aid; pay more than half their rent for housing; or live in bad conditions. More than a quarter of those with severe housing woes are elderly, nearly a third are unemployed and another 21 percent are only marginally employed. [4]

Some housing advocates are focusing their attention on the 3 million Americans among those with critical needs who earn up to 120 percent of the national median income by either working full time or by patching together part-time jobs. They spend more than half their wages for shelter, and many can only afford to live far from their jobs in cities. The number of working families in this category has increased sharply since 1991, according to HUD.

"The affordable-housing issue has moved from the cities to the suburbs," says Michael A. Stegman, director of the Center for Community Capitalism at the University of North Carolina and co-author of "Housing America's Working Families," a study released last June by the Center for Housing Policy.

Yet, at the same time, most Americans are more comfortably housed than at any time in U.S. history. The booming economy, low unemployment, low interest rates and improvements in the housing finance system have increased homeownership rates to record levels. The prosperity, while

From *The CQ Researcher*, February 2, 2001.

Affordable Housing at Low Point

*A family earning the median U.S. income could only afford 58.1 percent of the houses sold in the third quarter last year— the lowest percentage since fourth quarter 1992. The drop in the Housing Opportunity Index (HOI) since it peaked in third quarter 1999 reflected the fact that home prices rose faster than incomes.**

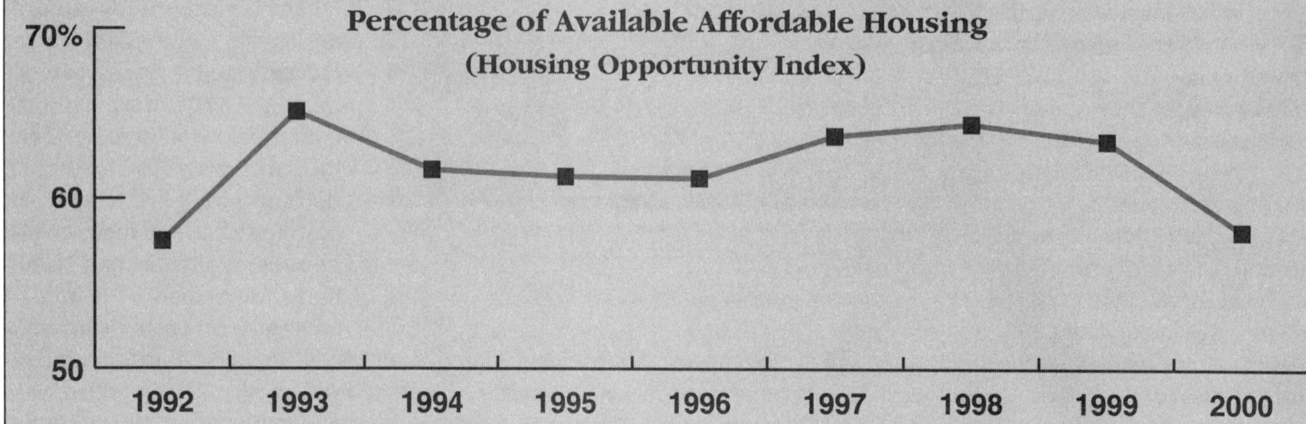

** The Housing Opportunity Index (HOI) measures the percentage of homes sold that a family earning the median income can afford to buy.*

Source: National Association of Home Builders; updated data is available at www.nahb.com/facts/economics/housingopindex.html

good for housing overall, has exacerbated difficulties for those in the bottom quarter of the wage scale because their pay has failed to keep pace with housing inflation.

It's easy to point to extremes, such as hot real estate markets where home values and rents have gone through the roof. These cases aren't alarming to housing economists and others who follow the industry; they see them as simply part of a repeating cycle.

"Seattle has been through boom and bust before," says Barry Zigas, senior vice president of housing and community development at the Federal National Mortgage Corporation, better known as Fannie Mae. "I can remember a time when you couldn't give away housing in Seattle, but now it's experiencing an unbelievable crunch."

Public sympathy probably would wear thin quickly if it were just a matter of high-wage workers struggling to find homes and apartments in hot markets. But in those very same communities cadres of lower-wage workers, who are integral to public services or general quality of life, are being shut out. [5]

Housing advocates are concerned that underlying problems in the nationwide housing market — such as increasing gentrification — are causing the shrinking supply of moderately priced and low-cost housing, especially apartments.

The situation is gravest for the poorest Americans, because the inventory of public housing is fast disappearing as HUD performs radical surgery on its properties. Since beginning to restructure its vast portfolio of properties in 1993, HUD has torn down about 33,000 public housing units, but it has built only 7,362 new ones to replace them, says HUD spokeswoman Donna White.

Under HUD's long-term plan, a total of 61,000 public housing units will be demolished across the country. But only about 42,000 units definitely will be replaced. The remaining units will be replaced by private developers, who will be encouraged, but not required, to provide subsidized units for low-income residents. Meanwhile, private landlords are opting out of HUD contracts, while in hundreds of local communities slow-growth initiatives are making it uneconomical to build low-cost housing.

To make matters worse, as the supply of low-cost housing has dwindled wages for those at the bottom quarter of the income scale have lagged behind housing inflation, making it impossible for them to compete.

Renters are ignored by federal subsidy programs. While the federal government eagerly subsidizes homeownership through mortgage interest tax deductions, renters can't take advantage of the hefty annual subsidy, which amounted to $55 billion in fiscal

2000. And while HUD focuses attention on the poorest of the poor, there has been little support for middle-to-lower-income renters.

Although affordable-housing issues haven't registered prominently on the national political scene, local and state officials are increasingly aware of how critical the lack of moderately priced housing is to the overall well being of their communities. Businesses feel the housing pinch acutely when they try to recruit workers. They must deal with the high cost of turnover, poor worker morale and low productivity because employees face long commutes or live in unstable housing conditions.

Besides the Mayo Clinic, a long list of well-known companies like Intel and Harley Davidson are now helping to provide housing for their employees. The U.S. Conference of Mayors has made housing a top priority, and late last year it successfully pressed Congress to increase funding for rent subsidies. In Massachusetts, rapid job growth has not been matched by the construction of vitally needed apartments and low-cost housing. To spur production, Republican Gov. Paul Cellucci ordered last January that cities and towns boosting their affordable housing units should have first dibs on discretionary state grant money.

As governments and nonprofit organizations confront a housing market in which many are comfortable but millions face a housing crisis, here are some of the questions being asked:

Is there a housing crisis?

Some of the urgency over housing is tied to a few extreme cases in hot markets where prices have been bid up. Traditionally, in such overheated instances the market addresses the shortages, says John Weicher, a senior fellow at the conservative Hudson Institute.

"People see an opportunity, and you get construction," says Weicher, a former assistant secretary for policy development and research at HUD under President George Bush. "Gradually, the market catches up to the demand."

Opponents of government housing subsidies, like Howard Husock, director of the case study program at Harvard University's John F. Kennedy School of Government, contend that most people can find satisfactory housing. "If you have two incomes at not much more than minimum wage," he says, "there's a good chance that you could afford a decent house."

"Can you find a place to live?" he asks. "I think the answer is largely, yes. Is it in the best school district? No, but that's a school problem. Is it close to work? No, but that's a transportation problem."

Indeed, much of the discomfort associated with high housing costs is tied to the fact that in order to find affordable housing people must commute long distances. Some companies have begun sending out daily shuttle buses to pull in workers from outlying areas. "We see that as a decent adaptation," Husock says. "It doesn't sound ideal, but it doesn't mean that it will continue forever."

Most housing advocates, however, say there is clearly an affordability crisis among those at the lower end of the pay scale, and they blame low wages. Many would like to see a tripling of the $5.15 minimum wage and more aggressive use of earned income tax credits, which provide lower-wage workers with significant tax refunds. Housing advocates also would like to see more public money available for housing allowances and rent vouchers.

But to some economists, such initiatives indicate more of a wage problem than a housing shortage. "We would prefer people had more income, but that's not a housing problem," says Ron Seldman, assistant vice president of the Federal Reserve Bank of Minneapolis. And if it's just that people can't afford what they'd like to have, "That's not a housing shortage," he adds.

Conventional wisdom holds that people should spend no more than 30 percent of their gross wages for housing, a benchmark used by HUD and most prime lenders. But real estate economists Richard Green and Stephen Malpezzi of the University of Wisconsin question just how a housing shortage should be defined. In a primer on U.S. housing markets, they contend that there is no affordability crisis "if households have the opportunity to spend a small fraction of their incomes on housing, but instead choose to spend a larger fraction." [6]

However, their calculations showed that even if people on the lower income rungs rented the lower-priced housing that is available, in many states they would have to spend more than 30 percent of their wages. "If low-income households are forced to spend a substantial amount of their incomes on housing," they wrote, "then we clearly have a housing-affordability problem." [7]

For renters, Green and Malpezzi found that those making the median income were not experiencing a severe housing-affordability problem, but the picture was grim for those in the lowest quartile of income distribution.

Many would argue that those at the very bottom rungs and the chronically homeless have not just a housing problem but also a litany of other chronic problems, such as addictions and mental illness.

Lately, the housing finance system has begun to open up considerably to families previously considered bad risks. Lenders are accepting more candidates from so-called "risky pools" that would have been shut out in the past. Plus, secondary markets, such as the quasi-governmental Fannie Mae and

Shuttles Go Where the Jobs Are

Last summer, Jackie Turner looked for a new job after a temporary stint with the Census Bureau. But the best-paying jobs were in the suburbs, 30 miles from her Baltimore neighborhood. Without a car and no public bus service, she figured those slots weren't options.

"I thought, there are a lot of nice-paying jobs, but how am I going to get there?" she says.

Then she learned about a free shuttle service to outlying Howard County and got a job with Home Depot in Columbia, Md. Now, Turner walks about seven blocks from the home she's renting in southeast Baltimore to pick up a shuttle to ride about 30 minutes to her $10-an-hour position.

She had briefly considered buying a home near work, but realized it would cost too much. "I want to buy my first home," she says, "but I don't want it to be $150,000."

In fact, the median price for homes in Howard County is $175,000. Besides, Turner says, she likes her neighborhood and doesn't want to live in the suburbs.

In 1999, a nonprofit, BWI Partnership, set up the Career Caravan shuttle between Baltimore's inner city and Howard County to address the mismatch between available jobs and workers like Turner.

"The inner-city workers couldn't find jobs in the city, and Howard County had all these jobs but couldn't find workers," says Janice Butler, transportation coordinator for BWI Partnership. About 120 workers use the free service to travel to 25 Howard County businesses from light manufacturing to call centers. One of the participating companies, Bagel Bin stores, had previously been providing its own private transportation because it had such difficulty finding employees.

The Career Caravan is free to both riders and businesses. It is funded largely by a $640,000 Federal Transit Administration (FTA) grant, but it also receives money through state reverse-commute money and private donations that should keep it going for another four years. In fact, the service is expanding to cover the entire city and expects to pick up several hundred more riders, Butler says.

Baltimore is not unique. "We've made these grants throughout the country — in virtually all the major urbanized areas," says Doug Birnie, the FTA's job-access coordinator. Some of the funds are used to promote car-pooling or other solutions.

Baltimore's Department of Social Services uses the job shuttle to help women who are looking for jobs get off welfare. When the department canvassed the region for potential jobs, it didn't consider neighboring Howard and Harford counties, where jobs are plentiful, because of the lack of low-cost transportation, says Cindy Theede, assistant contract manager. "We really gave up after a while. There either wasn't transportation when they needed it, or it was too costly."

Now, with the availability of Career Caravan and a similar service, Bridges to Work, women on welfare will be given the option of taking long-distance jobs. But Theede says the welfare clients may not want those jobs, because they are too far from their children's schools and daycare.

Meanwhile, taking its cue from the nonprofit shuttles, Baltimore may start to offer regular public transportation to suburban counties. As for Turner, the caravan has been a godsend, though she sometimes has to wait two hours after her shift for the shuttle to arrive. As soon as she can, she plans to buy a car.

Freddie Mac, are supporting expanded financing opportunities. * Nevertheless, people are still being shut out or are paying predatory fees.

Land-use regulations, which tend to benefit upper-income people, are also exacerbating the housing-affordability problem at the lower end of the wage scale. Green and Malpezzi don't argue that all such regulations are bad, just that they clearly push rents higher. Regulatory reforms are one way to address the affordability crisis, the two economists say. But localities should consider rules case by case to determine where their costs outweigh their benefits, they add.

Is prosperity bad for housing?

The long economic expansion in the United States pushed the homeownership rate to a record 67.7 percent in the third quarter of last year. The fact that more than two-thirds of Americans are homeowners is all the more impressive considering that homeownership as an apple-pie American aspiration only became a realistic possibility about seven decades ago. In addition, because Americans' homes constitute their single biggest source of net worth, pervasive home-value inflation has boosted the net worth of many.

Home sales and the value of residential construction set records during the late 1990s and hit record highs in 1999. Although the number of housing permits and starts cooled off a bit at the end of 2000, they still beat out a 19-year stretch from 1979 to 1997. [8]

"The United States is the best housed it has ever been in its history," says Nicolas Retsinas, director of the Joint Center for Housing Studies at Harvard University.

All the news, however, wasn't good. Thanks to basic economics, the good times wreaked havoc on the low-cost housing market. Prosperity brought in-

* The Federal National Mortgage Corporation, or Fannie Mae, and the Federal Home Loan Mortgage Corporation, or Freddie Mac, are stockholder-owned corporations chartered by Congress to provide liquidity in the housing market. They buy loans from banks and other lenders to free up funds for additional loans, and either sell loan packages as securities or keep them in their portfolios.

creased demand, which pushed prices higher. The median sales price of existing single-family homes jumped 13.5 percent from 1997 to October 2000, from $121,800 to $138,200, according to the National Association of Realtors (NAR).

"Clearly, we have a serious affordability issue for some people, which has been exacerbated by this prosperity," says Retsinas, who served as federal housing commissioner and assistant secretary for housing during the Clinton administration. Last October, when home sales were at near-record levels, NAR's Housing Affordability Index dropped to its lowest level since the second quarter of 1992. [9]

Gentrification has added to the affordability problem. According to a popular adage, housing becomes more affordable as it ages. But as wealthier buyers have snapped up modestly priced homes in older neighborhoods and renovated them, raising their value, they have taken moderately priced housing out of the trickle-down supply.

"You can go around the country and find gentrification of downtowns, and now it has gone into the suburbs," says housing economist Sheehan. "People are getting forced out." All of the gentrification has forced lower-income homebuyers farther and farther out into the distant suburbs, where commuting costs are higher.

In addition, now, bigger is better. Starter homes — small, low-cost houses designed for first-time buyers — are out of vogue, as new homes get bigger and bigger. In 1950, about 62 percent of all new homes were less than 1,200 square feet; last year only 7 percent were. [10] The same "mansionization" is happening to newly renovated homes.

Starter homes in strong markets sell for much higher prices. Near Tyson's Corner, Va., in the Washington suburbs, homes in a post-World War II temporary housing development, built during a shortage, are in hot demand. A For Sale sign at a house in the area last year read: "$250,000 as is, $750,000 with new house," Sheehan recalls.

Overall, the inventory of homes available for sale has shrunk. Near the end of last year, it was at the lowest level in a decade. The inventory was estimated to last only four months, compared with inventories throughout most of the 1990s that lasted six to nine months. [11] And the inventory of low-cost housing has been reduced as well. Between 1993 and 1995, for instance, the number of unsubsidized units affordable to very low-income households dropped 8.6 percent — a decrease of 900,000 units. [12]

Economic prosperity also has spurred the passage of slow-growth regulations around the country. They typically favor people at the higher income levels, because they tend to take land out of development, driving up land prices and restricting dense developments and apartments.

Meanwhile, good economic times have not closed the homeownership gap between minorities and whites. Seniors and renters have been particularly hard hit. The Joint Center's "State of the Nation's Housing: 2000" report found that the median net worth of older American minority renters was a dismal $600.

"In the midst of this remarkable prosperity, the homeownership gap between whites and minorities has hardly narrowed," the study said.

Housing advocates blame the fact that wages at the bottom quarter of the scale haven't kept pace with housing inflation. Even where employees are paid well above the current minimum wage, it's not enough.

Each year, the National Low Income Housing Coalition calculates the wage required to pay for a typical two-bedroom apartment if no more than 30 percent of a tenant's income is spent on rent. In New Jersey, which has some of the nation's highest-priced rental properties, a tenant in 2000 had to earn $16.88 an hour. In Georgia, which ranked in the middle, the required wage was $11.13, and in West Virginia, the lowest, a worker would have to make $8.12 an hour.

Some housing advocates would like to see the minimum wage increased, but others say that could just throw fuel on the fire. Sheehan, who is president of Catholics for Housing, a Northern Virginia nonprofit, says raising wages to a level at which all families could compete in the housing market would be wildly inflationary and only further elevate prices. Others warn that employment would go down as companies reduced hiring. [13]

"The more money you pour into the economy, the more prices rise," Sheehan says. "If you are going to give that worker a raise and there's no more productivity, you are going to have inflation. That would push housing costs out of reach if it were done on a large scale."

Many cities celebrated economic booms in the last decade, but often more jobs than housing were created, especially for people in the kind of lower-wage jobs that help fuel growth. The outcome has been obvious. In Boston, for instance, in 1998 there was potential demand for 30,791 one- or two-bedroom homes in the $100,000 to $125,000 price range, but only 1,255 were vacant or available for sale. [14]

At the end of 2000, signs of an economic slowdown were popping up with greater regularity. If the marketplace softens considerably, the affordable-housing crunch likely will ease. But experts like Retsinas don't think a slower economy will bring widespread relief. Prices are much stickier coming down than going up, he says, and a recession would hit people at the lower economic rungs hardest.

Is enough being done to solve the affordable-housing problem?

There is certainly no shortage of programs aimed at solving America's housing problem. Indeed, new programs

Where Can You Afford a House?

In Springfield, Ill., workers earning the median local income ($59,100) could buy 90 percent of the homes that sold there in the third quarter last year. In pricey San Francisco, workers earning the median local income ($74,900) could only afford 5.7 percent of the houses.

The 10 Most Affordable Cities

Metro Area	Homes Affordable in 2000* for Median-Income Families	2000 Median Family Income ($000s)	2000* Median Sales Price ($000s)	2000 National Affordability Rank
Springfield, Ill.	89.6%	59.1	95	1
Davenport, Iowa; Moline-Rock Island, Ill.	87.6	51.8	75	2
Elkhart-Goshen, Ind.	86.0	54.0	112	3
Rockford, Ill.	85.8	55.3	92	4
Mansfield, Ohio	85.5	46.1	83	5
Wilmington-Newark, Del.	85.0	69.0	137	6
Dayton-Springfield, Ohio	82.4	55.9	101	7
Vineland-Millville-Bridgeton, N.J.	81.9	47.2	85	8
Des Moines, Iowa	81.6	60.0	110	9
Kansas City, Mo./Kan.	81.2	57.7	106	10

The 10 Most Expensive Cities

Metro Area	Homes Affordable in 2000* for Median-Income Families	2000 Median Family Income ($000s)	2000* Median Sales Price ($000s)	2000 National Affordability Rank
San Francisco, Calif.	5.7	74.9	505	177
Santa Cruz-Watsonville, Calif.	8.7	61.7	371	176
San Jose, Calif.	13.0	87.0	448	174
Salinas, Calif.	13.0	50.3	275	174
Santa Rosa, Calif.	13.8	58.1	287	173
San Luis Obispo-Atascadero-Paso Robles, Calif.	17.8	48.0	235	172
Oakland, Calif.	23.5	67.6	310	171
Eugene-Springfield, Ore.	23.6	41.7	136	170
San Diego, Calif.	24.6	53.7	235	169
Vallejo-Fairfield-Napa, Calif.	24.9	53.3	220	168

** Data from third quarter 2000*

Note: The housing survey covered 177 cities.

Source: National Association of Home Builders; http://www.nahb.com/facts/hoi/2000_3Q/complete_ranking.htm

Where Can You Afford an Apartment?

When it comes to apartment living, New Jersey is the priciest state and West Virginia the most affordable. Workers would have to earn $16.88 an hour to rent a two-bed apartment in New Jersey without spending more than 30 percent of their wages. In West Virginia, they would only need $8.12 an hour.

10 Most Expensive States

State	Hourly Wage Needed to Rent Two-Bedroom Apt.
New Jersey	*$16.88*
District of Columbia	*$16.60*
Hawaii	*$16.52*
Massachusetts	*$16.43*
New York	*$16.04*
Connecticut	*$15.67*
California	*$15.22*
Alaska	*$15.18*
New Hampshire	*$14.15*
Maryland	*$13.42*

10 Most Affordable States

State	Hourly Wage Needed to Rent Two-Bedroom Apt.
West Virginia	*$8.12*
Mississippi	*$8.17*
Arkansas	*$8.27*
Alabama	*$8.61*
Oklahoma	*$8.62*
Kentucky	*$8.65*
North Dakota	*$8.98*
Louisiana	*$9.03*
Missouri	*$9.03*
Iowa	*$9.10*

Source: National Low Income Housing Coalition: http://www.nlihc.org/oor2000/table9.htm

and financing products are announced with great regularity and fanfare.

But while the number of strategies has proliferated, most have lacked firepower. "We don't need more tools, we've got all the tools we need," says Conrad Egan, executive director of the Millennial Housing Commission, which is expected this year to recommend expanding affordable-housing opportunities and improving public and subsidized housing. "We need more support, we need more oomph," says Egan, former policy director of the National Housing Conference. By "oomph" he means political clout, leverage for funding and legislation.

Yet, affordable housing has not been a high-profile issue. "How many times did you hear the presidential candidates talk about prescription drugs?" asks J. Michael Pitchford, senior vice president of community development at Bank of America. "A thousand times. How many times did they talk about affordable housing? Zero."

With historically high homeownership rates and a general level of comfort among the American public, few lawmakers are motivated to examine problems facing those at the lower end of the housing market, Egan says. In addition, many perceive housing development and preservation as being too complicated. People aren't going to throw support behind something they don't understand, he adds. Also, in many cases the connection between low-cost housing and general community well being hasn't been made, he adds.

Thus, despite the seemingly endless number of affordable-housing programs, "At the end of the day, there's not enough money," Egan says.

But clearly, low interest rates have the most powerful influence on making homeownership more affordable, and Federal Reserve Board Chairman Alan Greenspan seems committed to keeping rates low.

In addition, Fannie Mae and Freddie Mac have a strong hand to play in solving the affordability crunch. While both quasi-governmental agencies have ratcheted up their goals for influencing affordable-housing lending, the agencies have come under fire recently. A study commissioned by HUD suggests that the giant mortgage purchasers aren't doing enough to promote homeownership in low-income neighborhoods. [15]

Yet, both agencies boast scores of new innovative approaches. They also continue to offer new programs that reduce costs and dig deeper into pools of potential homeowners who may not have stellar credit but are nonetheless good risks.

A key to solving the problem, says Stegman of the Center for Community Capitalism, is to move away from tying housing issues to poverty and to recognize their impact on economic growth in cities and regions in general.

"As more and more communities realize that affordable housing is where jobs critical to their local economies go to sleep at night," he says, "we will begin to see the kinds of more broadly based coalitions of public and private stakeholders that will be required to deal with the problem."

In the meantime, there are increasing signs that affordable housing is drawing more attention and dollars. After a drought of significant legislation, Congress passed several bills at the end of 2000 described by housing advocates as a net gain for their cause.

For instance, year after year Congress had rejected attempts to increase the amount that states could allocate for federal Low Income Housing Tax Credits (LIHTCs), a key federal incentive program for boosting the supply of affordable housing. The program gives federal tax credits to banks and other investors in exchange for providing capital for new construction and the rehabilitation of low- and moderate-income apartment projects. The program had been losing steam, primarily because the amount states could allot in tax credits had been stalled at $1.25 per resident since 1987, when the program went into effect.

In a December tax measure, Congress and the White House agreed to increase the tax credit to $1.75 per person and link future increases to inflation. In addition, the cap on private bonds to fund new production was increased from $50 per resident to $75. [16]

Housing advocates also had pushed for significant legislation, such as the creation of a National Housing Trust Fund. Although no landmark laws were passed, Congress did expand homeownership and modify housing laws for seniors, the disabled and Native Americans. Lawmakers also gave manufactured homes more credibility with lenders by creating uniform, new installation regulations and enforcement provisions via the Home Ownership and Economic Opportunity Act of 2000.

Will affordable housing capture the attention of the 107th Congress and President George W. Bush? Most housing advocates hesitate to predict the future, but many suggest little new ground will be gained. Bush has pushed the idea of homeownership and likely will place his emphasis there.

On the other hand, housing insiders say apartments and multifamily projects are needed desperately, but apartments aren't as politically popular as individual homeownership.

"From a NIMBY ("Not In My BackYard") standpoint, it is easier to find support for homeownership than rentals," Egan says. "Some people think renters aren't like us, especially those getting assistance." ■

BACKGROUND

U.S. Gets Involved

Until the 1930s, the federal government generally stayed out of the housing business. When the public sector did step in, it was local governments — most often counties — that sheltered the poor at orphanages, poor farms and veterans' homes. But it wasn't equal-opportunity housing; the shelters were mostly for whites.

The country's first housing boom occurred during the prosperous 1920s. Initially, home loans were made for large amounts, on a short-term basis and required frequent refinancing. That meant that only Americans in the upper-income echelons could participate.

But when the banking system and stock market collapsed in 1929, even those homeowners were in jeopardy of losing their properties, and many did. It was in this climate that President Franklin D. Roosevelt began getting the federal government into housing.

Roosevelt's creation of new institutions—such as the Federal Home Loan Bank System and the Federal Housing Administration (FHA)—developed an infrastructure for long-term lending and a sense of security for lenders. Thus, the thrust in America toward individual homeownership was set in motion.

Meanwhile, desperate to stimulate the moribund Depression-era economy, Roosevelt used construction of public housing as a vehicle for employment. The Housing Act of 1937 made possible the creation of local public housing authorities to construct and manage housing for the poor, using federal money funneled to states and localities. The first public housing project ever built, Santa Rita Courts in Austin, Texas, still has residents.

Private builders and conservatives opposed public housing. "Recognizing that the special interests and the courts would block a national program to build and operate housing for the poor, the Roosevelt administration sought to define a housing policy around decidedly conservative approaches," according to the Texas Low Income Housing Information Service. "It would seek to link any low-income housing built directly to the elimination of slums in the cities and to the creation of jobs and local business opportunities." [17]

Nonetheless, in 1939, the National Association of Real Estate Boards weighed in, noting in one of its

Chronology

1920s-1950s

Federal housing policy begins promoting housing construction and homeownership.

1929
Collapse of the banking system triggers a national housing crisis. Only a small minority of higher-income Americans own homes, and they are on the verge of losing them. Mortgages are short-term and must be repeatedly refinanced.

1932
President Franklin D. Roosevelt creates the Federal Home Loan Bank System to create savings and loan associations to offer long-term mortgages in communities throughout the country.

1933
The Public Works Administration clears out slum housing and constructs apartment communities for the poor, in the process creating thousands of jobs.

1934
The Federal Housing Administration (FHA) is created to insure private residential mortgage loans. With lenders protected, mortgage lending expands. The creation of the FHA and Federal Home Loan Bank System mark a shift from an emphasis on rental housing to homeownership.

1937
The Housing Act of 1937 creates local public housing authorities to construct and manage housing for the poor with federal money funneled to states and localities.

1938
The Federal National Mortgage Corporation (Fannie Mae) is created to bolster the housing market by buying up FHA loans.

1949
Promising to create a "decent home and suitable living environment for every American family," the Housing Act prompts new waves of public housing production during the 1950s and early '60s.

1960s-1980s

Public housing is elevated in the political pecking order, even as the government turns to private markets to provide low-income housing.

1965
A number of housing agencies are consolidated into the Department of Housing and Urban Development (HUD).

1970
Congress charters the Federal Home Loan Mortgage Corp. (Freddie Mac) as a stockholder-owned corporation to create and maintain a national secondary market for conventional residential mortgages.

1971
Rent subsidies are introduced as an alternative to the construction of public housing.

1977
Under President Jimmy Carter, the Community Reinvestment Act (CRA) pushes banks to provide credit in low-income neighborhoods.

1986
As part of the Tax Reform Act, Congress creates Low-Income Housing Tax Credits, which encourage private investors to invest in affordable housing.

1990s-2000s

A new political agenda reduces the housing role of the federal government.

1993
HUD begins radical revamping of public housing properties, dubbed Hope VI. Aging and decrepit units are demolished and replaced with fewer units geared to mixed-income levels.

1994
A conservative Congress vows to dismantle HUD, but does not succeed. Congress holds static the number of HUD housing vouchers for the poor from 1994-1998.

1990s
No significant legislation on affordable housing is passed. Allocations for Low Income Housing Tax Credits, the key federal program to spur production of low-cost housing, remain at 1986 levels.

2000
Congress boosts federal tax credits to promote new construction of affordable housing and passes legislation in the 11th hour to expand homeownership. At the end of the year, President-elect George W. Bush taps Florida lawyer Melquíades Martinez as new HUD secretary.

newsletters: "United States Housing Authority projects now underway are undiluted socialism." [18]

Congress Acts

At the end of the Depression, Congress created a secondary market for government-insured loans by establishing Fannie Mae to stabilize and enhance lending.

The nation experienced an acute housing shortage after World War II. That not only triggered a boom in the private housing market but also prompted President Harry S Truman to push Congress to rev up construction of public housing once again. Despite opposition from Sen. Joseph McCarthy, Congress passed the Housing Act of 1949.

According to the landmark law's preamble:

"The Congress declares that the general welfare and security of the Nation and the health and living standards of its people require housing production and related community development sufficient to remedy the serious housing shortage, the elimination of substandard and other inadequate housing through the clearance of slums and blighted areas, and the realization as soon as feasible of the goal of a decent home and a suitable living environment for every American family, thus contributing to the development and redevelopment of communities and to the advancement of the growth, wealth, and security of the Nation."

The wave of public housing construction continued into the 1960s. By 1965, several housing agencies had been consolidated into the Department of Housing and Urban Development (HUD), which was elevated to a Cabinet-level agency.

Meanwhile, during President Lyndon B. Johnson's administration, with guidance from the 1968 Kaiser Commission on Urban Housing, housing policy shifted toward private-market solutions, such as offering subsidies to developers and guaranteed rent payments to private-property managers.

In 1969, HUD lowered income-eligibility requirements for public housing. This and similar policies eventually increased economic segregation and isolation in public housing. Today, HUD's early strategy of building large high-rise housing projects for the poor has been deemed a failure by observers and those involved in housing policy. Several crime-ridden projects have been razed, and HUD now is working hard to reverse its previous pattern by creating low-density, mixed-income housing that won't end up segregating subsidized tenants into substandard ghettoes.

Nixon's Legacy

During Richard M. Nixon's presidency, significant policy changes gave public housing residents more mobility and decreased reliance on publicly owned projects, which were riddled with cost overruns and corruption. Under Section 8 of the Nixon-proposed Housing and Community Development Act of 1974, poor families could receive subsidies to help them rent privately owned apartments. These vouchers have been popular with both political parties because they avoid the cumbersome bureaucracy of public construction and ownership of properties.

In 1977, during President Jimmy Carter's administration, the Community Reinvestment Act (CRA) pushed lenders to reach out to the poor by threatening to reject bank mergers and restrict bank growth if the institutions failed to serve the low-income and high-risk areas of their communities. CRA did not carry a lot of punch initially, and debate continues over how strictly it is enforced.

However, CRA's influence grew when bank mergers heated up in recent years. For instance, Charlotte-based NationsBank made its biggest CRA and community-development push just before it announced a merger with Bank of America.

President Ronald Reagan's administration continued to favor relying on the private sector to satisfy the nation's housing needs. In 1986, for example, Congress sought to motivate private investment in affordable housing in exchange for federal tax credits. Although the state-administered LIHTC program has been popular, funding didn't keep up with inflation for the program's first 13 years.

After the 1994 takeover of Congress by a Republican majority, conservatives began attacking large government-assistance programs, such as welfare and public housing. Some even advocated dismantling HUD altogether.

Amid those debates, funding for rent vouchers was frozen for four years, from 1994 to 1998. Since then, Congress has agreed to some voucher increases, but HUD is still under pressure to reform its operations.

HUD's New Approach

Large-scale, high-rise housing projects had come under fire for high-crime rates and the long tenure of many tenants, which sometimes went back three generations. Now, the agency has revised its blueprints to create public housing models more likely to improve the tenants' prospects for moving up to homeownership, by creating housing that supports a range of incomes in small-scale settings. Rather than isolating the poor together, the newer housing brings together people who are trying to im-

Factory-Built Homes on the Rise

It's not uncommon these days to see half a house barreling down the highway, open-faced like a dollhouse, as factory-built home sections are shuttled from plants to homeowners' lots. And the phenomenon is about to become even more common.

As the cost of homes continues to rise, some housing experts predict an increasing number of people will turn to factory-built homes as cheaper alternatives.

The potential was largely overlooked until recently. But it can no longer be ignored, since 20.7 percent of all housing starts in 1999 were manufactured homes, according to the National Conference of States Building Codes and Standards. Although the National Association of Home Builders calculates that only 17.2 percent of new homes that year were manufactured, either way you look at it, manufactured homes have captured a significant share of the new-home market.

To many consumers, manufactured homes conjure images of boxy metal trailers. But that's the old era. Technology has elevated the quality of manufactured homes dramatically, and new designs blend seamlessly into conventional neighborhoods. Some are two-story homes and in rare cases boast 6,000 square feet of interior space.

Today's factory-built homes are designed to blend in with traditional housing.

As middle- and low-income homebuyers find themselves increasingly priced out of the housing market, housing advocates are turning to assembly-line homes to address the affordability crunch. Nonprofits in Seattle and other cities are using manufactured homes for many projects, including urban infill — putting homes on small, often vacant, inner-city lots.

"People should think of using manufactured housing as part of the strategy," says Michael Savage, a Washington, D.C.-based community-development consultant. He helped implement a joint program of the National Coalition for Homeless Veterans and the Miss America Corp. to promote using manufactured homes to get disabled veterans off the streets.

Cost savings are considerable. The average manufactured home is 1,450 square feet and $43,300 without a lot. Conventional homes now average 2,190 square feet and cost $136,425 for the structure alone. [1] That means a manufactured home costs about $30 a square foot to build, compared with $62.30 for a conventional home.

In portions of Sun Belt states, such as Florida, Texas, California, Georgia and Alabama, factory-built homes are fairly well accepted. [2] But communities in many other states reject them outright. Often, neighbors fear their property values will decline, especially if the manufactured homes are the modest, boxy doublewides.

Most of the newer manufactured homes are stand-alone units on foundations — nothing like the tiny rectangular mobile homes in trailer parks. Yet many communities classify all manufactured homes as trailers, abiding by decades-old zoning laws that in essence specify "no trailers." As a result, when would-be buyers of manufactured homes seek zoning variances, neighbors rally to keep them out.

Although biases against pre-manufactured homes are powerful, acceptance is growing, albeit slowly. At the end of 2000, Congress hastened the process by passing legislation standardizing installation and other regulations for manufactured homes. And 16 states prohibit discrimination against factory-built homes. [3]

Economic trends may force the issue. The shortage of construction workers and diminishing skill levels eventually will push more production into factories. And thanks to economies of scale in purchasing, assembly-line efficiencies and automation, manufactured homes are a bargain.

Demographic shifts in the next 10 years will also favor manufactured housing. [4] Of the 12 million new households expected to form in the next decade, most will be headed by people under 25 and over 55 — the age groups that buy manufactured homes in the greatest numbers.

Mark Patton, chief executive officer of the Rural Housing Institute, predicts that by the end of the decade the only two jobs left for carpenters will be remodeling or building fancy homes. "Everything else is going to be built in a factory," says Patton, whose Wilton, Iowa-based nonprofit builds modular homes for low-income people.

[1] U.S. Department of Commerce, Bureau of the Census, www.census.gov.

[2] "Estimated Stock and Sale of Existing Manufactured Homes in 1999," Manufactured Housing Institute, 2000.

[3] *Ibid.*

[4] Eric S. Belsky, "2000-2010: The Decade for Manufactured Housing," Joint Center for Housing Studies, Harvard University, May 2000, p. 19.

prove their circumstances with residents who are already successful.

Under a program dubbed HOPE VI, which started as a pilot in 1993, HUD is well on its way to demolishing 61,000 public housing units and replacing them with 42,000 mixed income, low-density units. The remaining units will be replaced with private housing, but developers will not be required to include units for low-income residents.

The Homeownership and Economic Opportunity Act, passed in late 2000, should help ease affordability problems by allowing rent subsidies to be applied toward buying homes. The act especially targets elderly, disabled and Native Americans. Rep. Rick A. Lazio, R-N.Y., then chairman of the House Banking and Financial Services Housing and Community Opportunity Subcommittee, had pushed this and other housing legislation for many years.

"For regions of the country where real estate and rental costs are unusually high, such as my home state, our initiatives can mean the difference between renting and owning a home, helping thousands of New Yorkers and other Americans become homeowners," Lazio said when the bill passed in the House. [19]

By the late 1990s, the booming economy had generated record-breaking homeownership rates. But the strong marketplace, coupled with stagnant wages at the lower end of the pay scale, also contributed to the current crunch in affordable housing.

At the end of 2000, signs of a slowing economy had yet to hit the housing market, which continued to produce record housing starts. A cooling economy was expected to ease the affordable housing crunch, but not alleviate it to any great extent, partly because the supply of low-cost housing has been shrinking. ■

HUD Secretary-Designate Melquiades Rafael Martinez.

CURRENT SITUATION

Martinez to Head HUD

The new administration is bringing many changes at the federal level. At the end of 2000, President-elect Bush selected Melquiades Rafael Martinez as secretary of HUD. During his confirmation hearings, Martinez told a Senate committee on Jan. 17 that he would work to ensure that more minority families could buy their own homes.

"Despite record-high levels of homeownership, African-American and Hispanic-American homeownership rates remain below 50 percent," Martinez said. "That is not acceptable." [20]

Martinez, a wealthy personal-injury lawyer who fled to Florida from Cuba as a teenager, added, "I know the value of homeownership because I have witnessed its great power throughout my entire life."

Martinez, former chairman of the Orlando Housing Authority and the Florida Growth Management Study Commission under Gov. Jeb Bush, assured the committee that he was not part of the wing of the Republican Party that had tried to abolish HUD. "I intend to be a very active secretary," he said, suggesting that the department should take a leading role in managing the explosive urban growth precipitated by the recent economic prosperity.

The nation faces a looming housing problem in both rural areas and in cities, he said, pointing out that the number of affordable houses for sale had declined while the number of poor people seeking housing had grown.

"Unless we make sure that everyone is participating in this great economic expansion and until we ensure that barriers to home ownership are torn down for everyone . . . until then, our job is not done," he said.

Advocacy groups that once had been wary of Martinez, claiming he lacked significant experience in housing, now say they look forward to working with him. "We were encouraged that he understands the country is facing a serious problem that there is not enough affordable housing for low-income families," said Sheila Crowley, president of the National Low Income Housing Coalition.

Habitat for Humanity's Dilemma

Lori Vaclavik, head of the Habitat for Humanity affiliate in Denver, considers herself a friend of Mother Nature. Indeed, a book by noted Colorado nature photographer John Fielder adorns her coffeetable.

But last fall, in a surprising turn of events, Vaclavik found herself opposed to a proposed state constitutional amendment to slow growth and protect green space.

Vaclavik opposed the initiative because she feared it would have made it impossible for Habitat to continue its mission of building low-cost, interest-free-mortgage housing for Denver's working poor. "It's not that we are against growth management and in favor of sprawl," Vaclavik said. "It's the right problem, but the wrong solution."

Private builders and developers are vociferous opponents of the growing number of slow-growth and "smart growth" plans, contending they drive up the cost of housing by pulling land off the market and restricting housing density. Now, nonprofit affordable-housing builders like Habitat International, which otherwise have stayed outside local political machinations, are joining the fray on the side of developers.

AP Photo/Ric Feld

Habitat for Humanity built several homes for low-income residents in Atlanta's Edgewood neighborhood.

When the Colorado measure failed to pass muster with voters last November, the defeat was attributed by some observers and pollsters to public opposition by the local Habitat affiliate. Vaclavik, who appeared in anti-amendment commercials with Republican Gov. Bill Owens, says the ecumenical Christian housing ministry also would have been priced out of the land-purchase market by the measure. The average price Habitat pays for a 6,250-square-foot lot in Denver has risen from $5,000 three years ago to $20,000, she says.

Across the country, in a classic case of "strange bedfellows," other affordable-housing advocates also find themselves fighting alongside developers fending off slow-growth efforts. For example, the Sea Island Habitat for Humanity chapter, which builds housing on Johns and Wadmalaw islands outside Charleston, S.C., has been lobbying against Charleston County's comprehensive plan, which at one point required four-to-eight-acre lots for each new home. Habitat generally builds three homes to an acre in that area.

"With this regulation, it would have become another Hilton Head, where all the poor people have long commutes to jobs," says Chuck Swenson, Habitat's local executive director. "We're interested in preserving the rural nature, but the plan has to include low-income housing."

Habitat for Humanity was created in 1976 by Millard Fuller, a Georgia businessman and lawyer, who believed that poor people hungering for their own home would gladly work hundreds of hours to build it. The organization gets corporations, churches and individuals to donate building materials, and prospective owners and volunteers do the actual construction work. Since its creation, Habitat chapters have completed about 100,000 homes around the world.

The organization has also become a considerable force in U.S. housing. The typical Habitat house covers 1,000 square feet and costs about $46,600. In 1999, with 3,893 successful closings, Habitat was the 15th largest U.S. homebuilder in volume.[1] Fuller and other housing experts estimate it may eventually move into the top spot.[2]

Throughout the nation, most of the hundreds of proposed and already-enacted growth management plans are well-intentioned attempts to protect the environment and preserve quality of life. But the constraints they impose on affordable housing are often overlooked by those not involved in housing advocacy.

"Land-use and growth-management controls probably have the largest aggregate effects on housing," says Stephen Malpezzi, a professor of real estate economics at the University of Wisconsin at Madison. "Regulations raise prices."

Malpezzi says it's difficult to accurately measure the true costs and benefits of growth-management components and regulations. "Yet, any time we put a regulation in place, we're deciding that the benefits are worth the costs," he says.

When Vaclavik stepped into the growth management debate, her telephone voice mail quickly filled with angry calls. Some of her volunteers quit; some donors told her they'd never write another check to the cause. But Vaclavik says that by raising the red flag, she brought low-cost housing into the debate. "Now the environmental groups are going to consider affordable housing and the consequences," Vaclavik says. "I think they figured that out."

---

[1] *Builder* magazine, "Builder 100" ranking, May 2000.

[2] Howard Husock, "It's Time to Take Habitat for Humanity Seriously," *City Journal*, Manhattan Institute, summer 1995, p. 36.

"Suddenly You Belong Somewhere"

President George W. Bush made the following remarks about his support for homeownership in a speech in Cleveland in April during the campaign:

[In] the spirit of the Homestead Act, we will help many Americans to buy their first home. Just as Lincoln gave immigrants fresh from Europe a piece of land, we will help Americans to own a part of the American Dream.

Everyone who owns a home can remember that first day when the loan was approved, the check cleared and they stepped foot into their very own house.

It's different from renting. Suddenly you belong somewhere. Just like that, you're not just visitors to the community anymore but part of it — with a stake in the neighborhood and a concern for its future.

Looking at today's construction boom, it's easy to forget that many Americans are still waiting for this experience. The homeownership rate among whites in America is 73 percent. Among African-Americans and Hispanics, it is 47 percent.

AP Photos / Harry Cabluck

President George W. Bush

Right now the government offers help to low-income families, but mainly in the rental market. Through what's known as the Section 8 program, the federal government makes up the difference between fair-market rents and what a given family is able to pay.

This is a good aim, as far as it goes — but we should extend it further. Instead of receiving monthly voucher payments to help with the rent, I propose a path to ownership.

Under my plan, low-income families can use up to a year's worth of rental payments to make a down payment on their own house. And for five years after that, as they pay their mortgage and build equity, they can still receive housing support, just as they would if they were still renting.

It makes a lot more sense to help people buy homes than to subsidize rental payments forever. They are not only gaining property but independence and the sense of belonging that ownership brings.

For the millions of low-income families not enrolled in Section 8, we will create a new program — called the "American Dream Down Payment Fund." When a low-income family is qualified to buy a house but comes up short on the down payment, we will help them. If they and the bank can come up with 25 percent of the down payment, the government will pay the rest, up to $1,500.

This simple reform could help over 650,000 families in five years purchase homes.

I believe in private property. I believe in private property so strongly, and so firmly, I want everyone to have some.

"He also understands the need for more affordable rental units." [21]

Sen. Paul S. Sarbanes, D-Md., announced at the hearing that HUD had been removed from the government's "high-risk" category because of management changes made by departing Secretary Andrew M. Cuomo. "You're inheriting a better HUD," he told Martinez.

In October, Congress approved a $32.4 billion budget for HUD, including a record $1 billion in new grants to help the estimated 200,000 homeless people nationwide. Martinez indicated he would like to shift some HUD programs to state and local governments, partly to eliminate red tape that bedeviled him as a local official applying for HUD grants.

Echoing Bush's campaign theme of "compassionate conservatism," Martinez said he hoped to create partnerships with faith-based and non-profit organizations to help solve the nation's housing problems. He also said he would promote Bush's plan to provide tax credits to financial institutions that help low-income families finance houses.

Regardless of what happens at the federal level, state and local governments are already taking matters into their own hands. Realizing that only so much aid is going to trickle down from the federal government, many communities have created housing trusts to fi-

At Issue:

Should the government help poor people pay the rent?

ROBERT J. REID
EXECUTIVE DIRECTOR
NATIONAL HOUSING CONFERENCE

WRITTEN FOR THE CQ RESEARCHER, JANUARY 2001

yes

Federal rental assistance for lower-income households helps the impoverished, disabled and elderly. It also enables families to attain the stability, security and proximity to jobs they need in order to climb the ladder of success. Affordable housing contributes to health, education, economic growth and strong neighborhoods. It also attracts the involvement of private and government capital.

It is a normal, although painful, feature of real estate that lower-income households are priced out of the regular markets. Those households can find affordable housing only in soft real estate markets or in substandard properties. Government intervention is thus necessary to help develop and preserve good quality properties with long-term affordability.

Federal support comes in three forms: subsidies that contribute to equity or reduce debt service; default protection; and rental subsidies paid to public and private landlords, which make up the difference between the actual rent and the amount residents can pay with 30 percent of their income. Over 5 million households currently receive supports.

The supports almost always provide good quality housing. The cost to taxpayers is in line with the public benefits provided, and the end result is public-private partnerships, as well as partnerships between federal, state and local participants. However, the formulas for distributing supports are complex, and as a result they reach only about a third of America's households with critical housing needs.

Future rental assistance should include the following lessons gleaned from 70 years of experience: mixed-income developments compatible with their neighborhoods are more successful; subsidies should include both those tied to specific properties and those that move with the residents; high-quality landlords, who emphasize long-term viability, are crucial; and appropriate supportive services should be linked to the rental assistance.

To supplement federal assistance, local and state governments should be encouraged to reduce fees and taxes for affordable housing and expand development opportunities through inclusionary zoning. Local and state expenditures on affordable housing should be increased and leveraged with private contributions, using trust funds when appropriate.

Finally, we can only hope the growing recognition that at least 14 million American families still face critical housing needs — and that more than 3 million of those are working families — will build the broad public support necessary to continue these efforts.

HOWARD HUSOCK
CONTRIBUTING EDITOR
MANHATTAN INSTITUTE

WRITTEN FOR THE CQ RESEARCHER, JANUARY 2001

no

The $13 billion federal housing voucher program may look good at first blush, compared with public housing projects. But replacing an old failure with a new one should not be confused with success. Vouchers now serve 1.7 million households — more than are served by public housing. But they pose significant problems of their own.

For instance, in south suburban Chicago, middle-class minority homeowners are up in arms over the fact that inner-city households are being relocated, via vouchers, into their neighborhoods. "Their lifestyle doesn't blend with our suburban lifestyle," complains African-American hospital administrator Kevin Moore. His concern embodies many of the unforeseen consequences of vouchers.

By subsidizing poor households to relocate in lower-middle-class neighborhoods, we devalue the effort those newly emergent middle-class families have made to buy into such neighborhoods. We assume, wrongly, that moving families into "better" neighborhoods will encourage them to adopt better habits, rather than acknowledging that good lifestyle choices should come first in order for the poor to reach the middle class. In the Chicago case, two-parent minority families, who fought to leave the problems of too-often-troubled families behind, complain that the government now is paying those same families to move next door.

What's more, because 75 percent of vouchers must go to households earning 30 percent of the median income — a group dominated by unmarried mothers — 84 percent of vouchers go to female-headed households. Yet, contrary to welfare reform's time-limited approach to public assistance, there is no time limit on such support. Thus, we are providing unlimited assistance to single-parent families.

But what about the claims that housing costs everywhere are outstripping the ability of working families to pay? We should not confuse price spikes in a few hot markets with a generalized affordability crisis. Homeownership is at an all-time high. Even HUD figures acknowledge that two-income families do not face a housing crisis.

Thus the housing crisis is closely related to our illegitimacy crisis. It is bad social policy to provide the resultant single-parent households with unlimited housing vouchers in neighborhoods others have struggled to reach. If we feel we must provide support for such households, better to do so through existing public housing — coupled with job training and a time limit on their stay. Let's not undermine welfare reform through the back door in the name of a non-existent housing crisis.

nance low-cost housing projects and make loans and down-payment grants to individual homebuyers. At least 150 such housing trusts already have been launched throughout the country.

"They are becoming a prevalent strategy," says Egan of the Millennial Housing Commission

In Charlotte, where a population boom has put a squeeze on housing, the local housing authority plans to begin building its own apartments. Other local and state governments are making idle public lands available for affordable-housing developments. Massachusetts, for instance, recently put more than 1,000 acres of surplus state property on the market for private developers to build affordable housing. New York City is putting thousands of buildings acquired by the city through tax delinquencies back into private hands. Many of the buildings are targeted for moderate-income housing.

Mayor Rudolph Giuliani also promised on Jan. 8 to spend $600 million to build or renovate low-cost housing during the next four years. Housing advocates in New York were disappointed that none of the money is to be used for rental vouchers.

"We remain concerned about the ground that has been lost," said Mary Brosnahan, executive director of the Coalition for the Homeless. Previous administrations had spent $600 million to $700 million each year, she said, but Giuliani had let spending drop to $100 million to $200 million a year. [22]

In California, appropriations for affordable housing were increased by 800 percent last year, to $570 million. To deal with a boom in the population of low-wage earners in Colorado, the state created its own housing-credit program to allow investors in affordable housing to offset state tax liabilities.

And Baltimore, like many other cities, is encouraging workers — especially public servants — to move back into the city to be closer to their jobs. Two years ago, the city began offering cash incentives to help cover closing costs or down payments for police officers, teachers and others who buy homes in the city.

Public-Private Efforts

Preserving existing affordable housing is another priority for state and local governments. About a million rental units tied to federal rent subsidies will expire by 2004, and many housing experts fear that landlords, who now can make more money in the private market, may opt out of the federal program. Even though HUD is increasing the value of the vouchers given to the landlords to keep those properties in the program, it is unclear how many will stay.

Colorado did some creative financing in order to issue $96 million in housing bonds, many of which will be used to refinance and preserve more than 4,300 units of affordable rental housing in 22 counties. Recent federal laws increasing the cap on so-called private-activity bonds should help Colorado and other states raise more money for housing.

In Washington, D.C., the public housing agency also applied unconventional means to raise money. At the end of last year, it used the prospect of future funding from HUD as leverage for a $29 million loan to complete renovations started five years ago. Issued in conjunction with Bank of America and Fannie Mae, it is the first loan transaction ever made based on forthcoming federal funding.

Congress encouraged such public-private partnerships in 1998, when it passed legislation prodding HUD and local housing authorities to create more partnerships with the private sector and to structure loans so they would give more confidence to lenders.

"Housing authorities and communities around the country will benefit from loans of this nature, allowing them to accomplish in one year what would have otherwise taken several years," said William Cooper, president of Bank of America of Greater Washington. [23]

On another front, the National Equity Fund (NEF) — the country's largest nonprofit syndicator of low-income housing tax credits — is getting directly involved in preserving older buildings. NEF acts as a middleman between developers and bankers. Developers who need cash give their tax credits for building low-income housing to NEF, which sells them to banks and gives the money to the developers.

In Missouri, 12 properties that have been part of the federal rent-subsidy program were turned over to the NEF in exchange for tax credits offered by Missouri. "With tens of thousands of affordable homes at risk nationwide, innovative solutions like the Missouri model are becoming critical to preservation" of older buildings, said NEF President Joseph Hagan. [24]

Corporate Initiatives

Faith-based nonprofits are also getting more active in housing preservation. Sheehan of Catholics for Housing says such groups look for private multifamily housing units whose HUD contracts are poised to run out and make purchase offers to the landlords. "We're looking for opportunities to acquire property and preserve it," he says. "It's too difficult to buy land and build in cities."

In addition, employers are taking on more responsibilities for their employees' housing needs. In Northern California, the Silicon Valley Manufacturers Group, made up of 190 companies from tiny startups to Hewlett Packard and Intel along with government agencies and nonprofits, has made housing one of its key initiatives.

"With rents up so high, we are concerned that churches are seeing their members driven away and nonprofits and small businesses being forced out of the area," says Laura Stuchinsky, the group's director of transportation and land use.

The group's housing committee actively lobbies city and county commissions for approval of high-density housing projects near public transportation and other services. It also helped boost the Santa Clara Housing Trust's housing kitty to $20 million to help develop housing projects and provide loans to first-time homebuyers.

Companies like Bank of America, the nation's largest consumer bank, have begun to offer employees grants toward down payments or closing costs. If they stay on the job five years, the bank's grants of up to $5,000 are forgiven.

Predatory Lending

Meanwhile, the lending industry is reaching deeper into the pool of potential borrowers to find low-income families who will make good prospects for homeownership. Low- and zero down-payment mortgages are becoming more common. And so-called sub-prime lenders, who offer financing to people with poor credit histories but at higher than prime interest rates, have been playing a bigger role in the housing market. Sub-prime lending for home purchases in cities grew from 1 percent in 1993 to 5 percent in 1998. [25]

Although traditionally underserved populations are beginning to get financing, many housing experts are concerned about the higher rates and fees they are paying. Indeed, many note that some of the borrowers could have been accepted by prime lenders in the first place but were turned down, possibly because of racial or other forms of discrimination.

According to a 1996 study by Freddie Mac, between 10 percent and 35 percent of sub-prime borrowers could have qualified for a lower-cost loan. Lawmakers have pushed to restrict Freddie Mac and Fannie Mae from purchasing loans from predatory lenders. In recent years, the two secondary-market institutions have been helping more underserved populations get access to better credit.

At the end of the 1990s, the nation's immigrant population was the fastest-growing subset of new U.S. households; but in this decade, immigrants are expected to represent the largest share of population growth. [26] As a result, Freddie Mac has begun to tailor lending products to the new population. For example, instead of having to wait until they get green cards, immigrants now can qualify for homeownership as long as they are legal residents.

In addition, since many immigrants don't have bank accounts, they will be permitted to count cash on hand as part of their assets. And friends and family members living together — a common practice among immigrants — can contribute toward 30 percent of the down payment.

"When we looked at the immigrant issue, we realized that the whole environment had changed and we needed to change," says Craig Nickerson, vice president of community development lending at Freddie Mac. ■

OUTLOOK

President Bush's Focus

Retsinas at the Harvard Joint Studies program says he's relatively bullish about the prospects for the housing market in general over the next decade. His optimism is based in part on the likelihood that new immigrants are likely to fuel a strong housing market when they eventually reach home-buying age.

But on the affordable-housing front, Retsinas and others are not as sanguine. If there is an economic downturn, he notes, low-income people are the first to be affected. Moreover, federal support is likely to continue its retreat, he says, while the supply of existing low-cost housing will undoubtedly continue to shrink. In that event, state and local leaders will have to pull more weight and continue to direct resources to moderately priced housing.

If President Bush follows through on his campaign statements, he will focus on increasing homeownership rather than programs to boost rental housing. Among other things, he proposed allowing low-income families to use up to a year's worth of federal rental subsidies for down payments on a house. In addition, they would still receive subsidies during the first five years that they are paying mortgages.

"It makes a lot more sense to help people buy homes than to subsidize rental payments forever," Bush said in Cleveland on April 11. "It's different from renting. Suddenly you belong somewhere."

Another key component of Bush's housing agenda is boosting savings accounts for those in the lowest 20 percent of the income bracket. Under Bush's proposed individual development accounts program, banks would be encouraged to match up to $300 in savings put away by a low-income savings-account holder, in exchange for federal tax credits. Critics have pointed out that the plan would require education and counseling since many low-income Americans don't have banking experience.

The idea is to broaden welfare reform into asset building, says Stegman of the University of North Carolina's Center for Community Capitalism. "But all of this requires more sophistication among lower- and moderate-income working families," he says. "When you step back and look at the fact that one in 10 families have no bank account at all, financial education is hugely important to this."

For families that don't receive federal housing aid, Bush proposed that the federal government kick in up to $1,500 toward a down payment if would-be homeowners and their lenders could come up with at least 25 percent of the total down payment. Bush suggests the plan could help 650,000 families buy homes in the next five years.

Bush's proposals, and others, of course, depend on financial support from Congress. And with the nearly even split between Republicans and Democrats, it remains to be seen how much bipartisan cooperation will prevail.

Few who closely follow affordable-housing issues predict monumental shifts in the near future. Top housing experts expect only pilot programs to emerge in the next administration.

"It doesn't look like housing affordability is a priority for this administration," says Patrick Markee, senior policy analyst for New York City's Coalition for the Homeless, although he says it's a perfect time to make major investments. "It's an opportunity to use the benefits of the strong economy. It will be a shame if we don't see it as a priority." ■

FOR MORE INFORMATION

Joint Center for Housing Studies, Harvard University, 1033 Massachusetts Ave., Cambridge, Mass., 02138; (617) 495-7908; www.gsd.harvard.edu/jcenter. This collaborative center aligned with Harvard's Design School and the Kennedy School of Government analyzes housing policies, practices and demographic trends.

National Low Income Housing Coalition, 1012 14th St., N.W., Suite 610, Washington, D.C. 20005; (202) 662-1530; www.nlihc.org. Established in 1974, this nonprofit advocates for decent, affordable housing by disseminating information, formulating policy and providing public education programs.

National Housing Conference, 815 15th St., N.W., Suite 538, Washington, D.C., 20005; (202) 393-5772; www.nhc.org. Founded in 1931, the nonprofit advocacy group is made up of developers, lenders, nonprofits and public-sector housing agencies. It advocates housing policy changes.

National Association of Home Builders, 1201 15th St. N.W., Washington, D.C., 20005; (800) 368-5242; www.nahb.com. The NAHB represents some 800 state and local builders associations and 203,000 individual firms.

National Association of Realtors, 700 11th St. NW, Washington, D.C., 20001; (202) 383-1000; http://nar.realtor.com/. Founded in 1908, the association represents 750,000 residential and commercial Realtors and others engaged in the real estate industry. Its economists provide up-to-date reports and data useful in monitoring housing trends and home values.

Notes

[1] Quoted in Nina Bernstein, "Changing Course, Giuliani Proposes Rent subsidies for Homeless Families," *The New York Times*, Oct., 12, 2000.

[2] Luke Shockman, "Addressing the Workers Shortage," *Post-Bulletin*, Rochester, Minn., Jan. 19, 2000.

[3] "Rental Housing Assistance: The Worsening Crisis: A Report to Congress on Worst Case Housing Needs," U.S. Department of Housing and Urban Development, 1999.

[4] American Housing Survey, 1997.

[5] Michael A. Stegman, Roberto Quercia, and George McCarthy, "Housing America's Working Families," *New Century Housing*, Volume 1, Issue 1, The Center for Housing Policy, June 2000.

[6] Richard Green, and Stephen Malpezzi, draft, "A Primer on U.S. Housing Markets and Housing Policy," Center for Urban Land Economics Research, University of Wisconsin-Madison, Feb. 23, 2000.

[7] *Ibid.*

[8] U.S. Housing Market Conditions, U.S. Department of Housing and Urban Development, Office of Policy Development and Research. Third-Quarter 2000.

[9] National Association of Realtors. Up-to-date figures on median home prices and Housing Affordability Index can be found at http://nar.realtor.com/.

[10] Joint Center for Housing Studies, Harvard University, "The State of the Nation's Housing: 2000," June 2000.

[11] NAR, *op. cit.*

[12] *Ibid.*

[13] Michael Verespej, "Can Living Wage Work?" *Industry Week*, Sept. 18, 2000.

[14] American Housing Survey, 1998, along with calculations by Michael Stegman, *et al.*, in Stegman, *op. cit.*

[15] Patrick Barta, "Fannie Mae, Freddie Mac Are Chided On Low-Income Homeownership Effort," *The Wall Street Journal*, Nov. 30, 2000.

[16] Jean Cummings and Denise DiPasquale, "The Low-Income Housing Tax Credit: An Analysis of the First Ten Years," *Housing Policy Debate*, Volume 10, Issue 2, Fannie Mae Foundation, 1999.

[17] From their Web site, at www.texashousing.org.

[18] *Ibid.*

[19] From prepared statements by Lazio, Oct. 24, 2000.

[20] Quoted in Elizabeth Becker, "HUD Candidate Would Seek More Homes for Minorities," *The New York Times*, Jan. 18, 2001.

[21] *Ibid.*

[22] Quoted in Bruce Lambert, "Housing: Lowering Costs Seen as Crucial to Building Plan," *The New York Times*, Jan. 9, 2001.

[23] Quoted in Kovaleski, Serge F., "D.C. Housing Agency Lands Repair Loans: $29 Million Deal Uses Private Money," *The Washington Post*, Dec. 21, 2000.

[24] Quoted in "NEF Affiliate Acquires Sec. 8 Projects Donated in Return for State Tax Credit," *Affordable Housing Finance*, p. 54, Sept. 2000.

[25] Joint Center for Housing Studies, *op. cit.*

[26] *Ibid.*, p. 4.

Bibliography

Selected Sources Used

Articles

Bernstein, Nina, "Rent Subsidies Proposed for Homeless Families: Giuliani Changes View on Housing Aid," *The New York Times*, Oct. 12, 2000.
New York City Mayor Rudolph Giuliani proposes rent subsidies to ease crowding at emergency shelters, which increasingly house working parents and their children.

Oppel, Richard Jr., "Efforts to Restrict Sprawl Find New Resistance From Advocates for Affordable Housing," *The New York Times*, Dec. 26, 2000, p. A18.
Oppel documents opposition by Habitat for Humanity and other affordable-housing groups to anti-growth measures, which the nonprofits say would limit their outreach.

Shockman, Luke, "Addressing the Worker Shortage," *Post-Bulletin* (Rochester, Minn.), Jan. 19, 2000.
A shortage of health-care workers is tied to the lack of affordable housing.

Verespej, Michael, "Can Living Wage Work?" *Industry Week*, Sept. 18, 2000, p. 11.
There's little empirical data to indicate whether living-wage bills requiring employers to pay higher-than-minimum wages have improved the economic status of entry-level workers or led to fewer workers being hired, or both.

Reports and Studies

Burchell, Robert C., *et al.*, "Inclusionary Zoning: A Viable Solution to the Affordable Housing Crisis?" New Century Housing, The Center for Housing Policy, Vol. 1, Issue 2, October 2000.
The report advocates using inclusionary zoning ordinances to increase the affordable homes available in communities. Such ordinances typically set minimum percentages of affordable units required in new developments and give developers incentives to include low-cost housing, such as waiving zoning requirements.

Cummings, Jean, and Denise DiPasquale, "The Low-Income Housing Tax Credit: An Analysis of the First Ten Years," Housing Policy Debate, Volume 10, Issue 2, Fannie Mae Foundation, 1999.
The study generally concludes that low-income housing tax credit projects — the major federal program to produce affordable rental housing — fail to reach the very poor.

Green, Richard K., and Stephen Malpezzi, "A Primer on U.S. Housing Markets and Housing Policy" (draft), Center for Urban Land Economics Research, School of Business, University of Wisconsin-Madison, Feb. 23, 2000.
Housing economists conclude that Americans at the bottom quarter of the income ladder face the most difficulties in finding affordable housing.

"Out of Reach," National Low Income Housing Coalition, 2000.
The annual study determines that minimum-wage earners would be unable to rent a two-bedroom house in any city without spending over 30 percent of their income.

Pill, Madeleine, "Employer-Assisted Housing: Competitiveness Through Partnership," Joint Center for Housing Studies and Neighborhood Reinvestment Corporation, September 2000.
This study argues that housing is a crucial component of economic competitiveness and that employers should play a role in creating housing opportunities.

"Rental Housing Assistance: The Worsening Crisis: A Report to Congress on Worst Case Housing Needs," U.S. Department of Housing and Urban Development, 1999.
The housing-affordability crisis facing very-low-income renters continues to worsen as a record high 5.4 million renter households pay a disproportionately large share of their wages for housing or live in substandard conditions

Stegman, Michael A., *et al.*, "Housing America's Working Families," *New Century Housing*, The Center for Housing Policy, Vol. 1, Issue 1, June 2000.
This study argues that the critical housing needs of working families are growing and impacting suburban communities. It calls for increased emphasis on the housing needs of moderate- and middle-income families, instead of a narrow focus on the very poor.

"The State of the Nation's Housing: 2000," Joint Center for Housing Studies, Harvard University, June 2000.
In its annual report, the center explores the homeownership gap between whites and minorities and the affordability crisis for low-wage earners and renters.

13 Auto Industry's Future

DAVID MASCI

General Motors didn't begin the new millennium on a promising note. On Jan. 4, in what many are calling a desperate marketing ploy, the nation's largest automaker offered $500 "loyalty coupons" toward new purchases. The offer was extended not only to current owners of GM cars but even to car shoppers who had expressed interest in GM products.

American Honda Motor Co., Inc.

The move was clearly aimed at helping GM's sagging U.S. market share, which slipped below 29 percent last year, its lowest level since the company's early days in the 1920s. The decline prompted rare self-criticism from GM Vice Chairman Harry Pearce. "We have absolutely not delivered on our commitment on market share, and that's simply unacceptable," he said at a Dec. 10 news conference. "We're in the hot seat, where we ought to be." [1]

And the huge corporation may not be alone. Some analysts argue that the other two big U.S. automakers, Ford and DaimlerChrysler, also face increasingly potent foreign competition in the U.S. market. Perhaps most alarming for the Big Three, Honda, Toyota and other Japanese carmakers are beginning to move aggressively into the so-called light-truck market (minivans, SUVs and pickup trucks), which comprises more than half of all U.S. auto sales and is almost entirely controlled by Detroit.

"The Japanese are introducing some great products in this area, things that really meet consumer needs," says Brad Fox, an analyst at AutoPacific, an industry consulting firm in Detroit.

At the same time, the Japanese have a huge presence in the traditional passenger car market. Indeed, Toyota and Honda make the two top-selling automobiles in America. And that's unlikely to change any time soon, Fox says, in part because the Big Three don't have too much that can compete with the phenomenally successful Camry and Accord.

But, other analysts say, Detroit is not likely to lose any more of its nearly 70 percent market share. "The Big Three are no longer complacent about what Japan is doing," says Diane Swonk, chief economist at Bank One Corp. in Chicago.

Swonk and other analysts say all three companies have a host of new models in the pipeline — light trucks as well as passenger cars — that will be very competitive.

Besides, Swonk says, the Japanese "don't have the factory capacity in the United States to take that much market share away from the Big Three." And, she adds, they couldn't make up the shortages by exporting cars from plants at home without creating a political firestorm in the United States.

But concern about foreign encroachment in the auto industry may be fading as firms set up operations overseas, thus diluting their once coveted national identities. The trend toward globalization was given a boost in 1998, when German automaker Daimler Benz merged with Chrysler, America's No. 3 car company. Since then, other car companies — including Sweden's Volvo and Japan's Nissan — have been wholly or partly acquired by other firms. *

Indeed, on the same day Pearce was lamenting GM's declining market share, his company announced its plan to purchase a 20 percent stake in Japan's Subaru. GM hopes that the $1.4 billion deal will strengthen its presence in the huge Asian market, where it currently sells fewer than 5 percent of all vehicles. "For us, it's a further push in Asia, particularly the Japanese market," says Andrew Card, GM's vice president for government relations and former secretary of Transportation under President George Bush. But more broadly, he says, the move is just another example of the trend toward rationalization, or consolidation. "This industry has been ripe for [change] for the past eight to 10 years," Card says.

Many analysts and industry insiders agree. In fact, Ford CEO Jacques Nassar and Hiroshi Okuda, who heads Toyota, predict that in a relatively short time there will be only five or six large car companies around the world. Small and medium-sized firms, like Germany's BMW or South Korea's Daewoo, they say, will be gobbled up by other companies.

Those who predict an industry-wide consolidation argue that it is inevitable because only very large companies will have the resources and global reach to be competitive in what is fast becoming a cutthroat business. "It's just getting tougher and tougher out there, and you have to have size and reach to survive," says Ed Lewis, a spokesman for Ford.

Size is important, Lewis and others

From *The CQ Researcher*, January 21, 2000.

* On Jan. 10, 2000, GM announced that it was buying the half of the Swedish automaker Saab that it did not already own. The move could add new customers to the GM fold and reduce European production costs.

Japanese Firms Nibbling at U.S. Market

Japanese automakers have steadily increased their share of the U.S. car and light-truck market in the past 15 years while the Big Three U.S. firms saw their share fall below 70 percent in 1999 for the first time in more than 50 years.

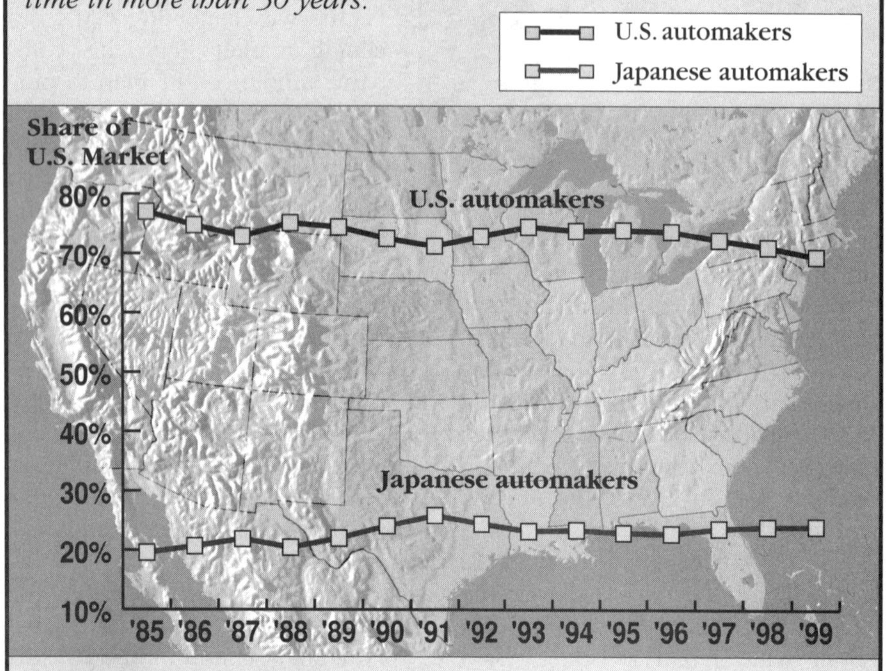

Source: Ward's AutoInfo Bank

say, because it allows automakers to lower the unit cost of manufacturing each car. And pressure to lower costs is increasing. That's because automakers can stay competitive only by bringing out new and redesigned models, a hugely expensive proposition. At the same time, consumers are getting more and more price conscious. The only way carmakers can keep prices as low as possible while spending the billions needed to develop new models is by realizing greater economies of scale. Thus, the more vehicles a carmaker produces, the more it can reduce its development and manufacturing costs.

In addition, proponents of consolidation say, car companies increasingly need a global presence — which also requires size. For one thing, they say, having access to all or most markets spreads risk, since a company can have a bad year in one or two regions and still make money if sales in remaining markets are steady. Global reach also helps to spread out development costs by allowing a firm to market the same or similar cars around the world. "You need to be able to sell everywhere these days in order to keep costs down," says Bank One's Swonk.

But other industry-watchers say that consolidation is not inevitable because some small-to-medium-size car companies, like Italy's Fiat or France's Renault, are often important symbols of national pride — which may militate against a merger even it makes good business sense. "People like the French are very nationalistic and may not want to see foreign ownership of their auto industry," says analyst Fox at AutoPacific.

In addition, some midsize auto companies, like Honda and BMW, have announced their intention to remain independent, arguing that giant auto manufacturers are actually at a competitive disadvantage. "We think our smaller size allows us to be more flexible and more responsive to changing preferences," says Barbara Ponce, a spokeswoman for Honda.

As companies gear up to meet the increasingly competitive global marketplace, these are two questions being asked:

Will the recent merger of Daimler Benz and Chrysler spark further consolidations leading to the creation of just five or six big car companies in the next few years?

When Germany's Daimler Benz and the smallest of America's Big Three carmakers, Chrysler, announced merger plans in May 1998, many observers saw the marriage as a Big Bang that would set off a wave of consolidations within the auto industry. DaimlerChrysler would be the rule not the exception, they said, because only huge companies would survive for long in what was fast becoming a hypercompetitive business.

"The industry landscape will need to change," said Ford's Nassar in January 1999, just two months after the merger became official. "For global players to be really competitive, their sales volumes will have to be over 5 million a year."[2] Toyota's Okuda echoed these sentiments: "In the next century, there will be [only] five or six automakers."[3]

In fact, GM Chairman John F. Smith Jr. said on Jan. 17 that in the future GM will rely more on partnerships with foreign carmakers and would better be described as "the General Motors group."

Speaking at the Automotive News World Conference in Detroit, Smith said, "This alliance strategy is our major thrust, and it is clearly a different approach to growth than most people have associated with General Motors — or with the rest of the industry, for that matter." [4]

According to Okuda, Smith and others, car companies will soon be unable to compete effectively in what has become a high-cost, low-margin global business unless they have a huge infrastructure and a presence in many markets. That means that only big players like Ford, GM, Toyota and now DaimlerChrysler will be able to stay afloat for long.

So far, a few companies have followed DaimlerChrysler's example to one degree or another. Last May, for instance, Ford agreed to buy Volvo. Late last year, GM announced its intention to buy 20 percent of Subaru and all of South Korea's Daewoo Motors. And in the most significant deal since the Daimler-Chrysler merger, France's Renault took a stake in Japan's ailing No. 3 carmaker, Nissan.

Big Three Have Biggest Share of U.S. Market

Led by GM, the Big Three U.S. automakers had just under 70 percent of the U.S. market of cars and light trucks in 1999. Foreign firms, led by Toyota, had nearly a third of the market.

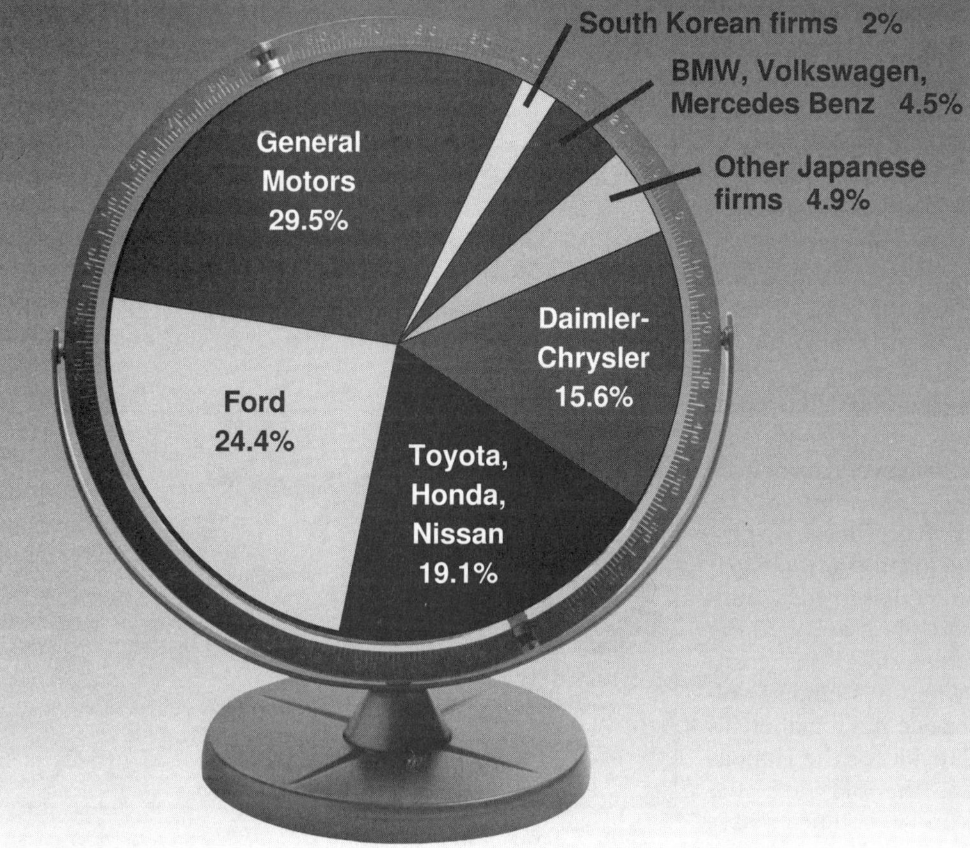

Source: Ward's AutoInfo Bank

But the auto industry is still largely made up of companies of all shapes and sizes. Midsized firms like Fiat and Peugeot remain independent. Indeed, some automakers, like BMW and Honda, have tried to dampen speculation by openly declaring that they are not interested in linking up with another car company.

Still, many analysts and industry insiders say, most of these midsize companies are unlikely to survive as individual entities for long. One of the biggest problems, they say, will be bringing out new models and redesigning old ones in order to keep competitive in today's glutted and cutthroat market. "Companies need to bring out new products all the time or they will be in trouble," says Robert Schnorbus, director of economic analysis for J.D. Power, an auto consulting firm that rates customer satisfaction. "New products generally do well their first year because people are usually excited about them."

But the cost of redesigning existing models or developing new ones is becoming prohibitively expensive for all but the largest firms. Currently, development costs have risen, on average, to about $3 billion per vehicle.

Much of the money is spent on outfitting redesigned or new models with the latest technology, such as satellite navigation systems or crash-avoidance radar. "People are expecting more and more when they buy a car these days," says Ford's Lewis. "That means the cost of developing cars is getting higher."

At the same time, intense competition is driving average vehicle prices down. According to J.D. Power, the average purchase price of a car or light truck in the United States fell 2 percent in 1999, and the trend is likely to continue for the foreseeable future.

"Today everyone is looking for ways to realize economies of scale," Lewis says. One approach is spreading the cost of developing new technology over a large number of different vehicles so that recouping an investment is not dependent on one or two models selling well, a strategy that plays to the strength of large companies producing a diversity of models and designs.

Another way to spread out costs is to sell the same or similar vehicles in many markets. Again, only large companies with a global presence — like Ford, which has a solid foothold in every major market — are able to offer a car everywhere. By producing the same or similar models in great numbers, big automakers reduce their unit costs. "When this kind of volume comes together, it's difficult for the Hondas and the BMWs of the world to compete," says David Cole, director of the University of Michigan's Office for the Study of Automotive Transportation.

Global presence also allows carmakers to spread the risk in another way. "If you're a niche player or a player in only one or two markets, it's OK so long as that market or niche is robust," Lewis says. "But what happens when there's a downturn in that market? You don't want all your eggs in one basket. You want to be in other niches, other markets, in order to stay afloat when one segment isn't performing."

But some auto-industry watchers dismiss the inevitability of the supposed rush to consolidate. "I think it's all humbug," says veteran auto analyst Maryanne Keller, now head of the auto services division for online auctioneer, Priceline.com. "We've been hearing the same thing since 1975, and it hasn't happened."

Ironically, automakers that might otherwise be ripe for acquisition are protected by a potentially powerful barrier — nationalism — that has more to do with politics than economics or technology. "Auto companies are very politically important in other countries, and they are huge employers," Keller says. "Do you think the Italians are going to accept Fiat being swallowed by a bigger company that would then shed 10,000 jobs? I don't think so." The same could be said for France's Peugeot or Germany's BMW, she says.

Ford Motor Co.

Ford's F-Series pickup is No. 1 in U.S. sales of all passenger cars, SUVs, minivans and light trucks.

In addition, Keller and others argue, consolidation isn't the panacea many auto-watchers think it is. To begin with, she points out, the idea that you sell the same car all over the world is generally not true. "There are not a lot of examples around the world where product commonality exists," she says. "Each market has fairly distinctive needs and wants and to maximize sales, which means you have to tailor the car for the country.

In addition, Keller argues, the much ballyhooed need for global presence has produced little but heartache and losses for those companies that are active in most markets. "GM and Ford are losing their shirts overseas, especially in the developing world," she says. "By buying auto companies in these other countries, they bought into every nation's crisis by exposing themselves to market volatility in developing countries like Brazil and Southeast Asia."

But even if greater size does lead to savings, there could be other negative effects. Honda's Ponce says her company wants to remain independent because going solo allows it to be a more "nimble competitor" than a corporate behemoth. "When you have a huge company with all its hierarchy, it's hard to respond quickly to market changes because every decision takes longer to make and implement," she says.

Are the Japanese and other foreign automakers once again poised to make serious inroads into the American car market?

For the past decade, Japan's share of U.S. auto sales has held steady, at roughly a quarter of the vehicle market. In 1999, for instance, the Japanese sold 24 percent of the new cars and light trucks purchased in the United States. By comparison, the U.S. market share for the Big Three was 69.5 percent.

During the late 1970s and the '80s, however, Honda, Toyota, Nissan and other Japanese companies seemed unstoppable. In less than a decade, the once-ignored Japanese automakers had grabbed more than a quarter of the U.S. market from stunned and reeling American manufacturers. Some experts were predicting that one or more of the Big Three would go bankrupt. Indeed, at one point, Chrysler required a $1.2 billion bailout from the federal government to stay in business.

But in the late 1980s, after years of complacency, the Big Three finally began to respond to the Japanese, by making better-quality cars that better met customer needs. In addition, American manufacturers were quick to pick up on consumers' passion for minivans, SUVs and pickup trucks, a rapidly growing market that the Japanese initially largely ignored. Americans also had a price advantage due to the then-strong yen, which made cars produced in Japan much more expensive to export to the United States. As a result, Japanese carmakers had to charge higher prices, which in turn made some consumers take a second look at cheaper American alternatives.

Now, analysts say, the situation appears to be changing once again, with many industry-watchers predicting that Japanese manufacturers could make serious, new inroads into the Big Three's home-market share. "If things continue as they are, I could see them taking 5 percent in the next five years, or even more," says Priceline.com's Keller. "I think the Japanese are doing exactly what they should be to gain share," agrees AutoPacfic's Fox. "It's a strategy that should work very well for them."

Not surprisingly, the strategy involves introducing more light trucks into their product line to compete in a market segment that now comprises half of all U.S. vehicle sales. Currently, GM, Ford, and Chrysler control more than 90 percent of the light-truck market — but not for long, Fox predicts. "First, the Japanese have a lot of vehicles — pickups, SUVs and minivans — coming that are going to plug the holes the Japanese have in this area," he says.

Chevrolet

Critics say the sleek Oldsmobile Alero (top) reflects forward thinking at General Motors while Chevrolet's family sedan, the Impala (bottom), exemplies GM's conservatism.

"Second," Fox says, "what they're doing so far has been great." He points to the Odyssey, a new minivan that is already in such demand that Honda cannot produce enough vehicles to satisfy dealers' needs. "It's exceeded all of our sales and customers' expectations," Ponce says. And Toyota's latest offerings in this market, the full-size Tundra pickup and a luxury SUV from the company's Lexus division, the RX300, have also been big hits. [5]

Even as they are aggressively moving into the light-truck market, the Japanese appear likely to maintain their strong hold on traditional cars, where their reputation for quality and reliability is unmatched. For the past five years, the two top-selling family sedans in the United States have been the Toyota Camry and Honda Accord. Honda's hot-selling Civic and Toyota's popular Corolla also have a sizable chunk of the small-coupe market. In both these market segments, Fox and others say, Japanese automakers are unlikely to cede any ground.

"Anyone who thinks that the Japanese are likely to walk away from this market is fooling himself," he says, because "their cars are perceived as better, and they are."

Meanwhile, other foreign auto-makers have been busy carving up smaller bits of the American market. At the low end, South Korean car companies like Hyundai and Daewoo have increased their market share by targeting the under-$10,000 market. And Germany's Mercedes, BMW, Audi and Volkswagen have made significant gains in the lucrative luxury car segment. "I fully expect these other foreign car makers to continue making inroads into the American market," Keller says.

Keller, Fox and other industry experts question whether the Big Three are taking the appropriate steps to fend off the challenge from overseas. General Motors is seen as par-

The Top 10 Models

The Toyota Camry and Honda Accord were the top-selling passenger cars in the United States in 1999, but pickup trucks and SUVs dominated the Top 10 list. Ford led the list with four models, including the No. 1 vehicle, the F-Series pickup.

Brand	Subseries	No. of Vehicles 1999 Sales
Ford	Ford F-Series	804,210
Chevrolet	Silverado	530,106
Toyota	Camry	448,162
Dodge	Ram Pickup	428,930
Ford	Explorer	428,772
Honda	Accord	404,192
Ford	Taurus	368,327
Ford	Ranger	348,358
Honda	Civic	318,308
Jeep	Grand Cherokee	300,031

Source: Ward's AutoInfoBank

ticularly vulnerable. "Right now, they don't have the right vehicles," Keller says, "and it's debatable, in this changing market, whether they will any time soon."

J.D. Power's Schnorbus agrees, pointing to Chevrolet's new family sedan, the Impala, as an example of what's wrong at the nation's No. 1 automaker. "It's not an innovative product and is conservative in its styling," he says. "It will get some buyers but won't be a big hit."

Even if GM had the right products, Schnorbus says, it would still be at a disadvantage, at least in the short term. "They have a big image problem," he says. "Our surveys point to concerns among customers that their quality and styling are a problem." Consequently, he says, innovative GM cars like Oldsmobile's Alero and Intrigue have trouble taking off. "These are great cars, but they're struggling because they're attached to a stodgy brand name."

Some analysts also criticize GM for having too many different versions of what is essentially the same car — a vestige of the days when the company had roughly half of the American car market. "They have too many products now, and it's confusing," Fox says, pointing to what he calls an almost countless number of four-door sedans. "There's the [Oldsmobile] Intrigue, [Chevrolet] Impala, [Chevrolet] Lumina, [Pontiac] Grand Am, [Chevrolet] Prism, [Chevrolet] Malibu and on and on."

On the other hand, No. 2 Ford is seen by some as better positioned than GM and DaimlerChrysler to face foreign competition. The company's redesigned flagship sedan, the Taurus, appears likely to sell well, while a smaller, cheaper new car, the Focus, has won rave reviews and may someday rival the Civic and Corolla.

Looming as a potential problem for the Big Three, and especially DaimlerChrysler, is the heavy dependence of U.S. automakers on the light-truck market for current and future sales. "U.S. automakers are committed to increasing light-truck capacity substantially, which could get them into trouble if the market bottoms out or declines," Keller says. All it would take, she says, is a big rise in gasoline prices, making large vehicles much more expensive to operate.

But others say the days of American complacency are over. "They were whipped badly in the '80s, but things are different now," says Bank One's Swonk. "The Big Three understand that competition is a moving target, and they're on it."

All three companies, including GM, now have a host of new, competitive products coming to market. "I really think that GM has killed its last dog and is no longer producing cars that aren't viable in the marketplace," says the University of Michigan's Cole.

Louis Lataif, dean of Boston University's School of Management, thinks the company is on track to attract new buyers, though he concedes that GM has an image problem. "I've seen some of their concept cars — some that are close to actual production — and I think they are moving in a very innovative direction," he says.

The Alero and Intrigue may not be selling as well as they should, he says, but their sleek styling and high quality reflect new thinking at GM. "I mean, look at the old Oldsmobile models, and you can see that these are a big step in the right direction."

And consumers will eventually respond if the positive trend continues, Lataif says. "It takes time for these things to sink in, but they will."

Meanwhile, Ford and DaimlerChrysler are also moving ahead with competitive, new models. Ford is especially optimistic about the first major changes in the Taurus — once the nation's best-selling sedan — since 1996. "They've made the styling more conservative, added more room inside and priced it more competitively," Fox says. "I think there will be some big sales improvements."

DaimlerChrysler's new lineup includes a redesigned Neon, the company's briskly selling standard-bearer in the small-car market. The recently redesigned Intrepid, the company's primary family sedan, sells well, too.

In the all-important light-truck market, the Big Three are also preparing for new pressure from the Japanese and others. "We understand that there's a lot of competition coming in light trucks, but we've been developing new products that we think are superior in some categories of that market," says GM's Card. Those include a new version of the Chevrolet Suburban, a very large SUV that has been a huge seller for GM. Card also points to the popularity of Ford's Excursion, which is currently the Suburban's only real competitor. And all three U.S. automakers are planning new models to compete with Toyota's RAV4 and Honda's CRX in the small-SUV market, the only part of the light-truck market the Japanese actually dominate.

In the final analysis, auto-industry experts say, even if the Japanese win the U.S. public's favor, limited production will prevent them from taking too much market share away from American companies. "They don't have enough capacity to kick butt," Swonk says. "They really can't even take advantage of this booming sales market, and so I think they may even lose market share, at least in the near term.

Moreover, she says, it is politically risky for Toyota, Honda and the others to try to make up the difference by exporting more vehicles from their factories in Japan, which are underutilized due to an almost decadelong recession. "They know they can't export their way out of this because it's politically unfeasible to do that." ■

Toyota Motor Sales, U.S.A., Inc.

Toyota's full-size Tundra pickup has been successful in the U.S. light-truck market.

BACKGROUND

Henry Ford's Genius

The automobile was not invented in America. That honor goes to Carl Benz, a German. But no country has done more to make the car a part of everyday life than the United States.

The first American automobile manufacturing company was begun in 1895, 10 years after Benz's breakthrough, by brothers Charles E. and J. Frank Duryea. Like all early cars, the Duryeas' flimsy-looking vehicle resembled a horse-drawn buggy. It was powered by a one-cylinder gasoline engine and started with an electric ignition.

Three years after the Duryeas set up shop, the number of automakers in the United States had swelled to 50. And a decade after that, in 1908, there were more than 250 firms producing cars. Some, like those founded by Ransom Eli Olds and James Ward Packard, became American institutions. Others, like the Duryeas' enterprise, would eventually fade from the scene.

In any event, carmakers sparked a consumer boom the likes of which had never been seen in the United States. In 1914, less than 20 years after the Duryeas began, more than 1.2 million cars were tooling along the nation's roadways. In 1929, there were more than 26 million cars, and annual U.S. auto production topped 5.5 million vehicles.[6]

Most of the credit for the boom goes to Henry Ford, an engineer from Dearborn, Mich., who set out to make a safe, reliable automobile that all Americans could afford. When Ford introduced his famous Model T in 1908, the car retailed for $850. Eight years later, mass production pioneered by Ford had brought the price down to just $360.

By building cheap and reliable cars, Ford dominated the American auto industry into the 1920s. In 1920, for example, the company had a 55.7

percent share of the American market, selling 845,000 cars a year. By contrast, its next biggest competitor, GM, sold fewer than 200,000. [7]

GM Overtakes Ford

But throughout the decade, GM, led by the brilliant Alfred P. Sloan, steadily overtook Ford. Sloan created five distinct brands within the company — Chevrolet, Pontiac, Oldsmobile, Buick and Cadillac. Each was targeted at different segments of the market, from first-time car buyers (Chevrolet) to the affluent (Cadillac).

Differentiating the various models from one another forced carmakers to shift the focus from quality and reliability to appearance. Sloan himself once said the "appearance of a motor-car is . . . perhaps the most important factor because everyone knows the car will run." [8]

As its market share shrank, Ford abandoned its policy of selling plain but high-quality cars at affordable prices. Along with the rest of the industry, Ford began mimicking Sloan's design strategy, and almost continual restyling became the norm.

The economic boom following World War II led carmakers to more ostentatious designs using abundant chrome trim, huge fins and other extravagances. During the 1960s, automakers introduced sporty vehicles like the popular Ford Mustang. But technical improvements were also being made, including automatic transmissions, power steering and power brakes.

Challenge From Japan

Luxury and sports cars from Europe have long been fixtures on American roads. Germany even had a mass-market breakthrough in the late 1950s and the '60s with the diminutive Volkswagen Beetle, an economical, distinctive-looking car that appealed to motorists seeking an alternative to chrome-laden Detroit, behemoths. But through the mid-1970s, U.S. manufacturers — largely today's Big Three — routinely sold more than 90 percent of all the cars driven in America.

In those days, Japanese auto companies barely dented the American market. In 1968, for instance, only 150,000 Japanese cars were sold in the United States, less than 1 percent of all U.S. sales. But that began to change in 1973, when an oil embargo by the major petroleum exporting countries drove gas prices way up.

All of a sudden, consumers began looking for alternatives to the oversized gas-guzzlers they had driven all their lives. What they found from companies like Toyota, Datsun (today's Nissan) and Honda were small, plain-looking cars with great fuel economy. What they also discovered, after a few years, was that Japanese cars were much more reliable than the American automobiles they had previously owned.

What was their secret? To a large extent, the Japanese built better cars because they gave their factory workers more responsibility in the manufacturing process — empowered them, in today's management jargon. At the most fundamental level, for example, any of the plant's workers could stop the assembly line if they found a defect in a car. In addition, cars were designed more simply, with fewer parts, making them easier to assemble. [9]

By the early 1980s, the Japanese had cornered fully a quarter of the U.S. auto market, sparking real fear that one or more of the Big Three might be put out business. Indeed, in 1980, Chrysler avoided bankruptcy only after the federal government agreed to guarantee a controversial $1.2 billion loan to the struggling automaker. Ford was also experiencing financial difficulties, although its fortunes never sank as low as Chrysler's.

For GM, the situation was less dire, at least at the start of the 1980s. GM had more than half the American car market throughout the 1970s, and it was financially solid.

But GM's next decade proved horrible. By 1985, it had lost 13 points of market share, or nearly a third of its sales. By 1990, the automaker's share of the U.S. market had shrunk to 36 percent. [10] The resulting losses from the company's shrinking North American automobile business were billions of dollars each year.

U.S. Automakers Respond

With a declining market share and increasing financial difficulties, American automakers began to take steps to regain momentum. Ford purchased 24 percent of automaker Mazda in 1979, a move that allowed it to gain firsthand access to Japanese manufacturing methods. By 1986, when Ford introduced the Taurus, the company had radically changed the way it designed and built cars. And in the early 1990s, the company introduced a number of highly competitive light trucks, including the Explorer, a hugely successful SUV, and a hot-selling minivan, the Windstar.

Chrysler also began to revive its sagging fortunes. Like Ford, the company used its minority stake in a Japanese automaker — in this case Mitsubishi Motors — to help improve its manufacturing methods. In 1987, the company purchased the floundering American Motors Corp. (AMC), a smaller automaker known for its

Chronology

1960s *Domestic automakers dominate the U.S. market, with European and Japanese firms taking only a small slice of car sales.*

1964
Ford introduces the Mustang, a popular sports car.

1968
Japanese auto manufacturers sell only 150,000 cars in America, less than 1 percent of the market

1970s *Successive oil shocks drive U.S. consumers to fuel-efficient Japanese cars.*

1973
An Arab oil embargo drives gas prices up.

1975
Nissan (then called Datsun) replaces Germany's Volkswagen as the leading exporter of cars in the United States.

1979
Ford buys a 25 percent stake in the Japanese automaker Mazda, which serves as a model for the No. 2 U.S. automaker in its quest to improve quality.

1980s *As the Japanese continue to gain market share, U.S. automakers begin instituting changes to improve the quality and desirability of their cars.*

1983
Chrysler introduces the minivan, creating a new market segment.

1985
GM launches the Saturn and builds a state-of-the-art plant in Tennessee that employs Japanese manufacturing methods.

1986
Ford introduces the Taurus, which becomes one of the nation's most popular cars.

1987
Chrysler buys American Motors Corp., a smaller automaker known for its Jeep division of light trucks. The move positions Chrysler to quickly take advantage of the growing demand for sport utility vehicles (SUVs).

1989
The Honda Accord becomes the nation's best-selling car.

1990s *The Big Three halt their market-share slide. The number of mergers within the industry begins to increase.*

1990
Ford enters the sport utility market with its instantly popular Explorer.

1991
GM announces it will close 21 factories and lay off 74,000 workers in the first of several attempts to streamline operations.

1992
Detroit gains market share for the first time since 1989 as the Taurus bumps the Accord from the No. 1 spot in U.S. car sales.

1993
Chrysler launches a critically acclaimed and popular line of sedans with innovative "cab-forward" design giving passengers more room.

1994
Chrysler introduces the Neon, a popular, small car.

May 1998
Germany's Daimler Benz and Chrysler agree to merge, becoming the fifth-largest automaker in the world and setting off a wave of mergers and acquisitions within the industry.

June 1998
UAW members walk off the job at GM to protest the proposed closing of a metal-stamping plant. The action leads to a bitter, 54-day strike.

January 1999
Ford agrees to pay $6.6 billion for Sweden's Volvo.

March 1999
French automaker Renault buys 36.8 percent of Japan's Nissan.

December 1999
U.S. automakers end the year with a bang, selling 17 million cars in the United States. GM announces that it will purchase 20 percent of troubled Japanese carmaker Subaru.

January 2000
GM announces that it will purchase the 50 percent of Swedish carmaker Saab that it doesn't own.

light trucks and jeeps. The acquisition proved a godsend for Chrysler, positioning the company to quickly take advantage of the growing demand for light trucks.

In addition, Chrysler introduced a slew of new models, starting in 1983 with the now popular minivan, a vehicle that created an entire market segment. In 1993, Chrysler again jolted the industry when it launched a critically acclaimed and popular line of sedans with its innovative "cab-forward design," which gives passengers more room inside.

General Motors was the last of the Big Three to change. But its shrinking market share spurred the auto giant into action. In 1984, the company launched a joint venture with Toyota to build cars together at a plant in Freemont, Calif. The following year, it started its cutting-edge Saturn division, using Japanese manufacturing techniques to produce high-quality, small cars at an affordable price. Both ventures proved successful — reliable cars were manufactured that sold well. But GM failed to use the lessons it had learned from Toyota and Saturn to transform its other divisions.

Ford Motor Corp.

Ford is hoping for a boost in sales after making styling changes to the Taurus and pricing it more competitively.

By 1990, GM's market share was down to just over one-third. Its factories were considered models of inefficiency and its cars were generally viewed as uninspired. Under Chairman Robert Stempel and now Smith, the company began improving its efficiency and profitability. In 1991, Stempel announced that GM would close 21 plants and lay off 74,000 workers. [11] In addition to streamlining operations, improvements in quality, such as reducing the number of parts in each car, were introduced.

In 1992, American automakers actually gained market share from the Japanese for the first time in four years. Over the next three years, the Big Three's share hovered around 73 percent. Some of the success grew out of the changes instituted in the 1980s. [12] All three companies had significantly improved the quality and reliability of their cars. In addition, GM, Ford and Chrysler were positioned to meet the growing demand for SUVs and other light trucks.

Meanwhile, Japanese automakers were struggling with handicaps of their own, including their failure to forecast the high demand for light trucks, which left them with few products to offer. In addition, a strong yen made exports to the United States more expensive, requiring Toyota and other manufacturers to raise prices in order to maintain profitability.

But, like the Americans a decade earlier, the Japanese have worked diligently to improve their prospects. With new factories in the United States and more light trucks to offer, Toyota, Honda and other Japanese makers once again are making inroads, albeit slowly, in the Big Three's market share. ■

CURRENT SITUATION

The Modular Revolution

Nearly a century after Ford's assembly line revolutionized auto manufacturing, automakers are launching another revolution in the way cars are made.

"Modular manufacturing" gives suppliers a much larger role in the car-making process. Instead of providing single parts that are added to the car at the assembly plant, suppliers deliver an entire section, or module. On the new Pontiac Bonneville, for example, the seats arrive at the assembly plant with belts and side air bags pre-installed by the supplier.

Many auto experts say that modular manufacturing will reduce automakers' costs because suppliers can do much of the assembly work for less. "When suppliers specialize in something, it's much cheaper for them to develop that part of the car, because of their expertise, than it would be for the auto manufacturer," Schnorbus says. Moreover, he adds, they can also make similar modules for a variety of different cars, cutting costs through the economy of scale.

It's Not Your Father's Oldsmobile

Judging by today's automotive developments, the pioneers of the horseless carriage were rather limited in their vision: After all, they simply saw the automobile as a mode of transportation. Today, thanks to high-tech marvels, the car is much more than a way of getting from Point A to Point B.

"Customers are increasingly using their cars as extensions of their workplace and their home," says David Cole, director of the Office for the Study of Automotive Transportation at the University of Michigan.

Carmakers are expanding the car's appeal by providing a host of new communications devices. The Big Three, Honda and Toyota either offer or plan to offer factory-installed wireless phones. With safety and convenience in mind, many of the new systems will be "hands-free" speakerphones, with voice-activated dialing. [1]

But voice communication is just the tip of the iceberg. Cars will also be equipped to send and receive faxes and even access the Internet. Flat screens will be mounted behind the front seats so that passengers in the back can watch television or use a computer without distracting the driver.

In addition, car companies are already installing navigation systems that use global-positioning satellites to allow a driver to get directions to any location. For instance, Honda is offering a screen-based navigational system on its new Odyssey minivan. The device will also be available on an upcoming luxury SUV from Honda's Acura division.

American Honda Motor Corp., Inc.

The new Honda Odyssey minivan features a satellite navigation system.

GM has developed a more wide-ranging system, called OnStar, and is already installing it on new Cadillac De Ville sedans and Escalade sport utility vehicles. OnStar is a one-stop communications and navigation system, offering drivers cell phone service in addition to navigation help. But OnStar is a platform for other offerings as well. According to Andrew Card, senior vice president for government relations at General Motors, "it also automatically calls a nearby service center if you've been in an accident or have broken down." Drivers can even use OnStar to make travel, restaurant and entertainment reservations.

OnStar is already operating on 100,000 vehicles. GM officials hope to increase that number to 3 million in the next two years. [2] Not to be left out, Ford says that a similar system will be available on its Lincoln line of luxury cars and light trucks later this year.

Carmakers are also developing more innovative safety systems. Air bags are becoming "smarter" — able to respond differently depending on the severity of the accident. "They inflate with a different level of force depending on the weight of the impact," says Brian Wallace, a safety expert with DaimlerChrysler. Smart air bags are already on some of the company's Mercedes Benz models and will be added to additional cars in coming years, he says.

Even an old technology like the seat belt is being improved. "You're going to see new seat belts that give a little in a crash instead of just tightening," Wallace says. The flexibility is intended to prevent cracked ribs in serious collisions.

Indeed, tomorrow's cars may even be able to avoid collisions. Carmakers are ready to begin making collision-avoidance systems standard equipment on some cars. Using sonar, the devices will send audio or even visual warnings when the driver is in danger of hitting another car. Some of these systems may even prevent a driver from falling asleep at the wheel, issuing a warning when driving becomes erratic.

Automakers are even taking a page from the military, using a heat-sensing, infrared detection system to "see" objects in the road at night — like people or dogs. Long before the headlights bring such hazards into view, their image is projected onto the front windshield.

"It's really amazing that many of these innovations will be on millions of cars in just a few years," Card says.

As Cole puts it, "We're moving out of the period of gradualism in the auto industry." Automakers are "at the edge of a revolution." [3]

---

[1] Warren Brown, "Cars Bringing More Information to the Superhighway," *The Washington Post*, Dec. 12, 1999.

[2] Figures cited in "GM Driving into Cyberspace," *The Washington Post*, Jan. 13, 2000.

[3] Quoted in Brown, *op. cit.*

According to a recent University of Michigan study, car companies could cut assembly costs by an average of 14 percent if they abandoned their current manufacturing process in favor of modular manufacturing. [13]

The new process will also allow carmakers to be flexible in the way they use their factories. In particular, plants will be able to switch to making different models much faster since the final assembly process will be much simpler and will require less retooling when changes are introduced.

Although most assembly plants, including those in the United States, use at least some modules, modular manufacturing has yet to become the industry norm. "To some extent, it's done everywhere now," says Dan Moore, a spokesman for DaimlerChrysler, which uses modules for seats, instrument panels and even engines.

And a number of factories in France, Brazil and England have converted completely to modular assembly. At a plant owned by BMW's English subsidiary, Rover, in Longworth, England, production nearly doubled since the introduction of a modular system. And the factory now makes three different models where it previously made one.

Most analysts argue that modular manufacturing will become more common in the near future. "This really is the way things are going," Keller says. "It's not going to happen overnight, but move in that direction gradually."

But some of the most efficient carmakers, especially among the Japanese, are not going modular. "Companies like Toyota and Nissan question why there is migration to modules because they find few suppliers that can meet their production requirements," said Ron Harbour, a manufacturing consultant in Troy, N.Y. [14]

The United Auto Workers (UAW) is also wary of modular manufacturing, arguing that the process is simply a way for automakers to replace their unionized work force with a supplier's non-union workers. "As far as I'm concerned, it's outsourcing . . . just another way to destroy good-paying jobs and benefits," said UAW President Stephen Yokich at a March 28 union convention in Detroit. Indeed, the University of Michigan report on modular manufacturing estimates that 74,000 union jobs would be lost if the Big Three instituted the approach on a broad scale.

Toyota Motor Sales, U.S.A., Inc.

The Toyota Camry (above) is the top-selling passenger car in America, reflecting Japanese automakers' big slice of the U.S. market. The Honda Accord is the No. 2 car.

Labor Peace Treaty

Labor negotiations between the nation's 400,000 unionized autoworkers and the Big Three ended last fall with a four-year deal that seemed to please everyone. According to auto analysts, the talks succeeded largely because both sides wanted to avoid what happened in 1998.

In June of that year, thousands of UAW members at GM went on strike in an effort to prevent the automaker from closing a metal-stamping plant in Flint, Mich. After 54 days, both sides reached an agreement that largely left things as they'd been before the dispute.

But some things had changed, and for the worse. While the UAW action kept the plant open, the strikers lost more than $1 billion in wages and benefits. GM not only lost an estimated $3 billion in after-tax profits but also precious market share that it has yet to fully recover. "It's safe to say it was a disaster for all involved," Keller says.

And so, in 1999, everyone was determined to avoid strikes, even rancor. "We entered the negotiations committed to building a good working relationship with the UAW," says GM's Card. "When we were finished, we felt like we had built that relationship, that it was much closer."

UAW representatives also sounded a positive note. Vice President Richard Shoemaker called the negotiations good for workers and management. "We look forward to building on those agreements to sustain a healthy and constructive relationship," he said.

Although the union negotiated separately with GM, Ford and DaimlerChrysler, the deals struck with all three automakers were virtually identical. For the union, the agreement offered significant gains in pay and other benefits. Workers won a 3 percent pay

At Issue:

Should the government impose limits on the production or sale of large sport utility vehicles?

yes

Joan Claybrook
President, Public Citizen

WRITTEN FOR *THE CQ RESEARCHER*

Government must address the hazards of sport utility vehicles by ensuring they meet key safety and fuel-economy standards. The massive SUVs are dangerously underregulated and threaten pedestrians and motorcyclists, people in passenger cars, the environment and even their own occupants because of their propensity to roll over, their heavy weight and their inefficiency. New rules must be put in place to make SUVs less polluting and safer for occupants and other roadway users.

The automobile manufacturers shrewdly took advantage of the absence of adequate government standards covering the performance of these behemoths. SUVs, originally designed for off-road, all-terrain driving and hauling, are advertised as urban assault vehicles for use like passenger cars — for trips to the grocery store or daily commutes on busy highways. However, they are incompatible with passenger cars in terms of weight and structure.

The Ford Expedition tips the scale at more than 5,000 pounds. Compare this with a Honda Civic (2,600 pounds) or a large passenger sedan (about 3,500 pounds). The heavy, high-riding SUVs create a deadly mismatch on the road with other passenger vehicles. SUVs are far too aggressive in weight and structure (built on a stiff truck chassis) and are unforgiving when they hit another vehicle.

SUVs also provide occupants with a false sense of security. While SUV occupants may presume protection in multivehicle crashes with cars, they are at risk of injury in single-vehicle rollover crashes — in which they are disproportionately involved. The single-vehicle rollover death rate in these vehicles in 1998 was more than five times as high as the rate in the largest cars (110 deaths per million registered vehicles compared with 22).

Single-vehicle rollover crashes accounted for 50 percent of occupant deaths in utility vehicles in 1998 compared with 35 percent of deaths in pickups and 19 percent of deaths in cars.

Fuel-economy standards for SUVs lag far behind the equivalent standards for passenger cars. The SUV standards have barely been changed since the 1980s. Fuel economy for SUVs has stagnated at about 20.5 miles per gallon, while the current standard for passenger cars is 27.5 miles per gallon. If these vehicles were required to achieve greater fuel efficiency, design changes would result in weight compatibility with passenger vehicles and less aggressive structures. And if meeting those standards reduces their advertising sex appeal, it is a small price to pay for ensuring the safety of owners and others who share the road.

no

Gloria Bergquist
Senior vice president, Alliance of Automobile Manufacturers

WRITTEN FOR *THE CQ RESEARCHER*

Some newspaper columnists, radio hosts and other professional provocateurs have enjoyed themselves by suggesting that this popular vehicle be banned or limited. This gambit may lead to stimulating dinner conversation, but it shouldn't lead to government action.

For some people, the popularity of SUVs is reason enough to limit them. In 1998, SUVs represented 18 percent of the vehicles sold. While more pickup trucks were sold than SUVs, the "sport utes" have been singled out for attention.

Whether used for sport or not, sport utility vehicles of all sizes are popular because of their utility. Even if SUV owners never take their vehicles off-road, they enjoy knowing that their vehicle could perform well in a snowstorm. They also enjoy the ample capacity for passengers or cargo. Many drivers simply enjoy the greater visibility of the road.

Across the country, we see millions of Americans using them for their work or family, or both.

In Washington, D.C., SUVs are very popular work vehicles. Because the vehicles provide so much utility, we see the Secret Service using SUVs to escort the president. We see media using SUVs to carry cameras and crew. We see members of Congress campaigning in SUVs.

From a public-policy perspective, there is no reason to impose production limits, quotas or special taxes on SUVs — or minivans or pickups or cars, for that matter.

Sport utility vehicles will meet tough new emissions standards — the same as for cars. In December 1999, the U.S. Environmental Protection Agency adopted new federal emission requirements called "Tier 2," which dramatically reduce tailpipe emissions for cars, minivans, pickups and all SUVs. Under Tier 2, automakers will provide even-cleaner cars and light trucks.

Over the past 20 years, fuel efficiency in all vehicles has been improved substantially. Today's pickup, minivan and SUV get better mileage than a subcompact car did in the 1970s. Manufacturers are now focused on developing advanced engine technologies — such as lean burn, hybrids and fuel cells that could dramatically increase fuel economy in the future, without sacrificing utility, affordability or safety.

Automakers are providing products that meet the needs of families, small businesses, farmers, ranchers, tradesmen and outdoor enthusiasts. The bottom line is consumer choice, and members of Congress should reflect the views of their constituents.

Millions of Americans have chosen SUVs.

The Amazing Fuel Cell

It's hard to believe: A power source that is non- or low polluting, powerful, quiet. And there's more: It doesn't require recharging or expensive fuel.

That, in a nutshell, is why the fuel cell is increasingly being seen as an eventual replacement for the internal combustion engine.

In essence, fuel cells generate electricity by combining the atoms of two of the most common elements: hydrogen and oxygen.

A fuel cell operates like a battery. It has a negative electrode (anode) and a positive electrode (cathode) with electrolyte material placed between them. When hydrogen atoms are fed through the anode they lose their electrons (and their negative charge). These lost electrons are fed into an external circuit where they produce electricity and hence power. Unused hydrogen atoms pass through to the cathode, where they combine with oxygen atoms to produce heat and water.

Fuel cells that use pure hydrogen make no pollution. Only heat and a little water drain out of the car's tailpipe. But hydrogen presents a number of problems. First, it is highly flammable, and thus hard to store and deliver. Second, setting up the infrastructure to fuel cars with hydrogen would cost tens if not hundreds of billions of dollars.

DaimlerChrysler/Randy Santos

DaimlerChrysler Co-chairman Robert Eaton and Jurgen Schrempp unveil the prototype NECAR 4 last March, calling it the first "drivable" hydrogen fuel-cell car in the United States.

But fuel cells can also operate using more traditional fuels, such as methane, ethanol, natural gas and even gasoline. In these cases, the hydrogen is extracted from the fuels before being fed to the fuel cell. This process produces some pollution, but still only a fraction of that released by internal combustion.

Surprisingly, the fuel cell is hardly a new technology. Sir William Grove, an Englishman, invented it in 1839. Grove's cell never was put to practical use, however, because it produced very little power. But 125 years later, it was a full-fledged partner in the Space Age: In 1965, NASA used fuel cells to help power internal systems on its Gemini spacecraft.

increase, plus cost-of-living allowances for each year of the contract. They also took home $1,350 bonuses and improved pension benefits.

"It's an expensive contract, but given the fact that the companies are making record sales and earnings and have a strong cash flow, it is hard for them to plead poverty," said David Healy, an auto analyst at Burnham Securities.[15]

Still, the pay increases will be costly for the Big Three. The average worker will earn an additional $30,000 over the contract's four years, which translates into a 4-5 percent rise in labor costs.[16] Plants owned by Japanese and other foreign automakers are not unionized and hence were not part of the negotiations.

But, many analysts note, the deal also offers opportunities for significant personnel cuts through attrition, replacing retiring workers on a one-for-two or even one-for-three basis in certain cases. "This gives them the flexibility they need to improve the efficiency of their operations by allowing them to shed workers," Schnorbus says. According to Saul Rubin, an analyst at Warburg, Dillon, Read, the pact should allow GM to make productivity gains of about 7-8 percent a year.[17]

Indeed, some see the deal largely as a victory for the Big Three because it allows them to drastically reduce their work forces. "This contract was basically a payoff or a bribe," says Bank One's Swonk. "The UAW got some nice face-saving pay and pension gains in exchange for letting the Big Three improve productivity." ■

OUTLOOK

Car of the Future?

DaimlerChrysler took a big step into the future last March 17, unveiling what it called the first "drivable" hydrogen fuel-cell car in the United States. "Today, the race to develop the fuel-cell car is over," said company Chairman Jurgen Schrempp. "Now we begin the race to lower the cost to the level of today's internal combustion engine." [18]

The prototype unveiled by Schrempp was a far cry from earlier experimental models — vans with most of their passenger space crammed full of fuel cells. The new model, the NECAR 4, is based on a Mercedes Benz A-class sedan. It seats five, cruises at up to 90 mph and travels 280 miles without refueling.

Like other carmakers, DaimlerChrysler has long been looking for low- or non-polluting alternatives to the traditional internal combustion engine. The industrywide search is driven by the realization among manufacturers that governments, especially in the industrialized world, are increasingly worried about the environmental impact of auto emissions. Indeed, California has passed a law requiring that zero-emission vehicles make up at least 10 percent of a carmaker's in-state sales by 2004. [19]

Attempts to find alternatives to traditional engines are already in the showrooms and on the road. GM, Ford, Honda and Toyota all sell battery-powered vehicles. And taxis and buses operating on natural gas ply streets in New York, Chicago and other cities around the country.

But most industry-watchers see these early attempts at cleaner cars as temporary or transitional solutions. Natural-gas vehicles are currently unrealistic for all but taxis or buses because there are almost no public refueling stations. "Resolving infrastructure issues is more important than building the car," said Ralf Frochtenicht, project manager for research and development at BMW. [20]

Automobiles running on electric batteries also have huge problems that make them unappealing to most consumers. Even the most advanced models can only travel about 140 miles before recharging, a process that takes hours. And that limitation is far from being overcome. [21] "There hasn't been the long-awaited breakthrough in batteries that was hoped for," says Ann Smith, advanced technologies communications manager at DaimlerChrysler.

Ford Motor Co.

The Ford Excursion (above) now competes with the Chevrolet Suburban, a large SUV that has been a big seller for GM.

As a result, batteries have gone from being a much-ballyhooed replacement for internal combustion engines to a disappointment. "Battery technology is clearly on the back burner for now," Smith says. Keller agrees. "You get the sense whenever they talk about electric cars these days that they're not really interested anymore," she says.

The "Hybrid" Alternative

But battery-driven cars have not been written off entirely. So-called hybrids use a small internal combustion engine to recharge the battery while the car is moving. Hybrids get more than 70 miles per gallon and produce very low emissions. "Right now, hybrids have the most support in the industry because there's little new invention involved," says the University of Michigan's Cole.

In fact, Honda and Toyota are already selling small hybrids in Japan and are planning to offer them in the United States later this year at around $20,000. [22]

Still, no one is predicting big hybrid sales any time soon, since low gasoline prices allow consumers to splurge on less than economical models. "Fuel is still cheaper than bottled water, so there's little incentive to buy [a hybrid or other alternative] car," Cole argues.

Another problem with hybrids is maintenance. "Hybrids are expensive to keep up because you have two power systems in the car, which means twice as much can go wrong," he says.

In addition, carmakers ultimately see hybrids and other alternative vehicles as transitional cars that they can offer until fuel-cell technology becomes good enough and cheap enough to be viable. "Hybrids are a near-term solution," says DaimlerChrysler's Smith. "While there may be some time when we're selling both [hybrids and fuel-cell cars], they will be phased out."

Smith and others say that fuel cells offer the best long-term hope for an environmentally friendly car. Fuel cells are much cleaner burning than traditional internal combustion engines, and some are completely non-polluting, emitting only heat and water. In addition, proponents say, cars powered by fuel cells will have good acceleration and long cruising ranges.

As a result, carmakers have thrown billions of dollars into fuel-cell research. "They've become the mainstream choice, and that's generated a real competition to get there first," Keller says. But even the biggest car companies are hedging their bets. GM and Toyota have joined forces to work on fuel-cell research. And Ford and DaimlerChrysler both have invested in a Canadian fuel-cell manufacturer, the Ballard Corp.

Still, while carmakers are confident about the future of fuel cells, many obstacles remain. Cells don't operate well in cold weather because they rely on water, which freezes and shuts down the whole system. Fuel cells are also very expensive, in large part because they contain platinum. They now cost roughly 10 times as much as conventional engines, or about $30,000.

But, Smith and others say, these obstacles will be overcome, and sooner rather than later. Scientists are working to reduce the platinum and other costly materials used in fuel cells. And costs are also expected to drop once cells are manufactured in large numbers.

DaimlerChrysler and other carmakers are so optimistic about overcoming the problems that they expect to have fuel-cell vehicles on the market by 2004 — just four years from now. "There are a lot of challenges with this technology, but we're progressing much faster than we ever thought we would," Smith says. ■

FOR MORE INFORMATION

Alliance of Automobile Manufacturers, 1401 H St., N.W., Suite 900, Washington, D.C. 20005; (202) 326-5500; www.autoalliance.org. The alliance represents the interests of major automakers in the United States.

Japan Automobile Manufacturers Association, 1050 17th St., N.W., Suite 410, Washington, D.C. 20036; (202) 296-8537; www.japanauto.com. The association works on behalf of Japanese automakers in the United States.

Office for the Study of Automotive Transportation, University of Michigan, Transportation Research Institute, 2901 Baxter Rd., Ann Arbor, Mich. 48109-2150; (734) 764-5592; www.osat.umich.edu. The office provides research and analysis, information resources and communication forums for international automotive and automotive-related industries.

United Auto Workers, 1757 N St., N.W., Washington, D.C. 20036; (202) 828-8500; www.uaw.org. The union represents more than 400,000 autoworkers in North America.

Notes

[1] Quoted in Joseph B. White and Gregory L. White, "GM's Pearce Pans Market-Share Efforts," *The Wall Street Journal*, Dec. 9, 1999.
[2] Quoted in Keith Naughton, "The Global Six," *Business Week*, Jan. 25, 1999.
[3] Quoted in *Ibid*.
[4] Robyn Meredith, "In Policy Shift, G.M. Will Rely On Alliances," *The New York Times*, Jan. 18, 2000, p. C1.
[5] Fara Warner and Joseph B. White, "U.S. Auto Sales Surge as Japan and Europe Gain Market Share," *The Wall Street Journal*, Dec. 2, 1999.
[6] Figures cited in Paul Johnson, *A History of the American People* (1998), p. 723.
[7] Figures cited in *Ibid*, p. 731.
[8] Quoted in *Ibid*.
[9] Mary H. Cooper, "U.S. Auto Industry," *The CQ Researcher*, Oct. 16, 1992, pp. 881-904.
[10] Figures cited in *Ibid*.
[11] Figures cited in *Ibid*.
[12] Wards Automotive.
[13] David Welch, "Modular Car Assembly Would Cut Jobs," *The Detroit News*, Aug. 3, 1999.
[14] Quoted in *Ibid*.
[15] Quoted in Robyn Meredith, "G.M. Agrees to 4-Year Pact with Union," *The New York Times*, Sept. 29, 1999.
[16] Figures cited in Nikki Tait, "Carmakers Strike Pay Agreement," *The Financial Times*, Dec. 3, 1999.
[17] *Ibid*.
[18] Quoted in: "The Fuel Cell Car Accelerates," *The Economist*, March 20, 1999.
[19] For background, see Mary H. Cooper, "Renewable Energy," *The CQ Researcher*, Nov. 7, 1997, pp. 961-984 and David Hosansky, "Traffic Congestion," *The CQ Researcher*, Aug. 27, 1999, pp. 729-752.
[20] Quoted in Sue Zesiger, "Reinventing the Wheel," *Fortune*, Oct. 25, 1999.
[21] See Mary H. Cooper, "Electric Cars," *The CQ Researcher*, July 9, 1993, pp. 577-600.
[22] Warren Brown, "Cars Bringing More Information to the Superhighway," *The Washington Post*, Dec. 12, 1999.

Bibliography

Selected Sources Used

Books

Maynard, Micheline, *Collision Course: Inside the Battle for General Motors*, Birch Lane Press, 1995.
Maynard chronicles GM's efforts during the late 1980s and early '90s to restore itself to profitability by laying off workers and closing factories.

Articles

Adams, David, "Suppliers Play Key Role in Carmakers' Use of Modular Manufacturing," *Akron Beacon Journal*, Jan. 10, 1999.
Adams examines the increasing use of modular manufacturing and determines that "carmakers are becoming car assemblers, just snapping together major parts and slapping their names on the back."

Ahrens, Frank, "Suburban Warriors," *The Washington Post Magazine*, Nov. 7, 1999.
Ahrens tries to figure out the reasons behind America's love affair with the sport utility vehicle (SUV).

Brown, Warren, "Cars Bringing More Information to the Superhighway," *The Washington Post*, Dec. 12, 1999.
Brown details various new technical developments within the auto industry that are either here now or coming soon. He says that cars in coming years will be safer and more environmentally friendly.

Cooper, Mary, "U.S. Auto Industry," *The CQ Researcher*, Oct. 16, 1992.
Cooper's survey of the auto industry tracks Japan's successful entry into the U.S. automobile market.

Meredith, Robyn, "Can G.M. Return to the Passing Lane?" *The New York Times*, Nov. 7, 1999.
The article catalogs the problems with G.M.'s products — from lackluster styling to low reliability.

Meredith, Robyn, "In Policy Shift, GM Will Rely on Alliances," *The New York Times*, Jan. 18, 1999.
Meredith describes the No. 1 automaker's decision to rely more on alliances and partnerships with other car companies in the future.

Muller, Joann, "The Auto Talks: Who Really Won," *Business Week*, Oct. 25, 1999.
Muller gives a good post-mortem of the latest round of negotiations between the Big Three and the United Auto Workers. She argues that even though the generosity of the deal might lead one to believe that it was a victory for the union, the car companies also came away with crucial productivity gains.

Naughton, Keith, "The Global Six," *Business Week*, Jan. 25, 1999.
The article gives a good overview of the trend toward greater consolidation within the auto industry, arguing that the need for companies to realize greater economies of scale will push them to acquire or merge with other firms.

"The Quiet Man," *The Economist*, May 8, 1999.
A profile of General Motors' current chairman, John F. "Jack" Smith Jr., reveals a man who is trying to change the company gradually instead of overhauling it completely.

Thornton, Emily, and Kathleen Kerwin, "Can Honda Go It Alone?" *Business Week*, July 5, 1999.
The piece examines the arguments for and against Honda remaining an independent car company.

Welch, David, "Japan's Automakers Hang Tough," *The Seattle Times*, Nov. 28, 1999.
Welch says that far from being in "full retreat," Japan's car companies remain fierce competitors. He argues that the Big Three may lose market share to Toyota, Honda and others as the Japanese bring new products and production facilities on line.

Zesiger, Sue, "Reinventing the Wheel: The Cars of Tomorrow — Hybrids, Natural Gas-Powered Sports Cars, and Fuel Cells — Are Here Today," *Fortune*, Oct. 25, 1999.
Zesiger details the pros and cons of each new alternative-fuel technology currently being considered by the auto industry. She concludes that automakers see fuel cells as the system that will ultimately replace internal combustion.

14 The Economics of Recycling

MARY H. COOPER

Reduce, reuse, recycle. Since the first Earth Day in 1970, the mantra of the environmental movement has prescribed a simple remedy for the country's growing mountain of waste: If Americans would simply reduce the volume of stuff they buy, reuse what they have and recycle the rest, the depletion of natural resources would be slowed and there would be fewer potentially toxic garbage dumps.

Nearly three decades into the war on waste, however, most Americans have proved reluctant soldiers. There is little evidence that we are reducing our consumption of goods. The U.S. economy is in its eighth year of uninterrupted growth, driven largely by domestic consumption. If Americans were heeding the call to reuse what they have, environmentalists argue, they wouldn't be buying so many new products or tossing so much out. Although the sheer volume of trash is growing more slowly today than it did in the past, the United States remains the world's leading throwaway society. [1]

"Our per-capita waste is just so out of whack," says Michele Raymond, whose firm, Raymond Communications Inc., tracks state recycling efforts. "We're just 20 percent of the people in the world, but we consume 80 percent of the world's resources. Our per-capita waste is the highest in the world and about twice the level of Germany and the United Kingdom. We're just trashing more than anyone else."

The only part of the anti-waste message that has taken hold to any noticeable degree is the call to recycle. Since 1988, when the Environmental Protection Agency (EPA) first set a recycling goal for the United States at 25 percent of total waste, communities across the country have introduced more than 8,000 curbside recycling programs and more than 3,000 composting facilities, all aimed at reducing the amount of household trash that ends up in landfills and incinerators. Colorful recycling bins are now a familiar sight on neighborhood streets.

PhotoDisc

From *The CQ Researcher*, March 27, 1998.

"When I announced the 25 percent goal, only about 12 percent of the nation's garbage was recycled," says former EPA Assistant Administrator J. Winston Porter, now president of the Waste Policy Center, a research and consulting firm in Leesburg, Va. "The recycling rate grew pretty rapidly, and our goal was reached in 1995." The nation's overall recycling rate today is 27 percent of the total municipal solid waste stream. Sixteen percent is burned, while the remaining 57 percent ends up in landfills. [2]

Communities have been recycling trash for decades. Most early programs used drop-off points where people could leave their used newspapers, glass bottles and metal cans for a recycler to pick up every week or so. More than 9,000 drop-off centers are still in operation. But lackluster participation in drop-off programs prompted many communities to begin adopting curbside programs in the late 1980s as a way to boost recycling rates. For several years, the supply of recyclable materials was adequate for the infant recycling industry. Indeed, newspaper publishers created such a demand for old newsprint that "garbage rustlers" prowled neighborhood streets to collect junked papers from curbside bins.

But markets for recycled materials, much like those for pork bellies, corn and other commodities, are notoriously volatile. Prices often gyrate when unusual weather, technological advances or other events cause sudden gluts or scarcities of a given commodity. When an oversupply of paper caused the booming market for recycled paper to collapse in the mid-1990s, a number of paper-processing facilities went under, and some recycling operators simply delivered the papers to the local landfill. Since then, recycling has come under closer scrutiny.

Critics blamed the collapse on state and local government goals and mandates for recycling. "Recycling may be the most wasteful activity in modern America: a waste of time and money, a waste of human and natural resources," wrote journalist John Tierney in a scathing criticism of recycling that appeared in *The New York Time Magazine* two years ago. [3] He and other skeptics charge that recycling programs fail to appreciably help the environment while imposing an unwarranted government intrusion into people's lives and disrupting the economy.

Tierney's criticism prompted a flurry of angry responses from readers and experts alike. "If we are serious about lowering the costs of recy-

Recycling Efforts Span Wide Range

More than half the states recycled at least 20 percent of their municipal solid waste in 1995. Thirteen states require recycling, and 16 states have set recycling goals of at least 50 percent by the year 2000.

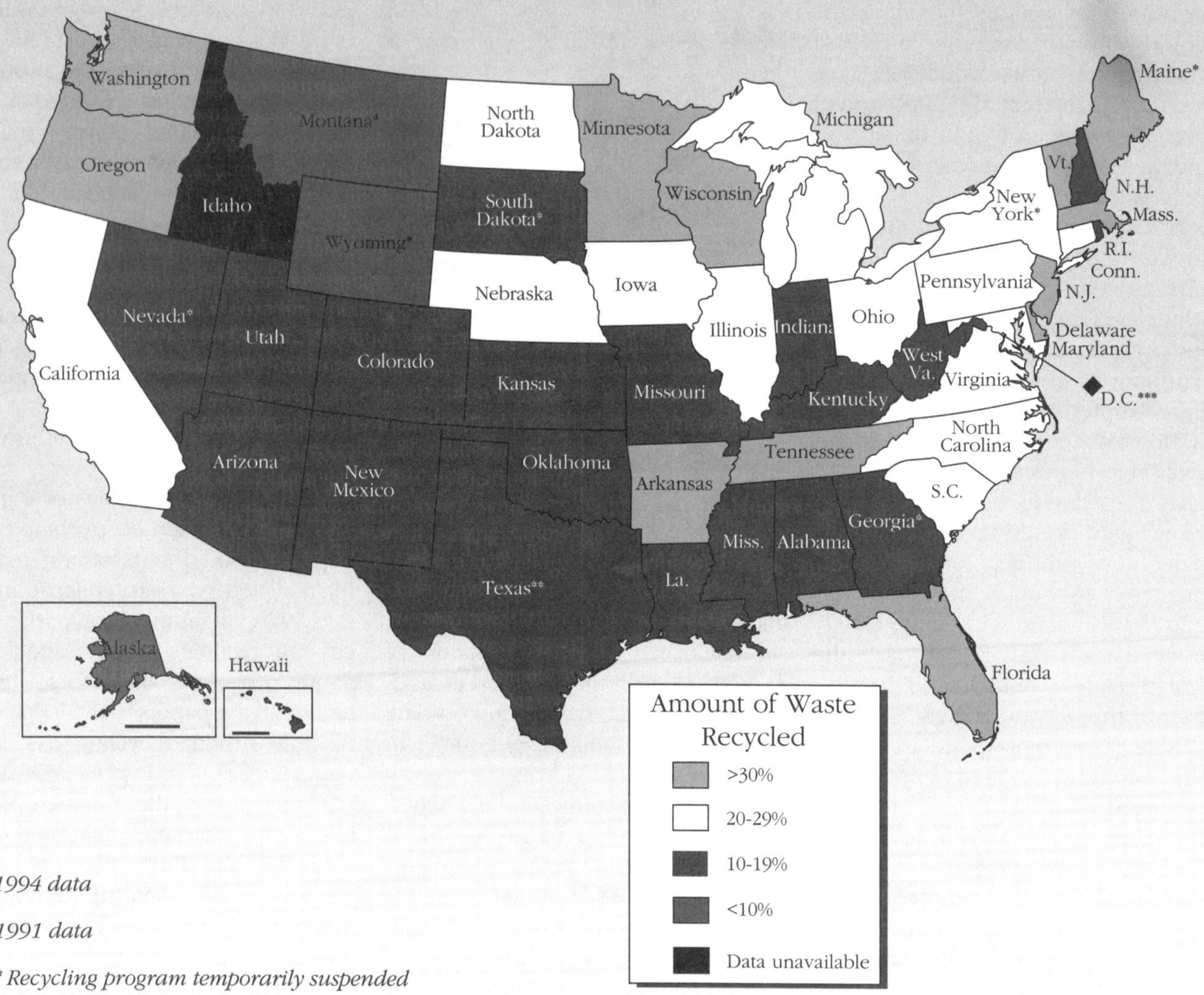

** 1994 data*

***1991 data*

**** Recycling program temporarily suspended*

Sources: ©Raymond Communications, 1997, State Recycling Laws Update, 1997 Year-End Edition; *Natural Resources Defense Council*

cling, the best approach is to study carefully how different communities improve efficiency and increase participation rates — not to engage in debating-club arguments with little relevance to the real-world problems these communities face," write Richard Denison and John Ruston of the Environmental Defense Fund (EDF). "By boosting the efficiency of municipal recycling, establishing clear price incentives where we can and capitalizing on the full range of environmental and industrial benefits of recycling, we can bring recycling much closer to its full potential." [4]

Polls indicate that public opinion favors the environmentalists when it comes to recycling. Sixty-three percent of respondents to a recent survey reported that they were "personally doing more now" to help the environment, mainly by recycling. [5]

Skeptics dismiss such statistics, however. "I don't buy them for a second," says Jerry Taylor, director of natural resource studies at the Cato

Institute, a Washington think tank that promotes free-market policies. "If you ask people if they recycle, you're basically asking them if they care about the Earth, or if they like animals. They're going to say 'sure' because they don't want to sound like cretins." Whatever the reason, however, the polls suggest a high degree of public interest in recycling.

Many experts in solid waste management say the debate over recycling has been cast in overly simplistic terms that fail to accommodate the complexities of the markets for different recyclable materials. Whether it makes economic or even environmental sense to recycle, they say, depends on the material in question. "Recycling is like a vacuum cleaner that sucks up dispersed materials and reuses them," says Lynn Scarlett, vice president for research at the Reason Foundation, a nonprofit think tank in Los Angeles, Calif. "Where the material is of uniform quality, collected in large quantities and easy to isolate from contaminants, there are net benefits to recycling."

Steel scrap is one such recycling success story. Used cars, appliances and other goods that end up in junkyards are broken apart to allow giant magnets to separate the steel from plastics and other contaminants; then crushers collapse and bale the metal. Electric arc mini-mills melt the metal down to produce high-quality recycled steel, at less cost than "virgin" steel and ready to be made into new products. Steel has been recycled profitably for years, without the benefit of government support, and now accounts for about half of all steel consumed, Scarlett says.

The economic picture for materials collected in curbside programs is mixed. "Tin" cans, which actually are largely steel, are profitably recycled like steel scrap. Recycled aluminum beverage cans also are a hot commodity because they can be processed into new cans at less cost — and with less pollution — than mining and processing bauxite into virgin sheet aluminum. And despite the market's volatility, there usually is strong demand for old newspapers and cardboard boxes.

But the case for recycled plastics is more complex. There are six major types of plastic resins found in consumer products, only two of which are relatively easy to recycle. Containers made with these resins often have to be manually separated out of the recycling bin and carefully washed to remove contaminants before they can be reprocessed, an expensive process that is not always cost-effective.

"If you ask people if they recycle, you're basically asking them if they care about the Earth, or if they like animals. They're going to say 'sure' because they don't want to sound like cretins."

—Jerry Taylor
Director, natural resource studies,
Cato Institute

"Environmentalists are right to say there are many opportunities for recycling," Scarlett says. "But for some products, it makes little sense to have any recycled content. Like any manufacturing process, recycling is a way of making products, an alternative to using virgin feed stocks. The question is whether you can do it and get the product you want at a cost you want. In many cases the answer is yes, in others no. Each product has its own story to tell."

Nonetheless, a growing number of Americans have incorporated recycling into their daily lives and expect curbside service as a basic amenity, like electricity and other utilities. Supporters predict that recycling will keep expanding if Americans are made more aware of the benefits of waste reduction. To that end, more than 1,000 communities participated in the first America Recycles Day last Nov. 15. Sponsored by the EPA and environmental organizations, the event was designed to encourage recycling and the use of products containing recycled materials.

"For many people across the United States, recycling is a matter of habit, something they do in the course of their daily lives, both in the office and at home," says Richard Keller, chief of recycling at the Maryland Environmental Service, a state agency that sorts and markets recycled materials. "But recycling is at a fairly critical crossroads right now. We're already recycling the materials that are easy to recycle. The next step is going to depend on whether we start dealing with materials that are hard to recycle." These include more grades of plastics, as well as organic materials such as food wastes, paper food wrapping, diapers and tissues, which could go to special composting facilities.

The success of recycling programs varies widely according to local conditions. In some highly populated regions of the Northeast and the West,

Our Throwaway Society

- *Every week more than 500,000 trees are used to produce the two-thirds of newspapers that are never recycled.*

- *Americans throw away enough office and writing paper annually to build a wall 12 feet high from Los Angeles to New York City.*

- *Every year Americans dispose of 24 million tons of leaves and grass clippings, which could be composted to conserve landfill space.*

- *Americans throw away enough glass bottles and jars to fill the 1,350-foot twin towers of New York's World Trade Center every two weeks.*

- *American consumers and industry throw away enough aluminum to rebuild our entire commercial air fleet every three months.*

- *Americans throw away enough iron and steel to continuously supply all the nation's automakers.*

- *Americans use up 2.5 million plastic bottles every hour, only a small percentage of which are now recycled.*

Source: Environmental Defense Fund

high fees for landfill dumping make recycling especially attractive. In rural areas of the Rocky Mountain West, the high cost of collecting materials and the low cost of land for dumping waste have hindered recycling efforts. Ultimately, it is up to consumers and their elected officials in state and local governments to decide how best to dispose of their trash. These are some of the issues that shape their decisions:

Do the environmental benefits of recycling outweigh the costs?

Some markets for recyclable materials are strong enough to pay for their collection and conversion into new products. Recycled steel from cars and appliances is one of the most profitable post-consumer materials. Recovery of steel and aluminum cans also tends to more than pay for itself.

But demand for other products is less predictable. Plastics are hard to recycle economically because there are so many types of materials, and most are costly to clean and return to a usable form for new consumer products. Paper is less difficult to recycle, but the market for recycled paper has fluctuated wildly in recent years. After peaking in 1995, prices of recycled newsprint sank so low that some recycling contractors simply dumped the paper they collected in landfills.

On average, curbside recycling programs tend to cost slightly more than they earn from the sale of collected materials. According to Franklin Associates Inc., a Prairie Village, Kan., research firm that conducts solid waste studies for the EPA, residential recycling programs cost on average $2 a month per household. "The cost varies widely from community to community," says Bill Franklin, the firm's chairman. "But recycling costs are a very small percentage of the total cost of solid waste removal, which averages $10 a month per household." Commercial recycling, which generally is contracted out by businesses to private haulers, probably makes more money than it costs. "We don't have good numbers on commercial recycling," Franklin says. "But it must be cost-effective, or they wouldn't bother to do it."

Environmentalists say the quantifiable financial costs of collecting, sorting and processing recyclable materials are far outweighed by an array of benefits to the environment. Nobody disputes the fact that recycling reduces the amount of trash that ends up in landfills or incinerators. Of the 208 million tons of municipal solid waste generated in the U.S. in 1995, 27 percent, or more than 56 million tons, was recycled. Fifty-seven percent ended up in landfills, and the remaining 16 percent was burned.[6]

But some critics dispute the importance of saving landfill space. "It's not in the least bit true that we're running out of places to put our garbage," Taylor says. He cites a Cato Institute estimate that all the trash generated in the United States over the next 1,000 years would fit into a single, 30-square-mile landfill 1,000 feet deep. "Of course, nobody is going to build that big a landfill," Taylor says. "But this shows the idea that we're running out of places to put garbage is just silly. Anyway, most landfills, when they're retired, are sodded over and turned into golf courses or other public facilities."

Many experts say recycling does far more to help protect the environment than merely preserve land that would otherwise be needed for waste disposal. "The more important goals of recycling are to reduce environmental damage from activities such as strip mining and clear-cutting and to conserve energy, reduce pollution and minimize solid waste in manufacturing new products," write Denison and Ruston of the EDF. "[R]ecycling is an environmentally beneficial alternative to the extraction and manufacture of virgin materials, not just an alternative to landfills."[7]

But some experts say the environmental benefits of recycling depend on the material in question. "Each material has its own tale to tell," Scarlett says. "It takes about 95 percent less energy to make a new can out of recycled aluminum than to make can sheeting by mining bauxite and smelting the ore. But the energy savings offered by recycled glass are very modest because it takes only slightly less heat to process cullet [recycled glass] than to make glass from silica. And if you have to transport the glass hundreds of miles to a reprocessing facility, those gains may be undone because glass is very heavy and consumes a lot of energy to transport."

©PhotoDisc

Lackluster participation in drop-off programs prompted many communities to adopt curbside collection programs to boost recycling rates.

Even aluminum recycling can harm the environment under some circumstances. "If you have to drive trucks far out into the countryside to pick up the cans, the air pollution generated by the trucks will outweigh the pollution saved by recycling," Porter says. "If you try to get the last squeal of the pig, you end up doing more environmental damage than good. While the environmental benefits of recycling outweigh the costs for most things, people who treat recycling as a religion haven't considered the whole picture."[8]

Some critics go further, saying the environmental benefits of recycling have been grossly exaggerated. "You'd be hard-pressed to find real environmental benefits in recycling under any circumstances," Taylor says. "If you're recycling glass, what commodity are you saving, sand? We're not running out of sand. We're also not running out of energy — energy prices are the lowest ever, adjusted for inflation. And while, as a general matter, you can argue that energy consumption is a precursor of industrial pollution, if we suddenly started recycling everything instead of using virgin materials, the reduction in energy use wouldn't be all that dramatic."

Do government recycling mandates impede the creation of efficient markets for recyclables?

Most curbside recycling programs now in effect were introduced in the wake of the "landfill crisis" of the late 1980s, when several cities in the Northeast appeared to be running out of space to bury their garbage. Although the perceived crisis never materialized, governments at all levels called for increased recycling. In 1988, when the nationwide recycling rate stood at about 12 percent, then-EPA Assistant Administrator Porter called for Americans to boost that rate to 25 percent by 1993. States followed suit by setting goals of their own, prompting local governments to create or expand curbside residential recycling programs.

Garbage Loaded With Paper, Lawn Trimmings

Cardboard boxes, newspapers and yard trimmings comprised nearly two-thirds of the nation's municipal solid waste recovered in 1995. Some recycled materials, such as batteries and aluminum cans, had high recovery rates but contributed only a small percentage of the total materials recovered.

Recovery of Products in Municipal Solid Waste, 1995

Product	Tons Recycled (in thousands)	Percent of Product Recycled	Percent of All Solid Waste Recovered
Corrugated boxes	*18,480*	*64%*	*33%*
Yard trimmings	*9,000*	*30*	*16*
Newspapers	*6,960*	*53*	*12*
Glass bottles and jars	*3,140*	*27*	*6*
High-grade office papers	*3,010*	*44*	*5*
Major appliances	*2,070*	*61*	*4*
Lead-acid batteries	*1,830*	*96*	*3*
Steel packaging	*1,550*	*54*	*3*
Aluminum beverage cans	*990*	*63*	*2*
Magazines	*670*	*28*	*1*
PET soft drink bottles	*300*	*46*	*1*
HDPE milk and water bottles	*190*	*30*	*<1*
All other products	*8,000*	*8*	*14*
Total recovery	**56,190**	**27%**	**100%**

Source: Environmental Protection Agency, "Characterization of Municipal Solid Waste in the United States," 1996 Update

The majority of recycling mandates are merely goals, with no enforcement provisions. "Most recycling in this country is voluntary," Raymond says. "Some states have mandatory curbside separation, and some have mandatory goals, but most of it is voluntary."

Some jurisdictions, however, including California and New York City, impose fines for non-compliance with recycling mandates. In addition to recycling goals, some governments require agencies to buy a specified percentage of recycled goods, such as office paper, plastic traffic cones or paving materials made of old tires. At the federal level, for example, President Clinton issued an executive order in 1993 requiring all federal agencies to buy printing and writing paper with at least 30 percent recycled content by the end of 1998.

There is little doubt that government mandates have spurred growth in recycling programs. About 40 states have set recycling goals, ranging from 15-70 percent of the waste stream, according to Keller. "Most programs call for 25-50 percent recycling over varying periods of time," he says. "I think that without those mandates, especially on the residential side, you'd see far lower rates of recycling than what you're seeing now."

But critics say mandates distort the markets for recycled materials, possibly impeding their development over time. "Post-consumer material is a resource just like water, energy or any other resource, and a certain amount of it is going to be reused because it makes economic sense to reuse it," Taylor says. "But there's a lot of it that it doesn't make economic sense to reuse, and that's where government mandates come in. It cannot make economic sense to mandate the use of a material that nobody would otherwise use. You can build a nice Potemkin village marketplace out of that, but it doesn't mean you're really helping the economy, because the money used to pay for recycling programs is money that would otherwise have gone to more productive uses."

Many critics blame recycling mandates for the collapse in recycled paper prices in 1995. By suddenly increasing the supply of recycled paper in the early 1990s, this argument goes, governments flooded the market with more material than reprocessors could absorb. But Keller, who finds buyers for his agency's recycled materials, says mandates do not significantly distort the market, at least over the longer term. "In Maryland, which has set recycling goals of 20 percent for large subdivisions and 15 percent for small ones, the marketplace is very resilient," he says. "There may have been some marketplace dislocations when the programs came on line, but as a matter of fact there are some industries that we're working with that are scrambling to find materials. You have to recognize that the markets fluctuate."

Most curbside programs collect recyclables from individual houses, making them most common in urban and suburban neighborhoods as well as residential areas in smaller communities. Typically, apartment houses and commercial businesses are not included in public recycling programs. Some experts charge that by focusing on households, which generate relatively small quantities of trash, governments targeted the least suitable population for efficient recycling programs. "If they had actually studied where the trash was coming from, they would have put the mandates on industrial plants first, then commercial businesses and then multifamily housing units," Raymond says. "Curbside recycling would have come last in order of priority."

Like many other experts, Raymond says mandates have a positive role to play in helping markets for recyclables get started. But in her view, the focus on curbside collection has actually stymied that effort. "Had they phased curbside collection in last, these markets might have stabilized, and they would know what makes sense to pick up and what doesn't," Raymond says. "With commercial re-

Ups and Downs of Newspaper Recycling

The amount of newspaper recovered for recycling or composting rose steadily from 1980 to 1995, but prices have fluctuated dramatically.

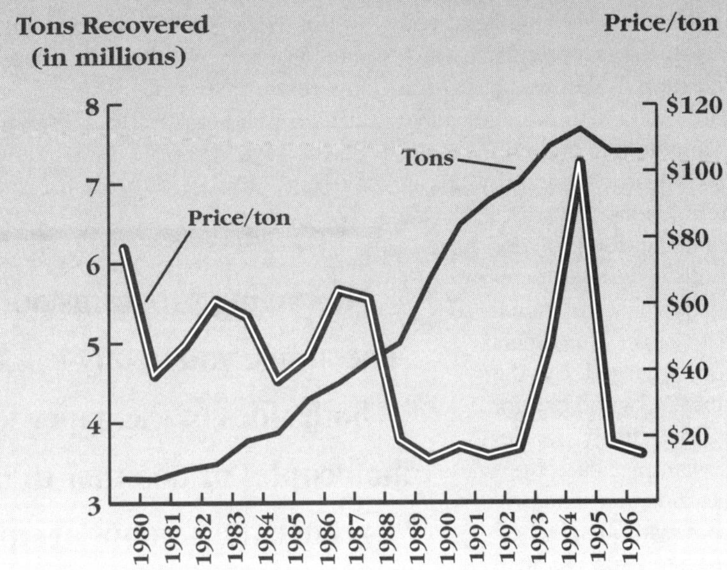

** Prices are adjusted for inflation*
Source: R.W. Beck

cycling, if the market goes bad for paper they simply stop recycling. But you can't do that with curbside recycling because it takes so long to educate people about what stuff to put in their bins. You can't just drop the glass and continue collecting the plastics, even though that probably would be better for the environment in the long run. With residential recycling, once you turn on that spigot you can't turn it off again."

Is a "pay-as-you-throw" system a more rational approach to waste management than other programs?

Experts agree that it is virtually impossible to educate consumers to periodically adjust the list of materials they leave for curbside pickup in response to fluctuations in the markets for recyclables. But program operators have found other ways to make recycling more cost-effective. Costs can be trimmed by shifting pickup schedules from weekly to every other week, investing in automated trucks to reduce labor costs or simply redesigning collection routes to use fewer trucks or reduce the time needed to complete collection.

But the most promising cost-saving measure may be variable-rate waste management. Also known as pay-as-you-throw, this approach replaces the flat fee typically charged households for waste removal, including recyclables, yard trimmings and other trash, with fees that vary according to the amount of trash destined for the landfill or incinerator. "Pay-as-you-throw is an excellent program that bears consideration in most communities," says Lisa A. Skumatz, president of Skumatz Economic Research Associates in Seattle, who found the system raised recycling rates by up to 10 percent in more than 500 communities she studied. [9] "It can be extremely cost-effective, the biggest-bang item you can get to improve recycling and yard-waste diversion." She estimates that more than 5,000 communities have adopted variable-rate programs to date.

Pay-as-you-throw works by charging households for the waste they generate, and so provides an economic incentive to recycle or compost as much trash as possible. Customers usually are charged by the garbage can or by the bag for non-recyclable trash. In Seattle, for example, customers pay by the container. The program is not without glitches: Customers often jam as much as they can into one container — a practice so common it's known as the "Seattle stomp." "Some guy actually hurt his back jamming stuff into his trash barrel and sued the city," Franklin says. "But in general, the pay-as-you-throw system does seem to work. If we know there's a penalty for the second barrel of trash, the economic incentive helps us manage waste better."

Some communities have made the system more accurate by using special trucks equipped with scales to weigh the trash they collect. "The variable-rates approach works for the customer because it says you can do what you want," Skumatz says, "but you'll save real dollars if you recycle."

By placing greater responsibility on the customer, variable rates not only encourage people to recycle but also to reduce their consumption. "Recycling programs, whether they're mandatory or not, in no way encourage source reduction in the first place," Skumatz says. "They don't encourage you to buy less, use both sides of the paper for photocopies or do other things to reduce the amount of stuff consumed. Variable rates does that — it adds something that even mandatory recycling can't accomplish."

But there is a downside to variable rate-systems. "While unit-based pricing rewards people who are more efficient, it's not a total panacea," Porter says. "People will haul their garbage to the Dumpster in the McDonald's parking lot on their way to work, or they'll sort their mail in the post office and throw away the junk mail before going home. So there's a lot of trash shifting going on."

"Recycling programs don't encourage you to buy less, use both sides of the paper for photocopies or do other things to reduce the amount of stuff consumed. Variable rates does that — it adds something that even mandatory recycling can't accomplish."

— Lisa A. Skumatz, president, Skumatz Economic Research Associates

Porter also questions the ability of most people to drastically reduce the amount of stuff they consume. "What exactly are you supposed to do, stop buying milk or feeding the dog?" he asks. "You may get a 10 percent reduction in consumption with pay-as-you-throw, but not much more. People can't change their habits that much."

Variable-rate programs also have limited impact beyond the supply side of the market for recyclables. "Pay-as-you-throw is the best idea we have now because it provides the correct signal to the consumer for wasting less," Raymond says. "The problem is, it doesn't solve the problems we have with recycling right now because it doesn't create markets. It just changes consumers' habits and improves their cooperation in putting all of their recyclables out. Now what are you going to do with them? You've got to have markets for them. Industry has to use recycled materials for the markets to operate properly."

Other critics object to pay-as-you-throw for the same reasons they object to all recycling programs. "I'm suspicious whenever governments at any level think they know exactly the right way to do things," Taylor says. "Some people will be annoyed at having to pay for each bag they throw out and would far rather pay a flat fee for trash removal. I don't think government should be involved in recycling at all. Each household should be allowed to make its own decisions about who's going to collect their garbage and under what terms." ■

BACKGROUND

Birth of a Movement

Throughout history, recycling has been the rule rather than the ex-

Chronology

1940s ***The first widespread residential recycling efforts emerge during World War II as consumers contribute scrap metals and paper to wartime industries.***

———•———

1960s ***Concern builds over the nation's mounting waste stream.***

1962
Author Rachel Carson warns of the dangers of toxic chemicals left in landfills in her best-seller *Silent Spring*.

1965
The Solid Waste Disposal Act launches federal research into the technology of waste disposal and provides technical and financial assistance for state and local waste programs.

———•———

1970s ***The environmental movement spurs interest in residential recycling.***

1970
The Resource Recovery Act extends federal assistance to recycling programs and waste incineration and requires states to come up with plans for managing their waste.

1975
More than 100 communities across the country have introduced curbside recycling, mostly for newspapers, in an effort to boost recycling. More than a quarter of all aluminum beverage cans, the most valuable post-consumer material, are recycled.

1976
The Resource Conservation and Recovery Act (RCRA) sets national standards for landfills and incinerators. By requiring the use of expensive landfill liners and smokestack scrubbers, the law indirectly encourages recycling.

1978
The Public Utilities Regulatory Policies Act (PURPA) encourages the development of waste-to-energy plants. Support for these alternatives to landfills later wanes, however, because of their emissions of toxic ash.

———•———

1980s ***Acting on fears that landfill space is running out, communities across the country step up curbside recycling programs.***

1987
The *Mobro 4000*, a garbage barge out of Long Island, attracts national attention as it sails down the East Coast to the Caribbean in the vain search for a place to dump its cargo. The incident prompts concern, largely unfounded, that the entire country faces a landfill crisis.

1988
The Environmental Protection Agency (EPA) sets a recycling goal for the United States at 25 percent of total waste.

1990s ***Recycling comes under scrutiny after a series of supply gluts causes upheaval in the markets for recycled materials.***

1991
Manufacturers' demand for recycled materials fails to keep pace with the supply following the sudden increase in curbside programs, causing the first major crash in the market for recyclables.

1993
President Clinton issues an executive order requiring all federal agencies to buy printing and writing paper with at least 30 percent recycled content by the end of 1998.

1995
The nationwide recycling rate reaches 27 percent, exceeding the EPA's 25 percent goal. Prices of recycled newsprint and some other materials reach historic peaks, prompting "garbage rustlers" to raid curbside bins for valuable materials. The Chicago Board of Trade sets up an electronic listing for recycled plastic, paper and glass that helps link buyers and sellers of these materials and thus improves the market's efficiency.

1996
Newsprint prices sink so low that some recycling contractors dump collected paper in landfills.

1997
The pace of new curbside programs begins to slow because most programs already collect the materials that are in demand by manufacturers.

How Germany Copes With Recycling Success

The United States may have launched the recycling movement, but other countries have embraced stricter recycling requirements, notably Germany. German manufacturers must take responsibility for collecting and recycling or reusing the packaging materials for the products they sell. Unlike U.S. recycling programs, which focus on consumers and for the most part rely on their cooperation, the German system embodies the "polluter-pays" principle. It holds that because industry is responsible for choosing what packaging it uses, it should bear the burden of recycling it.

The law was partly a consequence of the collapse of European communism. Before German reunification in 1990, West Germany had "solved" the problem of dwindling landfill space by exporting its trash to East Germany, where landfill regulations were minimal.[1] Meanwhile, West Germany's increasingly influential Green Party helped pass strong environmental protection regulations. With reunification, those regulations were extended to the whole country, and a new solution to Germany's waste problems had to be found.

The Ordinance on Avoidance of Packaging Waste, which took effect in June 1991, required industry to switch to reusable shipping cartons and reduce its use of non-essential "secondary" packaging, such as cardboard boxes containing bottles of aspirin or the plastic "blister" packs used to display many consumer goods. Beverage producers were able to comply with the law by using refillable bottles, a longstanding practice in much of Europe.

But problems quickly arose for essential, "primary" packaging materials, the countless pill bottles, toothpaste tubes and myriad other containers that manufacturers were required to take back and recycle or reuse under the law. Faced with a near-impossible obligation, German industries banded together and created a consortium — the Duales System Deutschland (DSD) — to provide collection and recycling services on their behalf. Manufacturers pay DSD for the right to place a green dot on their packaging, which exempts those items from the law's take-back provision. DSD then pays waste companies to collect those packaging materials from curbside bins or drop-off centers and sells the materials to industry for recycling.

The German system immediately boosted recycling rates. By 1994, DSD had grown into a multibillion-dollar business and was recycling two-thirds of the country's packaging materials. But the system has also been the victim of its own success, especially in the collection and recycling of plastics. Overwhelmed by a glut of collected plastic packaging, DSD exported much of the excess to other countries where it was often buried or burned.

Despite its drawbacks, the German recycling system is being emulated in other countries, particularly in Europe, where high population densities make landfills less feasible than in the United States. As part of an effort to harmonize regulations throughout the 15-member European Union, the EU in 1994 adopted a Packaging Directive setting both minimum and maximum recycling goals — the latter aimed at avoiding some of the German system's problems. By 2001, all member countries are to recycle from 25-45 percent of their packaging. Germany, which already exceeds the maximum quota for all materials, must either reduce its recycling rate or demonstrate that it can recycle its own materials.

A number of countries have adopted or are considering recycling programs based on the German green dot system. For example, Austria, Belgium and France have introduced similar programs, modified to allow incineration of recyclables as a way to avoid the oversupply of materials that has hampered the German program.

The German model may have little appeal, however, in the United States, where recycling has always been a largely voluntary effort based on individual participation. Additionally, the German approach owes much of its success to the country's high population density and limited geographical area. In the United States, with its vast distances and large tracts of undeveloped land, landfilling is still an option, while transportation costs discourage recycling in many parts of the country.

"Germany's packaging law is the most stringent in the world, and they spend up to $4 billion a year enforcing it," says Michele Raymond, publisher of *State Recycling Laws Update*. "It's a totally different system there."

[1] Information in this section is based on Frank Ackerman, *Why Do We Recycle?* (1997), pp. 108-109.

ception. Even after the Industrial Revolution ushered in the modern era of mass production and consumption of consumer products, many basic materials continued to be recycled. Until the late 19th century, for example, paper was made from rags, and the demand for rags upheld a robust market for used clothing and other textile scraps.[10] Scavengers picked garbage dumps for these and other materials that were routinely fed back into the production cycle. Today, the remnants of older types of recycling persist in the form of scrap dealerships where cars, appliances and other goods are broken up, sorted into their steel and other metal components and sold to mini-mills for use in new products.

Although recycling had always been a common business activity, it was not until the 1940s that people began collecting materials for reasons other than profit. During World War II, Americans voluntarily contributed metals, rubber and other materials for the war effort. More than a third of all paper and paperboard products, as well as other materials, were recovered and recycled by the war industries.

Recycling fell from view after the war, but re-emerged in the 1960s in response to a new concern — the environment. Lady Bird Johnson, the wife of President Lyndon B. Johnson, helped launch a campaign to clean up the trash strewn along the nation's roadways, and Rachel Carson, in her 1962 best-seller *Silent Spring*, warned of the dangers of toxic chemicals left in landfills. Largely unregulated at the time, landfills were frequently used as dumps for hazardous wastes, which leached into the groundwater. [11] Recycling was seen as a way to reduce the amount of trash and thus the need for more landfills.

By the early 1970s, thousands of grass-roots recycling centers had appeared where consumers could drop off newspapers, glass bottles and aluminum cans. In addition, by 1974 more than 100 communities had set up curbside collection services for recyclables, mostly newspapers. Newspaper collection fell off following a slump in the newsprint market in the mid-1970s. But the demand for recycled aluminum remained strong; by 1975, a quarter of all aluminum cans were being recycled.

Federal Role

Although recycling has always been a matter of state and local jurisdiction, the federal government has enacted several laws since the environmental movement's inception in the 1960s that have indirectly influenced the progress of recycling programs. [12] The 1965 Solid Waste Disposal Act launched federal research into the technology of waste disposal and provided technical and financial assistance for state and local waste programs. The 1970 Resource Recovery Act extended the federal effort to include recycling programs and waste incineration, including waste-to-energy facilities, which generate steam or electricity from burning garbage. [13] The law stopped short, however, of setting standards, and it required states to come up with plans for managing their waste as a condition for receiving the federal aid.

The 1976 Resource Conservation and Recovery Act (RCRA) set national standards for landfills and incinerators that were strengthened in 1984. While the law did not address recycling directly, its requirements of environmental safeguards, such as landfill liners and smokestack filters, made it more expensive to bury or burn waste and thus encouraged recycling indirectly.

Waste incineration gained support as an attractive source of energy in the wake of the energy crises of the 1970s. In 1978, Congress encouraged the development of waste-to-energy facilities with the Public Utilities Regulatory Policies Act (PURPA), which required utilities to buy power from these plants at favorable rates. Enthusiasm for waste-to-energy facilities soon cooled, however, out of concern over the toxic ash they generate, which must be disposed of in special landfills. As a result, only about 16 percent of municipal solid waste is incinerated. [14]

©PhotoDisc

Of the 208 million tons of municipal solid waste generated in the United States in 1995, 57 percent ended up in landfills.

Landfill "Crisis"

The administration of Ronald Reagan (1981-1989) enacted no major laws dealing with solid waste. But public perceptions that the country's mounting trash flow posed threats to the environment continued. These fears escalated in 1987, when the *Mobro 4000*, a garbage scow, sailed for days down the East Coast and into the Caribbean Sea in search of a port to dump its fetid cargo.

The widely publicized voyage came to symbolize the emergence of a landfill "crisis," in which cities, having run out of space to bury their own garbage, were desperately trying to export it to other jurisdictions.

As it turned out, the *Mobro's* problems had little to do with the lack of landfill space. The barge operator had simply set sail without signing any agreements with landfill operators to dump its garbage, and port authorities turned the scow away, not because local landfills were full but because they feared it carried hazardous wastes. [15] But the *Mobro's* wayward journey bolstered public support for recycling as a solution to the problem.

By this time, recycling operations had expanded in number and in the range of materials collected. Beginning in the early 1980s, recycling operators built "material-recovery facilities" where they could sort, bale and market the recyclable materials they collected in curbside programs. In the absence of federal standards for recycling, states set their own standards. Today, most states have passed laws aimed at reducing the total waste stream and encouraging recycling as well as composting of yard trimmings. [16] ■

CURRENT SITUATION

An Uncertain Market

Community recycling programs are just the first link in the recycling process. The next role is played by markets for recyclable materials — the paper mills, steel mills, aluminum smelters, glass container makers and plastics reprocessors that transform these materials into new products.

The 1990s have seen both unprecedented growth in recycling programs and volatility in the markets for recyclable materials. A glut in the supply of recyclables that followed the sudden increase in curbside programs in the late 1980s caused a crash in prices in 1991, as new manufacturing plants failed to keep pace with the supply of raw materials. A so-called "basket" of recyclables that fetched $70 a ton in 1989 went for just $25 a ton by 1992, prompting some communities to pay haulers to cart away the materials they had collected. [17]

Barely two years later, however, prices soared. Old corrugated cardboard rose in value from $25 to $150 a ton during the first six months of 1994, while mixed paper prices skyrocketed from $5 to more than $200 a ton. Prices for old newsprint, plastic soda bottles and milk jugs and aluminum cans also soared. [18] Boom again turned to bust in mid-1995, when prices for paper and plastics plummeted.

Such extreme swings in the market come as no surprise to recycling experts. "After all, these are market commodities, and how they fare depends on what is going on in the overall economy," Keller says. "If the economy goes south and people stop making as many houses and automobiles and buy less retail goods, you'll see a drop-off in the end market for recyclables."

Today, recycling in the United States is a $30 billion industry. As the industry has grown, the market for recyclables has become somewhat more stable, and while prices for most materials are nowhere near their peaks of three years ago, they are close to historical norms. According to R.W. Beck Inc., a consulting and engineering firm that tracks the market in recyclables, the value of a basket of nine materials it measures stood at an estimated $80 a ton in 1997, much lower than the $145 reported in 1995 but higher than the $68 reported in 1996. [19] A closer look shows how different market conditions are for the most commonly recycled materials:

Paper — Almost 40 million tons of paper were recovered from the waste stream in 1996, or nearly 85 percent of all recycled materials. More than half of that was corrugated containers, the single largest item in Beck's index. These are primarily boxes used for packaging and shipping goods from factories to retailers, and most are collected through privately contracted recycling programs. Demand for this material is generally strong.

The glut of old newspapers that sent the market into a tailspin three years ago has abated, in part because growth in newspaper circulation has slowed with the advent and growth of electronic news media. Mixed paper, one of the more recent items included in curbside collection, is expected to be in greater demand as an alternative to corrugated boxes for the production of paperboard, used to make shoeboxes, cereal boxes and other items. Likewise, high-grade paper is in demand, in part because of federal and state purchasing mandates requiring public agencies to buy writing and printing paper with recycled content.

Prices for recycled paper in 1997 ranged between $5.69 per ton for mixed paper to $109 per ton for high-grade paper. With the exception of old newspapers, which fell slightly in 1997 to $15 a ton, prices for recycled paper materials rose slightly from 1996 to 1997.

Although many deinking plants were built in response to the 1995 peak in paper prices, a number of paper recycling manufacturers have been in business for years. Marcal Paper Mills Inc., for example, has been using a variety of waste papers to make 100 percent recycled-content napkins, tissues and paper towels at its Elmwood Park, N.J., plant since 1947.

New deinking technology that can reprocess coated paper, such as old magazines and catalogs, has increased demand for a broader range of paper products than was once collected for recycling. But paper mills still report problems resulting from contamination of the materials, especially from "stickies," or adhesive notes, which raise the cost of producing recycled paper. [20]

Glass — After newspapers, glass containers are the most common item by weight found in residential waste. Although they are rapidly being replaced by plastics for soft drinks, glass bottles and jars are widely used to package beer, other drinks and food products. Recovery of glass containers has fallen slightly since it peaked in 1994. Prices for clear glass — the only type measured in Beck's analysis — fell 20 percent in 1997, to $37 a ton.

Clear, green and brown glass bottles have different properties and must be processed separately. In areas where they are collected together, breakage can quickly contaminate the recovered materials. Another obstacle to reprocessing glass is its weight, which makes it costly to ship, especially in sparsely populated regions such as the Mountain West. Transportation is becoming a greater factor in the cost of reprocessing glass because of consolidation: 127 regional plants have been replaced by 62 larger plants over the past 20 years. [21]

Steel cans — Scrapped appliances as well as steel cans collected curbside account for most steel and iron recovered from municipal solid waste. Almost 60 percent of all steel cans produced in the United States, mostly food cans, are recovered for recycling, and the percentage is growing steadily, thanks in part to the recent inclusion of aerosol cans in many curbside programs. Perhaps reflecting that trend, prices for baled steel cans fell to $50 a ton in 1997, the lowest level reported by Beck since 1980. However, given high demand for scrap steel by the steel industry in the United States and abroad and the recent increase in the number of electric-arc furnaces in operation, prices for recycled steel are expected to rise in coming months. [22]

©PhotoDisc

After peaking in 1995, prices for recycled newsprint sank so low that some contractors simply dumped the paper they collected in landfills.

Aluminum cans — At 64 percent, the 1997 recycling rate for aluminum beverage cans outstrips that for steel cans, and amounts to about a million tons a year. But the price of aluminum cans is much higher — $1,090 a ton in 1997 — and has risen by more than half since 1993, making these the most valuable items collected in most curbside programs. Unlike most recyclables, aluminum is relatively unaltered by reprocessing, so it can be recycled over and over again with little sacrifice in quality. Aluminum cans are unusual also because they typically emerge from the recycling process as new aluminum cans, completing the closed loop depicted in the universal symbol designating products with recycled content. Domestic demand for aluminum cans is so high that less than 1 percent of them are exported to overseas processors.

Plastic — More than half of the nation's roughly 32,000 communities have access to programs that collect one or more types of plastic. [23] But plastic recycling has been hampered by the difficulty of separating the different types of containers and packaging materials and reprocessing them into materials suitable for remanufacture. Of the scores of plastic resins used in manufacturing, six are most commonly found in everyday consumer products. Of these, only two have been widely included in recycling programs — polyethylene terephthalate (PET), used to make beverage bottles, and high-density polyethylene (HDPE), used in milk jugs and other containers.*

*Plastic containers are numbered from 1-7 depending on which resins they contain.

Prices for old PET bottles, much like those for recycled paper, have fluctuated in recent years, ranging from a record high of $354 per ton in 1995 to $40 per ton in 1996. The main reason for the crash in prices for PET bottles was the opening of numerous factories here and abroad producing virgin resin, which curbed demand for scrap PET. Last year, Beck reports, PET prices rebounded to $118 per ton. There is no lack of capacity to reclaim PET — 27 plants in 18 states processed more than 300,000 pounds of post-consumer PET in 1995. [24]

Both the recovery rate and prices for HDPE bottles have risen in recent years. Many recycling programs have expanded the list of eligible HDPE items to include water and juice bottles as well as pigmented bottles used for liquid detergents. Baled HDPE containers, which totaled 660 million tons, brought $421 a ton last year, almost as much as during the 1995 peak. Recycled HDPE is often used to make new containers, plastic plumbing pipes, leaf bags and plastic "lumber."

The complexity of plastics recycling makes it hard to develop stable markets for products made of resins other than PET and HDPE, however. New technologies are making it possible to break plastic materials down into their original state, so that they are virtually indistinguishable from virgin resins, but most resin producers have not invested in this technology. [25] "Remember, these producers are the Exxons of this world, large, traditional companies that are not likely to spend money for a small niche business like recycling," Raymond says. "Anyway, why should they want to use less virgin resin? They're selling more and more of it, 40 percent more over the past six years alone. Plastics surpassed steel in the 1970s in terms of volume. Today it's bigger than just about anything."

Most of the plastic that is recycled undergoes only partial reprocessing before it is transformed into new products, products that bear little resemblance to the bottles and packaging materials consumers tossed in the bin. In such an "open-loop" application, plastic bottles are washed, ground up and made into fiber for fleece jackets and carpets, or they are exported. Only about 16 percent is used to make new bottles. [26]

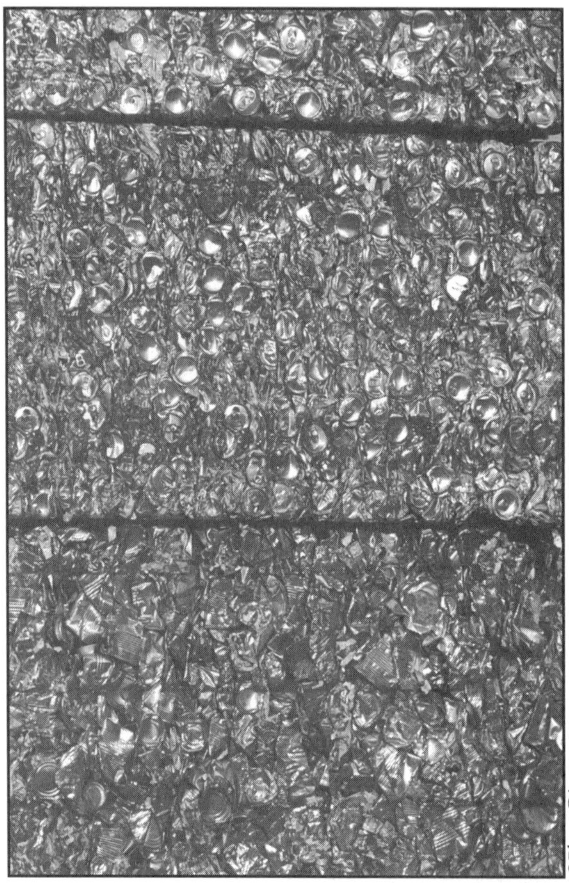

Nearly two-thirds of all aluminum beverage cans were recycled in 1997. About a million tons of aluminum cans are recycled each year.

Another obstacle to further plastic recycling is the growing popularity of single-serve PET drink bottles. Because they are often used and discarded away from home, these bottles often elude recycling programs and end up in the trash. Businesses and public agencies are beginning to install special bins to encourage recycling of these bottles.

Compost — Though it is collected separately from other recycled items, yard trimmings are commonly picked up curbside and hauled to a municipal composting facility. Once composted, leaves, grass clippings, branches and some food wastes produce a nutrient-rich soil additive that is purchased by nurseries, landscapers and residential gardeners. But because its value is so low in most parts of the country, the cost of collecting yard wastes is usually borne by consumers and embedded in the bill for solid waste removal.

Some communities provide special bins to encourage households to compost their own organic wastes and keep this material out of landfills. In the Northeast and other areas where landfill operators charge high "tipping" fees to dump trash, yard wastes are actually banned from the waste stream.

Communities Pitch In

The 1990s have seen rapid growth in recycling efforts. Today, about 27 percent of the nation's municipal solid waste is being recovered through recycling, up from just 17 percent in

At Issue:

Does recycling make economic sense?

Yes

Richard A. Denison and John F. Ruston

Denison is a senior scientist and Ruston is an economic analyst at the Environmental Defense Fund

FROM "ANTI-RECYCLING MYTHS," ENVIRONMENTAL DEFENSE FUND, JULY 18, 1996.

Recycling is not just an alternative to traditional solid waste disposal, it is the foundation for large, robust manufacturing industries in the United States that use recyclable materials. These businesses are an important part of our economy and provide the market foundation for the entire recycling process. . . .

Recycling provides manufacturing industries with raw materials that are less expensive than virgin sources, a long-term economic advantage that translates into value for consumers who ultimately spend less on products and packaging. For example, in the area of paper manufacturing, new mills making paper for corrugated boxes, newsprint, commercial tissue products and folding cartons have lower capital and operating costs than new mills using virgin wood. . . . Recycling has long been the lower-cost manufacturing option for aluminum smelters, and is essential to the scrap-fired steel "mini-mills" that are part of the rebirth of a globally competitive U.S. steel industry. . . .

In a recent study examining 10 Northeastern states, recycling was found to have added $7.2 billion in value to recovered materials through processing and manufacturing activities. These activities employed approximately 103,000 people, 25 percent of them in materials processing and 75 percent in manufacturing. . . .

Market prices for materials like polystyrene are set in the near term by supply and demand forces, underpinned by a host of production cost factors, many of which have nothing to do with environmental impact. An entire sub-discipline of environmental economics has developed to address a range of environmental damages, called externalities, that are not reflected in market prices even in the most regulated industries. . . . [When] a coastal wetland in the Carolinas is converted to a pine plantation and results in damage to estuarine fish hatcheries or reduced water quality, such impacts are certainly not captured in the market price of wood taken from the site.

Nor are any of the costs of disposal included in product prices. If someone drains motor oil from a car into the gutter, it may pollute surface water or groundwater. But the price originally paid for the oil does not anticipate its proper or improper disposal. Finally, another major obstacle to incorporating environmental factors into market prices is the difficulty or impossibility of assigning a meaningful economic cost to such "goods," for example, the value of preserving a rare animal or plant species.

No

Jerry Taylor

Director of natural resource studies at the Cato Institute and senior editor of* Regulation *magazine

FROM "MINIMUM CONTENT: MINIMUM SENSE," THE CATO INSTITUTE, April 25, 1997.

Ten years into America's holy war against garbage, the case for residential curbside recycling has run smack into the harsh realities of economics. If resources are indeed becoming more scarce, they have a funny way of showing it. Prices for energy, minerals and paper have continued to fall as they have over the course of the century. . . . Post-consumer material is less competitive with virgin material than ever before. . . .

"But," you might point out, "what about the environmental externalities of the mining, timber, paper and energy industries? If you accounted for that, wouldn't recycling be competitive?" Again, not necessarily. First, we have no reliable means by which we can "price" those externalities. Second, those industries do spend tens of billions of dollars annually to comply with federal and state environmental regulations. Are the environmental externalities they impose greater than, less than or equal to the regulatory costs they pay to do business? No one knows for sure, but a number of respected economists . . . strongly suspect the environmental externalities of those industries are more than paid for through the cost of regulatory compliance.

Nor are the externalities of recycling's alternative all that impressive. EPA regulations now ensure that solid waste landfills cause only one additional cancer risk every 13 years, and that's assuming we use such worst-case scenarios and assumptions that even that figure, according to most risk assessment specialists, probably overestimates the actual risk by 100 to 1,000 times the actual risk. Likewise, municipal waste incinerators, according to those same worst-case assumptions, pose less than a 1 in 1 million risk to neighboring communities. . . .

Finally, recycling has its own environmental externalities that must be put into the equation. After all, the actual process of extracting usable raw material from a product is an industrial activity every bit as involved as the process of combining various raw materials to make a product. Both are industrial activities. And both create waste. For example, recycling 100 tons of old newsprint generates 40 tons of toxic waste. Is this consequential? Sure. EPA has reported that 13 of the 50 worst Superfund sites are/were recycling facilities.

If recycling makes economic sense, we don't need to mandate it. And if it doesn't, we shouldn't. You can make a silk purse out of a sow's ear . . . but it's usually cheaper to use silk.

1990. But because materials that are relatively easy to recycle are already being collected by many programs, the pace of new program start-ups has slowed over the past year, a trend that experts predict will continue.

Recycling often pays for itself in peak years, such as 1995, when communities earn more from selling materials than they spend to collect them. But when the value of recyclables drops, as it did in 1996, recycling often poses a financial burden on local governments, undermining support for the programs.

State and local budget cuts also are forcing many communities to reassess recycling programs. Several cities, including beleaguered Washington, D.C., dropped residential recycling altogether. Miami's City Council planned to do the same until public protests against the move. Many localities have cut back on frequency of collection and taken other steps to reduce costs. [27]

Even in Washington state, one of the leaders in recycling efforts, budget cuts are taking a toll. The Clean Washington Center is a state agency that helped Seattle and Tacoma achieve recycling rates of about half their waste by developing markets for recyclables. But last year the center, which also provides information to recycling programs throughout the country, was cut from the state budget altogether and forced to become an independent organization. ■

OUTLOOK

No End of Trash

While recycling programs are not growing as fast as they did in the early 1990s, many experts predict that they will continue to expand. "The amount of trash out there is tending to grow at a slower rate than in the past," Franklin says. "Longer-term, we expect the recycling rate to reach 30 percent of the waste stream by 2000 and 35 percent by 2020." He predicts that most of the increase will result from expanding municipal composting facilities to include more yard waste and food waste rather than new materials collected for sale to manufacturers. "We'll see more composting of paper that's too contaminated for traditional recycling, such as food packages, paper napkins, food waste and even wood."

Consumer preference is likely to be a key determinant of recycling's future in the United States. Americans — both manufacturers and consumers — may embrace recycling on the supply side by participating in recycling programs, but they have been less enthusiastic consumers of recyclable materials and recycled-content end products. "Recyclables tend to be the last hired and the first fired," Keller quips. "If the economy is good, more recyclables get used, but if the economy is not going well, people go back to things they're more comfortable with."

In the absence of pressing consumer demand for recycled products, Raymond predicts, manufacturers are unlikely to boost production of these goods. "We don't have a crisis, virgin materials are cheap, energy is cheap and tip fees are very low, so industry has no incentive to use more recycled materials," Raymond says. "That's just corporate behavior as history has always shown it to be."

Many experts say the decade since curbside recycling took off, boosting the supply of recyclable materials, is too short a time to accurately assess the recycling market's full potential. Technological advances continue to broaden the range of materials that can be recycled cost-effectively, and new processing facilities can be expected to boost demand for post-consumer materials. "We will never reach the point where industries will be dependent on recycled materials alone," Keller says. "Although steel can be recycled an infinite number of times, paper loses a little fiber every time it's recycled, so we're going to still need virgin materials. But the technology will continue to improve, and we'll find ways to recycle materials now considered non-recyclable. There's no question that as technology changes, the variety of things we can recycle will improve over time."

Anticipating such an expansion, the Chicago Board of Trade in 1995 set up an electronic listing for recycled plastic, paper and glass that helps link buyers and sellers of these materials and thus makes the market more efficient. "It's not a full-fledged commodities market," Scarlett says, "but it's growing and provides another tweaking mechanism that helps increase information flows and improve recycling markets."

Of course, industry responds to consumer demand as well as the cost of raw materials. And for the most part, Americans remain unreliable end users of products made from recycled materials, which many view as inferior in quality.

"People in the food-processing industry will tell you that as a rule putting the green seal of approval on a product indicating it is environmentally benign is going to cost them market share," Taylor says. "People avoid it because they think it's flimsy, unsanitary or not up to standard performance."

Even active participants in recycling programs overlook recycled-content products. "Sure, there are some 'greens' out there, but the vast majority of us are more sensitive to price and quality than to environmental concerns," Raymond says. "Do I have the time to read the labels on all the products that I buy in the grocery store when I have only 30 minutes to get the shopping done? Get real."

Recent trends suggest those attitudes are slowly changing, however. Environmentally concerned consumers are driving growth in retail businesses such as the Fresh Fields-Whole Foods grocery chain, which specializes in environmentally benign products, including those with recycled content. In any case, consumer demand for recycled-content products may not be necessary for further expansion of this market, which Keller says already accounts for at least $10 billion in sales each year, because so many products include recycled materials even though they don't bear the green seal.

"There is no question that there are still remnants of the population who view recycled materials as inferior," Keller says. "But lots of recycled-content products have been quietly used for decades. There is no steel in the United States that doesn't have a minimum of 25 percent recycled content. There are no paper mills being built in the United States today that depend on virgin materials alone. Even *Air Force One* flies on retread tires." ■

FOR MORE INFORMATION

U.S. Environmental Protection Agency, Solid Waste and Emergency Response, USEPA Ariel Rios (S101) 1200 Pennsylvania Ave., N.W., Washington, D.C. 20460; (800) 424-9346 (in the Washington area, (703) 412-9810; http://www.epa.gov. EPA's Solid Waste Hotline offers information on how to contact recycling coordinators at the local level.

Reason Foundation, 3415 S. Sepulveda Blvd., Suite 400, Los Angeles, Calif. 90003; (310) 391-2245; http://www.reason.org. This nonprofit, nonpartisan public policy think tank advocates market solutions to environmental problems. It has done economic studies of recycling.

Waste Policy Center, 211 Loudoun St. S.W., Leesburg, Va. 20175; (703) 777-9800; www.recycle.net/assn/wpc.html. This independent consulting and research organization analyzes the costs and benefits of recycling.

Environmental Defense Fund, 257 Park Ave. South, New York, N.Y. 10010; (800) 684-3322; http://www.edf.org. EDF provides information on the economic and environmental benefits of recycling.

Solid Waste Association of North America, P.O. Box 7219, Silver Spring, Md. 20907; (800) 467-9262; http://www.swana.org. Representing government officials who manage municipal solid waste programs, this group provides information on recycling, combustion and other alternatives to waste disposal.

U.S. Conference of Mayors, Municipal Waste Management Association, 1620 I St. N.W., 6th floor, Washington, D.C. 20006; (202) 293-7330. This organization of local governments and private firms involved in waste collection and recycling helps communities plan recycling programs. www.usmayors.org/uscm/mwma

Notes

[1] See Franklin Associates Ltd., *Solid Waste Management at the Crossroads* (December 1997). For background, see "Garbage Crisis," *The CQ Researcher*, March 20, 1992, pp. 241-264.

[2] Franklin Associates Ltd., *op. cit.*, p. 1-16. Franklin Associates provides the EPA with data on recycling. See also J. Winston Porter, *Trash Facts IV*, Waste Policy Center, 1997.

[3] John Tierney, "Recycling Is Garbage," *The New York Times Magazine*, June 30, 1996.

[4] Richard A. Denison and John F. Ruston, "Recycling Is Not Garbage," *Technology Review*, October 1997.

[5] The poll, conducted by American Opinion Research for the now-defunct Council on Packaging in the Environment in 1996, was cited in Bill Noone, "'Closing the Loop' Remains a Priority for Packagers," *Packaging Technology & Engineering*, November 1996.

[6] Porter, *op. cit.*

[7] Denison and Ruston, *op. cit.*

[8] For background on air pollution, see "New Air Quality Standards," *The CQ Researcher*, March 7, 1997, pp. 193-216.

[9] Lisa A. Skumatz, "Nationwide Diversion Rate Study: Quantitative Effects of Program Choices on Recycling and Green Waste Diversion: Beyond Case Studies," Skumatz Economic Research Associates Inc., July 1996.

[10] Information in this section is based on Frank Ackerman, *Why Do We Recycle?* (1997), pp. 14-19.

[11] For background, see "Cleaning Up Hazardous Wastes," *The CQ Researcher*, Aug. 23, 1996, pp. 745-768 and "Water Quality," *The CQ Researcher*, Feb. 11, 1994, pp. 121-144.

[12] For background, see "Environmental Movement at 25," *The CQ Researcher*, March 31, 1995, pp. 288-311.

[13] For background, see "Renewable Energy," *The CQ Researcher*, Nov. 7, 1997, pp. 961-984.

[14] Ackerman, *op. cit.*, p. 18.

[15] *Ibid*, pp. 11-12.

[16] *Ibid*, p. 18.

[17] See Lynn Scarlett, "Roller Coaster Recycling Markets: Down, Up, and What's Next?" *MSW Management*, January/February 1996, p. 51.

[18] *Ibid.*

[19] See Jessica Lucyshyn and Robert Craggs, "A Five-Year History of Recycling Market Prices: 1997 Update," *Resource Recycling*, February 1998, p. 16.

[20] See Franklin Associates Ltd., *op. cit.*, p. 4-8.

[21] *Ibid.*, p. 4-14.

[22] *Ibid.*, p. 4-12.

[23] "'America Recycles Day' to Raise Awareness of Recycling and Buying Recycled Products," *PR Newswire*, Nov. 14, 1997.

[24] Franklin Associates Ltd., *op. cit.*, p. 4-9.

[25] See Susan Warren, "Environment: Polyester Trash Is Pure Plastic after an 'Unzip,'" *The Wall Street Journal*, Nov. 6, 1997.

[26] Franklin Associates Ltd., *op. cit.*, p. 4-9.

[27] See Jim Glenn, "Year End Review of Recycling and Composting," *BioCycle*, December 1997.

Bibliography

Selected Sources Used

Books

Ackerman, Frank, *Why Do We Recycle? Markets, Values, and Public Policy*, Island Press, 1997.
The author, a professor at Tufts University's Global Development and Environment Institute, reviews the history and market development of recycling. He argues that environmental as well as economic concerns must be included in any assessment of recycling's value.

Articles

"America's Recyclers: A Funny Sort of Market," *The Economist*, Oct. 18, 1997, pp. 63-64.
Government mandates have skewed the markets for recyclable materials, according to this article, by increasing supply with no concern for demand by industry.

Denison, Richard A., and John F. Ruston, "Recycling Is Not Garbage," *Technology Review*, October 1997.
In this response to an earlier critique of recycling, two researchers at the Environmental Defense Fund point out the economic and environmental benefits of recycling and call for efforts to improve the efficiency of community programs.

Lucyshyn, Jessica, and Robert Craggs, "A Five-Year History of Recycling Market Prices: 1997 Update," *Resource Recycling*, February 1998.
Two recycling analysts with R.W. Beck Inc., a national consulting and engineering firm, point out that markets for recycled materials have become less volatile in the past two years and suggest that program managers may be better prepared to avert the oversupply that buffeted the markets in 1996.

Scarlett, Lynn, "Roller Coaster Recycling Markets: Down, Up, and What's Next?" *MSW Management*, January/February 1996, pp. 50-53.
The gyrations in the markets for recycled materials seen in the mid-1990s are likely to continue, the author writes, because numerous events that are beyond the control of governments will continue to affect demand.

Skumatz, Lisa A., Erin Truitt and John Green, "The State of Variable Rates: Economic Signals Move into the Mainstream," *Resource Recycling*, August 1997, pp. 31-35.
By charging consumers for the amount of non-recyclable waste they generate, the authors write, communities can greatly increase recycling rates. More than 4,400 communities in the United States and Canada have integrated this approach into their waste collection programs.

Reports and Studies

Franklin Associates Ltd., *Solid Waste Management at the Crossroads*, December 1997.
This research firm, which provides recycling data to the EPA, predicts that the recovery of recyclable materials will continue to grow, though more slowly than in the past, reaching 35 percent by 2010.

Raymond Communications Inc., *State Recycling Laws Update*, Year-End Edition 1997.
State lawmakers enacted a total of 70 recycling bills in 1996, out of nearly 200 bills followed by this annual study. Local governments, however, maintained their commitment to recycling.

Scarlett, Lynn, Richard McCann, Robert Anex and Alexander Volokh, *Packaging, Recycling, and Solid Waste*, Reason Public Policy Institute, July 1997.
This study from a think tank in Los Angeles, Calif., examines the economic costs and benefits of recycling and concludes that government mandates for recycling rates or levels of recycled content in finished products are unlikely to help the environment.

U.S. Environmental Protection Agency, *The Consumer's Handbook for Reducing Solid Waste*, August 1992.
This overview of recycling includes a guide to help consumers understand what types of materials are commonly included in curbside programs as well as community drop-off centers.

U.S. Environmental Protection Agency, *Manufacturing from Recyclables: 24 Case Studies of Successful Recycling Enterprises*, February 1995.
Companies specializing in products containing recycled materials are profiled. Most are small manufacturers in or near the communities generating the recyclables. They include makers of paper, plastic, glass and other products.

U.S. Environmental Protection Agency, *Recycling Works! State and Local Solutions to Solid Waste Management Problems*, January 1989.
This dated but still relevant study examines innovative approaches to recycling — including programs that didn't work — in 14 states and communities.